The Keynesian Heritage
Volume II

Schools of Thought in Economics

Series Editor: Mark Blaug
Emeritus Professor of the Economics of Education, University of London and Consultant Professor of Economics, University of Buckingham

For greater convenience, a cumulative index to all titles in this series will be published in a separate volume number 12.

The Keynesian Heritage Volume II

Edited by

G.K. Shaw

Rank Foundation Professor of Economics
University of Buckingham

EDWARD ELGAR

Published by
Edward Elgar Publishing Limited
Gower House
Croft Road
Aldershot
Hants GU11 3HR
England

Gower Publishing Company
Old Post Road
Brookfield
Vermont 05036
USA

British Library Cataloguing in Publication Data

The Keynesian heritage. — (Schools of thought
  in economics; 1).
  1. Economics. Theories of Keynes, John
  Maynard, 1883–1946
  I. Shaw, G.K. (Graham Keith), *1938–*
  II. Series
  330.15'6

Library of Congress Cataloging-in-Publication Data

The Keynesian heritage.
  (Schools of thought in economics; 1)
  Includes indexes.
  1. Keynesian economics. I. Shaw, G.K.
(Graham Keith), 1938– II. Series.
HB99.7.K3955   1988
330.15'6   88–16528

ISBN 1 85278 067 3 (vol. II)
     1 85278 117 3 (2 volume set)

Printed and bound in Great Britain
by Bookcraft (Bath) Ltd.

for
Ursula Jancis Shaw

'Had the *General Theory* never been written, Keynes would nevertheless have deservedly been regarded as one of the great economists of all time – to be listed in the pantheon of great British economists along with Adam Smith, David Ricardo, John Stuart Mill, William Stanley Jevons, and Alfred Marshall.'

Milton Friedman – 'The Keynes Centenary:
A Monetarist Reflects', *The Economist*,
4 June, 1983

Contents

Acknowledgements

The editor and publishers wish to thank the following who have kindly given permission for the use of copyright material.

Academic Press Inc. (London) Ltd for article: Terry Baker (1980), 'The Economic Consequences of Monetarism: A Keynesian View of the British Economy 1980–90', *Cambridge Journal of Economics*, 4 (4), December, pp. 319–36.

American Economic Association for articles: R.M. Solow (1980), 'On Theories of Unemployment', *American Economic Review*, 70, March, pp. 1–11; J.L. Yellen (1984), 'Efficiency Wage Models of Unemployment', *American Economic Review*, 74, May, pp. 200–5; P.A. Samuelson and R.M. Solow (1960), 'Problem of Achieving and Maintaining a Stable Price Level: Analytical Aspects of Anti-Inflation Policy', *American Economic Review*, 50 (2), May, pp. 177–94; R.A. Musgrave and M.H. Miller (1948), 'Built-in Flexibility', *American Economic Review*, 38 (1), March, pp. 122–8; S. Rosen (1985), 'Implicit Contracts: A Survey', *Journal of Economic Literature*, 23, September, pp. 1144–75.

Basil Blackwell Ltd for articles: L. Tarshis (1939), 'Changes in Real and Money Wages', *Economic Journal*, 49, pp. 150–4; P.R.G. Layard and S.J. Nickell (1980), 'The Case for Subsidising Extra Jobs', *Economic Journal*, 90, March, pp. 51–73; F.H. Hahn (1987), 'On Involuntary Unemployment', *Economic Journal Supplement*, 97, pp. 1–16; J. Tobin (1981), 'The Monetarist Counter-Revolution Today: An Appraisal', *Economic Journal*, 91 (361), March, pp. 29–42; W. Beckerman and T. Jenkinson (1986), 'What Stopped the Inflation: Unemployment or Commodity Prices?', *Economic Journal*, 96, March, pp. 39–54; A.W. Phillips (1957), 'Stabilisation Policy and the Time-Forms of Lagged Responses', *Economic Journal*, 67, pp. 265–77; D. Currie (1985), 'Macroeconomic Policy Design and Control Theory: A Failed Partnership?, *Economic Journal*, 95, June, pp. 285–306.

Canadian Journal of Economics for article: R.G. Lipsey (1981), 'The Understanding and Control of Inflation: Is there a Crisis in Macro-economics?', *Canadian Journal of Economics*, XIV (4), November, pp. 545–76.

North Holland Publishing Co. for articles: A.S. Blinder and R.M. Solow (1973), 'Does Fiscal Policy Matter?', *Journal of Public Economics*, 2, November, pp. 319–37; W.H. Buiter (1977), ' "Crowding Out" and the Effectiveness of Fiscal Policy', *Journal of Public Economics*, 7, pp. 309–28.

Public Finance/Finances Publiques for article: M.H. Peston (1971), 'The Tax Mix and Effective Demand', *Public Finance*, XXVI (3), pp. 493–6.

Review of Economics and Statistics for article: William A. Salant (1957), 'Taxes, Income Determination, and the Balanced Budget Theorem', *Review of Economics and Statistics*, 39, pp. 152–61.

M.E. Sharpe, Inc. for article: S. Weintraub (1981–82), 'Keynesian Demand Serendipity in Supply-Side Economics', *Journal of Post Keynesian Economics*, IV (2) Winter, pp. 181–91.

Social Research for article: A.P. Lerner (1943), 'Functional Finance and the Federal Debt', *Social Research*, 10, February, pp. 38–51.

Tieto Ltd for article: R. Layard (1982), 'Is Incomes Policy the Answer to Unemployment?', *Economica*, 49, August, pp. 219–39.

John Wiley & Sons Inc. for articles: J. Tobin (1970), 'Money and Income: Post Hoc Ergo Propter Hoc?', *Quarterly Journal of Economics*, 84, pp. 301–17; G. Akerlof (1979), 'Irving Fisher on His Head: The Consequences of Constant Threshold-Target Monitoring of Money Holdings', *Quarterly Journal of Economics*, 93, pp. 169–87.

Every effort has been made to trace all the copyright holders but if any have been inadvertently overlooked the publishers will be pleased to make the necessary arrangement at the first opportunity.

In addition the publishers wish to thank the Library of the London School of Economics and Political Science and the British Library Document Supply Centre for their assistance in obtaining these articles.

Introduction

Volume I of the Keynesian Heritage focused primarily upon theoretical contributions which might be considered as essentially Keynesian in spirit in that they reflect an interventionist philosophy, believing that all was not necessarily for the best in the classical economic world. Precisely why Keynes believed that the classical macroeconomic model was fundamentally flawed and that the self adjusting and relatively painless process of restoring full employment income was not as simple or as inevitable as the classical postulates would suggest, is a matter of considerable dispute and controversy (as outlined in the introduction to Volume I). Nonetheless, whatever the reasons, they lead to the essentially Keynesian conclusion that macroeconomic performance can be improved by judicious government intervention.

The Keynesian revolution in macroeconomic theory was accompanied by a profound sense of optimism amongst economic practitioners and policy makers generally, who believed, perhaps naively, that the business cycle, which had plagued mankind from the time of Solomon, could be eliminated once and for all. The experience of the Second World War, and the maintenance of full employment in the immediate postwar years, (which were years of very strict controls, especially in the United Kingdom), served to convince many sceptics of the essential correctness of the Keynesian prescription and led to a climate of opinion conducive to interventionist measures, although it was later to be argued that full employment was more the consequence of good luck than good management (Matthews, 1968). In any event, it was probably the experience of war time controls which gave a certain fiscal orientation to macroeconomic policy formulation and led to a certain de-emphasizing of the importance of monetary forces. It was probably also the case that because within the United Kingdom, fiscal changes could be easily and swiftly implemented by the government of the day, there emerged a decided preference for fiscal, as opposed to monetary control.

On the policy front, therefore, Keynesianism became identified with the virtues of demand management and fine tuning through active interventionist fiscal policy and the monetary implications were effectively ignored. In this respect, at least, Keynesianism was arguably more Keynesian than Keynes had actually intended (see Leijonhufvud, 1968) and became identified with an open disdain for the tenets of monetarism and monetary control. Subsequent 'Keynesian' expositions recognizing the importance of the economics of the budget constraint were then to reconcile Keynesian demand management policies and the monetary implications of budgetary deficits by calling for prices and incomes controls, which equally became associated with the new Keynesian economics.

The contributions included in the present volume are all Keynesian in this broadest sense and moreover, they are all either directly related to policy issues or carry profound implications for macroeconomic policy. For convenience they are grouped under three general headings, namely the relationship between Wages and Unemployment, Money, Monetarism and Inflation and the Fiscal Implications stemming from Keynesian economics. Needless to say, these topics in no way exhaust the economics that might be aptly termed Keynesian in spirit; in particular, space limitations have dictated the need to omit consideration of open economy macroeconomics which might justifiably merit the consideration of a separate volume.

Precisely what to include has remained the subjective choice of the present editor and the editorial exercise has made me acutely aware that for every contribution selected here, an equally appealing or plausible alternative exists which could just as well have merited inclusion. As in the case of Volume I, however, a criterion invoked to justify exclusion has remained the wide availability of the relevant article in other collected readings and symposia.

It is now more than fifty years since the appearance of Keynes' *General Theory*. It is interesting to speculate upon what the contents of a volume such as this would be if there were to be a publication to mark the centenary of the *General Theory*. Undoubtedly, its composition would be vastly changed. For, whatever the real meaning of Keynes or the essence of the Keynesian revolution there can be little doubt that the spirit of Keynes continues to exert a profound and lasting influence upon the evolution of economic science.

Acknowledgements

The present collection of papers has benefited considerably from the comments of the General Editor to this series, Professor Mark Blaug, and equally by the perceptive suggestions of my former colleague, Rod Cross of St Andrews University. Neither, of course, bear any responsibility for any idiosyncratic inclusion on the part of the editor nor equally any responsibility for a glaring sin of omission. As always, I am especially indebted to Mrs Linda Waterman of Buckingham University for her unfailing efficiency in conducting the secretarial and typing chores associated with such a venture.

G.K. Shaw
July, 1988

Part I
Wages and Unemployment

[1]

NOTES AND MEMORANDA

Changes in Real and Money Wages

In this note I should like to present certain data which, I believe, amplify some of the conclusions reached by Mr. Dunlop in his article in the Economic Journal for September 1938.[1] In particular these data relate to the first section of his article and to the citation from Mr. Keynes' *General Theory*, quoted on p. 413 : " But in the case of changes in the general level of wages, it will be found, I think, that the change in real wages associated with a change in money wages, so far from being usually in the same direction, is almost always in the opposite direction. When money wages are rising, that is to say, it will be found that real wages are falling; and when money wages are falling real wages are rising." [2]

The materials on which my conclusions are based are these. Series to indicate the level month by month of money earnings per hour and real hourly earnings were prepared.[3] The figures relate to wage-earners and employees in the lower-salary groups in the United States. The series begin with January 1932 and extend to March 1938—75 months in all. The coverage is quite wide : the earnings of employees in manufacturing, mining, public utilities, retail and wholesale trade, laundries, dyeing and cleaning, hotels, railroads and building construction are provided for in the indices. Some important groups are, due to the lack of data, omitted, the most important of them being employees in the service of the Government—about 3·3 millions in all; wage-earners in agriculture—1·5 millions; employees in the professional services—nearly 1 million; domestic servants numbering about 1·75 millions; and other service industries—nearly 1 million. In all, into the calculation of these figures for money wages and real wages enter materials that relate to more than 16 of the 28 million employees in the United States.[4]

To allow for changes in the purchasing power of money wages, I used for my basic series the index of the cost of living that is

---

[1] John T. Dunlop, " The Movement of Real and Money Wages," Economic Journal, September 1938, pp. 413–34.

[2] *General Theory of Employment, Interest and Money*, p. 10.

[3] There are advantages in using monthly data, since we can thereby assume the existence of the conditions of the short period. Certainly Mr. Keynes, in writing the paragraph quoted above, assumed such a framework.

[4] And it is doubtful, in any case, whether we should *for this purpose* take account of the earnings of Government employees and of certain others—for obviously Mr. Keynes' arguments assume that the employing units make their decisions on the basis of profits.

published by the Bureau of Labor Statistics of the United States Department of Labor.   Since this index covers only four months—or fewer—a year, I secured estimates for the intervening months on the basis of the monthly index of living costs published by the National Industrial Conference Board.   Finally, I prepared what I shall in this note identify as the " corrected " index of real wages.   The corrections were made to allow for changes in the cost of living that were due to changes in the prices of agricultural products.[1]   A table containing the relevant data appears below.

Money Wages and Real Wages in the United States.

		Money Hourly Earnings (actual figures).	Real Wages per Hour (Index: 1932 = 100).	
			Uncorrected.	" Corrected."
1932	Jan.	53·0	102·6	104·0
	Feb.	52·2	102·7	103·2
	Mar.	51·0	100·6	101·0
	Apr.	50·6	100·6	100·9
	May	50·4	101·4	101·1
	June	49·6	100·6	100·1
	July	49·2	100·1	100·0
	Aug.	48·4	99·2	99·3
	Sept.	47·3	97·4	97·8
	Oct.	47·0	97·7	97·4
	Nov.	46·9	98·0	97·7
	Dec.	46·6	98·4	97·5
1933	Jan.	46·7	100·3	97·8
	Feb.	46·4	101·6	99·6
	Mar.	46·5	102·6	100·9
	Apr.	46·0	101·6	100·5
	May	45·8	100·5	102·0
	June	45·1	97·9	98·7
	July	45·9	96·4	99·1
	Aug.	50·5	104·4	106·5
	Sept.	52·2	107·1	109·2
	Oct.	53·3	109·9	111·7
	Nov.	53·2	110·4	112·4
	Dec.	52·6	110·2	111·9
1934	Jan.	54·7	114·3	117·0
	Feb.	54·6	113·0	116·4
	Mar.	54·4	112·3	115·7
	Apr.	55·2	114·3	117·3
	May	55·7	115·1	118·0
	June	55·9	115·2	119·3
	July	56·4	116·4	120·6
	Aug.	56·5	116·0	122·0
	Sept.	56·8	115·2	122·0
	Oct.	56·7	115·6	121·6
	Nov.	56·7	115·9	121·9
	Dec.	56·4	115·4	121·8

[1] For the United States, changes in the terms of trade between agriculture and industry are of some importance in determining the level of real wages; changes in the terms of trade in the international sense are relatively unimportant, and were here neglected.

		Money Hourly Earnings (actual figures)	Real Wages per Hour (Index: 1932 = 100).	
			Uncorrected.	"Corrected."
1935	Jan.	57·4	116·4	124·3
	Feb.	58·1	116·5	124·8
	Mar.	57·6	115·6	123·6
	Apr.	58·2	115·9	124·5
	May	58·2	116·4	125·0
	June	58·3	116·9	124·8
	July	58·0	116·7	124·4
	Aug.	57·6	116·0	124·2
	Sept.	57·6	115·7	123·9
	Oct.	57·6	115·4	123·3
	Nov.	57·7	115·2	122·8
	Dec.	57·6	114·4	122·3
1936	Jan.	58·6	116·5	124·5
	Feb.	58·4	116·9	125·4
	Mar.	58·5	117·5	125·2
	Apr.	58·3	117·0	124·8
	May	58·5	116·9	124·2
	June	58·6	115·6	123·5
	July	58·6	115·6	124·4
	Aug.	58·6	115·1	124·8
	Sept.	58·5	114·7	124·4
	Oct.	58·6	115·4	125·0
	Nov.	59·2	116·5	126·6
	Dec.	59·2	116·2	127·2
1937	Jan.	60·1	117·0	128·8
	Feb.	60·5	117·7	129·5
	Mar.	61·0	117·7	130·4
	Apr.	62·7	120·6	132·9
	May	63·7	121·9	133·5
	June	63·9	122·4	133·7
	July	64·5	123·5	135·4
	Aug.	64·9	124·0	135·2
	Sept.	64·9	123·5	134·5
	Oct.	65·4	124·3	133·5
	Nov.	65·4	124·8	132·3
	Dec.	64·2	122·9	129·8
1938	Jan.	64·6	125·0	131·7
	Feb.	64·5	125·6	131·9
	Mar.	64·2	125·1	131·1

Two scatter diagrams were prepared. In the first I measured along one axis percentage changes in the level of money wages, and along the other axis percentage changes—for the corresponding months—in the level of " uncorrected " real wages. In the second diagram the relations between the percentage changes in money wages and the percentage changes for corresponding months in the " corrected " index of real wages were indicated. The second diagram is presented below. There is no considerable difference in the results, whether we are concerned with the " corrected " or " uncorrected " index of real wages.

It is obvious that there is a rather high direct or positive

association between changes in money wages and changes in real
wages. Mr. Keynes appears to be mistaken, for when money
wages are rising, it is generally found that real wages are rising,
and when money wages are falling, real wages are usually falling.
The coefficient of association[1] is + 0·86. If we omit from our
calculations those changes for which there were changes of two-
tenths of one per cent. or less, the coefficient of association is
even higher : + 0·96. The coefficient of association between
changes in money wages and changes in the " uncorrected " index
of real wages on the same basis is + 0·94.

Mr. Keynes' conclusions, which are not borne out statistically

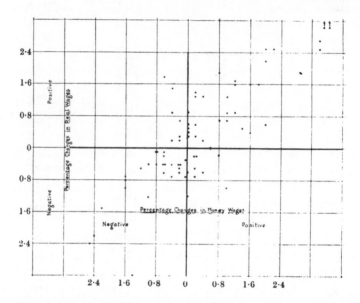

for this period, are based upon three assumptions which, in my
opinion, are not realistic. The first is that money wages only
begin to rise after unemployment has fallen to quite a low figure.
The second is that increases in output beyond this level—in the
region in which money wages are rising—are associated with
rising marginal costs, even in the absence of rises in money wages.
Finally, he assumes that the degree of competition does not
change appreciably as between slump and boom, and, more
important, that price revisions occur frequently. It is because
none of these assumptions truly portrayed conditions in the
United States, because there were many wage-goods the prices
of which were inflexible, and because marginal cost curves were

[1] G. Yule, *An Introduction to the Theory of Statistics*, p. 38.

not inclined positively, that we get a positive association when we should expect, on Mr. Keynes' assumptions, the association to be inverse and negative.

Postscript.—Further analysis of the material, undertaken after this note had been set up in proof, brought to light certain results relevant to this inquiry. These have to do with the relationship between changes in real wages per hour and changes in man-hours of employment.

The data for man-hours are derived from the industries, mentioned above, for which we have wage data. If changes in man-hours are related to changes in " real hourly wages, uncorrected " a rather high negative association is to be found. For the period of 75 months, considered above, the coefficient of association is —0·64, and with the exclusion of changes of two-tenths of one per cent. or less, the coefficient stands at —0·75. That is to say, changes in real hourly wages are in general opposite in direction from changes in man-hours of work. However, it is surprising that there is a less close association between changes in the " corrected " (cf. above) figures for real wages and man-hours. In this case, the coefficient stood at only —0·48. LORIE TARSHIS

Tufts College,
Massachusetts.

[2]

The Economic Journal, **90** *(March 1980)*, 51–73
Printed in Great Britain

THE CASE FOR SUBSIDISING EXTRA JOBS*

Unemployment is expected to remain high for some time. Given the well-known problems of general reflation, it is worth exploring other possible anti-unemployment measures. The one we shall consider in this paper is the marginal employment subsidy. Under such a scheme, any firm which expands its employment will be paid a subsidy of, say, £20 a week for each additional job it provides above its average level of employment during some base period.

Such a scheme was first proposed in Britain in Layard (1976) and Layard and Nickell (1976). A similar scheme was put forward in the TUC Economic Reviews for 1976 and 1977, and a mini version was introduced in the 1977 Budget. By January 1979 it had been extended to all firms with under 200 workers except for service industries outside the development areas.[1] The actual scheme differed from ours both in its limited coverage and because the subsidy is only paid for six months after the expansion occurs. The scheme which is analysed here visualises a take-up period of about two years, with the additional jobs being subsidised for a considerably longer period during which there is a gradual phasing out of the payments. We present the general arguments for the scheme in Section I, followed by a discussion of the analytical model in Section II. Section III assesses the likely impact of the scheme and compares it with a number of other possible policies; we conclude with more general remarks.

I. SOME GENERAL ARGUMENTS

A country with large-scale unemployment is in a familiar dilemma, which can be crudely depicted thus. General reflation, by tax cuts or expenditure increases, will have bad effects on the balance of payments, and on the budget deficit and prices. The balance of payments might be remedied by a devaluation – but this only helps if it is possible to reduce the real wage. For devaluation involves price increases. Without real wage resistance these price increases could be once-for-all; but if real wage resistance makes it impossible to reduce real wages, the price increases will only call forth wage increases which will obliterate the improvement in the balance of payments.[2] Moreover, however wages are determined, reflation is bound to worsen the budget deficit, which is bad for prices, investment or both.

These harmful effects would stem equally from ordinary tax cuts or from, say, a general employment subsidy. However, a subsidy to *marginal* employment or output offers a different range of opportunities. Since a marginal value-added subsidy is difficult to administer in a period of inflation, we shall confine

---

* We are grateful to David Allen, Lucien Foldes, Richard Jackman, Lord Kaldor and Gosta Rehn for helpful discussions, and to John Flemming, John Black and the referee for useful comments.

[1] The U.S. Employment Tax Credit is another version of the same basic idea. See Ashenfelter (1977).
[2] This has been used as an argument for import controls, but these involve other familiar problems.

ourselves to a marginal employment subsidy.[1] The ideal arrangement would be to *confine the subsidy to extra jobs provided as a result of the subsidy*. Such a 'marginal' job subsidy has enormous advantages over a general one. A given expenditure, if concentrated on marginal workers, will generate many more jobs than the same expenditure spread over all workers. We discuss the reasons more fully in the next section. But the basic idea is this. Any subsidy can have only a limited effect on domestic demand. For, taking wages as given, it has its effect mainly by reducing prices, and prices cannot fall below the average cost of the marginal firm. So, since the price elasticity of aggregate domestic demand is low, the effect of *any* subsidy upon domestic demand is limited. But with exports and import-substitutes matters are quite different, and a marginal subsidy can have a much bigger effect than an average subsidy costing the same amount. For many firms are price-takers in markets for internationally traded goods. Thus a large fall in the marginal cost of producing them will have a profound effect on the quantity sold, even if there is only a small fall in their average costs. Since exports and import-substitutes will rise, the balance of payments is likely to improve. And since the same expenditure generates more jobs this way than if it were spent on general reflation, the budget deficit is much less adversely affected. In fact, an ideal marginal job subsidy would pay for itself. For where an extra man was employed, the saving on unemployment relief plus additional taxes paid would exceed the subsidy, unless the subsidy were very large.

The advantage of a counter-cyclical marginal subsidy would be further strengthened if it were only paid out for additional jobs provided *within two years*. Such a device would encourage firms to bring forward their expansion plans so as to qualify for the subsidy, and quite substantial employment effects might be secured by relatively small expenditures of public money. Further dynamic gains might be secured if initially output grew faster than demand, inducing downward pressure on prices (Rehn, 1975). In addition, if the subsidy were at a flat rate for each extra worker, it would encourage firms to produce extra output by employing extra men, rather than by lengthening the hours of those already employed. So there would be fewer people unemployed at any given level of capacity utilisation, and thus, one hopes, less inflationary pressure at any particular level of unemployment.

We seem to have found the philosopher's stone. But is an ideal marginal wage subsidy administratively possible? Unfortunately not. For it requires that the government can get firms to report truthfully what their employment would have been in the absence of the subsidy. In principle this is what they are meant to do to obtain the UK Temporary Employment Subsidy.[2] To get this a firm has to 'prove' that it would have made redundant 10 or more workers in the absence of the subsidy. Having proved this, it qualifies for £20 per week for a year for each job preserved. But proving these claims has become an increasingly slippery business. It would be even more difficult to require expanding firms to

---

[1] If the word subsidy is unattractive, the same scheme could be conceived as a rebate to employers' National Insurance contributions.

[2] This is now being phased out.

prove that they would not have expanded their labour force but for the subsidy. And yet it is at least as important to induce expanding firms to expand more, as it is to induce contracting firms to contract less. The main reason why unemployment has risen in Britain is not that more people have become unemployed, but that those who are unemployed have remained unemployed longer. So what can be done?

We propose a perfectly general subsidy to *all* new jobs created, whether due to the subsidy or not. If introduced in year t, the scheme could be guaranteed to last in this form until the end of year $t+2$ and to go on being paid thereafter in relation to the average number of jobs in year $t+2$ or the then current level, whichever is the less. However, the subsidy per worker would fall progressively to zero over, say, four years. The reason for a six-year guarantee is that this will induce employers to act more strongly in taking on workers before year $t+3$, while the gradual reduction in the subsidy should discourage them from any precipitate layoffs as the subsidy is dismantled. If, of course, the gloomier forecasts of unemployment prove right, then the subsidy could be extended later.

The subsidy would have to relate to changes in employment at the level of the firm, not of the establishment. For, if it related to the latter, this would encourage firms to transfer jobs from one establishment to another and so obtain the subsidy without providing extra jobs. If two firms merged, the original calculated level of those employed in year t should include workers in both the constituent firms.[1] The subsidy would be paid at, say, £20 a week for full-time workers, and £10 for part-timers. The flat rate nature of the subsidy means, of course, that it raises the relative demand for unskilled workers. But its supreme virtue is its administrative simplicity. The firm would supply an easily checked record of its employment and be paid the relevant sum.[2]

Clearly it would be nice to analyse the effects of such a scheme in a fully dynamic model. However, economic science does not seem to be at the stage where such an analysis is possible. We therefore confine our analysis to the medium-term impact of the scheme as indicated by a relatively simple static macro model.

[1] The definition of 'firm' would be the same as for Corporation Tax.

[2] The idea is not new. It dates back to at least April 1932 when it was an important part of the German recovery measures announced by the then Chancellor Von Papen (Rustow, 1932). By the 'Papen Plan' employers were paid a large subsidy per week for each additional job created after the plan was announced, and the Chancellor said that he expected this to reduce unemployment by 1¾ million. Unfortunately, it is difficult to isolate the actual effects of the measure, partly because it was accompanied by a very large cut in business taxes. However, the actual course of German unemployment is striking. The number of unemployed (seasonally adjusted) was climbing steadily until it reached 5¾ million in August 1932. It then turned down quite sharply, falling by a quarter of a million within four months, over a million within a year, and nearly three million within two years. Meanwhile, of course, Hitler had come to power in January 1933, but his expansion of public expenditure can have had little impact within the first year of the Papen Plan. More important perhaps, the world recovery also began in 1933, but since German exports continued to decline, the German recovery must have occurred to some extent independently of trends elsewhere. Perhaps on the strength of this experience, the West Germans again operated a job-expansion subsidy in 1975. The fraction of the wage subsidised was over a half. But the payment lasted only six months, the period during which the extra jobs had to be created was short, the extra jobs had be be occupied by men already unemployed for over three months, and the scheme was confined to areas of high unemployment (about a third of the country). Given this, it is perhaps not surprising that the subsidy was only claimed for about 90,000 workers.

II. A MACRO MODEL

We start by presenting a Keynesian model and then consider a monetarist variant. Both of these models are simple-minded but we feel that they capture most of the crucial points. They are based on a fixed money wage and a fixed exchange rate, for reasons which we shall explain at the beginning of the next section.

Starting with the less controversial aspects of our model we first have the *ex ante* equilibrium condition

$$y = e\left[y^d, \frac{\Pi(1 - t_2)}{p}\right] + g + \frac{x}{p} - \frac{p_m\, m(p, y, p_m)}{p}. \tag{1}$$

y is real domestic value added and e is private expenditure which comprises both consumption and investment and is a function of personal real disposable wage income, y^d, and real after-tax profits, $\Pi(1 - t_2)/p$, where t_2 is the rate of profits tax and p is the domestic price level. g is real government expenditure, x is the value of exports, m is real imports, all of which are assumed to be inputs, and p_m is the price of imports in pounds. p_m is assumed to be normalised so that it is initially equal to p. It is worth commenting on the aggregation of private consumption and investment in the light of the fact that we are proposing a wage subsidy which will presumably have an adverse relative price effect on investment in the long run. Since the subsidy is only temporary, however, and applies to but a small proportion of the work force, it will only have a tiny relative price impact on total investment demand, which may safely be ignored.[1]

Disposable wage income, y^d, comprises real after-tax wages and unemployment benefits. We treat earnings as subject to a proportional tax, t_1, since, in the medium term with given wages, aggregate earnings vary mainly due to changes in the numbers employed. Real unemployment benefit is paid only to some fraction of the difference between full employment n^*, and the number currently employed, n. Thus when we say that the total of real unemployment benefit is $u(n^* - n)$, the coefficient u has to allow for cyclical variations in labour force participation as well as the fact that not all the unemployed receive benefits. Thus we have

$$y^d = \frac{wn(1 - t_1)}{p} + u(n^* - n), \tag{2}$$

where w is the exogenous money wage. Profits Π equal domestic value added less labour costs. The subsidy is, of course, a (negative) part of labour costs. If we assume that n_0 is base period employment, $\bar{n}$ is the number of workers who receive the subsidy minus the expansion of aggregate employment and s is the proportional subsidy, then the total government handout is $sw(n - n_0 + \bar{n})$. Profits are then given by

$$\Pi = \frac{py}{1 + t_3} - wn + (n - n_0 + \bar{n})\, ws, \tag{3}$$

---

[1] We have computed that a 30 % wage subsidy lasting for four years would affect private investment to the tune of less than ½ %. This computation was performed assuming a putty-clay world and an ex-ante elasticity of substitution of 0·77, an estimate taken from Hausman (1974).

where t_3 is the rate of indirect taxes. An important point to notice about the subsidy is that some firms which would have contracted in the absence of the subsidy will in fact expand in order to obtain it. This has two consequences. First, it implies that $\bar{n}$ is not equal to the total of gross expansions that would have occurred in the absence of the subsidy with aggregate employment unchanged. Second, it has the consequence that $\bar{n}$ is a function of the size of the subsidy. We shall henceforward assume that this effect is small (being mainly confined to firms in the export sector) and may therefore be ignored. (Its importance is in any case proportional to the level of subsidy s and therefore affects only the scale of the optimum subsidy.)

On the production side we assume the simple relationship

$$y = f(n), \tag{4}$$

where f' is assumed to be positive but we make no assumptions concerning f''. In order to close the model it remains for us to specify an export function and a relationship between prices, wages and employment. This latter function is of vital importance and, if we are to use this model to determine the order of magnitude of the impact of a marginal wage subsidy, we must choose a function which bears some relationship to known facts.

In textbook macroeconomic models of this type the function most commonly used is the equality between the marginal product of labour and the (marginal) real wage which is a necessary condition for profit maximisation by a price-taking firm.[1] So we have

$$f'(n) = w/p, \tag{5}$$

which determines aggregate employment as a simple function of the marginal real wage. Unfortunately there are two extremely strong objections to the use of such an equation in an aggregate model. First, it implies that the level of employment is inversely related to the real wage whereas we know that real wages (net of trend) do not move contra-cyclically during business cycles. Second, we are not aware of any satisfactory estimated aggregate labour demand function which is specified in terms of equation (5), or a dynamised version of it, without including output.[2] Since we are concerned to use our model to make rough predictions of the impact of policy changes, to use a relationship such as (5), which is completely at variance with observed facts, is clearly out of the question.

The rejection of equation (5) seems to neutralise what is, at first sight, one of the major arguments in favour of a *marginal* wage subsidy. A naïve microeconomic analysis might conclude that since a profit-maximising firm is solely concerned with the *marginal* wage in determining its output and employment levels, a large subsidy on the wages of marginal employees would have a dramatic effect on the firm's level of employment at very little cost. This argument is, however, grossly misleading at a more aggregate level at least in a closed economy. Suppose *all* the firms in a competitive industry in equilibrium

---

[1] See for example, Dernberg and McDougall (1960), chapter 11.
[2] Killingsworth (1970) discusses a very large selection. See also Hamermesh (1977).

are offered a marginal wage subsidy and there is a consequent dramatic éxpansion in industry output. This will immediately lead to an equally dramatic fall in price in this industry and since average costs will have fallen but a little, the firms will be making losses. The industry will then contract, and in the new equilibrium the price of output will be equal to average cost in the marginal firm. Aggregate employment in the industry will have risen only to the extent that average cost has fallen as a result of the marginal subsidy; that is, not very much. This is of course a long-run argument, and since the subsidy is but a short-term phenomenon it is difficult to say precisely what will happen in a short period. If all firms in the industry were of identical efficiency, we might argue that in the short run they would implicitly collude to avoid making losses, in which case the short-run expansion would be determined again on the basis of average cost pricing as in the long run. This is the *worst possible result* as far as the marginal policy is concerned. If the firms differ in efficiency, those which are most efficient would be able to expand output to maximise their profits without fear of making a loss due to the fall in price when all their competitors do the same. Temporary losses will, however, be inflicted on the marginal firm which might be borne in the short term. In this case industry output would be determined to some extent by marginal cost and the expansion would be greater than if output and price were determined exclusively on an average-cost basis. Nevertheless, we feel it is better to err somewhat on the side of caution and suppose that prices, at least in the home market, are determined by the average cost of the representative firm. We shall, therefore, assume an aggregate 'normal' cost pricing relationship which has some empirical support from Godley and Nordhaus (1972) and Sargan (1977). Prices are determined as a fixed mark-up on the 'normal' average cost of production where 'normal' means that inputs and outputs are taken to be on their trend paths. The resulting equation for the home price level is then given by

$$p = (1+\pi)[w\hat{n} + p_m\hat{m} - (n+\bar{n}-n_0)ws\alpha]/(\hat{y}+\hat{m}). \tag{6}$$

The 'hats' indicate trend levels, π is the mark-up including the indirect tax rate, t_3,[1] and α is the proportion of the subsidy which is 'passed on' in price reductions.[2] The denominator is equal to gross output, the sum of domestic value added, $\hat{y}$, and imports, $\hat{m}$, all of which are assumed to be inputs into some firm.[3]

It is worth noting, in the context of the marginal employment subsidy scheme, that in equation (6) we have made no distinction between expanding firms in receipt of the subsidy and contracting firms which receive nothing. Instead we have averaged over the two sets of firms to produce the aggregate price index p.

[1] Note that the total indirect tax revenue is given by $pt_3y/(1+t_3)$, where $p/(1+t_3)$ is the price before taxes are added. We implicitly assume that $(1+\pi) = (1+\pi')(1+t_3) \simeq (1+\pi'+t_3)$, where π' is the non-tax mark-up.

[2] It is worth emphasising again that even if all the subsidy is 'passed on', this is still somewhat pessimistic and ignores the fact that some firms in the home market will determine output on the basis of marginal cost. In this case we have $p = w(1-s)/f'(n)$ and the subsidy has a dramatic effect compared with (6), even when $\alpha = 1$.

[3] Remember that p_m has been normalised to be equal to the initial value of p and is, therefore, approximately equal to p throughout.

Within this index there will be some changes in relative prices which will lead to so-called displacement effects; that is, falling prices and expanding employment in some firms will directly contribute to contractions in others. This is another aspect of the dependence of $\bar{n}$ on s which we gave reasons above for ignoring. The displacement effects will be automatically netted out when we consider any expansions in demand due to falls in the aggregate price level p, and consequently they need trouble us no further.

The final equation we must specify in our model is the one which determines the value of exports, x. Pricing in export markets must be sharply distinguished from the policies employed by firms in the home market, particularly in so far as they relate to marginal costs. First, a firm which is a price-taker in export markets will export up to the point where marginal cost is equal to the price received, but with the difference that a subsidy on marginal units will lead to expansion of output *without* any corresponding fall in price, since foreign firms competing in the same markets will not be expanding their output simultaneously. Furthermore, a marginal subsidy may also enable a firm to enter a new export market where the price was originally too low to cover marginal costs.[1] Second, a monopolistic firm in an export market will use marginal costs to determine its optimal price, and any marginal subsidies are likely to have more of an expansionary effect than in the home market because elasticities of demand are generally likely to be higher.

Evidence that marginal considerations are deemed important by exporters is provided by the results of surveys described in Gribbin (1971) (particularly pp. 19–20) and in Rosendale (1973) (pp. 47–8). Rosendale notes that about one-third of the firms in her sample of 29 large engineering companies sell abroad at prices which do not fully cover overhead costs, and Gribbin records that 68 % of firms in his sample distinguish marginal costs in their accounting systems, with those firms making this distinction selling abroad at prices considerably lower relative to the home price than those that do not. Rosendale also reveals that over half of the products sold abroad by the firms in her sample are, in fact, sold in price-taking markets (Table 2, p. 47).

This analysis thus leads us to consider in our model three types of exports. Type (1): those sold by firms who simply charge a mark-up on average normal cost, which yields for them a total export revenue $px_1(p)$. Type (2): those sold by firms which equate marginal revenue to marginal cost in export markets, yielding a total revenue $p_2 x_2(p_2)$, where p_2 is the export price index for such firms. Type (3): those sold by firms which are price takers in export markets, giving a revenue $p_3 x_3(c)$, where p_3 is the world price level in export markets and c is the marginal cost of production. p_2, p_3 are both measured in pounds and hence the total value of exports is given by

$$x = px_1(p) + p_2 x_2(p_2) + p_3 x_3(c). \tag{7}$$

Our Keynesian macro model is now completely determined by equations (1), (2), (3), (4), (6) and (7). In the next section it will also be convenient to have a

---

[1] Such entry will, however, be restricted by the knowledge that the subsidy is only temporary, particularly if the fixed costs of entry are considerable.

monetarist model to hand, and here we go to the opposite extreme and simply add a quantity theory equation, based on domestic absorption, to equations (4), (6) and (7). Thus we have

$$M = pk\left(y + \frac{p_m\,m(y,\,p,\,p_m)}{p} - \frac{x}{p}\right),\tag{8}$$

M being aggregate nominal money balances.

III. THE IMPACT OF THE MARGINAL EMPLOYMENT SUBSIDY AND OTHER POLICIES

We are now ready to look at the effects of the marginal employment subsidy. Our main aim is to compare these with the effects of other policies generating the same number of extra jobs, in order to see which policy or mix of policies is the most desirable. For this purpose we need only look at the initial effect of each policy on the level of employment, the balance of payments,[1] the budget deficit and the short-run price level. The policies we consider are non-marginal employment subsidies, government expenditure changes, indirect tax changes and exchange rate changes (all other policy effects being computed for fixed exchange rates). The resulting effects (which we shall eventually show in Table 3) can be used to answer the following types of question.

(i) If the exchange rate is taken as fixed, are there policy mixes which dominate others in terms of their effects on the balance of payments, the budget deficit and the short-run price level?

(ii) If the exchange rate is flexible, so that the sum of balance of payments effects has to be zero, are there policy mixes which dominate others in terms of their effects on the budget deficit and the short-run price level?[2]

Notice that we do not need to trace through the longer-run effects of changes in the budget deficit and the short-run price level since these will be the same, independent of the policy mix that brought them about. All the formulae used are derived in the Appendix. We shall only consider impact effects since the multipliers in all these policies turn out to be approximately unity, as we also demonstrate in the Appendix.

The effect of the marginal employment subsidy on employment comes about via a number of distinct channels. Taking the Keynesian model first, it is clear that it will have a direct impact on expenditure via the changes in prices and profits consequent on the subsidy being paid for intra-marginal workers, who are $\bar{n}$ in number. This leads to the following proportional employment effects $(\Delta n/n)$.

Proportional effect via price reductions increasing real personal incomes

$$= \frac{\alpha e_1(1 - t_1)}{e(1 + \pi)(1 + b)}\frac{\bar{n}s}{n}.\tag{9}$$

[1] We assume no change in the capital account.

[2] If we wished to proceed formally we could find the optimal mix of three policies by finding for each combination of three policies what level each policy would need to be set at in order to achieve a given Δn and zero ΔB and ΔD. We would then choose that policy mix which gave the lowest Δp.

Proportional effect via profits $= \dfrac{[1 - \alpha/(1+b)]\,e_2(1-t_2)}{e(1+\pi)}\,\dfrac{\tilde{n}s}{n}.$ (10)

Proportional effect via price reductions leading to import substitution

$$= \frac{\alpha\tilde{m}e_{mp}}{e(1+\tilde{m})}\,\frac{\tilde{n}s}{n}.$$ (11)

Proportional effect via price reductions leading to increased

$$\text{type (1) exports} = \frac{-\alpha\tilde{x}_1(1+e^1)}{e(1+\tilde{m})}\,\frac{\tilde{n}s}{n}.$$ (12)

In these formulae, e_1 is the marginal propensity to consume out of personal disposable income, e_2 is the same out of profits, $\tilde{m}$, $\tilde{x}_1$ are the ratios of imports and type (1) exports to domestic value added and e_{mp} and e_1 are the elasticities of imports and type (1) exports with respect to the home price level. Finally b is the import bill divided by labour costs and $e = nf'(n)(1+b)/y(1+\tilde{m})$, where $nf'(n)/y$ is the elasticity of value added with respect to the labour input.[1]

There are a number of things worth noting about these results. First, these expansionary effects bear no relation to the marginality of the employment subsidy but arise solely from the lump sum subsidy, $\tilde{n}s$, received by firms. This aspect of the marginal employment subsidy is thus identical to any other policy which transfers funds directly to firms. Its effectiveness depends crucially on how much of the subsidy is 'passed on' in price reductions for, if it accrues entirely as profits, we have $\alpha = 0$ and effects (9), (11) and (12) are all zero because there are no price reductions. The only impact is via expenditure out of profits, which in the short term is generally considered to be rather low at the margin.

The impact on employment which is associated particularly with the marginal aspect of the policy, is that due to increases in exports, especially in markets where firms operate as price takers. Here we have the following.

Proportional effect via type (2) and type (3) exports

$$= \frac{s(1+b)}{e(1+\tilde{m})}\left[\tilde{x}_2(1+e^2)\frac{\partial \log p_2}{\partial s} + \tilde{x}_3 e^3 \frac{\partial \log c}{\partial s}\right].$$ (13)

$\tilde{x}_2$, $\tilde{x}_3$ are the ratios of type (2) and (3) exports to domestic value added and e^2, e^3 are the elasticities with respect to selling price p_2 and marginal cost c, respectively. The point to notice about this effect is that it operates completely at the margin, both p_2 and c being crucially affected by marginal changes. In this particular aspect, the policy is similar to an export subsidy, albeit of a rather special kind. In determining the size of the subsidy's impact on the selling price p_2 and marginal cost c, it is not necessarily the case that all exporting firms will be in receipt of the subsidy. If the exporting firm happens to be simultaneously contracting in the home market, it will only take up the subsidy if its export sales are a large enough proportion of its total output, so that its

---

[1] If the reader becomes confused by the number of symbols, their definitions are repeated in a compact form on pp. 61-2 together with Table 1.

induced expansion in exports outweighs the home market contraction and leads to a take-up of the subsidy. This we shall assume to be the typical case. The whole difficulty could, however, be avoided altogether if we took the baseline employment level beyond which the subsidy is paid as being, say, 90 % of the current employment level. In such circumstances nearly all firms would receive the subsidy, and this would have the additional advantage of discouraging contractions as well as encouraging expansions. It would, however, be more costly, as we shall see.

The fact that a particular policy is expansionary is, of course, of no particular interest unless it can also be demonstrated that it is particularly unsusceptible to the usual drawbacks of such policies. As we have already indicated, these drawbacks may be conveniently classified under the headings of balance of payments effects, budget deficit effects and price level effects, and we shall consider each in turn. Because one of the major expansionary effects of the policy comes via exports, it is to be expected that the balance of payments effect will be favourable. The change in the balance of payments, B, which is defined by

$$B = x - p_m m(y, p, pm) \qquad (14)$$

is given by

$$\frac{\Delta B}{py} = \frac{\alpha[\tilde{m}e_{mp} - \tilde{x}_1(1 + e^1)]}{(1 + b)}\left(\frac{\tilde{n}}{n} + \frac{\Delta n}{n}\right)s + \left[\tilde{x}_2(1 + e^2)\frac{\partial \log p_2}{\partial s} + \tilde{x}_3 e^3 \frac{\partial \log c}{\partial s}\right]s$$
$$- \frac{\tilde{m}e_{my}e(1 + \tilde{m})}{1 + b}\frac{\Delta n}{n}, \qquad (15)$$

$\Delta n/n$ being the proportional employment effect of the policy. The first term is the favourable effect of import substitution and type (1) export expansion brought about by the falling price level, and the second is the direct export expansion brought about by the fall in marginal costs. The last is the only negative effect, which is the rise in imports due to the expansion of domestic expenditure. As we shall see, this should generally be offset by the export terms. Turning now to the budget deficit, D, this may be written as

$$\frac{D}{p} = g + \frac{sw}{p}(n - n_0 + \tilde{n}) + u(n^* - n) - t_1 \frac{wn}{p} - \frac{t_2 \Pi}{p} - \frac{t_3 y}{1 + t_3}, \qquad (16)$$

where constant elements are omitted for convenience. In order to see the impact of the subsidy clearly, we make the not unreasonable assumption that falls in the price level affect the tax and expenditure elements of the government balance sheet in an identical manner. The one exception to this is that we shall include the loss in corporation tax due to the fall in profits following the fall in prices. The change in the budget deficit resulting from the policy is then given by

$$\frac{\Delta D}{py} = \left[\frac{(1 + b)(1 + \pi)}{(1 + \tilde{m})}\right]^{-1}\left(\left\{1 - t_2\left[1 - \frac{\alpha(1 + \pi)}{(1 + \tilde{m})(1 + t_3)}\right]\right\}\frac{\tilde{n}s}{n}\right.$$
$$\left. - \left[\frac{u}{w/p} + t_1 - s + t_2 k + \frac{t_3 e(1 + \pi)}{1 + t_3}\right]\frac{\Delta n}{n}\right), \qquad (17)$$

where
$$k = e\,\frac{(1+\pi)}{1+t_3} - (1-s).$$

The important point to notice here is that the impact of the policy depends crucially on the money paid out to firms which would have expanded without any increase in aggregate employment, $\bar{n}s$, compared with the expansion induced by the policy, Δn.

Finally, the impact effect of the policy on prices can be nothing other than favourable and is given by

$$\frac{\Delta p}{p} = -\frac{\alpha s}{(1+b)}\left(\frac{\bar{n}}{n} + \frac{\Delta n}{n}\right). \tag{18}$$

Here, of course, the extent to which the subsidy is 'passed on' in price reductions, as measured by α, is the vital factor.

Before considering the order of magnitude of these effects it is worth noting the employment changes which would ensue if the monetarist model was correct. The impact effect is given by

$$\frac{\Delta n}{n} = \frac{\alpha \bar{n}s}{en} + \frac{\alpha}{e}\left[\tilde{m}e_{mp} - \tilde{x}_1(1+e^1)\right]\frac{\bar{n}}{n}s + \frac{s(1+b)}{e(1+\tilde{m})}\left[\tilde{x}_2(1+e^2)\frac{\partial \log p_2}{\partial s} + \tilde{x}_3 e^3\frac{\partial \log c}{\partial s}\right]. \tag{19}$$

The similarities with the Keynesian model are most striking, with the first term corresponding to the domestic expenditure effects (9) and (10), the second to the import substitution and type (1) export effects (11) and (12), and the last being identical to the export effects of (13). The differences are in fact minimal and, unlike some other policies, such as changing government expenditure, it matters little whether one takes a Keynesian or a monetarist view of the world; the efficacy of the policy is unaltered. We shall hereinafter use the Keynesian model to analyse all policies.

In order to discuss the likely size of these policy impacts it is necessary to attach numbers to the parameters which appear in the formulae. Our plan here is to fix the relatively non-contentious ones and then consider variations in the less certain parameters, grouping them under pessimistic, reasonable and optimistic headings. The parameters considered as non-contentious are allotted values as follows.

$$b = \frac{\text{import bill}}{\text{labour costs}} = 0{\cdot}35;\ \tilde{m} = \frac{\text{import bill}}{\text{domestic value added}} = 0{\cdot}30,$$

$$\tilde{x}_i = \frac{\text{type } i \text{ exports}}{\text{domestic value added}};\ \tilde{x}_1 = 0{\cdot}15;\ \tilde{x}_2 = \tilde{x}_3 = 0{\cdot}075,$$

$e_{my} = $ elasticity of imports with respect to income $= 2,$

$t_1 = $ tax rate on personal incomes $= 0{\cdot}15,$

$t_2 = $ *marginal* tax rate on profits $= 0{\cdot}5,$

$\pi = $ mark-up $= 0{\cdot}25$ of which $0{\cdot}15$ is indirect taxes $(t_3),$

$$\frac{u}{w/p} = \frac{\text{marginal reduction in benefit payment}}{\text{wage}} = 0{\cdot}3,$$

$$\frac{f'(n)\,n}{y} = \text{elasticity of value added with respect to labour input} = 1\cdot5, \; \cdot$$

e_1 = marginal propensity to spend out of personal disposable income = $0\cdot8$,

$$\frac{\partial \log p_2}{\partial s} = \frac{\text{proportional change in type (2) export prices}}{\text{subsidy}},$$

$$= \frac{\text{proportional change in marginal cost}}{\text{subsidy}} \; \begin{array}{l}\text{(assuming constant}\\ \text{demand elasticity),}\end{array}$$

$$= -\frac{\text{wage costs}}{\text{total costs}} \text{ in export industries,}$$

$$= -0\cdot3.$$

It is worth noting that we have assumed half the exports to be priced at normal cost p, which is somewhat higher than the evidence suggests is correct. This may be thought of as adjusting for the fact that some price-taking exporters will not be in receipt of the subsidy because of home market contractions, by effectively lumping them in with the normal-cost pricing group. For the contentious parameters we have three sets of values and the details are set out in Table 1.

Table 1

Alternative Assumptions on Contentious Parameters

	Pessimistic	Reasonable	Optimistic
α = proportion of the subsidy passed on in price reductions	0	$0\cdot5$	1
e_2 = marginal propensity to spend out of profits	0	$0\cdot5$	$0\cdot5$
e_{mp} = elasticity of imports with respect to the home price level	0	$0\cdot5$	1
$e^1 = e^2$ = price elasticity of demand for type (1) and (2) exports	-1	-1	-2
e^3 = marginal cost elasticity of supply of type (3) exports	$-0\cdot5$	-1	-1

Given these parameters, we present in Table 2 the impact effect of the marginal employment policy on employment, the balance of payments, the budget deficit and the price level. In order to incorporate as much information as possible into the table, we show at the bottom the general formula containing $\bar{n}/n$, the proportion of the labour force in receipt of the subsidy when aggregate employment remains fixed, and at the top the actual numbers resulting if $\bar{n}/n$ is set at 3%, 6% and 10%. The derivation of the first two figures is discussed in the Appendix. The 10% figure would arise if the baseline was taken as 90% of the current employment level, assuming that no firms were going to contract naturally by more than 10%. It should be borne in mind that the export effects for this latter policy will be larger than those we have predicted.

Under the reasonable assumptions, a marginal employment subsidy equal to

Table 2

Effect of a Marginal Employment Subsidy at Rate s

	Employment $\Delta n/n$	Balance of payments surplus $\Delta B/py$	Budget deficit $\Delta D/py$	Price level $\Delta p/p$	Budget deficit cost per job $\Delta D/\Delta n$
		If $\bar{n}/n = 0 \cdot 03$			
Pessimistic	$0 \cdot 0075s$	$0 \cdot 006s$	$0 \cdot 008s$	0	$1 \cdot 6py/n$
Reasonable	$0 \cdot 022s$	$0 \cdot 0084s$	$0 \cdot 004s$	$-0 \cdot 014s$	$0 \cdot 18py/n$
Optimistic	$0 \cdot 046s$	$0 \cdot 017s$	$-0 \cdot 003s$	$-0 \cdot 033s$	$-0 \cdot 06py/n$
		If $\bar{n}/n = 0 \cdot 06$			
Pessimistic	$0 \cdot 0075s$	$0 \cdot 006s$	$0 \cdot 019s$	0	$3 \cdot 8py/n$
Reasonable	$0 \cdot 030s$	$0 \cdot 005s$	$0 \cdot 012s$	$-0 \cdot 026s$	$0 \cdot 40py/n$
Optimistic	$0 \cdot 062s$	$0 \cdot 015s$	$0 \cdot 006s$	$-0 \cdot 06s$	$0 \cdot 1py/n$
		If $\bar{n}/n = 0 \cdot 10$			
Pessimistic	$0 \cdot 0075s$	$0 \cdot 006s$	$0 \cdot 034s$	0	$0 \cdot 7py/n$
Reasonable	$0 \cdot 040s$	0	$0 \cdot 026s$	$-0 \cdot 042s$	$0 \cdot 64py/n$
Optimistic	$0 \cdot 085s$	0	$0 \cdot 020s$	$-0 \cdot 096s$	$0 \cdot 24py/n$
		General formula			
Pessimistic	$0 \cdot 0075s$	$0 \cdot 006s$	$(0 \cdot 37n/\bar{n} - 0 \cdot 0033)s$	0	
Reasonable	$(0 \cdot 015 + 0 \cdot 25\bar{n}/n)s$	$(0 \cdot 012 - 0 \cdot 11\bar{n}/n)s$	$(0 \cdot 36\bar{n}/n - 0 \cdot 01)s$	$-(0 \cdot 4\bar{n}/n + 0 \cdot 002)s$	
Optimistic	$(0 \cdot 03 + 0 \cdot 54\bar{n}/n)s$	$(0 \cdot 024 - 0 \cdot 24\bar{n}/n)s$	$(0 \cdot 36\bar{n}/n - 0 \cdot 016)s$	$-(0 \cdot 9\bar{n}/n + 0 \cdot 006)s$	

one-third of average weekly earnings would yield an increase in employment of between 0·7 and 1·0 %, improve the balance of payments by between 0·2 and 0·3 % of G.N.P., worsen the budget deficit by between 0·2 and 0·5 % of G.N.P. and lower prices by between 0·5 and 0·9 %. The budget deficit cost per job is between £1,100 and £2,500 per annum, this figure being obtained by setting py/n in the last column at £5,000.[1] One of the drawbacks of the policy is its minuscule effect under pessimistic assumptions, with all the subsidy disappearing into profits never to emerge again. This could lead to a budget deficit cost per job as high as £19,000 per annum (with $\bar{n}/n = 6\%$) although under these circumstances the government would have no trouble in borrowing the money back again to finance the deficit, with little impact either on the money supply or interest rates. It is worth noting how susceptible the change in the budget deficit is to assumptions about $\bar{n}/n$, and this implies that there is a high degree of uncertainty attached to estimates of the budget deficit cost per job. On the other hand, if a baseline of 90 % of current employment were used, the value of $\bar{n}/n$ is almost certain to be around 0·1, with results illustrated in the third row of Table 2. The employment effects are generally larger but the budget deficit cost per job rises to around £3,750 per annum.

We next consider some other possible policies for comparative purposes, and

[1] The cost per job would be greatly reduced if the subsidy were confined to manufacturing. For the effect on exports would be more or less the same but the deadweight loss much reduced. The effects of the subsidy would then be very approximately as indicated in the bottom section of Table 2, but with $\bar{n}/n$ replaced by $\frac{1}{2}\bar{n}/n$, where $\bar{n}$ refers to the value it would take in the case of an economy-wide subsidy.

the ones we have chosen are a proportional labour subsidy, s', on all jobs, an increase in government expenditure, Δg, a change in the exchange rate, $\Delta \eta$, where η is the price of pounds in terms of foreign currency and a change in indirect taxes, Δt_3. In order to compute the impact of a devaluation we assume that the elasticity of import prices with respect to the exchange rate is $-2/3$ and that of type (2) export prices (in pounds) is $-1/2$. The impact effects of all these policies, given the same parameter values, are shown in Table 3.

Comparing the marginal employment subsidy with an across the board employment subsidy (such as a cut in employers' National Insurance contributions) we can see that a proportional marginal wage subsidy of one-third is equivalent in its employment effect to a non-marginal subsidy of about 3 %. But this latter would lead to a worsening of the balance of payments and a larger budget deficit cost per job. It is, therefore, an inferior policy. Similar remarks apply to a cut in indirect taxes.

The obvious advantage of a government expenditure increase is the comparative certainty about its effects, for, as can be seen from the table, these are insensitive to those parameter values which are crucial in determining the effects of the other policies. It should be remembered, however, that if the world is as monetarists view it, marginal employment subsidies remain highly effective whereas *ceteris paribus* government expenditure increases make no impact whatever. Furthermore, the balance of payments effects of government expenditure increases are adverse and the budget deficit cost per job is about £3,250 per year, higher than all but the most pessimistic calculations for marginal employment subsidies.[1]

Turning to the effects of a devaluation, we can see that the balance of payments effect of a marginal subsidy of one-third of average earnings is equivalent to a devaluation of about $1\frac{1}{2}$%. Devaluation, as an instrument of employment expansion, appears to be rather effective but it does, of course, have an adverse impact on the price level. It is an overt 'beggar my neighbour' policy which invites retaliation, whereas the marginal employment subsidy whose action is, in part, that of an export subsidy, is more of a covert 'beggar my neighbour' policy and only partly one at that. Of course, the fact that one is doing down the rest of the world by subtle rather than obvious means is not necessarily something to be pleased about, but then if the economically stronger countries of the world had not pursued such contractionary policies in the recent past, papers such as this might well not have been worth writing.

So far we have compared the marginal employment subsidy with each alternative in turn. The question remains as to whether there does not exist some combination of policies which is superior to the marginal subsidy. The obvious candidate is devaluation linked to a non-marginal employment subsidy or a cut in indirect taxes to offset the adverse price effects. A non-marginal employment subsidy of 2·6 % plus a devaluation of 2·9 % will have precisely

---

[1] The preceding argument does not allow for possible forms of government expenditure that are either markedly less import-intensive than general expenditure on goods and services, or that employ low wage labour, e.g. the Job Creation Scheme. On the effects of special labour market measures other than employment subsidies, see Layard (1979).

Table 3

Effects of Various Possible Reflationary Policies ($\bar{n}/n = 0.03$)

	Employment $\Delta n/n$	Balance of payments surplus $\Delta B/py$	Budget deficit $\Delta D/py$	Price level $\Delta p/p$	Budget deficit cost per job $\Delta D/\Delta n$
Pessimistic					
MES*	0·0075s	0·006s	0·008s	0	1·6py/n
NMES	0·005s'	−0·003s'	0·32s'	0	0·42 py/n
Govt expenditure	0·66Δg/y	−0·60Δg/y	0·43Δg/y	0	0·65py/n
Devaluation	0	0·13(−$\Delta\eta/\eta$)	0	0·18(−$\Delta\eta/\eta$)	—
Cut in indirect taxes	0·34(−Δt_3)	0·3(−Δt_3)	0·45(−Δt_3)	−0·8(−Δt_3)	1·3py/n
Reasonable					
MES	0·022s	0·0084s	0·004s	−0·014s	0·18py/n
NMES	0·24s'	−0·075s'	0·29s'	−0·38s'	1·40py/n
Govt expenditure	0·66Δg/y	−0·60Δg/y	0·43Δg/y	0	0·65py/n
Devaluation	0·10(−$\Delta\eta/\eta$)	0·16(−$\Delta\eta/\eta$)	−0·06(−$\Delta\eta/\eta$)	0·18(−$\Delta\eta/\eta$)	−0·60py/n
Cut in indirect taxes	0·42(−Δt_3)	0·18(−Δt_3)	0·38(−Δt_3)	−0·8(−Δt_3)	0·90py/n
Optimistic					
MES	0·046s	0·017s	−0·003s	−0·033s	−0·06py/n
NMES	0·58s'	−0·02s'	0·21s'	−0·75s'	0·41py/n
Govt expenditure	0·66Δg/y	−0·60Δg/y	0·43Δg/y	0	0·65py/n
Devaluation	0·22(−$\Delta\eta/\eta$)	0·26(−$\Delta\eta/\eta$)	−0·10(−$\Delta\eta/\eta$)	0·18(−$\Delta\eta/\eta$)	−0·48py/n
Cut in indirect taxes	0·54(−Δt_3)	0	−0·3(−Δt_3)	−0·8(−Δt_3)	−0·55py/n

* MES = marginal employment subsidy, NMES = non-marginal employment subsidy.

the same balance of payments and price level effects as a one-third marginal employment subsidy and will generate about 20 % more employment, but at over four times the budget deficit cost or over three times the budget deficit cost per job. Similarly, a 1·3 percentage point cut in indirect taxes plus a 3·2 % devaluation will again have the same balance of payments and price level impact as the marginal subsidy generating 17 % more employment at about three times the budget deficit cost per job.

One of the possible problems with our analysis of these policies, in particular with the marginal subsidy, is our assumption of a fixed exchange rate. If the subsidy generates an improvement in the balance of payments there is always, of course, the temptation to allow the exchange rate to move up, thereby reducing its employment effect and improving its effect on the home price level. This can clearly be avoided by combining the marginal subsidy with, say, tax cuts which can be such a size as to nullify the balance of payments effect. Thus, for example, a one-third marginal employment subsidy combined with an indirect tax cut of some 1·6 percentage points will have a zero balance of payments effect and generate an increase in employment of 1·4 %, although increasing the budget deficit by some 0·7 % of G.N.P. The combination of devaluation and indirect tax cuts, which achieves the same employment and balance of payment effects, has a budget deficit effect which is about 20 % worse and a fall in the price level which is some 15 % smaller.

Finally, there are a number of further general points to be made about the marginal employment subsidy. First, as has been made clear. the deadweight cost incurred through the payment of the subsidy to workers in firms which expand even at constant aggregate employment is crucial in determining the budget deficit cost per job. This deadweight cost is extremely difficult to estimate, and although our analysis in the Appendix comes up with a rather low figure of about 3 % of the labour force, this estimate has a very high variance and it could be a great deal higher.[1]

Another problem which we have not mentioned is the possibility that the expanding firms in a particular industry will obtain such a cost advantage over the remainder in the home market that they will drive them out of business. This is a particular danger given that their cost advantage will grow as their market share increases. The upshot would be to raise the deadweight burden to an enormous size while driving a large number of firms out of business. Given the limited time horizon of the proposed subsidy, however, this seems a somewhat unlikely scenario given that the typical firm would have to expand fairly dramatically in order to gain an appreciable cost advantage.[2]

The scheme has also been criticised as being a charter for over-manning.

---

[1] If the subsidised employment growth had an upper limit, this would exclude the deadweight cost of some very large expansions that would happen anyway.

[2] The scheme *has* to be contracyclically operated. For imagine a permanent scheme with the base period being moved forward by one period each period. Knowing this, a firm evaluating the undiscounted present value of the stream of subsidy associated with alternative employment streams would find them all the same. So the incentive to expand earlier rather than later would be fairly weak. Notice also that the scheme has to be introduced in an unexpected way otherwise firms will rig their level of employment in the base period (unless this is made very long).

But it is difficult to see why firms should create jobs where nothing is produced if it costs them £50 a week to do so. Overmanning may be a problem in many existing jobs, but it is hardly encouraged by steps to bring forward the creation of new jobs.

IV. CONCLUDING REMARKS

So we conclude that there is much to be said for a scheme whereby firms are paid a subsidy proportional to their increase in employment over its level in some initial period. Compared to a general employment subsidy costing the same amount of money, this is bound to generate more jobs (mainly in the export sector) and thus a healthier balance of payments and a smaller budget deficit. Concentration of the subsidy at the margin gives it that much more leverage. Compared to an increase in government expenditure, the performance of the marginal employment subsidy depends on the size of the deadweight subsidy to additional jobs that would have been provided anyway. However, provided this is not too large, the budget deficit cost per additional job is less for the marginal employment subsidy, and the balance of payments effects are always more favourable. So are the price level effects. Devaluation is of course an attractive alternative on all counts other than its price level effects. If there were real wage resistance, so that price increases led to equivalent wage increases, devaluation could not work. But the marginal employment subsidy works even if there is real wage resistance, since real wages improve slightly.

The analysis leading to these conclusions uses a 'normal' cost theory of pricing over the cycle. Thus the model involves an essentially recursive approach to the cyclical behaviour of the economy: wages determine prices, real demand determines output, and output determines employment. But similar conclusions to ours have been reached by economists using a longer term approach to the labour market in which employment is always a unique negative function of the real wage.[1] According to this approach, recent unemployment has been due to an excessive real wage, and a marginal wage subsidy would be a good antidote. It is not always the case that opposed theories lead to the same conclusion, and the fact that they do here gives us added confidence in putting forward our proposal.

APPENDIX

The Keynesian Model

The basic model consists of the following equations.

$$y = e\left[y^d, \frac{\Pi(1 - t_2)}{p}\right] + g + \frac{x}{p} - \frac{p_m m(p, y, p_m)}{p}, \tag{A 1}$$

$$y^d = \frac{wn(1 - t_1)}{p} + u(n^* - n), \tag{A 2}$$

---

[1] Flemming (1976). General employment subsidies were advocated by Kaldor (1936), using the same model. Our model could also lead to the conclusion that too high a real wage would lead to unemployment, but by a different mechanism: the excessive real wage would make impossible the devaluation needed to maintain balance of payments equilibrium at full employment.

$$\Pi = \frac{py}{1+t_3} - wn + (n - n_0 + \bar{n})\,ws, \qquad\qquad\qquad \text{(A 3)}$$

$$y = f(n), \qquad\qquad\qquad\qquad \text{(A 4)}$$

$$p = (1+\pi)[w\hat{n} + p_m\hat{m} - (n + \bar{n} - n_0)\,ws\alpha]/(\hat{y} + \hat{m}), \qquad \text{(A 5)}$$

$$x = px_1(p) + p_2 x_2(p_2) + p_3 x_3(c). \qquad\qquad\qquad \text{(A 6)}$$

In order to compute the employment effects of any particular policy, it is necessary to differentiate these equations with respect to the appropriate policy variable and solve for the derivative of n. In the case of changes in government expenditure the model is as above except that $s = 0$. For an across-the-board wage subsidy we assume, for simplicity, that (A 3) and (A 5) are replaced by

$$\Pi = \frac{py}{1+t_3} - w(1-s')\,n, \qquad\qquad\qquad \text{(A 3}a\text{)}$$

$$p = (1+\pi)[w(1-\alpha s')\,\hat{n} + p_m\hat{m}]/(\hat{y} + \hat{m}). \qquad\qquad \text{(A 5}a\text{)}$$

When the exchange rate, η, is changed, it must be remembered that p_m, p_2 and p_3 are all functions of η and that $\dfrac{\eta}{p_3}\dfrac{\partial p_3}{\partial \eta} = -1$, by definition.

In order to obtain the formulae below, the partial derivatives are evaluated at the point where $n = n_0$, $y = \hat{y}$, $m = \hat{m}$ and the balance of payments deficit is zero. It is further assumed that $n_0 = \hat{n}$.

First we state the *multipliers* for all the policies. For the marginal employment subsidy it is given by K^{-1}, where

$$K = 1 + \tilde{m}e_{my} - \frac{e_1}{e(1+\pi)}\left[(1-t_1)\left(1 - \frac{\alpha s}{1+b}\right) - \frac{u}{w/p}\right]$$

$$- \frac{e_2(1-t_2)}{e(1+\pi)}\left[\frac{e(1+\pi)}{1+t_3} - (1-s) - \alpha s\right] + \frac{\alpha s}{e(1+\tilde{m})}[\tilde{m}e_{mp} - \tilde{x}_1(1-e^1)].$$

For the other three policies it is given by K_1^{-1}, where $K_1 = K$ when $s = 0$. It is easy to check that for the parameter configurations used in the paper, $K_1 \simeq K \simeq 1$ and so the impact effects are the primary concern.

The *impact effects on employment* are as follows.

Marginal employment subsidy:

$$\frac{\partial n/n}{\partial s} = \frac{\alpha e_1(1-t_1)}{e(1+\pi)(1+b)}\frac{\bar{n}}{n} + \frac{[1-\alpha/(1+b)]e_2(1-t_2)}{e(1+\pi)}\frac{\bar{n}}{n}$$

$$+ \frac{\alpha}{e(1+\tilde{m})}[\tilde{m}e_{mp} - \tilde{x}(1+e^1)]\frac{\bar{n}}{n} + \frac{(1+b)}{e(1+\tilde{m})}\left[\tilde{x}_2(1+e^2)\frac{\partial \log p_2}{\partial s} + \tilde{x}_3 e^3 \frac{\partial \log c}{\partial s}\right].$$

Change in government expenditure:

$$\frac{\partial n/n}{\partial g/y} = \frac{(1+b)}{e(1+\tilde{m})}.$$

Employment subsidy:

$$\frac{\partial n/n}{\partial s'} = \frac{\alpha e_1(1-t_1)}{e(1+\pi)(1+b)} + \frac{[1-\alpha/(1+b)]e_2(1-t_2)}{e(1+\pi)} + \frac{\alpha}{e(1+\tilde{m})}[\tilde{m}e_{mp} - \tilde{x}_1(1+e^1)]$$

$$+ \frac{(1+b)}{e(1+\tilde{m})}\left[\tilde{x}_2(1+e^2)\frac{\partial \log p_2}{\partial s'} + \tilde{x}_3 e^3 \frac{\partial \log c}{\partial s'}\right].$$

Devaluation:

$$\frac{\partial n/n}{\partial \eta/\eta} = \frac{1+b}{e(1+\tilde{m})}\left\{(1+\pi)\tilde{m}e_{p_m\eta}\left[\frac{\tilde{x}_1(1+e^1)}{(1+\tilde{m})} - \frac{e_1(1-t_1)}{(1+\pi)(1+b)}\right.\right.$$

$$+ \frac{e_2(1-t_2)}{(1+\pi)(1+b)} - \frac{\tilde{m}e_{mp}}{(1+\tilde{m})}\right] - \tilde{m}(1-e_{mp})e_{p_m\eta} + \tilde{x}_1 e^1$$

$$+ \tilde{x}_2[(1+e_{p_2\eta})(1+e^2) - 1] - \tilde{x}_3(1-e^3)\bigg\}.$$

Cut in indirect taxes:

$$\frac{\partial n/n}{\partial t_3} = -\frac{(1+b)}{e(1+\tilde{m})(1+\pi)}\left\{\frac{e_1(1-t_1)(1+\tilde{m})}{(1+\pi)(1+b)} + e_2(1-t_2)\left[(1+\pi) - \frac{(1+\tilde{m})}{(1+\pi)(1+b)}\right]\right.$$

$$+ \tilde{m}e_{mp} - \tilde{x}_1(1+e^1)\bigg\}.$$

Next we present the *balance of payments effects* of the policies where the balance of payments is defined as

$$B = x - p_m m(y, p, p_m).$$

Marginal employment subsidy:

$$\frac{\partial B/py}{\partial s} = \frac{\alpha[\tilde{m}e_{mp} - \tilde{x}_1(1+e^1)]}{(1+b)}\left(\frac{\tilde{n}}{n} + \frac{\partial n/n}{\partial s/s}\right) + \tilde{x}_2(1+e^2)\frac{\partial \log p_2}{\partial s}$$

$$+ \tilde{x}_3 e^3 \frac{\partial \log c}{\partial s} - \frac{\tilde{m}e(1+\tilde{m})e_{my}}{(1+b)}\frac{\partial n/n}{\partial s}.$$

Change in government expenditure:

$$\frac{\partial B/py}{\partial g/y} = -\frac{\tilde{m}e_{my}e(1+\tilde{m})}{(1+b)}\frac{\partial n/n}{\partial g/y}.$$

Employment subsidy:

$$\frac{\partial B/py}{\partial s'} = \frac{\alpha[\tilde{m}e_{mp} - \tilde{x}_1(1+e^1)]}{(1+b)} + \tilde{x}_2(1+e^2)\frac{\partial \log p_2}{\partial s'} + \tilde{x}_3 e^3 \frac{\partial \log c}{\partial s'}$$

$$- \frac{\tilde{m}e(1+\tilde{m})e_{my}}{(1+b)}\frac{\partial n/n}{\partial s'}.$$

Devaluation:

$$\frac{\partial B/py}{\partial \eta/\eta} = \tilde{x}_1\left[e^1 + (1+e^1)\frac{(1+\pi)}{(1+\tilde{m})}\tilde{m}e_{p_m\eta}\right] + \tilde{x}_2[(1+e_{p_2\eta})(1+e^2) - 1]$$

$$- \tilde{x}_3(1-e^3) - \tilde{m}\left[(1-e_{mp}) + \tilde{m}\frac{(1+\pi)}{(1+\tilde{m})}e_{mp}\right]e_{p_m\eta} - \frac{\tilde{m}e(1+\tilde{m})e_{my}}{(1+b)}\frac{\partial n/n}{\partial \eta/\eta}.$$

Cut in indirect taxes:

$$\frac{\partial B/py}{\partial t_3} = \frac{1}{1+\pi}[\tilde{x}(1+e^1) - \tilde{m}e_{mp}] - \frac{\tilde{m}e_{my}e(1+\tilde{m})}{(1+b)}\frac{\partial n/n}{\partial t_3}.$$

The following are the *budget deficit effects*, where we assume that pure price level effects net out. The budget deficit is defined as

$$\frac{D}{p} = g + \frac{sw}{p}(n - n_0 + \bar{n}) + u(n^* - n) - t_1\frac{wn}{p} - t_2\frac{\Pi}{p} - t_3\frac{y}{1+t_3}.$$

In the formulae, $k = e(1+\pi)/(1+t_3) - (1-s)$, where $s = 0$ in the second and fourth policies.

Marginal employment subsidy:

$$\frac{\partial D/py}{\partial s} = \frac{(1+\tilde{m})}{(1+b)(1+\pi)}\left(\left\{1 - t_2\left[1 - \frac{\alpha(1+\pi)}{(1+\tilde{m})(1+t_3)}\right]\right\}\frac{\bar{n}}{n}\right.$$
$$\left. - \left[\frac{u}{w/p} + t_1 - s + t_2k + \frac{t_3e(1+\pi)}{1+t_3}\right]\frac{\partial n/n}{\partial s}\right).$$

Change in government expenditure:

$$\frac{\partial D/py}{\partial g/y} = 1 - \frac{(1+\tilde{m})}{(1+b)(1+\pi)}\left[\frac{u}{w/p} + t_1 + t_2k + \frac{t_3e(1+\pi)}{1+t_3}\right]\frac{\partial n/n}{\partial g/y}.$$

Employment subsidy:

$$\frac{\partial D/py}{\partial s'} = \frac{(1+\tilde{m})}{(1+b)(1+\pi)}\left(\left\{1 - t_2\left[1 - \frac{\alpha(1+\pi)}{(1+\tilde{m})(1+t_3)}\right]\right\}\right.$$
$$\left. - \left[\frac{u}{w/p} + t_1 - s' + t_2k + \frac{t_3e(1+\pi)}{1+t_3}\right]\frac{\partial n/n}{\partial s'}\right).$$

Devaluation:

$$\frac{\partial D/py}{\partial \eta/\eta} = -\frac{(1+\tilde{m})}{(1+b)(1+\pi)}\left[\frac{u}{w/p} + t_1 + t_2k + \frac{t_3e(1+\pi)}{1+t_3}\right]\frac{\partial n/n}{\partial \eta/\eta} - \frac{t_2(1+\pi)\tilde{m}e_{pm\,\eta}}{(1+\tilde{m})(1+t_3)}.$$

Cut in indirect taxes:

$$\frac{\partial D/py}{\partial t_3} = -\frac{1}{1+t_3} + t_2\left[1 - \frac{1}{(1+t_3)(1+\pi)}\right]$$
$$- \frac{(1+\tilde{m})}{(1+\pi)(1+b)}\left[\frac{u}{w/p} + t_1 + t_2k + \frac{t_3e(1+\pi)}{1+t_3}\right]\frac{\partial n/n}{\partial t_3}.$$

The *price level effects* are as follows.

Marginal employment subsidy:

$$\frac{\partial p/p}{\partial s} = -\frac{\alpha}{(1+b)}\left(s\frac{\partial n/n}{\partial s} + \frac{\bar{n}}{n}\right).$$

Change in government expenditure:

$$\frac{\partial p/p}{\partial g/y} = 0.$$

Employment subsidy:

$$\frac{\partial p/p}{\partial s'} = -\frac{\alpha}{(1+b)}.$$

Devaluation:

$$\frac{\partial p/p}{\partial \eta/\eta} = \frac{(1+\pi)}{(1+\tilde{m})} \tilde{m} e_{p_m \eta}.$$

Cut in indirect taxes:

$$\frac{\partial p/p}{\partial t_3} = \frac{1}{1+\pi}.$$

Finally, in this section of the Appendix we consider the impact of the marginal employment subsidy in the context of a monetarist model. Such a model would consist of equations (A 4), (A 5) and (A 6) plus

$$M = pk\left[y + \frac{p_m m(y, p, p_m)}{p} - \frac{x}{p}\right].$$

The employment effect of the marginal employment policy is given by

$$\frac{\partial n/n}{\partial s} = \left\{\frac{\alpha}{e}\left[1 + \tilde{m}e_{mp} - \tilde{x}_1(1+e^1)\right]\frac{\bar{n}}{n} + \frac{1+b}{e(1+\tilde{m})}\left[\tilde{x}_2(1+e^2)\frac{\partial \log p_2}{\partial c} + \tilde{x}_3 e^3 \frac{\partial \log c}{\partial s}\right]\right\}$$

$$\left\{1 + \tilde{m}e_{mv} - \frac{\alpha s}{e}\left[1 + \tilde{m}e_{mp} - \tilde{x}_1(1+e^1)\right]\right\}^{-1}.$$

This analysis has been rather cryptic. A full derivation is available from the authors on request.

Spontaneous Labour Force Growth

The marginal employment subsidy is paid to all firms which experience labour force growth. As we noted in the main body of the paper, the amount of subsidy paid out, even when aggregate employment is fixed, is a crucial parameter in predicting the effects of the policy. Here we present a derivation of the likely size of this parameter.

There is evidence that in manufacturing industry, over a two-year period the sum of gross increases at the *establishment* level would be 6% of a constant labour force. But we are interested in increases at the *firm* level. There are two extreme cases. First, the percentage growth in all establishments within any given firm is the same. In this case the sum of gross increases at the firm level is 6%. At the other extreme there is perfect negative correlation between the growth of establishments in the same firm – one establishment grows by the transfer of workers from another establishment in the same firm. In that case the sum of increases at the firm level is roughly zero. An intermediate assumption is that there is no correlation between the growth of establishments in the same firm. Let us explore this case.

First, suppose each firm has n establishments. G_{ij} is the growth in the ith establishment of the jth firm. Then the growth of the firm, assuming it has n establishments, is $(G_{1j} + G_{2j} + \ldots + G_{nj})$. Call it Q_j. If all firms have n

establishments and G_{ij} is a random normal variable, then

$$\text{Var}\ (Q_j) = \text{Var}\ (G_{1j} + G_{2j} + \ldots + G_{nj}) = n\ \text{Var}\ (G_{ij})$$

and

$$\text{SD}\ (Q_j) = \text{SD}(G_{1j} + G_{2j} + \ldots + G_{nj}) = \sqrt{n}\ \text{SD}(G_{ij}).$$

So

$$\frac{\Sigma(Q_j | Q_j > 0)}{J\ \text{SD}\ (Q_j)} = \frac{\Sigma(G_{ij} | G_{ij} > 0)}{nJ\ \text{SD}\ (G_{ij})},$$

where J is the number of firms. Thus

$$\frac{\Sigma(Q_j | Q_j > 0)}{\Sigma(G_{ij} | G_{ij} > 0)} = \frac{1}{\sqrt{n}}.$$

However, not all firms have the same number of establishments. The Census of Production gives grouped data on firms according to their number of establishments and their total workforce. Suppose there are K groups. In the kth group each firm has n_k establishments. Now let us assume that the (known) ratio of gross employment increases at the establishment level to total employment is the same (0·06) in each group of firms. Then in size group k the sum of gross increases at the establishment level is 0·06 E_k, where E_k is total employment in the group. The sum of gross increases at the firm level, following the argument just developed, is 0·06 $E_k/\sqrt{n_k}$. So the ratio of the sum of gross increases at the firm level to the total labour force is

$$0 \cdot 06 \sum_k \left(\frac{1}{\sqrt{n_k}} \frac{E_k}{\Sigma E_k} \right).$$

Using data on manufacturing industries from the *Census of Production* (1968), volume 158, table 42, p. 158–60, this equals 0·06/2·5 (or 0·06/3·2 if only establishments with more than 100 workers are included). Thus on the assumptions given, the spontaneous sum of increases at the firm level in a static labour force would be about 2 %. To this must be added 1 % to allow for the natural rate of increase of the labour force. However, the resulting estimate of 3 % may be too low and we therefore also use the extreme estimate of 6 %.

London School of Economics and Political Science,   P. R. G. LAYARD

Centre for Labour Economics   S. J. NICKELL

Date of receipt of final typescript: June 1979

REFERENCES

Ashenfelter, O. (1977). 'Evaluating the effects of the Employment Tax Credit.' Princeton University mimeo (November).

Dernberg, T. E. and McDougall, D. M. (1960). *Macro-Economics*. New York: McGraw-Hill.

Flemming, J. (1976). 'The British Economy in 1977', *Financial Times*, New Year, 1977.

Godley, W. and Nordhaus, W. (1972). 'Pricing in the Trade Cycle.' ECONOMIC JOURNAL (September), pp. 853–82.

Gribbin, J. D. (1971). *The Profitability of U.K. Exports*. Government Economic Service Occasional Papers, No. 1.

Hamermesh, D. S. (1976). 'Econometric studies of labour demand and their application to policy analysis.' *Journal of Human Resources*, vol. 11, 4.

Hausman, J. A. (1974). 'A theoretical and empirical investigation of an aggregate putty-clay technology for Great Britain, 1946–1970.' M.I.T. mimeo.

Kaldor, N. (1936). 'Wage subsidies as a remedy for unemployment.' *Journal of Political Economy* (December).

Killingsworth, M. R. (1970). 'A Critical Survey of Neoclassical Models of Labour.' *Bulletin of the Oxford Institute of Economics and Statistics* (May), pp. 133–66.

Layard, P. R. G. (1976). 'Subsidizing jobs without adding to inflation.' *The Times* (28 January).

—— (1979). 'The costs and benefits of selective employment measures: the British case.' *British Journal of Industrial Relations* (July), pp. 187–204.

—— and Nickell, S. J. (1976). 'Using subsidies as a means of cracking the unemployment nut.' *The Guardian* (2 April).

Rehn, G. (1975). 'The fight against stagflation.' University of Stockholm, mimeo (August).

Rosendale, P. B. (1973). 'The short-run pricing policies of some British engineering exporters.' *National Institute Economic Review* (August), pp. 44–51.

Rustow, H. J. (1932). 'Stimulating the economy. The Reich government's economic programme.' *Reich und Staat* (September).

Sargan, J. D. (1977). 'The consumer price equation in the post war British economy. An exercise in equation specification testing.' L.S.E., S.S.R.C. Econometrics Programme Discussion Paper No. A.11.

Trades Union Congress (1976). *Economic Review*, Congress House, London (March).

Trades Union Congress (1977). *Economic Review*, Congress House, London (February).

[3]

Economica, **49**, 219–239

Is Incomes Policy the Answer to Unemployment?

By Richard Layard

Centre for Labour Economics, London School of Ec...

In Western Europe unemployment has remained obstinately high ever since 1975. What has prevented governments from reducing it? The answer is simple. If unemployment were reduced by normal methods, inflation would rise. It follows that the only way to cut the long-run level of unemployment is to find some other way of controlling inflation. No such device will be costless. But if we could find any method that was less costly than unemployment, we ought to adopt it. Maurice Chevalier was asked in later life what he thought of old age. "It's not so bad," he replied, "when you consider the alternative." That was a true economist talking, and it is also the spirit in which I shall approach the unhappy choices open to us.

My argument will proceed roughly as follows. First, imagine that a costless incomes policy is available. Then most people would probably agree that, if inflation was too high, a temporary incomes policy would be a good idea—in order to get inflation down. But what then, when it was down? We would still be left with far too high an unemployment rate. Only a permanent incomes policy can substantially reduce the non-inflationary level of unemployment. However, against these benefits have to be set the costs of an incomes policy. A conventional incomes policy, which permanently suspended collective bargaining, would be out of the question in a free society. So we have to have an incomes policy that works by incentive rather than by regulation. The best thing would be a tax on wage increases, levied on employers and proportional to wage increases above a prescribed norm. I shall spend some time discussing this tax using various different models of wage-setting to explain how it would have its effect. And finally, I shall try producing a first draft of the Operator's Manual.

I. The Case for a Permanent Incomes Policy

So let me start with the case for an incomes policy, assuming that it is costless. One must at once distinguish between the case for a policy designed to *reduce* inflation (which could be a temporary policy) and one designed to hold inflation *steady* (which would presumably be permanent). The case for a temporary policy is pretty obvious. The government wants to reduce inflation and can do this indirectly, by reducing the growth of total money spending, and possibly in addition by exerting direct control over wages or prices. We have only to look around us to see the problems of the indirect method. For if you control only money spending (which equals price times the quantity of output), there is in the short run no way of ensuring that what gets held down is price rather than quantity. In fact, comparing 1980 with 1979, about two-thirds of the reduced growth of money GNP went into a reduced growth of output rather than a reduced growth of prices.[1] By contrast if we use the direct method of control, we try to hold down unit costs as such, and leave quantity to be determined by the relation between money spending and unit costs. In this way, having two instruments instead of one, we can achieve two targets—a satisfactory inflation rate and a satisfactory level of employment.

We can formalize this argument using the standard inflation relation

(1) $\dot{p} = \dot{p}^e - \gamma(U - U^*)$

where $\dot{p}$ is price inflation, $\dot{p}^e$ expected price inflation and U is unemployment. This says that inflation will be less than expected only if unemployment is higher than some level U^*. If inflationary expectations depend on past experience of inflation, the inflation rate will fall only if unemployment exceeds U^*.

Now this relation holds in the absence of an incomes policy. Without an incomes policy any government that wants to reduce inflation has to raise unemployment, unless it can somehow reduce inflationary expectations by announcing monetary targets or other such tricks. By contrast, a government with an incomes policy can affect costs directly and may also in the process find that the inflationary pressure is itself reduced as expectations change.[2] Once inflation has been held down to a steady rate for long enough, inflationary expectations will come to equal inflation, and the level of unemployment will settle down at U^*.

That is how an incomes policy could ease the transition to a lower inflation rate. But could we then put incomes policy to bed? The answer to this question depends mainly on whether we are satisfied with the level of unemployment that would prevail with no incomes policy (which is U^*)—in the sense that it is the best that is open to us over a run of years.[3] Among what might be called *laissez-faire* economists, the usual line is that long-run unemployment can be reduced by microeconomic measures such as reducing benefits, but not by anything as macroeconomic-looking as an incomes policy. One line of reasoning is this. Long-run unemployment reflects an equilibrium where, apart from frictions, demand is in balance with effective supply. Those who want work at prevailing wages can get it. It follows that no form of wage control can increase the quantity of labour that is bought and sold, since, if wages are held down, fewer people will be willing to work.

This analysis can be challenged on theoretical and empirical grounds. First, a wage-inflation tax (though not a traditional incomes policy) could lower long-run unemployment even in a virtually competitive labour market, once one allows for the simultaneous existence of vacancies and unemployment. But second, and much more important, the labour market in Western Europe is not competitive. If all the main labour markets are affected by union monopoly, then any incomes policy can increase employment.[4]

I shall come back to these theoretical issues when I have developed my proposal. But first I have to establish the empirical evidence for the view that the competitive model is irrelevant in explaining Western European stagflation. To see this one has only to look at the data on labour shortage, which can be taken to reflect the tightness of the labour market. According to the competitive model, this tightness should not vary from one cycle to another, unless there is a major acceleration or deceleration of inflation. Yet in most Western European countries the labour market has been much more slack since 1975 than in any previous period since at least 1960. This is

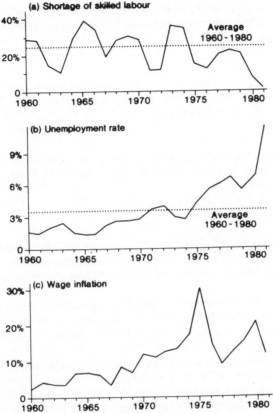

FIGURE 1. Labour shortages, unemployment rates and wage inflation, 1960–1981. Each observation is an annual average; 1981 observation is for June–July. (a) Shortage of skilled labour: percentage of firms in manufacturing expecting their output over the next four months to be limited by shortages of skilled labour (percentage is weighted by number of employees). *Source*: Confederation of British Industries, *Industrial Trends Survey*. (b) Unemployment rate, seasonally adjusted, excluding school-leavers. (c) Wage inflation: average weekly earnings, 12-monthly rate of increase.

illustrated for Britain in Figure 1(a), which shows that since 1975 the shortage of skilled labour was in every year below its 1960–1980 average. The official vacancy series for Germany, Belgium and the Netherlands tell an almost equally melancholy tale.[5] Yet if we compare early 1981 with 1976 there has been no net fall in the 12-monthly rate of wage inflation in the EEC, and very little even in Britain.[6] So evidently the labour market has to be much slacker nowadays in order to contain inflation than it did in earlier times.

II. THE CAUSES OF STAGFLATION

Some economists will say this cannot be. So let me help with a brief digression to explain how this wretched turn in our affairs has come about. This means we must investigate what determines the constant-inflation rate of unemployment U^* in equation (1). Contrary to what is often taught, this depends not only on the wage equation but also on the price equation. The wage equation is

$$(2) \qquad \dot{w} = \dot{p}^e - \gamma(U - U_0) + \dot{x}^*$$

where $\dot{w}$ is wage inflation and $\dot{x}^*$ is the target real-wage growth that would be embodied in settlements when unemployment was at U_0. This is pretty familiar. The price equation is, say,

$$(3) \qquad \dot{p} = \dot{w} - \dot{x}$$

where $\dot{x}$ is the feasible rate of real wage growth when unemployment is constant.[7] This also is pretty familiar. Yet substituting (2) into (3) we get something not so familiar:

$$(1') \qquad \dot{p} = \dot{p}^e - \gamma \left\{ U - \left(U_0 + \frac{\dot{x}^* - \dot{x}}{\gamma} \right) \right\}.$$

This says that the long-run unemployment rate will rise if the feasible rate of growth of real wages falls, assuming that this fall is not matched by a fall in the level of real wage settlements that would occur at a given unemployment rate.

Well, there has certainly been a fall in the rate of feasible real wage growth since 1973. Let me take Britain as an example and give some purely illustrative calculations. Comparing the period since 1973 with the 15 years before that, the long-run annual rate of growth of labour productivity has fallen by $1\frac{1}{2}$ percentage points. In addition, relative import prices, which improved by $1\frac{1}{4}$ per cent a year up to 1972, have worsened on average by $2\frac{1}{4}$ per cent a year since then. This, after allowing for the share of imports in GDP, implies a further fall in feasible real wage growth of nearly 1 percentage point a year. Thus, the feasible annual growth rate of real wages ($\dot{x}$) has fallen by nearly $2\frac{1}{2}$ percentage points altogether, implying a rise in the long-run unemployment rate of $2\frac{1}{2}$ points divided by γ. To find γ I have here estimated a highly simplified Phillips Curve, in which expected inflation is proxied by lagged inflation.[8] This indicates that γ is around $1\cdot6$. Thus the long-run unemployment rate rose by $1\frac{1}{2}$ percentage points, which helps to explain the increase in unemployment between the early 1970s and the late 1970s.

David Grubb, Richard Jackman and I have developed a somewhat more sophisticated version of this model and applied it to each of 19 OECD countries. We have found that it explains quite well the change in the relation between labour slack and inflation on a country-by-country basis.[9] Interestingly enough, most of these countries have pretty well-defined Phillips Curves. Of course, many of them, like Britain, have also experienced substantial increases in unemployment, owing not to increased slackness in the labour market, but rather to supply-side forces. For Britain this effect can be seen by comparing figures 1(a) and 1(b), which show how, from the mid-1960s onwards, the unemployment rate at a given level of labour shortage has risen. It can also be seen from the time trend in the wage equation.[10] Since there is no evidence of growing mismatch between workers and jobs (Nickell, 1982, Table 3), this increase in the degree of labour shortage at a given level of unemployment must mean that unemployed workers became, over the 1960s and 1970s, more choosey about what work they would accept—perhaps owing in part to a less stringent application of the work test (Layard, 1981, Table 1).

But the key point for today is that the rise in unemployment in the 1970s was due not only to supply side forces of this kind; it was also due to a failure of the wage-setting process, which has required more labour slack than ever before in order to contain inflation.

One would of course expect that in due course the target real-wage growth in the wage equation would change to reflect whatever changes had happened to the feasible rate of growth of real wages. But there is no reason why adjustment should be quick. Employers and workers may feel they have implicit long-term contracts guaranteeing significant real wage growth (see e.g. Okun, 1981). Or alternatively, if we think of the unions as the prime movers in real-wage determination, union members may misperceive the general rate of real wage growth in the economy. The model of union wage-setting that I shall develop later gives one a Phillips Curve just like equation (1′), with $\dot{x}^*$ corresponding to individual unionists' perception of what is happening elsewhere in the economy.

Thus my basic argument so far is this. Unemployment has to be high enough to prevent inflation from increasing. The required level of unemployment does not correspond to a competitive equilibrium. Long-run unemployment is higher the lower the real-wage increase that people have to be forced to accept (given their target). But unemployment could be permanently reduced if some other force in addition to unemployment could be brought to bear, which would help induce people to accept the rate of growth of real wages that is feasible. Incomes policy is the obvious candidate, and I would therefore without question support a permanent incomes policy, if it were costless.

III. REQUIREMENTS OF AN INCOMES POLICY

But, alas, no incomes policies are costless. So let me set out four required characteristics of an incomes policy and see how each can be achieved at least cost. As I have already argued, the first requisite is permanence. This immediately rules out traditional incomes policies. For the essence of these is that they prohibit the free bargaining of wages between employers and workers. This may be tolerable for short periods, but is intolerable on a permanent basis. It is not just that regulatory agencies or procedures are unlikely to produce an efficient pattern of wages. A more important cost is the politicization of an area of life that is best left to decentralized decision-making. Regulation in this area breeds frustration and discontent. The main cost of a permanent incomes policy is the loss of liberty that it involves. Any attempt to impose a permanent incomes policy of a traditional type would almost certainly, as in the late-1970s, lead to unrest and probably to the humiliation of the government. That is why both Tory and Labour Parties are now so leery of incomes policies. However, the answer to their fears lies in a policy that works by incentive rather than by regulation. The virtue of tax-based incomes policies is that individual agents have all the decision-making powers they had before. They just face an additional tax constraint, which forces them to take into account the interest that the public has full employment.

The second requisite of a policy is that it should not take away from workers any part of their gross pay. A scheme that did this would face impossible political opposition and would soon be dropped. So the tax must be levied on employers, and not on workers.[11] But there are also technical reasons. Employees could not be taxed on the basis of their own personal increases in earnings, since this would make it impossible to operate incremental scales and would discourage job mobility and promotion effort. So an employee tax would have to be levied on the basis of increases in group earnings, which would lead to endless arguments about what group an individual belonged to.

Third, the tax should be based on the money that employers actually pay out and not on the notional value of settlements. It is hourly earnings that determine the cost of labour, and these should be the tax base. If instead we used earnings per *worker*, we should penalize an employer who increased overtime and provide an incentive for employers to dilute their tax base by hiring lots of very part-time workers—perhaps ones who did practically no work at all.

Fourth, there is the issue of income distribution. Most incomes policies in the past have had some bias in favour of the low-paid—the clearest case being the £6 a week flat rate policy introduced by Denis Healey. Though I believe income distribution matters desperately, it should be dealt with through taxes and transfers and not through pay policy. There are three reasons for this (see Layard, 1980). First, there is the employment effect on the low-paid, for which there is some good evidence (see, for example, Hamermesh, 1981). Second, the relation between low pay and low income per family member is very weak, suggesting that fiscal policy should be the main instrument of redistribution. And, third, it is in any case very difficult by administrative fiat to alter the distribution of gross earnings when other forces are pulling in defence of the status quo: between April 1975 and April 1976, while the lowest decile got the prescribed £6 a week, the upper decile got £17.

So an incomes policy should be proportional in design. It should permit as much as possible of the medium-run adjustment of differentials that is dictated by market forces. But it would be no bad thing if it suppressed some of the random year-to-year variations in differentials, which are one of the most costly results of inflation, demoralizing the temporary losers more than they satisfy the temporary gainers. Perhaps as much as 80 per cent of the year-to-year changes in relativities that occurred in the 1970s were disfunctional. I arrive at this figure as follows. First take the annual wage increase in each bargaining group in each year and look at the dispersion of this across groups. Now, take the earnings increase in each group over the ten years 1970–1980 expressed as an annual average, and look at the dispersion of this across groups. The first figure is on average five times as large as the second (Ashenfelter and Layard, forthcoming, Table 4). In other words, most short-run changes in relativities get reversed soon after—and have no useful effect on the allocation of labour. Needless to say, the higher the level of inflation, the higher the dispersion of year-to-year pay increases. Low inflation, especially when linked to an incomes policy, tends to reduce the amount of pointless change in relativities.

IV. A Wage-inflation Tax and How It Has its Effect

So if you accept my four requirements, there is just about only one way of doing things, which is this. Each year the government would declare a norm for the rate of growth of hourly earnings. If an employer increased his average hourly earnings by more than this, all his excess payments would be subject to a tax; likewise, he could be rewarded for payment below the norm. The tax would have nothing to do with the pay of any individual—only with the average hourly earnings at the level of the firm.

The idea of an employer-based wage-inflation tax is not new.[12] The challenge is to find an appropriate design for the tax, and a satisfactory way of analysing it effects in the whole-economy context.[13] Let me first suggest an important additional feature of the design. We do not want the tax to increase the net tax burden on companies, for three reasons. First, we do not want to treat firms unfairly as compared with workers. Second, we do not want any net passing-on of the tax into prices. Third, we want a revenue-neutral scheme: we do not want a scheme that (like monetarism) automatically increases unemployment if wages go up faster than is expected. So I suggest that in each period the rate of social security contributions should be reduced (or "rebated") by an amount that would in aggregate just offset the tax proceeds from the wage-inflation tax. This "rebate" would be proportional to the firm's total wage-bill, while the tax was proportional to its excess wage bill.[14]

So what would be the effect of the scheme? Would it really reduce inflationary pressure at given unemployment and thus permit a lower long-run unemployment rate? My claim is that the tax in effect modifies the Phillips Curve by adding an extra term ($-\beta t$, where t is the tax rate):

$$\dot{w} = \dot{p}^e - \gamma(U - U_0) + \dot{x}^* - \beta t.$$

In this way, in the short run it permits *either* the same inflation path and lower unemployment *or* the same unemployment and a lower inflation path. This effect is, of course, strengthened if the tax also affects price expectations. In the long run, the inflation rate has to be determined by the rate of growth of money income (adjusted for potential output). So the inflation tax becomes exclusively a mechanism for raising the level of employment.

To establish my claim, let me first give some rather intuitive arguments before becoming more formal. Under the tax any firm that gives a £1 wage increase will lose not only the pound, but also £1 times the tax rate. If the tax rate were 100 per cent, it would lose £2; if the tax rate were infinite, it would lose everything. This affects inflationary pressure by modifying the behaviour of both employers and workers. It provides employers with a stronger incentive to resist wage claims. This is so even though the employer with an average wage increase receives roughly as much rebate as he pays tax (see n. 14). For the rebate is unaffected by his current wage increase, while the tax depends crucially upon it. If the firm can now save £2 by paying £1 less, it will be more likely than before to pay £1 less. Of course, if all firms conspired to give the same increase, then there would be no way in which they could affect their net tax liability by paying less. But British industry is fortunately not monolithic, and British firms will respond to a wage-inflation tax just as British drivers respond to a tax on speeding—even though British drivers, if they colluded, would notice that higher fines would be offset by lower taxes.

The tax will also discourage workers from pushing wage claims so far. For the tax reduces the employer's demand for labour at high wages (when he pays a net tax per worker) and increases the employer's demand for labour at low wages (when he recieves a net subsidy per worker). The union realizes this and concludes that an additional wage claim will now have more of an effect on unemployment than it would without the tax. It therefore chooses a lower wage claim.

To examine both these effects more rigorously, we have to specify some formal model of the economy and then work it through. I shall concentrate on the long-run level of employment. There are essentially three possible models of this, each of which has elements of truth in it, and in each of which we shall find that the inflation tax does reduce unemployment.

The first model is one in which workers are organized into unions but employers are fragmented. The unions are thus the prime-movers in wage determination and do the best they can for their members, after taking into account the employment effects of their actions. Let me briefly discuss a model of this kind that Richard Jackman and I have developed (published as an Appendix to this paper).

Each representative union faces a competitive demand curve for labour in its sector, illustrated as DD in Figure 2. Subject to this constraint, it maximizes the wage bill in its industry *plus* the income that members who cannot get work in this industry can expect to get elsewhere. This latter, of course, depends on the general national level of unemployment, which is why in this model unemployment has such a dampening effect on wage settlements. Point A shows the union's choice of wage and employment in the absence of an inflation tax. If we assume that *ex post* workers have to get paid the same wages as they think prevail elsewhere, then unemployment equals $\theta/(\eta - 1 + \theta)$, where η is the elasticity of demand and θ the fraction of workers in an industry hired from outside. Thus the unemployment rate is higher, the lower

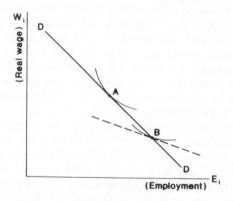

FIGURE 2. The labour market in the *i*th industry.

the elasticity of demand and the greater the consequent monopoly power of the unions.[15]

So how can one reduce the level of unemployment? Obviously, by making the effective demand curve faced by unions more elastic. This is exactly what the inflation tax does. If a firm gives more than the average wage increase, the firm is subject to a net tax per worker, while if it gives less than the average wage increase it is subject to a net subsidy. This reduces the demand for labour at high wages and raises it at low wages. Thus, tax-based incomes policy (TIP) works, appropriately enough, by tipping the demand curve—to the dotted line shown in Figure 2. Unemployment is now given by $\theta/\{\eta(1 + \delta t) - 1 + \theta\}$ where t is the rate of inflation tax and δ is the union's real rate of discount. So unemployment has fallen and employment risen. This is illustrated at point B.

This model seems to me quite powerful. Unlike many models of union-determined wages, it gives rise to a standard Phillips Curve wage equation. And this equation predicts that unemployment rises if unions have exaggerated impressions of real-wage growth elsewhere in the economy—a possible explanation of our equation (1'). But the basic point of this model is that an inflation tax works by confronting the unions with worse consequences if they raise wages. It thus reduces their monopoly power, but does this by a tax rather than by the thorny route of labour legislation.

A second model is one in which both employers and workers are actively involved in wage determination through a process of bargaining at industry level or below. Unfortunately, there is no very satisfactory model of bargaining outcomes, but a rather crude line of argument goes like this (see Seidmann, 1978). Wages are determined where the downwards push from the employers equals the upwards push from the workers. A unique wage bill will be determined, because, the higher the wage being considered, the more employers push down and the less hard workers push up. Now suppose a wage inflation tax is introduced. Even if employers expect it to have no effect on wages and prices in the rest of the economy, they will push harder for lower wages in their industry, because by paying lower wages they now save more money than they would have without the tax. Hence, even if the push from workers remains the same, a lower wage will be settled for. This analysis, of course, assumes that the general level of unemployment (which affects the bargaining power of the two sides) is the same in both cases. Thus, in a climate of given price expectations, the tax produces less wage inflation for a given unemployment. Hence, in a steady-state inflation, where price expectations are fulfilled, we must have less unemployment than we would if we had no tax.

This line of reasoning is rather casual and better models of bargaining outcomes are needed. Stephen Nickell and Christopher Pissarides have been working on the bargaining case and have found that the conclusions of the first model hold in a world of bargaining between firms and workers (Nickell, 1981; Pissarides, 1981 and 1982).

Finally there is a third model, where neither workers nor firms are organized, but where firms have complete control over wage determination. Christopher Pissarides (1981) has developed a useful model of this kind. The firms believe they can get more workers only by raising wages, but this monopsony power is only temporary, and does not lead to any permanent profit. This model is thus the nearest we can get to describing a competitive equilibrium, while assigning an explicit wage-setting role to firms. However, unlike normal competitive models, where employment is determined by supply or demand, whichever is the less, this model allows for the obvious fact that vacancies and unemployment co-exist. How, then, would unemployment change if a tax were introduced? Each firm now has an additional incentive to lower real wages, because it saves more money by doing so. This leads to a fall in real wages and an increase in vacancies. With more vacancies unemployed workers can find jobs more easily, so equilibrium unemployment falls. Thus, even in a purely competitive model, a wage inflation tax can work. Obviously, some labour markets in the economy are more like one of our three models and some are more like another. But the reassuring point is that the tax works whatever the model.

It is more difficult to analyse its effects in the short run than in the long run because the effects on expectations are not easy to model. However, there is every reason to suppose that the mechanisms I have described for the long run would also work in the short run, plus some added gain through effects on expectations.

I have not so far mentioned the public sector. Here one must distinguish between central government, local government and the nationalized industries. Only the last two would pay the tax. But all sectors would benefit from the tax, in two ways. First, if comparability is used as an argument in pay settlements, any scheme that helps in the private sector must contribute to the problem of public sector pay. I regard that as crucial. There is a strong tendency to suppose that it is one or two settlements in the public sector (especially the miners) that somehow determine the national inflation rate. That is absolutely wrong, as one can see from what is going on now. Broadly, private sector pay is determined by the economic forces at work in the private sector, and public sector pay follows the private sector inflation rate with some lurches in the name of catch-up.

Moreover, a sensible general norm could help to provide a frame of reference in public pay negotiations. In central government there could be a presumption that workers get the norm plus a catch-up equal to the difference between last year's norm and last year's actual wage increase in the private sector. This formula would be modified to allow extra increases for central government employees whose occupation was in shortage or whose comparator group had grown faster than the private sector average. Any extra payments of this type would of course be deducted when calculating the catch-up. In this way average pay in central government and the private sector would grow in line,[16] although individual occupations in the public sector would rise or fall relative to the national average, according to their shortage position or the movements in their comparator groups.

So much for public services. In the nationalized industries the tax would have an additional effect through the incentive that it provided to employers to resist wage increases (just as in the private sector). This incentive would obviously not hold if it was known that the cash limit would be reduced to pay the tax, and doubtless this would sometimes occur. Thus, it may be that the tax would have little effect on miners' pay. But if it affected the pay of the other 99 per cent of us, it would be well worth having.

V. INCIDENCE

Let me now turn to the incidence of the tax. Clearly, anything that increases employment benefits the genuinely unemployed. But would an inflation tax also benefit those who already have work? A common left-wing argument against incomes policy is that it will lower real wages. This is partly true and partly not. In the very short run, if wage inflation starts falling before price inflation does, real wages can fall quite sharply at the beginning of an incomes policy. But equally, under mark-up pricing, price inflation would go on falling after wage inflation had stopped falling, so real wages would at that stage be restored.

However, there is some evidence that mark-up pricing is not the whole story, and that in the medium term prices have to rise relative to wages if employment is to rise (Symons, 1981).[17] This is what I have been assuming in my earlier analysis. But, if it is true, then a successful inflation tax must lower real wages for a given capital stock. However, we must then allow for the fact that if employment is higher the tax rates needed to finance a given government expenditure will be lower, not to mention the reduced financing of unemployment benefit. Moreover, with higher activity there will be more investment. The capital stock will become larger and this will tend to raise the real wage. So workers have little to fear from incomes policy in the medium and long run. But union leaders inevitably have a short time-horizon, and may find it difficult to agree to a policy.[18] That is why it is so essential to have a policy that can, if necessary, be implemented without union agreement, although it is sincerely to be hoped that union leaders would prefer to have the necessary restraint imposed by a tax, rather than by unemployment, which is the only alternative.

VI. DESIGN

Let me now turn to some more nuts-and-bolts issues of tax design. Should one provide for a negative range of tax? Let met first put the argument in favour of providing for this. The reason is this. If firms that pay below the norm in any quarter get no credit for it in the form of a negative tax, then the tax penalizes those firms where wages grow in jumps relative to those with the same long-run wage growth but having a steadier growth path. If this is unacceptable, we have to have a negative range of tax, within which slow wage growth is rewarded. For the same reason, the rebate cannot be confined to firms paying below the norm or some other cut-off.

This leaves us with a positive and negative range of tax, and a rebate payable to all. Thus, taking the tax and rebate together, we have a net tax schedule in which firms paying above the average pay positive net tax and those paying below the average pay negative net tax. In such a set-up, what is the function of the norm? In terms of formal economic theory it has no role,[19] in which case we might just as well have a zero norm and tax all earnings growth.

This line of thought has its attractions. But against it one must allow for the psychological value of a realistic norm. The norm could have an important effect of its own if it could be chosen so that the ex post inflation rate was usually fairly near it. One must also allow for the massive political difficulties of rewarding firms for paying below the norm. So it would probably be best to have no negative range of tax and to aim at a realistic norm.

Turning to the tax rate, this would obviously have to be quite high. For when a firm raises its wage it pays a once-for-all tax. The true annual cost to the firm of raising it wage by £1 is (in pounds sterling) only the tax rate times the discount rate.[20] For this reason, the tax rate will need to be at least 50 per cent and probably 100 per cent.

As regards the definition of hourly earnings, earnings could probably be defined as for PAYE. Hours pose more problems. For the 90 per cent or so of workers whose pay varies according to their hours, there is no problem. We want to know the actual hours they worked (since these determine output). If we confine the tax-cum-rebate scheme to firms with over 100 workers (which is desirable on many grounds), we shall find that nearly all the firms have an automatic record of the hours worked by workers whose pay is related to hours worked. Problems arise with other workers, since firms will not normally know the hours that they actually worked. For workers who have contractual hours firms could be asked to enter in each quarter their annual contractual hours divided by 4. For workers like academics and some salesmen, who have no contractual hours, employers would be asked to enter a nominal figure. If in one year a firm recorded an increase in the average hours of workers not paid by time, it would have to supply detailed evidence to the Inland Revenue.

Next, the start-up problem. In the year after the announcement of the tax, firms may not have adequate records of earnings and hours for the previous year. But if the tax were announced in advance there would be a danger of firms conceding big wage increases before the tax came in, so as to reduce their tax liability in the following year. This suggests that the government might have to announce simultaneously the introduction of a one-year incomes policy of the old style, plus the fact that it would be followed in the second year and thereafter by a tax. Thus, when the tax eventually came in every firm would have a data base for the previous year.

As regards the problem of anomalies existing at the beginning of the scheme, the scheme should make no explicit allowance for them. They will of course be gradually rectified, at some cost to employers, but there is little more that can be done about them. No other incomes policy has found any successful method of handling this problem. There is also a problem connected with the timing of the wage round. To ensure that a firm's inflation tax liabilities do not vary wildly from quarter to quarter, the tax should relate to the excess of a firm's average payments in each quarter over their level in the corresponding quarter a year earlier.

VII. Costs of the Tax

These are the outlines of the scheme. I have already praised it for its benefits. What costs should be set against them? The main cost is the fact that the tax discourages adjustment in the labour market. It will discourage expanding firms from raising wages in order to attract more labour,[21] and thus slow down the redeployment of the workforce. The tax will also discourage productivity agreements, though less than might at first sight appear, since over a run of years pay rises no faster in industries of high productivity growth than in those of low productivity growth. These costs are important, but are worth bearing for the sake of substantially higher employment.

Next, since the tax bears on average hourly earnings irrespective of the skill composition of the workforce, it provides an incentive to firms to employ relatively more unskilled people, and by the same token penalizes firms that wish to move towards a relatively more skilled workforce. This is a more mild distortion, and some would regard it as a desirable boost to the demand for unskilled labour that could offset the inefficiency caused by too high wages for the unskilled. The tax also discourages overtime, which some would count as a virtue.

Third, there is the administrative cost. This would not be horrific. The tax would be paid quarterly to the Inland Revenue, and self-assessed by the company (like PAYE and national insurance). The company would send a tax cheque quarterly to the relevant computer centre, and receive its "rebate" as a quarterly cheque from the same computer centre. The company would be subject to a spot audit at one week's notice (as with PAYE and national insurance). At present the audit of the whole of PAYE and national insurance at the firm's end requires under 500 inspectors, so there is no reason why the audit of the inflation tax should require more than another 100 or so.[22]

VIII. DIVIDENDS AND PRICES

An incomes policy would of course have to control capital income as well as wages. The natural thing would be to have a similar scheme for dividends as for wages. There could be the same norm, and the same tax rate on increases above the norm. There would also of course have to be a share-out of the tax proceeds.

There would of course be complaints that reinvested profits were exempt from control. However, these are of distributional significance only if there are corresponding capital gains accruing to households; and the share of real capital gains in household income is rather small these days. In any case, capital gains can be handled by capital gains tax.

If it were felt politically necessary, one could operate a prices policy as well as a wages policy. This could be of the traditional kind, aiming to maintain a reasonable level of mark-up over cost. There are however notorious difficulties in controlling for changes in the quality of products, as well as efficiency costs even if you do. One thing is clear: a prices policy is certain to fail without a wages policy, whereas a wages policy can work without a prices policy.

IX. CONCLUSION

Before summing up I should like to thank most warmly my colleagues at the Centre for Labour Economics, and especially Richard Jackman, for the uncountable hours we have spent discussing these issues. The questions are enormously important, but also, alas, enormously difficult, involving as they do the whole question of how the labour market works. No one understands this very well, and if it were not for the magnitude of the issue I would hesitate to suggest another change in our social arrangements.

But suppose that such a tax enabled us permanently to reduce unemployment by 2 percentage points, as well as avoiding the horrors of the temporary unemployment required to change the inflation rate. What magnitude of costs should be set against these benefits? Some microeconomic inefficiency, without a doubt. But the whole cost of monopoly and tariffs is often estimated at less than 2 per cent of GNP (see for example Harberger, 1954, and Johnson, 1960). Surely the costs of an inflation tax will be trivial compared with the cost of monopoly and tariffs, and therefore far less than the benefits of lower unemployment. The more we actually experience of the real costs of unemployment, the more compelling becomes the case for fighting inflation some other way.

ACKNOWLEDGMENTS

This is a revised version of an inaugural lecture presented at the London School of Economics on 7 October 1981. I should like to thank the following for many helpful discussions and comments: O. Ashenfelter, J. Bray, D. Grubb, O. Hart, C. Huhne, R. Jackman, J. Kay, J. King, J. E. Meade, S. Nickell, D. Piachaud, C. Pissarides, C. Smallwood, A. Zabalza and A. P. Lerner, whose paper (Lerner, 1978) first aroused my interest in this subject.

APPENDIX

TRADE UNIONS, THE NAIRU AND A WAGE-INFLATION TAX[23]
By R. JACKMAN and R. LAYARD

Our aim is to analyse the effects of an inflation tax in a world in which unions set wages, and labour is in permanently excess supply. For this purpose we use two simple general equilibrium models. The first (Dunlop) model assumes that unions maximize the real-wage bill in their industry subject to the demand curve they face, in which case their choices are unaffected by the level of employment in the rest of the economy (Dunlop, 1944).[23] Our second model allows for mobility between industries. This implies that when workers settle wages in one industry they are affected by conditions elsewhere, since these affect the re-employment prospects of workers who are sacked. This explains why the general level of employment enters into the Phillips Curve, and suggests that the constant term in the wage equation (which helps to explain stagflation) reflects the real wage increases that workers expect to occur in the rest of the economy.

The Dunlop model

We shall assume throughout that the economy consists of N competitive industries, each with the same production function and the same quantity of capital. A fraction $(1/N)$ of the labour force is associated with each industry. There is some substitution in demand between the output of the different industries. After taking this into account,[24] as well as the diminishing marginal product of labour, there is a demand curve for labour in the ith industry which is locally given by

(A1) $E_i = a - bW_i.$

Here E_i is the employment rate in industry i (i.e. its employment as a proportion of $1/N$ of the labour force) and W_i is the real wage (i.e. the money wage relative to the general price level). The demand curve is illustrated as DD in Figure 2.

According to the Dunlop model, the unions maximize the real wage bill in their industry. Maximizing this $(E_i W_i)$ implies that

$$W_i = \frac{a}{2b}.$$

Thus employment is at point A (in Figure 2) with

$$E_i = \frac{a}{2}.$$

The NAIRU is $1 - a/2$.

We now consider the impact of an inflation tax. Suppose that firms pay tax at a rate t on that part of their wage-bill corresponding to wages in excess of W_0 (with negative tax for wages below W_0). They also receive a rebate at a rate s on their total wage-bill. Dropping the subscript i, the cost per worker becomes not W but

$$W + (W - W_0)t - sW = W(1 + t - s) - tW_0$$
$$= W(1 + t') - tW_0$$

where $t' = t - s$. Thus, the firm's demand curve is now

$$E = a - b\{W(1 + t') - tW_0\}.$$

As before, the union maximizes EW and therefore selects

$$W = \frac{a + btW_0}{2b(1 + t')}.$$

However, to ensure fiscal neutrality of the tax-cum-rebate, the government chooses the rebate rate so that the cost to it of the rebate exactly equals the tax proceeds. Thus, since all firms will be making exactly the same choices, it follows that $t(W - W_0) = sW$ or $t'W = tW_0$. Hence

$$W = \frac{a}{b(2 + t')}$$

and

$$E = a - bW \quad \text{(owing to fiscal neutrality)}$$
$$= a\frac{1 + t'}{2 + t'} > \frac{a}{2}.$$

This new optimum is shown at B in Figure 2. Employment is up. Note that the norm has no effect as such, since the lower the norm, the higher the rebate.

The analysis so far is inadequate because it does not take into account the fact that, if a firm raises its wages this period, it pays less tax next period (for any given wage that it pays in that period). For in each period firms are taxed on the excess of their wage growth over some norm. Since, as we know, the norm has no effect as such, we can for simplicity set it at a zero rate growth of wages. Thus the tax that firms pay per worker in the jth period is $t(W_j - W_{j-1}) - sW_j = t'W_j - tW_{j-1}$. For simplicity, assuming no productivity growth, employment in the jth period is therefore

$$E_j = a - b\{W_j(1 + t') - tW_{j-1}\}.$$

Subject to this constraint, unions maximize

$$\sum_{j=1}^{\infty} E_j W_j (1 - \delta)^j$$

where δ is the union's real discount rate. First-order conditions plus budget balance require

$$W_j = \frac{a - btW_{j-1} + (1 - \delta)btW_{j+1}}{2b}.$$

If employment is in a steady state, wages must be constant from period to period. Hence in each period

$$W = \frac{a}{b(2 + \delta t)}.$$

Thus the employment rate is

$$E = a\frac{1 + \delta t}{2 + \delta t}.$$

This is exactly analogous to our single-period result, except that the tax element is now represented by the annuitized value of the tax levied on a once-for-all wage increase.[25]

The proportional change in employment in response to a change in t is therefore

$$\frac{dE}{dt}\frac{1}{E} = \frac{\delta}{(2 + \delta t)(1 + \delta t)} = \text{(for small } t\text{) } 0.5\delta.$$

It is interesting (and commonsensical) that the tax has its maximum impact if people expect it to be abolished, which is equivalent to setting $\delta = 1$.

A more general model

As we have already said, the preceding model ignores the influence of the general economic climate on settlements in each particular industry. In fact, unions are influenced by whether workers dis-employed in their industry are likely to get jobs elsewhere, and at what wage. The chances of re-employment depend in part on the extent to which firms want to hire workers from outside their industry. We shall assume that this latter propensity is a constant, and that firms will in each period hire a fraction θ of their workers from outside their industry $(0 < \theta < 1)$. Hence the employment prospects of the workers initially associated with the ith (small) industry are:

probability of employment in ith industry: $E_i(1 - \theta)$

probability of employment elsewhere: $\{1 - E_i(1 - \theta)\}\dfrac{E\theta}{1 - E(1 - \theta)}$

where E is the national employment rate. The union's maximand is therefore

(A2) $E_i(1 - \theta)W_i + \{1 - E_i(1 - \theta)\}\dfrac{E\theta}{1 - E(1 - \theta)} W^e$

where W^e is the expected wage in the economy as a whole. We shall assume in this section a constant elasticity demand curve (which we could not assume before, since the Dunlop model has no interior solution in that case). By suitable choice of units, this is[26]

(A3) $E_i = W_i^{-\eta}.$

Maximization of (A2) subject to (A3) implies

(A4) $W_i = \dfrac{\eta}{\eta - 1}\dfrac{E\theta}{1 - E(1 - \theta)} W^e.$

This is positive because the elasticity of demand must exceed unity at an optimum, given that the non-employed can on average expect some income by finding work elsewhere in the economy.[27]

The wage chosen will be higher, the higher the national level of employment and the higher the wage level expected elsewhere. To determine the actual level of employment, we need to make some assumption about the relationship between W_i and W^e. If workers are well-informed W_i and W^e will be equal, since all industries are assumed identical. Thus, looking at (A4) we can see straight away that, the higher is the elasticity of demand η, the higher is the employment rate E. For the higher is the elasticity of demand the lower the wage W_i and the less unemployment is needed to hold it at a given level. In fact, E is given by[28]

$$(A5) \quad E = \frac{\eta - 1}{\eta - 1 + \theta}.$$

Once again, the way to raise employment is to make the demand curve more elastic by a tax-cum-rebate. For simplicity we shall confine ourselves to the single-period case. We shall assume that all firms pay a tax per worker equal to $t(W - W_0)$ and receive a rebate sW, where *ex post* $t'W = (t - s)W = tW_0$. The industry demand function is now

$$E = \{W(1 + t') - tW_0\}^{-\eta}$$

which gives a solution

$$(A4') \quad W = \frac{\eta(1 + t')}{\eta(1 + t') - 1} \frac{E\theta}{1 - E(1 - \theta)} W^e.$$

Setting $W = W^e$ gives an employment rate of

$$(A5') \quad E = \frac{\eta(1 + t') - 1}{\eta(1 + t') - 1 + \theta}.$$

The effect of the tax on the employment rate is given by

$$\frac{dE}{dt'} \frac{1}{E} = \frac{\eta\theta}{\{\eta(1 + t') - 1 + \theta\}\{\eta(1 + t') - 1\}}$$

$$= \text{(for small } t') \frac{\eta\theta}{(\eta - 1 + \theta)(\eta - 1)}.$$

To adapt this to the full intertemporal context we need to note that, if t' is the "effective tax rate", $t' = \delta T$ where T is the actual tax rate on once-for-all wage increases.

To get some feel for the relevant magnitudes, we can choose values of η and θ consistent with, for example, $E = 0\cdot9$. If $\theta = 0\cdot1$,[29] (A5) implies that $\eta = 1\cdot9$. So (with $\delta = 0\cdot1$) a 100 per cent tax rate would raise employment by about $1\cdot8$ per cent.

Finally, we turn to the implications of this model for the Phillips Curve wage equation. If we take equation (A4) in the logs and aggregate over the i industries, we have

$$\ln W = \ln \frac{\eta}{\eta - 1} + \ln \frac{E\theta}{1 - E(1 - \theta)} + \ln W^e.$$

Hence, subtracting $\ln W_{-1}$ (the previous period's wage) we have

$$(A6) \quad \dot{W} = f(E) + \dot{W}^e \qquad (f' > 0)$$

where $\dot{W}^e$ means $\ln W^e - \ln W_{-1}$. This is a Phillips Curve, expressed in real terms.[30] If we want to have on the left-hand side the nominal wage increase that will be given when prices are expected to rise by $\dot{p}^e$, we add $\dot{p}^e$ to each side:

$$(A6') \quad (\dot{W} + \dot{p}^e) = \dot{p}^e + f(E) + \dot{W}^e.$$

This is the standard Phillips Curve (if $\dot{W}^e$ is treated as a constant).

We can now investigate some additional forces affecting the NAIRU. So far we have assumed that expected real wages (W^e) and actual real wages (W) are the same. Hence the NAIRU was given by

$$f(E) = 0.$$

However, if the economy experienced a fall in the rate of productivity growth, workers might not realize that this had happened except in their own industry. Suppose, for example, that the rate of feasible real wage growth (at given employment rates) fell from $\dot{x}$ to $\dot{x}'$. Workers might continue to think of $\dot{W}^e$ as equal to $\dot{x}$. But in a steady state with fully anticipated prices workers cannot choose any growth rate of real wages.

They have to choose voluntarily the growth rate of real wages corresponding to the feasible growth rate of real wages $(\dot{x}')$. And the national level of employment (E) has to be such that they do choose it voluntarily. Hence (using (A6)),

(A7) $\dot{x}' = f(E) + \dot{x}$

and $f(E) = \dot{x}' - \dot{x} < 0$. Since $f' > 0$, the level of employment has to fall in order to force workers to accept a real-wage growth below that which they expect in the rest of the economy. We have explored the model of equation (A7) more fully in empirical work reported elsewhere (Grubb, Jackman and Layard, 1982).[31]

Let us clarify exactly how the natural rate (E) is arrived at. Suppose the rate of growth of nominal income is constant at $\dot{m}$, and the rate of feasible real wage growth is $\dot{x}'$. Then, an economy with a fixed labour force will converge on a stable employment level with prices growing at an anticipated rate of $\dot{m} - \dot{x}'$. Employment is determined (to produce zero net inflationary pressure) by equation (A7). Thus, in the steady state we can think of a recursive procedure under which employment is determined by equation (A7), and the real wage is determined by the demand curve—so as to be consistent with the non-inflationary level of employment.

NOTES

[1] If Y is log-nominal GDP, y log-real GDP and p the log GDP deflator, then $\Delta^2 Y \equiv \Delta^2 y + \Delta^2 p$. If Δ^2 is $\{1981(I)-1980(I)\}-\{1980(I)-1979(I)\}$, $\Delta^2 y = \frac{2}{3} \Delta^2 Y$.

[2] The legal effect of incomes policy would tend to supersede equation (1), but the effect of it on $\dot{p}^e$ would also help to reduce incentives to break the law. The evidence on effects on $\dot{p}^e$ is ambiguous. There is evidence of price expectations from the Gallup Poll, FT and CBI surveys and of wage expectations from the FT and CBI surveys. Only the Gallup Poll price series and the FT wage series show any sharp drop in late 1975.

[3] There is also the catch-up argument that, in the period *after* the temporary incomes policy, inflation will go back to its former level, partly because price expectations have never really altered and partly, perhaps, because of troubles over real wages. However, the econometric evidence on this in relation to past policies is not conclusive either way. Wadhwani (1982) suggests that the inflationary leap in 1978–1979 was not a straightforward catch-up. The main causes were the earlier price increases (owing to depreciation) and the increase in vacanices.

[4] Minford (1981) has a union sector *and* a competitive sector, and would therefore deny the potential effectiveness of incomes policy. However, his estimates imply a rise in the union mark-up from 10 per cent in 1963 to 74 per cent in 1979, which is not consistent with the evidence of the New Earnings Survey (Ashenfelter and Layard, forthcoming) or with other results (Layard, Metcalf and Nickell, 1978). The findings would imply massive falls in real wages in the competitive sector.

[5] In 1981 vacancies were down more in Britain than anywhere else.

[6] *Department of Employment Gazette*, July 1981, Table 5.9.

[7] (3) should be $\dot{p} = \dot{w} - \dot{x} - \delta \dot{U}$, but has been simplified for expositional purposes.

[8] Using annual data for 1960–1980 inclusive, I find

$$\dot{w} = \dot{p}_{-1} - 1 \cdot 61\ U + 0 \cdot 0054\ T - 0 \cdot 10\ D + 0 \cdot 098$$
$$\quad\quad\quad\quad (1 \cdot 9)\quad\ (2 \cdot 5)\quad\quad (4 \cdot 6)$$

where T is years since 1970 and D is an incomes policy dummy for 1976 and 1977. (t-statistics in brackets); $D-W = 2 \cdot 02$; s.e. $= 0 \cdot 027$. Chow-test compared with 1960–1974 is $F(5, 12) = 1 \cdot 66$. An incomes policy catch-up dummy for 1978 and 1979 was insignificant.

[9] Grubb, Jackman and Layard (1982).

[10] The wage equation implies that unemployment has been growing for supply-side reasons by $0 \cdot 34$ percentage points a year. If one regresses the percentage rate of unemployment on the pressure of demand and on time, we get, for 1960–1980,

$$U = 3 \cdot 63 - 0 \cdot 045\ S + 0 \cdot 217\ T + 0 \cdot 013\ T^2 \quad\quad D-W = 1 \cdot 22$$
$$\quad\quad (5 \cdot 0)\quad\ (16 \cdot 1)\quad\ (5 \cdot 5)$$

and

$$U = 4 \cdot 15 - 0 \cdot 0084\ V + 0 \cdot 229\ T + 0 \cdot 016\ T^2 \quad\quad D-W = 1 \cdot 41$$
$$\quad\quad (8 \cdot 0)\quad\quad (24 \cdot 6)\quad\ (9 \cdot 1)$$

where S is percentage of firms experiencing shortage of skilled labour, V is vacancies at employment exchanges ('000), and T is years since 1970. These regressions imply a rather slower average increase in supply-side unemployment over the period (0·22 points a year). We explain the difference in a moment.

We can compute the level of unemployment in 1980 that would correspond to the average level of labour market tightness in the period 1960–1980. Using either of the equations in this note, this comes out at about $6\frac{1}{4}$ per cent. We can now compare this with the constant-inflation rate of unemployment implied by the wage equation at the average rate of growth of real wages over the period 1960–1980 of 2·6 per cent. This gives a figure of $7\frac{1}{2}$ per cent. The reason for the difference is that, at the average level of labour market tightness, inflation increased by about 15 per cent over the period plus an additional 20 per cent which was "suppressed" by incomes policy. To eliminate this $1\frac{3}{4}$ per cent per annum acceleration of inflation would require an additional $1\frac{1}{8}$ per cent of unemployment.

As regards the constant-inflation rate of unemployment at the *current* rate of real wage growth of, say, $1\frac{1}{2}$ per cent (assuming no further rises in relative import prices), this would on the above reckoning be $8\frac{1}{4}$ per cent.

[11] For a useful discussion of various schemes see Blackaby (1980).

[12] A tax of this type was originally suggested by Wallich and Weintraub (1971). In their version, the firm's corporation tax rate was varied in relation to the rate of its excess wage increase. A whole issue of the *Brookings Papers* (1978, No. 2) was devoted to discussing the proposal. In Britain the tax was independently suggested by Wiles and Roberts (1971) and became Liberal Party policy in the early 1970s.

[13] For other analyses of the Wallich–Weintraub tax see Seidmann (1978), Meade (1982) and Kotowitz and Portes (1974). Seidmann's bargaining model and his monopsony model have no general equilibrium context, and his general equilibrium treatment makes the inflation tax work via reduced profits, in which case why not just have a profits tax? Meade offers a monopsony model in a general equilibrium context, but relies on a somewhat *ad hoc* effect of the tax in the wage equation (resulting in a reduced mark-up of prices over wages). Unemployment does not appear in his wage equation. An analysis that is explicitly partial equilibrium is that by Kotowitz and Portes, who look at one market with unions setting wages. The unions' "utility" depends on the rate of growth of money wages and the rate of growth of employment. If there is a tax, a union facing a demand curve rising at a given rate will choose a lower rate of growth of wages and a higher rate of growth of employment.

[14] Thus, the tax liability of a firm would be

$$t\left(\frac{g - \pi}{1 + g}\right)(EW)$$

and its rebate would be $s(EW)_{-1}$, where t is the tax rate, g the growth rate of hourly earnings, π the norm growth rate, and EW the wage-bill. The self-balancing character of the scheme ensures that

$$s = t\frac{\bar{g} - \pi}{1 + \bar{g}}$$

where $\bar{g}$ refers to the national average.

[15] Identical results would follow if the tax were levied on workers. It is natural to ask how inflation enters into our tax since it is essentially a marginal tax on wages. Given this, could not the same results be achieved by an ordinary proportional tax on labour, linked to an equal-yield flat-rate subsidy—such as we have in the present income tax? There are two insuperable difficulties. First, our proposal is for a tax on hourly earnings, whereas an income tax or social security tax is levied on weekly earnings and thus has a much greater efficiency cost in terms of labour supply. It *could not* be levied on individual hourly earnings because there are enough *individuals* for whom these can be defined only in an arbitrary way. Second, one would like to levy our tax at quite high marginal rates (e.g. 50–100 per cent on wages net of the tax). Such rates are politically unthinkable if levied on the base of *all* earnings, even though the latter (linked to an equal yield subsidy) is analytically equivalent to the same tax rate levied on all hourly earnings above a norm (linked to a much smaller subsidy).

[16] This is so only if inflation is stable. Rising inflation would hurt public sector workers and vice versa. Note that in the long run public and private sector pay do in any case grow at the same rate (*Department of the Employment Gazette*, December 1977, pp. 1338–1339).

[17] For the debate on this issue see the references in Symons (1981).

[18] As Isard (1973) pointed out, it is possible but not certain that the policy would lead to more strikes. But a few more strikes are surely more acceptable than mass unemployment. To investigate this question one might start from the model of Ashenfelter and Johnson (1969). If the tax left the workers' reaction function unchanged, it would lead employers to choose lower

wages and more strikes. But in the transition phase the tax could well lower the reaction function of workers. However, this whole model is based on wage-setting by employers rather than by workers, and the latter seems on the whole more relevant (see my first model above).

[19] A glance at Figure 2 shows that the level of W and E is determined only by the level of the marginal tax rate.

[20] For a similar argument using the union's discount rate see the appendix.

[21] For evidence that changes in relative wages are an important mechanism for redeploying labour, see Pissarides (1978).

[22] For further discussion of administrative issues see Jackman and Layard (1982).

[23] The same maximand is used by Hart (1981). But Hart is concerned to show how fiscal policy can alter the level of employment. Inflation does not appear in his model and it has no NAIRU.

[24] For an illustration of how this can be done see n. 26 below.

[25] In a later note we show that if there is productivity growth at rate λ, δ should be replaced (in the formula) by $\delta - \lambda$.

[26] Suppose that normalized output is $Q_i = E_i^{1-(1/\alpha)}$, so that the marginal productivity conditions (ignoring the multiplicative constant) give

(AA) $$\frac{W_i}{\pi_i} = E_i^{-1/\alpha}$$

where π_i is the price of output i relative to the general price level. The demand for good i is given by

(AB) $$\pi_i = Q_i^{-1/\gamma} = E_i^{(1-1/\alpha)(-1/\gamma)}.$$

Hence the demand for labour is, from (AA) and (AB),

$$W_i = E_i^{-(1/\alpha+1/\gamma-1/\alpha\gamma)} = E_i^{-1/\eta}.$$

[27] Second-order conditions for a maximum are satisfied if $\eta > 1$.

[28] Note that $0 < \theta < 1$. If $\theta = 0$, we have the Dunlop model and no interior solution. If $\theta = 1$, the maximand (A2) is a constant, and workers have no attachment to an industry. Note also that the model can easily be generalized to allow for unemployment benefits (B), in which case $E = (\eta - 1 - B/W)/(\eta - 1 + \theta - B/W)$.

[29] According to the 1976 *New Earnings Survey*, about 10 per cent of workers had changed employers within the previous 12 months. There are no data on change of bargaining group.

[30] It is interesting to note that

$$\frac{E\theta}{1-E(1-\theta)} = \frac{E\theta}{1-E+E\theta} = \frac{\text{vacancies}}{\text{unemployment}+\text{vacancies}}.$$

[31] To check the plausibility of the present method of obtaining equation (A7), note that

$$\frac{df}{dE} = \frac{1}{E\{1-E(1-\theta)\}}.$$

If $\theta = 0 \cdot 1$ and $E = 0 \cdot 9$, this is about 6—rather on the high side.

REFERENCES

ASHENFELTER, O. and JOHNSON, G. (1969). Bargaining theory, trade unions, and industrial strike activity. *American Economic Review*, **59**, 35–49.

ASHENFELTER, O. and LAYARD, R. (forthcoming). Incomes policy and wage differentials, *Economica*.

BLACKABY, F. (1980). An array of proposals. In *The Future of Pay Bargaining* (F. Blackaby, ed.). London: Heinemann.

DUNLOP, O. T. (1944). *Wage Determination under Trade Unions*. New York: Kelley.

GRUBB, D., JACKMAN, R. and LAYARD, R. (1981). Causes of the current stagflation. Review of Economic Studies, forthcoming.

HAMERMESH, D. (1981). Minimum wages and the demand for labour. National Bureau of Economic Research Working Paper no. 656.

HARBERGER, A. C. (1954). Monopoly and resource allocation, *American Economic Review*, **64**, 77–87.

HART, O. (1982). A model of imperfect competition with Keynesian features. Quarterly Journal of Economics, **97**, 109–138.

ISARD, P. (1973). The effectiveness of using the tax system to curb inflationary collective bargains: An analysis of the Wallich–Weintraub plan. *Journal of Political Economy*, **81**, 729–740.

JACKMAN, R. and LAYARD, R. (1982). An inflation tax. *Fiscal Studies*, **3**, 47–59.

JOHNSON, H. G. (1960). The cost of protection and the scientific tariff. *Journal of Political Economy*, **68**, 327–345.

KOTOWITZ, Y. and PORTES, R. (1974). The "tax on wage increases". *Journal of Public Economics*, **3**, 113–132.

LAYARD, R. (1980). Wages policy and the redistribution of income. In *Income Distribution: The Limits to Redistribution* (D. Collard, R. Lecomber and M. Slater, eds) Colston Society. Bristol: Bristol University Press.

—— (1981). Unemployment in Britain: Causes and cures. London School of Economics, Centre for Labour Economics Discussion Paper no. 87.

—— (1982). *Jobs without Inflation. The case for a counter-inflation tax*, London: Grant McIntyre.

LAYARD, R., METCALF, D. and NICKELL, S. (1978). The effects of collective bargaining on relative wages. In *The Economics of Income Distribution* (A. Shorrocks and W. Krelle, eds) and *British Journal of Industrial Relations*, **16**, 287–302.

LERNER, A. P. (1978). A wage-increase permit plan to stop inflation. *Brookings Papers on Economic Activity*, no. 2.

MEADE, J. E. (1982). *Stagflation*. Volume 1: *Wage-Fixing*, London: Allen and Unwin, Chapter X and Appendix C.

MINFORD, P. (1981). Labour market equilibrium in an open economy. Paper presented at the Cambridge Conference on Unemployment, University of Liverpool, mimeo.

NICKELL, S. (1982). The determinants of equilibrium unemployment in Britain. *Economic Journal*, forthcoming.

—— (1981). Some notes on a bargaining model of the Phillips Curve. London School of Economics, Centre for Labour Economics Working Paper no. 338.

OKUN, A. M. (1981). *Prices and Quantities*. Oxford: Basil Blackwell.

PISSARIDES, C. (1978). The role of relative wages and excess demand in the sectoral flow of labour. *Review of Economic Studies*, **45**, 453–467.

—— (1981). The effects of a wage tax on equilibrium unemployment. London School of Economics, Centre for Labour Economics Discussion Paper no. 118.

—— (1982). Trade unions and the number of jobs in a model of the natural rate of unemployment, London School of Economics, Centre for Labour Economics Discussion Paper No. 124.

SEIDMANN, L. S. (1978). Tax-based incomes policies. *Brookings Papers on Economic Activity*, no. 2.

SYMONS, J. (1981). The demand for labour in British manufacturing. London School of Economics, Centre for Labour Economics Discussion Paper no. 91.

WADHWANI, S. (1981). Wage inflation in the UK. London School of Economics, Centre for Labour Economics Working Paper no. 330.

WALLICH, H. C. and WEINTRAUB, S. (1971). A tax-based incomes policy. *Journal of Economic Issues*, **5**, 1–19.

WILES, P. J. and ROBERTS, B. C. (1971), *Evening Standard*, 8 March, 1971.

[4]

On Theories of Unemployment

By ROBERT M. SOLOW*

There is a long-standing tension in economics between belief in the advantages of the market mechanism and awareness of its imperfections. Ever since Adam Smith, economists have been distinguished from lesser mortals by their understanding of and —I think one has to say—their admiration for the efficiency, anonymity, and subtlety of decentralized competitive markets as an instrument for the allocation of resources and the imputation of incomes. I think we all know this; for confirmation one can look at the results of a paper (James Kearl et al.) presented at the last annual meeting, reporting the responses of professional economists to a sort of survey of technical opinion. The propositions which generated the greatest degree of consensus were those asserting the advantages of free trade and flexible exchange rates, favoring cash transfers over those in kind, and noting the disadvantages of rent controls, interest rate ceilings, and minimum wage laws.

Views on these policy issues did not seem to represent mere conservative ideology: half of the respondents agreed and another 30 percent agreed "with provisions" that redistribution of income (presumably toward the poorest) is a legitimate function of government policy. The profession's reservations about rent control, interest rate ceilings, and minimum wage laws do not appear to reflect a rejection of the goals of those measures, but rather a feeling that nonprofessionals simply do not understand fully the consequences, often unexpected and undesired, of messing around with the market mechanism. Most of us are conscious of a conflict that arises in our minds

*Presidential address delivered at the ninety-second meeting of the American Economic Association, December 29, 1979, Atlanta, Georgia. Like most people, I get by with a little help from my friends, in this case especially Paul Samuelson, George Akerlof, Arnold Kling, and James Tobin.

and consciences because, while we think it is usually a mistake to fiddle the price system to achieve distributional goals, we realize that the public and the political process are perversely more willing to do that than to make the direct transfers we would prefer. If we oppose all distorting transfers, we end up opposing transfers altogether. Some of us seem to welcome the excuse, but most of us feel uncomfortable. I don't think there is any very good way to resolve that conflict in practice.

Simultaneously, however, there is an important current in economics that focuses on the flaws in the price system, the ways that real markets fail because they lack some of the characteristics that make idealized markets so attractive. I think that outsiders, who tend to see economists as simple-minded marketeers, would be astonished to learn how much of the history of modern economic analysis can be written in terms of the study of the sources of market failure. The catalog runs from natural and artificial monopoly, to monopolistic competition, to the importance of public goods and externalities of many other kinds, to—most recently—a variety of problems connected with the inadequate, imperfect, or asymmetric transmission of information and with the likelihood that there will simply be no markets for some of the relevant goods and services.

Even the vocabulary can be revealing. Market "imperfection" suggests a minor blemish of the sort that can make the purchase of "irregular" socks a bargain. Market "failure" sounds like something more serious. To take a more subtle example, I mentioned that one kind of flaw in the system can be the absence of certain markets. The common generic term for the reason why markets are missing is "transaction costs." That sounds rather minor, the sort of thing that might go away in due course as accounting and information

1

processing get cheaper. But some of the cases of missing markets really go much deeper. The fact that distant future generations can not participate directly in the markets for nonrenewable resources will not be remedied by improvements in communication. Nor are the residents of densely populated areas ever likely to be able to dicker effectively with the dozens or hundreds of sources of barely traceable pollutants whose health effects, if any, cumulate over many years.

There is a large element of Rohrschach test in the way each of us responds to this tension. Some of us see the Smithian virtues as a needle in a haystack, as an island of measure zero in a sea of imperfections. Others see all the potential sources of market failure as so many fleas on the thick hide of an ox, requiring only an occasional flick of the tail to be brushed away. A hopeless eclectic without any strength of character, like me, has a terrible time of it. If I may invoke the names of two of my most awesome predecessors as President of this Association, I need only listen to Milton Friedman talk for a minute and my mind floods with thoughts of increasing returns to scale, oligopolistic interdependence, consumer ignorance, environmental pollution, intergenerational inequity, and on and on. There is almost no cure for it, except to listen for a minute to John Kenneth Galbraith, in which case all I can think of are the discipline of competition, the large number of substitutes for any commodity, the stupidities of regulation, the Pareto optimality of Walrasian equilibrium, the importance of decentralizing decision making to where the knowledge is, and on and on. Sometimes I think it is only my weakness of character that keeps me from making obvious errors.

The critics of the mainstream tradition are mistaken when they attribute to it a built-in Panglossian attitude toward the capitalist economy. The tradition has provided both the foundations for a belief in the efficiency of market allocations and the tools for a powerful critique. Economic analysis by itself has no way of choosing between them; and the immediate prospects

for an empirically based model of a whole economy, capable of measuring our actual "distance" from the contract curve, are mighty slim. The missing link has to be a matter of judgment—the Rohrschach test I spoke of a minute ago. For every Dr. Pangloss who makes the ink blot out to be of surpassing beauty, give or take a few minor deviations—the second-best of all possible worlds, you might say—there is a Candide to whom it looks a lot like an ink blot. Maybe there are more Panglosses than Candides. But that was true in Voltaire's time too—just before the French Revolution, by the way—and has more to do with the state of society than with the nature of economics.

The tension between market efficiency and market failure is especially pointed in discussions of the working of the labor market, for obvious reasons. The labor market connects quickly with everything else in the economy and its performance matters more directly for most people than that of any other market. Moreover, the labor market's own special pathology, unemployment, is particularly visible, particularly unsettling, and particularly frustrating. The fuse leading from theory to policy in this field is short, and has been known to produce both heat and light throughout much of the history of economics.

Contemporary macro-economic theory, though apparently full of technical novelties, has revived many of the old questions in only slightly different form. One of the points I want to make is that underneath the theoretical innovations—some of which are interesting and important—the basic controversial issues that come to the surface are the same ones that occupied earlier literature. The most important among them is really the old tension between market efficiency and market failure. Should one think of the labor market as mostly clearing, or at worst in the process of quick return to market-clearing equilibrium? Or should one think of it as mostly in disequilibrium, with transactions habitually taking place at non-market-clearing wages? In that case presumably the wage structure is either not receiving any strong signals to make it change in the right direction or is not responding to the signals it receives. My own belief in this case lies with the market-failure side. That is to say, I believe that what looks like involuntary unemployment is involuntary unemployment.

Of course that conclusion only leads to another question. If the labor market often fails to clear, we had better figure out why. There is no shortage of candidate hypotheses. Here I think it is worthwhile to insist on a commonplace: although it is natural for academic people to seek a single weighty Answer to a weighty Question, if only because it is so satisfying to find one, it is quite likely that many of the candidate hypotheses are true, each contributing a little to the explanation of labor-market failure. Now the second general point I want to make is one that I am surprised to hear myself making. While I find several of the candidate hypotheses entirely believable, I am inclined to emphasize some that might be described as noneconomic. More precisely, I suspect that the labor market is a little different from other markets, in the sense that the objectives of the participants are not always the ones we normally impute to economic agents, and some of the constraints by which they feel themselves bound are not always the conventional constraints. In other words, I think that among the reasons why market-clearing wage rates do not establish themselves easily and adjust quickly to changing conditions are some that could be described as social conventions, or principles of appropriate behavior, whose source is not entirely individualistic.

I said that I am a little surprised at myself. That is because I am generally stodgy about assumptions, and like to stay as close to the mainstream framework as the problem at hand will allow. In any case, I think that the unconventional elements in what I have to say are only part of the story. And I assure you that I am not about to peddle amateur sociology to a captive audience. All I do mean to suggest is that we may predispose ourselves to misunderstand important aspects of unemployment if we insist on modelling the buying and selling of labor within a set of background assumptions whose main merit is that they are very well adapted to models of the buying and selling of cloth. Far from advocating that we all practice sociology, I am pleasantly impressed at how much mileage you can get from the methods of conventional economic analysis if only you are willing to broaden the assumptions a little.

I

It might be interesting to have a history of the evolution of economic ideas about unemployment, and their relation both to the internal logic of the subject and to the parallel evolution of the institutions of the labor market. I am not sufficiently well read to provide that kind of survey. To make my point about the persistence of the market-efficiency market-failure tension, I took a short cut. I went back to reread Pigou's *Lapses from Full Employment*, a little book I remember having been assigned to read as a student just after the war. And that in turn sent me back to its parent book, Pigou's *Theory of Unemployment*. The Preface to *The Theory of Unemployment* is dated April 1933, after a decade of poor performance and relatively high unemployment in Great Britain, well into the Great Depression, and before the publication of the *General Theory*. The Preface to *Lapses from Full Employment* (another example of a revealing vocabulary) is dated November 1944, after five years of the war that put an end to the depression, and well after the appearance of the *General Theory*. That seemed like an interesting approach to the historical question, because current controversies in macro-economic theory are often described as a debate between "Keynesians" and others—"monetarists," "Classicals," or "equilibrium theorists" — and because Pigou, besides being a great economist, was in particular the embodiment of the Marshallian tradition, the leading figure in the "classical economics" that the Keynesian revolution was explicitly intended to overthrow.

Lapses makes interesting rereading. It emphasizes the money wage, whereas its predecessor was written almost entirely in terms of the real wage. The general macro-theoretic framework, in which the discussion of the labor market is embedded, clearly has an eye on Keynes. The underlying model could be *IS-LM* without doing much violence to the argument. There are little anachronisms: Pigou tends to think of the interest rate as being determined in the goods market (by Savings = Investment) and nominal income as being determined by the demand for money. Today we take simultaneity seriously, but the *General Theory* more or less speaks as if real output is determined in the goods market and the interest rate by liquidity preference. After what is to me a confusing description of a Keynesian low-level liquidity-trap equilibrium, Pigou invokes the Pigou effect to explain why the low level might not be as low as all that and then, characteristically, remarks that none of it is very important in practice anyway. All this is relevant here only as background for the treatment of the labor market.

Pigou says the obvious thing first, and I agree that it is the first thing to say: if there is "thorough-going competition" among workers, then the only possible equilibrium position is at full employment. That is little more than a definition of equilibrium. He is aware that he is taking a lot of dynamics for granted. Expectations of falling wages could perversely reduce the demand for labor; and he discusses the possibility that under some conditions, with the interest rate at its practical floor, nominal wage rates and prices may chase each other down and thus prevent the real-wage adjustment needed for an increase in employment. (This is where the Pigou effect makes its appearance, of course.)

It is what comes next that interests me. It is obvious to Pigou, writing in 1944, that the labor market does not behave as if workers were engaged in thorough-going competition for jobs. With the common sense that seems somehow to have escaped his modern day successors, he wonders why it does not. And he discusses three or four of the institutional factors that a reasonable person would mention even now as obstacles to the classical functioning of the labor market.

First of all, he realizes that the labor market is segmented. Not everyone in it is in competition with everyone else. I am not referring here to the obvious fact that abilities, experience, and skills differ, so that unemployed laborers can not compete for the jobs held by craftsmen. That fact of life merely reminds us that "labor" is not a well-defined homogeneous factor of production. Even within skill categories or occupational groups, however, workers have ties to localities, to industries, to special job classifications, even to individual employers. These ties can be broken, but not easily. It is interesting to me that even the *Theory of Unemployment* of 1933 devotes a lot of space to the analysis of a labor market in which there are many "centers of employment"—to use the neutral term chosen by Pigou to describe segmentation of the labor market—between which mobility is absent or slow. Of course he observes that even in a completely segmented labor market, if there is thorough-going competition within segments, full employment will be the rule, although there may be wage differentials between centers of employment for otherwise identical workers. I think that the fact of segmentation is very important, not only because it limits the scope of competition but because its pervasiveness suggests—though it can not prove—that habit and custom play a large role in labor market behavior. From the prominence that he gives it, I gather that Pigou might have agreed.

A second factor, which has been more often discussed, is trade unionism. Pigou does not have very much to say about collective bargaining, but what he says makes sense.

Of course, these agencies in their decisions have regard to the general state of the demand for labour; they will have no wish to set wage rates so high that half the people of the country are thrown out of work. Nevertheless, there is reason to believe that they do not have regard to demand conditions in such degree as would be necessary to secure, as thorough-going competition would do, the establishment of full employment.   [1945, p. 26]

Later on in the book, Pigou makes an observation that is not explicitly connected with collective bargaining. He does connect it with "actual life" however, and it fits organized workers very well, and perhaps others besides:

> In periods of expansion employers might be willing to agree to substantial advances in wage rates if they were confident that, when prosperity ended, they would be able to cancel them. They know, however, that in fact this will not be easy, that elaborate processes will have to be gone through, and that their work-people will put up a strong rear-guard action.... In periods of depression wage-earners, for precisely similar reasons, hold out against wage reductions, which they might be ready to concede if it were not for the difficulty that they foresee in getting them cancelled when times improve.... A widespread desire for 'safety first' helps to make wage rates sticky.
> [1945, p. 48]

These casual remarks raise more questions than they answer about the determination of nominal wages by collective bargaining. The first excerpt can be taken as a redefinition of full employment when the labor market is not competitive; the second, however, advances an account of wage stickiness and is therefore on a different footing. It would help to explain the failure of the labor market to clear on any reasonable definition, and thus provide a connection between nominal demand and real output.

The third institutional factor mentioned by Pigou has also been the subject of much analysis, past and present: the provision of unemployment insurance. There are several channels by which the availability of unemployment compensation can add to the recorded amount of unemployment. The prolongation of search is only the most obvious. My own impression is that this is currently a significant factor. As an indication of the complexity of the issues, let me just mention here that some recent research by my colleagues Peter Diamond and Eric Maskin suggests the possibility that in some environments search activity conveys a posi-

tive externality. So the optimal search strategy for the individual might provide less than the socially optimal amount of search, and unemployment compensation could be regarded as a corrective subsidy. This is a neat twist on the theme of the counterpoint between market efficiency and market failure. In any case, it can hardly be doubted that the unemployment compensation system is an important determinant of behavior on both sides of the labor market, and complicates even the definition of full employment.

The last comment of Pigou's that I want to cite is especially intriguing because it is so unlike the sort of thing that his present day successors keep saying. Already in the 1933 *Theory of Unemployment* he wrote: "...public opinion in a modern civilized State builds up for itself a rough estimate of what constitutes a reasonable living wage. This is derived half-consciously from a knowledge of the actual standards enjoyed by more or less 'average' workers.... Public opinion then enforces its view, failing success through social pressure, by the machinery of...legislation" (p. 255). A similar remark appears in *Lapses*. Such feelings about equity and fairness are obviously relevant to the setting of statutory minimum wages, and Pigou uses them that way. I think they also come into play as a deterrent to wage cutting in a slack labor market. Unemployed workers rarely try to displace their employed counterparts by offering to work for less; and it is even more surprising, as I have had occasion to point out in the past, that employers so rarely try to elicit wage cutting on the part of their laid-off employees, even in a buyer's market for labor. Several forces can be at work, but I think Occam's razor and common observation both suggest that a code of good behavior enforced by social pressure is one of them. Wouldn't you be surprised if you learned that someone of roughly your status in the profession, but teaching in a less desirable department, had written to your department chairman offering to teach your courses for less money? The fact that nominal wage rates did fall sharply during the early stages of the depression of the 1930's, and the fact that the Chrysler Corporation has been able to negotiate concessions from the UAW certainly show that wage rates are not completely rigid. But those very instances seem to me only to confirm the importance of social convention in less extreme circumstances. After all, people have been known to try to claw their way into a lifeboat who would never dream of cheating on a lift-line.

I think I have made the case that the most eminent representative of orthodox economics in the 1940's was fully aware of the many obstacles to "thorough-going competition" among workers, that is, of the many ways in which the labor market may "fail." In particular, one cannot under those circumstances expect the labor market always to clear. Pigou certainly drew that conclusion. He says, in the Preface to *Lapses*: "Professor Dennis Robertson...has warned me that the form of the book may suggest that I am in favour of attacking the problem of unemployment by manipulating wages rather than by manipulating demand. I wish, therefore, to say clearly that this is not so" (p. v).

Pigou clearly felt the tension between market efficiency and market failure. Nevertheless, he did not come down on the side of market failure, even after the 1930's. The very title of *Lapses from Full Employment* tells us that much. Evidently he concluded that the tendency of the capitalist economy to seek (and find) its full-employment equilibrium was strong enough so that departures from full employment could be regarded as mere episodes. Is that surprising? Well, to begin with, there is no accounting for Rohrschach tests. One person's ink blot is another person's work of art. But I think there is also something more systematic to be said.

In the *Theory of Unemployment*, Pigou gives an elaborate analysis of the short-run elasticity of demand for labor. He is very careful: he allows for the elasticity of supply of complementary raw materials; he allows for the (presumably very high) price elasticity of demand for exports; he discusses the effects of discounting future returns to labor. It is a masterly attempt to get a grip on orders of magnitude. It is all based on the presumption that the only possible starting point is the elasticity of the marginal-product-of-labor curve. Let me remind you that in the old standby, two-factor Cobb-Douglas case, the elasticity of demand for labor with respect to the real wage is the reciprocal of the share of capital. Everybody's back-of-the-envelope puts the capital share at $1/4$ and the elasticity of demand for labor at 4. This is not exactly the way Pigou proceeds, but he reaches the same conclusion: the initial estimate of the elasticity is "certain to be (numerically) much larger than -1 and may well amount to -5 or more." There follow some modifications, but the conclusion remains that in times of depression, the aggregate elasticity of demand for labor with respect to the real wage "cannot, on the least favourable assumption here suggested, be numerically less than -3 and may well be larger than -4" except perhaps in the very shortest run.

For practical purposes, one would want to know the elasticity of demand with respect to the nominal wage, taking account of the likelihood that prices will follow wages down, at least partially. (Obviously if product prices fall equiproportionally with wage rates, as Keynes thought might happen in unlucky circumstances, the real wage doesn't move at all and employment will not improve.)[1] The details of Pigou's calculations do not concern us, but his conclusion does: "...we may...not unreasonably put the elasticity of the money demand for labour in times of deep depression at not less numerically than -1.5."

If I could believe that, I too could believe that the labor market generally clears. To reduce the unemployment rate by 6 percentage points is to increase employment by about 6 percent, if we ignore for this purpose the side effects that go to make up Okun's Law. If that could be accomplished by a real-wage reduction of 2 percent, or even less, that is, by foregoing one year's normal productivity increase, than I could imagine that the labor market might easily

[1]Neither Pigou nor Keynes invoked Kaldor's notion that prices can be expected to fall faster than wages in a recession with the resulting rise in real wages providing the force for recovery from the demand side, through a distributional shift toward wage incomes which generate more spending per dollar than other incomes do.

learn to adjust smoothly to fluctuations in aggregate demand. I could even imagine that workers might accept the necessary 4 percent reduction in nominal wages, in the expectation that half of it would be offset by lower prices. The trouble is that Pigou's demand elasticities are way too high. A recent econometric study by Kim Clark and Richard Freeman, based on quarterly data for *U.S.* manufacturing. 1950–76, puts the real-wage elasticity of demand for labor at about one-half, a whole order of magnitude smaller than Pigou's guess.[2] And the Clark-Freeman work is presented as revisionist, a counterweight to other estimates that are typically *lower*, averaging out at about 0.15 according to a survey by Daniel Hamermesh. To my mind, smooth wage adjustment seems intrinsically unlikely in a world with such a small demand elasticity and institutions like those sketched earlier. Nothing I read in the newspapers suggests to me that 6 percent of nonfrictional unemployment produces a threat adequate to set off a quick 12–15 percent fall in the real wage, or a drop in nominal wage rates twice as large. Sellers facing inelastic demands usually try to discourage price cutting; why should workers be different?

The modern classical school seems curiously remote from all this. When they try to explain how the equilibrium volume of employment can fluctuate as widely as actual employment does in business cycles, their only substitute for Pigou's high elasticity of demand is a high elasticity of supply (of labor) in the face of a perceived temporary opportunity for unusual gains, which in this case reflects wages that differ from average expected (discounted) future wages. In other words, People who give the vague impression of being unemployed are actually engaged in voluntary leisure. They are taking it now, planning to substitute extra work later, because they think, rightly or wrongly, that current real wages are unusually low compared with the present value of what the labor market will offer in the future. They may be responding to changes in real wages or to changes in the real interest rate.

It is astonishing that believers have made essentially no effort to verify this central hypothesis. I know of no convincing evidence in its favor,[3] and I am not sure why it has any claim to be taken seriously. It is hardly plausible on its face. Even if the workers in question have misread the future, they are merely mistaken, not confused or mystified about their own motives. It is thus legitimate to wonder why the unemployed do not feel themselves to be engaged in voluntary intertemporal substitution, and why they queue up in such numbers when legitimate jobs of their usual kind are offered during a recession.[4]

When they face the market-clearing issue at all, Pigou's successors take a rather abstract line. They regard it as inherently incredible that unexploited opportunities for beneficial trade should be anything but ephemeral—which means merely that they ignore all those human and institutional facts of which Pigou was aware. Or else they argue that one cannot believe in the failure of markets to clear without having an acceptable theory to explain why that happens. That is a remarkable precept when you think about it. I remember reading once that it is still not understood how the giraffe manages to pump an adequate blood supply all the way up to its head; but it is hard to imagine that anyone would therefore conclude that giraffes do not have long necks. At least not anyone who had ever been to a zoo. Besides, I think perfectly acceptable

---

[2]The Clark-Freeman estimates are based on quarterly data for aggregate *U.S.* manufacturing. Their difference from other work appears to rest on allowing wage changes to operate with a lag different from other factor prices. According to their results the lag of employment behind wage changes is quite short; it is complete in about two quarters.

[3]Just after writing those words, I received a working paper by Robert Hall which (a) concludes that the elasticity of supply of labor required to make the inter-

temporal-substitution hypothesis work is actually in the ballpark suggested by other facts, but (b) rejects the whole theory on other empirical grounds. I have done some further experimentation on Hall's data (with the help of Mr. Sunil Sanghvi) with results that cast doubt on the reliability of even the first conclusion. On reflection, I stand by the words in the text.

[4]I have tried to phrase that carefully. For some direct evidence, see "Jobs and Want Ads: A Look Behind the Evidence," *Fortune*, Nov. 20, 1978.

THE AMERICAN ECONOMIC REVIEW   MARCH 1980

heories can indeed by constructed, as soon as one gets away from foolishly restrictive and inappropriate assumptions.

II

That brings me to the second and last general point I had hoped to make. Suppose one chooses to accept the apparent evidence of one's senses and takes it for granted that the wage does not move flexibly to clear the labor market. By the way, my own inclination is to go further and claim that commodity prices are sticky too, at least downward. But it is the persistence of disequilibrium in the labor market that I want to emphasize. How can we account for it?

There is, as I mentioned at the beginning, a whole catalog of possible models of the labor market that will produce the right qualitative properties. Since I have surveyed this literature elsewhere, I will just list a half-dozen possibilities now, with the reminder that they are not mutually exclusive alternatives.

(1) There is Keynes's idea that case-by-case resistance to wage reductions is the only way that workers can defend traditional wage differentials in a decentralized labor market. The net result is to preserve the general wage level or its trend, but that is an unintended artifact.

(2) There is a complementary hypothesis about the behavior of employers that I have proposed myself: if employers know that aggressive wage cutting in a buyer's market may antagonize the remaining work force, hurt current productivity, and make it harder to recruit high-quality workers when the labor market tightens, they will be less inclined to push their short-run advantage.

(3) Pigou realized that widely held notions of fairness, enforced by social pressure or by legislation, might have to be part of any serious account of wage determination. George Akerlof has pursued this trail further, documented the prescription of codes of good behavior in manuals of personnel practice, and showed formally that such codes of behavior can be self-enforcing if people value their reputations in the community. Obviously there are no Emily Post manuals to consult as regards the behavior

of laid-off workers, but you would certainly not be astonished to learn that self-esteem and the folkways discourage laid-off workers from undercutting the wages of their still-employed colleagues in an effort to displace them from jobs. Reservation wages presumably fall as the duration of unemployment lengthens; but my casual reading suggests that this pattern shows up more in a willingness to accept lower-paid sorts of jobs than in "thorough-going competition" for the standard job. The cost to the worker of this sort of behavior is diminished by the availability of unemployment insurance. It is worth remembering that the acceptance of lower-grade jobs is itself a form of unemployment.

(4) I need only touch on the Azariadis-Baily-Gordon implicit-contract theory, because it has been much discussed in the literature. Here wage stability is a vehicle by which less-risk-averse firms provide income insurance for more-risk-averse workers, presumably in exchange for a lower average wage.[5] It is now understood that the theory works well only when workers have some source of income other than wages, unemployment compensation for instance. This is not really a disadvantage in a world with well-developed unemployment insurance systems. In any case such implicit contracts do not themselves account for unemployment. Their effect is to reduce the average amount of unemployment below the level that would occur in a simple spot market. The theory belongs in my list because I suspect it does help to account for the habit of wage inertia and therefore the vulnerability of employment to unexpected fluctuations in aggregate demand.

(5) Wherever there is collective bargaining in our economy, the standard pattern,

---

[5]Unemployment generated by this mechanism is, in a sense, voluntary. Workers reveal a preference for steady wages over steady employment. But the aggregate welfare cost of the system can still be reduced by stabilization policies. This comment applies equally to the social customs described in the preceding paragraph of the text. One can ask why workers cling to such costly conventions. It is the job of sociology to answer that question. But it is the job of economics to point out that, whatever the reason, the narrowly economic cost of such conventions can be reduced by the stabilization of aggregate demand.

with few exceptions, is that wage rates are specified in the contract, and the employer chooses the amount of employment. This is not exactly simple monopoly, because the union cannot set the wage schedule unilaterally. To the extent that it can, another source of wage stickiness can be identified. Under a reasonable assumption about what the union maximizes, it turns out that the only aspect of the demand for labor that has any effect on the monopoly wage is its elasticity. So if the demand curve for labor shifts down nearly isoelastically in a recession, the contractual wage will change little or not at all, and the full effect of the fall in demand will bear on employment. The amount of unemployment compensation available plays a role here too. (There is much more to be said along these lines, and Ian McDonald of the University of Melbourne and I hope to say it on another occasion.)

(6) As a last example, I recall Pigou's observation that wage changes may be seen by the parties as hard to reverse without a struggle whose duration and outcome cannot be foreseen. The resulting uncertainty causes employers to drag their feet when demand increases temporarily and workers to reciprocate when demand falls. The result is wage stickiness in the face of fluctuating employment.

Only what Veblen called trained incapacity could prevent anyone from seeing that some or all of these mechanisms do indeed capture real aspects of the modern capitalist economy. Assessing their combined significance quantitatively would be a very difficult task, and I do not pretend to be able to do that. We are all interpreting this ink blot together. Obviously I would not be giving this particular talk if I did not think that wage stickiness is a first-order factor in a reasonable theory of unemployment.

To make my position plausible, I want to try to summarize the sort of general characteristics that the labor market should have if the particular mechanisms that I have enumerated are to be important. By the way, I have no reason to believe that my list is anything like exhaustive; you may think of others. Simply to narrow the field, I have deliberately left out of account factors relating specifically to age, sex, race, and other characteristics that normally form the basis for discussions of structural unemployment as distinct from cyclical unemployment.

The sort of labor market I have in mind is segmented. It often makes sense to think of an employer or definable group of employers as facing its own labor pool. Some members of the labor pool may be unemployed, but still belong to it. Although transportation, information, and transaction costs are possible sources of segmentation, they need not be among the most important. The buildup of firm-specific or industry specific human capital may be more fundamental, and equally a kind of mutual knowing-what-to-expect that gives both parties in the labor market a stake, a rent, in the durability of the relationship. This point is close to the distinction between auction markets and customer markets made by Arthur Okun in a different context. The labor market, at least the "primary" labor market, is a customer market; this may be one of the important facts that differentiates the primary from the secondary labor market.

A second general characteristic is the availability of some nontrivial source of nonemployment income. The obvious one is unemployment compensation, but I imagine that fringe activity ranging from hustling to home maintenance can function in much the same way. I suppose in some societies the possibility of returning temporarily to farming is now as important as it once was here. The presence of a second earner in the family can make an obvious difference. One consequence is that it becomes easier to maintain a labor pool in the presence of fluctuating employment. In addition, as I mentioned a few moments ago, several of the specific sticky-wage mechanisms in my catalog depend for their operation on this characteristic.

Third, the stability of the labor pool makes it possible for social conventions to assume some importance. There is a difference between a long-term relationship and a one-night stand, and acceptable behavior in one context may be unacceptable in the other. Presumably most conventions are adaptive, not arbitrary, but adaptiveness may have to be interpreted broadly, so as to include pecuniary advantage but not be limited by it. Critics who deride the notion of "economic man" have a point, but usually the wrong point. Economic man is a social, not a psychological, category. There are activities in our culture in which it is socially acceptable and expected that individual pecuniary self-interest will be the overriding decision criterion: choosing a portfolio of securities, for example.[6] There are others in which it is not: choosing a mate, for example.[7] The labor market is more complicated than either, of course, and contains elements of both. Perhaps in nineteenth-century Manchester labor was bought and sold by "thorough-going competition" but I think that is unlikely to be a good approximation to contemporary wage setting. In particular, as I have emphasized, there is nothing in the data or in common observation to make you believe that moderate excess supply will evoke aggressive wage cutting on either side of the labor market.

III

I draw two conclusions from this whole train of thought, one about economics and the other about the economy.

About economics: it need not follow that we old dogs have to learn a lot of new tricks. It still seems reasonable to presume that agents do the best they can, subject to whatever constraints they perceive. But in some contexts the traditional formulations of the objective function and constraints may be inappropriate. In the labor market, the participants are firms and groups of firms on one side, and individual workers, organized trade unions, and informally organized labor pools on the other. Grant me that all feel constrained, to some nontrivial degree, by social customs that have to

do with the wage and wage-setting procedures. The result is that factor prices turn up in our equations in unfamiliar ways. Let me just mention a few examples from my earlier list of hypotheses. If Keynes was right about the conventional significance of relative wages, then ratios of wage rates appear in the objective functions on the labor side. If the current or future performance of workers depends on their feelings that wage levels are fair, then wage rates appear in the production functions constraining firms. If the individual worker's utility function depends quite conventionally on current income, then the collective objective function of a labor pool of identical workers might reasonably be a weighted average of the utility of the wage and the utility achievable when unemployed, with weights equal to the employment and unemployment fractions. This objective function contains both wage and volume of employment as arguments; and it has the interesting property that the marginal rate of substitution between wage rate and employment can depend very sensitively on the size of the unemployment insurance benefit. Constrained maximization and partial or complete reconciliation in the market can still be the bread and butter of the macro theorist. Spread with more palatable behavior assumptions, they may make a tastier sandwich, and stick to the ribs.

About the economy: if the labor market is often not in equilibrium, if wages are often sticky, if they respond to nontraditional signals, then there is a role for macro policy and a good chance that it will be effective. Equilibrium theories that conclude the opposite may conceivably turn out to have the right answer, but they simply assume what they purport to prove. It is not my argument that standard textbook policy prescriptions are bound to be right. That has to be worked out case by case. All I do claim is that a reasonable theory of economic policy ought to be based on a reasonable theory of economic life.

REFERENCES

G. Akerlof, "The Case Against Conservative Macroeconomics: An Inaugural Lecture,"

[6]The emotion aroused by the case of South Africa strikes me as one of those extreme exceptions that proves the rule.
[7]In Gary Becker's defense, I should point out that he does not assume cash income to be the decisive motive in courtship.

Economica, Aug. 1979, *46*, 219–37.

C. Azariadis, "Implicit Contracts and Unemployment Equilibria," *J. Polit. Econ.*, Dec. 1975, *83*, 1183–202.

M. N. Baily, "Wages and Employment under Uncertain Demand," *Rev. Econ. Stud.*, Jan. 1974, *41*, 37–50.

K. Clark and R. Freeman, "How Elastic is the Demand for Labor," Nat. Bur. Econ. Res. work. Paper no. 309, Cambridge, Mass., Jan. 1979.

P. Diamond and E. Maskin, "Externalities and Efficiency in a Model of Stochastic Job Matching," working paper, Mass. Inst. Technology, forthcoming.

D. F. Gordon, "A Neo-Classical Theory of Keynesian Unemployment," *Econ. Inquiry*, Dec. 1974, *12*, 431–59,

R. Hal, "Labor Supply and Aggregate Fluctuations," Nat. Bur. Econ. Res. work paper no. 385, Stanford, Aug. 1979.

D. Hamermesh, "Econometric Studies of Labor Demand and their Applications to Policy Analysis," *J. Hum. Resources*, Fall 1976, *11*, 507–25.

J. Kearl, C. Pope, G. Whiting and L. Wimmer "A Confusion of Economists?," *Amer Econ. Rev. Proc.*, May 1979, *69*, 28–37.

A. Okun, "Inflation: Its Mechanics and Welfare Costs," *Brookings Papers*, Washington 1975, *2*, 351–90.

A. C. Pigou, *The Theory of Unemployment* London 1933.

———, *Lapses from Full Employment* London 1945.

R. Solow, "Alternative Approaches to Macroeconomic Theory: A Partial View," *Can. J. Econ.*, Aug. 1979, *12*, 339–54.

[5]

Journal of Economic Literature
Vol. XXIII (September 1985), pp. 1144–1175

Implicit Contracts: A Survey

By SHERWIN ROSEN

University of Chicago

I am indebted to Oliver Hart, Charles Kahn, Robert Lucas, Robert Topel and Yoram Weiss for comments and criticism. They do not necessarily concur with my interpretations. The National Science Foundation provided financial support.

I. *Introduction*

IDEAS associated with implicit contracts originate in the work of Martin Baily (1974), Costas Azariadis (1975)—who apparently coined the term—and Donald F. Gordon (1974) though certain pre-Keynesian views of the labor market such as the remarkably enduring work of John R. Hicks (1932) and later analyses by Armen Alchian (1969) and others are important predecessors. This line of research has been extremely active in the past decade and is notable for bringing microeconomic theory to bear on the problem of unemployment and employment fluctuations. Forty years ago Franco Modigliani (1944) identified the workings of the labor market as the weak link in understanding macroeconomic fluctuations. The promise of implicit contract theory lies in taking a step toward repairing that deficiency. Practical interest in this theory also has been promoted by a search for alternatives to the Phillips' Curve approach to labor market equilibrium, which was criticized for its inconsistencies with micro-theory by Milton Friedman (1968) and Robert Lucas (1973), and which failed em-

pirically in the inflationary environment of the 1970s.

The speed with which the term *implicit contracts* has entered the economics vocabulary is slightly astonishing, but perusal of the literature reveals considerable controversy and strongly held differences of opinion on the meaning of the term and its implications. It is natural enough that passions tend to be aroused by any model purporting to analyze employment security and stability, and professional disagreements in this area undoubtedly are not made less intense by intellectual tensions in the field of macroeconomics today. These debates will not be joined here. My goal is limited to presenting some elementary versions of the theory with sufficient clarity to reveal its main content and its relationship with more conventional ways of thinking about labor markets. For these reasons as well as the fact that research in this area is proceeding at a rapid pace, it is inevitable that this survey is incomplete. Additional material may be found in the surveys by Azariadis (1979), Azariadis and Joseph Stiglitz (1983), Oliver Hart (1983), Takatoshi Ito (1982) and Aba Schwartz (1983), which differ in style and perspective from what is presented here. The following serves as a summary and overview.

(1) Viewing labor market exchange in terms of contracts represents an interesting and novel methodological departure from conventional models in which market wage rates decentralize impersonal and unilateral labor demand decisions by firms on the one hand and labor supply decisions by workers on the other. In contrast, contracts are inherently bilateral negotiations between partners that are disciplined by external opportunities, making analysis of the labor market more akin to the marriage market than to the bourse. Contract markets are supported by frictions and specificity of employment relationships that tend to insulate contracting parties from short-run external shocks and which take current wage rates "out of competition" in allocating labor resources.

(2) A contract is a voluntary ex-ante agreement that resolves the distribution of uncertainty about the value and utilization of shared investments between contracting parties. The contract specifies precisely the amount of labor to be utilized and the wages to be paid in each state of nature, that is, conditional on information (random variables) observed by both parties. Wage payments in a contract reflect both allocative production decisions and risk-sharing and income transfer decisions jointly determined by both parties.

(3) Contract theory neither resolves nor illuminates questions of Keynesian unemployment based on nominal wage and price rigidities, money illusion and non-market clearing. Explanations for "sticky" wages and prices that impede efficient labor utilization must be sought in other quarters. Contracts allocate resources through a subtle and "flexible" nonlinear pricing mechanism, which sometimes gives the outward appearance of rigidities

in observed real wages and prices. But these observed rigidities signal little about market failure.

(4) The most important empirical implications of contract theory follow from the hypothesis that contract wages embody implicit payments of insurance premiums by workers in favorable states of nature and receipt of indemnities in unfavorable states. Contractual income transfers smooth consumption, which interacts with labor utilization by eliminating income effects. The prominence of substitution effects promotes an elastic labor utilization response to socially diversifiable external shocks. *Contracts tend to increase the volatility of employment*, but these effects are difficult to detect in structural econometric models because observed wages reflect more than production/labor supply efficiency margins in contract markets.

(5) Only socially diversifiable risks are contracturally insurable. Complete contracts and full risk-shifting imply that all ex post aspects of contracts, including possible layoffs and unemployment, are "voluntary": laid-off workers in a firm are no worse off than those remaining employed, distinctly non-Keynesian. Nondiversifiable and uninsurable risks, risk aversion of firms, information asymmetries and other costs that make contracts incomplete are needed to create ex post involuntary aspects into contract terms. Incomplete risk shifting qualifies the main empirical implications of contracts because income effects play a more prominent role under those circumstances: Consumption varies more and labor utilization varies less in response to demand shocks than when contracts are complete, similar to conventional theory.

The paper is organized as follows: The next section presents some background and contextual discussion of labor market contracts. An elementary contract is analyzed in Section III, where employment

1146   *Journal of Economic Literature, Vol. XXIII (September 1985)*

is modeled as an all-or-nothing affair. This model has some simple properties, but its special features obscure the relations between contract theory and conventional theories of labor markets. Section IV presents a more familiar model which clarifies these relationships. Section V takes up the distinction between layoffs and worksharing viewed as choices at the extensive and intensive margins. Section VI sketches some extensions to intertemporal problems and the relation between contract theory and intertemporal substitution theory. The models in Section II–VII are based on common information assumptions. Much research in this area has investigated asymmetric information models as sources of market failure. Discussion of that work necessarily requires more advanced methods and appears in Section VII. Conclusions are found in Section VIII.

II. Background

The first substantial treatment of the effects of unemployment on a labor market is Adam Smith's discussion of equalizing wage differences on unemployment risk. Smith recognized that workers exposed to such risks, e.g., bricklayers, would require higher wages while employed to compensate for less regular work patterns and to sustain consumption during periods of slack demand. An extra premium might be needed to compensate risk averse workers for bearing earnings risk.

Refined development of this idea has occurred only in recent years, beginning with the work of Michael Todaro (1969), John Harris and Todaro (1970), Arnold Harberger (1971) and Jacob Mincer (1976), which is notable for analyzing the effects of market controls and minimum wages on unemployment, viewed as an equilibrium phenomenon. Workers array their search activities across markets to equate expected earnings in each. If

wages are constrained as a clearing mechanism, something else must do the job and that is the probability of finding employment. In equilibrium workers queue up for high wage jobs in the regulated sector: greater unemployment and smaller job finding probabilities are observed in those markets where wages are highest to enforce the equilibrium supply condition. These models have had some success in explaining urban unemployment in less developed economies.

Robert Hall (1970) incorporated some novel inventory theoretic ideas into models of this type to account for persistent spatial differences in unemployment. Cities with greater equilibrium unemployment rates must pay wage premiums to attract workers. Higher wages support longer unemployment spells and more frequent transitions between jobs, and represent the implicit prices that firms must pay for the privilege of drawing on an inventory of ready labor. The advantage of this reserve army of the unemployed, as it were, lies in greater flexibility and quicker responses of employment decisions by firms facing shifting and uncertain demands. Robert Topel (forthcoming) extended the argument to incorporate intermarket mobility and found evidence of equalizing differences on local unemployment rates when unemployment insurance is properly accounted for. A full market equilibrium analysis in this vein was attempted, but incompletely realized by Hall (1979).

So far, the most complete micro-analysis of equalizing differences in the Smithian mode is by John Abowd and Orley Ashenfelter (1981, 1984), based on utility theory and rationing constraints on hours availability. This and related work by Robert Hutchens (1983) and Stephen Bronars (1983) find small, but persistent equalizing wage rate differences among jobs, but insignificant, if not perverse effects on the variability or risk elements. Small effects for mean differences might be expected when the value of leisure is taken into account, but the unsubstantial effects of risk are not consistent with this theory.

The literature reviewed here concentrates much more on the contractural features of labor market exchange than on implicit risk attributes of jobs. However, an important link between the two is provided in an unpublished paper by H. Gregg Lewis (1969) and more recently by Tomio Kinoshita (1985). Lewis analyzed a deterministic market in which both employers and employees care about hours worked per employee. The equilibrium that emerges out of this analysis looks much different than that of a traditional market: a single wage does not clear the market. Instead, each firm offers fixed wage-hours packages, insisting that its employees work a fixed number of hours in exchange for a fixed income or seek employment elsewhere. A nonlinear equalizing wage-hours locus across firms serves as the equilibrium concept. There is an important sense in which implicit contract theory extends these ideas to incorporate uncertainty, since a contract specifies wage-work package deals for each state of nature.

Professional interest in contract theory has been stimulated by a number of recent empirical observations on labor market institutions. Many features of labor markets bear little resemblance to impersonal Walrasian auction markets. Chief among them is the remarkable degree of observed worker-firm attachment. Martin Feldstein's (1975) surprising finding that over 70 percent of layoffs are temporary, with most laid-off workers ultimately returning to their original employers, was confirmed on similar aggregate data by David Lilien (1980) and by much different methods on micro-panel data in a recent study by Lawrence Katz (1984). The typical adult male worker spends twenty years or more on a single job (Hall 1982) and the proba-

bility of job turnover is a sharply declining function of job tenure (e.g., Mincer and Boyan Jovanovic 1981; William Randolph 1983). Most job changes in a worker's life occur at younger ages, and a person who has persisted in the same job for a few years is likely to continue employment in it for a long time to come. If tenure is de jure in academia, it is de facto in much of the labor market at large. These findings can be explained by search theory through "job shopping" (William Johnson 1978) or searching for the best "match" between a worker and a firm (Jovanovic 1979).

The rationale for observed employment continuity ultimately rests on Gary Becker's (1964) concept of firm-specific human capital, which formed the basis of the earlier quasi-fixed cost theory of employment fluctuations originated by Walter Oi (1962). Robert Hart (1984) presents an up-to-date discussion and prior references. Quasi-fixed cost theory and implicit contract theory share many of the same features and assumptions, as demonstrated in the recent book by Arthur Okun (1981), who attempted an integration of the two. Charles Schultze (1985) pursues this line. Fixed costs, firm-specific investments or match-specific capital create the equivalent of market frictions that render significant value to enduring employment relationships. Maintenance of existing employment attachments creates shared rents which introduce a wedge between the value of a current job and outside opportunities. Rents relax momentary arbitrage constraints between current wages, current fortunes of the firm, and general labor maket conditions, as in the economics of marriage (Becker 1973). Under these circumstances it is expected present values of wages that matter to firms and workers, not necessarily the current wage. Wage income is in part an installment payment on specific-investments: Hall (1980); James R. Millar (1971) presents an inter-

1148   *Journal of Economic Literature, Vol. XXIII (September 1985)*

esting early model along these lines which deserves to be pursued.

Fixed cost theory focuses on quantity adjustments of labor inputs to changing demand conditions. Implicit contract theory potentially provides a more complete description of wage adjustments as well. For if firm-specific investments are an important component of labor market exchange, employment specificity implies that the worker is effectively a partner in his enterprise. But the return on specific capital embodied in workers is inherently stochastic and its joint ownership raises deep questions of how this capital is utilized and how its risks are shared. An ex ante agreement, or contract, resolves these issues of utilization and risk-sharing.

Theoretical research on contracts has been propelled by recent developments in the economics of uncertainty and information. Feldstein's (1976) and Baily's (1977) analyses of the U.S. unemployment insurance system showed the practical relevance of applying insurance principles to certain labor market activities. Economists' increasing understanding of state-contingent claims theory (Kenneth Arrow 1964; Gerard Debreu 1959) has played its part as well.

However, the idea of implicit contracts goes back to Frank Knight's (1921) views of the entrepreneur as a residual income recipient and bearer of risk. Knight's entrepreneur makes contractual commitments to input suppliers and earns a risky return on the difference between stochastic receipts and fixed contractual and other costs (Friedman 1962). Contracts with workers are supported by human capital specificity. Occupational selection suggests that entrepreneurs are less risk averse than the average person (Richard Kihlstrom and Jean-Jacques Laffont 1979, 1983). Modern analysis also shows that entrepreneurs shift some of these risks to the capital market. Nonetheless, a firm's owners may have comparative advantage

at risk management through portfolio diversification, whereas a worker's main wealth is nonmarketable human capital. Specialized human capital, and firm-specific human capital in particular, is not diversifiable and does not collateralize consumption loans in modern economies. Furthermore, there are practical limitations, from moral hazard and adverse selection, on private unemployment insurance markets, because workers and employers share employment and wage decisions in any state of nature. The insurance features of contracts therefore manifest the gains from trade between effectively more and less risk averse agents, and, since employment and earnings decisions are internalized at the firm level, partially avoid direct monitoring by third parties. It is these risk-shifting gains from trade that intermingles insurance and productive efficiency considerations in observed contract wages, and which determines how risks on shared investments are allocated.

Casting employment arrangements in contractual terms leads to a fundamentally different analysis, conceptually, from that of a standard competitive market. In traditional theory the worker is presented with a market-determined wage and decides how much labor to supply to the market at large at that wage. The firm decides how much impersonal labor services to buy. A contract specifies, up front, exactly how much labor the worker must supply and exactly what the wage will be in various circumstances at some particular firm. When the state of nature is actually realized there is no further scope for free choice at some external, market-determined wage rate. Instead, the worker supplies precisely the agreed upon quantity of labor (possibly none) at the previously agreed-upon wage payment, even though he might ex post prefer something different. Sometimes the agreement even transfers the rights of employment and hours determination to the complete discretion of a specific employer. These aspects of ex ante bilateral negotiation and agreement inherent in a contract system have no counterpart in an idealized decentralized competitive market in which all decisions are impersonal and unilateral. This difference is well expressed by Okun's (1981) felicitous characterization of a contract market as the "invisible handshake" rather than the invisible hand.

An employment relationship represents a complex interaction of authority, delegation, personal interactions and monitoring, so complex that remakably few provisions are actually written down.[1] Yet the economic analysis of implicit contracts amounts to working out the details of an explicit contract concerning wages and employment under uncertainty. Hence an implicit contract must be intepreted in the "as if" sense of an explicit one, as a mutual understanding between worker and employer that the invisible handshake implies, as in commercial contracts. At one level applying this as-if principle is no different from most theorizing in economics. At another, we know that contracts do not contain all contingencies because many of them cannot be foreseen and there are so many possibilities that contracting costs are prohibitive. The extent to which formal consideration of these costs and benefits affects any as-if model which ignores them is an open question that can be answered only by the empirical usefulness of the simpler theory.

III. *Contracts with Layoffs*

The literature on implicit contracts has introduced some new language and tech-

---

[1] The common law doctrine of at-will governs employment contracts (Clive Bull 1983; Richard Epstein 1984) and allows termination without fault at the will of either party at any time. Union contracts and certain Equal Opportunity legislation are major exceptions to at-will contracts. Both stipulate for-cause provisions and extensive adjudication procedures.

nical paraphernalia that sometimes makes the fundamental ideas difficult to grasp. This section sets out a simple one-period model aimed at clarifying the essential concepts. Models of this timeless type were first introduced by Azariadis (1975) and much of the subsequent literature has followed in this vein.

The basic set-up is this: the firm contracts with a group of workers. For simplicity, they are assumed to be identical in talents and preferences. The firm produces an output with a production function that depends on the utilized labor of its contract employees. This production function has conventional properties, except that it is shocked by a random variable θ. The stochastic disturbance θ is meant to reflect demand uncertainty and shocks to technology or other input supplies that are produced by external forces not controlled by contracting parties. The term "common knowledge" refers to the assumption that all relevant information is available to all parties. The probability distribution function of θ and the actual ex post realization of θ is costlessly observed and agreed upon by all contracting parties. This assumption carries great force, for it implies that the contract can be conditioned on the realization, that is, on the "state of nature" that actually materializes ex post.

The contract is a set of conditions such as: "if θ turns out to have the value θ_i then the worker agrees to supply exactly xxxx units of labor in exchange for exactly xxxx dollars." Statements of this form cover every possible realization of θ. This, and the fact that information is complete means that there is no economic rationale for any ex post renegotiation of terms (no "new" information comes in). Of course, nature is random, so contracting parties might well regret certain ex post realizations, similar to the way a poker player might have ex post regret, though there is nothing to be done about it then. These informational assumptions seem severe, to be sure, but they are exactly the same as the Arrow-Debreu contingent claims market model. Much work has been and continues to be done on models in which information is not common in this sense. However, the basic ideas are most easily seen in the simpler common information models.

The key simplifying assumption in Azariadis' model is specifying worker preferences in the form $u = U(C + mL)$, where C is consumption, L is the fraction of time devoted to leisure, and m is a constant. Normalize L so that $0 \leq L \leq 1$. The worker is assumed to be risk averse: $U' > 0$ and $U'' < 0$. This utility function has linear indifference curves: C and L are perfect substitutes, with constant marginal rate of substitution m. Alternatively, imagine the worker dividing his available unit of time between market work and the production of an equivalent but nonmarketable good with production function mL. Here, m is the marginal product of time in producing nonmarket goods. In either case, m is the unique reservation price of time supplied to market work. The conventional labor supply problem has a very simple solution in this case: either the worker supplies his entire endowment of time to the market or to leisure. This feature carries over to a contract as well. It is natural to identify a contractual provision which stipulates $L = 1$ in some state of the world as a layoff in that state.

The firm's production function is assumed to be of the form $x = \theta f(N)$, where N is utilized labor services and $f'(N) > 0$ and $f''(N) < 0$—positive and decreasing marginal product of labor. Capital is ignored. The random variable θ is distributed with known distribution function $G(\theta)$ and density function $G'(\theta) = g(\theta)$. Its mean is $E\theta = \mu$, known at the time the contract is struck (alternatively, μ may be random, but the contract is conditioned on it). Because the contract will specify either $L = 0$ or $L = 1$, for workers

with preferences such as these, write $N = \rho n$, where n is the fixed number of workers under contract, ρ is the proportion of them who work, and $1 - \rho$ is the proportion who don't work or the layoff rate. Furthermore, $0 \leq \rho \leq 1$. Given some realization of θ, the contract specifies a wage payment C_1 to those employees instructed to work and possibly a layoff payment C_2 to those who are laid off. Work or nonwork assignments are drawn by lot, represented by the employment probability, ρ. Thus, the contract specifies a set of three numbers (C_1, C_2, ρ) for each possible outcome θ. Another way to describe it is by three functions of the outcomes: $C_1(\theta)$, $C_2(\theta)$ and $\rho(\theta)$.

An employed worker $(L = 0)$ receives no nonmarket goods and obtains utility $U(C_1(\theta))$ under the contract. This occurs with probability $\rho(\theta)$. A laid off worker $(L = 1)$ produces m units of the nonmarket good and has contracted for $C_2(\theta)$ of market goods, so utility is $U(C_2(\theta) + m)$. This occurs with probability $(1 - \rho(\theta))$. Therefore the ex ante, expected utility of a worker in this firm is

$$Eu = \int [U(C_1(\theta))\rho(\theta) + U(C_2(\theta) + m)(1 - \rho(\theta))]dG(\theta). \tag{1}$$

The contract $\{C_1(\theta), C_2(\theta), \rho(\theta)\}$ maximizes the worker's expected utility (1) subject to an expected profit or utility constraint for the firm. It is Pareto optimal by construction.[2] In state θ the firm produces output of value $\theta f(\rho(\theta)n)$ and incurs contractual costs of $n\rho(\theta)C_1(\theta)$ paid to employed workers and costs of $n(1 - \rho(\theta))C_2(\theta)$ paid to laid-off workers. The

[2] The origins of this problem lie in Wassilly Leonteif (1946). Contract curve approaches to trade union bargaining have been developed recently by Ian McDonald and Robert Solow (1981), Thomas MaCurdy and John Pencavel (forthcoming) and Orley Ashenfelter and James Brown (forthcoming). Implicit contract theory substantially differs from these in resolving the uncertainty in the distribution of utility among parties using the theory of optimal risk sharing.

managers of the firm have utility function $v(\cdot)$ defined over profits, so the expected utility of the firm is

$$Ev = \int v(\pi(\theta))dG$$

$$= \int v(\theta f(\rho(\theta)n) - n\rho(\theta)C_1(\theta) \qquad (2)$$

$$-n(1 - \rho(\theta))C_2(\theta))dG(\theta).$$

The equilibrium contract maximizes (1) subject to $Ev = \bar{v}$ and corresponds to one point on the Pareto frontier between Eu and Ev.

Think of an economy composed of many such firms with the disturbance θ independently distributed among them, so many in fact that the mean $E\theta = \mu$ is realized with probability 1 (the entire distribution $G(\theta)$ is realized across firms ex post—otherwise feasibility requires the contract to be conditioned on the sample mean). To justify the solution of the constrained maximum problem as a description of the observed contract, think of firms competing for contract workers and making their joint investments (not modeled in this literature) at the beginning of the period. Firms compete for workers by offering favorable contract terms, given investments, and, in devising these terms, manager/owners diversify their risks by trading residual profit claims on an asset market. Possible risk aversion of firms is justified by some incompleteness in risk markets. For example, there may be bankruptcy possibilities or agency problems between owners and managers that make complete managerial diversification undesirable. If managers' reservation utility level is $\bar{v}$ and they are supplied elastically, then the equilibrium contract transfers rents to workers and the proposed solution follows as a competitive market equilibrium.

Associating a negative-valued multiplier λ (from Pareto optimality) with constraint (2), setting up the Lagrangian function and differentiating, yields the first order conditions for C_1, C_2, and ρ, respectively:[3]

$$U'(C_1) = -\lambda nv'(\pi)$$

$$U'(C_2 + m) = -\lambda nv'(\pi) \qquad (3)$$

$$\rho(1 - \rho)[U(C_1) - U(C_2 + m)$$

$$-\lambda nv'(\pi)(\theta f'(\rho n) - C_1 + C_2)] = 0.$$

The arguments C_1, C_2, ρ and π (profits) in (3) should be understood as functions of θ, but this functional notation is suppressed to save space. The term in $\rho(1 - \rho)$ in the third condition takes care of the constraint $0 \le \rho \le 1$.[4]

The first two conditions determine optimal risk sharing among risk averse agents as in Karl Borch (1962), Arrow (1971), and Robert Wilson (1968): marginal utilities between agents are proportional in all possible realizations; or, $U'(C_1(\theta)) = U'(C_2(\theta) + m)$, which in turn implies $C_1(\theta) = C_2(\theta) + m$ and $U(C_1(\theta)) = U(C_2(\theta) + m)$. Therefore, when the firm provides layoff pay (C_2) contracts make no ex post utility distinctions between employed and unemployed workers for any given value of θ. Of course workers attached to firms with favorable realizations of θ are better off ex post than workers attached to firms with unfavorable realizations of θ (if the

---

[3] The method may be unfamiliar. Think of the integrals in (1) and (2) as the limits of sums across a large number T of discrete possible realizations of θ (the relation between a histogram and a continuous density). The discrete formulation is a gigantic multivariate optimization problem which, by the logic of the contracts, associates specific values of the C's and ρ with each possible realization. These $3T$ marginal conditions are compactly written as (3) in the limit. For the third equation in (3), note that a ρ is associated with each value of θ and that is why there are no integrals in these conditions. Some of the literature works with the dual problem, but the solution is equivalent by Pareto optimality.

[4] Something equivalent to U-shaped average cost curves is required to determine n. Contract theory adds no insights to the determination of firm size and this issue is ignored here. Hajime Miyazaki and Hugh Neary (1983) determine n as in a worker-managed firm. Rosen (1983) does it by a local public goods argument. These papers and one by Dale Mortensen (1983a) further elaborate models of this type.

1152   *Journal of Economic Literature, Vol. XXIII (September 1985)*

firm is risk averse and not all risk is shifted), but all workers in the same firm get the same ex post utility independent of employment status. Layoffs are voluntary in this sense, though workers attached to a low θ firm may envy those in a larger θ firm ex post.

The third condition in (3) determines $\rho(\theta)$ according to

$$\rho(\theta)(1 - \rho(\theta))[\theta f\,'(\rho(\theta)n) - m] = 0 \quad (4)$$

because $U(C_1) - U(C_2 + m) = 0$ and $C_1 - C_2 = m$ from the first two conditions. If θ is such that $0 < \rho < 1$, then $\rho(\theta)$ is determined so that the marginal product of a unit of labor equals its social opportunity cost: $\theta f\,'(\rho n) = m$. However, this marginal condition does not hold with equality at the corners. When θ turns out to be very large, the firm would like to employ a great deal of labor, but has contracted with only n workers. In this case $\rho = 1$ and $\theta f\,'(n) > m$. Similarly, when θ is small enough, the marginal value product of labor falls short of its opportunity cost, in which case the firm shuts down its operations and $\theta f\,'(0) < m$. This is illustrated in Figure 1. The elbow shaped curve is the firm's internal supply curve of contract labor. Labor utilization decisions have a reservation property: for $\theta \geq \theta^*$, ρ is set equal to 1, and all of the firm's workers are fully employed. θ^* is defined by $\theta^* f\,'(n) = m$. For $\theta \leq \theta^{**}$, the firm shuts down, and all workers are laid off. The condition $\theta^{**} f\,'(0) = m$ defines θ^{**}. For $\theta^{**} < \theta < \theta^*$, some of the firm's workers are fully employed and others are laid off. In this region the employment rate $\rho(\theta)$ is increasing in θ, and the firm's layoff rate is decreasing in θ.

Notice that the ex post marginal product of labor is not equated across all firms in a contract market. It is equated only for the fraction $G(\theta^*) - G(\theta^{**})$ which have a common shadow price of labor m. The marginal product of labor exceeds m for those firms experiencing outcomes

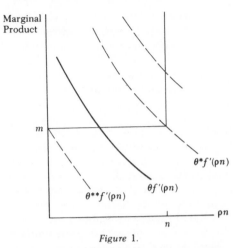

Figure 1.

more favorable than θ^*. This is not a sign of social inefficiency because employment specificity makes it too costly to move workers from one firm to another.

Nonetheless, those firms for which $\theta > \theta^*$ have ex post demands for temporary labor, and one might envision certain labor market institutions arising to take advantage of the situation. One possibility is a subcontract market of temporary workers (Melvin Reder 1962). The personal productivity of such workers would not be as large as that of contract workers due to less specific human capital, though movements across firms would help arbitrage differences in marginal values of labor across firms. It has been claimed that the Japanese labor market makes heavy reliance on this type of system, and perhaps guest workers in European economies (and use of illegal immigrants in the U.S.) can be partially explained in these terms. A temporary labor maket for laid off workers would also serve these purposes. Further, if workers differ in their reserve price of labor m, it is straightforward to show that the firm rationally contracts with several different classes of workers. Those with larger values of m are used as reserves, and are called to work only in the most favorable realiizations, similar to the way a power pool brings relatively inefficient generators on line only in periods of peak demand (Azariadis 1976; Rosen 1983). Finally, there may be incentives for firm mergers or product diversification that more easily accommodate worker transfers between operating units. The limits of the firm would then be determined by balancing the gains of internal reassignments of workers against the usual diseconomies of scale and lesser overall productivity of the firm's work force due to lesser labor specialization among divisions. This point is related to the gains to flexibility and adaptability in an uncertain environment (George Stigler 1939).

The implications of this model can be seen in an especially striking manner when firms are risk neutral [$v'(\pi) = 1$]. Then (3) implies complete consumption insurance for all workers in all firms. In this case the first two marginal conditions in (3) are independent of θ because the term in $v'(\pi(\theta))$ equals unity. Therefore $C_1(\theta)$ and $C_2(\theta)$ are constants for all value of θ, given μ. All employed workers in *all* firms receive the same incomes and so do all unemployed workers. Furthermore, the ex post utility levels $U(C_1) = U(C_2 + m)$ are independent of θ and the same for all workers. The labor utilization condition in (4) remains unchanged. This case is, in fact, equivalent to complete and costless contingent claims markets in which all socially insurable risks are diversified away, and is identical to the standard insurance result that risk averse people are completely insured when premiums are actually fair. It is as if firms contracted with an actuarially fair insurance company, turned over their entire output to the common fund and contracted to withdraw pro-rata shares.

To further clarify this strong result, write $\theta = \mu\epsilon$ where ϵ is an idiosyncratic, independent and identically distributed firm-specific random variable with distri-

bution function $Z(\epsilon)$ where $E\epsilon = 1$ and μ is a common economy-wide aggregate shock which strikes all firms equally. In a one-period model μ is an undiversifiable risk. (This is not necessarily true in a multiperiod dynamic model. See Section VI.) Given the information assumptions, all ex ante contracts must be conditioned on μ as well as on ϵ because of social budget constraints: feasible contracts cannot redistribute more market income than is actually produced.

A larger value of μ shifts the marginal value product curves to the right in Figure 1 for every possible value of ϵ and a smaller μ value shifts these curves down and to the left. Substituting $\theta = \mu\epsilon$ into (4), we see that given some realization μ, firms for which $\epsilon \geq \epsilon^* = m/\mu f'(n)$ fully utilize their work force. The value of ρ for firms on the interior of (4) is also increasing in μ. Consequently the utilization rate of labor in the work force as a whole is increasing in μ and the aggregate unemployment rate is decreasing in μ. Finally, when $v(\pi)$ is linear, (2) defines the social budget constraint for feasible contracts, given μ, as

$$\mu\int\epsilon f(\rho(\epsilon/\mu)n)dZ(\epsilon)$$
$$= n\int[C_1\rho(\epsilon/\mu) + C_2(1 - \rho(\epsilon/\mu))]dZ(\epsilon) \quad (5)$$
$$= n[C_2 + m\int\rho(\epsilon/\mu)dZ(\epsilon)].$$

National income per head (the left-hand side of (5) divided by n) is increasing in μ through its direct multiplicative effect and its indirect effect of increasing ρ. Therefore $C_1(\mu)$ and $C_2(\mu)$ are increasing in μ.

Diversifiable risk ϵ is shifted completely in this complete contracts case: consumption and utility are independent of local demand ϵ, suggestive of a form of "real wage rigidity" for these types of demand shocks. Laid off workers are no worse off than employed workers, and layoffs are voluntary. However, a contract market does not at all imply real wage rigidity

1154   Journal of Economic Literature, Vol. XXIII (September 1985)

for uninsurable risks: the consumption and utility levels of workers, be they employed or not, are strictly increasing functions of "aggregate demand" μ. Everyone is better off ex post when μ is larger and worse off when μ is smaller.[5]

The model sketched above has the undesirable prediction that laid off workers fare no worse than employed workers. It is the assumption that consumption and employment risk can be shifted without transactions costs that accounts for much of this result. By analogy, a person who can buy actuarial no-load insurance buys enough to be indifferent to whether his house burns down or not. But that is just a consequence of a simplifying assumption. Most people are worse off if their house burns because they are not fully insured. Incomplete insurance is rational when premiums are nonactuarial and when full insurance implies moral hazard. This is also true of the insurance in an implicit contract. The point gains greater force in this context because workers and firms jointly control layoff decisions, precisely the type of situation where coinsurance is known to be desirable. Therefore, incomplete insurance, or more generally some incompleteness in state contingent claims markets, is necessary to get involuntary layoffs into these models. John Bryant (1978) was the first to point this out; see also, Thomas Sargent (1979), Sanford Grossman and Hart (1981), and Bengt Holstrom (1981). While the point has created much controversy on the usefulness of common knowledge contract models, it seems to me that considerable insight is gained by analyzing actuarial cases, as in more conventional insurance problems.

It is by no means obvious how to incorporate nonactuarial elements into a formal model. The most straightforward way is to interpret the contract as a pooling arrangement with a risk-neutral, mutual insurance company and add an unemployment claims processing cost to the company's budget constraint, similar to the way load factors are calculated in conventional insurance premiums. Space limitations preclude extended development here. Consider, instead, an extreme case in which costs of providing private insurance to the unemployed are so large that none is provided at all. This adds the constraint $C_2(\theta) = 0$ to the problem above and is exactly Azariadis' (1975) original formulation.

The absence of indemnities to unemployed persons means that unemployed workers receive incomes of m alone, and the second marginal condition in (3) is irrelevant. But the first one remains. All employed workers receive the same wage C_1 if the firm is risk neutral ($v' = 1$) and their consumption is fully insured. The wage C_1 paid to employed persons must exceed m or else no one would be inclined to work. Therefore $U(C_1) > U(m)$ and employed persons in the same firm are better off ex post than the unemployed. Laid off workers have drawn the losing hand and definitely prefer employment.[6]

One might expect incomplete insurance to affect production efficiency. The third condition in (3) verifies this intuition. Substituting for $\lambda n v'$ from the first condi-

[5] Nor do contracts imply nominal wage rigidity because the price level would be a conditioning variable. Fixed duration nominal contracts (John Taylor 1980; Stanley Fischer 1977; and Jo Anna Gray 1976) must be rationalized on some other grounds, such as contracting costs and lags and errors in observing nominal price levels.

[6] Perceptive readers may have noticed that the complete contract could have been equivalently implemented by having all employees work ρ percent of the time and consume leisure $(1 - \rho)$ percent of the time rather than having a fraction ρ fully employed and a fraction $(1 - \rho)$ completely unemployed. These same possibilities arise in the incomplete contract, but are definitely not equivalent. The virtue of worksharing does not seem to have been noticed in this connection. Some factor that gives value to the continuity of a worker's employment time over the period is necessary to avoid pure worksharing solutions. See below.

tion in (3) and noting that $C_2 = 0$ by assumption, we have, for $\rho > 0$

$$\theta f'(\rho n) \geq$$
$$C_1 - [U(C_1) - U(m)]/U'(C_1). \tag{6}$$

This condition holds with equality on the interior ($0 < \rho < 1$), and with inequality for almost all firms whose workers are fully employed. It follows directly from risk aversion ($U'' < 0$) that the bracketed term on the right hand side of (6) exceeds $C_1 - m$, the difference in incomes between employed and unemployed workers. The shadow price of labor is the entire expression on the right hand and therefore falls short of m when insurance is incomplete. The horizontal portion of the internal supply curve in Figure 1 now lies below m. $\theta f'(\rho n)$ is compared with a smaller supply price in determining ρ, and the firm utilizes *more* of its contract labor compared with complete contracts. m is the social opportunity cost for firms with $0 < \rho < 1$. There is socially excessive employment in the incomplete contract equilibrium and social output would be greater if more people were unemployed!

This surprising result is part of a more general proposition in the economics of insurance. Availability of insurance promotes the undertaking of socially beneficial risks by separating the average benefits of actions from fear of risk. Risk averse persons act too cautiously and do not take enough good risks when insurance is unavailable. The only way a risk averse worker can partially insure against the utility loss of layoff and unemployment in this problem is by working in circumstances when it is socially inefficient to do so.

One more comparison must be made before concluding this section, and that is to a situation where employment relationships provide no insurance at all. This state of affairs is sometimes called an "auction market." George Akerlof and Miya-

zaki (1980) showed that an auction market can imply more unemployment than a contract market. The point is easy to see in this model when employers are risk neutral. Then workers in the firm must go it alone. Any incomes they receive must be distributed out of own firm's output, because claims on other firms' outputs are unavailable by assumption. In making its collective employment decisions, the firm could then do no better than to compare the marginal productivity of its own labor with the opportunity cost of its workers' time, which is m. Therefore, m again becomes the effective shadow price of labor as in Figure 1, employment decisions are socially efficient and identical to the full contract model. However, these workers are bearing consumption and wage risks, depending on their own realized value of θ, and some of these are socially diversifiable. Though efficient in production decisions, this solution is inefficient on risk sharing grounds. Clearly it is inefficient in the latter respect relative to a complete contract. However, it is not obviously less efficient than the incomplete contract, which is inefficient on the productivity account but possibly more efficient on the risk-sharing account. Therefore, no contracts at all may dominate an incomplete contract, depending on the extent of worker risk aversion.

IV. *Contracts and Labor Supply*

The unusual and unattractive assumptions about worker preferences in the model above conceals an intimate relationship between contract theory and the familiar theory of labor supply. Contracts embody an implicit nonlinear pricing mechanism that eliminates the income effects of insurable risks in the traditional consumption-leisure choice problem. They thereby smooth consumption which interacts with labor utilization and promotes elastic labor supply responses to ex-

1156   *Journal of Economic Literature, Vol. XXIII (September 1985)*

ternal stimuli. Contracts suggest much more volatility of employment to insurable risks than conventional models do.

To illustrate these important points in the most straightforward way, worker preferences in Section III are generalized, and the technology is simplified. Assume neoclassical worker preferences $u = U(C,L)$. The indifference curves of $U(C,L)$ are strictly convex and the worker is risk averse. As in the conventional labor supply problem, the quantity $(1 - L)$ is identified with time worked, and remaining time L is associated with nonmarket production (partial layoffs if one wishes). Assume that the firm consists of one worker ($n = 1$) with production function $x = \theta f(1 - L)$ where θ is the productivity shock. To simplify even more, assume $f(1 - L)$ is linear. Then the production function is $x = \theta(1 - L)$ and θ has the ready interpretation of the marginal product of the worker's labor, similar to a wage rate. Everything to be said here applies to a concave function $f(\cdot)$, a refinement that only adds expository noise to the main point.

Consider, first, the conventional problem of labor supply under uncertainty. Nature draws a ball out of the θ urn, the worker observes θ and makes the optimal labor-consumption decision. If an external market does not allow risks to be spread, the worker is constrained to consume out of own production (the "auction market" of Section III) and any source of non-earned income, say y. So given θ, the budget constraint is the standard one, $C = \theta(1 - L) + y$. The solution is described by the budget constraint and the first order condition $\theta = U_L/U_C$, which define demand functions $C = C(\theta, y)$ and $L = L(\theta, y)$. Assume that both C and L are normal goods and compare two alternative realizations of θ. A larger value of θ increases C, but has ambiguous effects on L. The substitution effect tends to induce greater labor supply $(1 - L)$ but the in-

come effect works in the other direction and may cause labor supply to fall. Substituting the demand functions into the utility function yields the indirect utility function $u(\theta, y)$. Indirect utility is increasing in θ (and y) irrespective of the labor supply response because full income is increasing in θ.[7]

An economy with many persons opens possibilities for mutually advantageous social arrangements that allow risk pooling. The conventional problem strictly ties a worker's consumption to current production, but a contract allows current consumption to be disassociated from current production for any given person if risks are diversifiable. The simplest way to model this is to replace the personal budget constraint with its expectation (over all workers), precisely what an actuarially fair insurance policy would do. Yet this is not standard insurance: the contract specifies exactly how much the person has to work for each possible realization of θ in order to eliminate adverse effects on work incentives that consumption insurance implies.

Assuming common knowledge, the contract specifies that the worker puts forth $(1 - L(\theta))$ hours of work in state θ and that the wage payment or consumption is $C(\theta)$ in state θ. Expected profitability of the firm is the difference between expected output and expected wage (consumption) payments

$$\int [x(\theta) - C(\theta)] dG(\theta)$$
$$= \int [\theta(1 - L(\theta)) - C(\theta)] dG. \tag{7}$$

---

[7] Increasing the spread of the distribution function $G(\theta)$ does not necessarily make the worker worse off, and Smithian risk compensation is more complex than would appear on the surface. Riskier distributions decrease welfare on risk aversion grounds, but have benefits in allowing workers to choose labor supply most advantageously in more probable high productivity states. John Hey (1979) summarizes this approach to uncertainty. Nonearned income is ignored in what follows because those issues are better treated in an intertemporal context.

Complete contracts (given μ) are analyzed in what follows, assuming risk-neutral firms, to bring out the connections between conventional theory and contract theory in the clearest possibly way. Competition in the market for contracts implies that the equilibrium contract solves:

$$\max_{L(\theta),C(\theta)} \int U(C(\theta), L(\theta))dG(\theta) \qquad (8)$$

subject to

$$\int [\theta(1 - L(\theta)) - C(\theta)]dG(\theta) = 0. \qquad (9)$$

The Lagrangian for this problem is

$$\int \{U(C,L) - \lambda[\theta(1 - L) - C]\}dG. \qquad (10)$$

The first order conditions for $L(\theta)$ and $C(\theta)$ given θ equivalent to (3) above are

$$U_C(C(\theta), L(\theta)) = -\lambda \qquad (11)$$

$$U_L(C(\theta), L(\theta)) = -\theta\lambda \qquad (12)$$

where $\lambda < 0$ as before. C and L are solved as functions of θ and λ from equations (11) and (12). Then the expected income constraint is used to solve for λ and hence the optimum contract $L(\theta)$ and $C(\theta)$. Notice that the conventional problem is completely nested in this one. It is feasible that $C(\theta) = x(\theta)$, but the contract surely will not specify equality of consumption and output for every realization of θ. True, (11) and (12) imply $U_L/U_C = \theta$—the marginal rate of substitution between leisure and consumption is equated with the marginal product of labor for any θ in a complete contract. However, now there is an extra degree of freedom: the expected income constraint allows the marginal utility of consumption to be equated in all states of the world: condition (11) is the Borch-Arrow-Wilson risk-sharing condition when one of the agents is risk neutral, equivalent to optimal choice of insurance in the actuarial, no-load case.

The properties of $L(\theta)$ and $C(\theta)$ in the contract are implicit in the first order con-

ditions (11) and (12). Since λ does not depend on θ, comparative statics on (11) and (12) show directly how C and L respond to θ in the contract. Equations (11) and (12) define marginal-utility-constant demand functions (Ragnar Frisch 1932), which prove useful when preferences are additively separable, as they are across states-of-the-world here. Martin Browning, et al. (forthcoming) contains an elegant statement of the method and gives prior references. Differentiating with respect to θ yields

$$U_{CC}C'(\theta) + U_{CL}L'(\theta) = 0$$

$$U_{CL}C'(\theta) + U_{LL}L'(\theta) = -\lambda$$

with solutions

$$L'(\theta) = -\lambda U_{CC} / \Delta \qquad (13)$$

$$C'(\theta) = \lambda U_{CL} / \Delta \qquad (14)$$

where $\Delta = [U_{CC}U_{LL} - U_{CL}^2] > 0$, by risk aversion.

From (13) we have $L'(\theta) < 0$, since $U_{CC} < 0$ by concavity and $\lambda < 0$. $d(1 - L(\theta))/d\theta = 1 - L'(\theta) > 0$. *The implicit contract always specifies that the employee works more hours in favorable states* (larger values of θ) and works less in less favorable states. There is no ambiguity due to opposing income and substitution effects in the optimal contract. Negativity of $L'(\theta)$ is basically a result of substitution effects. The worker is constrained by the expectation of output, not by realized output itself. A favorable or unfavorable drawing of θ carries no income effects because the good fortunes of one firm are counterbalanced by bad fortunes of another for diversifiable risks. Therefore, it is always efficient for the worker to work more when the marginal product of labor is larger (to make hay when the sun shines) and to redistribute consumption by insurance. If leisure is a normal good, contracts result in greater variance in hours worked than standard models and intuition based on them suggest.

Equation (14) shows that the total wage payments—identified with consumption under the contract—are rising, constant, or falling in θ as $U_{CL} \lessgtr 0$. Only when preferences are *strongly* separable in C and L it is true that $C'(\theta) = 0$ and consumption is completely smoothed, as in the permanent income hypothesis (Friedman 1957). Nonzero cross derivatives U_{CL} strongly link consumption behavior with labor supply.[8]

That a contract with full insurance does not necessarily imply full consumption smoothing suggests that the connection between complete insurance and income effects is more subtle than usual. Full insurance does not stabilize consumption except when preferences are strongly separable. More surprising, it does not stabilize ex post utility when leisure is a normal good. In this bivariate problem full insurance is completely described by condition (11) that the *marginal* utility of consumption is equalized in all states of the world, not necessarily equalization of total utility. Define $u(\theta)$ as ex post, indirect utility given θ in the optimal contract. Then

$$u'(\theta) = U_C C' + U_L L'$$
$$= -(U_C/U_{CC})[U_{CL} - (U_L/U_C)U_{CC}]L'(\theta). \qquad (15)$$

The second equality follows from (13) and (14). The bracketed term in (15) is familiar.

It determines the sign of the income effect in a conventional labor supply problem. Ex post utility is completely assured by the contract only if $u' = 0$, and this happens only when the income effect is zero, or when $U(C, L) = U(C + \psi(L))$ of which Section III is a special case. But if utility is completely assured, consumption $C(\theta)$ cannot be assured for it must compensate for the variation in L. The contract does not assure utility if the income effect is nonzero. $u'(\theta)$ is negative when the income effect is positive.[9]

A complete insurance contract makes a worker who has "suffered" an adverse draw of an insurable risk better off ex post than a worker who draws a more favorable value except when income effects are negative. Contracts underinsure ex post utility levels only when leisure is an inferior good. This strong result is a result of strong assumptions. It is not necessarily true when the firm is risk averse (then $v'(\cdot)$ multiplies the right hand side of (11) and (12)) so that risks are shared and insurance is incomplete. Nor is it necessarily true when information is private or when the shock is not diversifiable. A nondiversifiable risk affects μ, and has a powerful effect on the total amount of consumption produced and redistributed. It changes the marginal utility of consumption λ. Ex post utility necessarily increases in μ, as it did in Section III.

The consumption smoothing and insurance aspects of contracts have profound implications on the meaning of wage data in a contract market. Observed wages do two things in a contract: they allocate la-

---

[8] Notice that consumption is positively correlated with labor supply only when $U_{CL} < 0$ from (14). The sign of U_{CL} is determined by the degree of risk aversion as well as by the usual curvature restrictions in demand theory. A richer specification of nonmarket production yields more interesting implications. For example, those on short work schedules would substitute nonmarket goods production for market goods (Gilbert Ghez and Becker 1975). Michael Grossman (1973) and Daniel Hamermesh (1982) find these types of predictable differences in consumption (e.g., food prepared away from home) between the employed and the unemployed.

[9] This result is formally identical to a paradox found by James Mirrlees (1972) in an optimum spatial equilibrium problem. Mirrlees' paradox arises because of the nonconvexity that a person can occupy only one location (Richard Arnott and John Riley 1977). The "nonconvexity" here is that nonmarket production must be self-consumed. If it were possible to trade leisure on a competitive market then $u(\theta)$ is nondecreasing.

bor and shift risks.[10] These roles are best described by thinking of the observed wage as the outcome of a two-part variable tariff. The insurance aspect determines the equivalent of nonearned income in a conventional labor supply problem, conditional on the realized state θ. For risk pooling and insurance to have meaning, it must be that workers experiencing favorable realizations of θ subsidize those with unfavorable realizations. Given these "lump sum" taxes and subsidies, the contract allows workers to "choose" their optimal labor supply at the correct "marginal wage" θ, the marginal product of labor.

Define $s(\theta)$ as the worker's net debit position with the firm: $s(\theta) = C(\theta) - \theta(1 - L(\theta))$ is the difference between the wage payment and output in state θ. This equation is of the conventional budget form except that $s(\theta)$ has replaced the usual nonearned income term. A worker for whom $s(\theta) > 0$ is effectively subsidized by the contract ex post and one for whom $s(\theta) < 0$ is effectively taxed. Substituting $s(\theta)$ into the budget constraint (9) reveals that these subsidies and taxes balance each other, on average, across all workers in an actuarial system. Differentiate $s(\theta)$ with respect to θ and substitute from (13) and (14)

$$s'(\theta) = -(1 - L)$$
$$- (L'/U_{CC})[U_{CL} - (U_L/U_C)U_{CC}] \tag{16}$$

---

[10] The emerging literature on efficiency wages (Stiglitz' 1984 survey) also rests on the proposition that the wage performs more than one economic function. Multi-part pricing would allocate resources efficiently in these models (e.g., a lump-sum bond as well as a marginal wage rate in Carl Shapiro and Stiglitz' 1984 shirking problem), but two-part pricing is ruled out by assumption. Involuntary unemployment results because some margin is not satisfied when there are not enough prices available to perform all functions. Involuntary layoffs in contracts result from imperfections in state-claims markets, which is a different way of saying that there are not enough prices.

so $s(\theta)$ is decreasing in θ if leisure is noninferior.

The two-part tariff interpretation of contracts is shown in Figure 2. The first panel shows the solution to the conventional problem (assuming zero nonearned income). Two budget lines are shown. The realized marginal product θ_1 is assumed to be larger than θ_2, and comparison of equilibrium points involves the usual income and substitution effects. The second panel shows the effects of a contract, assuming $U_{CL} < 0$. For θ_1 above the mean we know from (16) that the worker is taxed and $s(\theta_1) < 0$. For θ_2 below the mean the worker is subsidized and $s(\theta_2) > 0$. The contract acts as if it puts the θ_1 worker "in the hole" by amount $s(\theta_1)$ and lets him work out of it by choosing L at (marginal) wage rate θ_1 along the altered budget constraint. The contract acts as if it gives the θ_2 worker a subsidy of $s(\theta_2)$ and then allows him to choose hours worked at marginal wage rate θ_2. The heavy curve labeled $C(L)$ is the locus of (C,L) pairs satisfying marginal condition (11), and $C'(L) < 0$ when $U_{CL} < 0$. The familiar marginal condition $U_L/U_C = \theta$ implied by (11) and (12) jointly is shown by the tangencies with the contract budget constraints. It is these adjustments in the "lump sum" portions of the two part tariff that ameliorate income effects, that promote consumption smoothing and elastic labor supply responses to diversifiable risks.

Figure 2 is useful for studying the observable wage consequences of contracts. The observed "average hourly wage rate" is measured by dividing total earnings (equals $C(\theta)$ in contracts) by hours worked:

$$W(\theta) = C(\theta)/(1 - L(\theta)). \tag{17}$$

This is how wage rates are measured in virtually all available data. Differentiating (17) and substituting from above yields

1160   Journal of Economic Literature, Vol. XXIII (September 1985)

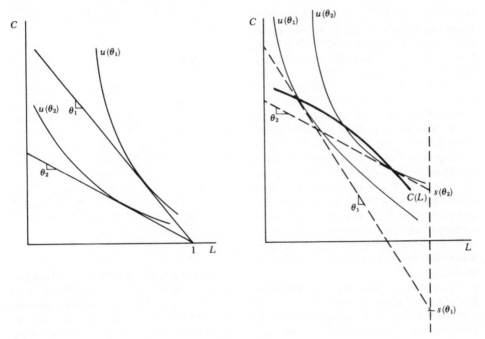

Figure 2.

$$W'(\theta)/W(\theta)$$
$$= [-(U_{CL}/CU_{CC}) + (1/(1-L))]L'(\theta). \tag{18}$$

The sign of this expression is unambiguous only when $U_{CL} \geq 0$, in which case $W(\theta)$ is actually decreasing in θ, given μ. The sign of $W'(\theta)$ is ambiguous when $U_{CL} < 0$ as in Figure 2. Figure 3 illustrates the construction of $W(\theta)$ for preferences without income effects. Here $C(L)$ coincides with an indifference curve because utility is constant in the contract, from (15). The points marked A and B correspond to large and small values of θ respectively. The measured average hourly wage rate is given by the slope of the line connecting either point with $L = 1$ and $C = 0$, from (17). The two values of θ have been chosen so that the wage rate is the same, illustrating nonmonotonicity of $W(\theta)$. In this case $W(\theta)$ is U-shaped. It is decreasing for θ sufficiently small and is increasing for θ sufficiently large. Two points follow from this.

First, there is no presumption that the measured average wage in a contract is positively correlated with the state θ, as the U-shaped pattern in Figure 3 shows, a possibility that could be confused with wage rigidity. This statement refers to real, average wage rates and to the diversifiable component of the state. If the economy experienced an adverse aggregate shock μ, the contract would have to be recalibrated. The equilibrium indifference curve in Figure 3 would be shifted down and the average hourly wage at each level of hours worked would be smaller than indicated. Average hourly wage rates should be positively correlated with noninsurable disturbances in a contract market.

The behavior of average real wages over the business cycle has been studied for many years. Manufacturing hourly wage rates show no obvious relationship with aggregate output (Salih Neftci 1978). Joseph Altonji and Ashenfelter (1980) suggest that the manufacturing real-wage rate resembles a random walk. However, panel and personal survey data indicate significant responses of measured personal wage rates to local labor market conditions (John Raisian 1983; Mark Bils, forthcoming; and Topel, forthcoming). James Heckman and Guilerme Sedlacek (1984) show that BLS manufacturing numbers may contain selection bias, because less productive workers are less likely to be employed in manufacturing during business cycle troughs, making measured wages fall less than a properly weighted index.

Second, using measured wage rates may lead to misleading inferences regarding unemployment or overemployment in personal surveys. Optimality of the contract means that ex post Pareto-improving recontracts are not possible. There is also no possibility of choosing hours worked ex post at some exogenously determined wage. In Figure 3 the worker is instructed to work $(1 - L_1)$ hours in the θ_1 state. Total earnings of C_1 go along with this, so the average hourly wage is $C_1/(1 - L_1)$ = W. If the worker could freely choose hours at an hourly wage rate W he would work up to point D rather than stay at A. In the θ_2 state, the contract specifies point B. Here the worker would choose to work more hours (point D) than the contract specifies if hours could be freely chosen at wage rate W. A survey respondent might indicate constraints on hours worked under these circumstances. The person who drew θ_2 might say that he would like more work than he is getting at the "going" wage rate and that he is involuntarily underemployed. The worker who drew θ_1 might respond that work hours are excessive and that he is involuntarily overemployed.

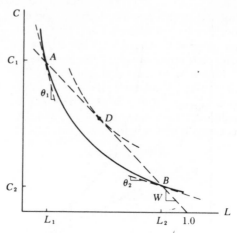

Figure 3. Measured Wage Rates

All this points out a significant problem for empirical analysis. Virtually all work on labor supply uses a model that assumes point D, that the worker is free to unilaterally choose hours at the *measured* wage rate W, whereas the insurance features of contracts disassociate the measured average wage rate from both the marginal product of labor and from the marginal rate of substitution. This point is conceptual and applies even if average wages were perfectly measured, so econometric techniques for dealing with measurement error does not dispose of it. This is not trivial because virtually all econometric work (in this field and elsewhere) lives or dies by the assumption that measured prices indicate efficiency margins. Contracts require that the data be adjusted for the lump sum components $s(\theta)$ to impute marginal wage rates. Some recent studies have attempted to include information on survey responses pertaining to whether or not the worker is constrained in the choice of hours, but this is generally viewed as a ration, not as an equilibrium phenomenon along contract lines (Shelly Lundberg, 1984, gives references and a related discussion).

This section concludes with an interest-

1162   Journal of Economic Literature, Vol. XXIII (September 1985)

ing and surprising comparative static experiment. Complete contracts imply that an *increase* in diversifiable risk increases expected utility of risk averse workers.

Following Michael Rothschild and Stiglitz (1970), parameterize the density function as $g(\theta) = \xi(\theta) + ar(\theta)$, where $\xi(\theta)$ is a density, a is a positive number, and $r(\theta)$ is a step function with properties:

$$R(\theta) = \int_0^\theta r(z)dz$$

$$R(0) = R(\infty) = 0 \qquad (19)$$

$$\int_0^\infty R(\theta)d\theta = 0$$

$$\int_0^\theta R(z)dz \geq 0.$$

Some reflection reveals that $r(\theta)$ is positive for large and small values of θ and is negative for intermediate values. Therefore an increase in a puts more weight in the tails of $g(\theta)$ and increases the spread of the distribution.

Differentiating the Lagrangian of the maximum problem in (8) with respect to a and using the envelope property gives

$$\partial Eu/\partial a = \int u(\theta)r(\theta)d\theta$$

$$- \lambda\int[\theta(1-L) - C]r(\theta)d\theta.$$

This expression may be signed by integrating by parts (twice) and exploiting the properties of (19): Peter Diamond and Rothschild (1978). Assuming $g(\theta)$ has bounded support, integration by parts gives

$$\partial Eu/\partial a = -\int[u'(\theta) + \lambda[\theta L'(\theta)$$

$$+ C'(\theta)]]R(\theta)d(\theta) + \lambda\int(1 - L(\theta))R(\theta)d\theta$$

$$= \lambda\int(1 - L(\theta))R(\theta)d\theta$$

since the first integral vanishes from first order conditions and (15). Integrating by parts again gives

$$\partial Eu/\partial a = -\lambda\int_0^\infty\int_0^\theta -L'(\theta)R(\tau)d\tau d\theta. \quad (20)$$

The sign of (20) is unambiguously positive because $\lambda < 0$, $L'(\theta) < 0$, from (13), and $\int^\theta R(z)dz > 0$, from (19). Greater diversifiable risk makes the worker better off.

This result is unexpected in light of the Smithian equalizing differences logic, but it is easily explained. Full insurance eliminates the adverse, direct consequences of risk aversion on expected utility. Increasing spread affords the worker superior opportunities of allocating work to the most favorable states and limiting losses of unfavorable outcomes by consuming more leisure. The opportune substitution of work effort toward more productive states has a value similar to that of an option: that less work is called for in the less favorable states serves to truncate the lower tail of the θ distribution.

V.   Layoffs or Worksharing?

Misconceptions about the nature of the price mechanism in contracts has led to the impression that contracts somehow rationalize layoffs through "sticky" wages and prices, and nonmarket clearing. This impression is wide of the mark because it confuses ex post contractual wages and prices with conventional "auction" market prices. Section IV clearly demonstrates that resources in contracts are really allocated by a sophisticated nonlinear price system. This nonlinear scheme is as flexible as one ordinarily supposes in competitive market theory and allocates resources as efficiently as the completeness of contingent claims markets permits. The true fact is that contracts per se have little to say about the split between changes in hours per head and layoffs. Contract outcomes fundamentally depend on preferences and technology, so the question of layoffs must rest on these same primitives. Section III produced layoffs by a peculiar assumption about preferences, that market and nonmarket goods are perfect substitutes. The conventional formulation in Section IV is not detailed enough to decide these issues.

Basically, there are two ways of introducing layoffs in contract (or any other' models. One links layoffs to capital utilization decisions based on capital heterogeneity and limited ex post substitution between labor and capital (Leif Johansen 1972). The idea is related to the "marginal firm." Marginal mines shut down completely when the price of ore falls because their quasi-rents are driven to zero. Production in marginal operations might begin when demand increases. Restricted ex post, capital-labor substitution and fixed operating costs create nonconvexities that make it advantageous to shut down inefficient facilities rather than operate them at excess capacity. These ideas could be extended to various divisions of a multiproduct or multiplant firm. The contract model must be extended to incorporate productivity differences among firms, perhaps based on vintage capital ideas (Solow 1960), differences in site-specific factors or in entrepreneurial capacities. This line has not been pursued much, and will not be developed here.

The other possibility is to directly introduce hours and employees (bodies) into the firm's technology (Feldstein 1967; Rosen 1968; Ray Fair 1969; M. Ishaq Nadiri and Rosen 1969; Ben Bernanke 1983), which serves to link the models of Sections III and IV above. Miyazaki and Neary (1983) and Murray Brown and Elmar Wolfstetter (1984) have constructed contract models along these lines.

Extend the production function of Section III to $x = \theta f(\rho n, h)$, where h is the intensity of work per employed person and $f(\cdot)$ is concave. Think of ρ as the fraction of contract labor who are employed. Then $1 - \rho$ is the layoff rate. Alternatively, maintain a timing convention in which the "period" is a year. Then h can be regarded as the length of the work week when employed and ρ as the fraction of the year (number of weeks) of employment. $h = 0$ during nonworking weeks spent on layoff. To simplify the presentation, I again assume complete contracts

(of course conditional on the mean μ of θ) and risk neutral employers.

Writing the utility function in terms of h rather than L, an employed worker receives contractual wage payment $C_1(\theta)$ and works $h(\theta)$ in state θ, receiving utility $U(C_1(\theta), h(\theta))$. A laid off worker receives payment $C_2(\theta)$ and h is zero, so utility is $U(C_2(\theta), 0)$. The probability of these events is ρ and $1 - \rho$ respectively, so

$$Eu = \int [U(C_1, h)\rho + U(C_2, 0)(1 - \rho)]dG(\theta). \quad (21)$$

The budget constraint is

$$\int [\theta f(\rho n, h) - n(C_1 \rho + C_2(1 - \rho))]dG(\theta) = 0. \quad (22)$$

The equilibrium contract $\{C_1(\theta), C_2(\theta), h(\theta), \rho(\theta)\}$ maximizes (21) subject to (22). First order conditions for C_1 and C_2 are familiar by now

$$U_C(C_1(\theta), h(\theta)) = U_C(C_2(\theta), 0) = -\lambda n \quad (23)$$

and imply that C_2 is independent of θ (because λn is independent of θ). C_1 depends on θ (unless $U_{CH} = 0$) only if h does. The intensive margin h is (note that $U_h < 0$)

$$-\rho(\theta)U_h(C_1(\theta), h(\theta)) = -\lambda \theta f_2(\rho(\theta)n, h(\theta)) \quad (24)$$

or, substituting from (23) and rearranging, $\theta f_2 = (\rho n)(-U_h/U_C)$: the marginal product of h in state θ equals its marginal cost, which is the shadow price $(-U_h/U_c)$ per employed worker times the number employed. The extensive margin ρ is, assuming $\rho > 0$ (the firm never closes)

$$U(C_1, h) - U(C_2, 0) - \lambda n[\theta f_1(\rho n, h) - (C_1 - C_2)] \geq 0 \quad (25)$$

so the shadow price of labor utilization ρ is

$$(C_1 - C_2) - [U(C_1, h) - U(C_2, 0)]/U_C(C_1, h)$$

Further analysis of these conditions is neither elementary nor illuminating. At this level of generality about all that can be said is that $d\rho/d\theta \geq 0$ and $dh/d\theta \geq 0$. Yet time-series data on employment and hours follow systematic patterns. Aggregate hours and employment variations are positively correlated with output growth rates (deviations about trend), and hours per week show variation of less than two hours peak to trough. Employment fluctuations account for the bulk of total labor utilization adjustments even in deep recessions. Indivisibilities appear necessary to account for this (Mortensen 1978; Kenneth Burdett and Mortensen 1980).

Consider an example: Assume $U(C, h) = U(C - \phi(h))$ where $U'' < 0$ and $\phi(h)$ is an increasing convex function. Then (23) implies equal utility in all states—there are no income effects—and $C_1(\theta) - C_2 = \phi(h(\theta)) - \phi(0)$. For production assume $f(\rho n, h) = F(\rho n \gamma(h))$, where $\gamma(h)$ has the interpretation of efficiency units of work hours. A long tradition of labor market research suggests that $\gamma(h)$ may have an ogive shape, due to set-up costs (Sidney Chapman 1909; Arthur C. Pigou 1920): productivity of a worker's time is small at small values of h, rises rapidly after some threshold is passed, and finally shows diminishing returns when h is very large. Indivisibilities due to fixed costs of market participation (John Cogan 1980, Giora Hanoch 1980) have similar implications. Hanoch includes both hours worked and weeks worked as arguments of utility functions, which generalizes (21). Then (24) and (25) become

$$\theta\gamma'(h)F'(\cdot) = \phi'(h)$$
$$\theta F'(\cdot) \geq [\phi(h) - \phi(0)]/\gamma(h). \tag{26}$$

When $0 < \rho < 1$, the second condition in (26) holds with equality. Dividing the two expressions yields

$$\gamma'(h)/\gamma(h) = \phi'(h)/[\phi(h) - \phi(0)] \tag{27}$$

which gives a unique solution for h, say h^*. At $h = h^*$ we must have diminishing returns, or $\gamma''(h^*) < 0$. Equation (27) is independent of both ρ and θ, so $h(\theta) = h^*$, a constant whenever *any* layoffs occur. Furthermore we have in this region

$$\theta F'(\rho n \gamma(h^*)) = \phi'(h^*)/\gamma'(h^*)$$
$$= [\phi(h^*) - \phi(0)]/\gamma(h^*), \tag{28}$$

so the shadow price of labor is $[\phi(h^*) - \phi(0)]/\gamma(h^*)$, a constant independent of θ. (28) defines $\rho(\theta)$ when layoffs are positive, and implies that $\rho(\theta)$ is increasing in θ. Fewer workers are laid off in more favorable states. Furthermore, wages $C_1(\theta)$ paid to employed workers are rigid and independent of θ whenever layoffs are positive.

Since $\rho(\theta)$ is increasing, there must be some critical value θ^* beyond which $\rho = 1$. The firm would like to hire more workers than it has contracted with in states more favorable than this. Therefore, for $\theta > \theta^*$ it is h that does all the adjusting. In this range $h(\theta)$ is defined by the first condition in (26) with ρ set equal to one. The firm's shadow price of labor is $\phi'(h)/\gamma'(h)$ here and is increasing in h on the assumptions above. Therefore $h(\theta)$ is increasing for $\theta \geq \theta^*$. $C_1(\theta)$ is increasing here as well.

The overall solution is pieced together in Figure 4. The employment rate does all the adjusting when θ falls short of θ^*. h is rigidly set at h^* here and the shadow price of labor to the firm is constant. For $\theta > \theta^*$, the shadow price of labor is rising, $\rho = 1$, and hours do all the adjusting. Furthermore, the wage paid to employed persons is "rigid" downward: C_1 is constant for $\theta \leq \theta^*$. The internal supply price of labor would be smaller than shown if contracts did not fully indemnify laid-off workers, and layoffs would be involuntary, as above. In either case the layoff rate is

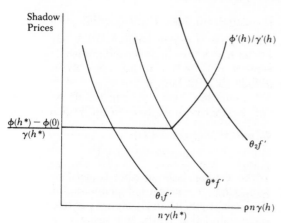

Figure 4.

decreasing in μ (the undiversifiable risk) because θ^* is decreasing in μ.

This example suggests the following interpretation of hours and employment data. In normal times (the mean of θ exceeds θ^*) hours per worker account for most total manhours variation (hours are a leading indicator). Workers are not laid off until conditions get sufficiently bad to pass beyond the threshold θ^*, at which point hours per head show downward rigidity that puts distinct limits on the use of worksharing.

This type of model can account for some of the broader features of the data, but recent international comparisons present interesting and important challenges. Robert J. Gordon (1982) compared the U.S. with Japan. Both countries exhibit about equal variance in total hours worked, but hours per worker varies more in Japan than in the U.S. and employment varies more in the U.S. The widespread use of bonuses makes for greater wage variability in Japan as well. Models of this type account for these differences on the basis of differences in preferences and technology and surely leave much unexplained. It appears as if some consideration of differences in firm-specific human

capital, labor mobility, and quasi-fixed factor ideas are required to fully account for these differences (Masanori Hashimoto 1979).

VI. *Intertemporal Contracts*

This survey follows the literature in expositing timeless single period models. There is a parallel intertemporal formulation, following Baily (1974) who suggested that contracts might exploit gains from trade due to capital market imperfections. The firm's greater access to capital markets allows it to save and dissave on the worker's behalf, and eliminates intertemporal uncertainty in consumption (James N. Brown 1982) that the worker cannot accomplish on his own. The contract again specifies consumption (wage payments) and labor utilization in each state and each time period, conditional on information available in that period. It mimics the solution to an intertemporal, expected utility maximization problem. Now the observed wage payments intermingle elements of intertemporal savings and dissavings as well as the usual productive efficiency considerations. Nonetheless, the formal analysis has many features in common with the one-period model. Under complete information the contract specifies (C_t, L_t) pairs conditional on the history of state realizations θ_t up to the present time t. In the leading model the worker has an intertemporally separable utility function of the form $E\Sigma U(C_t, L_t)D^t$, where D is the rate of time preference, similar to (8), and the firm is risk neutral. The budget constraint at time t equates the expected present value of future consumption to the expected present value of future production, conditional on the observed sequence $\{\theta_\tau\}$ at t, similar to (9).

The precise solution depends on the properties of $\{\theta_t\}$ and the extent to which capital consumption allows intertemporal

1166   Journal of Economic Literature, Vol. XXIII (September 1985)

diversification of aggregate disturbances (Richard Cantor 1983). Consider the simplest case in which θ is independently distributed over agents with a constant mean (Sanford Grossman and Laurence Weiss 1984). Then the insurance of Section IV is achieved by a consumption loan market, subordinated through firms. Those with adverse realizations borrow on their worker's behalf and those with favorable realizations are lenders. The loan market is cleared at a rate of interest equal to the rate of time preference (to satisfy intertemporal marginal conditions) and the analysis of Section IV carries through intact. Here the $s(\theta)$ terms of Figure 2 are the savings and dissavings components of observed earnings of workers, personal consumption is smoothed and personal labor supply is accentuated by substitution effects. "Capital market imperfections" introduce, ex post, involuntary elements in contract terms, as above.

More generally, write $\theta_{it} = \mu_t \epsilon_{it}$. Then the contract is conditioned on the history of the aggregate shock as well as on local disturbances. These aggregate shocks are undiversifiable if there are no stores of nonhuman wealth. An unanticipated adverse aggregate disturbance increases the demand for consumption loans. The rate of interest rises to ration reduced supply. Smaller aggregate consumption is redistributed out of the diversifiable risks, as before, but observed consumption and employment contain elements of Keynesian income effects. The optimal program embodies forecasts of permanent wealth to the extent that the μ-process is serially correlated and persistent. These redistribute planned consumption and labor supply over time through direct wealth effects and indirectly through their anticipated effects on interest rates. In the most general formulation, capital allows the aggregate disturbance to be partially diversified through capital accumulation in favorable aggregate conditions and

through decumulation in unfavorable circumstances (Truman Bewley 1980; William Brock 1982). These intertemporal trading possibilities reduce the income and wealth effects of aggregate shocks on consumption and employment behavior and accentuate pure substitution effects.[11]

This discussion makes clear that intertemporal contract models are closely related to the intertemporal substitution hypothesis (Lucas and Leonard Rapping 1970). A substantial practical difference is the role of measured wage rates in uncovering the structure of preferences and technology from actual data, because average wage rates do not index the true marginal product of labor or the marginal rate of substitution between C and L in contracts (Section IV). This point is important because almost all empirical studies of intertemporal substitution assume that measured wage rates fully reflect both margins in the data. Two notable exceptions are James N. Brown (1982), who attempted to estimate the optimal program directly on functional form restrictions, and Abowd and David Card (1983), who attempt to estimate the fraction of workers for whom wage rates reflect marginal conditions. The methods of Finn Kydland and Edward Prescott (1982) also rest heavily on functional forms and avoid the use of market price and wage data. But, on the conventional assumption, most recent estimates of intertemporal substitution on microdata are negligible for prime-age males (MaCurdy 1981; Joseph Altonji 1982); but they are much larger for those classes of workers, such as married women, who exhibit regular labor force transitions (Heckman and MaCurdy 1980). It is worth pointing out that in light of

[11] This general framework strongly links consumption and labor supply behavior unless one period preferences are strongly separable. Recent research has found excess volatility of consumption relative to permanent income and interest rates, but the extent to which this volatility can be explained by interactions with labor supply has not been studied.

the greater labor force and (contractual) job attachments traditionally exhibited by men, the maintained assumption that observed wage rates index marginal conditions is less likely to apply to them.

Studies by Finn Kydland and Edward Prescott (1982), Robert Barro and Robert King (1982), Kydland (1984), and Jisoon Lee (1984) conclude that the conventional intertemporal model cannot explain certain comovements in aggregate time-series data. The preferred specification is controversial and may require nonseparable preferences and technology. However, contract theory does not depend on these special assumptions. A contract can be written for any preferences and technology, but it always divorces measured wage rates from the production efficiency conditions of the optimum program that it embodies.

VII. *Contracts with Private Information*

As noted above, it is difficult to incorporate transactions costs and incomplete insurance in contract models. Interest in asymmetric information models has been sustained by their potential for doing this in an analytically tractable manner. The problem investigated most thoroughly so far is identical to that of Section IV with one bit of information removed: the firm is assumed to observe the realization of θ but the worker doesn't observe it (Guillermo Calvo and Edmund Phelps 1977; Hall and Lilien 1979). Recent work by Russell Cooper (1981) and John Moore (1984) consider two-sided private information models and cannot be reviewed here. Readers are forewarned that this section is more technically demanding than the rest of the survey. However, it may be skipped without significant loss of continuity.

The contract cannot be conditioned on θ because the worker cannot observe it, and since any rational employment deci-

sion must depend on the marginal product of labor, that decision must be delegated to the agent with the information, namely the firm. The contract takes the following form (Jerry Green and Charles Kahn 1983): the worker and firm agree ex ante on a compensation schedule $C(L)$ (equivalently $C(1 - L)$). The firm observes θ and instructs the employee to work $(1 - L)$ units of time in exchange for contractual compensation $C(L)$. Market competition takes the form of offering attractive compensation schedules $C(L)$, so the competitive contract maximizes expected utility of the worker subject to expected firm utility (or profit) and information constraints. The nonlinear contract pricing schedule $C(L)$ is closely related to the multipart-tariffs of Section IV. In fact the solution of the problem is formally identical to the theory of nonlinear pricing (Michael Mussa and Rosen 1978; Eric Maskin and Riley 1984).

Given any schedule $C(L)$, the firm observes θ and chooses L to maximize profit. The firm's ex post profit is $\pi(\theta, L) = \theta(1 - L) - C(L)$ so given $C(L)$ and θ, L is chosen to satisfy

$$\frac{\partial \pi}{\partial L} = -\theta - C'(L) = 0 \qquad (29)$$

so long as

$$\frac{\partial^2 \pi}{\partial L^2} = -C''(L) < 0.$$

The firm chooses L in (29) so that the marginal product of labor equals its marginal cost to the firm. Write the solution to (29) as $L(\theta)$. Comparative statics reveals

$$L'(\theta) = -1/C'' < 0.$$

The worker is always instructed to work more in favorable states and less in unfavorable states. Define $C(\theta) = C(L(\theta))$. Then $C'(\theta) = -\theta L'(\theta) > 0$, and compensation unambiguously increases in θ independently of worker preferences.

1168   *Journal of Economic Literature, Vol. XXIII (September 1985)*

The method of solution follows an idea of Mirrlees (1971). Given $C(L)$, the firm exploits its information through (29), which holds for every possible realization of θ. Therefore (29) may be regarded as a differential equation $dC/dL = -\theta$, or $dC = -\theta dL$. Integrating by parts will yield

$$C(\theta) - C(0) = -\theta L + \int_0^\theta L(\nu)d\nu \quad (30)$$

which is a convenient way of representing the information constraint (29).

The competitive equilibrium contract maximizes the worker's expected utility subject to the firm's expected utility, as before, and to the firm's exploitation of its information (30). Define the transformation $z(\theta) = \int_0^\theta L(\nu)d\nu$. Then $z'(\theta) = L(\theta)$ and (30) becomes

$$C(\theta) = C(0) - \theta z'(\theta) + z(\theta). \quad (31)$$

Furthermore, (assuming $f(1 - L) = 1 - L$ simplifies the presentation without affecting essentials):

$$\pi(\theta) = \max_L \pi(\theta, L)$$
$$= \max_L \theta(1 - L(\theta)) - C(\theta)$$
$$= \theta - \theta z' - C(0) + \theta z' - z$$
$$= \theta - C(0) - z(\theta).$$

Now the contract can be described as a variational problem in z and z'. Recalling that $Eu = \int U(C, L)dG$, and substituting for C from (31), we seek a function $z(\theta)$ and real numbers λ and $C(0)$ that maximize

$$\int U(C(0) - \theta z' + z, z')dG + \lambda[\bar{v} - \int v(\theta - z - C(0))dG] \quad (32)$$

where $v(\cdot)$ is the utility function of the firm. Once $z'(\theta) = L(\theta)$ has been found, (3) is used to calculate $C(\theta)$. Eliminating θ from these two expressions implies $C(L)$.

Two marginal conditions and a boundary condition characterize the solution.

Differentiating (32) with respect to $C(0)$, yields:

$$\int_0^\infty U_C dG = -\lambda \int_0^\infty v'dG. \quad (33)$$

The *average* marginal utility of consumption for the worker is proportional to *average* marginal utility of the firm. Marginal utilities are not necessarily equated state-by-state. An Euler equation gives the margin for z:

$$(U_C + \lambda v')g(\theta) = \frac{d}{d\theta}(U_L - \theta U_C)g(\theta). \quad (34)$$

Denote the upper and lower limits of θ in $G(\theta)$ by $\hat{\theta}$ and $\underline{\theta}$ respectively. Then multiplying (34) through by $d\theta$ integrating and exploiting (33) yields

$$U_L(\hat{\theta}) - \hat{\theta}U_C(\hat{\theta}) = U_L(\underline{\theta}) - \underline{\theta}U_C(\underline{\theta}). \quad (35)$$

The boundary condition sets (35) to zero, so the contract is production efficient ($\theta = U_L/U_C$) in the best and worst states (Cooper, 1983 gives an intuitive explanation in terms of the revelation principle: the firm cannot overstate the most extreme realizations to the worker if the distribution $G(\theta)$ is bounded and the bounds are common knowledge). Using this fact and integrating (34) yields the fundamental condition

$$\int_0^\theta (U_C + \lambda v')g(\theta)d\theta = (U_L - \theta U_C)g(\theta). \quad (36)$$

Equation (36) nicely illustrates the tension between insurance and efficiency under private information. The contract cannot be production efficient for $\underline{\theta} < \theta < \hat{\theta}$ unless there is efficient sharing of risks in the Borch-Arrow sense for each state. In addition the solution generally depends on $G(\theta)$. For example, it can be shown (Mussa and Rosen 1978; Kahn and Jose Scheinkman, forthcoming) that the firm may choose the same work hours $1 - L$ for a closed interval of states. The contract certainly doesn't achieve first-best efficiency in these regions.

Much effort has gone into analyzing the sign of the inefficiency implied by (36).

The interpretation plays heavily on a notion of contractual commitment and enforcement that does not arise in the common information case. For suppose the contract implies production inefficiency in some state. The worker and the firm have agreed to contractual terms $C(L)$ ex ante. When this state materializes, the worker generally can infer the realized value of θ by his implicit knowledge of (29): the production function and utility function are common knowledge in this formulation; Schwartz (1983), questions how this knowledge becomes common. At that point there are unexploited gains from trade and both parties could benefit by recalibrating L so that $\theta = U_L/U_C$ ex post. However, if recontracting is allowed, the contract must unravel, because it is written under the assumption that both parties bind themselves to its ex ante terms. The extent to which private information models produce "involuntary" unemployment and overemployment depends on how these ex ante commitments can be enforced ex post. While some authors are careful to recognize this important point (especially Oliver Hart 1983), a convincing description of labor market institutions that embody this enforcement mechanism in *implicit* contracts has not been forthcoming.

Three special cases of (36) have been analyzed. The method of proof is established by Green and Kahn (1983), to which the reader is referred for details. Denote the left hand side of (36) as a function of θ, say $\zeta(\theta)$. The sign of $\zeta(\theta)$ is established by calculating its derivatives and ascertaining whether it achieves a local maximum or minimum for some interior value of θ, using boundary condition (35). The results are sensitive to the nature of risk aversion and to income effects in worker preferences.

Case 1 (Hall and Lilien 1979). Assume firms are risk neutral, workers are risk averse and have preferences of the form $u = U(C + \psi(L))$—no income effects. Then the left hand side of (36) turns out to be identically zero, and the contract specifies $\theta = U_L/U_C$ for every θ. There is, furthermore, complete and optimal risk shifting: $u(\theta)$ is constant and the firms eats all risks. Here the $C(L)$ schedule coincides with an indifference curve, as in Figure 3 Section IV. Private and common knowledge contracts are identical in this case.

Case 2 (Grossman and Hart 1983; Azariadis 1983). Maintain the same assumptions about workers as Case 1, but let the firm be risk averse. Here Green and Kahn's proof may be extended to show that the left hand side of (36) is negative for almost all θ. Therefore, $U_L/U_C < \theta$ and the marginal social cost of labor is less than its ex post marginal product. The worker would like to recontract for more employment, ex post, in practically every state, and there is involuntary underemployment in the sense qualified above. Furthermore, the worker bears consumption risk and $u(\theta)$ is increasing in θ.

Case 3 (Green and Kahn 1983; V. V. Chari 1983). The firm is risk neutral, the worker is risk averse and has a positive income elasticity of demand for leisure (as in Section IV). Now the integral in (36) is positive for almost all θ. Therefore $U_L/U_C > \theta$, and the marginal cost of labor exceeds its marginal product. The contract leads to "involuntary overemployment" and the worker would like to recontract ex post for less work than the firm chooses. Here $u(\theta)$ is decreasing in θ and the worker is worse off in the more favorable states, as in Section IV.

The nature of these contracts is altered if workers have means to disassociate current consumption decisions from current earnings. Thus, consider the third case and assume that the worker can self-insure (Topel and Finis Welch 1983), for example, by borrowing and lending in a perfect capital market in the intertemporal context. Then the worker's self-insurance ac-

1170   *Journal of Economic Literature, Vol. XXIII (September 1985)*

tivities imply $U_C = -\lambda$ for each θ. Since the firm is risk neutral, the left side of (36) vanishes and the asymmetric information contract is perfectly efficient. Its employment and consumption properties duplicate that of Section IV. Oliver Hart (1983) adds the assumption that the firm is risk averse and gives an ingenious argument for the relevance of Case 2. Risk neutral stockholders would be reluctant to provide full insurance to the firm's management on moral hazard grounds. However, they would not be so reluctant to contract for consumption insurance with workers, because workers' labor supply is delegated through the manager in private information contracts and there are no direct moral hazards. Hence, these third parties could conceivably enforce the $U_C = -\lambda$ condition for workers. But then, risk aversion of managers ($v'' < 0$) implies that the left side of (36) must be negative for bad realizations, or involuntary underemployment. This argument is a delicate one, for it implies that the effect of third party insurance to workers is partially subverted by workers intermediating it and providing partial insurance to managers (because workers become, effectively, risk neutral). Income risks to managers are reduced by making the contractual $C(L)$ function steeper than when third party insurance is available. In favorable states the marginal cost of labor to the firm is increasing too rapidly in $(1 - L)$ and the firm does not employ as much labor as is socially desirable. In unfavorable states the marginal cost of labor is falling too fast and too much labor is released.

VIII. *Conclusion*

Not all marriages are made in heaven. Firms go bankrupt, demand shifts to other locations, supply shifts to other countries, products become obsolete and relative demands for goods have been known to change over time. Contracts call for permanent dissolutions when quasi-rents on firm specific human capital fall to zero. Serious critics of contract theory have built their case on the observation that quits rise noticeably during business cycle expansions (Herschel Grossman 1977, 1978). Contracts break down if workers accept insurance payments opportunistically in bad times and renege on premium payments by skipping out in good times. How much of observed, voluntary turnover reflects opportunism and how much of it is the rational outcome of moving workers from lower to higher valued uses?

These issues occupy much attention in current research, which is proceeding in a number of different directions too disparate to be usefully reviewed here. However, these problems are important for delimiting the scope for self-enforcing contracts that the at-will labor market, contracting institution requires, and for pointing out potential reasons why contracts might be incomplete. The common knowledge framework illustrates some of these ideas. Under these circumstances the contract would specify the conditions and terms of its dissolution up front.

A suitable reinterpretation of the model in Section III clarifies the point. Think of θ as a disturbance that permanently affects the fortunes of the firm, and interpret mL as the value of the worker's time in an alternative job in another market.[12] Then p has the interpretation of the probability of a permanent separation. The solution is exactly the same as shown above. The complete contract stipulates a severance payment C_2 to those workers who depart when θ falls short of θ^*. Turnover

---

[12] Holmstrom (1983) analyzes an offer-matching equilibrium when the outside opportunity is stochastic. Hall and Edward Lazear (1984) discuss two-sided uncertainty in which the bargaining costs preclude ex post renegotiation. Turnover is socially excessive in this case.

is efficient if the severance payment offers complete insurance, but is inefficient if severance payments are constrained and workers are not fully protected against permanent separations. For the same reasons as before, there is insufficient turnover in these latter circumstances. (See, especially, Ito 1984, also Herakles Polemarchakis and Laurence Weiss 1978; Arnott, Arthur Hosios and Stiglitz 1983; John Geanakoplos and Ito 1982; Barry Nalebuff and Richard Zeckhauser 1984.)

The need for interfirm mobility in a well functioning labor market suggests important reasons why contracts might be incomplete. A worker's knowledge and perception of outside opportunities do not materialize out of the blue. Information gathering and job search activities are costly and cannot be a matter of common knowledge by the idiosyncratic nature of job-worker matches. A worker must bear some residual job finding risks because of the moral hazard effects of personal actions on success probabilities (Steven Shavell and Laurence Weiss 1979). Furthermore, the nature of searchers' interactions gives rise to externalities that have only recently begun to be understood (Diamond 1982; Christopher Pissarides 1984). A contract must embody a delicate balance of encouraging mobility in response to permanent changes in demands and discouraging it for temporary shocks. Full insurance discourages mobility by subsidizing leisure and reducing job search intensity (Bronars 1983; Mortensen 1983b; Ito 1984). This is undesirable when severance is economically warranted, but not when demand and supply disturbances have a more transient character. Since inferences on the permanent-temporary decomposition of disturbances is itself uncertain, it appears as if contracts cannot provide complete insurance. We are driven back to conventional models to the extent that this is true.

REFERENCES

ABOWD, JOHN AND ASHENFELTER, ORLEY. "Anticipated Unemployment and Compensating Wage Differentials," in *Studies in labor markets.* Ed.: SHERWIN ROSEN. Chicago: U. of Chicago Press for NBER, 1981, pp. 141–70.

——. "Compensating Wage and Earnings Differentials for Employer Determined Hours of Work." U. of Chicago, 1984.

ABOWD, JOHN AND CARD, DAVID. "Intertemporal Substitution in the Presence of Long-Term Contracts." Working Paper 166, Industrial Relations Section, Princeton U., 1983.

AKERLOF, GEORGE AND MIYAZAKI, HAJIME. "The Implicit Contract Theory of Unemployment Meets the Wage Bill Argument," *Rev. Econ. Stud.,* Jan. 1980, *47*(2), pp. 321–38.

ALCHIAN, ARMEN. "Information Costs, Pricing and Resource Unemployment," *Western Econ. J.,* June 1969, *7*(2), pp. 109–28.

ALTONJI, JOSEPH G. "The Intertemporal Substitution Model of Labour Market Fluctuations: An Empirical Analysis," *Rev. Econ. Stud.,* Special Issue, 1982, *49*(5), pp. 783–824.

—— AND ASHENFELTER, ORLEY. "Wage Movements and the Labour Market Equilibrium Hypothesis," *Economica,* Aug. 1980, *47*(187), pp. 217–45.

ARNOTT, RICHARD AND RILEY, JOHN G. "Asymmetrical Production Possibilities, the Social Gains from Inequality and the Optimal Town," *Scand. J. Econ.,* 1977, *79*(3), pp. 301–11.

——; HOSIOS, ARTHUR AND STIGLITZ, JOSEPH E. "Implicit Contracts, Labor Mobility and Unemployment," Princeton U., 1983.

ARROW, KENNETH J. "The Role of Securities in the Optimal Allocation of Risk-Bearing," *Rev. Econ. Stud.,* Apr. 1964, *31,* pp. 91–96.

——. *Essays in the theory of risk bearing.* Chicago: Markham, 1971.

ASHENFELTER, ORLEY AND BROWN, JAMES. "Testing the Efficiency of Employment Contracts," *J. Polit. Econ.,* forthcoming.

AZARIADIS, COSTAS. "Implicit Contracts and Underemployment Equilibria," *J. Polit. Econ.,* Dec. 1975, *83*(6), pp. 1183–1202.

——. "On the Incidence of Unemployment," *Rev. Econ. Stud.,* Feb. 1976, *43*(1), pp. 115–25.

——. "Implicit Contracts and Related Topics: A Survey," in *The economics of the labour market.* Eds.: ZMIRA HORNSTEIN, *et al.* London: HMSO, 1979, 221–48.

——. "Employment with Asymmetric Information," *Quart. J. Econ.* Supplement 1983, *98*(3), pp. 157–72.

—— AND STIGLITZ, JOSEPH E. "Implicit Contracts and Fixed Price Equilibria," *Quart. J. Econ.* Supplement 1983, *98*(3), pp. 1–22.

BAILY, MARTIN N. "Wages and Employment under Uncertain Demand," *Rev. Econ. Stud.,* Jan. 1974, *41*(1), pp. 37–50.

——. "On the Theory of Layoffs and Unemployment," *Econometrica*, July 1977, *45*(5), pp. 1043–64.

BARRO, ROBERT AND KING, ROBERT G. "Time-Separable Preferences and Intertemporal-Substitution Models of Business Cycles." U. of Rochester, 1982.

BECKER, GARY S. *Human capital.* NY: Columbia U. Press for NBER, 1964.

——. "A Theory of Marriage, Part I," *J. Polit. Econ.*, July/Aug. 1973, *81*(4), pp. 813–46.

BERNANKE, BEN. "An Equilibrium Model of Industrial Employment, Hours and Earnings, 1923–39." Grad. School of Bus., Stanford U., 1983.

BEWLEY, TRUMAN F. "The Permanent Income Hypothesis and Long-Run Economic Stability," *J. Econ. Theory*, June 1980, *22*(3), pp. 377–94.

BILS, MARK. "Real Wages over the Business Cycle: Evidence from Panel Data," *J. Polit. Econ.*, forthcoming.

BORCH, KARL. "Equilibrium in a Reinsurance Market," *Econometrica*, July 1962, *30*(3), pp. 424–44.

BROCK, WILLIAM A. "Asset Prices in a Production Economy," *Economics of information and uncertainty.* Ed.: JOHN JOSEPH McCALL. Chicago: U. of Chicago Press, 1982, pp. 1–47.

BRONARS, STEPHEN. "Compensating Wage Differentials and Layoff Risk in U.S. Manufacturing Industries." Ph.D. diss., U. of Chicago, 1983.

BROWN, JAMES N. "How Close to an Auction Is the Labor Market?" *Res. Lab. Econ.*, 1982, *5*, pp. 182–235.

BROWN, MURRAY AND WOLFSTETTER, ELMAR. "Underemployment and Normal Leisure," *Econ. Letters*, 1984, *15*(1–2), pp. 157–63.

BROWNING, MARTIN; DEATON, ANGUS AND IRISH, MARGARET. "A Profitable Approach to Labor Supply and Commodity Demands Over the Life-Cycle," *Econometrica*, forthcoming.

BRYANT, JOHN. "An Annotation of 'Implicit Contracts and Underemployment Equilibria,' " *J. Polit. Econ.*, Dec. 1978, *86*(6), pp. 1159–60.

BULL, CLIVE. "The Existence of Self-Enforcing Implicit Contracts." C. V. Starr Center, NYU, 1983.

BURDETT, KENNETH AND MORTENSEN, DALE T. "Search, Layoffs and Labor Market Equilibrium," *J. Polit. Econ.*, Aug. 1980, *88*(4), pp. 652–72.

CALVO, GUILLERMO A. AND PHELPS, EDMUND S. "Indexation Issues: Appendix," *J. Monet. Econ.*, Supplementary Series 1977, *5*, pp. 160–68.

CANTOR, RICHARD. "Long-Term Labor Contracts, Consumption Smoothing and Aggregate Wage Dynamics." Ohio State U., 1983.

CHAPMAN, SIDNEY J. "Hours of Labour," *Econ. J.*, Sept. 1909, *19*(3), pp. 354–79.

CHARI, V. V. "Involuntary Unemployment and Implicit Contracts," *Quart. J. Econ.*, Supplement, 1983, *98*(3), pp. 107–22.

COGAN, JOHN. "Labor Supply With Costs of Market Entry," in *Female labor supply.* Ed.: JAMES P. SMITH. Princeton, NJ: Princeton U. Press, 1980, pp. 327–64.

COOPER, RUSSELL. "Risk-Sharing and Productive Efficiency in Labor Contracts Under Bilateral Asymmetric Information." U. of Pennsylvania, 1981.

——. "A Note on Overemployment/Underemployment in Labor Contracts Under Asymmetric Information," *Econ. Letters*, 1983, *12*(1), pp. 81–87.

DEBREU, GERARD. *The theory of value.* Cowles Foundation Monograph 17. New Haven: Yale U. Press, 1959.

DIAMOND, PETER. "Aggregate Demand Management in Search Equilibrium," *J. Polit. Econ.*, Oct. 1982, *90*(5), pp. 881–94.

—— AND ROTHSCHILD, MICHAEL. *Uncertainty in economics.* NY: Academic Press, 1978.

EPSTEIN, RICHARD A. "In Praise of the Contract at Will," *Univ. Chicago Law Rev.*, Fall 1984, *51*(4), pp. 956–82.

FAIR, RAY C. *The short-run demand for workers and hours.* Amsterdam: North-Holland Pub. Co., 1969.

FELDSTEIN, MARTIN. "Specification of the Labour Input in the Aggregate Production Function," *Rev. Econ. Stud.*, Oct. 1967, *34*, pp. 375–86.

——. "The Importance of Temporary Layoffs: An Empirical Analysis," *Brookings Pap. Econ. Act.*, 1975, *3*, pp. 725–44.

——. "Temporary Layoffs in the Theory of Unemployment," *J. Polit. Econ.*, Oct. 1976, *84*(5), pp. 937–57.

FISCHER, STANLEY. "Long-Term Contracts, Rational Expectations and the Optimum Money Supply Rule," *J. Polit. Econ.*, Feb. 1977, *85*(1), pp. 191–205.

FRIEDMAN, MILTON. "The Role of Monetary Policy," *Amer. Econ. Rev.*, Mar. 1968, *58*(1), pp. 1–17.

——. *Price theory: A provisional text.* Chicago: Aldine Pub. Co., 1962.

——. *A theory of the consumption function.* Princeton, NJ: Princeton U. Press, 1957.

FRISCH, RAGNAR. *New methods of measuring marginal utility.* Tübingen: J.C.B. Mohr, 1932.

GEANAKOPLOS, JOHN AND ITO, TAKATOSHI. "On Implicit Contracts and Involuntary Unemployment." Cowles Foundation Discussion Paper No. 640, 1982.

GHEZ, GILBERT AND BECKER, GARY S. *The allocation of time and goods over the life cycle.* NY: Columbia U. Press for NBER, 1975.

GORDON, DONALD F. "A Neo-Classical Theory of Keynesian Unemployment," *Econ. Inquiry*, Dec. 1974, *12*(4), pp. 431–59.

GORDON, ROBERT J. "Why U.S. Wage and Employment Behavior Differs from That in Britain and Japan," *Econ. J.*, Mar. 1982, *92*(365), pp. 13–44.

GRAY, JO ANNA. "Wage Indexation: A Macroeconomic Approach," *J. Monet. Econ.*, Apr. 1976, *2*(2), pp. 221–36.

GREEN, JERRY AND KAHN, CHARLES M. "Wage Employment Contracts," *Quart. J. Econ.*, Supplement, 1983, *98*(3), pp. 173–87.

GROSSMAN, HERSCHEL. "Risk Shifting, Layoffs and Seniority," *J. Monet. Econ.*, Nov. 1978, *4*(4), pp. 661–86.

——. "Risk Shifting and Reliability in Labor Markets," *Scand. J. Econ.*, 1977, *79*(2), pp. 187–209.

GROSSMAN, MICHAEL. "Unemployment and Consumption: Note" *Amer. Econ. Rev.*, Mar. 1973, 63(1), pp. 208–13.

GROSSMAN, SANFORD J. AND HART, OLIVER D. "Implicit Contracts, Moral Hazard and Unemployment," *Amer. Econ. Rev.*, May 1981, 71(2), pp. 301–07.

———. "Implicit Contracts under Asymmetrical Information," *Quart. J. Econ.* Supplement 1983, 98(3), pp. 123–56.

GROSSMAN, SANFORD J. AND WEISS, LAURENCE. "Saving and Insurance," in *Bayesian models in economic theory.* Eds.: M. BOYER AND R. E. KIHLSTROM. NY: Elsevier, 1984, pp. 303–11.

HALL, ROBERT E. "Why is the Unemployment Rate So High at Full Employment?" *Brookings Pap. Econ. Act.*, 1970, 3, pp. 369–410.

———. "A Theory of the Natural Unemployment Rate and the Duration of Employment," *J. Monet. Econ.*, Apr. 1979, 5(2), pp. 153–69.

———. "Employment Fluctuations and Wage Rigidity." *Brookings Pap. Econ. Act.*, 1980a, 1, pp. 91–123.

———. "Labor Supply and Aggregate Fluctuations," *Carnegie-Rochester Conference Series on Public Policy, 12,* 1980b, pp. 7–33.

———. "The Importance of Lifetime Jobs in the U.S. Economy," *Amer. Econ. Rev.*, Sept. 1982, 72(4), pp. 716–24.

——— AND LAZEAR, EDWARD P. "The Excess Sensitivity of Layoffs and Quits to Demand," *J. Lab. Econ.*, 1984, 2(2), pp. 253–58.

——— AND LILIEN, DAVID M. "Efficient Wage Bargains Under Uncertain Supply and Demand," *Amer. Econ. Rev.*, Dec. 1979, 69(5), pp. 868–79.

HAMERMESH, DANIEL. "Social Insurance and Consumption," *Amer. Econ. Rev.*, Mar. 1982, 72(1), pp. 101–13.

HANOCH, GIORA. "A Multivariate Model of Labor Supply: Methodology and Estimation," in *Female labor supply.* Ed.: JAMES P. SMITH. Princeton, NJ: Princeton U. Press, 1980, pp. 249–326.

HARBERGER, ARNOLD C. "On Measuring the Social Opportunity Cost of Labor," *Int. Lab. Rev.*, June 1971, 103(6), pp. 559–79.

HARRIS, JOHN R. AND TODARO, MICHAEL P. "Migration, Unemployment and Development: A Two-Sector Analysis," *Amer. Econ. Rev.*, Mar. 1970, 60(1), pp. 126–42.

HART, OLIVER D. "Optimal Labour Contracts Under Assymmetric Information: An Introduction," *Rev. Econ. Stud.*, Jan. 1983, 50(1), pp. 3–35.

HART, ROBERT A. *The economics of non-wage labour costs.* London: George Allen & Unwin, 1984.

HASHIMOTO, MASANORI. "Bonus Payments, On-the-Job Training and Lifetime Employment in Japan," *J. Polit. Econ.*, Part 1, Oct. 1979, 87(5), pp. 1086–1104.

HECKMAN, JAMES J. AND MACURDY, THOMAS. "A Life Cycle Model of Female Labor Supply," *Rev. Econ. Stud.*, Jan. 1980, 47(1), pp. 47–74.

——— AND SEDLACEK, GUILERMO. "An Equilibrium Model of the Industrial Distribution of Workers and Wages." U. of Chicago, 1984.

HEY, JOHN D. *Uncertainty in microeconomics.* NY: NYU Press, 1979.

HICKS, JOHN R. *The theory of wages.* London: Macmillan, 1932.

HOLMSTROM, BENGT. "Contractual Models of the Labor Market," *Amer. Econ. Rev.*, May 1981, 71(2), pp. 308–13.

———. "Equilibrium Long Term Contracts," *Quart. J. Econ.*, Supplement 1983, 98(3), pp. 23–54.

HUTCHENS, ROBERT M. "Layoffs and Labor Supply," *Int. Econ. Rev.*, Feb. 1983, 24(1), pp. 37–55.

ITO, TAKATOSHI. "Implicit Contract Theory: A Critical Survey." U. of Minnesota, 1982.

———. "Labor Contracts With Voluntary Quits." U. of Minnesota, 1984.

JOHANSEN, LEIF. *Production functions.* Amsterdam: North-Holland Pub. Co., 1972.

JOHNSON, WILLIAM R. "A Theory of Job Shopping," *Quart. J. Econ.*, May 1978, 92(2), pp. 261–78.

JOVANOVIC, BOYAN. "Job Matching and the Theory of Turnover," *J. Polit. Econ.*, Oct. 1979, 87(5), pp. 972–90.

KAHN, CHARLES M. AND SCHEINKMAN, JOSE. "Optimal Employment Contracts With Bankruptcy Constraints," *J. Econ. Theory*, forthcoming.

KATZ, LAWRENCE. "Layoffs, Uncertain Recall and the Duration of Unemployment." MIT, 1984.

KIHLSTROM, RICHARD E. AND LAFFONT, JEAN-Jacques. "A General Equilibrium Enterpreneurial Theory of Firm Formation Based on Risk Aversion," *J. Polit. Econ.*, Aug. 1979, 87(4), pp. 719–48.

———. "Implicit Contracts and Free Entry," *Quart. J. Econ.*, Supplement 1983, 98(3), pp. 55–106.

KINOSHITA, TOMIO. "Working Hours and Hedonic Wages in the Market Equilibrium." Musachi U., 1985.

KNIGHT, FRANK H. *Risk, uncertainty and profit.* Boston: Houghton Mifflin & Co., 1921.

KYDLAND, FINN E. "Labor Force Heterogeneity and the Business Cycle," *Carnegie-Rochester Conference Series on Public Policy,* Autumn 1984, 20.

——— AND PRESCOTT, EDWARD C. "Time To Build and Aggregate Fluctuations," *Econometrica,* Nov. 1982, 50(6), pp. 1345–70.

LEE, JISOON. "A Rational Expectations Model of Labor Supply." Ph.D. diss., U. of Chicago, 1984.

LEONTIEF, WASSILY. "The Pure Theory of the Guaranteed Annual Wage Contract," *J. Polit. Econ.*, Feb. 1946, 54(1), pp. 76–79.

LEWIS, H. GREGG. "Employer Interests in Employee Hours of Work." U. of Chicago, 1969.

LILIEN, DAVID. "The Cyclical Pattern of Temporary Layoffs in United States Manufacturing," *Rev. Econ. Statist.*, Feb. 1980, 62(1), pp. 24–31.

LUCAS, ROBERT E., JR. "Some International Evidence of Output-Inflation Trade Offs," *Amer. Econ. Rev.*, June 1973, 63(2), pp. 326–34.

——— AND RAPPING, LEONARD A. "Real Wages, Employment and Inflation," in *Microeconomic foundations of employment and inflation theory.* Eds.: EDMUND PHELPS, et al. NY: W. W. Norton, 1970.

LUNDBERG, SHELLY. "Tied Wage Hours Offers and

1174 *Journal of Economic Literature, Vol. XXIII (September 1985)*

the Endogeneity of Wages." NBER Working Paper no. 1431, 1984.

MACURDY, THOMAS E. "An Empirical Model of Labor Supply in a Life-Cycle Setting," *J. Polit. Econ.,* Dec. 1981, *89*(6), pp. 1059–86.

_____ AND PENCAVEL, JOHN. "Testing Between Competing Models of Wage and Employment Determination in Unionized Markets," *J. Polit. Econ.,* forthcoming.

MCDONALD, IAN M. AND SOLOW, ROBERT M. "Wage Bargaining and Employment," *Amer. Econ. Rev.,* Dec. 1981, *71*(5), pp. 896–908.

MASKIN, ERIC AND RILEY, JOHN. "Monopoly With Incomplete Information," *Rand J. Econ.,* Summer 1984, *15*(2), pp. 171–96.

MILLAR, JAMES R. "A Theory of On-the-Job Training." U. of Toronto, 1971.

MINCER, JACOB. "Unemployment Effects of Minimum Wages," *J. Polit. Econ.,* Aug. 1976, *84*(4, Part 2), pp. S87–S104.

_____ AND JOVANOVIC, BOYAN. "Labor Mobility and Wages," in *Studies in labor markets.* Ed.: SHERWIN ROSEN. Chicago: U. of Chicago Press for NBER, 1981, pp. 21–64.

MIRRLEES, JAMES. "An Exploration in the Theory of Optimum Income Taxation," *Rev. Econ. Stud.,* Apr. 1971, *38*(114), pp. 175–208.

_____ . "The Optimum Town," *Swedish J. Econ.,* Mar. 1972, *74*(1), pp. 114–35.

MIYAZAKI, HAJIME AND NEARY, HUGH M. "The Illyrian Firm Revisited," *Bell J. Econ.,* 1983, *14*(1), pp. 259–70.

_____ . "Output, Work Hours and Employment in the Short-Run of a Labor-Managed Firm." Stanford U., 1983.

MODIGLIANI, FRANCO. "Liquidity Preference and the Theory of Interest and Money," *Econometrica,* Jan. 1944, *12*(1), pp. 45–88.

MOORE, JOHN. "Contracting Between Two Parties with Private Information." London School of Econ., 1984.

MORTENSEN, DALE T. "On the Theory of Layoffs." Northwestern U., 1978.

_____ . "A Welfare Analysis of Unemployment Insurance: Variations on Second Best Themes," *Carnegie-Rochester Series on Public Policy,* Autumn 1983a, *19,* pp. 67–98.

_____ . "Labor Contract Equilibria in an 'Island' Economy." Northwestern U., 1983b.

MUSSA, MICHAEL AND ROSEN, SHERWIN. "Monopoly and Product Quality," *J. Econ. Theory,* Aug. 1978, *18*(2), pp. 301–07.

NADIRI, M. ISHAQ AND ROSEN, SHERWIN. "Interrelated Factor Demand Functions," *Amer. Econ. Rev.,* Sept. 1969, *59*(4, Part 1), pp. 457–71.

NALEBUFF, BARRY AND ZECKHAUSER, RICHARD. "Involuntary Unemployment Reconsidered: Second-Best Contracting with Heterogeneous Firms and Workers." Harvard U., 1984.

NEFTCI, SALIH N. "A Time-Series Analysis of the Real Wages-Employment Relationship," *J. Polit. Econ.,* Apr. 1978, *86*(2), pp. 281–91.

OI, WALTER Y. "Labor as a Quasi-Fixed Factor," *J. Polit. Econ.,* Dec. 1962, *70*(6), pp. 538–55.

OKUN, ARTHUR. *Prices and quantities.* Wash., DC: The Brookings Institution, 1981.

PIGOU, ARTHUR C. *The economics of welfare.* London: Macmillan, 1920.

PISSARIDES, CHRISTOPHER A. "Search Intensity, Job Advertising and Efficiency," *J. Lab. Econ.,* Jan. 1984, *2*(1), pp. 128–43.

POLEMARCHAKIS, HERAKLES M. AND WEISS, LAURENCE. "Fixed Wages, Layoffs, Unemployment Compensation and Welfare," *Amer. Econ. Rev.,* Dec. 1978, *68*(5), pp. 909–17.

RAISIAN, JOHN. "Contracts, Job Experience and Cyclical Labor Market Adjustments," *J. Lab. Econ.,* Apr. 1983, *1*(2), pp. 152–70.

RANDOLPH, WILLIAM C. "Employment Relationships: Till Death Do Us Part?" Ph.D. diss., SUNY, Stony Brook, 1983.

REDER, MELVIN W. "Wage Structure Theory and Measurement," in *Aspects of Labor economics: A conference of the Universities-National Bureau Committee for Economic Research.* Princeton, NJ: Princeton U. Press, 1962, pp. 257–318.

ROSEN, SHERWIN. "Short-Run Employment Variation on Class-I Railroads in the U.S., 1947–1963," *Econometrica,* July–Oct. 1968, *36*(3), pp. 511–29.

_____ . "Unemployment and Insurance," *Carnegie-Rochester Conference Series on Public Policy,* Autumn 1983, *20,* pp. 5–49.

ROTHSCHILD, MICHAEL AND STIGLITZ, JOSEPH E. "Increasing Risk: I. A Definition," *J. Econ. Theory,* Sept. 1970, *2*(3), pp. 225–43.

SARGENT, THOMAS J. *Macroeconomic theory.* NY: Academic Press, 1979.

SCHULTZE, CHARLES. "Microeconomic Efficiency and Nominal Wage Stickiness," *Amer. Econ. Rev.,* Mar. 1985, *75*(1), pp. 1–15.

SHAPIRO, CARL AND STIGLITZ, JOSEPH E. "Equilibrium Unemployment as a Worker Discipline Device," *Amer. Econ. Rev.,* June 1984, *74*(3), pp. 433–44.

SHAVELL, STEPHEN AND WEISS, LAURENCE. "The Optimal Payment of Unemployment Insurance Benefits Over Time," *J. Polit. Econ.,* Dec. 1979, *87*(6), pp. 1347–62.

SMITH, ADAM. *The wealth of nations.* Modern Library Edition. NY: Random House, [1776] 1947.

SOLOW, ROBERT M. "Investment and Technical Progress," in *Stanford symposium on mathematical models in the social sciences.* Eds.: KENNETH J. ARROW, SAMUEL KARLIN AND PATRICK SUPPES. Stanford: Stanford U. Press, 1960, pp. 89–104.

STIGLER, GEORGE J. "Production and Distribution in the Short Run," *J. Polit. Econ.,* June 1939, *47*(3), pp. 305–27.

STIGLITZ, JOSEPH E. "Theories of Wage Rigidity." Princeton U., 1984.

SCHWARTZ, ABA. "The Implicit Contract Model and Labor Markets: A Critique." Tel Aviv U., 1983.

TAYLOR, JOHN. "Aggregate Dynamics and Staggered Contracts," *J. Polit. Econ.,* Feb. 1980, *88*(1), pp. 1–23.

TODARO, MICHAEL P. "A Model for Labor Migration and Urban Unemployment In Less-Developed

Countries," *Amer. Econ. Rev.*, Mar. 1969, *59*(1), pp. 138–48.

TOPEL, ROBERT E. "On Layoffs and Unemployment Insurance," *Amer. Econ. Rev.*, Sept. 1983, *83*(4), pp. 541–59.

———. "Local Labor Markets," *J. Polit. Econ.*, forthcoming.

——— AND WELCH, FINIS. "Self-Insurance and Efficient Employment Contracts." U. of Chicago, 1983.

WILSON, ROBERT. "The Theory of Syndicates," *Econometrica*, Jan. 1968, *36*, pp. 119–32.

[6]

Efficiency Wage Models of Unemployment

By JANET L. YELLEN*

Keynesian economists hold it to be self-evident that business cycles are characterized by involuntary unemployment. But construction of a model of the cycle with involuntary unemployment faces the obvious difficulty of explaining why the labor market does not clear. Involuntarily unemployed people, by definition, want to work at less than the going wage rate. Why don't firms cut wages, thereby increasing profits?

This paper surveys a recent literature which offers a convincing and coherent explanation why firms may find it unprofitable to cut wages in the presence of involuntary unemployment. The models surveyed are variants of the efficiency wage hypothesis, according to which, labor productivity depends on the real wage paid by the firm. If wage cuts harm productivity, then cutting wages may end up raising labor costs. Section I describes some of the general implications of the efficiency-wage hypothesis in its simplest form. Section II describes four distinct microeconomic approaches which justify the relation between wages and productivity. These approaches identify four benefits of higher wage payments: reduced shirking by employees due to a higher cost of job loss; lower turnover; an improvement in the average quality of job applicants; and improved morale.[1] Section III explains how the efficiency-wage hypothesis, with near rational behavior, can explain cyclical fluctuations in unemployment.

I. The Efficiency Wage Hypothesis

The potential relevance of the efficiency-wage hypothesis in explaining involuntary unemployment and other stylized labor market facts can be seen in a rudimentary model.

*University of California, Berkeley, CA 94720. I am indebted to George Akerlof, David Estenson, Michael Reich, and James Wilcox for invaluable discussion and comments.
[1] For a previous survey of portions of this literature, see Guillermo Calvo (1979).

Consider an economy with identical, perfectly competitive firms, each firm having a production function of the form $Q = F(e(\omega)N)$, where N is the number of employees, e is effort per worker, and ω is the real wage. A profit-maximizing firm which can hire all the labor it wants at the wage it chooses to offer (see Joseph Stiglitz, 1976a; Robert Solow, 1979), will offer a real wage, ω^*, which satisfies the condition that the elasticity of effort with respect to the wage is unity. The wage ω^* is known as the efficiency wage and this wage choice minimizes labor cost per efficiency unit. Each firm should then optimally hire labor up to the point where its marginal product, $e(\omega^*)F'(e(\omega^*)N^*)$, is equal to the real wage, ω^*. As long as the aggregate demand for labor falls short of aggregate labor supply and ω^* exceeds labor's reservation wage, the firm will be unconstrained by labor market conditions in pursuing its optimal policy so that equilibrium will be characterized by involuntary unemployment. Unemployed workers would strictly prefer to work at the real wage ω^* than to be unemployed, but firms will not hire them at that wage or at a lower wage. Why? For the simple reason that any reduction in the wage paid would lower the productivity of all employees already on the job. Thus the efficiency-wage hypothesis explains involuntary unemployment.

Extended in simple ways this hypothesis also explains four other labor market phenomena: real wage rigidity; the dual labor market; the existence of wage distributions for workers of identical characteristics; and discrimination among observationally distinct groups. Concerning real wage rigidity, in the simple model just described, real shocks which shift the marginal product of labor alter employment, but not the real wage. In more elaborate versions of the model discussed below, such shocks will change the real wage, but not sufficiently to leave unemployment unaltered.

VOL. 74 NO. 2   INFORMATION AND MACROECONOMICS   201

Dual labor markets can be explained by the assumption that the wage-productivity nexus is important in some sectors of the economy, but not in others. For the primary sector, where the efficiency-wage hypothesis is relevant, we find job rationing and voluntary payment by firms of wages in excess of market clearing; in the secondary sector, where the wage-productivity relationship is weak or nonexistent, we should observe fully neoclassical behavior. The market for secondary-sector jobs clears, and anyone can obtain a job in this sector, albeit at lower pay. The existence of the secondary sector does not, however, eliminate involuntary unemployment (see Robert Hall, 1975), because the wage differential between primary- and secondary-sector jobs will induce unemployment among job seekers who choose to wait for primary-sector job openings.

Theorists who emphasize the importance of unemployment due to the frictions of the search process have frequently found it difficult to explain the reasons for a distribution of wage offers in the market. The efficiency-wage hypothesis also offers a simple explanation for the existence of wage differentials which might motivate the search process emphasized by Edmund Phelps and others. If the relationship between wages and effort differs among firms, each firm's efficiency wage will differ, and, in equilibrium, there will emerge a distribution of wage offers for workers of identical characteristics.

The efficiency-wage hypothesis also explains discrimination among workers with different observable characteristics. This occurs if employers simply prefer, say, men to women. With job rationing, the employer can indulge his taste for discrimination at zero cost. As another possibility, employers may know that the functions relating effort to wages differ across groups. Then each group has its own efficiency wage and corresponding "efficiency labor cost." If these labor costs differ, it will pay firms to hire first only employees from the lowest cost group. Any unemployment that exists will be confined to labor force groups with higher costs per efficiency unit. With fluctuations in demand, these groups will bear a disproportionate burden of layoffs.

II. Microfoundations of the Efficiency-Wage Model

Why should labor productivity depend on the real wage paid by firms? In the *LDC* context, for which the hypothesis was first advanced, the link between wages, nutrition, and illness was emphasized. Recent theoretical work has advanced a convincing case for the relevance of this hypothesis to developed economies. In this section, four different microeconomic foundations for the efficiency-wage model are described and evaluated.

A. *The Shirking Model*

In most jobs, workers have some discretion concerning their performance. Rarely can employment contracts rigidly specify all aspects of a worker's performance. Piece rates are often impracticable because monitoring is too costly or too inaccurate. Piece rates may also be nonviable because the measurements on which they are based are unverifiable by workers, creating a moral hazard problem. Under these circumstances, the payment of a wage in excess of market clearing may be an effective way for firms to provide workers with the incentive to work rather than shirk. (See Samuel Bowles, 1981, 1983; Guillermo Calvo, 1979; B. Curtis Eaton and William White, 1982; Herbert Gintis and Tsuneo Ishikawa, 1983; Hajime Miyazaki, forthcoming; Carl Shapiro and Stiglitz, 1982; and Steven Stoft, 1982.) The details of the models differ somewhat, depending on what is assumed measurable, at what cost, and the feasible payment schedules.

Bowles, Calvo, Eaton-White, Shapiro-Stiglitz, and Stoft assume that it is possible to monitor individual performance on the job, albeit imperfectly. In the simplest model, due to Shapiro-Stiglitz, workers can decide whether to work or to shirk. Workers who shirk have some chance of getting caught, with the penalty of being fired. This has been termed "cheat-threat" theory by Stoft because, if there is a cost to being fired, the threat of being sacked if caught cheating creates an incentive not to shirk. Equilibrium then entails unemployment. If all firms pay an identical wage, and if there is full employment, there would be no cost to shirking and it would pay all workers, assumed to get pleasure from loafing on the job, to shirk. In these circumstances, it pays each firm to raise its wage to eliminate shirking. When all firms do this, average wages rise and employment falls. In equilibrium, all firms pay the same wage above market clearing, and unemployment, which makes job loss costly, serves as a worker-discipline device. Unemployed workers cannot bid for jobs by offering to work at lower wages. If the firm were to hire a worker at a lower wage, it would be in the worker's interest to shirk on the job. The firm knows this and the worker has no credible way of promising to work if he is hired.

The shirking model does *not* predict, counterfactually, that the bulk of those unemployed at any time are those who were fired for shirking. If the threat associated with being fired is effective, little or no shirking and sacking will actually occur. Instead, the unemployed are a rotating pool of individuals who have quit jobs for personal reasons, who are new entrants to the labor market, or who have been laid off by firms with declines in demand. Pareto optimality, with costly monitoring, will entail some unemployment, since unemployment plays a socially valuable role in creating work incentives. But the equilibrium unemployment rate will not be Pareto optimal (see Shapiro-Stiglitz).

In contrast to the simple efficiency-wage model, the shirking model adds new arguments to the firm's effort function—the average wage, aggregate unemployment, and the unemployment benefit. The presence of the unemployment rate in the effort function yields a mechanism whereby changes in labor supply affect equilibrium wages and employment. New workers increase unemployment, raising the penalty associated with being fired and inducing higher effort at any given wage. Firms accordingly lower wages and hire more labor as a result. In a provocative recent paper, Thomas Weisskopf, Bowles, and David Gordon (1984) have used the presence of the unemployment benefit in the effort function to explain the secular decline in productivity in the United States; they

argue that a major part of the productivity slowdown is attributable to loss of employer control due to a reduction in the cost of job loss. The shirking model also offers an interpretation of hierarchical wage differentials, in excess of productivity differences (Calvo and Stanislaw Wellisz, 1979).

All these models suffer from a similar theoretical difficulty—that employment contracts more ingenious than the simple wage schemes considered, can reduce or eliminate involuntary unemployment. In the cheat-threat model, the introduction of employment fees allows the market to clear efficiently as long as workers have sufficient capital to pay them (see Eaton-White and Stoft). Unemployed workers would be willing to pay a fee to gain employment. Fees lower labor costs, giving firms an incentive to hire more workers. If all firms charge fees, any worker who shirks and is caught knows that he will have to pay another fee to regain employment. This possibility substitutes for the threat of unemployment in creating work incentives. Devices which function similarly are bonds posted by workers when initially hired and forfeited if found cheating, and fines levied on workers caught shirking. The threat of forfeiting the bond or paying the fine substitutes for the threat of being fired. Edward Lazear (1981) has demonstrated the use of seniority wages to solve the incentive problem. Workers can be paid a wage less than their marginal productivity when they are first hired with a promise that their earnings will later exceed their marginal productivity. The upward tilt in the age-earnings profile provides a penalty for shirking; the present value of the wage paid can fall to the market-clearing level, eliminating involuntary unemployment.

As a theoretical objection to these schemes, employers would be subject to moral hazard in evaluating workers' effort. Firms would have an obvious incentive to declare workers shirking and appropriate their bonds, collect fines, or replace them with new fee-paying workers. In Lazear's model, in which the firm pays a wage in excess of marginal product to senior workers, there is an incentive for the firm to fire such workers, replacing them with young workers, paid less than their pro-

VOL. 74 NO. 2   INFORMATION AND MACROECONOMICS   203

ductivity. The seriousness of this moral hazard problem depends on the ability of workers to enforce honesty on the firm's part. If effort is observable both by the firm and by the worker, and if it can be verified by outside auditors, the firm will be unable to cheat workers. Even without outside verification, Lazear has shown how the firm's concern for its reputation can overcome the moral hazard problem. Sudipto Bhattacharya (1983) has suggested tournament contracts that also overcome the moral hazard problem. The firm can commit itself to a fixed wage plan in which a high wage is paid to a fraction of workers and a low wage to the remaining fraction according to an *ex post*, possibly random, ranking of their effort levels. By precommitting itself to such a plan with a fixed wage bill, any moral hazard problem on the firm's part disappears.

B. *The Labor Turnover Model*

Firms may also offer wages in excess of market clearing to reduce costly labor turnover. (See Steven Salop, 1979; Ekkehart Schlicht, 1978; and Stiglitz, 1974.) The formal structure of the labor turnover model is identical to that of the shirking model. Workers will be more reluctant to quit the higher the relative wage paid by the current firm, and the higher the aggregate unemployment rate. If all firms are identical, one possible equilibrium has all firms paying a common wage above market clearing with involuntary unemployment serving to diminish turnover.

The theoretical objection to the prediction of involuntary unemployment in this model again concerns the potential for more sophisticated employment contracts to provide Pareto-superior solutions. As Salop explains, the market for new hires fails to clear because an identical wage is paid to both trained and untrained workers. Instead, new workers could be paid a wage equal to the difference between their marginal product and their training cost. A seniority wage scheme might accomplish this, although, if training costs are large and occur quickly it might prove necessary to charge a fee to new workers. In contrast to the shirking model, an employment or training fee scheme could be employed without the problem of moral hazard. It is no longer in any firm's interest to dismiss trained workers; explicit contracts could probably be written to insure that training is actually provided to fee paying workers. Although moral hazard thus appears to be a less formidable barrier to achieving neoclassical outcomes via fees or bonds than in the shirking model, capital market imperfections or institutional or sociological constraints may in fact make them impractical.

C. *Adverse Selection*

Adverse selection yields further reason for a relation between productivity and wages. Suppose that performance on the job depends on "ability" and that workers are heterogeneous in ability. If ability and workers' reservation wages are positively correlated, firms with higher wages will attract more able job candidates. (See James Malcolmson, 1981; Stiglitz, 1976b; Andrew Weiss, 1980.) In such a model, each firm pays an efficiency wage and optimally turns away applicants offering to work for less than that wage. The willingness of an individual to work for less than the going wage places an upper bound on his ability, raising the firm's estimate that he is a lemon. The model provides an explanation of wage differentials and different layoff probabilities for observationally distinct groups due to statistical discrimination if it is known that different groups have even slight differences in the joint distributions of ability and acceptance wages. However, for the adverse-selection model to provide a convincing account of involuntary unemployment, firms must be unable to measure effort and pay piece rates after workers are hired, or to fire workers whose output is too low. Clever firms may also be able to mitigate adverse selection in hiring by designing self-selection or screening devices which induce workers to reveal their true characteristics.

D. *Sociological Models*

The theories reviewed above are neoclassical in their assumption of individualistic maximization by all agents. Solow (1980) has argued, however, that wage rigidity may more plausibly be due to social conventions and principles of appropriate behavior that are not entirely individualistic in origin. George Akerlof (1982) has provided the first explicitly sociological model leading to the efficiency-wage hypothesis. He uses a variety of interesting evidence from sociological studies to argue that each worker's effort depends on the work norms of his group. In Akerlof's partial gift exchange model, the firm can succeed in raising group work norms and average effort by paying workers a gift of wages in excess of the minimum required, in return for their gift of effort above the minimum required. The sociological model can explain phenomena which seem inexplicable in neoclassical terms—why firms don't fire workers who turn out to be less productive, why piece rates are avoided even when feasible, and why firms set work standards exceeded by most workers. Akerlof's paper in this issue explores alternative sociological foundations for the efficiency wage hypothesis. Sociological considerations governing the effort decisions of workers are also emphasized in Marxian discussions of the extraction of labor from labor power (see, for example, Bowles, 1983).

III. Explaining the Business Cycle

Any model of the business cycle must explain why changes in aggregate demand cause changes in aggregate employment and output. A potential problem of the efficiency-wage hypothesis in this regard is the absence of a link between aggregate demand and economic activity. In an economy with efficiency-wage setting, there is a positive natural rate of unemployment and real wage rigidity. But the economy's aggregate output is independent of price at this natural rate. These models have no wage or price stickiness to cause real consequences from aggregate demand shocks. However, for a natural but subtle reason, the efficiency-wage model is consistent with nominal wage rigidity and cyclical unemployment. This reason (suggested by Stoft), is explored in depth by Akerlof and myself (1983), where we argue that sticky wage and price behavior, that will cause significant business cycle fluctuations, is consistent with near rationality in an economy with efficiency wage setting. Any firm that normally chooses its wage as part of an optimizing decision will incur losses that are only second-order if it follows a rule of thumb in adjusting nominal wages which leads to a real wage error. At the point of maximum profits, the profit function relating wages to profits is flat. Thus, in the neighborhood of the optimum wage, the loss from wage errors is second-order small. This implies that firms with sticky wages have profits that are insignificantly different from firms with maximizing behavior. Furthermore, if firms have price-setting power because of downward-sloping demand curves, for similar reasons, price-setting errors also lead to insignificant losses.

In the Akerlof-Yellen model, firms are efficiency-wage setters and monopolistic competitors. In the long run, wages and prices are set by all firms in an optimal way. In the short run, in response to aggregate demand shocks, some firms keep nominal wages and prices constant, while other firms choose these variables optimally. In this model, a cut in the money supply causes a first-order change in employment, output, and profits. But the behavior of nonmaximizers is near rational in the sense that the potential gain any individual firm could experience by abandoning rule of thumb behavior is second-order small. And thus the efficiency-wage hypothesis can be extended into a full-fledged Keynesian model of the business cycle generated by sticky prices and wages.

IV. Concluding Remarks

It has been widely observed that the existence of excess labor supply does not lead to aggressive wage cutting by workers and firms. Firms appear content to pay workers more than the wages required by their potential replacements. The models surveyed here offer several different and plausible explanations of this seemingly paradoxical fact. In addition to accounting for the persistence of involuntary unemployment in competitive markets, these efficiency wage models can explain why unemployment varies in response to aggregate demand shocks. In sum, these models provide a new, consistent, and plausible microfoundation for a Keynesian model of the cycle.

REFERENCES

Akerlof, George, "Labor Contracts as Partial Gift Exchange," *Quarterly Journal of Economics*, November 1982, *97*, 543–69.

_____, "Gift Exchange and Efficiency Wage Theory: Four Views," *American Economic Review Proceedings*, May 1984, *74*, 79–83.

_____ and Yellen, Janet, "The Macroeconomic Consequences of Near Rational, Rule of Thumb Behavior," mimeo., University of California-Berkeley, September 1983.

Bhattacharya, Sudipto, "Tournaments and Incentives: Heterogeneity and Essentiality," mimeo., Stanford University, March 1983.

Bowles, Samuel, "Competitive Wage Determination and Involuntary Unemployment: A Conflict Model," mimeo., University of Massachusetts, May 1981.

_____, "The Production Process in a Competitive Economy: Walrasian, Neo-Hobbesian and Marxian Models," mimeo., University of Massachusetts, May 1983.

Calvo, Guillermo, "Quasi-Walrasian Theories of Unemployment," *American Economic Review Proceedings*, May 1979, *69*, 102–07.

_____ and Wellisz, Stanislaw, "Hierarchy, Ability and Income Distribution," *Journal of Political Economy*, October 1979, *87*, 991–1010.

Eaton, B. Curtis and White, William, "Agent Compensation and the Limits of Bonding," *Economic Inquiry*, July 1982, *20*, 330–43.

Gintis, Herbert and Ishikawa, Tsuneo, "Wages, Work Discipline and Macroeconomic Equilibrium," mimeo., 1983.

Hall, Robert, "The Rigidity of Wages and the Persistence of Unemployment," *Brookings Papers on Economic Activity*, 2:1975, 301–35.

Lazear, Edward, "Agency, Earnings Profiles, Productivity, and Hours Restrictions," *American Economic Review*, September 1981, *71*, 606–20.

Malcolmson, James, "Unemployment and the Efficiency Wage Hypothesis," *Economic Journal*, December 1981, *91*, 848–66.

Miyazaki, Hajime, "Work Norms and Involuntary Unemployment," *Quarterly Journal of Economics*, forthcoming.

Salop, Steven, "A Model of the Natural Rate of Unemployment," *American Economic Review*, March 1979, *69*, 117–25.

Schlicht, Ekkehart, "Labour Turnover, Wage Structure and Natural Unemployment," *Zeitschrift für die Gesamte Staatswissenschaft*, June 1978, *134*, 337–46.

Shapiro, Carl and Stiglitz, Joseph, "Equilibrium Unemployment as a Worker Discipline Device," mimeo., Princeton University, April 1982.

Solow, Robert, "Another Possible Source of Wage Stickiness," *Journal of Macroeconomics*, Winter 1979, *1*, 79–82.

_____, "On Theories of Unemployment," *American Economic Review*, March 1980, *70*, 1–11.

Stiglitz, Joseph, "Wage Determination and Unemployment in L.D.C.'s: The Labor Turnover Model," *Quarterly Journal of Economics*, May 1974, *88*, 194–227.

_____, (1976a) "The Efficiency Wage Hypothesis, Surplus Labour, and the Distribution of Income in L.D.C.s," *Oxford Economic Papers*, July 1976, *28*, 185–207.

_____, (1976b) "Prices and Queues as Screening Devices in Competitive Markets," IMSSS Technical Report No. 212, Stanford University, August 1976.

Stoft, Steven, "Cheat-Threat Theory: An Explanation of Involuntary Unemployment," mimeo., Boston University, May 1982.

Weiss, Andrew, "Job Queues and Layoffs in Labor Markets with Flexible Wages," *Journal of Political Economy*, June 1980, *88*, 526–38.

Weisskopf, Thomas, Bowles, Samuel and Gordon, David, "Hearts and Minds: A Social Model of Aggregate Productivity Growth in the U.S., 1948–1979," *Brookings Papers on Economic Activity*, 1984, forthcoming.

[7]

The Economic Journal, **97** *(Conference* 1987), 1–16
Printed in Great Britain

ON INVOLUNTARY UNEMPLOYMENT

F. H. Hahn

The notion of involuntary unemployment is out of favour. Some argue that nothing is gained in distinguishing between voluntary and involuntary unemployment and that in any case the distinction cannot be made empirically. Others argue that 'involuntary' contradicts the hypothesis that agents are rational and that it is certainly incompatible with equilibrium. For these critics the unemployment which we observe is to be explained by search for the best wage offer and by the preference for leisure (with unemployment pay). Keynes's theory of equilibrium involuntary unemployment is, for these critics, not grounded in any recognisable economic theory of the actions and interactions of agents.

This paper sets out to show that, contrary to what these critics maintain, involuntary unemployment is well defined, compatible with rationality and not inconsistent with an equilibrium of the economy. I start with definitions.

I. DEFINITIONS

For Keynes a worker is involuntarily unemployed if the market wage for his labour exceeds his shadow wage. The shadow wage is that wage at which a worker would be indifferent between not accepting and accepting an offer of work. It then follows from the first Fundamental Theorem of Welfare Economics that Walrasian equilibrium of the Arrow–Debreu variety and involuntary unemployment are incompatible. But of course if a description of the economy is best approximated by such an equilibrium not only is the whole Keynesian opus irrelevant but search unemployment is also problematical.

Search theory[1] postulates a distribution of wage offers and a probability distribution of offers per unit time. The latter is usually taken to be Poisson and if one treats time as continuous then the parameter λ of the distribution is the instantaneous arrival rate of offers. Both distributions are known to the workers. The shadow wage w^* is now that smallest wage which must be offered if an offer is to be accepted (just as in Keynes). If workers are risk neutral, infinitely long lived and if they discount at the going rate of interest, elementary dynamic programming allows one to calculate w^*. In this calculation one assumes positive search costs per unit time and a fixed disutility of work. Let $K(w^*)$ be the present value of income when w^* is the accepted wage. Clearly

$$rK(w^*) = w^*,$$

---

* Frank Paish Lecture. I am grateful to Jim Mirrlees for many useful improvements and for reminding me that the concavity of a maximimand is of some importance.
[1] For an excellent survey of labour search theory see Mortensen (1984).

2   THE ECONOMIC JOURNAL

where r is the rate of interest. Let W be the maximum expected present net value of continued search. Then w^* must satisfy[1]

$$K(w^*) = W.$$

Hence $rW = w^*$. Clearly w^* must at least compensate for the disutility of work but since search costs are positive it may be higher than that.

Now the critical wage w^* will be below the highest wage in the distribution of wage offers. Employers know this and so the employer offering the highest wage will reduce it. It is easy to see how this line of argument, (Diamond, 1971), can lead to a collapse of the wage distribution. That is, in equilibrium there would be a single wage equal to the disutility of work. While there are ways of avoiding this conclusion none of them is consistent with Arrow–Debreu theory. So if one opts for search unemployment one also opts for a different description of the economy.

Suppose that we simply postulate the existence of a wage distribution. One can readily calculate the probability at which a searching worker becomes employed per unit time. It depends on λ and on w^*. Also λ and w^* are semi-positively related. There will then be $\bar\lambda > 0$ such that w^* is constant for $\lambda < \bar\lambda$. This is because w^* is bounded below and the support of the wage distribution does not extend below this lower bound. The expected duration of unemployment in that region will now be entirely governed by λ – the arrival rate of *any* offer. That is, the chance of receiving any offer is small enough to induce the worker to accept any offer even when he knows that better offers might be made subsequently. In these cases λ is small because unemployment is large. It will be obvious that in this situation the worker is involuntarily unemployed precisely in the sense of Keynes. Of course the question of whether this is compatible with any equilibrium is still open.

This is a somewhat extreme case forced on us by the interpretation of search and the implicit assumption that workers are alike. Suppose we think of workers as knowing the wage being paid by all hiring employers. Given employment exchanges and advertisements this is only mildly unreasonable. What workers do not know for certain is whether if they apply they will land the job. It is this which explains the probability distribution of wage offers. The worker calculates w^* as before but this now represents the lowest wage he will apply for. He will apply first for the job with the highest expected wage. But any job which he applies for he is willing to take. (An unemployed person cannot search.) Once again there is good reason to suppose that one cannot take the distribution as exogenously given. For instance we might suppose that it is such as to equalise the expected wage in each firm. In any event there will be a positive probability that the worker does not get the job which he applies for. In general the wage paid to successful applicants will exceed w^*, the reservation wage of the unsuccessful candidate.

While the unsuccessful candidate is in the strict sense involuntarily unemployed such unemployment may be unavoidable if applications cannot be

---

[1] If not then either the worker would not have accepted w^* or would have set a lower acceptance wage.

ON INVOLUNTARY UNEMPLOYMENT 3

co-ordinated.[1] One can calculate the expected duration of unemployment if the number of acceptable jobs on offer equals the number of searching workers. One may call this unavoidable unemployment. One then reserves the appellation involuntary for the case where the number of acceptable jobs falls short of the number of searching workers. Once again the question of whether this is possible in equilibrium is open.

Search as such then provides no obstacles to a coherent definition. But so far I have paid no attention to the heterogeneity of workers and of jobs. This is held by some to make Keynes's definition incoherent. For instance my shadow wage for a job in the Bank of England may be below the wage of the economists that are being hired but since my productivity as a theorist is low or negative one can hardly claim that I am involuntarily unemployed if the Bank does not hire me. That this objection lacks merit will be obvious to the naked eye.

Keynes, like so many of his successors and opponents to this day, was not explicitly distinguishing between different types of labour and jobs for the same reason that he did not distinguish between different types of goods. He was engaged in writing macro-economics. If we do distinguish then two cases arise. The first is the situation when a worker's productivity in each job is known to himself and to each employer. This full information case evidently means that there will be lots of different reservation wages and that each worker will only be concerned with the wages distribution over his productivity type. No new problem arises. When full information is lacking then workers must be sorted not by their productivity type but by the signal they emit. By that I mean things like age, education, previous job, references etc. The employer must be taken as being indifferent between workers with the same signal. Indeed in my interpretation he advertises for workers with a certain signal or a class of signals, for instance if he offers a wage schedule based on previous experience. No doubt on careful investigation one will find that no two workers have absolutely identical signals. But the cost of fine distinctions makes this irrelevant except for a very small subset of jobs where mistakes are also very costly. One is now concerned with the wage distribution over signal types and proceeds to the required definition as before.

This leaves one last question: is the distinction between types of unemployment operational? The first (perhaps debating) point is that the proposition that labour markets always clear must have the same question addressed to it. But in any case the answer is 'yes', provided it is remembered that a precise correspondence between theoretical and empirical categories is not to be had. For instance if we sample the search experience of sixteen-year-old school leavers of the same school and social class we shall find some getting jobs and others not getting jobs of the same type. We can easily establish whether they have turned down jobs and searched over jobs of the same type. But one can think of other ways of estimation also – after all, unemployment statistics broken down by type are available, as are job statistics similarly broken down.

In all of this a common mistake must be avoided. An involuntarily

---

[1] See Mortensen's (1984) discussion of this from the point of view of economic efficiency.

4   THE ECONOMIC JOURNAL

unemployed worker may not apply for a job below a certain wage. This of itself is not evidence against his being involuntarily unemployed. Involuntary unemployment refers to the absence of Walrasian market clearing. The worker in question may have a reservation wage below the wage paid to those of his type who are being hired.[1] Thus a thirty-year-old bricklayer with five years experience may not apply for a low-paid job washing up but have a reservation wage below that paid to a working, thirty-year-old, bricklayer with five years experience.

Involuntary unemployment if it occurs simply signals market failure. The question now is whether such failure is possible in an economy of rational self-seeking agents.

II. EQUILIBRIUM

Before I attempt to answer this question I must take a short detour to discuss equilibrium. It will be short since I have written on this matter elsewhere (1973) but it will have to be made because ghastly misconceptions remain.

I think of an equilibrium as a stationary (or critical) point of a dynamic process. Thus for instance the classical Walrasian equilibrium rests on the hypothesis that the auctioneer will change the price of a good unless its price is zero and the excess demand negative or the excess demand is zero. This dynamic process is not founded on the calculated actions of rational agents.

There has recently been much work to remedy this deficiency. (A good summary will be found in a recent paper by Wilson (1985).) Much of it is game theoretic and the equilibrium concepts derive from this approach. The central element of an equilibrium is that strategies are equilibrium strategies if no rational agent will wish to deviate from his strategy given those of the other players. This Nash characteristic of an equilibrium is not directly related to a dynamics. But it clearly accords with the general characterisation of equilibrium with which I started. In general trading games often have inefficient allocations in the set of equilibria.

Sometimes, as in the case of auctions, one can think of an agent designing the trading game. He may then be able to design one whose equilibrium is efficient. However, such control over the game is the exception. Wilson, however, proposes to understand existing trading arrangements by demonstrating that their equilibria efficiency-dominate the equilibria of all other possible such arrangements. This seems to be wrong. The logic of the approach requires that we think of the game actually played as the outcome of a prior game over games. This latter, we have no reason to suppose, will yield Wilson-efficient outcomes.

In all of this there is a long way to go before the rational actions of each agent in each stage of an appropriate game is clear. But it seems evident that equilibria may be Pareto-dominated by other possible outcomes which rational players obeying the rules of the game cannot reach. One only needs to recall the

---

[1] Partha Dasgupta and others regard involuntary unemployment as mainly a manifestation of horizontal inequity.

ON INVOLUNTARY UNEMPLOYMENT 5

Prisoner's Dilemma to make this point. In particular the observation that involuntary unemployment leaves Pareto-improving moves unexploited is not sufficient to demonstrate its incompatibility with equilibrium. This would be a point not worth making if it were not for the literature. In any event I now propose to illustrate it by some examples.

III. EQUILIBRIUM WITH INVOLUNTARY UNEMPLOYMENT

The common feature of the cases I shall now discuss is that involuntary unemployment (in a certain range) does not lead any agent to change his actions and in particular does not lead to a change in the wage. There are many ways of demonstrating such a possibility and the literature contains some interesting examples. They and what follows may appear anecdotal since so far no general and equally powerful alternative to Arrow–Debreu is available. But they suffice to make the main point and in any case it may well turn out that descriptively more satisfactory theories will lack generality.

(a) Bargaining and fairness

Recently Shaked and Sutton (1984) building on Rubinstein's work (1981) have examined a bargaining situation whose equilibrium is consistent with involuntary unemployment. I shall want to proceed somewhat differently than they did but first I summarise their work. In a Rubinstein process of alternating offers by firm and worker the latter is designated as an 'insider' if the firm is committed to negotiating with him for a prescribed number of nodes in the sequence. There are also outsiders who become insiders once they start negotiating. These assumptions together with discounting of future receipts give an insider some power relatively to the outsider. This ensures that they can obtain a wage above the reservation wage of the outsider which is a characteristic of involuntary unemployment. The algebra of this game is peculiarly simple and I do not reproduce it here.

Suppose now that we remove the restriction that the firm is committed to negotiating with the insider for a given number of moves. Instead let ϵ be a small unit of time which must elapse before a firm can turn from one worker to another. As we make ϵ smaller and smaller the equilibrium wage of the game will approach the reservation wage of all workers. Since there is common knowledge of everything relevant to all players this outcome can be calculated by everyone.

But now we notice that there is a strategy available to the ϵ-insider which we have not yet considered. That is to match any offer at or above the reservation wage made by the outsider and to accept any offer which is accepted by the outsider. For the insider this is a perfect equilibrium strategy. At no node would he gain by departing from it.[1] We now think of many outsiders and they are part of the game. If they take offers and if the firm is indifferent between workers making the same offer, then the outsiders, if for the moment we take the number of jobs as given, know that they will not be employed. They may

---

[1] I assume that insiders have the same reservation wage as outsiders.

6   THE ECONOMIC JOURNAL

therefore be indifferent between making an offer or not. On the other hand the firm has an incentive to make offers to outsiders. Once again, given the matching strategy of insiders, it is a matter of indifference to the outsiders whether they accept or not for the firm will offer the reservation wage, or rather a wage very close to the latter. If indifference or near indifference means that outsiders are willing to participate in the game then its outcome will be a wage very close to the reservation wage.

So competition between outsiders and insiders harms the latter without benefitting the former by more than an arbitrarily small amount. The main beneficiary is the firm. If workers could communicate with each other before the game they would, if they could, surely choose to play a different one.

Let a group of workers be choosing between two games. The first of these, which I shall call the *fair game* is a Rubinstein game without outsider competition. The other is a Rubinstein game in which outsiders can compete with so small a delay that the outcome is approximately the Walrasian wage w^*. I write $V(w)$ as the net utility of the wage w; that is net of the disutility of work and I let λ be the fraction of the work force that will be insiders in the fair game. I suppose that insiders negotiate as one man (say as a Union) and I write $\hat{w}(\lambda)$ as the equilibrium wage of the fair game when $\lambda\%$ of the workers are insiders. The choice of insider is random.

Then before a worker knows whether he will be an insider or outsider he will prefer the fair game if

$$\lambda V[\hat{w}(\lambda)] > V(w^*).$$

Since for $\lambda < 1$, $\hat{w}(\lambda) > w^*$, the fair game will always be preferred if the competitive game yields zero surplus to the worker. Otherwise it will be preferred if the probability of unemployment is not too high relatively to the gain from the fair game over the competitive one. Moreover since the insiders have the credible threat of matching, outsiders will abide by their Rawlsian agreement if $V(w^*) = 0$. But they may abide by it if some disutility attaches to acting 'unfairly' that is contrary to the implicit contract they are deemed to have made before they knew whether they were insiders or not. So one requires $V(w^*)$ to exceed something strictly positive before workers will renege on fairness. This seems to me eminently plausible and there is a good deal of historical and labour literature to support it.

However, I have left a loose end when I took λ as given. I do not think it reasonable to regard workers in the imaginary initial position acting as monopoly sellers of labour. By this I mean that I do not think they set λ in the light of a function $\hat{w}(\lambda)$, giving the wage of the fair game as a function of λ. I prefer to suppose that workers regard λ as a random variable so that the critical inequality is

$$E\lambda V[\hat{w}(\lambda)] > V(w^*).$$

The argument then proceeds much as before.

I have also excluded the possibility of side payments from insiders to outsiders. This could be justified by an appeal to moral hazard when it cannot be observed whether or not a worker has chosen not to be an insider. Historically some side

ON INVOLUNTARY UNEMPLOYMENT 7

payments (far short of full insurance) have been observed, but it does not seem worthwhile to pursue this in detail.

I have given a sketch of a stylised model which, nonetheless, seems to me to capture an important element of the labour market. It will now be objected that even if it has merit it is unjustified to think of the unemployed outsiders as involuntarily unemployed. After all they chose to play the game with the non-Walrasian outcome. It is this kind of argument which has bedevilled the subject and it was to avoid it that I spent so much time on definitions. Involuntary unemployment has nothing to do with free will. The outsiders would prefer to be in the position of the insiders for whom they are perfect substitutes. The fact that they cannot be if $V(w^*) = o$, or are for reasons of fairness unwilling to get there by direct competition with insiders, does not change that. A preference of A over B remains even if (i) one cannot reach A from B or (ii) the path from B to A involves too large a utility loss. Definitions are definitions and it remains to be seen whether these particular ones are useful.

(b) Efficiency wages

As my second example of an equilibrium with involuntary unemployment I shall briefly consider efficiency wages. This topic has been ably surveyed by Yellen (1984). I shall here follow a line which may be novel but is not meant to exclude others which have been pursued.

I start with the hypothesis that for every skill group, ability is negatively related to search costs. Higher ability always means higher productivity of labour for all firms but the relationship is different for different firms with different production sets. I have in mind the model already discussed in which the firm announces a wage and hires a certain fraction of the applicants who are all willing to accept. To this I add the assumption that workers come equipped with signals correlated to their ability. Take a firm i and let $\mathbf{w}_{-i}$ stand for the vector of wages paid by other firms and let μ be the unemployment ratio of the skill group in question. Then the firm knows that given $(\mathbf{w}_{-i}, \mu)$, the higher its own wage the greater (up to a point) will be the proportion of workers applying who have high ability signals. Strictly this should be formulated probabilistically but I shall not do so here.

If the firm hires n_i workers we can write $\theta(w_i, \mathbf{w}_{-i}, \mu) n_i$ as the expected number of workers in efficiency units which it hires. One takes θ to be increasing in w_i, at least over the range. If the firm, over the relevant range has more applicants than jobs then[1] when θ_1 is the partial differential coefficient of θ w.r.t. w_i

$$\frac{\theta_1 w_i}{\theta} = 1$$

is a condition for maximum expected profit. This equation yields

$$w_i(\mathbf{w}_{-i}, \mu)$$

[1] Necessary conditions for maximising

$$pF[\theta(w_i, \mathbf{w}_{-i}, \mu) n_i] - w_i n_i$$

(where $F(.)$ is the production function) are: $F'\theta = w_i$ and $F'\theta_1 = 1$. From this the conditions in the text follow. One can also think of setting w_i to maximise θ/w_i with the same result.

as the wage set by firm i. It will be clear that I am here assuming that for one reason or another (e.g. fairness or union pressure) all hired workers must be paid the same wage.

Now suppose that there exists a wage vector $\mathbf{w}^*$ and an unemployment rate $\mu^* < 1$ such that

$$w_i^* = w_i(\mathbf{w}_{-i}^*, \mu^*) \quad \text{for all } i.$$

This evidently would be an equilibrium. Nothing in its construction suggests that the unemployed are not involuntarily unemployed in the sense in which I defined it when discussing search. At least that is so if at equilibrium all firms have something to gain from the more able. Of course the model is not complete. Conditions of clearing in the market for goods will also be required and one must show that a solution with $\mu \leqslant 1$ exists. This can be done on the usual assumptions. The following points are worth noting: (a) there may be many equilibria and (b) it is not at all clear what the relation between μ and wages is. For as can be seen from the profit maximising condition, it is the elasticity of θ and its dependence on μ and wages which will determine the answer.

The assumption that the firm must pay all workers of a given skill the same wage is critical and not too well motivated. Firms after all could pay by 'results'. However one can argue as follows. Firms must invest in the training of their workers. The average overhead cost of this training will be lower for the able than for the less able if production is not under constant costs. In this way even if wages are paid by results the main thrust of this model can be preserved although its formal description would have to be changed somewhat.

(c) General remarks

There are many more routes one can take to the same goal. For instance one can consider economies where the past has determined the wage and employment of a number of workers. They are insiders in a different sense than the one I used when discussing bargaining. One now gets an insider/outsider story where the former have some power due to the training invested in them and due to the better information employers have of their quality. Here, quite crude use of the Nash-bargaining solution will yield an outcome in which the insiders' wage exceeds their opportunity cost. There are other models, by Negishi (1979) for instance, in which individual unemployed workers do not reduce their wage because the effect of such a reduction on the probability of gaining employment is too small. My colleague Sabourian has yet another story which turns on the plausible assumption that a firm needs a minimum number of workers if it is to produce at all. Lastly there are models which take account of the limits oligopolistic conditions in the goods market impose on the elasticity of the demand for labour.

All of these arguments, as well as the ones I have sketched, are designed to fill in the gap in our notion of equilibrium which exists when we have not specified the actions agents can take in *each* state of the economy, in particular, of course, action with respect to price. When viewed in this, the correct, way it is misleading to speak of the examples giving an explanation of 'wage rigidity'. They are no more rigid than an optimally chosen price of a monopolist

ON INVOLUNTARY UNEMPLOYMENT   9

is 'rigid'. The terminology of rigidity takes an unexplained auctioneer as a reference point and not the rational agent. It leads to tautologies of the sort that unemployment is to be *explained* by rigid wages when rigidity is *defined* by a non-clearing labour market. There are few better examples of sloppy language leading to sloppy thinking. In any case if it is a condition of equilibrium that no agent finds it feasibly to his advantage to change a price under his control then I hope it will by now be crystal clear that an equilibrium with involuntary unemployment is a perfectly coherent concept.

IV. A SIMPLE COMPLETE MODEL

One can also now see why the distinction between voluntary and involuntary unemployment matters a good deal. For instance in the latter case it is not true that real wages must be lower if employment is to be higher. Moreover, it may be that involuntary unemployment arises from avoidable co-ordination failures and externalities.

I want first to illustrate this in the context of the example of the efficiency wage. I emphasise that this is an illustration in an example simple enough for presentation.

Suppose that there are only two kinds of firms and labour (of the same skill) is of differing efficiency. Then from $\theta^1(w_1, w_2, \mu)$ the firm can calculate its best wage offer given (w_2, μ) by maximising θ/w_1. By varying w_2 one can then obtain the reaction function of firm 1: $R_i(w_2, \mu)$. One can proceed similarly for firm 2. For definiteness, (and not for realism), I assume

$$\theta^i = (w_i - w_j \beta_i/\mu + 1)^{\alpha_i}, 1 > \alpha_i > 0 \quad (i, j = 1, 2). \tag{1}$$

The idea of this is that the adverse effect of a higher w_j, (given w_i), on the productivity of i's recruits is smaller the higher the unemployment rate.

Proceeding as outlined above[1] (i.e. maximising $\log \theta_i - \log w_i$) we find

$$w_i = R_i(w_j, \mu) = (w_j)^{(\beta_i/\mu + 1)/(1 - \alpha_i)} \quad (i, j = 1, 2).$$

From which we can solve for w_i^*, w_j^* which satisfies

$$w_i^* = R_i(w_j^*, \mu); \quad w_j^* = R_j(w_i^*, \mu),$$

and we can now write (1) as

$$\theta_i = \hat{\theta}_i(\mu) \tag{2}$$

[1] Since θ_i is concave in w_i the picture for a given w_j is

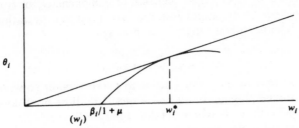

giving its equilibrium value as a function of the unemployment rate. If the production functions are

$$Y_i = a_i \theta_i n_i \quad (i = 1, 2) \tag{3}$$

then when q_i is the product wage in firm i we have in equilibrium

$$q_i = a_i \hat{\theta}_i(\mu) \quad (i = 1, 2).$$

Assume that labour (N) is supplied inelastically. Then the demand for each good will depend on (q_1, q_2, μ) and on real cash balances $\bar{m}$. In view of (2) we can write the reduced form demand function as

$$\xi_i(\mu, \bar{m}).$$

In equilibrium demand equals supply:

$$\xi_i(\mu, \bar{m}) = Y_i \quad \text{all } i.$$

These equations will determine the demand for labour i.e. (by 3)

$$n_i = \frac{Y_i}{a_i \theta_i} = \frac{\xi_i(\mu, \bar{m})}{a_i \theta_i} \quad \text{all } i.$$

Let $n_i(\mu, \bar{m})$ be the value of employment determined in this way. Then in equilibrium the unemployment rate μ must be consistent with that determined by the clearing of the market for goods, i.e.

$$1 - \frac{\Sigma n_i(\mu, \bar{m})}{N} = \mu.$$

By a proper choice of parameters one can ensure that there exists a solution

$$\mu(\bar{m}) \geqslant 0$$

which is decreasing in $\bar{m}$.

Now here is the point of the exercise. There are many equilibria depending on $\bar{m}$. There cannot, in this model, be a wage adjustment equation to clear the labour market. If we are in an equilibrium with $\mu > 0$ then there is no way rational agents can reach one with lower unemployment when they act on their own. If however, they all co-ordinated a reduction in money wages and so a higher $\bar{m}$, then an equilibrium with lower unemployment is possible. That is the essence of the co-ordination failure here.

If instead we look at the same economy with a higher money stock its unemployment could be unchanged (because of homogeneity) or it could be less. To predict we need a dynamics and some attention to expectations. This, however, would take me further than I can now go.

V. REAL WAGES

Before I leave this part of the story I want to make a point concerning the relations between unemployment and real wages. I shall be brief since I have made it already more fully elsewhere (Hahn, 1984).

I now forget all about the special features of the labour market and take a

ON INVOLUNTARY UNEMPLOYMENT   II

purely Walrasian stance. Indeed we shall follow Mrs Thatcher and consider a world in which unemployment occurs because money wages are too high. Production takes place by means of produced goods and labour, the latter is the only non-produced input and there are constant returns to scale and there is no joint production. Then if r is the rate of interest and $\mathbf{p}$ is the price vector of goods in terms of labour, the steady state equilibrium price vector can be written as an increasing function of r: $\mathbf{p} = \mathbf{p}(r)$.

The money wage is fixed by the likes of Mr Scargill and the nominal money stock by the likes of Mr Lawson. Consequently $\overline{m}$, the money stock in terms of labour is given exogenously. In view of what has already been said we can write the demand for $\overline{m}$ as a function of r and μ and we obtain the equilibrium condition

$$m(r,\mu) = \overline{m}. \tag{4}$$

The demand for goods depends on $(r,\mu,\overline{m})$. Since for each r the labour requirement per unit of output of each good is known we can write

$$\mu = \psi(r,\overline{m}) \tag{5}$$

provided $\overline{m}$ is not so large as to create an excess demand for labour. I here assume that (4), (5) can be solved for $r(\overline{m})$, $\mu(\overline{m})$ with $\mu(\overline{m}) > 0$.

The following signs of the relevant partial co-efficients can be justified by the reader. They are not of course in the nature of laws;

$$m_r < 0, \quad m_\mu < 0, \quad \psi_r < 0, \quad \psi_{\overline{m}} < 0.$$

Differentiating (4), (5) with respect to $\overline{m}$ we obtain

$$\frac{d\mu}{d\overline{m}} = \frac{m_r \psi_{\overline{m}} + \psi_r}{m_r + m_\mu \psi_r} < 0 \tag{6}$$

as Mrs Thatcher maintains. Also

$$\frac{dr}{d\overline{m}} = \frac{1 - m_\mu \psi_{\overline{m}}}{m_\mu - m_\mu \psi_r} < 0 \quad (\text{if } m_\mu \psi_{\overline{m}} < 1). \tag{7}$$

Now m_μ is connected with the income elasticity of demand for money and $\psi_{\overline{m}}$ with the wealth elasticity of demand for goods. The product is invariant to units and the condition of (7) can be satisfied by perfectly ordinary functions and production sets. In that case however since $\mathbf{p}(r)$ is monotone increasing in r it follows that in the steady state with the lower money wage and higher employment the real wage *is higher*. So it is not workers who have priced themselves out of a job but Mr Lawson who has priced them out by keeping the money stock too low. Of course that does not imply that had the money stock increased employment would also have increased. That would only be true if we could continue to take the money wage as given.

The result that real wages can be higher when employment is higher did not depend on increasing returns. What it did depend on is the abandonment of a habit of so much of current macro-economics, namely to write output as a function of labour only. Even if a short period interpretation is put on this the habit is unsatisfactory as is the complementary habit of not distinguishing investment expenditure from total expenditure. But so much of the new macro-economics is steady state economics that I do not pursue the faults which remain in the short-period interpretation. The result which I have been discussing does not crucially depend on the assumed technology although it is much more complicated to establish for more general cases. The result itself is however easy to understand. Lower money wages and higher real cash balances may lead to lower interest rates when the increased transaction demand for money from more employment is less than the increase in real balances. The lower interest rate is then associated with higher capital intensity and so a higher real wage.

VI. DYNAMICS

I now leave relatively simple problems and turn to much more difficult ones to which my answers will be correspondingly weak. Much of what follows arises out of joint work with Robert Solow.

One starts with a fact of the history of our subject. Keynes did not maintain that money wages must be regarded as fixed. He held that their determination was beyond the economist's grasp and that the honest thing was to take them as exogenous. But he also maintained that if it were the case that money wages responded rapidly to the state of the labour market it would be extremely bad for the economy. These simple points may be wrong but it is difficult to understand why they have been so consistently bowdlerised in so many textbooks and papers.

Now the new macro-economics has no fear of stepping in where Keynes feared to tread. They suppose that the money wage at each date is always such as to clear the labour market. If Keynes was right then this should certainly become evident in models making this assumption. And so it does in a somewhat indirect way.

Like everyone else, Solow and I have investigated the matter in the context of an overlapping generation model with production, money and perfect foresight. The equations become quite complicated and one needs the computer for explicit solutions. Our preliminary conclusion is this:

(*a*) generally the equilibrium paths are not unique,

(*b*) in the vicinity of the steady state there are parameter choices which yield deterministic Grandmont cycles,

(*c*) globally little can be deduced *a priori* but we would be surprised if the computer does not yield cycles for some range of parameter values. It is known that in models of this kind one can demonstrate (again for a range of parameter values) the existence of sunspot equilibria.

It is certainly not the case that all perfect foresight equilibrium paths are Pareto-efficient and there is no reason to suppose that the efficient ones will be picked. Further, it is known that in models with infinitely lived individuals who discount the future sufficiently, cyclical equilibria are also possible.

The literature on all of this is now very large and this is not the occasion for

ON INVOLUNTARY UNEMPLOYMENT   13

dotting the i's and crossing the t's. What we can do is to help our economic intuition of some of these results.

Suppose an economy is in steady state at t when everyone becomes aware that the labour supply from next period onwards will be higher than it has been hitherto. Since they expect the labour market to clear at every date one can try the plausible case that everyone expects wages to be lower at $t+1$ than they are now. If capital investment has to be undertaken one period in advance of its use then if the real wage next period is to be the same as now more must be invested now. But that, by market clearing, may imply that prices are higher now and are expected to fall. But then holding money now becomes relatively more attractive and investment now will not be such as to maintain the real wage. In general one would therefore have the expectation of a lower real wage at $t+1$ but that may rationally be combined with an expectation of lower prices which may be required to clear the higher output. The role of real balances here is crucial. If agents were promised higher cash balances in the future it might have been possible to start on a perfect foresight path with constant money wages and rising prices. The difference is considerable since it affects what happens to real interest rates and so to investment.

If we start along a path of higher real interest rates then the real wage will have to be falling while this persists. But the new steady state with more labour has the same real wage as before. So we will start off by moving away from steady state. This will not go on indefinitely since real cash balances are rising. When the path turns round, real interest rates again become favourable to investment. The latter will feed rising prices which are required to clear goods markets. The steady state may be overshot and so on. But here intuition gives out as it always does with even moderately complicated dynamics.

What I have said must be taken as provisional since not all the calculations are in. But work by Grandmont (1985), Woodford (1984) and Solow and myself suggests that the story is approximately correct. One thing I believe to be quite certain: there are many perfect foresight paths (indeed generally a continuum) and at present we have no reason to believe that they all seek the steady state. Keynes, who was much preoccupied with the real interest rate and bankruptcy effects of falling prices, probably correctly followed his intuition that the market clearing models would be ill behaved. In the example I have been considering the new labour is an innovation and bankruptcy cannot be excluded by perfect foresight before and after the innovation. But I have not studied this.

I now want to make a simple point concerning all of this. Whatever the precise outcome of future research it is clear that the market clearing model leaves great uncertainty for any policy maker. There are many paths and many of them cannot be easily computed. Suppose instead that money wages were in fact rigid. Does there now exist a policy which will ensure steady convergence to the steady state? In some of the models (e.g. Grandmont (1985) and Hahn and Solow (1985)) the answer is yes. It is too early to say how general this is. It depends crucially on agents foreseeing the policy. If this turns out to be generally the case then Keynes gets support in the following sense. Rigid money wages combined with policy allow us to avoid the turbulent and unknown voyages of perfect equilibrium ever changing money wage paths. This is more subtle than the text books but it is also nearer the truth.

VII. DISEQUILIBRIUM

I want to conclude with a brief look at the problems of disequilibrium. By the latter I shall want to designate states of the economy in which agents are in the process of learning. For instance workers who had expected to find a job with a certain probability find that they were mistaken. Mistakes, or if you like, new information, lead to an updating of beliefs but also to a change in actions. In particular one wants to include amongst the latter, changes in prices which were announced. Throughout there will be trading and production at 'false' prices, that is at prices which are different from what they would have been if agents when setting them had they had the expectations they have now. But there may also be unplanned inventory accumulation and decumulation. A serious economist will be dismayed by our ignorance of these processes and baffled by their complexity. The analysis of the invisible hand in motion is still well beyond us.

I have given various reasons why fully anticipated involuntary unemployment may be consistent with equilibrium and so constant money wages. In the tendentious language which has been adopted, the 'natural' rate of unemployment may be an interval rather than a number. But now I am concerned with the case in which involuntary unemployment is higher than anticipated. I want to consider only one fairly narrow aspect of this situation that arises if wages do fall and firms can correctly anticipate that fall. I must emphasise that I do not know by what means or with what delay and at what rate money wages will fall. The money wage equations of the econometricians have not impressed me as providing evidence on these matters.

However, it seems to be very widely agreed that workers' price expectations enter into this story. Given these expectations one is to suppose that wages in the situation envisaged will fall at a rate so as to lead to a decline in real wages if expectations turn out to be correct. Again I stress that it is the unexpected increase in involuntary unemployment that is driving this show and not some gap between 'the natural' and actual rate of unemployment.

Now Keynes believed that falling money wages were bad for the economy, in particular for stability, and that they would only doubtfully be accompanied by falling real wages. That is if workers correctly foresee price changes then they cannot change money wages relatively to these since the price changes are governed by the wage changes themselves. No doubt he was somewhat cavalier with lags here. But it was also soon pointed out that he had ignored the real cash balance effect. However, the latter's operation in this setting seems to be a good deal more complicated than the literature suggests.

To fix ideas suppose our economy has a unique long run equilibrium. We are now to imagine a once over unanticipated innovation which leads to the unexpected increase in unemployment when it becomes known. We can work out the new long run equilibrium. It is certainly possible that in this new long

ON INVOLUNTARY UNEMPLOYMENT   15

run equilibrium real cash balances are the same or lower than before. Now if agents had perfect foresight of this new long run equilibrium but not of the path and if they held firmly the optimistic view now so common amongst us that the economy will be carried to the new long run equilibrium then with a constant money stock, they must regard any windfall gain in real cash balances as purely transitory. Following Friedman it is reasonable to suppose that these gains will have a low effect on demand. Given transaction costs it is also unlikely that transitory increases in real balances will cause portfolio rearrangements leading to lower nominal interest rates. So the more confident the public is that the path is rapidly convergent the less likely is it to converge if it requires an initial fall in real wages to do so. It is when agents believe that some of the real-balance gains are permanent so that they no longer hold the view that the new steady state with lower real cash balances will be reached, that paradoxically convergence is more likely.

All of this is extremely informal and it neglects some important features of any actual process. One can write down a simple model with a simple dynamic structure which supports the argument but it is not much better than the verbal sketch. But once again my main contention that Keynes was right in distrusting money wage adjustments as satisfactory does not require me to be more precise. If money wages were rigid and real wage reductions were brought about by higher prices then in the case which I have discussed the economy would from the start be moving towards the steady state and not away from it. In the example prices and wages are bound to fluctuate at least for some time while that is not so with fixed money wages. Keynes' insight was that the wage mechanism would work via real balance effects on interest rates. He invented the liquidity trap to block that route. But even without the latter and even taking account of Pigou-effects two things stand out;

(a) the effects are tenuous and the more so when a change in real balances is regarded as transitory,

(b) it always seems more direct to operate on real cash balances by a change in nominal balances.

This is really as far as I can now go although I hope that Solow and I will have some precise and not too remote cases worked out in due course. But there is one more remark that needs making here. It will be obvious that my espousal of the Keynesian line on this matter will be met by the charge that it is a counsel to 'fine tune' and that fine tuning is impossible. It must have become clear to many people that this is not a very impressive argument. Economists are trained not to say that A is good but rather that A is better than B. Certainly a model of policy often gives the government more knowledge of the economy than it has or can have although the same is done for private agents by rational expectation models. Certainly therefore in practice the government can by policy make mistakes which are reflected in undesirable behaviour of the economy. But it is my contention that the invisible hand may not only tremble but mislead, indeed that it is almost bound to do so with flexible money wages. I have only argued about what would be possible without government ignorance and delays. I have not proposed that it is possible. But the case between the two sides is not decided by the observation that one of them may not deliver what is promised. Far subtler arguments and far more knowledge is needed to decide the case.

VIII. A FINAL COMMENT

I want now to conclude with a final, somewhat methodological comment.

To suppose that rational agents only have preferences over goods and leisure, that they have rational expectations, that all markets are Walrasian and that they clear at every instant is not only logically coherent but may also give interesting insights, although some of the insights recently claimed are wrong. To maintain that the models of this kind have not been falsified by econometrics is very weak. I am hard put to think of any model or theory which has been falsified. Moreover there are many theories, for instance astrological ones, which are not regarded as falsified although they are false. To maintain that the models give good predictions seems of doubtful validity but even if not, that circumstance has, Friedman notwithstanding, very small epistemological weight.

The world plainly can be conceived to be different than this model and to many of us it plainly is different in important aspects, some of which I here argued for. But I want to make only a weak claim. It is surely too soon to be certain and it surely is important to try alternative ways of seeing the world. I do not mean that we should abandon the rational calculating agent. That would leave us too much at sea. I do not mean that we should be uninterested in equilibrium. But we should realise that this leaves us great latitude in the manner in which we attempt to understand the world.

Churchill College, Cambridge

REFERENCES

Diamond, P. A. (1971). 'A model of price adjustment.' *Journal of Economic Theory*, vol. 3, pp. 156–68.
Grandmont, J. M. (1985). 'On endogenous competitive business cycles.' *Econometrica*, vol. 53, no. 5, pp. 995–1046.
Hahn, F. H. (1973). *On The Notion of Equilibrium in Economics*. Cambridge: Cambridge University Press.
—— (1984). 'Wages and employment.' In *Economic Theory and Hicksian Themes* (ed. D. A. Collard, D. R. Helm, M. FG. Scott and A. K. Sen). Oxford: Oxford University Press.
—— and Solow, R. M. (1985). 'Is wage flexibility a good thing?' (to appear in Proceedings of a Conference – ed. W. Beckerman).
Mortensen, D..T. (1984). 'Job search and labour market analysis.' In *Handbook of Labour Economics* (ed. R. Layard and O. Ashenfelter). Amsterdam: North-Holland.
Negishi, T. (1979). *Microeconomic Foundations of Keynesian Macroeconomics*. Amsterdam: North-Holland.
Rubinstein, A. (1981). 'Perfect equilibrium in a bargaining model.' *Econometrica*, vol. 50, pp. 97–110.
Shaked, A. and Sutton, J. (1984). 'Involuntary unemployment in a perfect equilibrium in a bargaining model.' *Econometrica*, vol. 52, pp. 1351–64.
Wilson, R. (1985). 'Game-theoretic analyses of trading processes.' Technical Report No. 474. Institute For Mathematical Studies in the Social Sciences: Stanford.
Woodford, M. (1984). 'Indeterminacy of equilibrium in the overlapping generations model: a survey.' Mimeo, Columbia University.
Yellen, J. L. (1984). 'Efficiency wage models of unemployment.' *American Economic Association Papers and Proceedings*, vol. 74 (2), pp. 200–5.

Part II
On Money, Monetarism and Inflation

[8]

MONEY AND INCOME:
POST HOC ERGO PROPTER HOC? *

JAMES TOBIN

An ultra-Keynesian model, 303. — A Friedman model, 310. — Comparisons of timing implications, 314.

Milton Friedman asserts that changes in the supply of money M (defined to include time deposits) are the principal cause of changes in money income Y. In his less guarded and more popular expositions, he comes close to asserting that they are the unique cause.[1] In support of this position Friedman and his associates and followers have marshaled an imposing volume of evidence, of several kinds.

Historical case studies are one kind of evidence. For example, in their monumental *Monetary History of the United States 1867–1960*,[2] Friedman and Anna Schwartz carefully analyze and interpret the role of money and monetary policy in the important episodes of American economic history since the Civil War. Summary regressions of time series of economic aggregates are a second type of evidence. Presumed effects are simply regressed on presumed causes; the single equations estimated are something like the econometrician's "reduced forms." In a study with David Meiselman,[3] Friedman concluded that his monetary explanation of variations in money income fits the data better than a simple Keynesian multiplier model. More recent studies in the same vein claim that monetary policy does better than fiscal policy in explaining postwar fluctuations of money income.[4]

* The research described in this paper was carried out under grants from the National Science Foundation and from the Ford Foundation. I am grateful to Milton Friedman for helpful comments on an earlier draft of this paper.

1. See, for example, his column in *Newsweek*, Jan. 30, 1967, p. 86, "Higher Taxes? No." He says, "To have a significant impact on the economy, a tax increase must somehow affect monetary policy — the quantity of money and its rate of growth. . . . The Federal Reserve can increase the quantity of money by precisely the same amount with or without a tax rise. The tax reduction of 1964 . . . encouraged the Fed to follow a more expansionary policy. This monetary expansion explains the long-continued economic expansion. And it is the turnabout in monetary policy since April 1966 that explains the growing signs of recession."
2. National Bureau of Economic Research, *Studies in Business Cycles*, No. 12 (Princeton: Princeton University Press, 1963).
3. Friedman and David Meiselman, "The Relative Stability of Monetary Velocity and the Investment Multiplier in the United States 1897–1958," Commission on Money and Credit, *Stabilization Policies* (Englewood Cliffs, N.J.: Prentice-Hall, Inc., 1963), 165–268.
4. Leonall Anderson and Jerry Jordan, "Monetary and Fiscal Actions: A

A third type of evidence relates to timing, specifically to leads and lags at cyclical turning points. Much of the work of Friedman and his associates at the National Bureau of Economic Research has been devoted to this subject.[5] Turning points in the rate of change of money supply, M',[6] show a long lead, and turning points in the money stock, M, itself (relative to trend) a shorter lead, over turning points in money income, Y. A great deal of the popular and semiprofessional appeal of the modern quantity theory can be attributed to these often repeated facts.

However, the relevance of timing evidence has been seriously questioned.[7] Friedman himself says, "These regular and sizable leads of the money series are themselves suggestive of an influence running from money to business but they are by no means decisive." [8] The apparent leads may "really" be lagged responses — either positive or negative ("inverted") — of money to previous changes in business activity. Friedman cautiously rejects this possibility. He finds that the M series conforms more closely to the NBER reference cycle on a positive basis with money leading than on an inverted basis with money lagging, and he regards the business-money causal nexus as very likely to be inverted. Having satisfied himself that the dominant association of M' and business activity is positive, Friedman concludes, ". . . it is not easy to rationalize positive conformity with a lead as reflecting supply response," [9] i.e., response of the supply of money to changes in business activity.

The purpose of the present paper is to spell out the lead-lag timing implications of alternative theoretical models of the relation

Test of their Relative Importance in Economic Stabilization," *Federal Reserve Bank of St. Louis Review* (Nov. 1968), 11–24.

5. See Friedman, "The Lag in the Effect of Monetary Policy," *Journal of Political Economy*, LXIX (Oct. 1961), 447–66; Friedman and Schwartz, "Money and Business Cycles," *Review of Economics and Statistics*, Feb. 1963 Supplement, 32–64; Friedman, "The Monetary Studies of the National Bureau," *Annual Report of the National Bureau of Economic Research 1964*.

6. Throughout this paper x' will denote the time derivative of x, $\frac{dx}{dt}$, and x'' the second derivative of x with respect to time.

7. By, among others, J. Kareken and R. Solow, "Lags in Monetary Policy," Commission on Money and Credit, *Stabilization Policies* (Englewood Cliffs, N.J.: Prentice-Hall, Inc., 1963), 14–25. They pointed out that a rate of change like M' will generally lead a level like Y, in the manner that a cosine series "leads" a sine series. Friedman replied in "The Lag in the Effect of Monetary Policy," *loc. cit.*, that both M' and Y have the dimension of a flow and that in any case he finds M' leading Y' and trend-corrected M leading Y. Kareken and Solow found little lead, if any, of M' over the rate of change of the industrial production index, but they should have used a monetary rather than a real measure of business activity.

8. In "The Monetary Studies of the National Bureau," *loc cit.*, 13.

9. *Ibid.*, 14.

MONEY AND INCOME   303

between money and money income. In one model, a version of the ultra-Keynesian theory that Friedman is so often attacking, monetary developments are just a sideshow to the main events. In the other model, one of Friedman's own, monetary developments are of decisive causal significance. What kinds of observed relations between money and money income and their rates of change do the opposing models generate? Do they imply different lead-lag patterns?

In the ultra-Keynesian model, changes in the money supply are a passive response to income changes generated, via the multiplier mechanism, by autonomous investment and government expenditure. This makes it possible to see what kinds of observations of money stock M and its rate of change M' would be generated in an ultra-Keynesian world. These can then be compared with the observations that would be generated by a Friedman economy. Here it is necessary to express Friedman's hypothesis with more precision and simplicity than it is usually expounded. However, this can be done with the help of the model of the demand for money set forth in his article with Anna Schwartz, "Money and Business Cycles." [1]

I hasten to say that I do not believe the ultra-Keynesian model to be exhibited (nor would Keynes), any more than I believe Friedman's. I do think, nevertheless, that the exercise points up the dangers of accepting timing evidence as empirical proof of propositions about causation. [2] I shall show that the ultra-Keynesian model — in which money has no causal importance whatever — throws up observations which a superficial believer in *post hoc ergo propter hoc* would regard as more favorable to the idea that money is causally important than does Friedman's own model. What is even more striking and surprising is that the ultra-Keynesian model implies cyclical timing patterns just like the empirical patterns that Friedman reports, while the Friedman model does not.

AN ULTRA-KEYNESIAN MODEL

The ultra-Keynesian multiplier model has

(1) $Y = m(G + K')$

where Y is net national product, G is the current rate of government expenditure, and K' is net capital accumulation, all in nominal units.

---

1. *Loc. cit.*
2. The same methodological lesson is given by the simulations of more complicated models in William C. Brainard and James Tobin, "Pitfalls of Financial Model Building," *American Economic Review* (*Papers and Proceedings*), May 1968, 19–122.

304   *QUARTERLY JOURNAL OF ECONOMICS*

(The division of cyclical fluctuations in income between real output and prices is inessential to the argument of the paper and is ignored throughout.) The multiplier m is derived routinely from the identity:

Saving + Taxes = Government Expenditure + Net Investment

(2) $s(1 - t)Y + tY = G + K'$

where s is the marginal propensity to save from income after taxes and t is the constant tax rate (net of transfers). Therefore the multiplier,

(3) $m = \dfrac{1}{s(1 - t) + t}$.

The determination of income by equation (2) is illustrated in the familiar textbook diagram, Figure I.

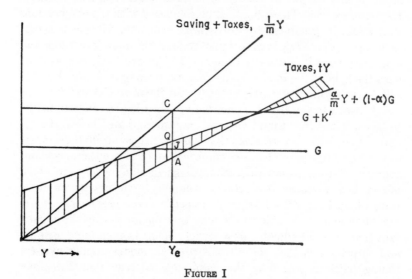

FIGURE I

Private wealth W is the capital stock K plus the government debt D (whether monetized or not), the cumulative total of past deficits, $G - tY$. Saving, the change in private wealth, is

(4) $s(1 - t)Y = W' = K' + G - tY = (K' + G)(1 - tm)$.

In Figure I government deficit is AB, and net capital accumulation is BC. JC $\overset{AJ}{}$

The public's balance sheet is

(5) $W = K + D = K - L + M + B$

where B is the public's holdings of the nonmonetary debt (bonds) of the government, L is the debt of the public to the banking system, and M is the public's holdings of the monetary liabilities of the government and the banking system. To be consistent with Friedman's model and his empirical findings, M includes time deposits as well as demand deposits.

The portfolio behavior of the public in this ultra-Keynesian world is very primitive. Real investment is autonomous; indeed, exogenous fluctuations in the pace of capital formation are the source of the business cycle. This implies that there are autonomous shifts in the proportions in which the public wishes to allocate its wealth among the available assets. During investment booms, capital becomes more attractive relative to money and bonds; during investment recessions, the reverse occurs.[3] By the same token, borrowing from banks rises in booms and falls in recessions. Specifically, the public's debt to the banking system is taken to be a fixed proportion of the capital stock:

(6) $\qquad L = a\,K \qquad\qquad (0 < a < 1).$

The only portfolio decision left is the allocation of the remainder of the public's net worth — $(W - K + L)$, which is equal to $(D + a\,K)$ — among the two remaining assets, money (currency and bank deposits) and bonds (interest-bearing government debt). This is the choice of Keynesian liquidity preference theory. The demand for money can be written as the sum of two components, an asset demand related to the interest rate and to allocable wealth and a transactions demand proportional to income:

(7) $\qquad M = a_0(r)\,(D + a\,K) + a_1 Y$

where r is the interest rate on bonds and the derivative $a'_0(r)$ is negative. By subtraction, public demand for bonds is

$(1 - a_0(r))\,(D + a\,K) - a_1 Y.$

The main point of the exercise can be made by assuming that the monetary authority provides bank reserves as necessary to keep r constant, so that a_0 is a constant. The monetary system responds to the "needs of trade." With the help of the monetary authority, banks are able and willing to meet the fluctuating demand of their borrowing customers for credit and of their depositors for money. In Friedman's terms, this is a "supply response" with "positive conformity" of money to business activity. It is indeed a response which he regards as all too common in central banking, one for which he has severely criticized the Federal Reserve. If these criticisms are justi-

3. It might seem more Keynesian to let bonds alone bear the brunt of the autonomous shifts to and from capital. But "money" here includes time deposits.

fied, then this endogenous response must have played an important role in generating monetary time series.

The relation among flows corresponding to (7) is

(8) $\quad M' = a_0(D' + a K') + a_1 Y'$
$\qquad\quad = a_0(G - tY + a K') + a_1 Y'.$

Using (1) converts (8) into

(9) $\qquad M' = a_0[G(1 - a) + Y(\frac{a}{m} - t)] + a_1 Y'.$

Thus, for given G, M' is a linear function of Y and Y', and these vary in response to autonomous changes in investment K'. The relationship to Y' is, of course, positive. Consider now the relationship to Y. In Figure I, at income level Y_e, D' is represented by AJ. Let JQ equal aJC, the amount of real investment covered by new indebtedness to banks. Then AQ represents $D' + a K'$, the quantity which the public divides between accumulations of money and of bonds. Imagine that G is held constant, while K' varies autonomously and carries Y with it. Then the vertical distance through the shaded area, of which AQ is an example, is $D' + a K'$. This declines with Y, as illustrated, provided the line through Q has a slope smaller than t, i.e., that a/m is smaller than t. (For example, if the multiplier is 2–1/2 and the tax ratio is 1/5, the loan-to-investment ratio a must be smaller than 1/2.) In this case $D' + a K'$ will become negative, as illustrated, at sufficiently high values of Y, where the government budget is in large surplus.

The financial operations of the government and the banks are as follows: The government and the monetary authority divided the increase of debt D' between "high-powered money" and bonds in such manner as to keep the interest rate on target. If we assume no change in currency holdings by the public, the increase M' in money requires an increase of kM', where k is the required reserve ratio, in bank reserves. Banks' loan assets increase by $L' = a K'$. The difference $(M'(1 - k) - L')$ the banks allocate between excess reserves and bond holdings, in proportions that depend on the interest rate. Thus the monetary authority provides enough new high-powered money to meet increased reserve requirements and any new demand for excess reserves. The remainder of the increase in public debt D' takes the form of bonds, and it is just enough to satisfy the demands of the banks and the public. This can be seen as follows: The increase in public demand for bonds is $W' + L' - K' - M' = D' + aK' - M'$. The increase in the banks' demand for bonds is $M' - L' - H' = M' - a K' - H'$, where H' is the increase in required and excess reserves. Adding the two together, we see that the increase in demand for bonds is $D' - H'$, just equal to the supply. In short, Walras' law guarantees that if the money market is cleared, the bond market is also cleared.

A dollar increase in government spending has the same effect in raising income and tax receipts as a dollar increase in private investment. Both raise income Y by the multiplier m, and taxes by tm. However, they have different effects on $D' + a K'$ and thus on M'. An increase in government expenditure raises $D' + a K'$ by $1 - tm$; an increase in private investment, by $a - tm$. Since a is less than 1, the demand for money is raised more by an increase of government expenditure. This fact is clear from (9). For given Y, a dollar increase in G (replacing a dollar of K') increases M' by $1 - a$.

A tax cut sufficient to create the same increase in income would entail an even larger rise in $D' + a K'$ and in the demand for additional money. Our ultra-Keynesian would not be surprised to find the money supply rising especially fast in an income expansion propelled by deficit spending. He would not even be surprised if some observers of the accelerated pace of monetary expansion in the wake of a tax cut conclude that monetary rather than fiscal policy caused the boom.[4]

Let us return, however, to a model cycle generated by fluctuation in private investment K', with government expenditure and the tax rate constant. The model abstracts from trends in Y and its components. However, private wealth grows over the model cycle, and this growth is responsible for an upward trend in M. What will be the cyclical behavior of the money supply M and of its rate of change M', in reference to the cycles in money income Y and its rate of change Y'?

There are two components of M', one related to Y and one to Y'. The Y-component has already been discussed. Its relationship to Y is shown in Figure II, as the downward sloping line. Y_{tr} and Y_{pk} are the trough and peak of the cycle. In the illustration, M' for stationary Y does not become negative, even at Y_{pk}. The second or transactions component is simply proportional to Y': $a_1 Y'$ in equation (8) or (9) above. This can be added to Figure II, provided we know the relation of Y' to Y. That relation is illustrated in Figure III, on the assumption that the cycle in K' and Y is a sine wave. The circle, with arrows, shows Y' zero at the trough of Y, Y' at its own peak, Y at its peak with Y' again zero, Y' at its trough, and so on.

4. Note Friedman's comment in *Newsweek* quoted above, note 1, page 301.

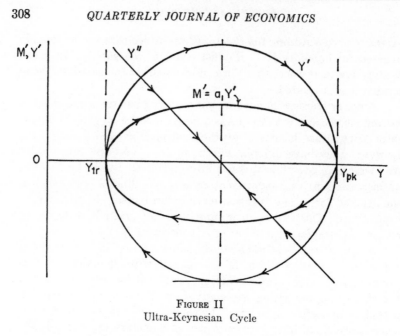

FIGURE II
Ultra-Keynesian Cycle

The ellipse within the circle represents the corresponding cycle in the second component of M'.

In Figure II, this component is added vertically to the line representing the first component. The squashed ellipse in Figure II shows the cycle of M' as income moves from Y_{tr} to Y_{pk} and back. The order of events in the cycle can be read by following the perimeter of the squashed ellipse clockwise. In Figure II there is a brief period of the cycle when M' is negative. Thus M has a late peak and early trough, and grows on balance over the cycle. It can easily be imagined, however, that the ellipse in Figure II lies entirely above the axis, so that M grows continuously but at varying rates. Or, if the first or level component of M' became negative before Y reached its peak, then M would lead Y at the peak as well as at the trough. In any case, it is clear that M' not only has a long lead over Y, more than a quarter of a cycle, but also leads Y'.

The horizontal line through the squashed ellipse represents the average value of M'. The stock of money M, corrected for trend, will reach its peak and trough when actual M' is equal to average M'. These points are also indicated in Figure II. They precede turning points in Y but not in Y''.

It is easy to modify Figure II to allow for a rise in interest rates during expansions of money income and a decline in contractions. In an ultra-Keynesian world this "leaning against the wind" by the monetary authorities would be irrelevant to stabilization. But it might occur nonetheless, because the monetary authorities mistakenly believe in their own powers or are just operationally conservative in changing the supply of high-powered money, or because they worry about the balance of payments. Anyway, it would be represented in Figure II by a steepening of the central line. This would result in a still longer lead of M' with respect to Y' and Y.

Equation (8) would read

$$(8') \qquad M' = a_0(r) \ (D' + a K') + a'_0(r) \ (D + a K)r' + a_1 Y'.$$

As r rises with Y, the decline in a_0 reinforces the decline in $D' + a K'$. Assuming that r' is positively related to Y', and given that $a'_0(r)$ is negative, the second term contributes a negative relation of M' to Y'. This would make the ellipse of Figure III flatter, as well

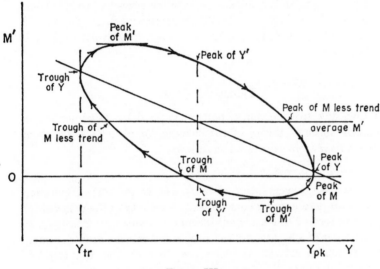

FIGURE III

as distorting its shape. Indeed, it could conceivably reverse the net effect of Y' on M' and therefore reverse the order of events in the cycle. But the central bank surely does not lean against the wind so hard as that, especially in an ultra-Keynesian world.

The results would also be reinforced if a term in Y', with a positive coefficient, were added to the basic demand for money equation (7). The logic of such a term would be that changes in wealth are in the first instance absorbed in cash balances, with more permanent portfolio allocations following later. Thus demand for money would be especially high when income and saving are rapidly increasing. This, after all, is what one would expect of money as "a temporary abode of purchasing power," to use Professor Friedman's famous phrase.

A Y' term in expression (7) for M means a Y''' term in expression (8) for M'. In a cycle of the type illustrated in Figure III, Y'' is inversely related to Y. Therefore a Y'' component of M' will be high at low levels of Y and low at peak levels. Like the interest rate effect, this will increase the slope of the central line in Figure II and accentuate the lead-lag pattern there depicted.

There is nothing sacred about sine waves, and neither is a sine-curve cycle crucial for the timing pattern shown in Figure II. The reader is invited to experiment with noncircular shapes of the relation of Y' to Y in Figure III. He will find it easy to change the lengths of the lags and leads, and in extreme cases to produce some coincidences and ambiguities. But the essential message of Figure II comes through, provided that M' is related negatively to Y and positively to Y'.

A FRIEDMAN MODEL

I turn now to the cyclical pattern implied by Friedman's own "permanent income" theory of the demand for money. For present purposes this may be expressed as follows:

$$(10) \qquad 1nM = A + \delta \, 1n \, Y^*_p.$$

Here M is the same quantity of money as in the ultra-Keynesian model; Y^*_p is permanent income; δ is the elasticity of the demand for money with respect to permanent income, estimated by Friedman to be of the order of 1.8. Income and permanent income grow secularly at an exponential rate β. As above, we abstract from this trend of income and consider the deviations from trend, Y_p and Y. Since $1n \, Y_p = 1n \, Y^*_p - \beta t - C$, equation (10) can be restated as

$$(11) \qquad 1n \, M = B + \delta \, 1n \, Y_p + \delta\beta t.$$

For rates of change, (11) implies

$$(12) \qquad M'/M = \delta(Y'_p/Y_p) + \delta\beta.$$

Permanent income, corrected for trend, is a weighted geometric average of current and past actual incomes, also corrected for trend, with the weights receding exponentially. Thus when actual and permanent income differ, the public changes its estimate of permanent income by some fraction of their relative difference. Specifically,

(13) $Y'_p/Y_p = w(\ln Y - \ln Y_p)$, or

$$\ln Y = \frac{1}{w}(Y'_p/Y_p) + \ln Y_p.$$

Friedman has estimated, mainly in connection with his work on the consumption function, that revision of permanent income eliminates about one-third of its deviation from actual income within a year. In other words, the weight of the current year's income is one-third, and the weights of past years' incomes two-thirds, in the calculation of permanent income. If the revision is taken to be continuous, as in (13), rather than discrete, these weights imply a value of 0.40 for w.

In this model the supply of money and its rate of change are autonomous. The demand for money must adjust to the supply at every point of time. Permanent income is the only variable involved in the demand for money; so it must do the adjusting. But much of permanent income is past history; the only part that can adjust is current income. Roughly speaking, Friedman's numerical estimates imply that permanent income must rise 0.55 per cent to absorb a 1 per cent increment in the supply of money. But in the short run money is much more powerful. Current year's income must rise by 1.65 per cent to make permanent income rise 0.55 per cent. Thus in a cyclical boom, in which the supply of money keeps rising, current income must rise even faster. In this way the theory explains why the velocity of money moves up and down with income in business cycles and reconciles this observation with Friedman's finding that secularly velocity declines as income rises.

An explicit relation of income to money supply can be obtained from (13) by using (11) to express $\ln Y_p$ in terms of $\ln M$ and (12) to express Y'_p/Y_p in terms of M'/M:

(14) $$\ln Y = \frac{M'/M}{\delta w} + \frac{\ln M}{\delta} - \beta t - \frac{\beta}{w} - \frac{A}{\delta}$$

(15) $$Y'/Y = \frac{g'_M}{\delta w} + \frac{g_M}{\delta} - \beta ,$$

for convenience letting g_M *denote* M'/M and g'_M, its time derivative. Equation (15) will be used for the analysis of cyclical timing patterns. It relates the rate of change of income, abstracting from trend, to the rate of change of the money stock and to the change in that rate. Note that if g_M is held steady at $\delta\beta$ then Y'/Y will be zero and income will be on trend.

This exposition is based on Friedman's theory as set forth in his

312   QUARTERLY JOURNAL OF ECONOMICS

article with Anna Schwartz.[5] I have used continuous rather than discrete time, and I have related money demand to money income, ignoring the complication that real income and price level enter Friedman's formula somewhat differently. These simplifications do not impair the essential message of the theory for the present purpose.[6]

Consider a business cycle generated by a sine wave in g_M. What will be the resulting movement of Y'/Y? This is, according to (15), the sum of two components, one linear in g_M itself, the other proportional to g'_M. The first is indicated by the positively sloped line in Figure IV. The trough and peak of g_M are indicated by g_{Mtr} and g_{Mpk}.

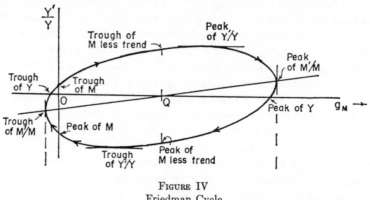

FIGURE IV
Friedman Cycle

The average value of g_M over the cycle is positive, specifically $\delta\beta$, while the average value of Y'/Y is, of course, zero. These average values are shown as point Q in Figure IV. To show the second component on the same diagram, we must use the relationship between g'_M and g_M, depicted by the circle in Figure V. The large ellipse in which the circle is inscribed is $g'_M/\delta w$, where $1/\delta w$ exceeds one, in keeping with Friedman's theory and numerical estimates. It is this which must be added vertically to the line of Figure IV to exhibit the total change in income Y'/Y. As in the case of Figure II, the order of events in the cycle may be read by following the perimeter of the misshapen ellipse in Figure IV clockwise.

5. "Money and Business Cycles," *loc. cit.*, 56–59.
6. Elsewhere, with Craig Swan, I have considered the permanent income theory in full detail and tested the model and Friedman's numerical estimates of the parameters against postwar U.S. data. See J. Tobin and Craig Swan, "Money and Permanent Income: Some Empirical Tests," *American Economic Review*, LIX (May 1969), 285–95.

MONEY AND INCOME   313

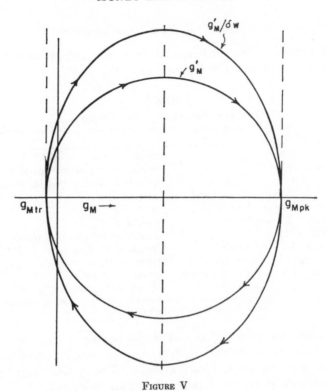

FIGURE V

In this monetary model of business fluctuations, M'/M *lags* Y'/Y and has only a short lead over Y itself. The money stock itself lags Y at peak and trough. However, as in the other model, there might be no cycle in M at all: M'/M might never be negative. This would be shown in Figure IV by moving the vertical axis entirely to the left of the ellipse. If it were moved part way, the trough in M might precede the trough in Y. But the major conclusions remain.

As in Figure II, it is also possible to indicate in Figure IV the peak and trough in the deviation of the money stock from trend. The average level of M'/M is shown by the dashed vertical line through Q. When actual M'/M equals this average, trend-corrected M reaches its peak and trough. Figure IV shows that these turning points lag the corresponding turning points in Y.

As in the case of the ultra-Keynesian model, the cycle does not need to be a sine wave in order to produce the basic order of events over the cycle.

314   QUARTERLY JOURNAL OF ECONOMICS

COMPARISONS OF TIMING IMPLICATIONS

In Table I, I have summarized the timing implications of the two models, as indicated in Figures II and IV.

TABLE I
ORDER OF EVENTS IN MODEL CYCLES

Ultra-Keynesian	Friedman
trough of Y	trough of Y or [trough of M]
peak of M'	[trough of M] or [trough of Y]
peak of Y'	trough of M corrected for trend
peak of M corrected for trend	peak of Y'/Y
peak of Y or [peak of M]	peak of M'/M
[peak of M] or peak of Y	peak of Y
trough of M'	peak of M corrected for trend
trough of Y' or [trough of M]	trough of Y'/Y or [peak of M]
[trough of M] or trough of Y'	[peak of M] or trough of Y'/Y
trough of M corrected for trend	trough of M'/M
trough of Y	trough of Y or [trough of M]

Note: events in brackets [ ] need not occur at all.

Clearly the monetary-causal model implies a much less impressive lead of money over business activity than its opposite.

Consider now the empirical evidence. The cyclical timing patterns reported by Friedman and Schwartz are as follows: [7]

(a) For "mild depression cycles" they find no cycle in M.

(b) For "deep depression cycles" they find a cycle in M, mildly lagging the NBER reference cycle, with which money income is roughly coincident, at peaks.

(c) They find that the rate of change of the money stock leads at peaks and troughs. This lead is dramatically long, so much so "as to suggest the possibility of interpreting the rate of change series as inverted, i.e., as generally declining during reference expansion and rising during reference contraction."

(d) They show a generally procyclical behavior of velocity Y/M, but with some tendency for velocity to start declining before the reference peak.

Friedman has also summarized the evidence in an earlier article, as follows:

. . . peaks in the rate of change of the money stock precede reference cycle peaks by 16 months (on the average) . . . peaks in the deviation of money

7. Friedman and Schwartz, "Money and Business Cycles," *loc. cit.*, especially Charts 2, 4, and 6, and p. 36.

MONEY AND INCOME   **315**

stock from its trend do so by five months . . . such absolute peaks as occur in the money stock precede reference cycle peaks by less than five months and may even lag . . . peaks in the rate of change of income precede such peaks as occur in the stock of money . . . they probably also precede peaks in the deviation of the money stock from its trend . . . they probably also follow peaks in the rate of change of money.[8]

In comparing these findings with the patterns of Figures II and IV, it is helpful to recall that sixteen months is roughly three-eighths and five months roughly one-eighth of a complete cycle. Figure II agrees with the empirical summary not only in order of events but also in the lengths of these leads or lags.

Every single piece of observed evidence that Friedman reports on timing is consistent with the timing implications of the ultra-Keynesian model, as depicted in Figure II. This evidence actually contradicts his own "permanent income" theory and lends support to the ultra-Keynesian model.

As the quotation in (c) above indicates, Friedman himself has worried whether the very long lead of M' over Y and the reference cycle may not prove altogether too much. It might be a lag instead of a lead. "An inverse relation," he says elsewhere, "with money lagging would be much easier to rationalize in terms of business influencing money than of money influencing business. . . ."[9]

It is only fair to notice, however, that there are two Friedmans when it comes to describing the causal mechanism from money to money income. One is the Friedman of the permanent income hypothesis, with the implications set forth above. The logic is that the demand for money is quite insensitive to current income, because current income has only a fractional weight in permanent income. This has the virtue of explaining why the monetary multiplier in the cyclical short run is so large and why velocity varies procyclically. But the cost of this explanation, as we have seen, is that it implies an immediate response as well as a powerful response. What is gained from the hypothesis in explaining amplitude is lost in explaining timing.

Friedman recognizes some of the limitations of the permanent income model. He sees that it cannot be applied without modification to quarterly as well as annual data. Since the current quarter of income experience has presumably even less weight in determining permanent income, and thus the demand for money, than the cur-

8. "The Lag in the Effect of Monetary Policy," *loc. cit.*, 456.
9. *Ibid.*, 458.

rent year of income experience, the money multiplier should be much larger (three to four times as large) on a quarter-to-quarter application of (15) than on a year-to-year application.[1]

Faced by this sort of *reductio ad absurdum*, Friedman says:

> In generalizing to a quarterly basis, it will no longer be satisfactory to suppose that actual and desired money balances are always equal. It will be desirable to allow instead for a discrepancy between these two totals, which the holders of balances seek to eliminate at a rate depending on the size of the discrepancy. This will introduce past money balances into the estimated demand equation not only as a proxy for prior permanent incomes [as in (14) and (15)] but also as a determinant of the discrepancies in the process of being corrected.[2]

The second Friedman explains the money-income causal nexus, and the reason that it takes some time to operate, in much more conventional and less controversial terms. This description relies heavily on discrepancies of the type just discussed. Excessive money balances, for example, are not immediately absorbed by mammoth spurts of money income. They are gradually worked off — affecting interest rates, prices of financial and physical assets, and eventually investment and consumption spending.[3] This account, though not yet expressed with the precision of the permanent income hypothesis, can doubtless be formulated so as to be consistent with the observed evidence on timing. But at a cost. It cannot attribute to money a large short-run multiplier or explain the procyclical move-

---

1. When the model is formulated in discrete rather than continuous time, equation (14) becomes (here interpreting M, as well as Y, as trend-corrected)

$$\ln Y(t) = \frac{1}{\delta w} \ln M(t) - \frac{(1-w)}{\delta w} \ln M(t-1) - \text{const.}$$

Since w, the weight of current period income, varies inversely with the length of the period, the multiplier of $\ln M(t)$ is larger the shorter the period.

A formulation free of this paradox would relate trend-corrected "permanent money balances" to trend-corrected "permanent income":

$$\ln M_p(t) = \sum_{-\infty}^{t} v(1-v)^{t-\tau} \ln M(\tau)$$

$$= \delta \sum_{-\infty}^{t} w(1-w)^{t-\tau} \ln Y(\tau) = \delta Y_p(t)$$

$$v \ln M(t) + (1-v) \ln M_p(t-1) = \delta w \ln Y(t)$$
$$+ \delta(1-w) \ln Y_p(t-1)$$

$$\ln Y(t) = \frac{v}{\delta w} \ln M(t) + \frac{w-v}{\delta w} \ln M_p(t-1).$$

Since v/w is presumably independent of the time period chosen, this formulation avoids the *reductio ad absurdum*. But it also has different implications both for policy and for estimation.

2. "Money and Business Cycles," *loc. cit.*, 59.

3. Passages describing this mechanism may be found in each of the Friedman articles previously cited.

MONEY AND INCOME   317

ment of velocity. Indeed it leaves room for interest rates and other variables to affect velocity. Therefore it cannot have those clear-cut implications regarding monetary and fiscal policy with which Professor Friedman has so confidently identified himself.

YALE UNIVERSITY

[9]

PROBLEM OF ACHIEVING AND MAINTAINING A STABLE PRICE LEVEL

ANALYTICAL ASPECTS OF ANTI-INFLATION POLICY

By PAUL A. SAMUELSON *and* ROBERT M. SOLOW
Massachusetts Institute of Technology

I

Just as generals are said to be always fighting the wrong war, economists have been accused of fighting the wrong inflation. Thus, at the time of the 1946-48 rise in American prices, much attention was focused on the successive rounds of wage increases resulting from collective bargaining. Yet probably most economists are now agreed that this first postwar rise in prices was primarily attributable to the pull of demand that resulted from wartime accumulations of liquid assets and deferred needs.

This emphasis on demand-pull was somewhat reinforced by the Korean war run-up of prices after mid-1950. But just by the time that cost-push was becoming discredited as a theory of inflation, we ran into the rather puzzling phenomenon of the 1955-58 upward creep of prices, which seemed to take place in the last part of the period despite growing overcapacity, slack labor markets, slow real growth, and no apparent great buoyancy in over-all demand.

It is no wonder then that economists have been debating the possible causations involved in inflation: demand-pull versus cost-push; wage-push versus more general Lerner "seller's inflation"; and the new Charles Schultze theory of "demand-shift" inflation. We propose to give a brief survey of the issues. Rather than pronounce on the terribly difficult question as to exactly which is the best model to use in explaining the recent past and predicting the likely future, we shall try to emphasize the types of evidence which can help decide between the conflicting theories. And we shall be concerned with some policy implications that arise from the different analytical hypotheses.

History of the Debate: The Quantity Theory and Demand-Pull. The preclassical economists grew up in an environment of secularly rising prices. And even prior to Adam Smith there had grown up the belief in at least a simplified quantity theory. But it was in the neoclassical thought of Walras, Marshall, Fisher, and others that this special version of demand determination of the absolute level of money prices and costs reached its most developed form.

We can oversimplify the doctrine as follows. The real outputs, inputs, and relative prices of goods and factors can be thought of as determined by a set of competitive equations which are independent of the absolute level of prices. As in a barter system, the absolute level of all prices is indeterminate and inessential because of the "relative homogeneity" properties of these market relations. To fix the absolute scale factor, we can if we like bring in a neutral money. Such money, unlike coffee or soap, being valued only for what it will buy and not for its intrinsic utility, will be exactly doubled in demand if there is an exact doubling of all prices. Because of this important "scale homogeneity," fixing the total of such money will, when applied to our already determined real system of outputs, factors, and relative prices, fix the absolute level of all prices; and changes in the total of such money must necessarily correspond to new equilibria of absolute prices that have moved in exact proportion, with relative prices and all real magnitudes being quite unaffected.[1]

As Patinkin and others have shown, the above doctrines are rather oversimplified, for they do not fully analyze the intricacies involved in the demand for money; instead they ignore important (and predictable) changes in such proportionality coefficients as velocity of circulation. But by World War I, this particular, narrow version of demand-pull inflation had more or less triumphed. The wartime rise in prices was usually analyzed in terms of rises in the over-all money supply. And the postwar German inflation was understood by non-German economists in similar terms.

But not all economists ever agree on anything. Just as Tooke had eclectically explained the Napoleonic rise in prices partially in terms of the war-induced increase in tax, shipping, and other costs, so did Harold G. Moulton and others choose to attribute the World War I price rises to prior rises in cost of production. And it is not without significance that the great neoclassical Wicksell expressed in the last years of his life some misgivings over the usual version of wartime price movements, placing great emphasis on movements in money's velocity induced by wartime shortages of goods.

Of course, the neoclassical writers would not have denied the necessary equality of competitive costs and prices. But they would have regarded it as superficial to take the level of money costs as a predetermined variable. Instead, they would argue, prices and factor costs are

---

[1] But as Hume had early recognized, the periods of rising prices seemed to give rise to at least transient stimulus to the economy as active profit seekers gained an advantage at the expense of the more inert fixed-income, creditor, and wage sectors. The other side of this Hume thesis is perhaps exemplified by the fact that the post-Civil War decades of deflation were also periods of strong social unrest and of relatively weak booms and long periods of heavier-than-average depressions—as earlier National Bureau studies have suggested.

simultaneously determinable in interdependent competitive markets; and if the level of over-all money supply were kept sufficiently in check, then the price level could be stabilized, with any increases in real costs or any decreases in output being offset by enough backward pressure on factor prices so as to leave final money costs and prices on the average unchanged.

Many writers have gone erroneously beyond the above argument to untenable conclusions such as the following: A rise in defense expenditure matched by, say, excise taxes cannot raise the price level if the quantity of money is held constant; instead it must result in enough decrease in wage and other factor costs to offset exactly the rise in tax costs. Actually, however, such a fiscal policy change could be interpreted as a reduction in the combined public and private thriftiness; with M constant, it would tend to swell the volume of total spending, putting upward pressure on interest rates and inducing a rise in money velocity, and presumably resulting in a higher equilibrium level of prices. To roll back prices to their previous level would take, even within the framework of a strictly competitive neoclassical model, a determined reduction in previous money supply. (This illustrates the danger of going from the innocent hypothesis, that a balanced change in all prices might in the long run be consistent with no substantive changes in real relations, to an overly simple interpretation of a complicated change that is actually taking place in historical reality.)

While the above example of a tax-induced price rise that takes place within a strict neoclassical model might be termed a case of cost-push rather than demand-pull, it does not really represent quite the same phenomena that we shall meet in our later discussion of cost-push. This can perhaps be most easily seen from the remark that, if one insisted on holding prices steady, conventional demand reduction methods would work very well, within the neoclassical model, to offset such cost-push.

Demand-Pull à la Keynes. Aside from the neoclassical quantity theory, there is a second version of demand-pull associated with the theories of Keynes. Before and during the Great Depression, economists had become impressd with the institutional frictions and rigidities that made for downward inflexibilities in wages and prices and which made any such deflationary movements socially painful. Keynes's *General Theory* can, if we are willing to oversimplify, be thought of as a systematic model which uses downward inflexibility of wages and prices to convert any reduction in money spending into a real reduction in output and employment rather than a balanced reduction in all prices and factor costs. (This is overly simple for at least the following reasons: in the pessimistic, depression version of some Keynesians, a hyperdeflation of wages and prices would not have had substantive effects in restoring employment and output, because of infinite elasticity of liquidity preference and/or zero elasticity of investment demand; in the general form of the *General Theory,* and particularly after Pigou effects of the real value of money had been built in, if you could engineer a massive reduction in wages and costs, there would have been some stimulating effects on consumption, investment, and on real output; finally, a careful neoclassical theory, which took proper account of rigidities and which analyzed induced shifts of velocity in a sophisticated way, might also have emerged with similar valid conclusions.)

While the Keynesian theories can be said to differ from the neoclassical theories with respect to analysis of deflation, Keynes himself was willing to asume that attainment of full employment would make prices and wages flexible upward. In *How to Pay for the War* (1939), he developed a theory of inflation which was quite like the neoclassical theory in its emphasis upon the demand-pull of aggregate spending even though it differed from that theory in its emphasis on total spending flow rather than on the stock of money. His theory of "demanders' inflation" stemmed primarily from the fact that government plus investors plus consumers want, in real terms among them, more than 100 per cent of the wartime or boomtime available produceable output. So prices have to rise to cheat the slow-to-spend of their desired shares. But the price rise closes the inflationary gap only temporarily, as the higher price level breeds higher incomes all around and the real gap reopens itself continually. And so the inflation goes on, at a rate determined by the degree of shifts to profit, the rapidity and extent of wage adjustments to the rising cost of living, and ultimately by the extent to which progressive tax receipts rise enough to close the gap. And, we may add, that firmness by the central bank in limiting the money supply might ultimately so increase credit tightness and so lower real balances as to bring consumption and investment spending into equilibrium with available civilian resources at some higher plateau of prices.

Cost-Push and Demand-Shift Theories of Inflation. In its most rigid form, the neoclassical model would require that wages fall whenever there is unemployment of labor and that prices fall whenever excess capacity exists in the sense that marginal cost of the output that firms sell is less than the prices they receive. A more eclectic model of imperfect competition in the factor and commodity markets is needed to explain the fact of price and wage rises before full employment and full capacity have been reached.

Similarly, the Keynes model, which assumes stickiness of wages even in the face of underemployment equilibrium, rests on various assumptions of imperfect competition. And when we recognize that, considerably before full employment of labor and plants has been reached, modern prices and wages seem to show a tendency to drift upward irreversibly, we see that the simple Keynesian system must be modified even further in the direction of an imperfect competition model.

Now the fact that an economic model in some degree involves imperfect competition does not necessarily imply that the concepts of competitive markets give little insight into the behavior of relative prices, resources allocations, and profitabilities. To some degree of approximation, the competitive model may cast light on these important real magnitudes, and for this purpose we might be content to use the competitive model. But to explain possible cost-push inflation, it would seem more economical from the very beginning to recognize that imperfect competition is the essence of the problem and to drop the perfect competition assumptions.

Once this is done, we recognize the qualitative possibility of cost-push inflation. Just as wages and prices may be sticky in the face of unemployment and overcapacity, so may they be pushing upward beyond what can be explained in terms of levels and shifts in demand. But to what degree these elements are important in explaining price behavior of any period becomes an important quantitative question. It is by no means always to be expected that by observing an economy's behavior over a given period will we be able to make a very good separation of its price rise into demand and cost elements. We simply cannot perform the controlled experiments necessary to make such a separation; and Mother Nature may not have economically given us the scatter and variation needed as a substitute for controlled experiments if we are to make approximate identification of the casual forces at work.

Many economists have argued that cost-push was important in the prosperous 1951-53 period, but that its effects on average prices were masked by the drop in flexible raw material prices. But again in 1955-58, it showed itself despite the fact that in a good deal of this period there seemed little evidence of over-all high employment and excess demand. Some holders of this view attribute the push to wage boosts engineered unilaterally by strong unions. But others give as much or more weight to the co-operative action of all sellers—organized and unorganized labor, semimonopsonistic managements, oligopolistic sellers in imperfect commodity markets—who raise prices and costs in an attempt by each to maintain or raise his share of national income, and who, among themselves, by trying to get more than 100 per cent of the available output, create "seller's inflation."

A variant of cost-push is provided by Charles Schultze's "demand-shift" theory of inflation. Strength of demand in certain sectors of the economy—e.g., capital goods industries in 1955-57—raises prices and wages there. But elsewhere, even though demand is not particularly strong, downward inflexibility keeps prices from falling, and market power may even engineer a price-wage movement imitative in a degree of the sectors with strong demand. The result is an upward drift in average prices—with the suggestion that monetary and fiscal policies restrictive enough to prevent an average price rise would have to be so very restrictive as to produce a considerable level of unemployment and a significant drop in production.

II

Truths and Consequences: The Problem of Identification. The competing (although imperfectly competing) theories of inflation appear to be genuinely different hypotheses about observable facts. In that case one ought to be able to distinguish empirically between cost and demand inflation. What are the earmarks? If I believe in cost-push, what should I expect to find in the facts that I would not expect to find were I a believer in demand-pull? The last clause is important. It will not do to point to circumstances which will accompany any inflation, however caused. A test must have what statisticians call power against the main alternative hypotheses.

Trite as these remarks may seem, they need to be made. The clichés of popular discussion fall into the trap again and again. Although they have been trampled often enough by experts, the errors revive. We will take the time to point the finger once more. We do this because we want to go one step further and argue that this problem of identification is exceedingly difficult. What appear at first to be subtle and reliable ways of distinguishing cost-induced from demand-induced inflation turn out to be far from airtight. In fact we are driven to the belief that aggregate data, recording the *ex post* details of completed transactions, may in most circumstances be quite insufficient. It may be necessary first to disaggregate.

Common Fallacies. The simplest mistake—to be found in almost any newspaper discussion of the subject—is the belief that if money wages rise faster than productivity, we have a sure sign of cost-inflation. Of course the truth is that in the purest of excess-demand inflation wages will rise faster than productivity; the only alternative is for the full increase in the value of a fixed output to be siphoned off into profits, without this spilling over into the labor market to drive wages up still further. This error is sometimes mixed with the belief that it is possible over long periods for industries with rapid productivity increase to pay higher and increasingly higher wages than those where output per man-hour grows slowly. Such a persistent and growing differential is likely eventually to alter the skill- or quality-mix of the labor force in the different industries, which casts doubt on the original productivity comparison.

One sometimes sees statements to the effect that increases in expenditure more rapid than increases in real output necessarily spell demand inflation. It is simple arithmetic that expenditure outrunning output by itself spells only price increases and provides no evidence at all about the source or cause of the inflation. Much of the talk about "too much money chasing too few goods" is of this kind.

A more solemn version of the fallacy goes: An increase in expenditure can come about only through an increase in the stock of money or an increase in the velocity of circulation. Therefore the only possible causes of inflation are M and V and we need look no further.

Further Difficulties. It is more disconcerting to realize that even some of the empirical tests suggested in the professional literature may have little or no cutting power in distinguishing cost from demand inflation.

One thinks automatically of looking at the timing relationships. Do wage increases seem to precede price increases? Then the general rise in prices is caused by the wage-push. Do price increases seem to precede wage increases? Then more likely the inflation is of the excess-demand variety, and wages are being pulled up by a brisk demand for labor or they are responding to prior increases in the cost of living. There are at least three difficulties with this argument. The first is suggested by replacing "wage increase" by "chicken" and "price increase" by "egg." The trouble is that we have no normal initial standard from which to measure, no price level which has always existed and to which everyone has adjusted; so that a wage increase, if one occurs, must be autonomous and not a response to some prior change in the demand for labor. As an illustration of the difficulty of inference, consider average hourly earnings in the basic steel industry. They rose, relative to all manufacturing from 1950 on, including some periods when labor markets were not tight. Did this represent an autonomous wage-push? Or was it rather a delayed adjustment to the decline in steel wages relative to all manufacturing, which took place during the war, presumably as a consequence of the differential efficiency of wage control? And why should we take 1939 or 1941 as a standard for relative wages? And so on.

A related problem is that in a closely interdependent economy, effects can precede causes. Prices may begin to ease up because wage rates are expected to. And more important, as wage and price increases ripple through the economy, aggregation may easily distort the apparent timing relations.

But even if we could find the appearance of a controlled experiment, if after a period of stability in both we were to notice a wage increase to a new plateau followed by a price increase, what could we safely conclude? It would be immensely tempting to make the obvious diagnosis of wage-push. But consider the following hypothetical chain of events: Prices in imperfect commodity markets respond only to changes in costs. Labor markets are perfectly competitive in effect, and the money wage moves rapidly in response to shifts in the demand for labor. So any burst of excess demand, government expenditure, say, would cause an increased demand for labor; wages would be pulled up; and only then would prices of commodities rise in response to the cost increase. So the obvious diagnosis might be wrong. In between, if we were clever, we might notice a temporary narrowing of margins, and with this information we might piece together the story.

Consider another sophisticated inference. In a single market, price may rise either because the demand curve shifts to the right or because the supply curve shifts to the left in consequence of cost increases. But in the first case, output should increase; in the second case, decline. Could we not reason, then, that if prices rise, sector by sector, with outputs, demand-pull must be at work? Very likely we can, but not with certainty. In the first place, as Schultze has argued, it is possible that certain sectors face excess demand, without there being aggregate pressure; those sectors will indeed show strong price increases and increases in output (or pressure on capacity). But in a real sense, the source of inflation is the failure of other sectors, in which excess capacity develops, to decrease their prices sufficiently. And this may be a consequence of "administered pricing," rigid markups, rigid wages and all the paraphernalia of the "new" inflation.

To go deeper, the reasoning we are scrutinizing may fail because it is illegitimate, even in this industry-by-industry way, to use partial equilibrium reasoning. Suppose wages rise. We are led to expect a decrease in output. But in the modern world, all or most wages are increasing. Nor is this the first time they have done so. And in the past, general wage and price increases have not resulted in any decrease in aggregate real demand—perhaps the contrary. So that even in a single industry supply and demand curves may not be independent. The shift in costs is accompanied by, indeed may bring about, a compensating shift in the subjectively-viewed demand curve facing the industry. And so prices may rise with no decline and possibly an increase in output. If there is anything in this line of thought, it may be that one of the important causes of inflation is—inflation.

The Need for Detail. In these last few paragraphs we have been arguing against the attempt to diagnose the source of inflation from aggregates. We have also suggested that sometimes the tell-tale symptoms can be discovered if we look not at the totals but at the parts. This suggestion gains force when we recognize, as we must, that the same general price increase can easily be the consequence of different causes in different sectors. A monolithic theory may have its simplicity and style riddled by exceptions. Is there any reason, other than a desire for symmetry, for us to believe that the same reasoning must account for the above-average increase in the price of services and the above-average increase in the price of machinery since 1951 or since 1949? Public utility prices undoubtedly were held down during the war, by the regulatory process; and services ride along on income-elastic demand accompanied by a slower-than-average recorded productivity increase. A faster-than-average price increase amounts to the corrective relative-price change one would expect. The main factor in the machinery case, according to a recent Joint Economic Committee study, appears to have been a burst of excess demand occasioned by the investment boom of the mid-fifties. And to give still a third variant, Eckstein and Fromm in another Joint Economic Committee study suggest that the above-average rise in the wages of steelworkers and the prices of steel products took place in the face of a somewhat less tight labor and product market than in machinery. They attribute it to a joint exercise of market power by the union and the industry. Right or wrong, it is mistaken theoretical tactics to deny this possibility on the grounds that it cannot account for the price history in other sectors.

Some Things It Would Be Good to Know. There are at least two classical questions which are relevant to our problem and on which surprisingly little work has been done: One is the behavior of real demand under inflationary conditions and the other is the behavior of money wages with respect to the level of employment. We comment briefly on these two questions because there seems to us to be some doubt that ordinary reversible behavior equations can be found, and this very difficulty points up an important question we have mentioned earlier: that a period of high demand and rising prices molds attitudes, expectations, even institutions in such a way as to bias the future in favor of further inflation. Unlike some other economists, we do not draw the firm conclusion that unless a firm stop is put, the rate of price increase must accelerate. We leave it as an open question: It may be that creeping inflation leads only to creeping inflation.

The standard way for an inflationary gap to burn itself out short of hyperinflation is for the very process of inflation to reduce real demands. The mechanisms, some dubious, some not, are well known: the shift to profit, real-balance effects, tax progression, squeeze on fixed incomes. If price and wage increases have this effect, then a cost-push inflation in the absence of excess demand inflicts unemployment and excess capacity on the system. The willingness to bear the reduced real demand is a measure of the imperfectness of markets permitting the cost-push. But suppose real demands do not behave in this way? Suppose a wage-price rise has no effect on real demand, or a negligible one, or even a slight positive one? Then not only will the infliction not materialize, but the whole distinction between cost-push and demand-pull begins to evaporate. But is this possible? The older quantity theorists would certainly have denied it; but the increase in velocity between 1955 and 1957 would have surprised an older quantity theorist.

We do not know whether real demand behaves this way or not. But we think it important to realize that the more the recent past is dominated by inflation, by high employment, and by the belief that both will continue, the more likely is it that the process of inflation will preserve or even increase real demand, or the more heavily the monetary and fiscal authorities may have to bear down on demand in the interests of price stabilization. Real-income consciousness is a powerful force. The pressure on real balances from high prices will be partly relieved by the expectation of rising prices, as long as interest rates in an imperfect capital market fail to keep pace. The same expectations will induce schoolteachers, pensioners, and others to try to devise institutions to protect their real incomes from erosion by higher prices. To the extent that they succeed, their real demands will be unimpaired. As the fear of prolonged unemployment disappears and the experience of past full employment builds up accumulated savings, wage earners may also maintain their real expenditures; and the same forces may substantially increase the marginal propensity to spend out of profits, including retained earnings. If there is anything to this line of thought, the empirical problem of verification may be very difficult, because much of the experience of the past is irrelevant to the hypothesis. But it would be good to know.

The Fundamental Phillips Schedule Relating Unemployment and Wage Changes. Consider also the question of the relation between money wage changes and the degree of unemployment. We have A. W. Phillips' interesting paper on the U. K. history since the Civil War (our Civil War, that is!). His findings are remarkable, even if one disagrees with his interpretations.

In the first place, the period 1861-1913, during which the trade-union movement was rather weak, shows a fairly close relationship between the per cent change in wage rates and the fraction of the labor force unemployed. Due allowance must be made for sharp import-price-induced changes in the cost of living, and for the normal expectation that wages will be rising faster when an unemployment rate of 5 per cent is reached on the upswing than when it is reached on the downswing. In the second place, with minor exceptions, the same relationship that fits for 1861-1913 also seems to fit about as well for 1913-48 and 1948-57. And finally Phillips concludes that the money wage level would stabilize with 5 per cent unemployment; and the rate of increase of money wages would be held down to the 2-3 per cent rate of productivity increase with about $2\frac{1}{2}$ per cent of the labor force unemployed.

Strangely enough, no comparably careful study has been made for the U.S. Garbarino's 1950 note is hardly a full-scale analysis, and Schultze's treatment in his first-class Joint Committee monograph is much too casual. There is some evidence that the U.S. differs from the U.K. on at least two counts. If there is any such relationship characterizing the American labor market, it may have shifted somewhat in the last fifty to sixty years. Secondly, there is a suggestion that in this country it might take 8 to 10 per cent unemployment to stabilize money wages.

But would it take 8 to 10 per cent unemployment forever to stabilize the money wage? Is not this kind of relationship also one which depends heavily on remembered experience? We suspect that this is another way in which a past characterized by rising prices, high employment, and mild, short recessions is likely to breed an inflationary bias—by making the money wage more rigid downward, maybe even perversely inclined to rise during recessions on the grounds that things will soon be different.

There may be no such relation for this country. If there is, why does it not seem to have the same degree of long-run invariance as Phillips' curve for the U.K.? What geographical, economic, sociological facts account for the difference between the two countries? Is there a difference in labor mobility in the two countries? Do the different tolerances for unemployment reflect differences in income level, union organization, or what? What policy decisions might conceivably lead to a decrease in the critical unemployment rate at which wages begin to rise or to rise too fast? Clearly a careful study of this problem might pay handsome dividends.

III

A Closer Look at the American Data. In spite of all its deficiencies, we think the accompanying scatter diagram in Figure 1 is useful. Where it does not provide answers, it at least asks interesting questions. We have plotted the yearly percentage changes of average hourly earnings in manufacturing, including supplements (Rees's data) against the annual average percentage of the labor force unemployed.

The first defect to note is the different coverages represented in the two axes. Duesenberry has argued that postwar wage increases in manufacturing on the one hand and in trade, services, etc., on the other, may have quite different explanations: union power in manufacturing and

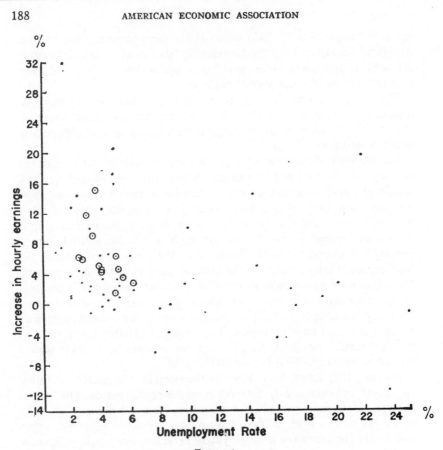

FIGURE 1

PHILLIPS SCATTER DIAGRAM FOR U.S.
(The circled points are for recent years.)

simple excess demand in the other sectors. It is probably true that if we had an unemployment rate for manufacturing alone, it would be somewhat higher during the postwar years than the aggregate figure shown. Even if a qualitative statement like this held true over the whole period, the increasing weight of services in the total might still create a bias. Another defect is our use of annual increments and averages, when a full-scale study would have to look carefully into the nuances of timing.

A first look at the scatter is discouraging; there are points all over the place. But perhaps one can notice some systematic effects. In the first place, the years from 1933 to 1941 appear to be *sui generis:* money wages rose or failed to fall in the face of massive unemployment. One may attribute this to the workings of the New Deal (the 20 per cent wage increase of 1934 must represent the NRA codes); or alternatively one could argue that by 1933 much of the unemployment had become structural, insulated from the functioning labor market, so that in effect the vertical axis ought to be moved over to the right. This would leave something more like the normal pattern.

The early years of the first World War also behave atypically although not so much so as 1933-39. This may reflect cost-of-living increases, the rapidity of the increase in demand, a special tightness in manufacturing, or all three.

But the bulk of the observations—the period between the turn of the century and the first war, the decade between the end of that war and the Great Depression, and the most recent ten or twelve years—all show a rather consistent pattern. Wage rates do tend to rise when the labor market is tight, and the tighter the faster. What is most interesting is the strong suggestion that the relation, such as it is, has shifted upward slightly but noticeably in the forties and fifties. On the one hand, the first decade of the century and the twenties seem to fit the same pattern. Manufacturing wages seem to stabilize absolutely when 4 or 5 per cent of the labor force is unemployed; and wage increases equal to the productivity increase of 2 to 3 per cent per year is the normal pattern at about 3 per cent unemployment. This is not so terribly different from Phillips' results for the U.K., although the relation holds there with a greater consistency. We comment on this below.

On the other hand, from 1946 to the present, the pattern is fairly consistent and consistently different from the earlier period. The annual unemployment rate ranged only narrowly, from 2.5 per cent in 1953 to 6.2 per cent in 1958. Within that range, as might be expected, wages rose faster the lower the unemployment rate. But one would judge now that it would take more like 8 per cent unemployment to keep money wages from rising. And they would rise at 2 to 3 per cent per year with 5 or 6 per cent of the labor force unemployed.

It would be overhasty to conclude that the relation we have been discussing represents a reversible supply curve for labor along which an aggregate demand curve slides. If that were so, then movements along the curve might be dubbed standard demand-pull, and shifts of the curve might represent the institutional changes on which cost-push theories rest. The apparent shift in our Phillips' curve might be attributed by some economists to the new market power of trade-unions. Others might be more inclined to believe that the expectation of continued full employment, or at least high employment, is enough to explain both the shift in the supply curve, if it is that, and the willingness of employers (conscious that what they get from a work force is partly dependent on its morale and its turnover) to pay wage increases in periods of temporarily slack demand.

This latter consideration, however, casts real doubt on the facile identification of the relationship as merely a supply-of-labor phenomenon. There are two parties to a wage bargain.

U.S. and U.K. Compared. A comparison of the American position with Phillips' findings for the U.K. is interesting for itself and also as a possible guide to policy. Anything which will shift the relationship downward decreases the price in unemployment that must be paid when a policy is followed of holding down the rate of wage and price increase by pressure on aggregate demand.

One possibility is that the trade-union leadership is more "responsible" in the U.K.; indeed the postwar policy of wage restraint seems visible in Phillips' data. But there are other interpretations. It is clear that the more fractionated and imperfect a labor market is, the higher the over-all excess supply of labor may have to be before the average wage rate becomes stable and the less tight the relation will be in any case. Even a touch of downward inflexibility (and trade-unionism and administered wages surely means at least this) will make this immobility effect more pronounced. It would seem plausible that the sheer geographical compactness of the English economy makes its labor market more perfect than ours in this sense. Moreover, the British have pursued a more deliberate policy of relocation of industry to mop up pockets of structural unemployment.

This suggests that any governmental policy which increases the mobility of labor (geographical and industrial) or improves the flow of information in the labor market will have anti-inflationary effects as well as being desirable for other reasons. A quicker but in the long run probably less efficient approach might be for the government to direct the regional distribution of its expenditures more deliberately in terms of the existence of local unemployment and excess capacity.

The English data show a quite clearly nonlinear (hyperbolic) relation between wage changes and unemployment, reflecting the much discussed downward inflexibility. Our American figures do not contradict this, although they do not tell as plain a story as the English. To the extent that this nonlinearity exists, as Duesenberry has remarked, a given average level of unemployment over the cycle will be compatible with a slower rate of wage increase (and presumably price increase) the less wide the cyclical swings from top to bottom.

A less obvious implication of this point of view is that a deliberate low-pressure policy to stabilize the price level may have a certain self-defeating aspect. It is clear from experience that interregional and interindustrial mobility of labor depends heavily on the pull of job opportunities elsewhere, more so than on the push of local unemployment. In effect the imperfection of the labor market is increased, with the consequences we have sketched.

IV

We have concluded that it is not possible on the basis of a priori reasoning to reject either the demand-pull or cost-push hypothesis, or the variants of the latter such as demand-shift. We have also argued that the empirical identifications needed to distinguish between these hypotheses may be quite impossible from the experience of macrodata that is available to us; and that, while use of microdata might throw additional light on the problem, even here identification is fraught with difficulties and ambiguities.

Nevertheless, there is one area where policy interest and the desire for scientific understanding for its own sake come together. If by deliberate policy one engineered a sizable reduction of demand or refused to permit the increase in demand that would be needed to preserve high employment, one would have an experiment that could hope to distinguish between the validity of the demand-pull and the cost-push theory as we would operationally reformulate those theories. If a small relaxation of demand were followed by great moderations in the march of wages and other costs so that the social cost of a stable price index turned out to be very small in terms of sacrificed high-level employment and output, then the demand-pull hypothesis would have received its most important confirmation. On the other hand, if mild demand repression checked cost and price increases not at all or only mildly, so that considerable unemployment would have to be engineered before the price level updrift could be prevented, then the cost-push hypothesis would have received its most important confirmation. If the outcome of this experience turned out to be in between these extreme cases—as we ourselves would rather expect—then an element of validity would have to be conceded to both views; and dull as it is to have to embrace eclectic theories, scholars who wished to be realistic would have to steel themselves to doing so.

Of course, we have been talking glibly of a vast experiment. Actually such an operation would be fraught with implications for social welfare. Naturally, since they are confident that it would be a success, the believers in demand-pull ought to welcome such an experiment. But, equally naturally, the believers in cost-push would be dead set against such an engineered low-pressure economy, since they are equally convinced that it will be a dismal failure involving much needless social pain. (A third school, who believes in cost-push but think it can be cured or minimized by orthodox depressing of demand, think that our failure to make this experiment would be fraught with social evil by virtue of the fact that they expect a creep in prices to snowball into a trot and then a gallop.)

Our own view will by now have become evident. When we translate the Phillips' diagram showing the American pattern of wage increase against degree of unemployment into a related diagram showing the different levels of unemployment that would be "needed" for each degree of price level change, we come out with guesses like the following:

1. In order to have wages increase at no more than the 2½ per cent per annum characteristic of our productivity growth, the American economy would seem on the basis of twentieth-century and postwar experience to have to undergo something like 5 to 6 per cent of the civilian labor force's being unemployed. That much unemployment would appear to be the cost of price stability in the years immediately ahead.

2. In order to achieve the nonperfectionist's goal of high enough output to give us no more than 3 per cent unemployment, the price index might have to rise by as much as 4 to 5 per cent per year. That much price rise would seem to be the necessary cost of high employment and production in the years immediately ahead.

All this is shown in our price-level modification of the Phillips curve, Figure 2. The point *A*, corresponding to price stability, is seen to involve about 5½ per cent unemployment; whereas the point *B*, corre-

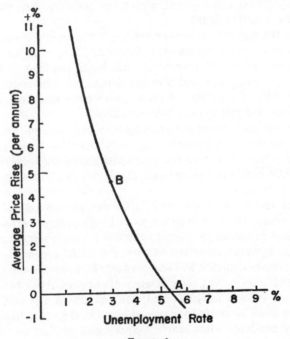

FIGURE 2

MODIFIED PHILLIPS CURVE FOR U.S.

This shows the menu of choice between different degrees of unemployment and price stability, as roughly estimated from last twenty-five years of American data.

sponding to 3 per cent unemployment, is seen to involve a price rise of about 4½ per cent per annum. We rather expect that the tug of war of politics will end us up in the next few years somewhere in between these selected points. We shall probably have some price rise and some excess unemployment.

Aside from the usual warning that these are simply our best guesses we must give another caution. All of our discussion has been phrased in short-run terms, dealing with what might happen in the next few years. It would be wrong, though, to think that our Figure 2 menu that relates obtainable price and unemployment behavior will maintain its same shape in the longer run. What we do in a policy way during the next few years might cause it to shift in a definite way.

Thus, it is conceivable that after they had produced a low-pressure economy, the believers in demand-pull might be disappointed in the short run; i.e., prices might continue to rise even though unemployment was considerable. Nevertheless, it might be that the low-pressure demand would so act upon wage and other expectations as to shift the curve downward in the longer run—so that over a decade, the economy might enjoy higher employment with price stability than our present-day estimate would indicate.

But also the opposite is conceivable. A low-pressure economy might build up within itself over the years larger and larger amounts of structural unemployment (the reverse of what happened from 1941 to 1953 as a result of strong war and postwar demands). The result would be an upward shift of our menu of choice, with more and more unemployment being needed just to keep prices stable.

Since we have no conclusive or suggestive evidence on these conflicting issues, we shall not attempt to give judgment on them. Instead we venture the reminder that, in the years just ahead, the level of attained growth will be highly correlated with the degree of full employment and high-capacity output.

But what about the longer run? If the per annum rate of technical progress were about the same in a low- and high-pressure economy, then the initial loss in output in going to the low-pressure state would never be made up; however, in relative terms, the initial gap would not grow but would remain constant as time goes by. If a low-pressure economy could succeed in improving the efficiency of our productive factors, some of the loss of growth might be gradually made up and could in long enough time even be more than wiped out. On the other hand, if such an economy produced class warfare and social conflict and depressed the level of research and technical progress, the loss in growth would be compounded in the long run.

A final disclaimer is in order. We have not here entered upon the important question of what feasible institutional reforms might be introduced to lessen the degree of disharmony between full employment and price stability. These could of course involve such wide-ranging issues as direct price and wage controls, antiunion and antitrust legislation, and a host of other measures hopefully designed to move the American Phillips' curves downward and to the left.

[10]

THE
QUARTERLY JOURNAL
OF ECONOMICS

| Vol. XCIII | May 1979 | No. 2 |

IRVING FISHER ON HIS HEAD: THE CONSEQUENCES OF CONSTANT THRESHOLD-TARGET MONITORING OF MONEY HOLDINGS*

GEORGE A. AKERLOF

I. INTRODUCTION

The monetary theory of Irving Fisher [1911], and also of the inventory theorists, Baumol [1952], Tobin [1956], and Miller and Orr [1966], views money holding as the consequence of two types of decision. The first type of decision concerns payments that are made independent of money holdings and that are, for this reason, denoted *autonomous*. The second type of decision concerns the monitoring rule which determines the payments that are made dependent on the level of the bank account, which payments prevent the bank account from becoming either too high or too low. Because of their dependence on the bank account, such payments will be denoted *induced*.

It makes sense to dichotomize the determinants of money holding

* The author would like to thank the National Science Foundation for supporting this research under grant number SOC 75-23076, through the Institute of Business and Economic Research, University of California, Berkeley. This paper was revised while the author was Visiting Research Economist, Board of Governors of the Federal Reserve System. The author would also like to thank Janet Yellen, Robert Dorfman, the editor of this *Journal*, and an anonymous referee for valuable comments.

in this fashion because these decisions are made for essentially different motives. Autonomous payments are made to take advantage of opportunities for sale or purchase of goods, factors, or securities; the monitoring rule is selected to balance costs relative to benefits of cash holding. Because these two types of decision are made with essentially different motives, they will be made with different lags in response to changes in such variables as income and interest, which affect both decisions in the long run.

In the model of Irving Fisher the monitoring policy is the average lag with which an induced payment follows an autonomous inpayment. According to Fisher, these average lags will have only a slow response to changes in payment flows and interest, for which reason they may be considered (roughly) constant in the short run.

Baumol, Tobin, and Miller and Orr, on the other hand, explicitly derive the demand for money as the result of the optimal monitoring policy and assumed payments flows. But the returns to complete optimization compared to near optimization in such models can be typically calculated to be small to the point of triviality, even though money holdings in percentage terms may be quite different. For example, consider the Baumol model for a person with an annual income of \$12,000, with transactions costs of \$10 per transaction, and an annual interest rate of 6 percent. If such a person holds 20 percent more money than prescribed by the Baumol model, he loses only \$2 per year, the loss being smaller still if transactions costs are less than \$10 per transaction.

The trivial magnitude of the returns from optimization makes a *short-run* model of money holding with constant monitoring rule (in the style of Irving Fisher) preferable to a model of complete optimization (in the style of Baumol, Tobin, and Miller and Orr). Generalizing Fisher permits the demand for money to be written as

(1) $$L = L(P,S),$$

where P is a vector of the probabilities of nonzero autonomous payments and S is a vector representing the policies whereby bank accounts are monitored. The policies S are assumed constant in the short run in this paper, partly because of the preceding argument regarding the magnitude of short-run returns to optimization, but also to contrast the results obtained in this paper with the conventional approach, in which the policies S result from optimal responses to changes in income and interest. Of course, I have no quibble with the notion that in the long run the policies of monitoring are adjusted to be at least roughly consistent with optimization, given the costs of purchasing assets, interest rates, and payments flows. Indeed, some such optimization is seen as historically responsible for the monitoring rules that in the short run are taken as fixed rules of thumb for controlling money holdings.

Irving Fisher's S is a vector of time intervals that represent the average lag with which induced purchases follow autonomous receipts in different bank accounts. According to Fisher, with S constant, a doubling of all autonomous payments causes a doubling of the demand for money. The added assumption that all autonomous payments are proportional to money income yields a quantity theory in the macro sense.

In contrast to Fisher, let S be a vector representing constant targets and thresholds whereby bank accounts are monitored; that is, each bank account, upon exceeding an upper threshold h, is returned to a target z; similarly, upon reaching a lower threshold 0, the bank account is returned to the target z.[1] S is the vector of (h,z) pairs for all bank accounts. Let P represent the probability distribution of nonzero autonomous payments and receipts of all bank accounts. In the example below in which bank accounts receive \$1 with probability p, lose \$1 with probability q, and experience no transaction with probability s, P is the vector of different (p,q) pairs (the probabilities of *nonzero* transactions) of all bank accounts. With constant target-threshold monitoring this paper shows that a proportionate increase in the probabilities of all nonzero transactions (e.g., p and q in the example above) results in no change in expected aggregate money holdings. The added assumption that the probabilities of nonzero transactions vary proportionally with income yields a velocity that, rather than being constant, is totally passive.[2] Furthermore, if the *amounts,* rather than the *probabilities* of nonzero transactions, change proportionately with income, with S constant, there is no presumption as to whether the expected demand for money will rise or fall with income. Under special (symmetric) conditions, however, as will be discussed in Section III below, the demand for money will be unchanged.

This passivity of velocity is a phenomenon with a simple explanation. The total expected additions to money holdings in any period are the sum of expected net autonomous payments and expected net induced payments. In equilibrium, with constant money supply, net desired autonomous payments and net induced payments must exactly balance. With constant threshold-target monitoring, a proportionate increase in the probabilities of nonzero autonomous payments produces a proportionate increase in the probabilities of nonzero in-

duced payments. If prior to the increase in the probabilities of autonomous payments expected net autonomous and expected net induced payments exactly balance, then subsequent to the increase the
expected values of these two types of payments will continue to balance. A cinematographic analogy makes this proposition clear. A
proportionate increase in the probabilities P of nonzero autonomous
payments with threshold-target monitoring acts in the same way as
if a movie of the payments made in the whole economy were being
projected at a proportionately faster speed. If prior to the increase
in probabilities the net autonomous and the net induced payments
exactly balance, then subsequent to the increase in the "speed of the
movie projector" these two types of payments will continue to balance.
No excess demand for money will result, provided, of course, that the
targets and thresholds remain unchanged. For this reason velocity
will be passive with constant targets and thresholds.

A simple example does not quite capture the generality (or,
therefore, the subtleties) in the preceding argument, but it is nevertheless illustrative. Consider an individual bank account with constant
inpayments at the rate of x dollars per period. Suppose that every λ
periods this bank account is monitored and money holdings are reduced to 0 (by an induced purchase of securities); average money
holdings will be $\lambda x/2$ and velocity will be a constant $2/\lambda$. Suppose, on
the contrary, the bank account is monitored so that upon reaching
a threshold h, a security is bought, and the bank account is reduced
to 0; then the average level of money holdings is $h/2$, independent of
x, and velocity will be $2x/h$, exactly proportional to x. In this simple
model the change from constant-lag to constant threshold-target
monitoring totally changes the behavior of velocity. In the one case,
it is constant; in the other, it is exactly proportional to payment
flows.

Let Y denote aggregate income, r the rate of interest, and E a
vector of exogenous expenditures. Let the probabilities of nonzero
transactions depend on Y, r, and E so that $P = P(Y,r,E)$. Then a
short-run expected aggregate demand for money function can be
written in the form,

(2) $L = L(Y, P(Y,r,E)/Y, S).$

The first argument denotes the dependence of the demand for money
on income insofar as the probabilities of payment are proportional
to income; the second argument represents the dependence of the
demand for money on payments flows insofar as the probabilities of
nonzero autonomous payments are *not* proportional to income.[3]

According to (2) with S constant, $dL/dY|dE = dr = 0$ has two components:

$$(3) \qquad \frac{dL}{dY}\Bigg|_{dE = dr = 0} = \frac{\partial L}{\partial Y} + \frac{\partial L}{\partial (P/Y)}\frac{\partial (P/Y)}{\partial Y};$$

and

$$(4) \qquad \frac{dL}{dr}\Bigg|_{dE = dY = 0} = \frac{\partial L}{\partial (P/Y)}\frac{\partial (P/Y)}{\partial r}.$$

With constant-lag monitoring in the style of Irving Fisher and with the probabilities P proportional to Y, the first term of (3) is a positive constant, and (4) vanishes, thus yielding a quantity theory.

In contrast, with threshold-target monitoring the first term of (3) vanishes so that the short-run income elasticity of the demand for money is zero if P is proportional to Y. It is well-known that empirical studies have found low short-run *interest* elasticities of the demand for money. However, these studies cannot be used to infer the ineffectiveness of fiscal policy in the short run, as would be suggested by constant velocity theory; with threshold-target monitoring the short-run income elasticity of the demand for money is also low.

As will be discussed in Section IV, the constant threshold-target model of this paper is at least roughly consistent with the empirical evidence regarding the demand for money. This evidence shows short-run income elasticities of the demand for money that are an order of magnitude less than the short-run income elasticity of approximately unity predicted by Irving Fisher's theory. As a result, in the usual econometric models fiscal policy is effective in changing aggregate income not because the short-run interest elasticity of the demand for money is high but rather because the short-run income elasticity of the demand for money is low. This low income elasticity has escaped the notice of monetary economists, presumably because Irving Fisher's arguments concerning the proportionality of the transactions demand for money and income have seemed so convincing.[4] According to this paper, those arguments are much more sensitive to the exact nature of Irving Fisher's assumptions than has previously been supposed. A precise explanation for low short-run income elasticity of the demand for money is given.

II. Relation between Payments Flows and Money Demand with Threshold-Target Monitoring

This section presents and analyzes an economy with threshold-target monitoring It is divided into four parts: Part A, which describes the microeconomic model of payments flows with threshold-target monitoring; Part B, which defines equilibrium in the money market; Part C, which derives the microeconomic consequences of changes in the probabilities of payments; and Part D, which states the consequences of this model for the aggregate demand for money.

A. Payments Flows and Monitoring

The model of payments flows and monitoring and its notation is adapted from Miller and Orr. Each bank account, subscripted by the letter i, has an upper threshold h_i, whose attainment triggers an induced purchase of goods or securities in amount $h_i - z_i$, thereby returning the bank account to the target z_i. Similarly, on reaching zero, a sale of either goods or securities in amount z_i is triggered, and the bank account also goes to the target z_i. Autonomous payments in each bank account are probabilistic, with three exhaustive outcomes: an inpayment of \$1 between t and $t + 1$ with probability p_i, no inpayment or outpayment between t and $t + 1$ with probability s_i, and an outpayment of \$1 between t and $t + 1$ with probability q_i.

B. Nature of Equilibrium: Short Run and Long Run

If $f_i(m_i,t)$ denotes the probability that bank account i has m_i money holdings at time t, the expected value of money holdings at t, denoted $E(m)_t$ is

$$(5) \qquad E(m)_t = \sum_i \sum_{m_i} m_i f_i(m_i,t).$$

Let M_t denote the money supply at t, and assume that it is exogenously determined. Assume, also, that the probabilities p_i, q_i, and s_i depend upon endogenous and exogenous variables (such as Y, r, and E). $E(m)_t$ is determined by p_i, q_i, and s_i, given the distributions of money holdings m_i at $t - 1$ and given the h_i and z_i.

A short-run equilibrium condition is therefore given by

$$(6) \qquad E(m)_t = M_t,$$

where $E(m)_t$ is given by (5); where $f_i(m_i,t - 1)$ is given; and where $f_i(m_i,t)$ can be derived from the assumed probabilities of payments and receipts, and the thresholds h_i and targets z_i by equations (7) and (8):

$$(7) \quad f_i(m_i,t) = p_i(\cdot)f_i(m_i - 1,t - 1) + s_i(\cdot)f_i(m_i,t - 1)$$
$$+ q_i(\cdot)f_i(m_i + 1,t - 1)$$
$$1 \leqq m_i \leqq h_i - 1 \qquad m_i \neq z_i;$$

and

(8) $\quad f_i(z_i,t) = p_i(\cdot)f_i(z_i - 1, t - 1) + s_i(\cdot)f_i(z_i, t - 1)$
$\qquad + q_i(\cdot)f_i(z_i + 1, t - 1) + p_i(\cdot)f_i(h_i - 1, t - 1)$
$\qquad + q_i(\cdot)f_i(1, t - 1).$

Values of the endogenous variables with payments probabilities $p_i(\cdot)$, $q_i(\cdot)$, and $s_i(\cdot)$, such that (5), (6), (7), and (8) are satisfied, cause the money market to be in equilibrium at time t. (Microeconomic Proposition II in the Appendix shows that this equilibrium condition can also be expressed in flow terms: that the expected value of desired autonomous payments between $t - 1$ and t plus the expected value of induced payments between $t - 1$ and t must equal the change in the money supply.)

Conditions (5), (6), (7), and (8) also yield a long-run equilibrium condition if the money supply is constant. For, if p_i, q_i, and s_i are constant, as they will be in a long-run equilibrium with their functional arguments constant, $f_i(m_i,t)$ will approach a long-run stationary distribution (denoted $f_i(m_i)$), with the property,

(9) $\qquad\qquad f_i(m_i, t - 1) = f_i(m_i, t) = f_i(m_i).$

Because of this stationarity property (9), $f_i(m_i)$ is given by the system (10) and (11):

(10) $\quad f_i(m_i) = p_i(\cdot)f_i(m_i + 1) - s_i(\cdot)f_i(m_i) + q_i(\cdot)f_i(m_i + 1)$
$\qquad\qquad\qquad\qquad 1 \leq m_i \leq h_i - 1 \qquad m_i \neq z_i;$

(11) $\quad f_i(z_i) = p_i(\cdot)f_i(z_i - 1) + s_i(\cdot)f_i(z_i) + q_i(\cdot)f_i(z_i + 1)$
$\qquad + p_i(\cdot)f_i(h_i - 1) + q_i(\cdot)f_i(1).$

In addition to (10) and (11),

(12) $\qquad\qquad\qquad\qquad f_i(0) = 0$

(13) $\qquad\qquad\qquad\qquad f_i(h_i) = 0$

(14) $\qquad\qquad\qquad\qquad \sum_{m_i=1}^{h_i-1} f_i(m_i) = 1,$

so that the system (10) to (14) consists of two second-order difference equations from 1 to $z_i - 1$ and from $z_i + 1$ to $h_i - 1$ (equation (10)), with four boundary conditions, (11) to (14). Miller and Orr [1966, pp. 434–35] have found that

(15) $\quad f_i(m_i) = \dfrac{1 - y_i^{z_i-h_i}}{z_i(1 - y_i^{z_i-h_i}) + (h_i - z_i)(1 - y_i^{z_i})}(1 - y_i^{m_i})$

$\qquad\qquad\qquad\qquad\qquad\qquad\qquad\qquad 0 \leq m_i \leq z_i$

$$(16) \quad f_i(m_i) = \frac{1 - y_i^{z_i}}{z_i(1 - y_i^{z_i - h_i}) + (h_i - z_i)(1 - y_i^{z_i})} \times (1 - y_i^{m_i - h_i})$$

$$z_i \leqq m_i \leqq h_i,$$

where $y_i = p_i(\cdot)/q_i(\cdot)$.

Consequently, the long-run equilibrium condition in the money market with constant money supply $\overline{M}$ is given by

$$\sum_i \sum_{m_i} f(m_i) = \overline{M},$$

where $f(m_i)$ is the distribution defined by (15) and (16).

C. Basic Microeconomic Propositions

The definition of long-run equilibrium just given is now used in the statement of the key "microeconomic propositions" of this paper. These propositions are called microeconomic because the relation between payments probabilities (p_i, q_i, s_i) and endogenous macroeconomic variables remains unspecified. Such a specification will be given in subsection D, which also gives a parallel "macroeconomic proposition." (Proofs of these propositions are provided in the Appendix.)

MICROECONOMIC PROPOSITION I. If money holdings in an initial period, denoted $t = 0$, are a random variable with a probability distribution in long-run equilibrium relative to the p_i's, q_i's, s_i's, h_i's, and z_i's in that initial period, as defined by (15) and (16), an equiproportionate change in all p_i's and q_i's will cause no expected change in money holdings, as long as the h_i's and z_i's remain constant.

Proposition I, of course, is the antithesis to the conventional wisdom of the quantity theory. According to Irving Fisher, velocity being constant, an equiproportionate increase in transactions will produce an equiproportionate increase in money holdings. According to Proposition I, an equiproportionate increase in the probabilities of transactions produces no change in money holdings.

MICROECONOMIC PROPOSITIONS II AND III. Microeconomic Propositions II and III verify the two key assertions of the introduction regarding the "cinematographic" image of payments flows. According to Microeconomic Proposition II, *the expected additions to money holdings of a bank account are the sum of net expected induced payments plus net expected autonomous payments.* Consequently, if the money supply is constant and equal to the expected sum of induced and autonomous flows, these two expectations must also sum to zero. According to Microeconomic Proposition III, *in long-run equilibrium an equiproportionate increase in the probabilities of nonzero autonomous payments causes an equiproportionate increase in the probabilities of induced payments.* Thus, following the analogy, in long-run equilibrium an increase in the "speed" of autonomous payments causes an equal increase in the "speed" of induced payments; and, using Microeconomic Proposition II, since the two flows balance in a long-run equilibrium with constant money supply, so they will continue to balance after an increase in the "speed" of the autonomous flows; there will be no increase in the demand for money.

D. Basic Macroeconomic Proposition

Microeconomic Proposition I has as counterpart its respective macroeconomic proposition.

MACROECONOMIC PROPOSITION. Let p_i, q_i, and s_i at time t depend upon income Y_t, interest r_t, and other exogenous variables E_t, as $p_i(Y_t,r_t,E_t)$, $q_i(Y_t,r_t,E_t)$, and $s_i(Y_t,r_t,E_t)$. Given the distribution of money holdings in each bank account in an initial period, denoted 0, the expected demand for money, denoted L_t in each subsequent period t is a function of the paths of Y_τ, r_τ, E_τ. In particular, if Y, r, and E are constant between 0 and t, it is possible to write

$$L_t = L_t(Y,r,E).$$

In general, such L_t is of the form,

$$(17) \quad L_t = L_t(p_1(Y,r,E), \ldots, p_N(Y,r,E), \ldots, q_N(Y,r,E);$$
$$h_1, \ldots, h_N, z_1, \ldots, z_N; f_1(1,0), \ldots, f_N(h_N - 1,0)),$$

where there are N bank accounts in the economy.

It follows from Microeconomic Proposition I that (17) can be written in such a way that

$$(18) \quad L_t = L_t(Y,p_1(Y,r,E)/Y, \ldots, p_N(Y,r,E)/Y,q_1(Y,r,E)/Y, \ldots,$$
$$q_N(Y,r,E)/Y;h_1, \ldots, h_N,z_1, \ldots, z_N;$$
$$f_1(1,0), \ldots, f_N(h_N - 1,0)),$$

and such that, if each $f_i(m_i,0)$ is given by (15) and (16), which is its long-run value, given p_i, q_i, h_i, and z_i, then

(19)
$$\frac{\partial L_t}{\partial Y} = 0.$$

Property (19) is, in fact, quite special; it is a precise yet general antithesis to the quantity theory; it states that, except insofar as the probabilities of nonzero transactions change relative to income, the income elasticity of the demand for money is zero; this property is true with constant threshold-target monitoring, provided that prior to the change in income, the distribution of money holdings was in its long-run stationary state.

III. Comments on the Model

The specificity of the model of the last section makes it easy to pinpoint the most important of the ways in which the model violates reality, of which some are intrinsic and others not. The most glaring violation of reality in the model of the last section occurs in the assumed probability distributions of payments and receipts with no payment or receipt having absolute value more than \$1. This feature of the model, however, is not intrinsic. If there is a probability p_l of receiving l dollars and a probability q_j of paying j dollars, an equiproportionate change in the p_l and q_j for all positive values of l and j and all bank accounts i will still cause no change in the expected value of money holdings, provided that the distributions of money holdings prior to this equiproportionate shift were stationary. This, of course, is the generalization of Microeconomic Proposition I, and it is easy to prove. Also, in addition to having a greater range of payment size, the generalized model should let this payment size depend upon the type of transactions being made; i.e. some purchases (for example, ice cream cones) involve greater probabilities of \$1 payments than other purchases (for example, automobiles) so that each p_l and q_j should depend upon the specific autonomous purchase being made.

A second feature of the last section concerns the nature of the comparative static change; increased nominal income is assumed to induce proportionate increases in the probabilities of receipts and payments, the *size* of those payments being fixed. An alternative representation of changes in nominal income would leave the probabilities of transactions unchanged but let their *size* increase in proportion to income. It is possible to do some analysis of this type of change in transactions probabilities, although the results are a bit less clean than with changes in probabilities. The independence of money demand and income generalizes in the following sense: with constant targets and thresholds, only insofar as the economy deviates from a certain type of symmetry, which will be described, will the demand for money shift as income shifts. Furthermore, there is no presumption in general as to whether increased income will cause increased or decreased demand for money.

Let the size of transactions be uniformly λ dollars so that a bank account receives λ dollars with probability p and loses λ dollars with probability q. Let the targets and thresholds be fixed at z dollars and h dollars, respectively; making the approximation which ignores that h and z are no longer integral multiples of λ, the expected demand for money in terms of units of size λ (following formula (A4) in the Appendix) is $E(y,h/\lambda,z/\lambda)$ and in terms of dollars is

$$(20) \qquad E(m) = \lambda E(y,h/\lambda,z/\lambda).$$

Use of (A4) and a particular type of symmetry reveals an economy in which the demand for money is independent of λ. Consider an economy in which bank accounts can be grouped in pairs, so that for a bank account with probability p of gaining λ dollars, probability q of losing λ dollars, with threshold h and target z, there is a dual bank account with probability q of gaining λ dollars, probability p of losing λ dollars, threshold h and target $h - z$. Such a symmetry makes sense because it is possible to think of the two bank accounts as being mutually payer and payee in a single transaction. The relative values of targets and thresholds also make dimensional sense, since both bank accounts have equal average durations between induced transactions. Use of (20) and (A4) shows that the sum of the demand for money of two paired bank accounts is h, independent of λ. Microeconomic Proposition IV, whose proof is given in the Appendix, states that

$$E(y,h,z) + E(1/y,h,h - z) = h$$

where

$$y = p/q.$$

As a result, only insofar as the bank accounts deviate from such symmetric pairing will changes in the size of transactions (i.e., in λ) yield changes in the demand for money. Furthermore, in the absence of such symmetry, increases in λ can result in either increases or decreases in the demand for money. In these two preceding senses the 0-income elasticity of the demand for money with constant targets and thresholds is robust to changes in the specification of the model of the preceding section.

The assumption regarding the independence of payments between different time periods also violates reality, as is evident from the monthly cycle of wage payments and bills, but again it does not appear that this assumption is intrinsic. A separate paper by Ross Milbourne and myself [1977] explores the extent to which periodic autonomous inflows from wage payments with constant targets and thresholds will modify the conclusions of this paper regarding low income elasticities of the demand for money. Constant targets and thresholds will cause bank accounts to be monitored more frequently as income increases. The increased frequency of monitoring tends to reduce money holdings and can more than offset the increased money holdings that occur because of larger payments flows, so that income elasticities of the demand for money, even with periodic payments, might actually be slightly negative.

Finally, of course, threshold-target monitoring is intrinsic for our conclusion. But that is indeed our point. There should be little doubt that an economy with constant threshold-target monitoring will have a low income elasticity of the demand for money.

IV. Agreement with Empirical Evidence

It remains to examine how well the predictions of the short-run constant threshold-target model agree with empirical evidence concerning the demand for money. In this regard, it is worthwhile to compare two possible specifications of money demand; the first of these specifications is consistent with a theory of money demand in which bank accounts are periodically monitored and habits, which are reflected in the periodicity of this monitoring, respond slowly to changes in the costs and benefits of holding cash balances. According to this model (in differential, as opposed to difference, form),

$$(21) \qquad \dot{v} = \alpha(v^* - v)$$

where
> v is current velocity
> v^* is a target (optimum) velocity

and
> α is a speed-of-adjustment parameter.

In contrast, the usual equation used in empirical estimates of the demand for money is

$$(22) \qquad \dot{m} = \alpha(m^* - m)$$

where

　　m is real balances demanded

　　m^* is a targeted (optimum) value of real balances

and

　　α is again a speed-of-adjustment parameter.

These two possible money-demands behave quite differently in the short run (which in the limit is zero time elapsed since the occurrence of a change). According to (21), velocity is constant in the short run, and money demand is proportional to income; conversely, according to (22), money demand is constant in the short run, and velocity is proportional to income. The model of constant targets and thresholds in the short run is roughly consistent with specification (22), with money demand independent of income; correspondingly, it is inconsistent with equation (21), with constant velocity. Economies in which money demand is described by these two equations are in consequence, quite different in terms of the effectiveness of fiscal policy in the short run. With (21) fiscal policy is totally ineffective in changing income even in the short run; with (22) fiscal policy is quite effective, but not for the usual reason: not because $\partial L/\partial r$ is large but rather because $\partial L/\partial Y$ is small.

　　Empirical estimates of the demand for money usually use (22) in difference equation form as their specification; in particular such stock adjustment equations have been estimated by Laidler [1966], Chow [1966], and Goldfeld [1973], among others. The famous Goldfeld "preferred" equation has a one-quarter income elasticity of 0.193, which is considerably less than the elasticity of nearly unity predicted by a theory of the demand for money with constant velocity in the short run. The correctness of this estimate is partly argued by its goodness of fit and also its robustness, as tested by Goldfeld in many ways. Still, the low income elasticity of 0.193 might be at least partially due to the constraint imposed by the stock adjustment equation that the money demand responds to changes in both income and interest with the same speed of adjustment (given by the parameter α). However, estimates of the demand for money (Goldfeld [1973, pp. 598–607]) using Almon lags without a constraint on income and interest elasticities to adjust at the same rate show that these two elasticities do adjust at approximately the same rate. If anything, money demand adjusts slightly more slowly to changes in income than to changes in interest. The one-quarter income elasticity of M_1 with Almon lags is 0.146.

　　Of course, it has been noticed (Enzler, Johnson, Paulus [1976], Goldfeld [1976]) in recent years that the Goldfeld equation, as estimated from 1952 to 1972 has predicted quite "badly," so that the empirical evidence is at least a bit ambiguous. Several explanations have been given for this phenomenon, of which the most convincing is the large increase in the size of the immediately available funds market; the market has grown from $1 billion net purchases by all commercial banks in 1967 to about $35 billion in June 1955.[5] Since Federal Funds are quite liquid and therefore a substitute for money, the dramatic increased importance of this market should alter the demand for money function. Furthermore, the poor predictive powers of the Goldfeld equation should not affect confidence in this paper's prediction of low income elasticities of the demand for money, since the predictions erred on the side of letting money demand follow income too closely.

Finally, of course it should be noted that the behavior of velocity in the short run in the constant target-threshold model explains at least one half of Milton Friedman's dilemma [1959], which is why velocity is covariant with income over the course of the business cycle. The second part of this dilemma, which was to explain why velocity was contravariant with income over the long run, as was observed prior to World War II, can be explained presumably by the adjustments of targets and thresholds by holders of money balances, who weigh the costs and benefits of different targets and thresholds and ultimately choose the optimum.

V. SUMMARY AND CONCLUSION

Economic theorists have usually assumed that the short-run income elasticity of the transactions demand for money is quite large, being approximately unity. The logic behind this supposition is that persons have "average rates of turnover" that reflect their habits of cash holding. These habits respond slowly to changes in income and interest. This paper shows that if habits are defined differently, in terms of threshold-target monitoring, velocity is not constant in the short run, but instead is proportional to income. This prediction is, in fact, consistent with the empirical evidence. Thus, fiscal policy is effective in the short run, not for the reason usually given by Keynesians that the interest elasticity of the demand for money is large, but rather because the income elasticity of the demand for money is small.

APPENDIX

MICROECONOMIC PROPOSITION I. If money holdings in an initial period, denoted $t = 0$, are a random variable with a probability distribution in long-run equilibrium relative to the p_i's, q_i's, s_i's, h_i's, and z_i's in that initial period, as defined by (15) and (16), an equiproportionate change in all p_i's and q_i's will cause no expected change in money holdings, as long as the h_i's and z_i's remain constant.

Proof of Microeconomic Proposition I. It will be shown that an equiproportionate rise in the p_i's, q_i's, and $(1 - s_i)$'s, the h_i's and z_i's being constant, causes no change in the distribution of money holdings under the assumed conditions. Therefore, there is no change in expected money holdings.

The proof will proceed by induction.

By definition, $f_i(m_i,0) = f_i(m_i,0)$.

It remains to show that if $f_i(m_i,t) = f_i(m_i,0)$, then $f_i(m_i,t + 1) = f_i(m_i,0)$.

Let p_i, q_i, and s_i be the initial probabilities of autonomously receiving \$1, of autonomously paying \$1, and of making no transaction, respectively.

Let p_i', q_i', s_i' be the corresponding probabilities subsequent to the equiproportionate shift.

By definition, there is a scalar λ, such that

(A1) $p_i' = \lambda p_i$

(A2) $q_i' = \lambda q_i$

(A3) $s_i' = 1 - \lambda(1 - s_i)$.

We now make two calculations which show that $f_i(m_i,t + 1) = f_i(m_i,0)$. By (7), for

$$1 \le m_i \le h_i - 1, \qquad m_i \ne z_i,$$
$$f_i(m_i,t + 1) = p_i'f_i(m_i - 1,t) + q_i'f_i(m_i + 1,t) + s_i'f_i(m_i,t);$$

by (A1), (A2), and (A3)

$$= \lambda p_i f_i(m_i - 1,t) + \lambda q_i f_i(m_i + 1,t) + \{1 - \lambda(1 - s_i)\}f_i(m_i,t);$$

by induction assumption

$$= \lambda p_i f_i(m_i - 1,0) + \lambda q_i f_i(m_i + 1,0) + \{1 - \lambda(1 - s_i)\}f_i(m_i,0);$$

by rearrangement of terms

$$= \lambda\{p_i f_i(m_i - 1,0) + q_i f_i(m_i + 1,0) + s_i f_i(m_i,0)\}$$

$$-\lambda f_i(m_i,0) + f_i(m_i,0);$$

by stationarity of $f_i(m_i,0)$ (equation (10))

$$= \lambda f_i(m_i,0) - \lambda f_i(m_i,0) + f_i(m_i,0)$$
$$= f_i(m_i,0).$$

184   *QUARTERLY JOURNAL OF ECONOMICS*

Similarly,

$$
\begin{aligned}
f_i(z_i,t+1) &= p_i' f_i(z_i - 1,t) + q_i' f_i(z_i + 1,t) + p_i' f_i(h_i - 1,t) \\
&\quad + q_i' f_i(1,t) + s_i' f_i(z_i,t) \\
&= \lambda\{p_i f_i(z_i - 1,0) + q_i f_i(z_i + 1,0) \\
&\quad + p_i f_i(h_i - 1,0) + q_i f_i(1,0) \\
&\quad + s_i f_i(z_i,0)\} - \lambda f_i(z_i,0) + f_i(z_i,0) \\
&= \lambda f_i(z_i,0) - \lambda f_i(z_i,0) + f_i(z_i,0) \\
&= f_i(z_i,0).
\end{aligned}
$$

Q.E.D.

COROLLARY TO MICROECONOMIC PROPOSITION I. If money holdings in an initial period are a random variable with a probability distribution in long-run equilibrium, an equiproportionate change in all p_i's and q_i's will cause no change in the probability distributions of money holdings in subsequent periods, provided the h_i's and z_i's remain constant.

MICROECONOMIC PROPOSITION II. Expected additions to money holdings are the sum of net expected induced payments, plus net expected autonomous payments. (Subscript i will be omitted in Microeconomic Propositions II, III, and IV, since these propositions apply uniformly to all bank accounts.) In symbols,

$$
\sum_m mf(m,t+1) - \sum_m mf(m,t)
$$
$$
= -p(h-z)f(h-1,t) + qzf(1,t) + p - q.
$$

Proof.

$$
\sum_m mf(m,t+1) - \sum_m mf(m,t)
$$

$$
= \sum_{m=1}^{h=1} smf(m,t) + \sum_{m=1}^{h-1} qmf(m+1,t) + \sum_{m=1}^{h-1} pmf(m-1,t)
$$
$$
+ qzf(1,t) + pzf(h-1,t) - \sum_{m=1}^{h-1} mf(m,t)
$$

$$
= \sum_{m=1}^{h-1} smf(m,t) + \sum_{m=1}^{h-1} q(m+1)f(m+1,t)
$$
$$
+ \sum_{m=1}^{h-1} p(m-1)f(m-1,t)
$$
$$
- \sum_{m=1}^{h-1} qf(m+1,t) + \sum_{m=1}^{h-1} pf(m-1,t) + qzf(1,t)
$$
$$
+ pzf(h-1,t) - \sum_{m=1}^{h-1} mf(m,t)
$$

$$
= \sum_{m=1}^{h-1} smf(m,t) + \sum_{m=1}^{h-1} qmf(m,t) + \sum_{m=1}^{h-1} pmf(m,t) - qf(1,t)
$$

$$- p(h - 1)f(h - 1,t) - \sum_{m=1}^{h-1} qf(m,t) + \sum_{m=1}^{h-1} pf(m,t)$$

$$+ qf(1,t) - pf(h - 1,t) + qzf(1,t) + pzf(h - 1,t)$$

$$- \sum_{m=1}^{h-1} mf(m,t),$$

and since $p + q + s = 1$ and $\sum_{m=1}^{h-1} f(m,t) = 1$,

$$= - p(h - z)f(h - 1,t) + qzf(1,t) + p - q.$$

MICROECONOMIC PROPOSITION III. An equiproportionate increase in the probabilities of autonomous payments causes an equiproportionate increase in the probabilities of induced payments.

Proof. The probability of a net induced inflow into a bank account in amount z is $qf(1)$. The probability of a net induced outflow from a bank account in amount $(h - z)$ is $pf(h - 1)$. According to the Corollary to Microeconomic Proposition I, an equal increase in p and q leaves $f(1)$ and $f(h - 1)$ unchanged; thus if p and q each change by a factor λ, the probability of an induced inflow in amount z becomes $\lambda qf(1)$ and the probability of an induced outflow in amount $(h - z)$ becomes $\lambda pf(h - 1)$.

Q.E.D.

MICROECONOMIC PROPOSITION IV. Let $E(y,h,z)$ represent the expected value of money holdings of a bank account with upper threshold h, target z and $p/q = y$.

$$E(y,h,z) + E(1/y,h,h - z) = h.$$

Proof. By (15) and (16)

$$E(y,h,z) = \left(\sum_{m=0}^{z} m(1 - y^{z-h})(1 - y^m) + \sum_{m=z+1}^{h} m(1 - y^z) \right.$$
$$\left. \times (1 - y^{m-h}) \right) \bigg/ \left(z(1 - y^{z-h}) + (h - z)(1 - y^z) \right).$$

A bit of algebraic labor produces the sum (A4):

(A4)

$$E(y,h,z) = \frac{1}{2} \left\{ \frac{1 + y}{1 - y} + h + z - \frac{hz(1 - y^{z-h})}{z(1 - y^{z-h}) + (h - z)(1 - y^z)} \right\}.$$

Use of (A4) with the value of the first argument of E equal to $1/y$, of the second argument equal to h, and of the third argument equal to $h - z$, yields

(A5) $E(1/y,h,h - z)$

$$= \frac{1}{2} \left\{ - \frac{1 + y}{1 - y} + 2h - z - \frac{h(h - z)(1 - y^z)}{(h - z)(1 - y^z) + z(1 - y^{z-h})} \right\}.$$

Addition of (A4) and (A5) yields

$$E(y,h,z) + E(1/y,h,h - z) = h.$$

Q.E.D.

London School of Economics

Notes

1. There is a natural generalization of this monitoring in which money holdings upon exceeding an upper threshold are returned to one target z_h; upon falling below a lower threshold, money holdings are returned to a different target z_l. Boylan [1967] has explored the optimality of such "multiple (S,s) policies."

2. The basic proposition of this paper, that insofar as probabilities of nonzero transactions are proportional to income, demand for money is independent of income may seem to have limited application, since this proportionality assumption must be violated for income sufficiently great. Otherwise the probabilities of nonzero transactions would exceed unity. It should be remembered, however, that if the unit of time is very short, the probabilities of making any transaction will be correspondingly small. In the limiting continuous case the probability of nonzero transaction in an interval dt is a differential Pdt, while the probability of making no transaction is unity.

3. This paper concentrates its attention on the implications for the demand for money of the proportionality of expected payments flows and income. Two earlier papers, Akerlof [1975] and [1976], examined the consequences for the demand for money of payments flows that are not proportional to income.

4. For example Keynes's argument in *The General Theory* [1936] concerning the proportionality of the transactions demand for money and income is a restatement of Irving Fisher's arguments for the constancy of velocity in *The Purchasing Power of Money* [1911].

5. See Porter and Mauskopf [1978] and Tinsley and Garrett [1978].

References

Akerlof, G. A., "The Microfoundations of a Flow of Funds Theory of Demand for Money," Working paper, University of California, Berkeley, March 1976.
——, "The Questions of Coinage,. Trade Credit, Financial Flows and Peanuts: A Flow-of-Funds Approach to the Demand for Money," Working paper, University of California, Berkeley, September 1975.
—— and R. D. Milbourne, "The Sensitivity of Monetarist Conclusions to Monetarist Assumptions," Board of Governors of the Federal Reserve System, November 1977.
Baumol, W. J., "The Transactions Demand for Cash: An Inventory Theoretic Approach," this *Journal*, LXVI (Nov. 1952), 545–56.
Boylan, E. S., "Multiple (S,s) Policies and the n-Period Inventory Problem," *Management Science*, XIV (Nov. 1967), 196–204.
Chow, G. C., "On the Long-Run and Short-Run Demand for Money," *Journal of Political Economy*, LXXIV (April 1966), 111–31.
Enzler, J., L. Johnson, and J. Paulus, "Some Problems of Money Demand," *Brookings Papers on Economic Activity*, 1 (1976), 261–80.
Fisher, I., *The Purchasing Power of Money* (New York: Macmillan, 1911).
Friedman, M., "The Demand for Money: Some Theoretical and Empirical Results," *Journal of Political Economy*, LXVII (Aug. 1959), 327–51.
Goldfeld, S. M., "The Demand for Money Revisited," *Brookings Papers on Economic Activity*, 3 (1973), 577–638.
——, "The Case of the Missing Money," *Brookings Papers on Economic Activity*, 3 (1976), 683–730.
Keynes, J. M., *The General Theory of Employment, Interest and Money* (New York: Macmillan, 1936).

Laidler, D., "The Rate of Interest and the Demand for Money: Some Empirical Evidence," *Journal of Political Economy*, LXXIV (Dec. 1966), 543–55.

Miller, M. H., and D. Orr, "A Model of the Demand for Money by Firms," this *Journal*, LXXX (Aug. 1966), 413–35.

Porter, R. D., and E. Mauskopf, "Some Notes on the Apparent Shift in the Demand for Demand Deposits Function," unpublished manuscript, Board of Governors of the Federal Reserve System, May 1978.

Tinsley, P. A., and B. Garrett, "The Measurement of Money Demand," preliminary unpublished manuscript, Special Studies Section, Board of Governors of the Federal Reserve System, April 1978.

Tobin, J., "The Interest Elasticity of the Transactions Demand for Cash," *Review of Economics and Statistics*, XXXVIII (Aug. 1956), 241–47.

[11]

The understanding and control of inflation: is there a crisis in macro-economics?

RICHARD G. LIPSEY / Queen's University

Abstract. The thesis is that the crisis of current macro-economics lies in the intractability of the economy which our theories reveal, not in any major failure of Keynesian macro theories to explain the behaviour of the economy. The first part outlines the market underpinnings of the neo-Keynesian model where markets do not clear in the sense that agents would be willing to sell more at the prevailing price if demand were forthcoming, but prices remain stable. The reasons are outlined for the basic Keynesian asymmetry: the short-term effect of increases in aggregate demand is mainly on prices but of decreases is mainly on output. The second part assesses the neo-Keynesian model against the last fifty years of evidence and suggests its record is surprisingly good. The third part reviews competing paradigms. The fourth part considers policy implications.

Résumé. Le point de vue défendu dans l'article est que la crise de la macroéconomique contemporaine réside dans la difficulté intrinsèque de maîtriser l'économie telle que la révèle nos théories plutôt qu'en un échec de la théorie keynésienne à expliquer le comportement de l'économie. La première partie décrit les structures sous-jacentes des marchés du modèle néo-keynésiens où les marchés ne sont pas en état d'équilibre de l'offre et de la demande dans le sens où les agents seraient disposés à vendre plus au prix actuel si la demande existait. De plus, les causes de l'asymétrie keynésienne (l'effet à court terme d'un accroissement de la demande se fait surtout ressentir sur les prix tandis qu'une diminution de la demande affecte surtout la production) sont analysées dans cette partie. La deuxième partie évalue la performance du modèle néo-keynésien dans les quinze dernières années et il en ressort qu'il s'est étonnamment bien comporté. La troisième partie revoit des paradigmes rivaux. Enfin la quatrième partie examine les implications politiques.

... the sweeping indictment [that orthodox Keynesian theory is 'wildly incorrect' and 'fundamentally flawed'] confuses two kinds of crises. One is the crisis of whether these [orthodox] models have captured the world itself. The second crisis which I believe is the real problem is that the world we capture is extremely hard to tame, to cure from

Presidential address, annual meeting of the Canadian Economics Association / l'Association Canadienne d'économique, Halifax, May 1981.

I am indebted to Scott Gordon, David Laidler, Milton Moore, Douglas Purvis, and David Smith for many helpful comments and suggestions. I am also indebted to Gernot Kofler and David McGechie for valuable research assistance as well as for valuable comments.

Canadian Journal of Economics / Révue canadienne d'Economique, XIV, No. 4
November / novembre 1981. Printed in Canada / Imprimé au Canada.

546 / Richard G. Lipsey

inflationary shocks ... So the crisis is right there in the structure of the world, not in our ability to capture that structure. Franco Modigliani (1978, 195)

My thesis is that Keynesian macro-economics is a 'progressive research programme' within Lakatos's definition of the term (Lakatos, 1978, especially chap. 1). As such it is fulfilling two criteria. First, it is continuing to prove resilient in explaining new observations which at first seemed in conflict with its basic tenets. It incorporates and explains what we see within its broad hypothesis without having to explain away inconvenient facts on a totally ad hoc basis. Thus it provides a coherent, evolving explanation of the macro economic behaviour of the Canadian and American economies (which like all coherent theories however, may, be wrong). Second, it continues to make strong predictions which conflict with those of its principal rivals. So far these predictions have a pretty good track record.

The picture of the world which is evolving from the progressive Keynesian research program, however, is one in which it is extremely difficult to reduce entrenched inflation. A crisis therefore does exist, not in the inability of Keynesian theory to explain the world we see, but in the inability of traditional policy instruments to influence the world described by that theory. *The crisis is real, but it is a crisis of policy, not a crisis of our theoretical understanding of the world of our experience.*[1]

THE NEO-KEYNESIAN PARADIGM

I am not interested here in the history of thought. What Keynes really meant and who critically reinterpreted his model to put it on the tracks again do not

---

1 Although there is, in my view, no crisis in neo-Keynesian macro-economics, some of the problems of macro-economics stem from an endemic complaint which afflicts all of economics. In the classic story of scientific method the 'awkward fact' is king. The number of theories which provide possible explanations for a finite number of observations is infinite. When in practice several competing theories provide more or less equally good explanations of existing observed facts, a new awkward fact is to be welcomed, since it provides a potential test among existing competitors, and it will constrain further theories by the requirement that any new theory explain the earlier known observations and the new awkward fact. From this point of view, awkward facts are to be welcomed as the vehicle which facilitates learning and constrains our theorizing.
    Economists, however, at least until the recent interest in the testing of non-nested hypotheses, have sometimes had little respect for the awkward facts or interest in the comparitive testing which is required by respect for them. Instead, our methodological criterion has more often been merely that a theory track the existing data 'reasonably well.' Since we are usually free to pick our lag structures ad hoc and to redefine variables at will (is 'the' inflation rate to be measured by the CPI, the wholesale price index, the private expenditure component of the GNE deflator, or the whole deflator; and what on earth is 'the' quantity of money?), making some specific version of the general theory track the data reasonably well is not a very strict criterion. This procedure also demotes the awkward fact to nothing more than a modest embarrassment which lowers the R^2 only slightly. In addition, t-statistics become meaningless when a dozen alternatives are 'tested' and the one that gives the highest t statistic is the only one reported. I have discussed this matter in more detail along with other relevant methodological issues in Lipsey (1979).

The understanding and control of inflation | 547

concern me in this paper, fascinating questions though these are. I am interested only in the *neo*-Keynesian view of the world which starts with the Swedes, blossoms in the *General Theory* and grows under the care of generations of economists on both sides of the Atlantic. Let us isolate the key characteristics of that paradigm.

Disequilibrium dynamics
Keynesian economics allowed us to escape from the strait-jacket of the Walrasian auctioneer. Comparative-static and general equilibrium theory have a place to play in dealing with some lines of enquiry. But when one is concerned with the day-to-day behaviour of the economy and its short-term ability to produce unemployment and / or inflation, it is helpful to recognize that real processes take place in real time and that transactions certainly take place out of equilibrium. Keynesian economics can be seen as a basic attempt to deal with this problem. This, of course, is the interpretation of Clower (1965) and Leijonhufvud (1968), and it was the interpretation taught to me by Bill Phillips when I was a junior staff member at the London School of Economics in the mid-1950s.[2]

Although Keynesian economics is best interpreted as an analysis of economies in disequilibrium, Keynes himself, unlike the Swedes whose dynamic, macro-economic, process analysis pre-dated the *General Theory*, analysed equilibrium states.[3] Indeed, what seemed so novel and so shocking in the *General Theory* was the concept of underemployment equilibrium, where desired expenditure equals income at less than full employment. Subsequent theorizing suggested that there are forces at work to push the economy back towards full employment. So Keynesian underemployment equilibrium is better viewed as a slowly changing disequilibrium where the fast-acting forces which equate output to aggregate demand have produced some persistent unemployment, while the slow-acting forces which create full employment have not had sufficient time to exert a major influence. (For further discussion see Tobin (1975).)

When the economy is in a situation of substantial unemployment, prices are not acting quickly to clear markets. *Indeed, the basic Keynesian paradigm is designed to explain how markets can come to rest in situations where sellers of goods and factors are willing to sell more at the current prices but cannot because the demand is not forthcoming, while there is simultan-*

2 Historians of thought argue that there is little evidence to support the view that this was Keynes's understanding of his own model. I am content, therefore, to interpret it as a development of the Keynesian paradigm rather than a deeper understanding of what Keynes really thought.
3 The interpretation of the behaviour of the Keynesian macro models out of equilibrium leads to some monumental confusions between equilibrium conditions and definitional identities. For a view that the entire stock of text books is wrong on this matter see Lipsey (1972), and for a suggestion that my view does not seem insane to at least one philosophically sophisticated observer see Hutchison (1973).

548 / Richard G. Lipsey

eously no pressure for prices of goods and factors to fall.[4] This situation leads
to the basic asymmetry which, then and now, distinguishes Keynesian models
from major competing paradigms: in the Keynesian model, fluctuations in
demand bring predominantly quantity responses below full-capacity output
and predominantly price responses at or above full-capacity output.[5]

To study this absolutely fundamental asymmetry we look first at goods
markets and then at factor markets.

Goods markets
The neoclassical model of the short run gives firms falling marginal product
curves and hence rising marginal cost curves, because the operation of
diminishing returns as a variable quantity of labour is applied to a fixed
quantity of capital.

To see the contrast with the Keynesian paradigm model consider the
example of a 'rag trade' factory which consists of a shed full of n sewing
machines each with its operator. In the short run the only variable cost is the
labour cost of the operators; capital has no short-run user cost. Nevertheless,
when the owner wishes to reduce production in the short run by $1/n$, he finds it
is cheaper to lay off one sewing machine and one operator, leaving the ratio of
employed capital, K^e, to employed labour, L^e, at 1 machine/1 operator, rather
than having $n - 1$ employees dash about trying to tend n machines. What this
commonly encountered example shows is that the marginal product of capital

4 Keynes himself clearly assumed market clearing in perfectly competitive goods markets and
   non-market clearing only in labour markets. But my concern is with the neo-Keynesian
   paradigm rather than with what Keynes himself thought.
5 Economists are generally concerned – one might even say obsessed – with consistency
   in models. The danger is that this concern may lead them to prefer the consistent but
   utterly incorrect model to the messy, less integrated model which contains much of
   the truth. Current theorizing is dominated by maximizing models. To relate all observed
   behaviour to maximizing behaviour is a research program which must be allowed to
   run its course. It is frustrating, however, to those not wholly caught up in it, to see others
   acting as if hard facts which cannot be rationalized in the currently accepted version
   of the maximizing model do not exist, and also acting as if behaviour shown to be
   consistent with some maximizing model, but blatently inconsistent with observed
   facts, must nonetheless exist. The neoclassical model is a beautifully coherent model in
   its original form, and in its reincarnation as the new-Classicism. Believers in this
   model castigate neo-Keynesians and others for not having coherent theories and therefore by implication having nothing interesting to say. But post-Popperian philosophy
   of science has shown us that any progressive research program always lives with both
   theoretical anomalies and inconsistent facts. A really progressive research program
   will often be a necessary mixture of theory plus factual assumptions not incorporated
   into the theory but well substantiated by observation. Lack of tight theoretical consistency is often a hallmark of a progressive research program, while a really tight, wholly
   logically consistent theoretical structure is often the hallmark of a degenerating research program. Such a program is mainly concerned with internal consistency and will
   have abandoned serious attempts to incorporate a constantly developing body of
   awkward facts. Of course, a tight, logically consistent theory is a useful goal to set
   ourselves. But to choose among competing theories on the grounds of beauty and
   consistency rather than empirical relevance is to become scholastic in the extreme.
   Readers can fill in their own list of critics who castigate neo-Keynesian theory because it lacks the theoretical purity of the neoclassical model and who care little about
   the test of empirical relevance of both assumptions and predictions.

The understanding and control of inflation / 549

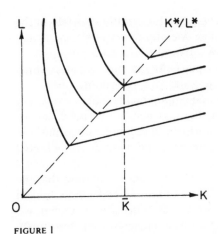

FIGURE I

is negative whenever the ratio of employed capital to employed labour exceeds the value it takes at normal-capacity output.

Next, assume that the owner wishes to produce more than normal capacity output before he can install new machines, sheds etc. He finds that an $n + 1^{th}$ person can contribute to output by doing some peripheral jobs which the operator used to do. Adding further ancillary workers does increase output but at a rapidly diminishing rate. In this case the marginal product of labour is positive (but diminishing), even though the ratio of employed capital to employed labour is less than at normal capacity output.

The same situation occurs when a refrigerator manufacturer chooses to cut his output by closing one of several parallel plants or by putting one plant on short time. In each of these cases the firm is electing to unemploy labour *and* capital. It would never do the latter if the marginal product of fixed capital were positive.

Thus we have our first micro underpinning hypothesis.

Hypothesis 1: The short run marginal product of capital is negative whenever the ratio of employed capital to employed labour exceeds the ratio at which the plant was designed to operate when producing normal capacity output. The short run marginal product of labour is everywhere positive.

The isoquants of firms of this sort are shown in figure 1. Our neoclassical indoctrination makes them look odd, even bizarre, yet evidence suggests that they do describe many empirical technologies.

For this technology to matter economically it is necessary that capital be divisible in the sense that it is subject to an inequality constraint $K^E \leq \bar{K}$ where $\bar{K}$ is the capital available. If the capital is utterly indivisible in the sense that it is subject to an equality constraint, $K^E = \bar{K}$, then variable proportions and diminishing returns are technologically dictated in the short run. In fact much short-run capital is physically divisible, as in the rag-trade

550 / Richard G. Lipsey

example given above, while almost all capital is temporally divisible in the sense that it and its associated labour can be used for fewer hours in the day or fewer days in the week, thus reducing K^E to hold K^E/L^E constant.

If firms of this type wish to reduce output below normal capacity, they disemploy both labour and capital and encounter constant, short-run, marginal cost. The capital utilization rate and employment of labour will vary directly with each other. If, in addition, there is some 'overhead' labour whose employment does not vary with short-run fluctuations in output, the firm will encounter constant marginal cost and declining average variable cost as it *raises* output towards normal capacity.

What is the evidence on hypothesis 1? The evidence is strong that the marginal cost curves of many plants are flat up to normal-capacity output. If plant cost curves are flat, then a fortiori cost curves of firms are flat wherever plants are replicated. The locus classicus for this evidence is Johnston (1960), but many other studies confirm this view.[6]

There is less direct testing on the fundamental underpinning of the nature of the production function than of its consequence of flat marginal cost curves. There is, however, a great deal of evidence that firms prefer to close down one plant of many or to put one plant on short time (which in both cases holds the ratio K^E/L^E constant), rather than try to spread a smaller labour force more thinly over a fixed amount of *employed* capital.

According to the neoclassical model of the short run, with falling marginal product as a changing quantity of variable labour is applied to a given quantity of fixed capital, capital utilization figures should not vary. The variations which do occur, however, are consistent with the Keynesian paradigm.[7]

Now we have firms with flat marginal cost curves for given input prices, and for the moment we assume these input prices do remain constant as output is varied.

Next we add:

Hypothesis 2: In most goods markets firms face downward-sloping demand curves. The evidence here is very strong. Most firms in manufacturing, retailing, and services do not operate as price takers in their output markets. Many industries are obviously oligopolistic in that they contain only a few firms. The spatial dispersion of firms in other industries imparts a strong oligopolistic element to the industry even when the number of firms is large (see Eaton and Lipsey, 1977 and 1978).

6 See, e.g., Dean (1976) and Wiles (1961, appendix to chapt. 13). For a textbook summary see Mansfield (1975, 188–91). The only major empirical dissent as far as I am aware is Walters (1963). Most subsequent commentators do not accept that the voluminous evidence cited by Walters justifies his own concluding remark that the evidence for flat cost curves is inconclusive.

7 Capacity utilization figures such as Department of Finance (1977, 37) or Department of Industry, Trade and Commerce (1980) display actual output as a percentage of capacity output and are neutral with respect to the classical model, where $K^E = \bar{K}$, and the Keynesian model, where $K^E \leq \bar{K}$ in the short run. (See Perry, 1973 for a description of alternative U.S. measures.) I know of much isolated but not systematically assessed data showing that $K^E < \bar{K}$ when output falls cyclically below normal capacity output.

The understanding and control of inflation / 551

Next, we need a pricing hypothesis; it can take either of two forms.

Hypothesis 3A: Firms price on a target-return, full-cost basis, as described by Eckstein and Wyss (1972); prices are set as mark-ups over full costs at normal output to achieve a target rate of return (which may be the profit-maximizing one) when production is at normal capacity. Notice three important implications of this hypothesis.

1. Cyclical fluctuations in demand will be met by quantity rather than price adjustments.
2. Changes in input prices will be met by changes in output prices.
3. The allocation of resources works qualitatively as in the neoclassical model, but the first signal that the firm gets of a change in demand for its output is a change in its rate of sales whereas the first signal the firm gets of a change in the market demand for its inputs is a change in their prices.

Hypothesis 3B: Firms with flat marginal cost curves (hypothesis 1) are profit maximizers. Cyclical shifts of individual demand curves are *on average* iso-elastic.

The implications of hypothesis 3B are the same as those of 3A, except that there may be some changes in relative prices as demands vary cyclically. However, the average level of prices, P, remains constant as with hypothesis 3A.

The evidence is very strong that many firms follow some short-run, normal-price policy so that in the short run they are quantity rather than price adjustors.[8] Even if they were short-run profit maximizers, hypothesis 3B shows we could still get a constant average price in the face of cyclical fluctuations in demand as long as hypothesis 1 is correct.

There is also strong direct evidence that manufacturing prices do not respond strongly to cyclical changes in demand. The attack by Stigler and Kindahl (1970), who tried to show that contract prices were more variable than list prices, is met by Phillip Cagan in his superb book *Persistent Inflation* (1979) in which he extensively documents the asymmetric response of prices to rising and falling demand. In any case, Moore (1972) always seemed to me to be a sufficient refutation.

The working of the model is illustrated in figure 2. Firms set price, p, to yield target profits at normal capacity output, q_c. If demand varies cyclically between D_0 and D_1, output varies between q_c and q_1, while price remains constant at p. If demand were to rise temporarily to D_2, firms would hold price at p. If they cannot profitably meet all the demand, they let order books rise and ration by queues rather than by price. (Order-book data gives solid evidence of this behaviour). Of course, if demand were to remain at D_2 persistently (i.e., D_2 were not merely a temporary cyclical high), firms might consider raising price.

It is important to note that the Keynesian paradigm of price rigidity refers

8 See, e.g., Cagan (1979), Coutts, Godley, and Nordhaus (1978), Eckstein and Wyss (1972), Moore (1970), Neild (1963), Okun (1981), and of course Hall and Hitch (1939).

552 / Richard G. Lipsey

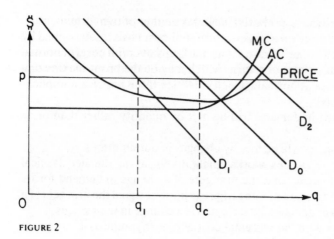

FIGURE 2

only to the cyclical component of prices. Firms price on costs at full capacity output. Cyclical fluctuations in demand are taken up by changes in output. Long-term changes in costs (as when, over the product cycle costs fall as the product is developed) are matched by changes in prices. Also large non-cyclical shifts in demand may be met by price reactions. An example was manufacturers' rebate schemes when shifts in demand towards high mileage cars left producers with large inventories of unsold gas-guzzlers.

Factor markets

So far we have a theory where firms hold prices constant over the cycle when demand fluctuates, *providing* that input prices remain constant. Since the major domestic component of input costs are labour costs, the important remaining part of the explanation is:

Hypothesis 4: Wage rates are relatively insensitive to the cyclical emergence of excess supplies of labour.

Downward inflexibility of money wages seemed a mystery to most of Keynes' critics. 'Money illusion!' they shouted. Those who believed that money wages were relatively inflexible downwards never were able to mount a reply which persuaded those in the middle ground who were amenable to rational argument. Furthermore, in the form just stated the hypothesis is ambiguous in ways that will be clarified below.

Yet the hypothesis was always there clearly stated in Keynes (1936, chap. 2). In the neoclassical paradigm model there is a single homogeneous labour supply which sells its services for the real wage W/P. Rejecting this model, Keynes used the correct hypothesis that there are many, many different kinds of labour selling services in many, many imperfectly linked labour markets. To this he added the hypothesis to which every economist I know who first came back from an arbitration assignment finds himself accepting with more or less surprise and reluctance: relative wages are an important argument in the utility functions of wage earners.[9]

Keynes argued that in the world of multiple markets with lagged adjustments, a 10 per cent fall in the real wage W/P accomplished by a 10 per cent fall in

$$W = \sum_{i=1}^{n} \alpha_i w_i, i = 1, \ldots n,$$

(where w_i and α_i are the wage and the employment weight in the ith labour market) is very different in its transitional effects from a 10 per cent fall in W/P caused by a 10 per cent rise in P. The latter preserves wage relatives in the transition, the former does not. Consider a disequilibrium requiring a fall in W/P. No one can be quite sure in advance how much the fall must be. Thus if one w_i falls too much, the affected workers will lose until the wage can be raised to its correct position. (With a three-year wage bargain the loss can be substantial.) Also, those who adjust sooner will lose more than those who adjust later. For these and many other reasons it pays a person who has influence over one w_i to resist its adjustment so that others adjust first and overshooting can be identified. Furthermore, before the full adjustment is accomplished, conditions may change again, requiring, say, that real wages return to their initial levels. Then those who have not yet made the first adjustment will have lost nothing. If, however, the adjustment is through P, all wage relatives are preserved and all gain or lose equally from temporary over- or undershooting of W/P.[10]

Proposition: In the neoclassical, homogeneous labour market it is a sign of money illusion to resist a fall in W/P accomplished by a fall in W while accepting it when accomplished by a rise in P; in a set of disaggregated labour markets where transactions occur out of equilibrium for a long time, the real effects of a fall in W/P accomplished by a fall in W are not the same as the real effects of the same fall in W/P accomplished by a rise in P, and it is not necessarily a sign of money illusion to accept the operation of the latter while fiercely resisting the former.[11]

9 For just one of hundreds of such expressions see Jones (1973, 87–8) and for a richer study of data in the same general spirit see Mitchell (1980). For some illustrative fireworks, however, consider an experiment removed from the wage bargain. Try giving one of two young children three chocolates and the other one chocolate, which is a clear gain to both, but one which upsets relatives. Someday we shall know if the enormous sense of equity and justice which experiments such as this one illustrate is innate or is acquired during very early experience. Whatever its origins, it is a matter of common observation that relatives really do matter to many people and that people will pay significant amounts to avoid what they apprehend to be unjust relatives. See Trevithick (1976) for reference to direct tests.

10 In understanding the workings of the wage bargaining process on money and real wages it is also important to realize that the price level is exogenous to the individual wage bargain but endogenous to the whole macro set of bargains (see Laidler, 1975, 48–9 and 90–1).

11 For more detailed discussion see Keynes (1936, Chap. 2), Trevithick (1976), and Solow (1979).

554 / Richard G. Lipsey

Modern implicit contract theory has tried to rationalize fixed-wage, variable employment contracts in terms of risk-sharing between risk-averse labour and risk-neutral firms. Early theories of this type, which assumed homogeneous labourers who were unemployed by lottery, did not succeed in the task set. To follow out Keynes's ideas, non-homogeneous labour is required, and relative wages need to be in workers' utility functions. Although some interesting work has been done, the theory has not yet produced a testable rationalization of the Keynesian view.

So the Keynesian paradigm makes wages downwardly rigid, owing to concern over relatives in a dynamic, uncertain, non-homogeneous world. Given constant input prices, marginal costs of producers are constant, owing to the technology of capital in goods production. Given this situation, output fluctuates cyclically with demand, while prices remain rigid.

We must now consider what kind of wage rigidity we need for the neo-Keynesian model. Keynes talked about downward rigidity in *money* wages because he was working in a non-inflationary world. The logic of his argument, however, easily extends to an inflationary world. If workers expect an x per cent general wage inflation, they will be reluctant to allow their own wage w_1 to rise by less than x per cent. No doubt early Keynesians typically thought in terms of downward inflexibility of money *wages*. No doubt it was the monetarists with their expectations-augmented Phillips curve who really jolted Keynesians into thinking about rates of change of individual prices relative to expected rates of change of all prices. But once that point was absorbed – and it took nearly half a decade for the absorption to happen fully – it became clear that the logic of Keynes's argument extends to this situation. Workers resist reductions in their relative wage, which means they resist *increases* in their own wage which are lower than expected increases in either the general wage level or a closely associated set of particular wages.

This behaviour causes 'inertial inflation.' The clearest modern statement is to be found in the writings of James Tobin (see, e.g., Tobin, 1980, 62–3). For illustrative Canadian evidence see Christofides et al. (1980a, b) and Wilton (1980, chap. 6.)

Tobin's inertial theory is Keynes of chapter 2 of the *General Theory* in a modern setting. Tobin claims that wage setters are concerned about their wages relative to other closely related wages. He adds that wage bargains are made only infrequently, say, typically every one to three years. Thus when a particular wage is set, all other closely related wages are predetermined and on average for a period of one-half the length over which the wage in question is now to be set. Thus whatever decision-makers' expectations are about the overall rate of wage or price inflation, they will resist setting their wages at a level which will alter their relation to other existing relevant wages.

This theory of inertia makes any given inflation rate hard to change. We can also add to it an asymmetry between raising and lowering relative wages. For example, workers don't mind getting ahead of other closely related groups, but they fiercely resist falling behind. Therefore the wage stickiness is mainly on the down side of reducing inflation. For further strong evidence which is couched in expectational terms but understandable in inertial terms see Eckstein (1981).

It is important to distinguish between Tobin's inertial inflation and the monetarists' expectational inflation. In the monetarist theory firms are concerned to set their own profit-maximizing, relative price and workers to demand their real-income-maximizing, relative wage. Thus over the contract period decision-makers are concerned with the relation between their own money price or wage and their expected price level. If they revise downwards the rate of inflation which they expect, they revise downwards the money wage or price which they require. Thus expectational inflation is forward-looking, since money price and wage behaviour depends on expectations about the future price level. A revision downwards of the expected rate of inflation makes individual wage and price setters respond in an inflation-reducing manner. Inertial theories are backward-looking, since labour, in particular, cares about existing wage relatives. Even if workers come to expect a lower rate of inflation, they will be reluctant to moderate their own individual wage demands, because such behaviour would upset relatives with contracts already agreed on to other labour markets. Any complete theory of inflation is likely to contain both forward-looking expectational, and backward-looking inertial forces. (For an early recognition of this point see, e.g., Laidler, 1976.)

Thus the basic Keynesian paradigm of asymmetries extends to an inflationary world; it is hard to force the rate of wage and hence price increases below those compatible with the current rate of inflation merely by depressing aggregate demand, although it is easy to force them above the current rate of inlation by raising demand. As a special case (and assuming zero productivity growth for simplicity), it is hard to reduce the level of money wages or prices by reducing demand when the current expected rate of inflation is zero.

Closure
Keynes actually closed his system with an aggregate supply curve as a function of the volume of employment, N. Implicit in this system, however, is a rising aggregate supply curve as a function of P/W because Keynes accepted the neoclassical theory of the firm rather than the neo-Keynesian, paradigm theory outlined above. This position led him into some serious empirical difficulties, and Keynes's method of closure was quickly forgotten in the core macro model.[12] It was replaced by the perfectly elastic aggregate

12 The empirical problems with Keynes's neoclassical goods market are stated by Okun (1981, 16) as follows: 'According to the [Keynes-neoclassical] model, the movement of both productivity and real wages should be countercyclical. Combined with a Cobb-Douglas production function, the model also implies that labour's share of income should be non-cyclical. In sharp contrast, empirical research suggests that real wages are essentially non-cyclical, productivity procyclical and labour's share countercyclical.' The neo-Keynesian paradigm model just outlined explains these facts, not by denying

556 / Richard G. Lipsey

supply curve for which the theory described above provides the micro under-pinnings.[13] Experience of World War II quickly reminded economists of full-employment demand inflation, and the vertical portion was added, yielding the kinked, upward-ratcheting, aggregate supply curve.

By the early 1950s Bill Phillips was already closing the models of short-run stabilization policy with a version of the 'price-Phillips curve,' which related the *GNP* gap to the rate of change of the price level (see Phillips, 1954 and 1956). Later (Phillips, 1958) he provided the factor market underpinning to his price-Phillips curve by relating the rate of change of wages to unemployment, which was a proxy for the excess demand for labour.

It is worth noting that the Phillips curve was persistently misunderstood on this side of the Atlantic as a cost-push phenomenon. See, e.g., Samuelson (1964), Meiselman (1968), Anderson and Carlson (1972), and Cagan (1979). In fact, as can be seen from Phillips (1954, 1956) and as is discussed in detail in Lipsey (1978), the Phillips curve closed the model in a very orthodox fashion, which left excess demand as a major cause of increases in the price level and monetary expansion as the only cause of permanent inflations. Friedman's (1975a, 18) assertion that the IS-LM model cannot be closed by the Phillips curve is therefore incorrect. This conclusion is discussed in detail in Lipsey (1978). (See especially n. 16 and surrounding text discussion.)

Neo-Keynesians always saw the Phillips curve as representing the pressure of excess or deficient demand on wages.[14] Starting with Phelps (1968) and Mortensen (1970), the new-Classicists tried to reinterpret the curve as a labour supply phenomenon where unemployment was a result of voluntary search activity which varied over the cycle, because of persistent misperceptions of labour market signals on the part of labour. This supply-side interpretation has been largely discredited, owing to empirical work on the relative unimportance of voluntary search activity as a contributor to total unemployment.

The wage-unemployment Phillips curve together with the firm behaviour just discussed provided the micro underpinnings to the two-equation Keynesian model so beloved of econometricians then and now. In this model the

the law of diminishing returns, but by saying it is irrelevant, because production is varied in the short run by changing the employment of both capital and labour. Thus, as demand rises out of a slump, wages and prices are constant (or rise at the same rate), holding real wages constant; overhead labour is spread over more units of output, raising measured labour productivity, and according to 'Okun's law,' output rises more than employment, so that labour's share of output falls.

13 The short-run neoclassical model still has an extraordinarily tenacious hold on economists, possibly because of the early indoctrination in the short-run competitive theory of the firm or possibly because Keynes himself accepted it and only the subsequent neo-Keynesians saw its error. For example, it is popular these days to close Mundell-Fleming international models with a neoclassical upward-sloping aggregate supply curve as a function of P / W. Given the Keynesian production conditions, the demand for labour is perfectly elastic over a wide range because marginal costs are constant. The downward-sloping real demand for labour is derived by varying the amount of labour applied to a fully employed capital stock, which experiment has few if any counterparts in the real world.

14 See Lipsey (1960, 13, n. 3, 1974, sections I and II and 1978, section III), and Hansen (1970).

The understanding and control of inflation / 557

transmission mechanixm for demand inflation is as follows: a rise in aggregate demand leads to an increase in desired output in the goods sector, which leads to an increase in the derived demand for factors, which bids up factor prices, which raises cost curves in the goods sector, which leads to an increase in goods prices. The model also allows for supply-side inflations which arise from any exogenous forces which increase input prices.

Friedman's essay on closure (reprinted as Friedman, 1974) seemed to neo-Keynesians to put the clock backwards. Of course he was right to emphasize the importance of the supply side, but the allegation that Keynesians closed their model with a perfectly elastic aggregate supply curve was several generations of closure out of date.

In the 1970s, accelerating inflation led economists to abandon the original Phillips curve. However, with very little evidence many accepted the symmetrical expectations-augmented Phillips curve, where inflation accelerates continually if national income, Y, exceeds full employment income Y_F, and decelerates continually if Y is less than Y_F.

Misunderstanding of the Keynesian paradigm may have been responsible for this unfortunate, non-empirically based change of view. *The Keynesian model was always asymmetrical.* [15] Consider the two ranges separately.

In its kinked-aggregate-supply version, the Keynesian model was totally silent about what would happen if excess aggregate demand prevailed continuously (except that P would certainly rise). The founders of its Phillips-curve version also gave remarkably little thought to what would happen in these circumstances. [16] Thus, neo-Keynesians could accept the acceleration of the inflation rate when $Y > Y_F$ (since it merely filled a hole in the Keynesian paradigm). They should not, however, accept the continued deceleration of inflation when $Y < Y_F$, since this conflicts both with the Keynesian paradigm and with much strong evidence of how the price level actually behaves when $Y < Y_F$.

Today the Keynesian model can be tentatively closed by a kinked, or non-linear, expectations-augmented Phillips curve. The expectations term reflects the strong evidence that expectations of inflation do influence the actual inflation rate. The steep short-run curve above Y_F reflects the evidence that increasing aggregate demand can increase output somewhat above Y_F, at least in the short run, while increasing the inflation rate greatly. The flat short-run curve below Y_F reflects inertial inflation and the evidence that

---

15 Among monetarists, Laidler (1975, 48–9 and fig. 6-1, 124) and Cagan (1979, chaps 1 and 3) were two who clearly did not accept this symmetry.

16 I presume I can speak with some authority on this subject. Phillips himself was interested only in analysing the potentially destabilizing effects of fine tuning (and this in the early 1950s!). In modern context his models clearly assumed a constant expected rate of inflation. When I tried to theorize on Phillips's relation I warned (Lipsey, 1960, 31–2) 'the fitted relation may not be a very good guide to the relation between W and U if U were to remain substantially unchanged for a long time,' which clearly implied that our interest was in short-run disequilibrium dynamics. Later, however (Lipsey, 1965), I followed the lead of Samuelson and Solow (1960) in treating the Phillips curve as if it provided a stable long-term menu of choice between inflation and unemployment.

558 / Richard G. Lipsey

reducing aggregate demand has only a small retarding effect on inflation in the short run.[17]

EXPLANATION AND PREDICTION

In this section I consider how well the Keynesian model has stood up to the evidence for the last half-century. For brevity I confine myself to Canadian and American experience but similar surveys would produce analogous stories for other advanced industrial countries. Notice that the Keynesian model includes the propositions that sustained inflations require monetary validation and that short bursts of inflation may be caused by short bursts of monetary expansion. Thus on many of the episodes mentioned below there is no major conflict between the Keynesian IS, LM and monetarist models.

The Keynesian model with a perfectly elastic aggregate supply curve explained the 1930s relatively well. With the addition of the full-employment, kinked, aggregate supply curve, it also explained the wartime inflations of the 1940s and the failure of wage-price controls to affect the price level permanently, when all they were doing was suppressing the effects of excess aggregate demand. The early Keynesian model failed utterly by predicting a post-war recession which never materialized. This failure pointed out the weakness of the simple Keynesian consumption function, led to the important distinction between cross-section and time-series functions, and led eventually to Friedman's (1957) permanent income and Modigliani and Brumberg's (1954) life-cycle consumption functions.[18]

The rising trend of unemployment in the late 1950s and early 1960s was well explained by the Keynesian model augmented by a growing Y_F which created fiscal drag. The Kennedy-Johnson tax cut was a triumph of Keynesian economics in restoring full employment in the United States. The first serious challenge for empirical explanation, however, came with observation that

17 John Cornwall (1981) restates and supports the fundamental Keynesian asymmetry in terms which leave me little to object to. He appears to believe it is a new idea and this claim is accepted, by for example, Donner (1981). The apparent novelty is achieved by taking issue with my 1960 paper on the micro underpinnings of the wage-Phillips curve. I plead guilty to ignoring in that paper the asymmetry problem in order to concentrate on the link between the aggregate wage-Phillips curve and micro labour markets. Indeed, by linking the Phillips curve to competitive but non-instantaneously clearing labour markets I was outside of the neo-Keynesian tradition, and Cornwall is quite right to take issue with me on this point. Note, however, that neither Phillips nor myself, nor anyone else whom I know of in the early Phillips-curve tradition, ever drew an empirical Phillips curve which did not display the asymmetry that wages could rise fast in the face of excess demand and would fall only slowly in the face of excess supply. Phillips, for example, calculated the asymptotic rate of decrease in U.K. money wages as unemployment went to 100 per cent as 1 per cent per annum! For a specific recognition and analysis of the implications of this asymmetry see Gray and Lipsey (1974). For a further study of neo-Keynesian underpinnings which puts more emphasis on maximizing behaviour than is given here see Gordon (1981).
18 By switching from the Keynesian concept of consumption expenditure on durables to the classical concept of consumption of the flow of services yielded by durables, Friedman caused some confusion. He writes (1957, 238) as if the multiplier was related to the latter concept, when of course it relates to the former. The importance of the distinction was fully explored in Tobin (1968).

The understanding and control of inflation | 559

before the tax cut the price level continued to rise from $\frac{1}{2}$ to 2 per cent per year in the face of what by anyone's definition, then or now, was less than full employment.

The Keynesian explanation was suggested by Schultze (1959). This was his theory of structural inflation. Relative downward inflexibility of wages and prices implies that when relative prices changed, as they must continually do in the face of the disturbances caused by economic growth, the general price level would rise. If such a rise was not validated by an increase in the money supply, one would expect a secular upward drift in the unemployment rate and in the price level. Schultze's theory is an early supply-shock theory of stagflation. It is also consistent with the basic neo-Keynesian paradigm of upward flexibility but relative, downward inflexibility of prices and wages. To the best of my knowledge no competing paradigm – monetarism or new-Classicism – has tried to meet the challenge of explaining the inflation at less than full employment of the late 1950s and early 1960s.

Then in 1968–70 a temporary tax surcharge was used in an attempt to dampen rising inflationary pressures. The measure failed and was widely held to be a refutation of the Keynesian model. Subsequent debate has not reached a final conclusion, partly because each side is able to show some version of their model can track the facts tolerably. My own reading of the exchange suggests that both the zero model (temporary tax changes have no effect on aggregate demand) and the 100 per cent model (temporary tax changes have the same effect on aggregate demand as do permanent ones) are inferior to the intermediate model (about half the effect on aggregate demand as permanent ones). Also, the failure to influence inflation rates now seems quite understandable in terms of either the monetarist model of expectational inflation or the neo-Keynesian model of inertial inflation. Even if aggregate demand had been influenced to the maximum predicted amount, we now see it as hopelessly naive to have expected that the inflation rate rather than the level of activity would have borne the primary impact effect.[19] In any case no revolutionary overthrow seems required, although the Keynesian model is made more powerful by the addition of modern life-cycle or permanent income theories of the consumption function that were held to be vindicated by this experiment.

In Canada the Mundell-Fleming version of the Keynesian model extended to cover an open economy explained the boom which occurred in the mid-1960s, when the resolution of the 'Coyne affair' led to an expansionary fiscal policy in a fixed exchange rate regime. It also explains fully the failure to contain the Canadian inflation rate below the u.s. rate by using tight

19 There seems no point in providing a full bibliography here. A careful analysis of the experiment would require a complete paper on its own. It is interesting, however, to compare the amount of attention paid by economists to some purely theoretical issue such as a neoclassical growth theorem with that paid to what was undoubtedly a key empirical experiment pertaining to a very important body of theory. For the key works in support of the view expressed in the text see Okun (1971), Blinder and Solow (1974), and Modigliani and Steindel (1977). For dissent, see Springer (1975).

560 / Richard G. Lipsey

monetary policy in a world of fixed exchange rates in 1969–70. This model also explained how the U.S. inflation was transmitted to Canada when the Bank of Canada decided on a policy of a dirty float to stabilize the Canadian dollar at about par with the U.S. dollar soon after the exchange rate had been freed. (On these episodes see Courchene, 1976.)

In the United States the Keynesian model (as well as most major competitors) predicted the failure of Nixon's wage-price controls to contain a demand-inflation permanently. The only apparent problem was the setting in of inflationary pressures at a higher level of unemployment than had previously been experienced, which posed a problem if there was a unique relation between full-employment national income and the associated volume of frictional unemployment.

Subsequent research has shown that the amount of unemployment associated with inflationary demand pressures had risen in the early 1970s. At the time policy-markers did not perceive this development and hence the force of excess demand present in 1972–3 was underestimated. After all, the unemployment rate suggested some labour-market slackness by historical standards. More recent research has shown that a combination of demographic changes and changes in unemployment insurance and minimum wage laws meant that full employment in the sense of excess demand pressures on capacity set in at a higher unemployment level than it had in the past. (In short, the unemployment-vacancy relation had shifted upwards.) In Canada a given vacancy rate was associated with 2–3 per cent more unemployment than in the past. Here again, what looked like a crisis in the theory turned out to be quite easily explained within the paradigm when some more attention was paid to disaggregated behaviour and supply-side phenomena. The theory was enriched and made more powerful as a result. (For evidence see Reid and Meltz, 1979, Fortin and Phaneuf, 1979, and Wilton, 1980.)

The boom in 1972–3 was fairly typical, although it took the inflation rate to an unprecedented high level. It was followed by the recession of 1974, during which the stagflation problem was first felt in its full strength. For about a year inflation remained approximately in the two-digit range, while the recession deepened with rising unemployment.

The prophets of theoretical doom announced the end of all conventional wisdom. Subsequent research has fairly well established that these prophets were misguided. There were some new phenomena which needed incorporation into the standard theory during this period of time (and there were also some fairly conventional occurrences merely exacerbated by the magnitude of the problem). In either case the Keynesian macro economic research program was able to incorporate them.

The neo-Keynesian explanation of the stagflation of the mid 1970s in the United States is to be found in Alan Blinder's excellent book *Economic Policy and the Great Stagflation* (1979). (See also the fine treatment by Eckstein, 1978 and the more eclectic but still basically neo-Keynesian treatment in McCracken, 1977.) The key to understanding what seemed so perplexing in

The understanding and control of inflation | 561

the mid-1970s is that a typical demand-shock inflation in the early 1970s turned into a supply-shock inflation in the mid-1970s with rising prices and falling output. The supply shocks were rises in the price level due to (1) increasing energy prices (2) temporary increases in food prices, and (3) (in the United States) the general post-controls bubble. The first two causes illustrate a newly important inflationary phenomenon which must be recognized if sensible policy is to be formed: *relative price inflation*. Strong increases in some prices can and do cause the measured price level to rise.[20]

The Canadian case is not as well documented as the U.S. experience, but it is clear that the neo-Keynesian model handles the supply-shock inflation in Canada and also predicts the different inflation-unemployment experiences of the two countries in response to the much greater degree of monetary accommodation which occurred in Canada.

At the time, the experience of stagflation seemed perplexing, because economists were unused to thinking of supply-shock inflations which, by shifting the aggregate supply curve upward along a fixed aggregate demand curve, are predicted by the neo-Keynesian model to cause stagflation. The experience required that economists open their minds to new shocks which could impinge on the economy; it required no change in the Keynesian model, which handled the experience without requiring any significant change in its structure (see Lipsey 1981).

By 1976 the exogenous, supply-shock inflation had receded and excess demand was clearly not a problem. The major problem which then emerged was the persistence of high underlying rates of inflation in spite of the deepest and most prolonged recession since the 1930s. It was clear that the experience of 1975–8 could be explained neither by external supply shocks pushing up the aggregate supply curve nor by excess demand.

The basic neo-Keynesian asymmetry, however, provided an explanation: although increases in aggregate demand raise the price level, reductions in aggregate demand lower output and employment but have only a minor effect on slowing the inflation rate. Indeed, neo-Keynesians such as Tobin (1974) predicted this phenomenon well in advance of its occurrence. Recent evidence on a well-defined but fairly flat Canadian short-run Phillips curve (see, e.g., Fortin and Newton, 1980 and Riddell, 1979) supports the Keynesian view that it is very difficult and costly in terms of lost output to force the inflation rate down by restrictive policies which act on aggregate demand.

So the diagnosis of the 1970s by neo-Keynesian economists such as Blinder, Eckstein, and Tobin is that the early 1970s saw a traditional demand inflation, the mid 1970s a supply-shock inflation, and the late 1970s an inertial inflation which is difficult to control.

I have argued that there is no current crisis of theory which will necessitate the replacement of the neo-Keynesian, macro-economic paradigm. Constant

20 For a criticism of the attempt of some monetarists to define away as not being inflation any price rise that does not have monetary causes, see Lipsey (1979).

562 / Richard G. Lipsey

challenge and rapid evolution has been the history of neo-Keynesian economics; replacement by a superior alternative currently does not seem on the cards. Two developments which have been necessary are much more attention both to the supply side in general and to disaggregated supply effects in particular.

ALTERNATIVE PARADIGMS

It is often alleged that the experience of the 1970s tipped the balance of evidence against Keynesianism and towards monetarism. I find it difficult to sustain this belief. Consider the two main events which posed problems for explanation. First, the stagflation of 1974–6 easily fits into the Keynesian model where, because of its asymmetry, supply shocks raise the price level and lower output. In contrast, some monetarists predicted that supply shocks would not raise the price level.

> ... what of oil and food to which every government official has pointed? Are they not the immediate cause of the price explosion? Not at all. It is essential to distinguish changes in *relative* prices from changes in *absolute* prices. The special conditions that drove up the prices of oil and food required purchasers to spend more on them, leaving less to spend on other items. Did that not force other prices to go down or to rise less rapidly than otherwise? Why should the *average* level of prices be affected significantly by changes in the prices of some things relative to others? (Friedman, 1975b).

To Friedman's last question the neo-Keynesian answers 'because the asymmetry between upward and downward adjustments means that when some prices are forced up other quantities rather than other prices will fall at least in the short run.' Surely, here is a clear test. Friedman predicted no change in the price level and hence no change in aggregate output and employment following an unaccommodated supply shock. (With the paths of P, M and V unaffected, the path of Y must be unaffected as well.) Neo-Keynesians predicted a rise in the price level and a fall in output and employment. Is it too optimistic to believe that the late Arthur Okun was right when he wrote shortly before he died (Okun, 1981), 'No professional economist will ever again insist (as some did in 1974) that a major rise in the price of oil cannot raise the price level since it merely pushes other prices down'? I hope Okun is right, but I for one am going to keep my eyes on *Newsweek* just to be sure!

Second, the experience of 1976–9 is predicted by the Keynesian asymmetric model. Writing in 1974, Tobin, for example, predicted that it would take a very long time for sustained aggregate demand restraint to reduce the inflation rate: 'The short-run Phillips curve is flat at high rates of unemployment. Since it is steep at low rates, a much longer time is required to unwind an inflation than to generate one. In the circumstances, neither monetary policy nor aggregate-demand policy is in general a useful tool.' (231–2). He could hardly

The understanding and control of inflation / 563

TABLE 1

Rates of Growth of $M1$ and the CPI in
Canada, 1975–80

Year	Per cent increase in $M1$	Per cent increase in CPI
1975	13.8	10.8
1976	8.0	7.9
1977	8.4	8.0
1978	10.2	9.0
1979	7.0	9.1
1980	6.4	10.1

SOURCE: *The Bank of Canada Review*,
April 1981 and *The Consumer Price
Index*, March 1981

be said to have been proved wrong by events. On the other hand, I suspect
that any monetarist who believed that $M1$ was an appropriate monetary
magnitude to control and who was given in 1975 an advance look at the
Canadian $M1$ data for the next six years, would have seriously underpredicted
the 1980–1 Canadian inflation rate.[21]

So the belief that the 1970s upset the Keynesian paradigm is wide of the
mark. It is not my purpose to argue that the Keynesian model has come out
superior to all contenders on all counts. I wish to argue only the bare minimum
claim, that it is still alive and well and not doing too badly – thank you very
much.[22] Lucas (1981) takes an opposite view, which he supports by assuming that the stable Phillips curve was the control assumption of Keynesian
economics, which of course it was not (see Lipsey, 1978).

The major current challenge to the neo-Keynesian paradigm is the
new-Classical model, where markets always clear and individual agents are
always in equilibrium, and where the theory of rational expectations requires
that people do not make systematic errors. This new-Classicism is a serious –
indeed revolutionary – idea. It holds that the whole Keynesian disequilibrium
approach was a blind alley. From the point of view of the sociology of
knowledge this new theory is a fundamentalist call for a return to the purity of
the past. From the point of view of economic science its claims must
eventually be judged in comparison with neo-Keynesian models against the

21 If monetarist theorists were not surprised, one of their chief practitioners, the governor
of the Bank of Canada, certainly was (see Bank of Canada, 1981).
22 Not only is it alive and well, but its American version lives as much as anywhere else in
the Brookings Institution in Washington, D.C. That institution has done much of the
empirically oriented research which has helped to maintain the neo-Keynesian paradigm
as a progressive research program. Their research is almost exclusively confined to American
data, however, so that tests which arise from different national responses to similar stimuli
are seldom made. Also, their bibliographies are almost exclusively confined to U.S.
sources, thus tending to isolate American neo-Keynesian research somewhat from its British and European counterparts.

564 / Richard G. Lipsey

only finally important test, the ability to explain and predict factual observations.[23]

The major contribution of the new-Classicism which is here to stay is rational expectations. This theory has substantially altered neo-Keynesian views on expectations.[24] First, we are much more aware than we ever were in the past of the importance of expectations in our models. Second, there will be no going back to such ad hoc theories of expectations formation as the naïve adaptive expectations model. The Keynesian model will no doubt be enriched by better and it is hoped more empirically oriented theories of expectations formation.

Conflicts between the two models arise mainly with the market-clearing assumption in which misperceptions are the sole explanation of deviations from long-run equilibrium. The Keynesian model of the firm with flat marginal cost curves and downward-sloping demand curves yields non-market-clearing in the sense that firms can be willing to sell more at the going price if there is more demand for their product while prices do not fall. (Can anyone doubt that there are firms in this position today?) The Keynesian model of labour market behaviour allows labour markets not to clear in the sense of the existence of unemployed workers who would be willing to work at the going wage rate while existing unions would not be willing to moderate their wage demand by 3 per cent even if their best *revised* estimate were that the rate of inflation was going to moderate by 3 per cent. The difficulty that rational expectations theorists have in accepting the significance of the Keynesian assymetry is well illustrated in McCallum (1980, 740).

The other major challenge comes from monetarism in its more general guise (without full new-Classicism and rational expectations). Here the differences are smaller.[25] Neo-Keynesians no longer deny the transmission

23 Real comparative testing and judgment lies in the future. Meanwhile, I find Okun's (1980) listing of empirical observations which conflict with the new-Classical model persuasive.

24 Historians of thought correctly point out that Keynes himself laid very heavy emphasis on expectations. Hence, it might be said that rational expectations returned neo-Keynesians to Keynesian orthodoxy! But in the flow of the development of ideas the rational expectations theorists certainly changed the thinking of most current theorists including neo-Keynesians.

25 Possibly monetarists find neo-Keynesians hard to pin down, in which case I for one offer to reply to any serious challenge to be pinned down. Keynesians certainly find some monetarists frustratingly hard to pin down; the exchange between Laidler (1981) and Tobin (1981) is an example. Reading and rereading Laidler I find several places where we are agreed on propositions which he claims are monetarist (I thought they were Keynesian, but no matter, as long as we agree on their substance). But I find no statement of where monetarism makes predictions about future policies or disturbances which differ from Keynesian predictions.

I find myself allied with Tobin (1981) in being baffled by Laidler's attempt to argue that there are no major differences left between the two groups.

As Tobin says (1981, 57), 'At the present time, the big policy issue is not whether we can get permanently lower unemployment at finite inflation cost, but whether we can get permanently lower inflation by monetary disinflation, and if so, at what cost in higher unemployment incurred for how long. I do not see the basis for Laidler's optimism about the speed and ease of disinflation.' Although I agree that many monetarists do have such optimism, I hasten to add that I admire Tobin's ability to extract so specific a

The understanding and control of inflation / 565

mechanism from changes in 'the' money supply, M, to changes in aggregate demand, AD. They are inclined to define the transmission mechanism as going from money to aggregate demand and to leave the separate closure mechanism to divide the effects of shifts in aggregate demand between real national income and the price level. Monetarists are inclined to define the transmission mechanism as going from money to money national income (PY). As Laidler (1978) shows, this definition gets them into some real problems, since the relation is not a unique one.[26]

More important is the question of symmetry with respect to expansionary and contractionary monetary shocks. Neo-Keynesians accept the link from M to AD but then allow for an asymmetrical influence of AD on P. Monetarists, by linking M directly to PY, sometimes implicitly assume a symmetrical influence. Here ought to be the makings of a critical test.

A second possible asymmetry is also worth mentioning. Both Keynesians and monetarists agree that rapidly increasing the money supply is a sure way to increase aggregate demand. On the downside they are not so unanimous. Surely one of the hallmarks of monetarism is that monetary restraint will effectively reduce aggregate demand. Some neo-Keynesians are not so sure; they fear that the flexibility of institutions and general human ingenuity may make it difficult to exert sustained pressure for aggregate demand to fall by using the traditional levers of monetary policy. For example, money substitutes may be invented to circumvent the restrictive policy that is applied.

In summary, Keynesians accept (and here some of them needed to learn from early monetarists) that changes in M exert a strong influence on AD in an expansionary direction and possibly also in a contractionary direction (although there is less agreement among Keynesians on the downside). They are clear, however, that changes in AD have asymmetric effects: when $Y = Y_F$, increases in AD mainly raise P, while decreases in AD mainly reduce Y. There tends to be less asymmetry in the monetarist model; increasing the rate of monetary expansion will raise the inflation rate; reducing monetary expansion will lower inflation.

The observed empirical relation is clearly asymmetrical, at least in the short term. So monetarists must specify time horizons. How much asymmetry do they allow and for how long? Not many of them seem to me to have committed themselves to statements which would provide tests. Neo-Keynesians are clear; they say it would take a long time and calculate the lost output needed to cut inflation (see, e.g., Tobin, 1980, 66–70).[27,28]

---

statement from all of the generalized wisdom in Laidler's paper. On several readings I am unable to do so. Also, as mentioned in footnote 15, I believe that in other contexts Laidler has accepted the neo-Keynesian asymmetry.

26 If V is constant, the relation is unique. But monetarists (see Friedman, 1974) work with a model where the demand for money is interest sensitive, so velocity is not constant.

27 Two important critiques of current Canadian economic policy are to be found in Donner and Peters (1979) and Barber and McCallum (1980) and (1981). On the former two authors I have little to add to what Fortin (1981) has to say. On the latter two I confess to being uncertain. Their 1980 piece gives much important evidence which is consistent with the

566 / Richard G. Lipsey

POLICY IMPLICATIONS

The public is understandably impatient with economists' ignorance on how to reduce inflation. The ignorance itself is understandable, however, and we should not develop any professional inferiority complexes about it.

We have plenty of historical experience on how to create an inflation. Any economist could create 20 per cent inflation in Canada given nothing more than control of the monetary levers. This is impressive evidence that we do know something. For the first time in modern industrial countries, however, we have tried to eliminate (or at least greatly reduce) an ongoing, entrenched, peacetime inflation. Also, we are trying to do so under much altered institutional settings. For a long time people believed in the dollar standard, in which a dollar was a dollar today and a dollar tomorrow. Rational firms were willing, for example, to make long-term contracts stated in nominal money units. This belief is now completely gone and many accommodating institutional changes have been made.[29] The stabilizing force of belief in an approximately constant price level is gone, and we have little experience of how the economy will actually respond to restrictive measures designed to reduce the inflation rate in these circumstances. Competing paradigms make different predictions. The degree of ignorance, uncertainty and conflict among inflation-control theories today is, I believe, no more than in any other empirical science when a wholly new phenomenon is encountered or a novel experiment is tried which produces unexpected results. Without doubt, five years from now the balance of evidence will be more clearly tilted towards one or another of the theories of how the economy behaves on the downside of inflationary pressures when confidence in the dollar standard is absent. Meanwhile we make educated guesses based on our reading of how well competing models fit the facts already available to us.

---

position I have argued here. I cannot, however, accept their dismissal of demand inflation in the 1970s. At the level at which they are operating the behaviour of the *real* supply of $M1$ tells us nothing about monetary impulses to inflation (for more detail see Courchene, 1981, 240). I find myself also largely in agreement with Courchene's criticism of their discussion of recent policy (1981). Their 1980 book is serious and deserves careful assessment, but in the present state of uncertainty about the policy implications of this work (does Courchene, 1981, give a reasonable or an unreasonable description of their position?) I can only hope that future debate will clarify what I perceive to be the unclear link between their positive analysis and their policy recommendations.

28 In this paper I accept a social policy objective of reducing to a very low level. In practice I am inclined to agree with Tobin (1980, 70) when he writes, ' "Inflation" has become the national obsession, the catchall scapegoat for individual and societal economic difficulties, the symptom that diverts attention from the basic maladies.' But the demand to control inflation clearly exists and as a 'social engineer,' I therefore set myself the task of discovering how to meet this demand.

29 It is difficult to document fully the institutional changes, but a flavour of them can be obtained from Flowers (1978), Hussey (1976, chap. 12), Okun (1975, 381–2), Simmonds (1978) and the *Wall Street Journal* (1974). The main message is that firms have greatly shortened the lag between upward shifts in their cost curves and increases in their quoted prices. An interesting research study is waiting to be done on how this fact affects inflation on the upside and on the downside within the neo-Keynesian paradigm.

The understanding and control of inflation / 567

What would I do in this situation? First, monetary restraint must be maintained. To give in to the clamour to drive down interest rates below their free-market levels would lose control of the money supply, fulfil the sufficient condition for rising inflation, and remove at least one necessary condition for reducing inflation. Further, the Bank of Canada should stop supporting the Canadian dollar and follow the basic monetarist tenet that it must target on the money supply and let interest rates and the exchange rate fall out where they may. This practice, incidentally, would have permitted interest rate to be at least two points lower than they were at the time of writing.

Second, we should continue with the gradualist monetarist experiment of slowly reducing the rate of monetary expansion on the assumption that this is the major requirement for reducing the inflation rate. Indeed, the policy should become less gradual.

We have in Canada today a purely monetarist experiment. The Bank of Canada has met its targets for reduced rates of $M1$ growth quite consistently since 1975. But the winding down has been so gradual that a couple of policy errors, a shift in the demand for money, and a less than perfect ability to control $M1$ have almost swamped the overall effects of the very gradual reduction in the rate of monetary expansion. Many monetarists are thus able to argue quite plausibly that monetarism hasn't yet been tried in Canada (Courchene, 1981). Extremists on either side will never be convinced by evidence. But it would be a tragedy if after, say, seven years of monetarism there was not enough evidence to allow those who wish to learn from experience to take an informed view on the experiment.

Third, the Bank of Canada should get some strong support currently totally absent from fiscal policy. Expenditures could be cut drastically. Then we might be able to restrain demand with means which exert temporary pressure to lower rather than to raise interest rates. Such action might also influence inflationary expectations by persuading people that the government is serious about the anti-inflationary battle. In addition, the government could try to get more control over public sector wage settlements. All current wage settlements give a gloomy outlook for inflation control, but the spectre of public sector wage settlements running well ahead of those in the private sector is highly disturbing. At the same time the government might think about de-indexing that portion of public sector pensions which arise from that portion of contributions made after the de-indexing date. How can the private sector feel the government has a real stake in controlling inflation when the public sector alone has an absolutely secure escape route if control proves impossible?

Finally, the government should understand that if it forces the Bank of Canada to follow a policy of lowering interest rates to the point where control over the money supply is lost, it will have abandoned the fight against inflation. The government should let Governor Bouey stick by his guns. I don't think he will halt inflation on his own, but all major competing paradigms

568 / Richard G. Lipsey

join in predicting that if monetary restraint is abandoned, accelerating inflation will result.

I have no clear way to foresee the future, but if I have to guess, I think the judgment will be that the present monetary policy is not sufficient. I believe that the two Keynesian asymmetries may be operating. Consider first the possible asymmetry between the effect of monetary expansiveness and monetary restraint on aggregate demand. At the outset of the decade Kaldor (1970) predicted that *whatever* the monetary magnitude the central bank tried to control, effective control would lead to institutional innovations which would allow this magnitude to be economized on, because uncontrolled close substitutes would be used instead. The evidence is certainly consistent with Kaldor's view on the endogeneity of monetary institutions (see, e.g., Porter et al. 1979). But we would expect high inflation rates alone to induce financial innovations by increasing the negative yield on $M1$ balances. What we don't yet know is how much of this innovative activity is exogenous to monetary policy (caused by high inflation rates alone) and how much is, as Kaldor predicted, endogenous to monetary policy – a response to tightness of the $M1$ supply.

My guess, however, is that monetary policy will have to be altered to target on some broader monetary magnitude than $M1$. Otherwise, the clear tendency for the Canadian velocity of circulation of $M1$ to rise every year since 1975 will end up with the bank controlling a variable whose magnitude goes to zero and whose velocity goes to infinity. In this respect I agree with Courchene (1979).

Now consider the second and more fundamental Keynesian asymmetry. Keynesians believe that even if monetary restraint does succeed in reducing aggregate demand, the effects will be mainly for output and employment to fall, while substantial reduction in the inflation rate will be slow in coming. So we should not wait forever for the monetarists' long run which may come, according to neo-Keynesian theory, when we are all dead. What if we have to conclude two or three years down the line that gradual monetary restraint of the sort that is feasible in Canada leaves the underlying inflation rate almost unaffected?

One alternative is to induce, à la Margaret Thatcher, a large enough recession to do the job: really fierce restrictive monetary and fiscal policy to sustain a 1930s-style recession long enough to bring the inflation rate down. The neo-Keynesian paradigm is pessimistic on this policy. It predicts that the cumulated loss in output would be very large indeed. For those who, like myself, tentatively accept the neo-Keynesian evidence, this is not the next line of defence but the last desperate measure when all others have been tried and have failed.

To a neo-Keynesian the preferred alternative may be to try some form of incomes policy. I am persuaded that the administrative difficulties for

The understanding and control of inflation | 569

tax-related incomes policies (TIPS) would be fierce.[30] I have been a long-term opponent of wage-price controls. I opposed them in 1975 because the government had not yet tried traditional monetary and fiscal policies (Lipsey, 1976, 39–42) and because I thought it would be an excuse, as it was for two decades in the United Kingdom, for doing little else by way of anti-inflationary policy (Lipsey, 1977a and 1977b). Alone they are clearly not sufficient, and since they do involve major costs, they should not be used as *the* anti-inflationary instrument.

But if present policies do not work, I would be prepared to try controls as a part of a full policy package which I shall outline in a moment. There would of course be constitutional problems and labour's hostility would be understandably strong. The late AIB's philosophy was based on the assumption that because under normal market conditions prices tend to follow wages, the same thing would happen under the abnormal conditions of enforced wage restraint. The AIB had some modest restraining the effect on wages, but that prices did not fully follow wages is a good example of Lucas's warning that the empirical relations of one policy regime cannot be expected to stand up under another policy regime (Lucas, 1976.)[31] It was also predictable on past evidence. For example, in 1976 I wrote, 'There seems to be more evidence of some modest restraining effect on wages than on prices, and, thus, that incomes policies may sometimes be more effective in redistributing incomes from wages to profits than in restraining price inflation' 54). Given past experience, labour's voluntary co-operation will be difficult to obtain, and its enforced adherence should not be asked for unless strong price and profit controls accompany wage control. It should be made clear that the controls are solely an anti-inflationary policy, and we expect to come out of controls with an unchanged distribution of national income between wages and profits.

What, then, is my package?

First, and as its centrepiece, there is a tight monetary policy directed at a monetary magnitude more comprehensive than $M1$. The rate of monetary expansion would be reduced rapidly over two to three years to levels consistent with a very low rate of inflation.

Second, there is increased fiscal restraint. This policy would be partly psychological, since there is not much evidence that current budget deficits are fuelling current inflationary fires. But psychology is an important element of inflationary inertia. The government must be seen to be willing to bear its share of the burden, and some kind of Reaganesque budget-slashing (although without the bias against the poor of Reagan's measures) would be an

30 See, for example, Dildine and Sunley (1978), although President Carter's outgoing Council of Economic Advisors (1981, 60–8) believed that such a scheme was feasible.
31 On the AIB's effect on wages see Auld et al. (1979), Christofides et al. (1979), Fortin and Newton (1980), and Reid (1979, 1980). For the effect on prices see Letourneau (1979) and Wilson and Jump (1979).

570 / Richard G. Lipsey

important part of the package. The government would be saying, 'This time it is an emergency and we are prepared to take drastic fiscal measures rather than use wage-price controls as an excuse for doing nothing else as we did last time.' The reduction of government expenditure would also make possible the tax cuts referred to in the fourth and sixth points below. They would also be key ingredients of the supply-side measures referred to in the fifth point. Finally, they would help monetary policy by putting some modest downward pressure on market rates of interest.

Third, wage-price controls can then be used in an attempt to cut through the inflationary inertias and accomplish what the Keynesian view says the free market cannot easily do – get wage inflation down *rapidly* in line with the much lower inflation rate, which is all that is being validated by monetary and fiscal policy. (We have no experience to tell us how these controls might work as part of a total package, although we have ample experience to tell us that on their own they have no lasting effect on the price level.)

Fourth, once-for-all measures such as cutting indirect taxes which give downward supply-side shocks can also be employed to begin the program and thus lend credence to the view that the policy actually is working.

Fifth, some supply-side incentive measures should also be a part of the package. They will not have a large moderating effect on the current inflation rate, but anything which aids productivity growth will help matters in the future.

Sixth and finally, the package should include some post-controls policy. Post-controls, wage-price guidelines should be used. If they are made consistent with the existing rate of monetary expansion, they may help in forming more reasonable expectations in a world where most employers and employees do not look primarily to monetary factors when forming expectations on the inflation rate. The guidelines may also provide a warning that the reimposition of controls is being risked if the guidelines are seriously breached. A temporary TIP might even follow the removal of controls to be used for two or three years. These measures are designed to attack any upward-bounding of inflationary expectations. Also some supply-side measures should be held in reserve to counter the inevitable burst of structural inflation which will occur when distorted relative prices and wages are adjusted in the post-controls period, leading to a burst of structural, relative-price inflation.

Let me be clear that I am not advocating wage-price controls immediately. But we cannot sit by forever. If within a reasonable period of time monetary restraint does not appear to be having any noticeable effect on the inflation rate, then the next line of defence seems to be a neo-Keynesian package. Let me be clear also that incomes policies are useless (as well as costly) on their own. The package must include tighter monetary and fiscal restraint to ensure that the expansion of aggregate money demand will be consistent with the much lower rate of inflation temporarily brought about by the controls.

The understanding and control of inflation / 571

If this package doesn't work, it is 'back to the drawing board' to design an even more drastic and more costly policy package, but on the principle of one thing at a time, speculation on what that package would be can be left till a later date.

One final word of caution is in order. Even if the policy worked and we found ourselves back to a 3 per cent inflation rate (dare I say 1 or 2 per cent?), there is no guarantee that this level could be sustained. The Keynesian paradigm suggests that once people stop believing in the dollar standard, the inflation rate may tend to show a long-term upward bias. Tobin (1972) gives reasons in the micro behaviour of the economy which are akin to Lipsey's (1960) explanation of the loops around the Phillips curve, to Schultze's structural inflation, and to Keynes's views on the rational origin of the asymmetry between raising the price level and lowering the wage rate. Gray and Lipsey (1974) give further reasons connected with a cycling economy. When the economy cycles around its static natural rate of unemployment, the non-linearity of the short-run Phillips curve implies that the price level rises in booms, while output and employment fall in slumps. Thus if the natural rate is our target in a fluctuating economy, we must expect a rise in the price level over each cycle. As soon as this rise comes to be expected, the cycle may produce more inflation with each cycle, since the boom will be associated with inflation rates above the expected rate and the slump (assuming a nearly horizontal Phillips curve above the natural rate) with inflation rates at the expected level. Finally, I do agree with Barber and McCallum (1980) that some supply-shocks are likely to become endemic over the next few decades and that this development will help to impart an inflationary bias to the world's economies.

However, it is a long time before we will have much evidence on that matter. Meanwhile, if we economists are not to be dismissed as irrelevant, we must be prepared to learn from experience. We cannot sit idly by and advocate old policies long after it is clear that in their present form they cannot do the job within an acceptable time frame. But it also seems to me that caution is required; as one policy is tentatively discredited, we should try the next least costly policy and so on, learning as we go.

These are hard times to be an actor in the economic drama. We can, however, take some consolation in the fact that they are exciting times to be an economist, because the pace of events is willy-nilly testing many forms of our theories.

The Keynesian paradigm seems to me to be alive and well, but it tells a relatively gloomy story about inflation control. Maybe it is wrong.[32] In many ways I hope it is, or at least mistakenly gloomy about inflation. But whether

---

32 One urgent research task for neo-Keynesians who accept the Keynesian asymmetry is to study cases throughout the world where inflation rates have been reduced drastically over relatively short time periods. We learn by exposing our theories to the possibility of refutation by awkward facts. The most exposed and therefore most potentially informative

572 / Richard G. Lipsey

our particular pet theories are right or wrong, we can only try to go on learning
from evidence and alter our theories, rather than defend our preconceptions
in the face of new conflicts between theory and observation.

REFERENCES

Anderson, L.C. and K.M. Carlson (1972) 'An econometric analysis of the relation
    of monetary variables to the behaviour of prices and unemployment.' In *The
    Econometrics of Price Determination* (Washington, D.C.: The Federal Reserve
    System and the SSRC)
Auld, D. et al. (1979) 'The impact of the Anti-Inflation Board on negotiated wage
    settlements.' This JOURNAL 12, 195–213
Bank of Canada (1981) *Annual Report of the Governor to the Minister of Finance and
    Statement of Accounts for the Year 1980* (Ottawa: Bank of Canada)
Barber, C.L. and J.C.P. McCallum (1980) *Unemployment and inflation: the Canadian
    Experience* (Toronto: James Lorimer and the Canadian Institute for Public Policy)
— (1981) 'The failure of monetarism in theory and policy.' *Canadian Public Policy*,
    Supplement, 7, 221–32
Blinder, A. (1979) *Economic Policy and the Great Stagflation* (New York: Academic
    Press)
Blinder, A.S. and R.M. Solow (1974) 'Analytical foundations of fiscal policy.' In *The
    Economics of Public Finance* (Washington: The Brookings Institution)
Cagan, P. (1979) *Persistent Inflation: Historical and Policy Essays* (New York:
    Columbia University Press)
Christofides, L.N. and D.A. Wilton (1979) *Wage Controls in Canada (1975:3–
    1988:2): A Study of Their Impact on Negotiated Base Wage Rates* (Ottawa:
    Ministry of Supply and Services)
Christofides, L.N., R. Swindinsky, and D.A. Wilton (1980a) 'A microeconomic
    analysis of spillovers within the Canadian wage determination process.' *The
    Review of Economics and Statistics* 62, 213–21
— (1980b) 'A microeconometric analysis of the Canadian wage determination
    process.' *Economica* 47, 165–78
Clower, R.W. (1965) 'The Keynesian counter-revolution: a theoretical appraisal.' In
    F.H. Hahn and F.P.R. Brechling, eds, *The Theory of Interest Rates* (London:
    Macmillan)
Cornwall, J. (1981) 'Do we need separate theories of inflation and unemployment?'
    Canadian Public Policy, Supplement, 7, 165–78
Council of Economic Advisors (1981) *Economic Report of the President* (Washington:
    U.S. Government Printing Office)
Courchene, T.J. (1976) *Money, Inflation, and the Bank of Canada* (Montreal: C.D.
    Howe Research Institute)
— (1979) 'On defining and controlling money.' This JOURNAL 12, 604–15
— (1981) 'The attack on monetarism: muddled and misdirected?' *Canadian Public
    Policy*, Supplement, 7, 239–48
Coutts, K., W. Godley, and W. Nordhaus (1978) *Industrial Pricing in the United
    Kingdom* (Cambridge: Cambridge University Press)
Dean, J. (1976) *Statistical Cost Estimation* (Bloomington: Indiana University Press)
Department of Finance (1977) *Economic Review* (Ottawa: Queen's Printer)

---

flank of the neo-Keynesian theory seems to me to be its universal prediction that inflation
will only fall slowly in the face of demand restraint which pushes national income below its
full employment level.

The understanding and control of inflation / 573

Department of Industry, Trade, and Commerce, Micro-Economic Analysis Branch (1980) (Quarterly) *Capital Expenditures Group. Rate of Capacity Utilization: Canada* (Ottawa: Department of Supply and Services)

Dildine, L.L. and E.M. Sunley (1978) 'Administrative problems of tax-based incomes policies.' *Brookings Papers on Economic Activity*, 363–400

Donner, A. (1981) 'Market imbalances may weaken policies.' *Globe and Mail*, Toronto, 8 June, B3

Donner, A. and D. Peters (1979) *The Monetarist Counter-Revolution: A Critique of Canadian Monetary Policy, 1975–1979* (Toronto: Canadian Institute for Economic Policy)

Eaton, B.C. and R.G. Lipsey (1978) 'Freedom of entry and the existence of pure profit.' *Economic Journal* 88, 455–69

— (1977) 'The introduction of space into the neo-classical model of value theory.' In M.J. Artis and A.R. Nobay, eds, *Studies in Modern Economic Analysis*, (Oxford: Basil Blackwell)

Eckstein, O. (1978) *The Great Recession with a Postscript on Stagflation* (New York: North Holland Publishing Company)

— (1981) *Core Inflation* (New Jersey: Englewood Cliffs, Prentice-Hall)

Eckstein, O and D. Wyss (1972) 'Industry Price Equations. In O. Eckstein, ed., *The Econometrics of Price Determination* (Washington, D.C.: Federal Reserve System and the SSRC)

Flowers, J.F. (1978) 'Pricing and payment terms in an inflationary era.' In D.I. Fisher, ed., *Managing in Inflation*, (Ottawa: The Conference Board of Canada)

Fortin, Pierre (1981) A review of *The Monetarist Counter Revolution*. This JOURNAL 14, 358–60

Fortin, Pierre and Newton, K. (1980) 'Labour market tightness and wage inflation in Canada.' Forthcoming in the proceedings volume of a Conference on Labor Market Tightness and Inflation held at the Brookings Institution in November 1980 (Martin N. Bailey, ed)

Fortin, Pierre and L. Phaneuf (1979) 'Why is the unemployment rate so high in Canada?' Mimeograph

Friedman, Milton (1957) *A Theory of the Consumption Function* (Princeton: Princeton University Press)

— (1974) 'A theoretical framework for monetary analysis.' In R.J. Gordon, ed., *Milton Friedman's Monetary Framework* (Chicago: University of Chicago Press)

— (1975a) *Unemployment versus Inflation?* (London: Institute of Economic Affairs)

— (1975b) 'Perspectives on inflation.' *Newsweek* 24 June, 73. Quoted in D.R. Vining Jr and T.C. Elwertowski (1976) 'The Relationship between Relative Prices and the General Price Level.' *American Economic Review* 66, 699–708

Gordon, R.J. (1981) 'Output fluctuations and gradual price adjustment.' *Journal of Economic Literature* 19, 493–530

Gray, M.R. and R.G. Lipsey (1974) 'Is the natural rate of unemployment compatible with a steady rate of inflation?' Queen's University Institute for Economic Research, Discussion Paper no. 147

Hall, R.L. and C.J. Hitch (1939) 'Price theory and business behaviour.' *Oxford Economic Papers* 2, 12–45

Hansen, B. (1970) 'Excess demand, unemployment vacancies, and wages.' *Quarterly Journal of Economics* 84, 1–23

Hultgren, T. (1965) *Costs, Prices and Profits: Their Cyclical Relations* (New York: NBER)

Hussey, D.E. (1976) *Inflation and Business Policy* (London: Longman)

Hutchison, T.W. (1973) 'A review of *Essays in Honour of Lord Robbins*.' *The Economic Journal* 83, 534–5

574 / Richard G. Lipsey

Johnston, J. (1960) *Statistical Cost Analysis* (New York: McGraw-Hill)
Jones, A. (1973) *The Politics of Prices and Incomes: The New Inflation* (Harmonds-worth, England: Penguin)
Kaldor, N. (1970) 'The New Monetarism.' *Lloyds Bank Review*, 97, 1–18
Keynes, J.M. (1936) *The General Theory of Employment, Interest and Money* (London: Macmillan)
Laidler, D. (1970) 'Expectations and the Phillips curve trade off: a commentary.' *Scottish Journal of Political Economy* 23, 55–72
— (1975) *Essays on Money and Inflation* (Manchester: University of Manchester Press)
— (1978) 'Money and money income: an essay on the transmission Mechanism.' *Journal of Monetary Economics* 4, 151–92
— (1981) 'Monetarism: an interpretation and an assessment.' *The Economic Journal* 91, 1–28
Lakatos, I. (1978) *The Methodology of Scientific Research Programes* (Cambridge: Cambridge University Press)
Leijonhufvud (1968) *On Keynesian Economics and the Economics of Keynes* (London: Oxford University Press)
Letourneau, R.S. (1979 *The Impact of the Anti-Inflation Programme: A Framework for Analysis* (Ottawa: the Conference Board of Canada)
Lipsey, R.G. (1960) 'The relation between unemployment and the rate of change of money wage rates in the United Kingdom, 1862–1957: a further analysis.' *Economica* 27, 1–31
— (1965) 'Structural and deficient demand unemployment reconsidered.' In A.M. Ross, ed., *Employment Policy and the Labour Market* (Berkeley: University of California Press)
— (1972) 'The foundations of the theory of national income: an analysis of some fundamental errors.' In M. Preston and B. Corry, eds, *Essays in Honour of Lord Robbins* (London: Weidenfeld and Nicolson)
— (1974) 'The micro underpinnings of the Phillips curve: a reply to Holmes and Smyth.' *Economica* 46, 62–70
— (1976) 'Appendix to the Factum of the Canadian Labour Congress, in the matter concerning the validity of the anti-inflation act' (Supreme Court of Canada), 1–64
— (1977a) 'Control and decontrol.' In *Which Way Ahead?* (Vancouver: The Fraser Institute)
— (1977b) 'Wage-price controls: how to do a lot of harm by trying to do a little good.' *Canadian Public Policy* 3, 1–13
— (1978) 'The place of the Phillips curve in macroeconomic models.' In A.R. Bergstrom et al., eds, *Stability and Inflation* (Chichester, England: Wiley and Sons)
— (1979) 'World Inflation.' *The Economic Record*, 55, 283–96
— (1981) 'Supply-side economics: a survey.' In *Policies for Stagflation: Focus on Supply* (Toronto: Ontario Economic Council, forthcoming)
Lucas, R.E., Jr (1976) 'Econometric policy evaluation: a critique.' *Journal of Monetary Economics* Supplement, 2, 19–46
— (1981) 'Tobin on Monetarism.' *Journal of Economic Literature* 19, 558–67
Mansfield, E. (1975) *Microeconomics: Theory and Applications*. Second ed. (New York: W.W. Norton)
McCallum, B.J. (1980) 'Rational expectations and macroeconomic stabilization policy: an overview.' *Journal of Money, Credit and Banking* 12, 716–46
McCracken, P. et al. (1977) *Towards Full Employment and Price Stability* (Paris: OECD)
Meiselman, D. (1968) 'Comment: is there a meaningful trade-off between inflation and ur employment?' *Journal of Political Economy* 76, 743–50

The understanding and control of inflation / 575

Mitchell, D.J.B. (1980) *Unions, Wages and Inflation* (Washington: the Brookings Institution)

Modigliani, F.C. (1978) 'Discussion of inflation and unemployment in a macroeconomic model by R.C. Fair.' In *After the Phillips Curve: Persistence of High Inflation and High Unemployment* (Boston: Federal Reserve Bank of Boston)

Modigliani, F. and R.E. Brumberg (1954) 'Utility analysis and the Consumption Function.' In K.K. Kurihara, ed., *Post-Keynesian Economics* (New Brunswick, N.J.: Rutgers University Press)

Modigliani, F. and R. Steindel (1977) 'Is a tax rebate an effective tool for stabilization policy?' *Brookings Papers on Economic Activity*, 175–209

Moore, M. (1970) *How Much Price Competition?* (Montreal: McGill-Queen's University Press)

— (1972) 'Stigler on Inflexible Prices.' This JOURNAL 5, 483–93

Mortenson, D.T. (1970) 'A theory of wage and employment dynamics.' In *Microeconomic Foundations of Employment and Inflation Theory* (New York: W.W. Norton) 167–211

Neild, R. (1963) *Pricing and Employment in the Trade Cycle* (Cambridge: Cambridge University Press)

Nordhaus, W. (1982) 'Macroconfusion: the dilemmas of economic policy.' In *Symposium in Honour of Arthur Okun* (Washington: Brookings Institute)

Okun, A.M. (1971) 'The personal tax surcharge and consumer demand.' *Brookings Papers on Economic Activity*, 167–211

— (1975) 'Inflation: its mechanics and welfare costs.' *Brookings Papers on Economic Activity*, 351–401

— (1980) 'Rational-expectations-with-misperceptions as a theory of the business cycle.' *Journal of Money, Credit and Banking* 12, 817–25

— (1981) *Prices and Quantities: A Macroeconomic Analysis* (Washington, D.C.: The Brookings Institution)

Perry, G.L. (1973) 'Capacity in Manufacturing.' *Brookings Papers on Economic Activity*, 701–42

Peters, D.D. and A.W. Donner (1981) 'Monetarism: a costly experiment.' *Canadian Public Policy*, Supplement, 7, 233–8

Phelps, E.S. (1968) 'Money wage dynamics and labor-market equilibrium.' *Journal of Political Economy* 76, 678–711

Phillips, A.W. (1954) 'Stabilization policy in a closed economy.' *Economic Journal* 64, 290–323

— (1956) 'Some notes on the estimation of time-forms of reactions in interdependent dynamic systems.' *Economica* 23, 99–113

— (1958) 'The relation between unemployment and the rate of change of money wage rates in the United Kingdom, 1861–1957.' *Economica* 25, 283–99

Porter, R.D., T.D. Simpson, and E. Mauskopf (1979) 'Financial innovation and the monetary aggregates.' *Brookings Papers on Economic Activity*, 213–29

Reid, Frank (1979) 'The effect of controls on the rate of wage change in Canada.' This JOURNAL 214–27

— (1980) 'Unemployment and inflation: an assessment of Canadian macroeconomic policy.' *Canadian Public Policy* 6, 283–99

Reid, F. and N. Meltz (1979) 'Causes of shifts in the unemployment-vacancy relationship: an empirical analysis for Canada.' *Review of Economics and Statistics* 61, 470–5

Riddell, W.C. (1979) 'The empirical foundations of the Phillips curve: evidence from Canadian wage contract data.' *Econometrica* 47, 1–24

Samuelson, P.A. (1964) *Economics: An Introductory Analysis*. Sixth ed. (New York: McGraw-Hill)

576 / Richard G. Lipsey

Samuelson, P.A. and R.M. Solow (1960) 'Analytical aspects of anti-inflation policy.'
     American Economic Review 50, 177–94
Schultze, C.L. (1959) 'Recent inflation in the United States,' materials prepared in
     connection with Study of Employment, Growth and Price Levels, Joint Economic
     committee (Washington, D.C.: U.S. Government Printing Office)
Simmonds, G.R. (1978) 'A corporate strategy for combatting inflation.' In D.I. Fisher,
     ed., Managing in Inflation (Ottawa: The Conference Board of Canada)
Solow, R. (1979) 'Alternative approaches to macroeconomic theory: a partial view.'
     This JOURNAL 12, 339–54
Springer, W.L. (1975) 'Did the 1968 surcharge really work?' American Economic
     Review 65, 644–59
Stigler, G.J. and J.K. Kindahl (1970) The Behaviour of Industrial Prices (New York:
     NBER)
Tobin, J. (1968) 'Consumption function.' In David L. Sills, ed., International
     Encyclopedia of the Social Sciences (New York: Macmillian)
— (1972) 'Inflation and unemployment.' The American Economic Review 62, 1–18
— (1974) 'Monetary policy in 1974 and beyond.' Brookings Papers on Economic
     Activity, 219–32
— (1975) 'Keynesian models of recession and depression.' American Economic
     Review (Papers and Proceedings) 65, 195–202
— (1980) 'Stabilization policy ten years after.' Brookings Papers on Economic
     Activity, 19–71
— (1981) 'The monetarist counter-revolution today – an appraisal.' The Economic
     Journal 91, 29–42
— (1981a) 'Comment on the paper by Professor Laidler.' The Economic Journal
     91, 56–7
Trevithick, J. (1976) 'Money Wage Inflexibility and the Keynesian Labour Supply
     Function.' Economic Journal 86, 327–32
Walters, A.A. (1963) 'Production and cost functions: an econometric survey.'
     Econometrica 31, 1–66
Wall Street Journal (1974) article on financial innovation, 31 Oct.
Wiles, P.J.D. (1961) Price, Cost and Output. Second ed. (Oxford: Basil Blackwell)
Wilson, T.A. and G.V. Jump (1979) The Influence of the Anti-Inflation Programme on
     Aggregate Wages and Prices (Ottawa: A/B)
Wilton, D.A. (1980) Wage Inflation in Canada 1955–75 (Ottawa: Economic Council
     of Canada)
Wirick, R.G. (1981) 'The battle against inflation: Bank of Canada and its critics.'
     Canadian Public Policy, Supplement, 7, 249–59

[12]

The Economic Journal, **91** *(March 1981)*, 29–42
Printed in Great Britain

THE MONETARIST COUNTER-REVOLUTION
TODAY – AN APPRAISAL

The oft-quoted concluding note of Keynes' *General Theory* sings of the power of 'the ideas of economists and political philosophers, both when they are right and when they are wrong'. 'Practical men', 'madmen in authority', 'civil servants and politicians and even agitators' – all are unconscious 'slaves of some defunct economist' or 'academic scribbler of a few years back'. The power of his own ideas fulfilled his prophecy, and he was right too that 'the gradual encroachment of ideas' 'came not immediately', but 'after a certain interval'. The monetarist counter to his own revolution is another confirmation. But the transmission of ideas to the world of affairs has speeded up, like so many communications in modern society. The insatiable appetite of the media for novelty assures an audience for intellectual revolutionaries who can convey their ideas in plausible and homely language. The monetarist economists and 'scribblers' whose theories are coming to rule the world are by no means defunct.

Another giant of a generation past, Joseph Schumpeter, reassured our profession about its inevitable compound of 'Science and Ideology'.[1] 'Vision or Intuition' guides the observations and interests that motivate our work, and is inherently ideological. Though the economist cannot purge his own scientific work of the ideological bias stemming from his initial vision, Schumpeter was optimistic that the collective intercourse of scientists gradually cumulates the durable truths distilled from successive waves of ideologically contaminated inquiries. He concludes, 'That prescientific cognitive act which is the source of our ideologies is also the prerequisite of our scientific work. No new departure in any science is possible without it. Through it we acquire new material for our scientific endeavours and something to formulate, to defend, to attack. Our stock of facts and tools grows and rejuvenates itself in the process. And so – though we proceed slowly because of our ideologies, we might not proceed at all without them'. Schumpeter's address takes Smith, Marx and Keynes as examples. Following his precedent, I intend nothing pejorative in stressing that monetarism is both science and ideology.

That point was made with characteristic eloquence and perception by Harry Johnson ten years ago in his Ely Lecture to the American Economic Association.[2] He observed that the Keynesian revolution and the monetarist counter-revolution shared characteristics essential for the success of revolutionary theory: a vulnerable orthodoxy to attack and to blame for contemporary economic reverses and policy failures; novel socially relevant conclusions

---

[1] The title of his 1948 Presidential address to the American Economic Association, *American Economic Review* (March 1949), pp. 345–59.
[2] The Keynesian revolution and the monetarist counter-revolution, *American Economic Review* (May 1971), pp. 1–14.

[29]

reached by professionally respectable techniques; focus on the salient economic evil of the era; intellectual and methodological excitement for the most talented young scientists and plenty of applied work for the journeymen. The forms these conditions took in the two cases are pretty obvious: I will not repeat or update Johnson's descriptions.

Johnson's 1970 prediction that monetarism will 'peter out' – the same words as Schumpeter's 1948 judgement of Keynesianism – was premature at best. Today it is interesting to see why. He gave two reasons. One was that the monetarists' Evil, inflation, 'is far less a serious problem than mass unemployment', the Evil of Keynesian ideology. But in the 1970s prevailing professional and lay opinion has not rendered this verdict.

Johnson's second reason was 'that monetarism is seriously inadequate as an approach to monetary theory, judged by prevailing standards of academic economics, and in the course of repairing its intellectual fences and achieving full scientific respectability it will have to compromise irretrievably with its Keynesian opposition'. His indictment made two specific charges. One was 'the abnegation of the restated quantity theory of money from the responsibility of providing a theory of the determination of prices and of output,' i.e. 'for analysing the supply response of the economy to monetary impulses, ... whether monetary changes affected prices or quantities.' The second was 'reliance on the methodology of positive economics', i.e. the appeal to simple reduced-form statistical correlations that do not contradict the theory, without specification of the structural mechanisms that could have produced them. Johnson predicted that to maintain academic respectability, and therefore ultimately public influence, monetarists would have to grapple with hard theoretical and empirical questions, losing in the process their sharp differentiation from mainstream Keynesians and eclectics.

The flaws Johnson detected have not yet proved fatal. The problems remain, but the failure to solve them has never been an embarrassment. To the contrary, it has become a virtue. In the ten-year interim monetarists, instead of being absorbed into a bland and messy synthesis, have pulled the centre of gravity of the profession toward their positions and their methodology. The credit goes to a second wave of monetarism, a second counter-revolution that has absorbed and breathed new life into the first, a movement both more reactionary and more revolutionary than its precursor. I shall return to this development, the new classical macroeconomics, later in my talk. It is very much an academic and intellectual development, and first I want to review the triumphs and trials of monetarism in the public arena since Harry Johnson's lecture.

I. MONETARISM, POLICY, AND PERFORMANCE IN THE 1970S

It is not surprising that the central banking fraternity embraced monetarism. Central bankers feel the need of an orthodoxy to which they can appeal in defence against the pressures of Presidents and Prime Ministers, Congresses and Parliaments. With the gold standard long gone and Bretton Woods moribund, money stock targets – their legitimacy and necessity scientifically attested – became the vehicles of discipline.

In the United States, the Federal Reserve began formulating its policies in these terms in 1970. The monetary oversight Committees in both Houses of Congress, influenced by monetarist staff, insisted on targets for monetary aggregates. These Committees examine the 'Fed' Chairman quarterly and grade him on his marksmanship. Elsewhere in the Capitol other Committees struggle, along with the President's agents, with the budget. The operations are

Table 1

U.S. Monetary Aggregates and Measures of Macroeconomic Performance 1951–1979 Means and Standard Deviations for Selected Periods

| | | Quarterly Changes of Seasonally Adjusted Series at Annual Percentage Rate | | | | | |
| | | Monetary aggregates | | | Macroeconomic outcomes | | |
		Base	M1	M1 B	Real GNP (1972 dollars)	GNP price Deflator	Unemployment rate quarterly average Percentage of Labour Force)
	Means						
(1)	1951:1 to 1960:4	1·71	2·20	n.a.	2·81	2·24	4·55
(2)	1961:1 to 1969:4	5·10	4·14	4·10	4·32	2·79	4·69
(3)	1970:1 to 1979:4	7·97	6·06	6·40	2·94	6·63	6·19
(4)	1951:1 to 1979:4	4·92	4·13	n.a.	3·33	3·92	5·16
	Standard deviations						
(5)	1951:1 to 1960:4	1·80	2·27	n.a.	4·76	2·32	1·28
(6)	1961:1 to 1969:4	1·66	2·40	2·42	2·57	1·68	1·09
(7)	1970:1 to 1979:4	1·36	2·31	2·14	4·50	2·35	1·17
(8)	1951:1 to 1979:4 from grand means, row 4	3·07	2·82	n.a.	4.13	2·91	1·40
(9)	1951:1 to 1979:4 from decade means, rows 1–3	1·62	2·33	n.a.	4.11	2.15	1·19

Note: 1961:1 and 1970:1 were chosen as beginnings of periods with explicitly different macroeconomic policies.

disjoint, in keeping with monetarist premises. That monetary policy should be different with different budgets, that fiscal and monetary policies should be concerted for common macro-economic objectives – these ideas are not effectively entertained.

What have been the results of the monetarist turn in U.S. demand-management policies? Following the reduced-form methodology to which Johnson alluded, we may seek proof of the pudding in the eating. As we all know, real outcomes have been less satisfactory on average than in the two previous decades and less stable than in the 1960s. Inflation has accelerated and its variance has risen too. After a decade without recession, we have suffered three in the last ten years, including the one now in progress. The two most recent recessions are the most severe of post-war history. All three recessions were deliberate acts of policy, especially monetary policy. As Table 1 indicates, there was somewhat greater stability in monetary growth rates in the 1970s, but considerably less stability in the macro variables of real importance. The decade of activist policy, the 1960s, looks better than the years before or after.[1]

Monetarists complain, of course, that the players on the field did not faithfully follow their coaches' game plan. True enough, and quite normal. Neither did Lyndon Johnson follow his 'Keynesian' coaches' game plan when he escalated the Vietnam war without raising taxes in 1966, but the 'New Economics' of the period has not thereby escaped blame for the resulting inflation. The Federal Reserve has not been wholly monetarist since the 1970 conversion. The 'Fed' moved its short-run money growth targets with eyes on national and international economic variables, actual and projected, and did not completely abandon its old strategy of 'leaning against the wind' but not too hard.

The 'Fed's' imperfect marksmanship did not prevent strong swings in demands for money and credit from showing up in money supplies. Sometimes these were 'IS' shocks whose accommodation intensified boom or recession. Sometimes they were 'LM' shocks that, according to William Poole's paradigm[2], should be accommodated. By the same principles, the Fed's corrective responses to errors of marksmanship were sometimes stabilising and sometimes not. Lacking any levers at its operations desk marked M_1 or M_2, the 'Fed' has to control these quantities indirectly, by reference to a related variable it can control. Until recently, this was the market interest rate on overnight interbank loans, 'Federal Funds'. Every month, sometimes more frequently, the Federal Open Market Committee reconsidered its Funds rate target and moved it up or down as thought necessary to return money stocks to the desired track or keep them there.

Monetarists criticised this procedure – pegging nominal interest rates! – for allowing excessive swings in money supplies. The Federal Open Market Committee, the critics said, adjusted the instrumental Funds rate target too little and too late. In October 1979 the Fed surrendered, announcing that henceforth its week-to-week operations would be guided by quantitative targets for bank reserves, subject to broad and adjustable interest rate limits. Unfortunately the short run relation of Ms and MVs to reserve stocks is, as subsequent events illustrate, no tighter than their relation to the Federal Funds rate.

More basic practical difficulties of single-minded monetarism were exemplified in the summer of 1980 by the dilemma of the American central bank. Demand for new bank credit had dwindled, and for the time being the 'Fed's' money growth targets seemed unattainable without short-term rates so low compared to those

---

[1] See also M. N. Baily, 'Stabilisation policy and private economic behaviour,' *Brookings Papers on Economic Activity* (1: 1978), pp. 11–50.

[2] W. Poole, 'Optimal choice of monetary policy instruments in a simple stochastic macro model,' *Quarterly Journal of Economics* (May 1970), pp. 197–216.

on this side of the Atlantic that the dollar would plummet once again. Apparently this pragmatic consideration prevailed over faithful pursuit of the targets.

Though not purely monetarist, demand management policies in the 1970s have been increasingly influenced by monetarist principles and sensitive to monetarist criticisms. Real outcomes have not been good, and might well have been worse if the authorities had followed less compensatory and accommodative policies. The 1970s were tough for demand management of any brand. But monetarists are in a poor position to shift blame to the inflationary legacy of the 1960s, or to OPEC, or to fiscal policies. Their own doctrines – stressing sharp dichotomies between real and monetary shocks, between relative and absolute prices, and between past trends and future expectations – disqualify as vulgar fallacies these popular explanations of inflation and stagflation.

The dismal record has not yet appreciably diminished the appeal of monetarism to central bankers, statesmen, and influential citizens. The doctrine has survived recent economic reverses much better than the so-called New Economics of the early 1960s weathered the failures for which it was, rightly or wrongly, held responsible at the end of that decade. The claim that current travails are the fault of the old orthodoxy, indeed further proof of its errors and dangers, has not lost credibility. Monetarism gains still from poor economic performance. Moreover, the inevitable short-run pro-cyclical elasticity of money supplies gives ready alibis to those monetarists who are not actually running central banks. Having defined policy by stochastic endogenous variables rather than by operationally controllable instruments, monetarist critics can always complain that 'policy' has been too unstable and accommodative. The more wilful deviations of practical central bankers, previously noted, add to the credence of these criticisms.

But there are signs that the honeymoon is coming to an end. The redefinition of monetary aggregates to catch up to financial innovations and substitutions, the persistence of endogenous swings in the aggregates after the authorities abandoned even temporary stabilisation of overnight interest rates, and recent gyrations of other interest rates inspire critical questions even within the naturally loyal financial constituencies of the central bank. As Johnson observed intellectual and operational responses to such questions are bound to impair the appealing simplicity of monetarist doctrine and policy.

II. MONETARISM AS CONSERVATIVE IDEOLOGY

In public political and economic debate, monetarism has become a central part of conservative, that is to say nineteenth-century liberal, ideology. These days the other principal elements are most easily summarised as oppositions to Government: to public operation or regulation of economic activities, to redistributions of income and wealth, to collective consumption and investment, and to budget deficits. 'Supply-side economics' is a more positive theme of contemporary right-wing ideology, stressing tax reductions and deregulation as incentives for work, saving, enterprise and efficiency.

The logical connections of the monetarism of the 1960s to its ideological partners remain obscure. Their unity was less in logic than in the person of Milton Friedman, the powerful and persuasive protagonist of the several ideas. In principle a monetarist could favour big and active government, advocate public interventions to correct market failures, or – like Friedman's Chicago precursor Henry Simons – urge redistribution by progressive taxation.

In principle monetarism provides no support for the traditional and ever-popular conservative warning that deficit spending is inflationary. Monetarist doctrine says that deficits increase aggregate nominal spending only as they lead to increases of money supply. In countries with underdeveloped financial systems, printing money may be the only feasible way to finance deficits. But in countries like the United States and United Kingdom, any linkage must be political choice rather than technical necessity. The allegation that political pressure forces the central bank to monetise deficits has dubious empirical foundation, especially in recent years. Some non-causal correlation between base money growth and deficits will be observed when both move counter-cyclically, money for policy reasons, deficits endogenously.

Monetarists frequently charge deficit spending with 'crowding out' productive private investment. Popular versions of this charge are particularly disingenuous in failing to distinguish cases in which real output is supply-constrained from those in which it is merely money-constrained. In the former cases, any new draft on resources, however financed, is bound to crowd out other uses. Allocational priorities are an important consideration in the mix of monetary and fiscal policies, but judgement about them is not a specifically monetarist issue. In cases of the second kind, to crowd out or not to crowd out is a choice of monetary policy. With employable resources available, deficit-financed demands could be accommodated by money supply to the degree they are not naturally accommodated by velocity.

Professional debate on the macro-economic efficacies of fiscal and monetary policies contains, after all, little ideological excitement. First principles of free enterprise do not say which will be the more effective or useful or hazardous. Both public finance and monetary management are embarrassing exceptions to the ideological rule that competitive pursuit of private interests will handle all society's economic problems. For just that reason many conservatives find the unmanaged gold standard more congenial than the controlled fiat money of the monetarists.

Monetarism is more in tune with the wider ideology in its insistence on stability in macro-economic policy. Activist demand management, 'fine tuning' compensatory counter-cyclical policies – monetarists identify these as the sources of instability in overall economic performance. With stable policies, they say, the economy itself will be stable. Exogenous non-policy shocks, including entrepreneurial expectations and spirits, are assigned comparatively little empirical importance. To those shocks that do occur market adjustments are swift and convergent. Policy variations are more likely to amplify than to dampen natural fluctuations, misallocating resources in the process. The logic of this view applies to all policy instruments, fiscal as well as monetary. Friedman himself so applied it, before he became so exclusively monetarist, in his 'Fiscal and Monetary Framework for Economic Stability'.[1]

This is a more fundamental theme than the technical sovereignty of any monetary aggregate and it is more congenial to free enterprise ideology. It is also the theme of the second wave of the monetarist counter-revolution, the new classical macro-economics. The new doctrine has given a theroetical rationale for propositions that were previously matters of faith and empirical judgement. The grasp of the Invisible Hand is extended beyond micro-economic resource allocation to macro-economic optimality – market competition produces not just a tendency towards long-run optima but a continuous sequence of equilibria. Friedman himself is the link between the old monetarism and the new. The 1968 message of his 'natural rate of unemployment'[2] was that demand management policies can only temporarily alter real economic outcomes, that under stable policies the economy will reach equilibrium employment on its own.

Nevertheless I doubt that the new wave will establish a permanent place for monetarism in conservative ideology. The popular success of monetarism arose along with Inflation, the Evil that could be plausibly blamed on the errors and excesses of the reigning orthodoxy, the Evil for which monetarist rules of policy were the specific remedy. As ideology monetarism profited from the substantial real disappointments of the decade, notably OPEC shocks, because the public identified all personal, national, and worldwide reverses of economic fortune in the 1970s as ravages of Inflation. Professional economists of all schools know that such disappointments and reverses could not be avoided by less accommodative monetary policies, any more than their first-order costs could be escaped by more accommodative policies. Printing money does not produce oil, and neither does not printing it.

There has always been tension between ideological monetarism, which promises to rescue us from Inflation, and theoretical monetarism, which says that Inflation has little or no effect on the real performance of the economy. The tension is accentuated in monetarism mark II, which relies heavily on the neutrality of money, even on super-neutrality, and applies the 'classical dichotomy' to continuously moving equilibrium. The message of the new classical macro-economics is not so much that Keynesian policies do Evil as that they do Nothing. Not quite: an alleged evil is that capricious shifts in policy rules confuse private agents and cause allocational distortions. Whatever its intrinsic merit, this point is not the stuff of ideology; its lay appeal is as limited as that of the 'shoe-leather' costs of economising cash during anticipated inflations.

The tension is likely in time to become a telling weakness in monetarism as conservative ideology, if only because it attenuates the evangelical fervour of leading new classical theorists. In the face of monetarism II, some more old-fashioned conservative economists steadfastly maintain that deficits, debt, easy money, and inflation do serious positive harm.

Both wings can agree on macro-economic policies. It is therefore likely that

[1] *American Economic Review* (June 1948), pp. 265–74.
[2] 'The role of monetary policy', *American Economic Review* (March 1968), pp. 1–17.

the public focus of conservative political economy will shift away from macro concerns to the size of government, regulation, progressive taxation, the welfare state, and related 'supply-side' issues. Government is a currently popular Evil, and probably an easier target than Inflation.

III MONETARISM AS PROFESSIONAL ECONOMICS

I return now to the intellectual inadequacies that Harry Johnson detected in monetarism in 1970. Why have they not proved as damaging as he predicted? How have the monetarists, especially those riding the second wave, handled them? Where does the professional debate between the old Keynesian revolution and the counter-revolution stand today? Johnson mentioned two problems, which I paraphrase as the output-price responses of the economy to variations of monetary demand, and the structure of the process by which measures of monetary control are transmitted to aggregate demand. I shall discuss them in turn.

The 'missing equation': money, output, and prices. 'The supply response of the economy to monetary impulses' is still the central issue, for both theory and policy. A monetary impulse can be regarded as a change, however generated, in the nominal rate of spending on final goods and services – nominal GNP or M times V. The roles of monetary policies and aggregates, fiscal policies, and velocity shocks in determining the path of MV are separable and secondary questions, deferred to the second part of this section. The division of monetary impulses between prices and quantities is the crucial matter today in assessing the real consequences and counter-inflationary prospects of the restrictive macro-economic policies your government and mine are pursuing.

In his 'Theoretical Framework'[1] Friedman referred to this division as the 'missing equation' of short-run models. He claimed that both Keynes and the classics relied on arbitrarily assumed rigidities, at one pole the money wage and at the other aggregate supply. His own candidate, a short-run adjustment equation, was not different in spirit from the wage/price/output mechanisms of mainstream eclectic Keynesian theory and econometrics. These included Okun's Law and Phillips-type equations for money wages and mark-ups, along with competitive pricing in 'flex-price' sectors.

The salient proposition underlying this approach is that labour and product markets in the dominant 'fixprice' sectors are in disequilibrium most of the time. That is, they are characterised by excess supply or demand at existing wages and prices. A large share of short-run adjustment occurs via quantities rather than prices. Wages and prices are insufficiently flexible to keep markets continuously cleared.

The adjustment process itself has not, in general, been successfully described as optimising behaviour, the only paradigm that carries theoretical conviction in our profession. This failure, neither surprising nor discreditable in view of the

[1] 'A theoretical framework for monetary analysis', *Journal of Political Economy* (March/April 1970), pp. 193–238.

intrinsic difficulties of the task, is the root of the chronic crisis in macro-econo-mics.

Monetarism II has not solved this problem, but has evaded it. The new classical macro-economists,[1] bolder than their pre-Keynesian forebears, just assume that product and labour markets are continuously in supply–demand equilibrium. They know and admit, of course, that this is not literally true. But the 'methodology of positive economics' protects them from empirical examina-tion of their premises: let's see, they say in effect, if macroeconomic observations behave 'as if' generated by price-cleared markets.

They further assume, of course, that participants in those markets make future-oriented decisions on the basis of rational expectations of relevant variables, including government policies. The substantive thrust of this impor-tant assumption is to eliminate the inertia that adaptive expectations imparted to earlier models of wage and price adjustments. The implication is that real outcomes will be invariant to anticipated monetary policies, as indeed to any events that do not change real endowments, current and expected.

By defining away the problem of the 'missing equation', the monetarists have escaped the messy grubwork in which Johnson expected them to lose their identity. Thus liberated, Monetarism II mobilises the power of general equili-brium theory and the eager young talent its apparatus naturally attracts.

But the facts of business fluctuations remain, challenging the theorists to explain in their equilibrium terms the cyclical variability of real macro-econo-mic variables. I find neither of the two lines of explanation so far advanced convincing. One is to attribute cyclical swings to basic real data: tastes, technologies, resource endowments. For example, swings in employment could reflect intertemporal choices between leisure and other consumption. Besides being an inherently implausible account of the variations of unemployment of labour and capital capacity since 1946, not to mention pre-war experience, this version of equilibrium theory omits monetary variables altogether.

The second approach attempts to explain the well-documented short-run positive association of nominal prices and real quantities. Superficially this correlation appears to refute the asserted neutrality of monetary policy. Robert Lucas's celebrated reconciliation[2] is that the correlated observations arise wholly from monetary surprises – for example, suppliers mistakenly interpret an economy-wide increase in absolute prices as a rise in their own relative prices. This theory invites two decisive objections. First, it requires, in addition

  [1] The leading protagonists are Robert Lucas, Thomas Sargent, and Robert Barro. See, for example, Lucas and Sargent, 'After Keynesian macroeconomics', in After the Phillips Curve (Federal Reserve Bank of Boston Conference Series 19, June 1978); Lucas, 'Understanding business cycles', in Brunner and Meltzer, eds., Stabilization of the Domestic and International Economy, Journal of Monetary Economics Supplement (1977). T. Sargent and Neil Wallace, 'Rational Expectations, the optimal monetary instru-ment, and the optimal money supply rule,' Journal of Political Economy (April 1975), pp. 241–54. For a critique of these developments see my Jahnsson lectures: Tobin, Asset Accumulation and Economic Activity: Reflections on Contemporary Macroeconomic Theory (London: Blackwell, 1980) chapter 2; also, 'How dead is Keynes?', Economic Inquiry vol. XV, no. 4 (October 1977), pp. 459–68.
  [2] Robert E. Lucas, Jr, 'Econometric testing of the natural rate hypothesis', in Otto Eckstein, ed., The Econometrics of Price Determination Conference, sponsored by the Board of Governors of the Federal Reserve System and the Social Science Research Council (Washington: Federal Reserve System, 1972).

to the basic assumptions of market-clearing and rational expectations, an arbitrary and empirically far-fetched specification of imperfections and asymmetries in the information available to various economic agents, for example sellers and buyers.

Second, the theory fails to account for many observed regularities of cyclical fluctuations. I do not have time to catalogue them here. My dear friend Arthur Okun, in a paper I heard him give only a couple of weeks before his tragic death, gave a thorough and admirable list[1]. These phenomena are quite consistent with the modern Keynesian view, and indeed the old monetarist view as well, that unemployment and idle capacity reflect excess supply in non-cleared markets. They are not consistent with the new classical view.

Inertia of wage and price paths could be attributed either to sluggishness in adaptation of expectations or to institutional rigidities. The rational expectations revolution, discrediting adaptive expectations, has focused the profession's attention on the second source of inertia. Contracts, explicit and implicit, are an obvious institutional rigidity. They are particularly important in United States labour relations, where collective bargaining contracts are made for as long as three years. Workers' concern for relative status is, as Keynes argued, another important factor, again especially in the United States, where collective bargaining is both decentralised and unsynchronised in time. Since contracts do not cover all contingencies, as they would if made by Arrow and Debreu, it is possible for compensatory policies following well-understood rules to be effective for good or ill by responding to macro-economic information that becomes available during the tenure of contracts.

The big policy debate today, certainly in our two countries, concerns the effectiveness and the side effects of a sustained and determined programme of monetary disinflation.[2] Will such a programme succeed in eliminating or significantly reducing our current inflations, and if so how fast? How much damage to real economic variables, employment, output, and investment, will occur in the process? How rapidly will local prices adjust downward if the monetary authorities resolutely refuse to accommodate OPEC boosts and other specific price shocks?

Past experience, including the previous recession and the current one, yields pessimistic answers. In the United States, up to 90 % of reductions in monetary spending for a year goes into output rather than prices. Two or three point-years of extra unemployment bring down the inertial core inflation by only one point.

Monetarists contend that the observations that generated these unpromising estimates of short-run trade-offs were coloured by the expectations of private agents – workers, unions, managements – that compensatory policies would relieve them of the necessity to lower money wages and prices to restore normal employment and sales volumes. Consequently, they contend, disin-

---

[1] A. M. Okun, 'Rational-expectations-with-misperceptions as a theory of the business cycle,' prepared for the American Enterprise Institute Seminar on Rational Expectations (February 1980).

[2] I have discussed the issues at more length in 'Stabilization policy ten years after', *Brookings Papers on Economic Activity* (1:1980), pp. 19–72.

flation will occur much more rapidly, and with much less real transitional damage, if the determination of the authorities to 'stay the course' this time is well advertised and well understood.[1]

This is a highly speculative prospect to bet on. Can such a threat really be credible in a democracy, where governments cannot bind their successors? Perhaps the chances of policy reversal are, and will be perceived to be, less in a Parliamentary system like your own than in our Congressional–Presidential structure. Even if the threat is credible, how will it be read by individual workers, unions, and enterprises? Each group might well prefer to let the rest of the economy do the disinflating, thus making sure that its relative status is protected whatever the other groups do. Unfortunately, monetarist propaganda has undermined the monetarist programme, by spreading the notions that inflation is wholly the responsibility of government and that disinflation can be achieved solely and costlessly by governmental financial reform while private agents conduct business as usual.

The main point is that the experiment is novel, the subjects are national and world economies, and the stakes are very high. For this reason, I personally think it would be only prudent to coordinate monetary disinflation with an incomes policy designed to disinflate nominal income claims at a pace consistent with the deceleration of aggregate monetary demand. A coordinated programme would combine threat with promise – promise that jobs and sales will be maintained and promise that no union or other interest will be going it alone. Given mutual consistency of the policies, wage/price controls would not be trying to hold the lid on a kettle boiling with excess demand. At the end of several transitional years, the inflationary legacy of existing contracts and status comparisons would have been overcome. Both expectations and policies would then support the continuation of less inflationary patterns without controls.

A coordinated programme of this kind presumes that the society enjoys or can reach rough basic consensus on division of the social product. If there is irreconcilable conflict, the society's maladies are deeper than their inflationary symptoms and certainly beyond the reach of any central bank. And it is gratuitously optimistic to think that fundamental distributional conflict can be resolved by shrinking the pie over which the parties are contesting.

Monetarists, of course, fervently oppose controls of any kind, even flexible varieties based on tax penalities or rewards or on the negotiable ration tickets devised by the ever-inventive Abba Lerner.[2] Monetarists commonly say that incomes policies are not sufficient, which is true; they must be accompanied by suitably disinflationary demand management. They commonly say that they were not necessary, which is a highly debatable assertion of faith. They always say they are allocationally inefficient, which is true as far as it goes. But these inefficiencies must be compared with the real costs of recession and stagflation

---

[1] William Fellner, *Towards a Reconstruction of Macroeconomics* (Washington: American Enterprise Institute, 1976).

[2] See Arthur M. Okun and George L. Perry (eds.), *Curing Chronic Inflation* (The Brookings Institution, 1978). For an elegant alternative with the same properties of flexibility, see Abba P. Lerner, 'A wage-increase permit plan to stop inflation,' *Brookings Papers on Economic Activity* (2:1978), pp. 491–505.

resulting from unassisted monetary disinflation. Ultimately, I suspect, monetarist objection to controls is based not on such cost-benefit analysis but on
ideological preference for a 'free' economy however badly it may perform. But
if the monetarist prescription exhausts the public's tolerance of real hardships
without visible abatement of inflation, the reaction will damage not only the
credibility of monetarism and the economy's freedom from controls but also
some more important social values.

Structural modelling of money and monetary policy. The second scientific deficiency
mentioned by Johnson in 1970 was the failure to provide structural models,
either theoretical or econometric. Johnson attributed this failure to excessive
reliance on the 'as if' methodology of positive economics.

For example, Friedman and other monetarists were impatient with requests
to define conceptually the 'money' whose quantity was the alleged fulcrum
of the economy. What properties of liabilities payable in the unit of account are
essentially monetary? What characteristics matter? The identity of the debtor –
government, commercial banks, other intermediaries? The term of the liability
– demand, notice, term? The bearing of nominal interest – zero, otherwise
fixed, market-determined? Transferability and acceptability in transactions?
Safety and predictability of nominal value? Monetarists have preferred not to
hear these questions but to reason in theoretical models 'as if' there were an
unambiguous unique monetary store of value, and to identify as its real world
counterpart whatever aggregate correlated best with nominal GNP. However
persuasive the R^2s of these simple regressions were to laymen, Johnson was right
that neither the theory nor the statistics satisfied the canons of the profession as
of 1970.

On the theoretical side, it seemed to critics, myself included, that monetarists
made quantum leaps from general asset preference theory to special monetarist
propositions. However stable 'the' money demand function may be, equating
it to money supply cannot describe the whole economy if the function contains
more than one endogenous variable. How Friedman and Brunner–Meltzer[1]
could turn multi-asset systems of equations into single equation monetarism
remains a mystery I do not fathom. Nor did Friedman's 'Theoretical Framework', evidently written in belated response to complaints of this genre, provide
a structural model supporting his strong propositions and policy recommendations. Certainly that work has not proved nearly so seminal and influential as
his 'natural rate' Presidential address.

However, on this score too the second wave of the counter-revolution has
saved monetarism from much of the embarrassment and absorption Johnson
foresaw. For example, Barro's revival of the Ricardian theorem[2] of the equivalence of public borrowing and taxation has provided an intellectually tight, if

---

[1] For an exposition of their monetary theory, see K. Brunner and A. Meltzer, 'An aggregate theory
for a closed economy', in J. Stein, ed., *Monetarism* (Amsterdam: North Holland, 1976), ch. 2. Benjamin
Friedman points out that the model does not differ significantly in its structure from other macro
models of asset stocks and flows: B. Friedman, 'The theoretical non-debate about monetarism', in
T. Mayer, ed., *The Structure of Monetarism* (New York: Norton, 1978), pp. 94–112.

[2] Robert Barro, 'Are government bonds net wealth?', *Journal of Political Economy*, vol. 82 (November/
December 1974), pp. 1095–117.

empirically implausible, rationale for monetarist dismissals of the macro-economic importance of fiscal policies. (At the same time, however, it exonerates government borrowing of the charge of crowding out private investment.) On the empirical front, Lucas's critique of econometric policy evaluation[1] has called existing structural models into question, on the ground that their behavioural equations will not be invariant to policy rules and regimes. Given the hazards of *a priori* classification of variables as exogenous or endogenous, Sims and others seek to infer causation from nonstructural systems.[2] So the pseudo-reduced-form empiricism of Monetarism 1 seems less illegitimate now than it did ten years ago. In any event, the question whether money causes income or income money or both is still undecided.

In some respects the new monetarism is as vulnerable to Johnson's objection as the old. Popular rational expectations macro-models, from which strong propositions about policy are derived, are underdeveloped on the financial side. They too neglect to describe the monetary transmission process. They assume a single sovereign M, unspecified as to concept, properties, and measure. They assume it to be directly controllable by the authorities; they do not explicitly relate it to instruments of monetary control, government budgets, or financial institutions and markets. They assume neutralities that would not survive in richer models, which would take account of such phenomena as rigidities of nominal interest rates on currency, deposits, and central bank discounts and as the different wealth and portfolio effects of monetisation of government deficits, central bank open-market operations, credit creation by financial intermediaries, and other money-supply processes. A related mone-tarist oversimplification is the common two-way classification of shocks as monetary or real, ignoring the monetary–real combination in a shock, for example, to the marginal efficiency of capital. These deficiencies are remediable as the new monetarism drops the primitive dogmas of the old, but as Johnson said, the process will involve some loss of distinctive identity.

The synthesis of revolution and counter-revolution that Harry Johnson expected in 1970 has not yet occurred. Instead the gulf has widened, as the advent of Monetarism II prolonged the life of the counter-revolution. I think nonetheless that the synthetic phase of the dialectic is beginning. The synthesis will not be, to the extent that Johnson predicted, the disappearance of mone-tarism into an eclectic neoclassical neo-Keynesian mainstream. The ideas of the second counter-revolution are too distinctive and too powerful to be lost in the shuffle. They are bound to shape whatever orthodoxy emerges. The durable ideas are more methodological than substantive – internally consistent deriva-tion of rational expectations and rational behaviour, embodied in the structural equations of a general equilibrium macro-economic model. These ideas are already being mobilised not just to exalt the Invisible Hand but to explain the

---

[1] Robert E. Lucas, 'Econometric policy evaluation: a critique', in Karl Brunner and Allan H. Meltzer (eds.), *The Phillips Curve and Labor Markets*, Carnegie-Rochester Conference Series on Public Policy, vol. 1 (Amsterdam: North-Holland, 1976), pp. 19–46.
[2] Christopher Sims, 'Macroeconomics and reality', *Econometrica*, (January 1980), pp. 1–48.

42   THE ECONOMIC JOURNAL   [MARCH 1981]

causes and effects of informational imperfections, long-term contracts and other commitments, incompleteness of capital markets, liquidity constraints, and many other phenomena of common observation. As the process bears fruit, Keynesian problems will be interpreted in a new light but will not disappear or be dismissed as theoretical impossibilities. There will be plenty of room for compensatory demand management, both in theoretical models and in real economies, and improved understanding how to use it. As this scientific synthesis proceeds, monetarism will lose the polar simplicity essential to its ideological appeal, which will in any case be eroded by disillusionment with the results of policies identified with monetarism. If I am right in these guesses, Joseph Schumpeter's faith in the fruitful interaction of science and ideology will be once more vindicated.

Yale University   JAMES TOBIN

Date of receipt of final typescript: September 1980

[13]

Cambridge Journal of Economics 1980, **4,** 319–336

The economic consequences of monetarism: a Keynesian view of the British economy 1980–90

Terry Barker*

Distinctively monetarist policy recommendations stem less from theoretical or even empirical findings than from distinctive value judgements. The preferences revealed consistently in those recommendations are for minimising the public sector and for paying a high cost in unemployment to stabilise prices. (James Tobin, 1976, p. 336).

I. Introduction

The British economy is in the throes of probably the deepest recession since the last war and possibly the deepest so far this century. The recession has been generated, at least in part, by deliberate Government policy, as a supposedly temporary by-product of monetarism. This article sets out to measure the lost output and employment which would be incurred by continuing to pursue present policies over the next decade. It does so by comparing the likely outcome for the economy under monetarism, as it has been adopted by the Conservative government, with that under Keynesian policies of demand management aimed at achieving full employment through fiscal expansion.

The consequences of monetarism have been estimated using the Cambridge multi-sectoral dynamic model† of the British economy. This is a structural model which does not impose the assumption of long-run full employment on the results. Indeed it has the property that the automatic forces tending to return the economy to full employment after a disturbance are very weak since it assumes that money wages are inflexible downwards. This is in contrast with monetarist or neo-classical models which usually *assume* full employment in the long-run (and in some extreme models in the short-run as well).

The purpose of present policies is of course to reduce the rate of inflation. The monetarist view is that inflation is purely a monetary phenomenon and originates in government failure to control the money supply. In this view, it is enough to gain this control and the problem is solved.

In contrast, the theoretical position adopted here is that inflation is the result of an administrative process in which industries pass on costs to prices. Cost inflation in turn is attributable to import costs, which are affected by the exchange rate, and wage costs

* Department of Applied Economics, University of Cambridge.
† The Cambridge model MDM is a large scale model of the British economy built by the Cambridge Growth Project to study the structure and prospects of the British economy. The model is described by Barker (1978) and Barker *et al.* (1981). Since it is a co-operative venture, I wish to acknowledge the contributions of the other members of the project.

0309–166X/80/040319 + 18 $02.00/0

320   T. S. Barker

which are determined by wage rates, employment and output. Wage rates are negotiated between trade unions and employers and the outcome depends on actual or expected increases in the cost of living, prospective job security and the desire for some target increase in real earnings. However present levels of unemployment, let alone expected future levels, are such that it is difficult to be precise about the magnitude of their effect on job security and wage bargaining, although not the direction. Unemployment will tend to depress the rate of growth of money wages.

Hence present policies may be expected to work in reducing the rate of wage inflation, not directly through the control of the money supply (which has been defective in any case), but through a high exchange rate and high interest rates which contribute to much higher unemployment. It is the fear of unemployment which may substantially lower rates of wage inflation, not any hypothetical or actual reduction in the money supply.

The approach adopted here is to give monetarist policies the benefit of the doubt as far as their effect on inflation is concerned, and assume that wage inflation is rapidly reduced as unemployment rises. Nominal wage rates are assumed to continue rising however—though at less than 10% per annum—even if unemployment rises to over three million. With this assumption, the consequences of Conservative monetarism *for economic variables except wage inflation* are measured by comparing simulations of the government's medium-term financial strategy (UK Treasury, 1980A) with two alternatives, a high public expenditure scenario with money supply targets but higher interest rates and a low tax scenario in which such targets are abandoned and an incomes policy is successful.

The study shows the enormous potential costs of continuing with monetarist policies for a benefit, the reduction of inflation, which is far from assured and which might well be achieved with alternative policies involving less unemployment but more intervention.

II. The doctrine of monetarism

There are a number of brands of monetarism. The relevant one here is the one espoused by the present British government and made evident in policy statements, interviews, and in budgetary and other economic measures. It is close to the policies advocated by Friedman (1968, 1969, 1977) but has its own distinctive emphasis. At the risk of over simplification the doctrine is as follows.

Money is a unique asset which is held, in the long run, on a predictable and stable ratio to aggregate monetary expenditure. The government gives money its status and controls its supply so that proper control will determine aggregate expenditure. Since in the long run the economy will return to a natural full employment level from any temporary disturbance, monetary control will effectively determine the price level. The lag in this process is variable, with its most likely value between 1 and 2 years. In reducing the rate of inflation by this mechanism, some costs of adjustment are manifested as unemployment. But these costs will be reduced the more rapidly trade unions and workers adjust their expectations and accept lower wage increases.

The doctrine has already been superseded in monetarist literature with the 'new classical economics' (Sargent, 1976) which is yet more extreme, denying even the possibility of short-term involuntary unemployment.

The doctrine involves many theoretical problems as well as practical problems of implementation. The theoretical problems centre upon the substitutability of money, the failure of markets to clear through price changes and the way expectations are formed—the very issues Keynes examined in the *General Theory*. The new classical economics has already provoked an impressive reaction from Keynesians. The reaction revives many of the arguments of the 1930s—and provides a case which applies to the British official version of monetarism as well as to the more sophisticated version to-which it is directed.†

However the purpose of this paper is not to pursue these lines of criticism but to examine the consequences of accepting the doctrine as a basis for policy. Here the practical problems of implementation come to the forefront. The British government's version of monetarism as a practical policy has the following additional features (again at the risk of over-simplification).

Inflation is brought down by controlling the money supply measured by sterling M3, whose rate of increase is to be steadily reduced over a 4-year period. The exchange rate must be allowed to float or M3 will go out of control via purchases and sales of sterling by the Exchange Equalisation Account. The only sure way of controlling M3 in the long-term, without unacceptable rates of interest, is for the government to reduce the public sector borrowing requirement (PSBR). If it does this then it will need to borrow less from the private sector and the rest of the world and so will be able to reduce the rate of interest. With a commitment to reduce the tax burden, the only way of reducing the PSBR is to reduce public expenditure.

It is this doctrine which is manifested in the Public Expenditure White Paper and the Financial Statement and Budget Report (UK Treasury, 1980A, B). It is a mixture of monetarist theory, practical implementation and political judgement.‡

The dilution of pure monetarism can be seen in the emphasis placed on reducing the PSBR in official policy. As long as monetary targets are reached, there seems to be no strict monetarist reason why the PSBR should be reduced via expenditure cuts rather than tax increases or indeed why the PSBR should be reduced at all. Of course reduction in the PSBR does make it easier to reduce the growth in money supply. And there is a considerable literature on 'crowding out' (e.g. Stein, 1977) where it is argued that public expenditure will pre-empt private expenditure by forcing up interest rates and making credit less available. Furthermore much play has been made of lower taxes improving incentives and raising employment (Eltis, 1980).

Particular weaknesses in the authorities' control of the money supply have been exposed in the literature. The money supply is difficult to define and there is a low correlation between different measures of 'money' (Smith, 1978); the methods of control are unpredictable in their effect (Savage, 1979, 1980) since the money supply is not determined by fiat as is an income tax rate; and there is the phenomenon that attempts to control one part of the monetary system tend to be undermined by developments elsewhere. All this is demonstrated by the successive attempts by British governments to extend and reform the system of control, the next possible reforms being previewed in the Green Paper (UK Treasury, 1980C).

† One of the most cogent theoretical critiques is by Tobin (1980); others are by Modigliani (1979) putting the case for stabilisation policies, Akerlof (1979) and Solow (1980) emphasising the weakness of the monetarist theory of employment. The 'rational expectations' argument for the ineffectiveness of fiscal policy assumes that first the monetarist model is the true one and second that economic agents have full information (B. Friedman, 1979). Neither assumption is necessarily correct. (See also Buiter, 1980.)

‡ For an excellent comprehensive critique of the policy, the reader is referred to Kaldor's Minutes of evidence to the House of Commons Treasury and Civil Service Committee (1980), part of which is published in a revised form in this journal.

322   **T. S. Barker**

At a more general level, the arguments linking the money supply closely to the PSBR, postulating the existence of 'crowding out' and recommending tax cuts for their incentive effects 'are not readily supported by the facts' (Jackson, 1980). Monetarism as practised in the UK is more of an act of faith than a well-supported empirical judgement of appropriate policy.

III. A Keynesian view

There are many claims to the label of Keynesian. Here it is taken to define views, models, policy prescriptions and theories in which there is a central role for stabilisation or demand management to maintain full employment, certainly in the short-run and possibly in the long-run as well.

The Cambridge multisectoral dynamic model is Keynesian in this sense. The effective demand for domestic output from consumption, investment or exports is not necessarily sufficient to employ all those seeking to work at the ruling wage rates. If unemployment is generated in the model, it does not automatically reduce the rate of growth of money wages. (Indeed in the projections it is usually assumed that there is a floor to wage inflation of 7% per annum, no matter how high unemployment.)

Lower rates of inflation do increase effective demand in the model through a wealth effect in the consumption function, and through the real trade balance, always provided that the exchange rate does not appreciate to compensate. There are further increases in effective demand through the automatic stabilisers of unemployment benefits and social security payments. However these increases are not necessarily sufficient in principle nor, under policies severely restricting government expenditure, in practice, to offset a growth in effective demand for labour which is less than the expected growth in supply. Unemployment in the model can easily rise to three million and does so by 1983 in one of the scenarios presented below, the high level lasting to the end of the decade. Demand expansion is therefore required to reach full employment.

The monetarist position is that though unemployment will result from the initial reduction in monetary growth, it will be temporary. And the more quickly those setting wage rates and prices adjust to lower monetary growth the more quickly will the real economy move back to full employment. This is the theory, but the structural mechanisms by which this is to happen are less clear.

Two such mechanisms by which the economy moves to full employment are suggested by the official monetarists (UK Treasury, 1980D). The first is that the 'volume of expenditure and output will be able to recover as the real value of the private sector's holdings of money and other financial assets fixed in money terms will be restored' (p. 4). Certainly it is *able* to recover, but is it likely to recover via this mechanism? And what does the statement mean? In the Cambridge model, and indeed in the Treasury's own model (1980E, p. 11.1), consumers' expenditure responds to the cumulated real value of personal wealth, which will increase if the consumer price index rises more slowly. This is presumably the reflationary possibility implied in the Treasury statement, because investment studies have so far revealed no systematic influences of inflation on investment (Savage, 1978). (Indeed, such influences are seldom even considered, let alone measured.)

The wealth effect in the Cambridge model suggests that each 1 percentage point fall in consumer prices raises consumers' expenditure by 0·30%. This is certainly worth taking into account, but even if inflation fell 10 percentage points it is just about enough to compensate for the effect on consumption of reductions in government spending proposed for 1980–83.

The other mechanism identified in the Treasury's paper is that 'the slower growth in costs and prices will also gradually reverse any loss of competitiveness of UK industry in relation to overseas competitors which occurred as a result of the exchange rate floating upwards' (UK Treasury, 1980D, p. 4). This is hard to believe under a free exchange rate policy. First the inflation rates of UK competitors have been much less than that of the UK, so that the slower growth of costs has to compensate for this as well as for the appreciation of the exchange rate. Second, the exchange rate may well appreciate further in response to declining UK inflation, so that there is no net effect on UK export prices measured in foreign currency. Third, the exchange rate is high as a result not only of monetarist policy, but also of North Sea oil production and reserves. Starting from the position in mid-1980, UK wage rates would have to *fall in nominal terms* by at least 40% just to restore UK cost competitiveness to its 1978 level. Any fall at all seems out of the question.

In summary, when the structural details of the mechanism are examined, it becomes clear that neither of the influences expected by the monetarists to restore full employment is sufficient to do so.

The treatment of the exchange rate and the interest rate in the Cambridge model is Keynesian in that each price is seen to be fixed in a highly speculative market and that such prices are certainly not those which will automatically ensure full employment of resources.

The floating exchange rate is determined by current and capital flows on the balance of payments. The current flows are expected to go into chronic surplus during the present domestic recession with reduced imports combined with increased net exports of oil being more than sufficient to offset reductions in exports due to the world recession and higher relative prices. Capital flows respond to expected movements in the exchange rate and to interest rate differentials between the principal world financial centres. Other things being equal a higher interest rate differential will raise the exchange rate but the effect of expectations is much less easy to predict. In the face of such difficulties the model treats the exchange rate as given in relation to a given path of interest rates, relative inflation and the current balance of payments such that higher interest rates or lower inflation or higher balance of payments surpluses are associated with a higher exchange rate.

Interest rates are assumed to be determined by government policy through its borrowing requirement, its funding policy and its influence on market expectations. Normally a higher borrowing requirement financed by bond issue will require a higher rate of interest to persuade the private sector to hold the additional debt instead of other financial instruments, but the extent of the increase depends on the extra savings ensuing when the government spends more or taxes less and the willingness of overseas institutions to take up extra British securities. Again the model takes the rate of interest as an exogenous variable, to be set in relation to the exchange rate assumption and the outcome of the projection for the PSBR.

The purchasing power parity theory of exchange rates and the law of one price invoked by the monetarists is firmly rejected in this treatment. UK import prices and export prices are both partly determined by domestic costs as well as world prices in

324   T. S. Barker

the model† and the exchange rate is not necessarily at that level which would keep British output competitive at full employment. Indeed to a large extent the expectations of the speculators leading to a high exchange rate are self-fulfilling, particularly under monetarist policies in an oil economy where oil output is fixed: the high rate exacerbates any depression which in turn raises the associated balance of payments surplus; this extra surplus exerts further upward pressure on the exchange rate, deepening the depression.

There is a strong case for management of the exchange rate, using the reserves and inter-government loans and borrowing to achieve an exchange rate consistent with full employment. In this event monetary policy would have to become much more flexible than it is. One proposal, which is in fact fully consistent with the government's policies, would be the introduction of a tax on interest payments to foreign holders of sterling debt. This would disengage the domestic interest rate from the exchange rate: it would allow the pursuit of a tight monetary policy, while permitting the reduction of the exchange rate.

IV. Monetarism versus demand management: some scenarios

To return to the original question: What are the economic consequences of the pursuit of monetarist doctrine? In order to give an answer, some credible alternative policy must be stated. Two alternatives are explored here. The first is the kind of monetarism which the last Labour government might have pursued if it had been returned to office. Money supply targets are formulated and achieved while public expenditure is increased and the PSBR contained by keeping tax rates at a high level. This is modelled by assuming that public expenditure rises in line with the 1979 White Paper plans (Cmnd 7439). This could give rise to a higher PSBR than current policies and presumably higher longer-term interest rates in order to reach a given money supply target.

The second alternative is one in which monetarism is jettisoned in favour of a return to demand management policies coupled with a fixed exchange rate. This would entail a deliberately-induced increase in the PSBR during the recession by means of tax cuts. This is orthodox Keynesian deficit-financing with a difference: instead of being increased, public expenditure would continue to be squeezed as planned. The short-term increase in PSBR is assumed to arise entirely from substantial cuts in income tax rates.

Table 1 shows a few characteristics of present official monetarism and its alternatives.

Table 1. *Some characteristics of monetarism and demand management*

	Monetarism		Demand Management	
	'Conservative'	'Labour'	'Conservative'	'Labour'
Control of the money supply	Yes	Yes	No	No
Control of the rate of interest	No	No	Yes	Yes
PSBR	Reduced via expenditure cuts	Reduced via tax increases	Increased via tax cuts	Increased via expenditure increases
Exchange rate	Floating	Floating	Fixed	Fixed
Incomes policy	No	Yes	Yes	Yes

† For an empirical analysis of the law of one price as it applies to UK export prices see Ormerod (1980). This study confirms the influence of domestic costs on export prices.

The policies are of course far more complicated than these caricatures and the table is intended only as a set of labels. A third alternative is shown for completeness in the last column of the table, 'Labour' demand management characterised by a higher PSBR induced by extra short-term public expenditure. This alternative is not considered further, being ruled out as too unlikely in the near future.

One point which the table brings out is that policies of monetarism and of a reduction in the public sector can be separately distinguished. Although the two policies are being pursued together as a policy package at present, there is no reason why the public sector should not be reduced in size whilst at the same time demand management policies increase the PSBR through tax cuts.

The consequences of the alternative policies have been measured against a recent forecast,† taken as a standard for comparison. Henceforth the MDM projection with the government's medium-term financial strategy is labelled as MTFS and taken as the 'Conservative' monetarist view. The important Keynesian assumptions discussed in Section III above for this and the other alternatives are quantified and compared with those of the standard projection in Table 2. In the projections with lower unemployment and a lower exchange rate, wage inflation is correspondingly higher and in the projections with higher PSBR, the rate of interest is also higher. In the projections which would otherwise show a worsened balance of payments, the exchange rate is depreciated. Note that in the two alternatives to present policies, in which unemployment is substantially less, some form of permanent incomes policy is assumed such that the rate of wage inflation is given.

The credibility of all these assumptions should be judged partly from their outcome in the simulations. For example in all the projections, the balance of trade and payments is very similar 1981–86. Thus there would be little pressure from the current flows of the balance of payments for a rate of exchange different from that assumed. Another outcome is the rate of increase of real incomes. In both the alternatives to monetarism, real incomes grow appreciably faster (2% per annum 1980–90 for the low tax view, 1·45% per annum for the higher expenditure view). Thus real wage targets will be wholly or partly reached in these views and the pressures to break any incomes policy will be correspondingly weaker.

The medium-term financial strategy (MTFS)

Although the economy is expected to be in recession for the next few years, the MTFS incorporates planned reductions in public expenditure and a deflationary fiscal stance which is unprecedented since the 1931 measures introduced by the National Government under Ramsey MacDonald. This is indeed a counter-revolution to Keynesian demand management. The government is adding a further deflationary squeeze at a time when the economy is expected to go into recession anyway because of the high exchange rate and slow-down in world trade.

The MTFS is very similar to the standard projection except that the latter assumes higher public expenditures on the grounds that either the authorities may not be able to achieve the cuts planned or some relaxation of the plans may occur if they do have the severe consequences expected here.

† This forecast is provided by Cambridge Econometrics which uses MDM to provide regular projections of the economy over the next ten years. Details of the forecast, CEISS8, were presented at a conference on Industry, Energy and the Economy, at Christ's College, Cambridge, June 1980 and are available on request.

Higher government expenditure

If government expenditure followed the last government's plans, increases would have taken place in each year 1980–83. This would have required more borrowing and a higher interest rate and so the rates in the model have been raised by 40% over the medium-term in order to achieve the money supply targets. The higher spending implies higher balance of payments deficits, so the exchange rate is depreciated. The worsened inflationary prospects are exacerbated by the assumption of higher wage increases, at least over the period 1981–83. In this projection, the rate of increase in government expenditure has been reduced in later years to slow down output growth and prevent the balance of trade going into serious deficit.

Table 2. *The alternative policy scenarios*

		Standard projection	'Conservative' monetarism or MTFS	'Labour' monetarism or higher government expenditure	'Conservative' demand-management or lower tax rates
Public	1980	0·9	0·2	0·2	0·9
expenditure	1981	−0·8	−1·5	0·8	−0·8
(% pa)	1982	0·8	−2·1	1·5	−2·8
	1983	1·0	−1·0	1·7	−1·9
	1984–90	1·4	1·7	1·4	1·7
Income tax,	1980	29			29
standard rate	1981	30	See	See	26
(%)	1982	28	standard	standard	21
	1983	25	projection	projection	20
	1984–90	25			20
Average	1980	18·9		18·9	18·9
wage (% pa)	1981	15·8	See	19·3	19·3
	1982	11·8	standard	15·0	15·0
	1983	9·7	projection	12·8	12·8
	1984–90	9·2		9·2	9·2
Rate of interest	1980	14·2		14·2	14·2
(industrial	1981	12·7	See	15·2	15·2
debentures	1982	10·4	standard	13·5	13·5
%)	1983	9·8	projection	13·7	13·7
	....				
	1990	9·3		12·9	12·9
Exchange	1980	2·20		2·11	2·11
rate	1981	2·17	See	2·02	2·02
($s per £)	1982	2·15	standard	1·91	1·91
	1983	2·07	projection	1·76	1·76
	....				
	1990	1·88		1·60	1·60

Lower tax rates

The demand management policy is one where the standard rate of income tax is reduced to 25% in the 1981 Budget and 20% in the 1982 Budget with comparable reductions in the higher rates. The low rates are then held through the decade. In order to pay for this huge reduction, the proposed public spending cuts (UK Treasury,

1980B) are assumed to be fully implemented, but with a lag. The departure from monetarist 'discipline' and the higher prospective trade deficits will undoubtedly provoke reactions in the same direction as the high government expenditure scenario. The same assumptions as shown in Table 2 have been made for convenience and in the absence of much knowledge about the exact magnitude of such reactions.

V. Policy alternatives and the economy

Public sector finances
Figure 1 shows the PSBR as a percentage of GDP at factor cost for the policy alternatives. It also shows the official estimate as published in the Budget documents which falls to about 1·5% in 1983–84. This is appreciably smaller than the results given by putting the assumptions of the MTFS into our model, which is not surprising since the official assumptions about growth (on average 1% per annum 1980–84) are much more optimistic. The notable feature of the MTFS and standard projections is that the PSBR falls relative to GDP throughout the recession. This is the Government's aim,† but it is counter to some monetarist advice. The other scenarios show the ratio rising as the recession deepens then falling with the recovery. The low tax projection provides an exact counter-cyclical pattern 1980–84.

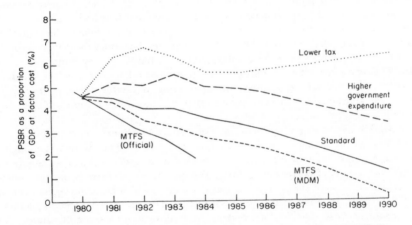

Fig. 1. *The public sector borrowing requirement (PSBR) in the policy scenarios, UK 1980–90*

† Official statements have shown some movement on this point. The November 1980 expenditure plans stated that 'Government borrowing must . . . be firmly controlled' (UK Treasury, 1979, p. 1) and this was followed by the 1980 Budget Report that 'the Budget is intended to achieve a real level of public sector borrowing in 1980–81 significantly lower than in 1979–80' (1980A, p. 3). This was at the same time as GDP was predicted to fall by 2½% 1979 to 1980 (p. 25). However the July Progress Report (1980D, p. 4) says that 'A reduction in the PSBR as a proportion of national output over the next few years is a crucial element in the Government's strategy . . . In any particular year, there is some scope for varying the mix of PSBR and interest rates consistent with a given target for the money stock.' In fact such is the depth of the depression and the weakness of the government's control over public spending, that the PSBR may well rise in 1980–81 over 1979–80 both in nominal terms and as a proportion of GDP.

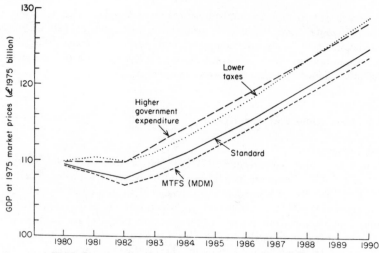

Fig. 2. *Gross domestic product (GDP) in the policy scenarios, UK 1980–90*

Figure 2 shows the GDP implications of the policies 1980–90. They all have the same long-term growth, about 2% per annum, but the main alternatives to present policies hold the economy stationary 1980–82, rather than depressing it further after the 1980 recession. These affect public sector finances because the higher levels of activity mean more tax revenue and lower expenditure on unemployment benefits.

The effects of the policies on the details of the public sector finances are given in Table 3. Here the whole of the public sector is analysed including the public corporations which are planned to make a substantial contribution to any reduction in the PSBR. The figures are all in current prices, expressed as differences from the standard projection. The general expectations in interpreting this table are first that more employment and activity will raise tax revenues and second that more inflation will raise costs as well as revenue.

The MFTS, by sticking to government expenditure plans, reduces expenditure but half or more of the saving is lost by reductions in tax and other revenue. The higher expenditure projection expands activity so much that current revenue rises to pay for current expenditure. However part of the expansion comes from extra public investment (the second last row of the table) and this extra cost, which is mainly investment in dwellings, results in additional public borrowing. The low tax projection increases activity sufficiently so that the total revenue from all taxes increases quite sharply (by nearly £5 billion in 1984). Income tax revenue is nevertheless reduced, the cut in tax rates not being totally offset by the increases in the income tax base. The higher inflation in this projection coupled with the higher debt interest payments mean that expenditure is above revenue and again public borrowing must rise.

Unemployment and the balance of trade
Figure 3 shows unemployment in the scenarios from 1980 to 1990. All the projections show unemployment rising until 1982, but with higher government expenditure (and an assumed *pro rata* increase in government employment) unemployment peaks at two million before declining at first very slowly and then rapidly at the end of the

Table 3. *Public sector incomes and expenditures in the policy scenarios, UK 1980–1984 (£ billion differences from standard projection)*

Flow	Medium-term financial strategy[a]					Higher government expenditure					Lower taxation				
	1980	1981	1982	1983	1984	1980	1981	1982	1983	1984	1980	1981	1982	1983	1984
Incomes															
Gross trading profits	—	—	—	—	—	0·1	0·4	1·0	1·8	2·1	0·1	0·5	1·1	1·9	2·2
Income tax	-0·1	-0·1	-0·4	-0·6	-0·7	-0·1	0·8	1·9	3·1	4·5	—	-2·8	-6·0	-4·1	-3·7
Other taxes	-0·1	-0·2	-0·7	-1·1	-1·3	—	1·8	4·0	6·9	9·2	0·3	2·3	4·3	6·3	8·5
Other income	-0·1	-0·2	-0·5	-0·8	-0·9	0·2	1·4	2·7	4·1	4·6	0·1	1·4	2·2	3·0	3·3
Total income	-0·2	-0·5	-1·6	-2·6	-2·9	0·2	4·5	9·6	15·8	20·4	0·4	1·3	1·6	7·1	10·3
Current Expenditures															
Goods and services	-0·4	-0·8	-2·6	-4·2	-4·7	-0·1	2·2	4·9	8·2	10·0	0·2	1·8	1·6	2·0	3·0
Transfers (net)	—	—	0·2	0·3	0·2	0·2	1·0	2·4	4·1	4·9	0·2	0·9	2·2	4·2	5·0
Subsidies	—	—	-0·1	-0·2	-0·3	—	0·2	0·4	0·7	0·9	—	0·2	0·3	0·4	0·5
Debt interest (gross)	—	—	-0·1	-0·2	-0·4	0·1	1·6	2·4	3·7	4·7	—	1·7	2·9	5·1	7·0
Total expenditure	-0·3	-0·8	-2·6	-4·3	-5·2	0·1	5·1	10·2	16·7	20·3	0·4	4·5	7·0	11·7	15·6
Current savings	0·1	0·3	1·0	1·8	2·2	0·1	-0·6	-0·5	-0·9	-0·1	0·2	-3·2	-5·4	-4·6	-5·2
Investment	—	—	—	-0·1	-0·1	0·1	1·0	2·4	4·0	5·2	0·2	0·5	1·2	2·1	1·7
NAFA[b]	0·1	0·3	1·1	1·9	2·3	—	-1·6	-2·9	-4·9	-5·2	-0·2	-3·7	-6·4	-6·7	-6·9

[a] These are the projections of MDM using assumptions derived from the Public Expenditure White Paper and the Financial Statement and Budget Report (UK Treasury, 1980A and B).
[b] Net Acquisition of Financial Assets, equals public sector financial balance.

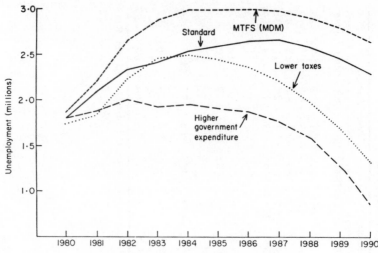

Fig. 3. *Unemployment in the policy scenarios, UK 1980–90*

decade. Reflation through tax cuts is considerably less employment intensive and unemployment soon rises to about half a million more than with higher government expenditure. Until 1984 this lower tax projection is similar to the standard because the extra employment from higher consumption in the former is balanced by that from higher government expenditure in the latter. The MFTS view is decidedly more pessimistic about unemployment which rises to about three million in 1984 and without further reflation stays at that level.

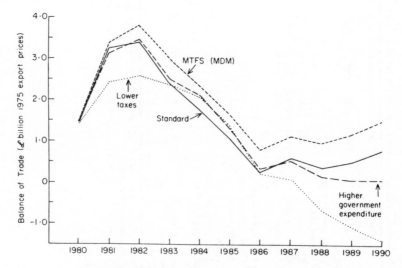

Fig. 4. *The balance of trade in the policy scenarios, UK 1980–90*

Table 4. *The use of resources in the policy scenarios*

	Consumers' expenditure	Government consumption	Gross fixed investment	Stock building	Exports of goods and services	Imports of goods and services	GDP at market prices
(£ billion 1975 prices)							
1979	69·4	24·0	20·0	1·9	32·7	35·1	112·8
(% per annum)							
1974	−2·3	1·4	−2·3	—	7·0	1·0	−1·5
1975	−0·8	6·1	−0·4	—	−2·4	−7·2	−0·9
1976	0·2	1·9	0·3	—	9·1	4·2	3·7
1977	−1·3	−1·0	−2·1	—	6·6	1·0	1·3
1978	5·5	2·0	1·9	—	1·9	3·7	3·1
1979	4·1	1·1	−2·7	—	2·0	11·0	0·1
Standard projection							
1980	−1·9	0·9	−7·8	—	−2·3	−5·5	−3·2
1981	−1·6	−0·8	−2·5	—	−0·5	−5·3	−0·9
1982	0·7	0·8	−4·6	—	0·1	1·5	−0·7
1983	3·3	1·0	−1·8	—	0·7	4·8	1·5
1984	1·5	1·7	8·4	—	1·7	5·4	1·6
1985	1·8	1·0	5·6	—	3·1	5·8	1·8
1986	1·9	1·0	4·0	—	3·9	5·3	1·8
1987	1·7	1·0	2·0	—	5·6	4·1	2·0
1988	1·6	1·7	2·2	—	5·5	4·6	2·1
1989	1·4	1·7	1·7	—	6·0	4·2	2·1
1990	1·2	1·7	1·6	—	6·2	4·1	2·0
Medium term financial strategy (MDM)							
1980	−2·0	0·2	−7·8	—	−2·3	−5·7	−3·3
1981	−1·7	−1·5	−2·5	—	−0·4	−5·5	−1·0
1982	0·4	−2·1	−4·7	—	0·2	0·7	−1·3
1983	3·0	−1·0	−2·2	—	0·8	4·2	1·1
1984	1·5	1·7	8·8	—	1·9	5·6	1·7
1985	1·8	1·7	5·8	—	3·2	6·0	2·0
1986	1·9	1·7	4·1	—	3·9	5·5	1·9
1987	1·7	1·7	2·1	—	5·6	4·2	2·1
1988	1·5	1·7	2·2	—	5·5	4·5	2·0
1989	1·2	1·7	1·6	—	6·0	4·1	2·0
1990	1·2	1·7	1·5	—	6·2	4·1	2·0
Higher government expenditure							
1980	−2·3	0·2	−7·4	—	−1·1	−6·2	−2·9
1981	−1·1	0·8	−1·0	—	0·8	−3·8	0·1
1982	0·5	1·5	−3·0	—	1·6	1·8	−0·1
1983	3·2	1·7	−0·2	—	2·1	5·4	2·2
1984	2·0	1·7	8·7	—	2·2	5·8	2·0
1985	2·5	1·0	5·6	—	3·1	6·3	2·1
1986	2·4	1·0	3·3	—	3·6	5·3	1·3
1987	2·1	1·0	1·4	—	5·1	4·1	2·0
1988	1·9	1·0	1·8	—	5·0	4·6	1·9
1989	1·7	1·7	1·5	—	5·4	4·3	2·0
1990	1·5	1·7	1·4	—	5·4	4·2	1·9
Lower income tax							
1980	−2·2	0·9	−7·4	—	−1·1	−6·0	−2·8
1981	1·6	−0·8	−1·7	—	0·6	−1·9	0·5
1982	2·0	−2·8	−3·7	—	1·6	2·3	−0·4
1983	1·9	−1·8	−1·6	—	2·5	3·1	1·1
1984	2·1	1·7	5·8	—	2·7	5·7	1·8
1985	2·7	1·7	3·7	—	3·4	6·1	2·1
1986	2·8	1·7	3·5	—	3·6	5·8	2·1
1987	2·6	1·7	2·1	—	5·1	5·8	2·3
1988	2·5	1·7	2·5	—	5·0	5·4	2·3
1989	2·2	1·7	2·1	—	5·4	4·9	2·2
1990	2·1	1·7	1·9	—	5·5	4·8	2·2

Sources: UK Central Statistical Office, *National Income and Expenditure*, 1979 and Cambridge Econometrics.

Figure 4 shows the balance of trade. The exchange rate has been deliberately manipulated so that the balance is similar in all projections for 1983–86. In the earlier period the lower tax projection, with its high consumer imports, has a significantly lower trade surplus. The same projection has a deteriorating trade balance towards the end of the period, indicating that some increase in taxation or further depreciation of sterling may be necessary. In any case the implications for the balance of trade are sufficiently similar for all the views to be feasible ones.

The use of resources and 'crowding out'

Table 4 shows the use of resources in the standard projection and the three policy alternatives expressed as annual changes in the expenditure components of GDP. Both higher government expenditure and lower taxes prevent the decline in GDP 1981–83 which is a notable feature of the standard and MTFS projections.

These results show little evidence of any 'crowding out' from higher public expenditure. Indeed the opposite is the case in the first years, when the higher public expenditure stimulates higher private expenditure as a whole. Any 'crowding out' must come through higher interest rates and a pervasive lack of liquidity. In the high PSBR projection, the rate of interest is raised by 40% or about 3 or 4 percentage points, but the main effect of this is to increase interest payments and receipts between institutional sectors. The only noticeable long-term effect of the high interest rate is to depress the level of industrial investment, although at worst this is only by 5% in 1990 in the higher government expenditure projection.

More generally the econometric work on the structure of the British economy is hard pressed to find any evidence of 'crowding out'. A recent survey (Savage, 1978) concludes that 'hardly any British research has been able to show that interest rates are an important influence on aggregate business investment'. Analysis of investment at a disaggregated level has also found that the effects of interest rates are weak and uncertain (Peterson, 1976). (It is a later version of this work which is included in the Cambridge model.)

Research on consumers' expenditure has generally ignored interest rate and liquidity effects as insignificant. The main monetary effects on consumption in the Cambridge model come through the wealth term. This is in nominal values deflated by the consumer price index so that higher inflation reduces net wealth and therefore consumers' expenditure. However the relatively small difference in inflation between the MTFS and the other projections (only about $\frac{1}{2}$% a year) is unlikely to have much effect.

The conclusion on 'crowding out' is that it would only occur on a significant scale if the extra public spending caused a substantial increase in inflation. The pressure to reduce consumption via a reduction in the real wealth of consumers must be more than sufficient to offset the higher consumption as a result of higher income. Higher interest rates associated with tight money supply targets and a higher PSBR are not likely to bring this about when there is plenty of unused capacity in the economy.

VII. The costs and benefits of conservative monetarism

Some of the costs of the present government's monetarist policies, cumulated for the years 1981 to 1990 are shown in Table 5. The costs, expressed as £ billion 1975 prices and millions of employed person-years, are measured by comparing the outcomes for the higher government expenditure and lower tax policies against the MDM version

Table 5. *Some cumulated costs of conservative monetarism (£ billion 1975 prices and million)*

	Higher government expenditure	Lower taxes
GDP costs of MTFS compared with higher government expenditure and lower taxes		
1981	2·1	2·9
1982	5·0	6·1
1983	9·2	9·3
1984	18·4	12·7
....	....	....
1990	41·3	38·7
Consumption costs of MTFS compared with higher government expenditure and lower taxes		
1981	−0·1	1·5
1982	0·5	4·2
1983	1·2	6·8
1984	2·3	8·8
....	....	....
1990	13·4	39·6
Fixed investment costs of MTFS compared with higher government expenditure and lower taxes		
1981	0·4	0·3
1982	1·1	0·7
1983	2·1	1·1
1984	3·1	1·0
....	....	....
1990	8·5	−1·6
Employment costs of MTFS compared with higher government expenditure and lower taxes (millions of employed-person years)		
1981	0·4	0·6
1982	1·0	1·0
1983	2·0	1·4
1984	3·0	1·9
....	....	....
1990	11·0	7·2

Table 6. *Reduced inflation under conservative monetarism*

	Higher government expenditure	Lower taxes
Percentage differences in the growth of money wages: MTFS compared with higher government expenditure and lower taxes		
1981	−3·5	−3·5
1982	−3·2	−3·2
1983	−3·1	−3·1
1984	−1·0	−1·0
1985–90	0·0	0·0
Percentage differences in the growth of consumer prices: MTFS compared with higher government expenditure and lower taxes		
1981	−3·3	−2·9
1982	−3·7	−3·1
1983	−3·7	−3·7
1984	−1·0	−1·0
1985–90	−0·5	−0·4

334   T. S. Barker

of the Medium Term Financial Strategy. The figures are extremely uncertain and should be taken as indicating orders of magnitude only. The results reflect the assumptions discussed in Sections III and IV above.

By 1984 the cumulated GDP costs of the MTFS are £18 billion at 1975 prices or about 18% of 1979 GDP at factor cost, if the higher government expenditure projection is taken as a comparison. If the lower tax projection is taken as the benchmark, the cost is about £12·7 billion at 1975 prices or 13% of 1979 GDP. If the recovery does no more than restore the long-term 2% growth of the economy, then the loss of GDP will continue to cumulate, more than doubling by the end of the decade.

The consumption and investment costs are similarly substantial, though they differ according to which alternative is used for comparison. By 1984 the cumulated costs of the MTFS compared to the lower taxes projection are £8·8 billion at 1975 prices of consumers' expenditure or 13% of 1979 levels, but only 3% of 1979 levels compared to the higher government expenditure projection. In contrast the investment costs of the MTFS are 5% and 15% of 1979 levels by 1984 for lower tax and higher government expenditure projections respectively. (Cumulated investment is actually lower by 1990 in the lower tax view so here there is a small benefit to the MTFS.)

The employment costs are inevitably very serious. By 1984 there will be a cumulative loss, compared with the alternatives, of between 1·9 and 3·0 million employed-person-years if the MTFS were to be followed. Unless major employment-creating policies were followed by later governments the cumulated loss of employment would continue to rise through the decade.

So much for the costs of Conservative monetarism, but what about the benefits? The most obvious one is of course a cut in inflation. Table 6 shows the reductions in the rate of wage inflation which have been assumed for the MTFS as against the alternatives. In the three years 1981–83 there is a reduction of over 3 percentage points. Thereafter it is much less because an incomes policy is assumed, supported by similar assumptions to the MTFS on the exchange rate and a long-term growth in real income much closer to previous growth than that under monetarism. The table also shows the implications of the MTFS for consumer prices from the lower wage inflation and lower import prices (as a result of the higher exchange rate). Price inflation is reduced by 3–4 percentage points 1981–83 and less than 1 percentage point thereafter.

Any more direct effect on prices, other than through the exchange rate or the fear of unemployment reducing wage rates, is more controversial. Inflation is partly determined by expectations and the monetarist arguments rely on these being adjusted rapidly. If this is not so, then as prices rise faster than the money supply, money will become increasingly expensive and money with its near substitutes (credit cards, trade credit) will be used more and more intensively. The speed of any reaction will depend on institutional factors, but it seems far more likely that the eventual adjustment would come through decreased real incomes than through lower prices.

There is a small further technical benefit. The MTFS generates a larger cumulated balance of trade surplus of £1·8 billion at 1975 export prices by 1984 compared with the lower tax view. This could be used to further appreciate the exchange rate or to increase consumer spending.

Finally the recession, compounded by the high value of sterling, might be regarded as a means of thinning out the less competitive and unprofitable firms in British industry —an economic survival of the fittest. The problem here is that the process may go on for far too long and may incur intolerable social costs.

VIII. Conclusions

The present policies and their outcome for the British economy can be regarded as an experimental test of practical monetarism. This paper has concentrated on one aspect of the potential failure of these policies, the prospect of considerable long-term unemployment and a protracted recession, with a loss of output which is not made up in the subsequent recovery. From a Keynesian standpoint this waste of resources holds only an uncertain hope of restraining inflation temporarily through mass unemployment so that the monetarist policies may also fail in their main purpose, the control of inflation.

The Keynesian objection is not to the achievement of monetary targets *per se*, but to the way this is being done by reducing public borrowing during a recession and doing so with policies which create unemployment.

Bibliography

Akerlof, G. C. 1979. The case against conservative macroeconomics: an inaugural lecture, *Economica*, Vol. 46

Barker, T. S. 1978. Towards strategic paths in economic planning, in Stone, R. and Peterson, W. (eds) *Econometric Contributions to Public Policy*, London, Macmillan

Barker, T. S., Borooah, V. K., van der Ploeg, F. and Winters, L. A. 1981. The Cambridge Multisectoral Dynamic Model: an instrument for national economic policy analysis, *Journal of Policy Modelling*, forthcoming

Buiter, W. H. 1980. The macroeconomics of Dr Pangloss: a critical survey of the New Classical Economics, *Economic Journal*, Vol. 90

Friedman, B. M. 1979. Optimal expectations and the extreme information assumptions of 'rational expectations' macromodels, *Journal of Monetary Economics*, Vol. 5

Friedman, M. 1968. The role of monetary policy, *American Economic Review*, Vol. 58

Friedman, M. 1969. *The Optimum Quantity of Money and Other Essay*, London, Macmillan

Friedman, M. 1977. *Inflation and Unemployment*. Institute of Economic Affairs, Occasional Paper 51 (The 1976 Nobel Lecture)

Jackson, P. M. 1980. The public expenditure cuts: rationale and consequences, *Fiscal Studies*, Vol. 1

Kaldor, N. 1980. Memorandum of Evidence on Monetary Policy to the Select Committee on the Treasury and Civil Service, *Memoranda on Monetary Policy*, London, HMSO

Modigliani, F. 1977. The monetarist controversy or, should we forsake stabilisation policies? *American Economic Review*, Vol. 67

Ormerod, P. 1980. Manufactured export prices in the United Kingdom and the 'law of one price', *The Manchester School*, September

Peterson, A. W. A. 1976. Investment, in Barker, T. S. (ed.) *Economic Structure and Policy*, London, Chapman and Hall

Sargent, T. J. 1976. A classical macroeconomic model for the United States, *Journal of Political Economy*, Vol. 84

Savage, D. 1978. The channels of monetary influence: a survey of the empirical evidence, *National Institute of Economic Review*, No. 83

Savage, D. 1979. Monetary targets and the control of the money supply, *National Institute Economic Review*, No. 89

Savage, D. 1980. Some issues in monetary policy, *National Institute Economic Review*, No. 91

Smith, D. 1978. The demand for alternative monies in the UK: 1924–77, *National Westminster Bank Review*, November

Solow, R. M. 1980. On theories of unemployment, *American Economic Review*, Vol. 70

Stein, J. L. editor, 1976. *Monetarism*, Amsterdam, North-Holland

Tobin, J. 1976. Is Friedman a Monetarist? in Stein, J. L. (ed.), *Monetarism*, Amsterdam, North-Holland

Tobin, J. 1980. *Asset Accumulation and Economic Activity*, Oxford, Blackwell

336   T. S. Barker

UK Treasury, 1979. *The Government's Public Expenditure Plans 1980–81.* Cmnd. 7746, London, HMSO, November

UK Treasury, 1980A. *Financial Statement and Budget Report 1980–81.* London, HMSO

UK Treasury, 1980B. *The Government's Expenditure Plans 1980–81 to 1983–84.* Cmnd. 7841, London, HMSO

UK Treasury, 1980C. Green Paper on *Monetary Control.* Cmnd. 7858, London, HMSO

UK Treasury, 1980D. Monetary policy and the economy. *Economic Progress Report*, No. 123, London, July

UK Treasury, 1980E. *The E.F. Unified Model Specification of Equations and Listing of Variables.* HM Treasury, August

[14]

Supply-side economics

Keynesian demand serendipity in supply-side economics

SIDNEY WEINTRAUB

Supply-side economics (SSE) gained great mileage out of a massive dose of ideological sloganeering sprinkled with a pinch of analysis. Its proponents qualify as the undiluted "capitalist roaders," although, in the domestic context, they appear not unwilling to wreak damage on the economy in the guise of repairing it. Fortunately the SSE fanfare seems to have melted like a spring snow in Washington, and in far faster time than during its blustering storm of distraction. Over the interval of the Reagan election in November 1980 to March 1981, the SSE avalanche blanketed the media and buried serious discussion. Dawning awareness that its chief plank, built out of the Kemp-Roth tax cut of 10 percent in each of three successive years, would not stem inflation and would not revitalize the economy, the SSE mystique vanished from the spotlight that generates economic policy.

Still, even if the SSE noise is destined to list among the more ephemeral marvels of the age, its concrete substance should be disentangled, for any set of slogans that can beguile the nation even once has some phoenix attributes to fit it for resurrection: there may be another election in it, not unconnected to its exaltation of the glories of a tax cut as the miracle potion for all our national ills. Exaggeration ultimately punctures the SSE myth as irrelevant to our stagflation mess of excessive inflation, superfluous unemployment, depression in the new housing sector, exorbitant interest rates tantamount to legalized loan sharking, and bond market debacles. The bewildering instability in our ongoing macroeco-

The author is Professor of Economics at the University of Pennsylvania and Distinguished Kennedy Professor at the University of the South (Fall 1981).

182   JOURNAL OF POST KEYNESIAN ECONOMICS

nomic farce satirizes the orthodox portrait of an immanent automatic stabilization lock in the private sector. The monumental dis-
order constitutes our madcap stagflation crisis and our ineffable
slide into *The Economics of Derision.*

SSE betrays one major head and several lesser atavistic features.
The main seizure is in: (1) the liberating force of a tax cut, ten-
dered as an unflagging energizer of business activity. A tax rate
slash is invoked as a lure to motivate (i) individuals to lend greater
work efforts in response to lower marginal tax rates, and likewise
(ii) to animate entrepreneurs and (iii) to generate a wave of optimism and thereby stimulate a burst of plant investment and modernization. Appended to (iii), as point (iv), the fresh technology
would revive our productivity trend, nudging it from its doleful
slump in the 1970 lapses to nearly nil, and sometimes negative
figures.

In its tax cut miracles the strident SSE rhetoric gulled a public
always ready to hear of salvation by a tax cut. Faith comes naturally in a country founded on a tax rebellion and now suffering
from stagnating productivity and wretched inflation. Under the
price siege it is particularly easy to believe that we will be better
served if the government shared as a less avid partner in our income. The ground is always fertile for SSE demagoguery, especially under inflationary anguish and real income frustrations.

Nontax aspects

Mingled with the SSE tax-cutting fever was a matching fervor for
government outlay slashing to trim the size of government. Here
the SSE crowd gave professional "respectability" to President
Reagan's predilections, rationalized now in the proposition that
the budget was the primary cause of inflation. On this the president and his advisers have deluded themselves and confused the
country. Government size, as measured by its outlays, scarcely
overlaps, and hardly coincides, with the dimensions of the inflation web. For example, we could well debate the matter of government size even in a stable price level and full employment economy: the issue of the proper preserve of government is ideological
or judgmental among "reasonable" people. Thus it is possible to
accept many aspects of the Reagan agenda while denying its relevance for our stagflation mess.

Too, if the president winds up preserving only his rock-bottom programs, and eliminating everything else, the cost of budget outlays will inevitably escalate as the price of government purchases from the private sector rockets. Every time the price of airplanes, missiles, and military hardware goes up, and civil servant salaries follow private sector tendencies, the budget outlay will reflect the inflationary trends. Government outlays are in this sense a prisoner of inflation, a *consequence* far more than a cause. The Reagan people read this relation backwards. If expenditures are the inflationary culprit, the president should advocate a cut in *all* expenditures, private as well as public, and thereby insist on a tax hike, and not a tax cut.

Confusion is even more rife over the effect of a deficit as an inflation-maker. Any serious analysis should have pointed up the strange composition of a government budget which lists, on the outlay side, a mass of operating outlays, as for paper clips, with a complex of capital sums, as for Trident submarines, lumped together indiscriminately. No private business mixes income and glaring capital investment charges in such profusion. Our most profitable growth companies would always report stupendous losses if they abided the arcane accounting practices of our federal government. Yet so many SSE proponents, among others, flay deficits and paint them as tantamount to business losses.

Always there has been the ritualistic SSE dirge of "steady and slower" money growth, holding a lax Federal Reserve money stance as the root of all inflation. At this point SSE doctrine merges with monetarist convictions, with exactly the same ideological overtones. Apparently monetary policy is never tight enough, and the unemployment havoc induced by money tautness is never high enough, but always "unnaturally low."

The other arrow in the SSE quiver is its condemnation of the various regulatory directives adopted for safety, health, consumer protection, and ecological and environmental objectives. These are to be marked for extinction, though there is the usual mumbo jumbo and pseudoscientific jargon that directives be made subject to vague pecuniary cost-benefit criteria, even when they do not lend themselves to specific dollar measurement. While many directives have undoubtedly surfaced from bureaucratic zeal and judgmental dysfunction, it is hard for less doctrinaire analysis to fault an objective of making our economic system more humane, beyond the bottom line of private income accounts.

Tax relief, investment, and productivity

On (i) SSE trumpets bellowed too loudly, for most employees are hired for standard workweeks; opportunities for marginal exertion in response to a minimal carrot are virtually nonexistent. A priori analysis has always been ambivalent over whether a rise in real income, via a tax cut, will pave the road to more income or, instead, to more leisure. For executives the plaintive story that those in the $100,000 or $500,000 or higher brackets crave "extra incentive" relies on a maudlin "old wives' tale" with ideological patches; SSE doctrines bemoan the economic system as somehow being loaded against the "haves" rather than the "have-nots" at the bottom of the income totem pole.

On (iii) the self-serving entreprenurial myth that the only obstacle to plant modernization was the corporate tax levy has been palpably false in its neglect of the inflationary climate and the high interest rates coming from the amalgam of the price binge and the Federal Reserve money pinch. Mortgage rates of 16 percent or higher, and the prime rate in the 20 percent range, block plant modernization more than the prevailing tax rates. Further, if there was a burst of new investment, given the Fed's adamant stance to damp down borrowing, the normal stimulating effect of the corporate tax cuts could be aborted by an even tougher monetary response.

In this respect the SSE advocates can be judged as either fools or knaves, demanding a tighter money flow to repress the economy and tax measures to revive it, or an injunction to go slow and to go fast, simultaneously. The left arm of government was to be driven out of sync with the right hand. Illogic, commonplace among politicans filling up vacuous air space on TV talk shows, is less forgivable in academic economists.

Furthermore, it is in the context of (iv) that the worst confusions are sown, for it was widely argued that boosting labor productivity would dispel inflation. This has been the paramount deception for, since Marshall if not well before, it has been elementary that supply prices, or the supply side of the price equation, is dominated by the two aspects: (1) the productivity of utilized productive factors, and (2) the prices of the productive factors. To site any supply curve, given the productivity facts, we would have to know "factor prices." Largely, the words "factor productivity" are a conventional circumlocution for talking about labor's marginal and average product, while the reference to "factor prices" is the economist's subterfuge for signifying money wage rates.

Yet supply-roaders *invariably* concentrated on productivity aspects with nary a reference to money wages. Cognizance was entirely lacking that in the unit labor cost calculus, the annual movements in productivity have been the junior partner, with money wages dominating the unit cost trend. At no time have the Reagan-supporting Economic Regulars pointed out that productivity facts, divorced from money wage facts, amount to a misstatement of the price equation. This has been a strange pathological episode by economists, sloppy in the simplest of fundamentals. Marshall never lived, microeconomics texts were never printed, thought was suspended, as jejune economics achieved the political pinnacle.

Even an empirical mind, much less an analytical one, should have sensed the folly. Productivity, over our best years, has advanced in the 2 to 3 percent pace per annum. In the 1970s the movement was under 1 percent, and negative in 1974 and 1979–80. In regaining the historic guide, the uplift would be from, say, the recent average annual 1 percent gain to 2 to 3 percent. But money wages have been rocketing on a 9 to 12 percent joyride. Inevitably inflation fills the gap. Not suprising, the former Democratic chairman of the Joint Economic Committee, Lloyd Bentsen and the ubiquitous Congressman Kemp, who has made the huge pole vault from football to economic eminence on a tax pass, could churn out economic "reports," at taxpayer expense, indicating how the productivity bursts of "supply-side economics," without ever mentioning money wages or salaries, would ward off inflation.

A further SSE oddity might be noted. It would not have been amiss if somewhere, some SSE proponent expressed alarm at the proliferation of billion-dollar corporations and a prospect of undue exercise of monopoly or oligopoly power, or uttered a call for resumption of more competitive markets to thereby *lower* market prices and check the price orgy. It would be most difficult to isolate even one such condemnation of potential, if not actual, monopoloid abuse. And yet, to the ideologically unwary, SSE "might" be surmised to be concerned with eliminating monopoly abuses. But supply-side economics never intended to seek objectivity; it was a pell-mell lunge for tax cuts, tailored mainly to big business and upper-income groups, and with only polite conventional curtseying toward mitigating the stagflation malaise.

186   JOURNAL OF POST KEYNESIAN ECONOMICS

The supply side of the macromodel

Having said so much in cynicism to puncture the SSE myth, we might sort out among the rubble for what may be valid in the idea. Just as the "supply side" has been in economics since the earliest conjectures on economics phenomena—for it would have been vapid otherwise to contemplate production phenomena, even more implausible than an unstriped zebra—SSE is an integral part of macrotheory. Keynes discerned this in his formulation though, to be sure, demand aspects swallowed up the supply aggregate which became lost among many gulled Keynesian followers. My own expositions of Keynes' thinking have always inserted Aggregate Supply in juxtaposition with Aggregate Demand (1955, 1969). Lawrence Klein noted this in his presidential address to the AER (1979); his thoughtful paper, incidentally, probably originated the "supply-side" vogue, maybe giving an unintended boost to the "school" which took it to a frivolous joy ride.

A linear macrotheory model (Weintraub, 1980) that makes supply-side phenomena explicit will be helpful, with qualifying amendments capable of being inserted later on.

(1)   Aggregate Supply: $Z = kwN$, where

Z = total proceeds or Gross Business Product (GBP);
k = the average price markup in GBP or the reciprocal of the GBP wage share;
w = average wage;
N = total private sector employment.

(2)   Aggregate Demand: $D = D_c + D_{ig} = awN + D_{ig}$, where

D_c = consumer market demand;
a = consumption coefficient linking D_c and the wage bill (wN).
D_{ig} = money investment outlay and government purchases from the private sector.

Equations (1) and (2) allow us to solve for N at the equilibrium of $D = Z$:

(3) $N = D_{ig}/w(k - a)$.

The equilibrium equation (3) contains the interesting result at this stage, to wit, that if w, k, and a are held constant, movements in business sector employment (N) depend entirely on investment and government purchases from the private sector. One further remark: if empirically $k = 2$, and $a = 1$, then it is entirely the nominal D_{ig} versus the money wage that establishes the private sector job outcome. Practically this result is not too far-fetched. (Perhaps k is closer to 1.85 and a about 1.04 in recent years, according to unrefined but not wholly uneducated guesses [Weintraub, 1978, chap. 3].)

Jobs and supply-side economics

What would SSE have to contribute to the growth in jobs, according to this simple linear model? Recall our interpretation of SSE as entailing tax relief and regulatory reticence by substantial deletion of industrial operating rules.

The effect might presumably be to lower k, either by technological speed-ups and lower unit costs over time, and to lower regulatory compliance costs mitigating the size of the former markups realized either in competitive markets or prices consciously dropped in more oligopolistic parts of the economy. For example, if k fell, say, from 2 to 1.75, and a was stuck at 1.04, then the $(k - a)$ term in the denominator of (3) would be lower, thus enlarging employment.

Theoretically, therefore, SSE could enlarge employment through $\Delta k < 0$, *provided* that a and D_{ig} held fairly constant. Analytically this seems to be the *only* SSE channel for improving the job outcome. Any other impact on N would have to come via a, w, or D_{ig}. Disregarding Δw, which involves other considerations, both a and D_{ig} involve *demand*, not supply, considerations. This is the curious *Keynesian* serendipity aspect of the SSE commotion.

Militating against any optimistic surmise that there can be any *strong* effect on k are the empirical findings on this ratio. If k hardly changes year to year, and drifts down slowly over the long period, then it is possible to be skeptical about any *important* job lift from this channel. Direct supply-side job miracles are thus vastly overrated.

Demand-side impacts

Tax cuts can most certainly work through the *demand* side, as Keynesians contend, SSE rhetoric notwithstanding. According to (3), the numerator D_{ig} is an obvious candidate for takeoff.

A corporate tax cut, for example, could bring on an investment binge, *provided* that the investment climate is propitious. Entailed here are clauses on Federal Reserve policy, interest rate phenom-

188   JOURNAL OF POST KEYNESIAN ECONOMICS

ena, and the inflation trend. In the ongoing price trauma, expensive new equipment, which must amortize its capital investment, has to compete against technologically *obsolete* equipment that long ago recovered its capital costs. Further, temporary borrowing at the current historic high interest rates adds enormously to the capital charges burden. From both sides there is a big edge imparted to staying with technically obsolete layouts, and the tilt against new equipment becomes stronger the higher the price balloon flys. One would think that the SSE school would give more attention to curbing inflation to obviate the manifest interest and amortization impediments to new plant installation. Investment booms are an unlikely practical outcome in an inflationary tight money environment. Herein is a damper on D_i buoyancy.

Ideologically, SSE generally argues vociferously for a variety of government outlay slashes. This drive must, if successful, compress the D_g component of D_{ig}. From this standpoint there is bound to be some canceling out: if D_i jumps and D_g drops, results can be something of a standoff. Actually, however, it will mainly be the time pace of $(\Delta D_g/D_g)$ that will be restrained, for in an inflationary situation, government outlays rise as a *consequence* of inflation. Unless the D_{ig} magnitude rises at least proportionately with $(\Delta w/w)$, jobs will trend down.

As to the demand effects via the D_{ig} numerator of (3), it is thus possible to doubt any important job assistance from the corporate tax and regulatory cut, accompanied by a government outlay slowdown. Because of the politics of the matter, and by some farfetched wishful thinking on how "savings" will be generated, the SSE group generally advocates personal income tax cuts.[1] This must tend to raise the a-term modifying the wage bill wN in $D_c = awN$.

As personal income taxes constitute a *compulsory* bit of "savings," in that the individuals transfer part of their income to the government and thus must tend to restrain consumption outlays, and thereby compel wage earners to forego some consumption, the tax cut on income recipients should tend to *raise a* to $(a + \Delta a)$. According to (3) this should tend to enlarge job opportunities.

---

[1] In utter disregard of data on the 0.9 average propensity to consume out of disposable income, the SSE rationalization is that the tax cuts will be "saved." Further, there is the stress on personal savings despite their relative unimportance in gross savings. Finally, and most shocking at this late date after Keynes, the SSE "analysts" have savings *preceding* investment.

An SSE smokescreen?

Skepticism about any important drop in k suggests that it must be in *demand* aspects that SSE becomes a persuasive article of faith for expanded jobs. Employment opportunities would come from either ΔD_i or Δa, negated to some degree by cutbacks in D_g. Supply-side economics peers out of the cave as orthodox Keynesian demand-side macrotheory.

Inflation

It is in its inflation analysis, or the lack of it, that SSE betrays its theoretical bankruptcy.

From (3) we can write $Z = PQ$, where $P =$ the price level and $Q =$ output volume. This establishes the wage-cost (*WCM*) price level equation:

(4) $P = kw/A$, where $A = Q/N =$ average product of labor.

In those rare, elusive, and futile moments when SSE analysis is directed to inflation, there is the assertion of a price deflation from a growth in A following an investment splurge. Experience reveals that productivity improvements are unlikely to leap ahead in a great splash; the older trend was in the 2 to 3 percent range, more recently to the 1 percent slide. Athletic records are mainly shaved fractionally; spectacular breakthroughs are not more probable at the workbench. A productivity improvement from 1 to 2 percent per annum is a 100 percent explosion, and from 2 to 3 percent is on the order of 50 percent, etc. With current energy bottlenecks, big productivity breakouts are unlikely to rival the past, when the story of technological progress was one of mechanical instruments supplanting human muscle. Not to be neglected is the time lag; today's capital gestation comes on stream two to five years from now, with the productivity increment deferred to the future.

While economics casts only small enlightenment on the future of technology, SSE uses mainly puffery over an A takeoff from plant modernization, despite Federal Reserve adamancy in opposing any investment boomlet, much less a boom, in their sadistic use of monetary rituals which perform marvelously in decimating jobs.

The SSE possible nibbling of k is likely to be minuscule. In the United States, over 1950 to 1978 it seems that k trended down by about 12 percent. From this score the price level should have been

190   JOURNAL OF POST KEYNESIAN ECONOMICS

below 1950, rather than over 200 percent higher! Thus SSE policies will confer scant price relief unless k plunges and A soars. Neither outcome is plausible.

On the Δw movements, which vastly transcend the pace of A and k over time, the SSE herd is thunderously silent. Deference is paid to monetary policy or the calloused hope that the Fed will make the Marxian army of unemployed so abundant as to dampen money wage progression. Of course, the magnificent contradiction in the simultaneous belief in monetary policy, Phillips curve accompaniments, and a profession of an investment boom and Laffer-curve GNP expansion is evaded and passed over by SSE advocates.

The SSE assertions come out naked on the critical subject of inflation. Yet it is this issue that must be solved to allow jobs, tax cuts, investment, and government size to fall in proper place.

Regulatory relief and inflation

Regulatory relief might, as remarked earlier, yield a—tiny?—downtrend in k and some bolstering of A by eliminating personnel from jobs mainly devoted to regulatory compliance.

But these are primarily one-shot gains. After the regulatory charges are relaxed, there is no scope for an encore. Measured against some deserved rebuke and discontinuous benefits from curbing overzealous bureaucrats, there is an abatement of worthy endeavors toward making the workplace and products more humane and satisfying. The antiregulation clamor naively ignores the steady, heady stuff of which inflation is made, namely, the persistent mismatch between $(\Delta w/w)$ leaps and $(\Delta A/A)$ creeps, in which the former has been the undisputed victor over the last thirteen years.

Output advances

From $Z = PQ$, obviously, if Z vastly outpaces P, Q will rise. Turning to $AN = Q$, what must be entailed for ΔQ is an expansion in N and a forward thrust in A. The SSE blessings for N have already been shown as a Keynesian *demand*-oriented package, with only some snatches of supply-side tinsel. Bursts in A are apt to be limited in the high interest rate climate. Any important growth in Q will have to wait a more perceptive solution of our stagflation malaise.

Conclusion

Rarely has any set of doctrines, with so little substantive content, ever enjoyed so rapt a hearing as supply-side theory.[2] Shake it out and turn it over, mostly demand propositions pour out. SSE would be a natural medium for exploring monopoly behavior. But in the ideological SSE framework, any intimation of monopoly prevalence is taboo, an unmentionable. Blindness comes easily to those already practiced at shutting their eyes.

[2] In some recent pompous blather about a "new macroeconomic supply-side model" (p. 33), Michael Evans, who has emerged as the solemn statistics-churning guru of the SSE movement, is described as discovering econometrically (!) that "stimulating investment is a key to supply-side policy because it will both increase real growth *and* moderate inflation" (p. viii). Murray Weidenbaum, Chairman of the Reagan Council of Economic Advisers, whose former Study Center sponsored the papers, declared, in peroration: "We need not and should not choose between tax reform and regulatory reform," for "the two go together" (p. 245). (See Meyers, ed., 1981.)

No other "revolution" in economics has ever been built on such platitudes or has been promoted so spectacularly as profound gospel through the eager uncritical media and receptive ideologues in economics. The SSE farce must set economics back in what Keynes once thought was an aspiration to become about as useful, say, as dentists.

REFERENCES

Klein, Lawrence R. "The Supply Side." *American Economic Review, 68*(1), March 1978.

Meyer, Laurence H. ed. *The Supply-Side Effects of Economic Policy.* Proceedings of the 1980 Economic Policy Conference, Cosponsored by the Center for the Study of American Business and the Federal Reserve Bank of St. Louis. St. Louis, May 1981.

Weintraub, Sidney. *An Approach to the Theory of Income Distribution.* Westport, Conn.: Greenwood Press, 1958.

_____ *A Keynesian Theory of Employment Growth and Income Distribution.* Chilton Book Co., 1966.

_____ *Capitalism's Inflation and Unemployment Crisis.* Addison-Wesley, 1978.

_____ "The Missing Theory of Money Wages." *Journal of Post Keynesian Economics,* Winter 1978-79, *1*(1), 59-78.

[15]

The Economic Journal, **96** (March 1986), 39–54

Printed in Great Britain

WHAT STOPPED THE INFLATION? UNEMPLOYMENT OR COMMODITY PRICES? *

Wilfred Beckerman and Tim Jenkinson

The main object of this paper is to argue that most of the deceleration of inflation in the OECD countries in general (including Britain) that took place between 1980 and 1982 should be attributed not to the direct impact of higher unemployment on the labour market but to the fall in 'commodity' (i.e. primary product) prices from 1980 to 1982, following their very sharp rise (accompanying the second 'oil shock') between 1978 and 1980. This led to a dramatic turn-round of about 50–60 % in the prices of primary products imported into the OECD countries from the rest of the world (and from other OECD countries), which, in turn, can account for the deceleration of about 20–25 % in the import prices for the average industrialised country. And our econometric estimates show that the pace of wage inflation is closely correlated with import prices. By contrast, our estimates for a variety of model specifications and choice of data do not show statistically significant correlations between aggregate unemployment and wage inflation.[1]

We have not attempted to establish statistically that the turn-round in commodity prices was caused mainly by the strength and duration of the post-1979 recession in the industrialised countries *as a whole*, but – like most commentators – we assume that this is the case. Given this assumption, therefore, our results imply that the recession in the industrialised world did not – as is widely believed – slow down the inflation by acting directly on the labour market (e.g. by crushing the unions or bringing a 'new breath of realism' into wage negotiations). Instead it worked by inducing a collapse of commodity prices (or, in the case of oil, inducing a slight fall by comparison with the preceding sharp rise).

Insofar as our results are valid there are various obvious implications for some central topical economic debates. First, if there is no stable direct relationship between unemployment within any country and its own rate of wage inflation then there would be no 'NAIRU' and no clearly identifiable Phillips curve – as some other investigators have found. Hence, debates as to whether and how far individual economies have unemployment rates above or below their NAIRUs and so on are irrelevant. In the Conclusions we summarise what seem to be the main policy implications for individual countries.

But, secondly, insofar as levels of demand in the industrialised countries taken *as a whole* influence commodity prices which feed back on wage inflation via

* The authors wish to acknowledge the various constructive suggestions made by Professor Stephen Nickell and two anonymous referees. The usual disclaimer applies.

[1] This is the case not merely when we use our own model but also when we carry out similar calculations with other investigators' models for individual countries. For details, see Jenkinson, T., 'Recent international comparisons of NAIRUs: a critique' (forthcoming).

import prices, then the Phillips curve for these countries *as a whole* may slope down to the right. Although we sketch out below the sort of model that would be implied by a relationship between demand in the industrialised countries as a whole and commodity prices we have not attempted to estimate this relationship econometrically.

There is, of course, nothing surprising about the proposition that national price levels are influenced by commodity prices. Few would deny the inflationary effects of the sharp rise in commodity prices (including oil) in 1972–4, at a time when the notion of 'imported inflation' was very popular. Hence, there is nothing paradoxical in the proposition that the turn-round in commodity prices after 1980, should have led – if not to 'imported deflation' – to at least a significant slowing down of inflation in the last two or three years. Various studies – such as several produced by the OECD – have also emphasised the role of import prices in general in explaining inflation and, in particular, the contribution that the slower rise in import prices made to the deceleration of inflation in the mid-1970s.[1] What is at issue is whether the deceleration of import prices in OECD countries after 1980 reflected (*a*) merely the pass-through into the prices of their exports to each other of their domestic deceleration of inflation caused, say, by the impact of unemployment on their own labour markets or (*b*) the turn-round in commodity prices, a large proportion of which are imported from non-OECD countries. As indicated above, it is difficult to identify any significant role played by the former and in the absence of any clearly defined relationship between aggregate unemployment and wage inflation. Instead, the deceleration of import prices for the average OECD country can be accounted for by the sharp turn-round in commodity prices.

I. PRICE RIGIDITY AND MACRO-MODELS

The notion that price rigidities can lead to (*i*) unemployment equilibria, (*ii*) large variations in output and employment in response to disturbances such as those arising out of changes in total monetary demand, and (*iii*) greater difficulty in reducing inbuilt inflation inertia, has, of course, a long tradition in macro-economic models. Every economics student is familiar with the debate over whether the only reason that Keynesian models lead to unemployment equilibrium is the assumption that wages are inflexible and so do not adjust to ensure that the labour market clears.

During the last decade or so much attention has been given in the academic literature to the implications, for macro-economic adjustment and policy, of the distinction between 'fix-price' and 'flex-price' markets (to use Sir John Hicks's terminology, or 'auction' markets and 'customer' markets, to use Arthur Okun's terminology).[2] Although it is an inevitable characteristic of most 'fix-price'

---

[1] See, in particular, OECD *Economic Outlook*, July 1980, p. 41 ff. and p. 123; Turner (1982); Larsen *et al.* (1983); Bruno (1980); *The Economist*, 'Inflation is down but not out', 7 May 1983.

[2] Hicks (1975); Okun (1975). The difference in price flexibility between primary products, on which the LDCs rely heavily for their export earnings, and other forms of output plays a key role in Kaldor (1976) and is discussed there in a context that is closely linked to the main theme of this paper.

macro-models that displacements from equilibrium in response to exogenous shocks – such as changes in total monetary demand – will affect mainly the quantity variables, this result may be mitigated if some relevant flexible price is introduced into the model.[1] One well-known elementary example is the two-sector labour market model, in which one sector only is unionised, and in which, therefore, wages are assumed to be inflexible. And if the wages in the non-unionised sector are assumed to be flexible downwards such labour as is displaced from the unionised sector on account of high real wage can be absorbed in the non-unionised sector. Hence, unions will not cause any *overall* unemployment, merely a differential between unionised and non-unionised wages.

It is widely believed that, in the industrialised countries, most wages and prices (except of such primary products that they produce) are more or less inflexible. It is also widely accepted that the prices of primary products are relatively flexible. And most of the output of LDCs is of this kind as are most of their exports to the industrialised countries. Hence, insofar as industrialised countries import primary products ('commodities') from the Third World, and produce some themselves, not all the burden of adjustment to, say, restrictive fiscal and monetary policies needs fall on output and employment. The 'external' sector for the industrialised countries taken as a whole, plus their own primary product output insofar as the prices of these are not stabilised, can act as the mitigating flex-price addition to the model, like the non-unionised sector in the example given above.

Although we concentrate here on the contribution of commodity price flexibility to the recent deceleration of inflation and we have not addressed ourselves to the question of how far it helps the industrialised countries to stabilise output, our results suggest the following possible mechanism:

(*a*) although there may be no identifiable, stable, Phillips curve for an individual country if (*i*) other industrial countries as a whole are deflating and (*ii*) commodity prices do respond to demand changes in the industrialised countries as a whole, such relationship as may exist at any time between aggregate unemployment and wage inflation will change in a manner that makes it easier for the authorities of an individual country to take discretionary action to raise demand without sacrificing its price stability objectives;

(*b*) the improvements in the terms of trade of the industrialised countries resulting from general contraction would exert some automatic expansionary influence on their economies, either through some rise in real wages, or the fall in real product wages, or the stimulus to investment – particularly investment at home – resulting from the rise in profits.

On the other hand, as Lord Kaldor has argued (Kaldor, 1976), the gains to the industrialised world from the flexibility of commodity prices may be offset by various disadvantages including, for example, the fall in exports to the Third World when these prices fall. In short, the contractionary effects on an individual country of a contraction in the rest of the world – via direct and indirect effects

[1] Of course, with respect to wages in particular, the proposition that more flexibility would attenuate quantity fluctuations is often disputed – e.g. by Keynes. For a recent discussion of the desirability of greater wage flexibility see Hahn and Solow (1986).

on its exports – may offset the demand–expansionary possibilities arising out of the improvement in its terms of trade and the reduction in its cost inflation.

Of course, the role of the external sector in providing an endogenous stabilising element in an otherwise fix-price model cannot be fully discussed without reference to flexible exchange rates, the potential role of which in macro-economic adjustment has been a common object of theoretical and empirical analysis. In this paper, however, we are not directly concerned with how far exchange rate changes affected import prices for individual industrialised countries. Differential changes in exchange rates would mainly influence the *relative* increases in import prices among individual industrial countries and hence their relative rates of inflation. But an explanation of the deceleration of inflation in the industrialised countries *as a whole* in terms of the deceleration of import prices would be no explanation at all – or would be a circular explanation – unless one can explain the deceleration of import prices. For much of their imports consist of imports from each other of goods produced within the industrialised countries. Hence, the strong relationship that we find between wages and import prices for a representative industrialised country could be consistent with any time path of inflation or deflation in these countries taken *as a whole*. In other words, in order that our estimated relationship between wages and import prices for individual industrialised countries can help explain the deceleration of inflation in the industrialised countries as a whole it has to be put into the context of what has actually happened to 'commodity' prices as a whole and the prices of imports into these countries as a whole. At the same time, although it is argued here that the deceleration of wage inflation in the OECD countries *as a whole* can be explained by the collapse of 'commodity' prices after their sharp rise from 1978 to 1980, the relative degree of inflation among individual OECD countries will still vary on account of other factors, of which their particular exchange rate experience will be one.[1]

II. THE TURN-ROUND OF COMMODITY PRICES

Table 1 shows various indicators of the changes in commodity prices and in the indices of unit values of exports from the LDCs and of imports into the industrialised countries as a whole. The latter are relevant partly because changes in commodity prices could have been greatly attenuated in final trade prices as a result of changes in exchange rates, exporters' margins, commodity control schemes, and so on. But, as can be seen in the table, all the indices moved in a similar manner over the period in question. The 'swing' in the final column is the difference in the percentage growth rates, allowing for the signs, between 1978 and 1980 and between 1980 and 1982. As can be seen from rows 1 to 5 below, whichever index one uses commodity prices swung round from a sharp rise in the first two years to some fall in the second two years gives a total 'swing' of around 50–60 %.

---

[1] As Hicks pointed out, in his original discussion of the flex price/fix price distinction (Hicks, 1975), the exchange rate constitutes an important potential flex price even in the industrialised countries.

Given the turn-round of about 50–60 % in commodity prices it is not surprising that there was a significant deceleration in the import prices of the industrialised countries. For imports of commodities (SITC groups 0–4) account for 45 % of total merchandise imports into the OECD area from all sources. Hence, if the prices of all primary products imported into OECD countries moved more or less in line with those imported from non-OECD countries the swing in commodity import prices indicated above would induce a swing in total import prices of about 25 % or more (i.e. 45 % of a swing of about 50–60 %). And, as Table 2

Table 1

Selected Commodity Price Indices (1980 = 100)

	1978	1979	1980	1981	1982	'Swing'
1 Export unit values of non-oil LDCs	70	81	100	95	88	55
2 Unit value imports of developed market economies	69	82	100	98	93	52
3 IMF 'all commodities' price index	78	91	100	92	83	45
4 UNCTAD commodity price index (SDRs)	78	87	100	93	83	45
5 UNCTAD commodity price index ($US)	76	87	100	84	71	61
6 Main OECD countries average price of commodity exports	66	80	100	115	121	30
7 Main OECD countries average price of manufactured exports	81	90	100	110	118	5

Notes: The IMF commodity price index in row 3, which is in dollars, 'includes 34 wholesale price series chosen as representative of the 30 commodities exported by primary producing countries' (see IMF, *International Financial Statistics, Supplement on Price Statistics*, no. 2, 1981, pp. 1, 19 and 24, and monthly issues of *IFS*), the weights corresponding to average export earnings excluding industrial and major oil-exporting countries (oil is excluded from the commodities selected in this index, but is, of course, included in row 2). The UNCTAD commodity price index is an index of market prices of the principal commodity exports of developing countries, the weights being 'proportional to the value, in terms of US dollars, of exports from developing countries in the years 1975–77' (see UNCTAD Monthly Commodity Price Bulletin, May 1983, Annex, page 25). These indices are shown in US dollars and SDRs in the quarterly *National Institute Economic Review*. The indicators of average export prices of ten industrialised OECD countries, distinguishing between 'commodities' (SITC 0–4) and manufactures have been based on the detailed data in OECD *Monthly Statistics of Foreign Trade*, weighted together by the value of each country's exports of the categories in question in 1980.

below shows, this is not much above the swing (22 %) that was actually experienced in the period in question. The slight discrepancy may be explained in various ways. One of the most obvious is that 40 % of total OECD imports of commodities are imported from other OECD countries and the prices of these traded commodities may not have decelerated as rapidly as those imported from non-OECD sources. In particular, the prices of foodstuffs are stabilised to a large extent under the European Community's CAP. But the prices of other indigenously produced commodities will tend to move sympathetically with world prices.[1] Coal, natural gas, and even oil prices are obvious examples. In fact,

[1] Apart from the fact that the above mentioned method of estimation is very approximate, the strengthening of the dollar after 1980 meant that for most countries in our sample the exchange rates declined so that their import prices in national currencies – which is what has been measured here – fell less than these prices in foreign currencies.

the swing in the prices of commodities exported by the aggregate of the main OECD countries (weighted by their respective values of exports of SITC groups 0–4) was only 30·3 % – from a rise of 51·3 % from 1978 to 1980 to a rise of only 21·0 % from 1980 to 1982. But this is far greater than the swing in the prices of their manufactured exports, which, for the aggregate of these countries was only 5·2 % – a deceleration from a 23·1 % rise, 1978–80, to a 17·9 % rise, 1980–82. This provides further confirmation of the view that the deceleration of import prices in the average industrialised country did not reflect any significant independent deceleration in the prices of the manufactured goods exported to each other. Finally, concentration on commodities that are traded probably under-estimates the contribution of the fall in commodity prices to the deceleration of inflation, since many commodities do not enter into intra-OECD trade at all, so that the ratio of commodity imports to GNP will understate the contribution of commodity prices to final prices.

Table 2

Summary of Changes in Wages and Prices and 'Swing' in Rates of Change, 1978–83 (% Change; Averages of 12 OECD Countries)*

	% increase in 2-year period				'swing' (all negative)		
	78/80	79/81	80/82	81/83	78/80 to 80/82	79/81 to 81/83	Average
Import prices	35·6	35·0	19·1	7·5	16·5	27·5	22·0
Consumer prices	20·4	22·9	18·3	13·1	2·1	9·8	6·0
Wages	23·0	22·8	19·7	14·0	3·3	8·8	6·0

* Data relate to the 12 countries to which our econometric estimates refer, namely United States, Canada, Japan, France, Germany, Italy, United Kingdom, Austria, Belgium, Netherlands, Norway, and Sweden. Wages refer to average hourly earnings in manufacturing; consumer prices are retail prices indices and import prices are average value indices.

All in all, therefore, as can be seen in the last column of Table 2 above, there was a sharp deceleration in import prices, of about 20 % or more, that can be accounted for approximately by the turn-round in commodity prices, and insofar as total imports constitute about 16 % of the GDP of total OECD and 25 % of the GDP of OECD Europe, one would expect a deceleration of final prices of about 5 %. Again, as Table 2 shows, this is almost precisely what occurred.

As can also be seen in Table 2, the deceleration of nominal wages was, at 6 %, about the same as the deceleration of consumer prices. It is, of course, difficult to say exactly how much deceleration our econometric equations would predict, given the dynamic structure of the full model and hence, for example, the role of the 'catch-up' variable which, in turn, will depend partly, in any given year, on how far profit margins were in fact constant. However, if all such other influences had remained constant, given the coefficient, in our model, of wage changes on import price changes in the same period of about 0·25, the average deceleration of import prices of about 22 % would have implied a deceleration of wages of about 5–6 % in two years, which is more or less equal to the actual deceleration of 6·0 %.[1] Of course, the fact that nominal wages decelerated by about the same amount as prices tells one nothing, by itself, about the actual course of real wages, and, in fact, real wages in the average OECD industrialised country rose very slightly in the post-1980 years.[2]

III. STATISTICAL VERIFICATION

One reasonable starting point in any attempt to estimate the relative role of import prices and unemployment in determining wages is to re-estimate wage and price equations for individual countries. Very many such estimates have been made, of course, and they tend to produce a wide variety of results. This may be largely because, with a single set of time series data, identifying the quantitative impacts of import prices and unemployment on wages could be flawed, since, as is generally accepted, the two are likely to be inter-related. One alternative procedure that has been adopted by some commentators is to use cross-country data on rates of change of wages and import prices in specific short time periods in a number of countries, together with observations of their relative levels of unemployment.[3]

However, this approach could seriously understate the role of unemployment. For it is highly likely that – even without taking account of statistical incomparabilities – the equilibrium level of unemployment, insofar as such a concept is relevant, differs between countries in line with differences in labour market conditions, social security provisions, and other factors. At the same time changes over time in unemployment within individual countries could still have an impact on wage inflation. If this is the case, the absence of any correlation between international differences in unemployment *levels* and in inflation rates would mean that too much of the variation in inflation rates would be caught up by the import price variable.

Hence, it seemed desirable to use rather more sophisticated econometric techniques in order to preserve the advantages of cross-section data without sacrificing the advantages of time series data for estimating the role of the unemployment variable within individual countries. The methods set out below have been applied to data for twelve OECD countries over the period 1963–83, and for the sub-periods preceding and following 1973.

The basic wage and price equations for the model are as follows:

$$W_t = a_0 + a_1 P_t + a_2 P_{t-1} + a_3 W_{t-1} + a_4 f(U_t) + a_5 g(Z_t), \tag{1}$$

$$P_t = b_1 W_t + b_2 M_t + b_3 Z_t + c, \tag{2}$$

[1] Not too much importance should be attached to this remarkably close concordance. Not only may other factors have changed, but the data relating to average hourly earnings in manufacturing (which we have used as our 'wage' variable) in the 12 industrialised countries covered are of uneven quality as well as of limited coverage.

[2] See OECD, *Economic Outlook*, July 1982, Table 17, and December 1983, Table 19.

[3] Some of the studies referred to in footnote 1 on p. 40 use cross-country data in connection with this problem, notably Bruno (1980) and Turner (1982).

where

W = hourly earnings in manufacturing;
P = domestic price index;
U = percentage of labour force unemployed;
Z = normalised output per manhour;
M = unit values of imports;
c = constant unit mark up over costs.

All variables are in logs, except the unemployment rate U_t. Equation (1) is a general dynamic wage equation but is clearly open to the criticism that price expectations do not enter as an explanatory variable. However, we capture the idea that real wages may be more or less inflexible, while allowing for short-term variations, by imposing the homogeneity restriction:

$$a_1 + a_2 + a_3 = 1. \tag{3}$$

This can be interpreted as a 'no long run money illusion' restriction, or that nominal wages are dynamically homogeneous of degree one in prices. This is clear since applying condition (3) in equation (1) yields:

$$W_t = a_0 + a_1 P_t + (1 - a_1 - a_3) P_{t-1} + a_3 W_{t-1} + a_4 f(U_t) + a_5 g(Z_t)$$

and hence,

$$\Delta W_t = a_0 + a_1 \Delta P_t + (1 - a_3)(P_{t-1} - W_{t-1}) + a_4 f(U_t) + a_5 g(Z_t). \tag{4}$$

This is simply an error correction model with the wage response to the price level providing a proportional error correction towards the real wage. Rather than model the error correction as acting towards some desired, or target, level of real wages, with all the consequent problems of determining real wage targets, we instead include a productivity variable and a measure of the slackness of the labour market explicitly (cf. Nickell, 1982). The question of which unemployment variables should be included in such models has been the subject of much debate, and we sidestep such questions by formulating the model both in terms of *changes* in unemployment, and *levels* of unemployment. Our results suggest that such dispute is largely misplaced: whichever formulation is used, the unemployment effect on wages is not statistically significant.

The inclusion of a productivity measure can be justified along simple neoclassical lines. Alternatively, within a bargaining approach it might be expected that wage increases claimed on the basis of productivity changes would be granted to some extent. Productivity levels are also included as an explanatory variable since in equilibrium we would expect the real wage to be related to output per manhour.

Wages are thus modelled as follows:

$$\Delta W_t = a_0 + a_1 \Delta P_t + (1 - a_3)(P_{t-1} - W_{t-1}) + a_4 \Delta U_t + a_5 \Delta Z_t + a_6 Z_t. \tag{5}$$

The steady-state properties of equation (5) show that nominal wages are homogeneous of degree one with respect to price changes since, in a steady state:

$$W = a_0/(1 - a_3) + P + (a_6 Z/1 - a_3)$$

that is, across steady states with different price levels, the real wage is constant, for a given level of labour productivity.

The influence of import price movements is introduced when we substitute our simple mark-up pricing rule into (5). We restrict ourselves to the constant profit margins case with

$$b_1 + b_2 = 1.$$

Taking first differences and substituting yields:

$$\Delta W_t = k_0 + k_1 \Delta M_t + k_2 (M_{t-1} - W_{t-1}) + k_3 \Delta U_t + k_4 \Delta Z_t + k_5 Z_t \tag{6}$$

where

$$k_0 = [a_0 + (1 - a_3) c]/(1 - a_1 b_1),$$
$$k_1 = a_1 b_2/(1 - a_1 b_1),$$
$$k_2 = (1 - a_3) b_2/(1 - a_1 b_1),$$
$$k_3 = a_4/(1 - a_1 b_1),$$
$$k_4 = [a_5 - (1 - a_3) b_3]/(1 - a_1 b_1),$$
$$k_5 = [(1 - a_3) b_3 + a_6]/(1 - a_1 b_1).$$

The 'disequilibrium factor' $(M_{t-1} - W_{t-1})$ will clearly become insignificant if a_3 tends to unity. In this case in equation (6) the *level* of the real wage would have no influence. The experience of the 1970s suggested that there was a significant 'catch up' effect in wage bargaining, with workers concerned about previous changes in their real wages, in which case the error correction term should capture this effect.

Given the model and the data there is still a choice of method. As indicated, one of the reasons for using pooled cross-section and time series data to investigate the impact of unemployment and import price changes on wages was that much information could be acquired by directly comparing how different economies behaved over a period of time. This is especially the case when all the countries in our sample have been influenced, but to different degrees no doubt, by the considerable instability of commodity prices and exchange rates in the last decade. Also, of course, since this instability has been more time-period specific than country specific, it might be expected that considerable information could be obtained from the inter-temporal variations in wages, import prices and unemployment for the countries considered in aggregate. These sources of information are utilised in determining the Variance Components estimates shown below, but they are excluded, of course, in the Least Squares Dummy Variables techniques, for which estimates are also shown. The relative properties of these methods, as well as of the Ordinary Least Squares method as applied to this form of pooled data, are discussed briefly in the Appendix.

The results obtained by applying the different estimation techniques to equation (6) for the period 1963–83 are presented in Table 3. The results reported treat unemployment as an endogenous variable, which is instrumented using current and one period lagged average unemployment in the remaining eleven countries as additional instruments. The results when U is not instrumented are very similar and are available upon request. In all calculations the coefficient on the import price term is highly significant, and implies that – other things being equal – a 10 % change in the price of imports into the OECD as a whole would result in roughly a 2·5 % change in the wages in the representative OECD country. This corresponds very closely to the average propensity to import (from all sources) of the representative OECD country. The results obtained when using levels of unemployment, rather than changes, as an explanatory factor were very similar, with again no significant unemployment effect on wage movements.

In addition to the results referred to earlier concerning the relative roles of import prices and unemployment, it will be observed that the disequilibrium or 'catch-up' factor $(M - W)_{t-1}$ is well defined and has the sign we would expect *a priori*. The fact that it is only around 0·04 reflects, presumably, the fact that a large portion of the period under consideration, i.e. 1963–72, was rather stable in terms of inflation and unemployment.

Table 3

The Effects on Wages of Import Prices, Changes in Unemployment and Productivity, 1963–83

(Coefficient of proportionate change in wages on variable indicated.*)

Method†	ΔM	$(M - W)$	ΔU	ΔZ	Z	a	mse (100)
VC	0·23	0·04	−0·28	0·59	0·003	0·04	0·093
	(6·4)	(2·3)	(0·9)	(2·8)	(0·1)	(0·3)	
LSDV	0·28	0·04	−0·21	1·41	0·07	—	0·127
	(9·7)	(2·1)	(0·6)	(5·7)	(3·3)	—	
OLS	0·29	0·02	−0·04	0·80	0·03	−0·09	0·151
	(10·1)	(1·2)	(0·1)	(5·6)	(1·8)	(1·3)	

* t values in parentheses.
† VC = Variance Components.
LSDV = Least Squares Dummy Variables.
OLS = Ordinary Least Squares.
mse = Mean Square Error of equation.

Considering the performance of the different estimation techniques shows that in terms of error variance the Variance Components method produces somewhat more reliable estimates for this period. The mean squared error for the same model is 27 % lower using Variance Component techniques compared to LSDV, and the latter itself has an MSE approximately 16 % less than that resulting from using Ordinary Least Squares. Clearly this result has no general implications other than that it is important to compare possible estimation techniques when combining data from many different countries, and that the simple OLS procedures that have been applied to such data in the literature may, in some cases, be relatively very inefficient. Table 4 (a) shows the results obtained for the post-Bretton Woods period 1973–83. As can be seen, the qualitative conclusions are unchanged, although the importance of the disequilibrium 'catch-up' effect is now increased significantly. This result is clearly in accordance with the observed events of the 1970s and early 1980s, when a significant factor in wage negotiations appeared to be claims based on previous reductions in real wages caused by rapid unanticipated inflation.

It can be seen that by comparison with the whole period 1963–83 the direct import price effect on wages, and hence inflation, in the OECD countries is slightly lower at 0·17 but the catch-up from previous import price changes is slightly greater and hence adds more significantly to the overall elasticity of wages with respect to import prices. The importance of the error correction term may also reflect the possibility that prices were not simply set as a constant mark-up over normal unit costs. Since 1973 there has been exceptional instability of commodity prices and exchange rates as well as in overall inflation rates, so that firms' conceptions of 'normal' costs, and employees' asssessments of what is happening to wage–good prices have become much more variable. In this situation one would expect the error correction term to be more important, and it may also be capturing the movement towards a target rate of mark-up.

As in the results for the whole twenty year period 1963–83 changes in rates of unemployment have little or no explanatory power: using both VC and LSDV techniques the unemployment coefficient is not statistically significant, and

Table 4 (a)

The Effects on Wages of Import Prices, Changes in Unemployment and Productivity, 1973–83

(Coefficient of proportionate change in wages on variable indicated.)

Method	ΔM	$(M - W)$	ΔU	ΔZ	Z	a	mse (100)
VC	0·17	0·10	0·06	0·56	−0·16	0·05	0·0845
	(4·7)	(2·8)	(0·2)	(1·8)	(4·3)	(4·5)	
LSDV	0·17	0·11	0·03	0·56	−0·17	—	0·0847
	(5·5)	(3·9)	(0·9)	(1·7)	(4·8)	—	

indeed appears with the wrong sign. The results thus provide no support for the belief that inflation has been reduced largely through any direct impact on the labour market of the rise in unemployment. Changes in productivity, measured by normalised output per manhour, do have considerable explanatory power, however, with productivity increases being rewarded by wage increases.

For this sub-period, the Variance Components and LSDV methods perform very similarly in terms of their respective mean squared errors, and this is reflected in the similar parameter estimates. Ordinary Least Squares, however, again produced markedly less reliable estimates, with a Mean Squared Error more than twice as large as that obtained using the other techniques. Hence they are not reported here.

In Table 4 (b) below we report the results obtained when the level of un-employment is substituted for unemployment changes. As can be seen, the results are robust to this change in specification, which has been suggested as most appropriate by some authors, with the unemployment variable again having no significant effect on wage movements.

Whilst in the above model we allow each country to have a different equi-librium rate of unemployment, we do not allow for changes in this rate over time.

This is a problem for which there is no simple solution, since it would be reason-able to assume that the equilibrium levels of unemployment have been increasing at different rates in each country. Modelling changes in equilibrium unemploy-ment in twelve countries is clearly outside the scope of this paper, but we did experiment with the inclusion of a time trend to pick up possible trended increases in equilibrium unemployment, and found that this made no difference to the results.[1]

However, the method used did not allow for possible inter-country differences in the trend rates of change of equilibrium unemployment. Hence we also experimented with the replacement of the unemployment variable by vacancies, which might be thought to allow for differential rates of change in the equilibrium levels of unemployment in the different countries. However, this, too, did not change the results. As can be seen in the following equations, which were estimated using LSDV (and excluding Italy for which no vacancy data are

Table 4 (b)

*The Effects on Wages of Import Prices, Unemployment Levels,
and Productivity, 1973–83*

(Coefficient of proportional change in wages on variable indicated.)

Method	ΔM	$(M-W)$	U	ΔZ	Z	a	mse (100)
VC	0·17	0·09	0·09	0·56	−0·17	0·88	0·0842
	(4·7)	(2·8)	(0·6)	(1·8)	(4·1)	(4·4)	
LSDV	0·17	0·12	−0·07	0·65	−0·14	—	0·0852
	(5·63)	(4·34)	(0·4)	(2·0)	(3·4)	—	

available), the coefficients on vacancies have the wrong sign and are statistically insignificant at the 5 % level. The first equation reported uses the simple vacancy rate (VR), and the second includes the log of the vacancy rate, as has been suggested by various authors. Indeed, the estimated coefficients on the other variables in our model were not significantly affected by replacing unemploy-ment by vacancies.

$$\Delta W_t = 0\cdot18\,\Delta M_t + 0\cdot11\,(W-M)_{t-1} - 2\cdot27\,VR_t + 0\cdot55\,\Delta Z_t - 0\cdot20\,Z_t$$
$$\quad\;\;(5\cdot7)\qquad(3\cdot8)\qquad\qquad(1\cdot8)\qquad(1\cdot6)\qquad(5\cdot0)$$

DW $= 1\cdot6$; mse(100) $= 0\cdot0824$.

$$\Delta W_t = 0\cdot19\,\Delta M_t + 0\cdot10\,(W-M)_{t-1} - 0\cdot02\log VR_t + 0\cdot55\,\Delta Z_t - 0\cdot20\,Z_t$$
$$\quad\;\;(5\cdot7)\qquad(3\cdot8)\qquad\qquad(1\cdot7)\qquad\quad(1\cdot6)\qquad(4\cdot9)$$

DW $= 1\cdot6$; mse(100) $= 0\cdot0829$.

Of course, this negative result may reflect to some extent the quality of the vacancy data which, for many countries, do not appear to behave like most other economic time series (in developed countries).

[1] For a discussion of the problems involved in estimating 'equilibrium' unemployment, see Beckerman and Jenkinson (1986).

IV. CONCLUSIONS AND POLICY IMPLICATIONS[1]

According to our estimates there is no identifiable relationship between aggregate unemployment and wage inflation in most individual industrialised countries. Nevertheless the slowdown in inflation in the industrialised countries taken together since 1980 can be attributed to the recession, on account of its impact on commodity prices, which fell after having risen sharply in the previous two years. Thus, although individual industrialised countries may all be characterised as mainly 'fix-price' markets, a fall in their aggregate demand can slow down inflation via the impact on the prices of commodities, a substantial proportion of which are imported from the Third World.

Our results imply, of course, relatively little scope for *an individual country* to influence its inflation rates by directly operating on its rate of wage inflation. If the rest of the OECD area is expanding, the best an individual country can do is to neutralise this rise in the foreign prices of its imports by engineering an appreciation of its exchange rate – a policy that a few countries followed with some success during the 1970s. However, given the change in commodity prices, variations in exchange rates can only influence the *relative* rates of inflation among the individual industrialised countries. The more some countries appreciate, the more the imported inflation in other countries. They cannot all simultaneously avoid inflation by exchange rate manipulation if they are all expanding.

Insofar as an individual country attempts to influence its import prices by exchange rate manipulation and insofar as this requires a tight fiscal and/or monetary policy, the link between unemployment and inflation is restored. How far such a quasi-Phillips curve shifts up or down, in the face of expansion or contraction in the rest of the industrialised world, must obviously depend on various coefficients, such as those relating the aggregate demand changes to commodity prices, and those relating its individual demand level *relative* to the aggregate of the other countries to its foreign balance and thence to its exchange rate, and so on. But these obvious theoretical extensions of the model lie outside the scope of this paper.

In essence, therefore, the above results imply that:

(*a*) it is not futile for the industrialised countries as a whole to deflate in order to reduce inflation. It is just that if they do so the inflation will be reduced by the resulting fall in commodity prices, not by moving out along their national Phillips curves, insofar as there are any;

(*b*) it would, however, be futile for all the industrialised countries to seek to avoid importing inflation from rising commodity prices, at times of general expansion, by appreciating their currencies;

(*c*) for an individual country, however, as long as the others are deflating, what it needs do (purely from the point of view of containing inflation) is to combine its own expansion with a monetary policy designed to prevent its exchange rate depreciating to the point where the resulting rise in import prices

[1] A more ex~   ~ve discussion of policy implications is contained in Beckerman (1985*a*, *b*).

on account of any exchange rate depreciation would offset the fall in primary product prices in foreign currency;

(*d*) conversely, when the rest of the world is expanding and commodity prices rising, the best the individual country can do is to follow a monetary/demand pressure policy such that the resulting appreciation of its currency offsets the rise in commodity prices in foreign currency terms;

(*e*) but this policy is not one that can succeed if followed by ALL the industrialised countries, since they cannot all appreciate their exchange rates against each other. Nor do the above policy options take account of the effects on competitiveness.

Although there are several major differences between the economic circumstances of the two countries, a comparison between the 'go-it-alone' expansionary policies of the USA between 1981 and 1984, and of France in 1981–2, illustrates some features of the model set out above. Apart from its relatively low dependence on imported commodities – though not on commodities in general – the expansion of the US economy (using old-fashioned fiscal stimulus) did not cause much inflation (which, in fact, continued to slow down) partly because, owing to the still contractionary stance adopted by the rest of the industrialised world, commodity prices did not rise sharply, if at all. At the same time the exchange rate appreciated largely because the tight monetary policy in the United States in conjunction with the budget deficit kept interest rates high enough to attract in foreign capital. By contrast, during the French expansion of 1981–2, which was also accompanied by a very sharp deterioration in the current external account, interest rates fell instead of rising, leading to a large devaluation of the franc *vis à vis* the rest of the world and hence to imported inflation.

Balliol College, Oxford

Merton College, Oxford

Date of receipt of final typescript: August 1985

Appendix A.
The pooled cross-country time series methods

When using cross-section and time-series data it is important to allow adequately for differences in behaviour of cross-sectional units in addition to time-series variation within countries. It may also be desirable to allow for time-period specific effects that have an impact on all cross-sectional units, and would suggest either the introduction of dummy variables or allowing the residuals of different countries to be correlated in a given time period. It is generally not advisable to apply simple OLS techniques to such panel data as it can easily be shown that such estimators have unbounded asymptotic variances.[1]

The approach normally taken to address some of these problems is to assume

[1] See e.g. Wallace and Hussain (1969).

that the error term corresponding to the ith country in the tth time period can be decomposed into three mutually uncorrelated elements:

$$e_{it} = u_i + v_t + w_{it}.$$

The u_i components pick up country specific effects, the v_t components capture country-invariant time specific effects, and the w_{it} are the remaining residuals. Two different approaches have been proposed for modelling the u_i and v_t terms. The first is to treat them as fixed parameters and estimate them using conventional dummy variable techniques. This Least Squares Dummy Variables (LSDV) approach is equivalent to running the model in terms of deviations from appropriate means, without the dummy variables or constant term.[1] Using LSDV techniques only the variation within each country, and within time periods if time dummies are also included, is utilised in estimating the regression coefficients.[2] If a significant proportion of the variation among the variables is between countries and between time periods then LSDV techniques may lead to inefficient estimates.

Following the work of Balestra and Nerlove (1966) more extensive use has been made of cross-section time-series data where the u_i and v_t terms are treated as random variables. The distribution of these 'random effects' is then of interest.

In this case we have the following model for the ith country:

$$\mathbf{Y}_i = \mathbf{b}\mathbf{X}_i + u_i\mathbf{j}_T + \mathbf{I}_T\mathbf{v} + \mathbf{w}_i$$

where $\mathbf{j}_T$ is the $T \times 1$ vector with all elements unity, $\mathbf{v}$ is the vector of time period specific effects $\mathbf{v}' = (v_1, v_2, \ldots, v_T)$, $\mathbf{I}_T$ is the $T \times T$ identity matrix, and $\mathbf{w}_i$ is the $T \times 1$ vector of residuals for the ith country. It is normally assumed that u_i and v_t are distributed independently $(0, s_u^2)$ and $(0, s_v^2)$ respectively, and that the u_i v_t and w_{it} are independent. A further important assumption is that the random effects are uncorrelated with the exogenous variables.

The covariance matrix for the composite disturbance is given by:

$$\mathbf{Q}_{ii} = \mathrm{E}(\mathbf{e}_i\mathbf{e}_i') \quad \text{where } \mathbf{e}_i \text{ is the } T \times 1 \text{ vector with elements } e_{it}$$

Then,

$$\mathbf{Q}_{ii} = \mathrm{E}[(\mathbf{u}_i\mathbf{j}_T + \mathbf{I}_T\mathbf{v} + \mathbf{w}_i)(\mathbf{u}_i\mathbf{j}_T + \mathbf{I}_T\mathbf{v} + \mathbf{w}_i)']$$
$$= s_u^2\mathbf{j}_T\mathbf{j}_T' + (s_v^2 + s_w^2)\mathbf{I}_T$$

and

$$\mathbf{Q}_{ij} = \mathrm{E}[(\mathbf{u}_i\mathbf{j}_T + \mathbf{I}_T\mathbf{v} + \mathbf{w}_i)(\mathbf{u}_j\mathbf{j}_T + \mathbf{I}_T\mathbf{v} + \mathbf{w}_j)']$$
$$= s_v^2\mathbf{I}_T,$$

under the assumption that the random effects are independent. Thus, disturbances of different countries in a given time period are correlated, as are disturbances in different time periods for the same country. The 'Variance Components' estimate of $\mathbf{b}$ is then arrived at via Generalised Least Squares:

$$\mathbf{b}_{vc} = (\mathbf{X}'\mathbf{Q}^{-1}\mathbf{X})^{-1}\mathbf{X}'\mathbf{Q}^{-1}\mathbf{Y}$$

[1] For details see e.g. Judge *et al.* (1980).

[2] No time dummies were included in the LSDV estimates reported in the main text, since world commodity prices being common to all countries, would be completely collinear with such time dummies.

where all variables are now aggregated for all cross-sectional units. The interesting result is that the estimator $\mathbf{b}_{vc}$ is an efficient matrix weighted average of the regression estimates obtained from (i) considering only variations in variables between countries, i.e. a purely cross-sectional approach; (ii) considering only variation between time periods, i.e. averaging over the countries in the data sample for each time period, and using only the resultant time-series, and (iii) considering only the residual variation.[1] In all practical applications these variances have to be estimated, and a transformation matrix $\mathbf{T}$ found such that $\mathbf{T'T} = \mathbf{Q}^{-1}$. When variance estimates are used rather than the actual unknown variances, $\mathbf{b}_{vc}$ is an estimated Generalised Least Squares (EGLS) estimator of $\mathbf{b}$. In these respects we follow the approach of Fuller and Battese (1974) who give sufficient conditions for this EGLS estimator to be unbiased and possess the same asymptotic distribution as the GLS estimator, although many alternative approaches have been suggested (e.g. Amemiya, 1971 and Nerlove, 1971).

REFERENCES

Amemiya, T. (1971). 'The estimation of variances in a variance components model.' *International Economic Review*, vol. 12, pp. 1–13.
Balestra, P. and Nerlove, M. (1966). 'Pooling cross section and time series data in the estimation of a dynamic model: the demand for natural gas.' *Econometrica*, vol. 34, pp. 585–612.
Beckerman, W. (1985a). 'How the battle against inflation was really won.' *Lloyds Bank Review*, No. 155, pp. 1–12.
—— (1985b). 'Stagflation and the third world.' In *Theory and Reality in Development: Essays in Honour of Paul Streeten* (ed. S. Lall and F. Stewart). London: Macmillan.
—— and Jenkinson, T. (1986). 'How rigid are wages anyway?' In *Wage Rigidity, Employment and Economic Policy*, (ed. W. Beckerman). London: Duckworth.
Bruno, M. (1980). 'Import prices and stagflation in the industrialised countries: a cross section analysis.' ECONOMIC JOURNAL, vol. 90, pp. 479–91.
Fuller, W. A. and Battese, G. E. (1974). 'Estimation of linear models with crossed-error structure.' *Journal of Econometrics*, vol. 2, pp. 67–78.
Hahn, F. H. (1984). 'Wages and employment.' In *Oxford Economic Papers* (Nov., Special Issue on Economic Theory and Hicksian Themes) (ed. D. A. Collard et al.) pp. 47–58.
—— and Solow, R. M. (1986). 'Is wage flexibility a good thing?' In *Wage Rigidity, Employment and Economic Policy* (ed. W. Beckerman). London: Duckworth.
Hicks, Sir John (1975). *The Crisis in Keynesian Economics*. Oxford: Oxford University Press.
Judge, G. et al. (1980). *The Theory and Practice of Econometrics*. New York: John Wiley.
Kaldor, N. (1976). 'Inflation and recession in the world economy.' ECONOMIC JOURNAL, vol. 86 (December), pp. 703–14.
Larsen, F., Llewellyn, J. and Potter, S. (1983). 'International economic linkages.' *OECD Economic Studies*, No. 1, pp. 43–91.
Maddala, G. S. (1971). 'The use of variance components in pooling cross section and time series data.' *Econometrica*, vol. 39, pp. 341–58.
Nerlove, M. (1971). 'Further evidence on the estimation of dynamic economic relations from a time series of cross sections.' *Econometrica*, vol. 39, pp. 359–82.
Nickell, S. (1982). 'A bargaining model of the Phillips curve.' Discussion paper 130, Centre for Labour Economics, London School of Economics.
Okun, A. (1975). 'Inflation: its mechanics and welfare costs.' *Brookings Papers on Economic Activity*, no. 2.
Turner, P. (1982). 'International aspects of inflation.' *OECD Economic Outlook*, pp. 5–27.
Wallace, T. D. and Hussain, A. (1969). 'The use of error components models in combining cross section with time series data.' *Econometrica*, vol. 37, pp. 55–72.

[1] For details see, for example, Maddala (1971).

Part III
Fiscal Policy
Implications

[16]
FUNCTIONAL FINANCE AND THE FEDERAL DEBT

BY ABBA P. LERNER

A PART from the necessity of winning the war, there is no task facing society today so important as the elimination of economic insecurity. If we fail in this after the war the present threat to democratic civilization will arise again. It is therefore essential that we grapple with this problem even if it involves a little careful thinking and even if the thought proves somewhat contrary to our preconceptions.

In recent years the principles by which appropriate government action can maintain prosperity have been adequately developed, but the proponents of the new principles have either not seen their full logical implications or shown an over-solicitousness which caused them to try to save the public from the necessary mental exercise. This has worked like a boomerang. Many of our publicly minded men who have come to see that deficit spending actually works still oppose the permanent maintenance of prosperity because in their failure to see *how* it all works they are easily frightened by fairy tales of terrible consequences.

I

As formulated by Alvin Hansen and others who have developed and popularized it, the new fiscal theory (which was first put forward in substantially complete form by J. M. Keynes in England) sounds a little less novel and absurd to our preconditioned ears than it does when presented in its simplest and most logical form, with all the unorthodox implications expressly formulated. In some cases the less shocking formulation may be intentional, as a tactical device to gain serious attention. In other cases it is due not to a desire to sugar the pill but to the fact that the writers them

FUNCTIONAL FINANCE   39

selves have not seen all the unorthodox implications—perhaps sub-consciously compromising with their own orthodox education. But now it is these compromises that are under fire. Now more than ever it is necessary to pose the theorems in the purest form. Only thus will it be possible to clear the air of objections which really are concerned with awkwardnesses that appear only when the new theory is forced into the old theoretical framework.

Fundamentally the new theory, like almost every important dis-covery, is extremely simple. Indeed it is this simplicity which makes the public suspect it as too slick. Even learned professors who find it hard to abandon ingrained habits of thought have complained that it is "merely logical" when they could find no flaw in it. What progress the theory has made so far has been achieved not by simpli-fying it but by dressing it up to make it more complicated and accompanying the presentation with impressive but irrelevant sta-tistics.

The central idea is that government fiscal policy, its spending and taxing, its borrowing and repayment of loans, its issue of new money and its withdrawal of money, shall all be undertaken with an eye only to the *results* of these actions on the economy and not to any established traditional doctrine about what is sound or unsound. This principle of judging only by *effects* has been applied in many other fields of human activity, where it is known as the method of science as opposed to scholasticism. The principle of judging fiscal measures by the way they work or function in the economy we may call *Functional Finance*.

The first financial responsibility of the government (since no-body else can undertake that responsibility) is to keep the total rate of spending in the country on goods and services neither greater nor less than that rate which at the current prices would buy all the goods that it is possible to produce. If total spending is allowed to go above this there will be inflation, and if it is allowed to go below this there will be unemployment. The government can in-crease total spending by spending more itself or by reducing taxes so that the taxpayers have more money left to spend. It can reduce total spending by spending less itself or by raising taxes so that taxpayers have less money left to spend. By these means total spending can be kept at the required level, where it will be enough to buy the goods that can be produced by all who want to work, and yet not enough to bring inflation by demanding (at current prices) *more* than can be produced.

In applying this first law of Functional Finance, the government may find itself collecting more in taxes than it is spending, or spending more than it collects in taxes. In the former case it can keep the difference in its coffers or use it to repay some of the national debt, and in the latter case it would have to provide the difference by borrowing or printing money. In neither case should the government feel that there is anything especially good or bad about this result; it should merely concentrate on keeping the total rate of spending neither too small nor too great, in this way preventing both unemployment and inflation.

An interesting, and to many a shocking, corollary is that taxing is *never* to be undertaken merely because the government needs to make money payments. According to the principles of Functional Finance, taxation must be judged only by its effects. Its main effects are two: the taxpayer has less money left to spend and the government has more money. The second effect can be brought about so much more easily by printing the money that only the first effect is significant. Taxation should therefore be imposed only when it is desirable that the taxpayers shall have less money to spend, for example, when they would otherwise spend enough to bring about inflation.

The second law of Functional Finance is that the government should borrow money only if it is desirable that the public should have less money and more government bonds, for these are the *effects* of government borrowing. This might be desirable if otherwise the rate of interest would be reduced too low (by attempts on the part of the holders of the cash to lend it out) and induce too much investment, thus bringing about inflation. Conversely, the government should lend money (or repay some of its debt) only

FUNCTIONAL FINANCE   41

if it is desirable to increase the money or to reduce the quantity of government bonds in the hands of the public. When taxing, spending, borrowing and lending (or repaying loans) are governed by the principles of Functional Finance, any excess of money outlays over money revenues, if it cannot be met out of money hoards, must be met by printing new money, and any excess of revenues over outlays can be destroyed or used to replenish hoards.

The almost instinctive revulsion that we have to the idea of printing money, and the tendency to identify it with inflation, can be overcome if we calm ourselves and take note that this printing does not affect the amount of money *spent*. That is regulated by the first law of Functional Finance which refers especially to inflation and unemployment. The printing of money takes place only when it is needed to implement Functional Finance in spending or lending (or repayment of government debt).[1]

In brief, Functional Finance rejects completely the traditional doctrines of "sound finance" and the principle of trying to balance the budget over a solar year or any other arbitrary period. In their place it prescribes: first, the adjustment of total spending (by everybody in the economy, including the government) in order to eliminate both unemployment and inflation, using government spending when total spending is too low and taxation when total spending is too high; second, the adjustment of public holdings of money and of government bonds, by government borrowing or debt repayment, in order to achieve the rate of interest which results in the most desirable level of investment; and, third, the printing, hoarding or destruction of money as needed for carrying out the first two parts of the program.

II

In judging the formulations of economists on this subject it is difficult to distinguish between tact in smoothing over the more stag-

[1] Borrowing money from the banks, on conditions which permit the banks to issue new credit money based on their additional holdings of government securities, must be considered for our purpose as printing money. In effect the banks are acting as agents for the government in issuing credit or bank money.

gering statements of Functional Finance and insufficient clarity on the part of those who do not fully realize the extremes that are implied in their relatively orthodox formulations. First there were the pump-primers, whose argument was that the government merely had to get things going and then the economy could go on by itself. There are very few pump-primers left now. A formula similar in some ways to pump-priming was developed by Scandinavian economists in terms of a series of cyclical, capital and other special budgets which had to be balanced not annually but over longer periods. Like the pump-priming formula it fails because there is no reason for supposing that the spending and taxation policy which maintains full employment and prevents inflation must necessarily balance the budget over a decade any more than during a year or at the end of each fortnight.

As soon as this was seen—the lack of any guarantee that the maintenance of prosperity would permit the budget to be balanced even over longer periods—it had to be recognized that the result might be a continually increasing national debt (if the additional spending were provided by the government's borrowing of the money and not by printing the excess of its spending over its tax revenues). At this point two things should have been made clear: first, that this possibility presented no danger to society, no matter what unimagined heights the national debt might reach, so long as Functional Finance maintained the proper level of total demand for current output; and second (though this is much less important), that there is an automatic tendency for the budget to be balanced in the long run as a *result* of the application of Functional Finance, even if there is no place for the *principle* of balancing the budget. No matter how much interest has to be paid on the debt, taxation must not be applied unless it is necessary to keep spending down to prevent inflation. The interest can be paid by borrowing still more.

As long as the public is willing to keep on lending to the government there is no difficulty, no matter how many zeros are added to the national debt. If the public becomes reluctant to keep on lend-

FUNCTIONAL FINANCE   43

ing, it must either hoard the money or spend it. If the public hoards, the government can print the money to meet its interest and other obligations, and the only effect is that the public holds government currency instead of government bonds and the government is saved the trouble of making interest payments. If the public spends, this will increase the rate of total spending so that it will not be necessary for the government to borrow for this purpose; and if the rate of spending becomes too great, *then* is the time to tax to prevent inflation. The proceeds can then be used to pay interest and repay government debt. In every case Functional Finance provides a simple, quasi-automatic response.

But either this was not seen clearly or it was considered too shocking or too logical to be told to the public. Instead it was argued, for example by Alvin Hansen, that as long as there is a reasonable ratio between national income and debt, the interest payment on the national debt can easily come from taxes paid out of the increased national income created by the deficit financing.

This unnecessary "appeasement" opened the way to an extremely effective opposition to Functional Finance. Even men who have a clear understanding of the mechanism whereby government spending in times of depression can increase the national income by several times the amount laid out by the government, and who understand perfectly well that the national debt, when it is not owed to other nations, is not a burden on the nation in the same way as an individual's debt to other individuals is a burden on the individual, have come out strongly against "deficit spending." It has been argued that "it would be impossible to devise a program better adapted to the systematic undermining of the private-enterprise system and the hastening of the final catastrophe than 'deficit spending.' "[3]

These objections are based on the recognition that although every dollar spent by the government may create several dollars of

<hr/>

[2] An excellent example of this is the persuasive article by John T. Flynn in *Harper's Magazine* for July 1942.

[3] Flynn, *ibid.*

14   SOCIAL RESEARCH

income in the course of the next year or two, the effects then disappear. From this it follows that if the national income is to be maintained at a high level the government has to keep up its contribution to spending for as long as private spending is insufficient by itself to provide full employment. This might mean an indefinite continuation of government support to spending (though not necessarily at an increasing rate); and if, as the "appeasement" formulation suggests, all this spending comes out of borrowing, the debt will keep on growing until it is no longer in a "reasonable" ratio to income.

This leads to the crux of the argument. If the interest on the debt must be raised out of taxes (again an assumption that is unchallenged by the "appeasement" formulation) it will in time constitute an important fraction of the national income. The very high income tax necessary to collect this amount of money and pay it to the holders of government bonds will discourage risky private investment, by so reducing the net return on it that the investor is not compensated for the risk of losing his capital. This will make it necessary for the government to undertake still more deficit financing to keep up the level of income and employment. Still heavier taxation will then be necessary to pay the interest on the growing debt—until the burden of taxation is so crushing that private investment becomes unprofitable, and the private enterprise economy collapses. Private firms and corporations will all be bankrupted by the taxes, and the government will have to take over all industry.

This argument is not new. The identical calamities, although they are now receiving much more attention than usual, were promised when the first income tax law of one penny in the pound was proposed. All this only makes it more important to evaluate the significance of the argument.

III

There are four major errors in the argument against deficit spending, four reasons why its apparent conclusiveness is only illusory.

FUNCTIONAL FINANCE   45

In the first place, the same high income tax that reduces the return on the investment is deductible for the loss that is incurred if the investment turns out a failure. As a result of this the *net* return on the risk of loss is unaffected by the income tax rate, no matter how high that may be. Consider an investor in the $50,000-a-year income class who has accumulated $10,000 to invest. At 6 percent this would yield $600, but after paying income tax on this addition to his income at 60 cents in the dollar he would have only $240 left. It is argued, therefore, that he would not invest because this is insufficient compensation for the risk of losing $10,000. This argument forgets that if the $10,000 is all lost, the net loss to the investor, after he has deducted his income tax allowance, will be only $4,000, and the rate of return on the amount he actually risks is still exactly 6 percent; $240 is 6 percent of $4,000. The effect of the income tax is to make the rich man act as a kind of agent working for society on commission. He receives only a part of the return on the investment, but he loses only a part of the money that is invested. Any investment that was worth undertaking in the absence of the income tax is still worth undertaking.

Of course, this correction of the argument is strictly true only where 100 percent of the loss is deductible from taxable income, where relief from taxation occurs at the same rate as the tax on returns. There is a good case against certain limitations on permissible deduction from the income tax base for losses incurred, but that is another story. Something of the argument remains, too, if the loss would put the taxpayer into a lower income tax bracket, where the rebate (and the tax) is at a lower rate. There would then be some reduction in the net return as compared with the potential net loss. But this would apply only to such investments as are large enough to threaten to impoverish the investor if they fail. It was for the express purpose of dealing with this problem that the corporation was devised, making it possible for many individuals to combine and undertake risky enterprises without any one person having to risk all his fortune on one venture. But quite apart from corporate investment, this problem would be met almost entirely if the maximum rate of income tax were reached at a relatively low level, say at $25,000 a year (low, that is, from the point of view of the rich men who are the supposed source of risk capital). Even if all income in excess of $25,000 were taxed at 90 percent there would be no discouragement in the investment of any part of income over this level. True, the net return, after payment of tax, would be only one-tenth of the nominal interest payments, but the amount risked by the investors would also be only ten percent of the actual capital invested, and therefore the net return on the capital actually risked by the investor would be unaffected.

In the second place, this argument against deficit spending in time of depression would be indefensible even if the harm done by debt were as great as has been suggested. It must be remembered that spending by the government increases the *real* national income of goods and services by several times the amount spent by the government, and that the burden is measured not by the amount of the interest payments but only by the inconveniences involved in the process of transferring the money from the taxpayers to the bondholders. Therefore objecting to deficit spending is like arguing that if you are offered a job when out of work on the condition that you promise to pay your wife interest on a part of the money earned (or that your wife pay it to you) it would be wiser to continue to be unemployed, because in time you will be owing your wife a great deal of money (or she will be owing it to you), and this might cause matrimonial difficulties in the future. Even if the interest payments were really lost to society, instead of being merely transferred within the society, they would come to much less than the loss through permitting unemployment to continue. That loss would be several times as great as the *capital* on which these interest payments have to be made.

In the third place, there is no good reason for supposing that the government would have to raise all the interest on the national debt by current taxes. We have seen that Functional Finance permits taxation only when the *direct* effect of the tax is in the social interest, as when it prevents excessive spending or excessive invest-

FUNCTIONAL FINANCE   47

ment which would bring about inflation. If taxes imposed to prevent inflation do not result in sufficient proceeds, the interest on the debt can be met by borrowing or printing the money. There is no risk of inflation from this, because if there were such a risk a greater amount would have to be collected in taxes.

This means that the absolute size of the national debt does not matter at all, and that however large the interest payments that have to be made, these do not constitute any burden upon society as a whole. A completely fantastic exaggeration may illustrate the point. Suppose the national debt reaches the stupendous total of ten thousand billion dollars (that is, ten trillion, $10,000,000,-000,000), so that the interest on it is 300 billion a year. Suppose the real national income of goods and services which can be produced by the economy when fully employed is 150 billion. The interest alone, therefore, comes to twice the real national income. There is no doubt that a debt of this size would be called "unreasonable." But even in this fantastic case the payment of the interest constitutes no burden on society. Although the real income is only 150 billion dollars the money income is 450 billion—150 billion in income from the production of goods and services and 300 billion in income from ownership of the government bonds which constitute the national debt. Of this money income of 450 billion, 300 billion has to be collected in taxes by the government for interest payments (if 10 trillion is the legal debt limit), but after payment of these taxes there remains 150 billion dollars in the hands of the taxpayers, and this is enough to pay for all the goods and services that the economy can produce. Indeed it would do the public no good to have any more money left after tax payments, because if it spent more than 150 billion dollars it would merely be raising the prices of the goods bought. It would not be able to obtain more goods to consume than the country is able to produce.

Of course this illustration must not be taken to imply that a debt of this size is at all likely to come about as a result of the application of Functional Finance. As will be shown below, there is a natural tendency for the national debt to stop growing long before it comes anywhere near the astronomical figures that we have been playing with.

The unfounded assumption that current interest on the debt must be collected in taxes springs from the idea that the debt must be kept in a "reasonable" or "manageable" ratio to income (whatever that may be). If this restriction is accepted, *borrowing* to pay the interest is eliminated as soon as the limit of "reasonableness" is reached, and if we further rule out, as an indecent thought, the possibility of *printing* the money, there remains only the possibility of raising the interest payments by taxes. Fortunately there is no need to assume these limitations so long as Functional Finance is on guard against inflation, for it is the fear of inflation which is the only rational basis for suspicion of the printing of money.

Finally, there is no reason for assuming that, as a result of the continued application of Functional Finance to maintain full employment, the government must always be borrowing more money and increasing the national debt. There are a number of reasons for this.

First, full employment *can* be maintained by printing the money needed for it, and this does not increase the debt at all. It is probably advisable, however, to allow debt and money to increase together in a certain balance, as long as one or the other has to increase.

Second, since one of the greatest deterrents to private investment is the fear that the depression will come before the investment has paid for itself, the guarantee of permanent full employment will make private investment much more attractive, once investors have got over their suspicions of the new procedure. The greater private investment will diminish the need for deficit spending.

Third, as the national debt increases, and with it the sum of private wealth, there will be an increasingly yield from taxes on higher incomes and inheritances, even if the tax rates are unchanged. These higher tax payments do not represent reductions of spending by the taxpayers. Therefore the government does not have to use these proceeds to maintain the requisite rate of spending, and it can devote them to paying the interest on the national debt.

FUNCTIONAL FINANCE   49

Fourth, as the national debt increases it acts as a self-equilibrating force, gradually diminishing the further need for its growth and finally reaching an equilibrium level where its tendency to grow comes completely to an end. The greater the national debt the greater is the quantity of private wealth. The reason for this is simply that for every dollar of debt owed by the government there is a private creditor who owns the government obligations (possibly through a corporation in which he has shares), and who regards these obligations as part of his private fortune. The greater the private fortunes the less is the incentive to add to them by saving out of current income. As current saving is thus discouraged by the great accumulation of past savings, spending out of current income increases (since spending is the only alternative to saving income). This increase in private spending makes it less necessary for the government to undertake deficit financing to keep total spending at the level which provides full employment. When the government debt has become so great that private spending is enough to provide the total spending needed for full employment, there is no need for any deficit financing by the government, the budget is balanced and the national debt automatically stops growing. The size of this equilibrium level of debt depends on many things. It can only be guessed at, and in the very roughest manner. My guess is that it is between 100 and 300 billion dollars. Since the level is a result and not a principle of Functional Finance the latitude of such a guess does not matter; it is not needed for the application of the laws of Functional Finance.

Fifth, if for any reason the government does not wish to see private property grow too much (whether in the form of government bonds or otherwise) it can check this by taxing the rich instead of borrowing from them, in its program of financing government spending to maintain full employment. The rich will not reduce their spending significantly, and thus the effects on the economy, apart from the smaller debt, will be the same as if the money had been borrowed from them. By this means the debt can be reduced to any desired level and kept there.

The answers to the argument against deficit spending may thus be summarized as follows:

The national debt does not have to keep on increasing;

Even if the national debt does grow, the interest on it does not have to be raised out of current taxes;

Even if the interest on the debt is raised out of current taxes, these taxes constitute only the interest on only a fraction of the benefit enjoyed from the government spending, and are not lost to the nation but are merely transferred from taxpayers to bond-holders;

High income taxes need not discourage investment, because appropriate deductions for losses can diminish the capital actually risked by the investor in the same proportion as his net income from the investment is reduced.

IV

If the propositions of Functional Finance were put forward without fear of appearing too logical, criticisms like those discussed above would not be as popular as they now are, and it would not be necessary to defend Functional Finance from its friends. An especially embarrassing task arises from the claim that Functional Finance (or deficit financing, as it is frequently but unsatisfactorily called) is primarily a defense of private enterprise. In the attempt to gain popularity for Functional Finance, it has been given other names and declared to be essentially directed toward saving private enterprise. I myself have sinned similarly in previous writings in identifying it with democracy,' thus joining the army of salesmen who wrap up their wares in the flag and tie anything they have to sell to victory or morale.

Functional Finance is not especially related to democracy or to private enterprise. It is applicable to a communist society just as well as to a fascist society or a democratic society. It is applicable to any society in which money is used as an important element in the economic mechanism. It consists of the simple principle of

'In "Total Democracy and Full Employment," *Social Change* (May 1941).

FUNCTIONAL FINANCE   51

giving up our preconceptions of what is proper or sound or traditional, of what "is done," and instead considering the *functions* performed in the economy by government taxing and spending and borrowing and lending. It means using these instruments simply as instruments, and not as magic charms that will cause mysterious hurt if they are manipulated by the wrong people or without due reverence for tradition. Like any other mechanism, Functional Finance will work no matter who pulls the levers. Its relationship to democracy and free enterprise consists simply in the fact that if the people who believe in these things will not use Functional Finance, they will stand no chance in the long run against others who will.

[17]

Built-in Flexibility*

I

The essence of compensatory fiscal policy lies in adjusting the level of government receipts and expenditures so as to stabilize total income (and employment) in the economy. This requires an increase in expenditures and a reduction in tax revenue during periods of deflation and a decrease in expenditures and increase in tax revenue during periods of inflation. Such compensatory movements may be brought about by properly timed changes in expenditure programs and in tax rates, but to some extent they occur automatically. Certain public expenditures, such as unemployment benefits, are geared to move in a countercyclical fashion. Similarly, tax yields under given statutory rates will fluctuate with changes in the national income since the size of the tax base usually varies directly with the level of income. Recently, the automatically compensatory movement of tax revenues—generally referred to as "built-in flexibility"—has received increasing attention. The purpose of this note is to appraise its importance as a stabilization device.

II

The magnitude of the automatically compensatory adjustment will depend of course upon the dollar change in tax revenue resulting from a given dollar change in the national income, that is, upon the "marginal tax rate" and the problem might be formulated in terms of this marginal rate.[1] There is, however, a more detailed and for our purposes more useful way of stating the problem. The fiscal planner, from year to year, is confronted with setting an "average tax rate," that is, a rate which will raise the desired amount of tax revenue at the expected level of income. This total revenue can be raised by various combinations of statutory rates and tax sources, and different combinations will result in tax systems which possess different degrees of sensitivity of yield in response to changes in income. It is the selection of one of these combinations and of the rates necessary to produce the desired yield from the expected level of income that determines the extent of "built-in flexibility" or the marginal tax rate for the system as a whole. Consequently, the degree of flexibility will be analyzed in this note in terms of the level of taxation (average tax rate at the expected level of income) and the sensitivity to changes in income of the selected combination of tax sources.

To measure the effect of "built-in flexibility," it is useful to start with a simplified model which assumes that public expenditures are fixed and wholly for goods and services, that all taxes are in the form of a personal income tax, that there are no corporate savings in the economy and that the level of investment is independent of taxation. The expression for the *change* in income be-

---

*The authors are indebted to Mr. Alfred Sherrard for his helpful suggestions and criticisms in the preparation of this note.

[1] For a statement of the problem in terms of the marginal rate see note 2 below.

tween two periods may then be written as

(1) $$\Delta Y = \Delta I + c\Delta Y - c(r_1 Y_1 - r_2 Y_2)$$

where ΔY equals $Y_1 - Y_2$ or the change in income from the first to the second period and ΔI equals $I_1 - I_2$ or the change in investment; (c) is the marginal propensity to consume out of disposable income which is assumed to remain constant; and (r_1) and (r_2) are the *average* rates of tax in the two periods.

The income elasticity (E) of the tax yield (T) is the ratio of the percentage change in tax yield to a given percentage change in income and may be expressed as

(2) $$E = \frac{(\Delta T) Y_1}{(\Delta Y) T_1}$$

Solving for ΔT and substituting the result for $(r_1 Y_1 - r_2 Y_2)$ in equation (1) gives

(3) $$\Delta Y = \Delta I \frac{1}{1 - c + cE \dfrac{T_1}{Y_1}} .$$

and by substituting (r_1) for $\left(\dfrac{T_1}{Y_1} \right)$ we obtain[2]

(4) $$\Delta Y = \Delta I \frac{1}{1 - c(1 - Er_1)}$$

As a convenient measure for the compensatory effectiveness of "built-in flexibility" we may then write

(5) $$\alpha = 1 - \frac{\Delta Y}{\Delta Y_a}$$

where ΔY refers to the change in income in the particular tax system under discussion (with its specific positive value for Er_1) and ΔY_a refers to a system where (E) is set equal to zero. That is. $\dfrac{\Delta Y}{\Delta Y_a}$ is the ratio of the decline (or increase) in income in the particular tax system under analysis to the decline (or increase) in income if the system had no "built-in flexibility"; and (α), which is one minus this ratio, is the *fraction of the change in income which is prevented because of the existence of "built-in flexibility."* If

---

[2] Expressing the relationship in terms of the marginal tax rate or (m) equation (1) is rewritten as

(1a) $$\Delta Y = \Delta I + c\Delta Y - cm\Delta Y$$

and solving for Y,

(1b) $$\Delta Y = \Delta I \frac{1}{1 - c(1 - m)}$$

which of course is the same as (4) above because $(E) = \dfrac{m}{r_1}$.

$\alpha = 0$, there is no built-in flexibility; if $\alpha = 1$, built-in flexibility is perfect, *i.e.*, total income remains unchanged.

Substituting (4) in (5) we have

(6)
$$\alpha = 1 - \frac{1 - c}{1 - c(1 - Er_1)} = \frac{cEr_1}{1 - c + cEr_1}$$

Given the community's propensity to consume, (α) will thus vary directly with (r_1) and (E), the level of taxation and the income elasticity of the selected combination of tax sources. But "built-in flexibility" can never be so effective as to eliminate all change in income. However high the values for (E) and (r_1), (α) will be less than one in any economy whose propensity to consume is less than unity. As a practical matter, of course, (Er_1) could not exceed 1, that is a marginal tax rate of 100 per cent. At this extreme (α) would be equal to (c) and the investment multiplier would be fully offset (equation 4). The change in income before tax would be limited to the change in investment and income after tax would be stabilized.

In interpreting the concept (α) as here developed, it should be noted that (c) is not a variable in the same sense as (E) or (r_1). While the numerical value of (α) will increase as (c) increases, the absolute amount of the remaining change in income will also be larger (equation 4). Consequently (α) has relevance only for comparing the effect of different tax systems in a single economy, all of whose other basic relations (including the value of [c]) are held constant.

III

Turning now to a consideration of the magnitude of (α) for various tax structures under ordinary conditions, the assumptions in the simplified model must be revised to take account of transfer payments, excise taxes and most important, corporate savings and taxes.

The introduction of transfer payments presents no particular difficulties. They may be handled either by introducing into equation (1) a new term which expresses consumption out of transfer payments or they may be treated as "negative taxes" reducing (r_1).[3] By extending the analysis in this fashion a new equation (4) may be derived which allows for "built-in flexibility" on both the revenue and expenditure sides of the budget.

The introduction of excise taxes raises no serious difficulty if they can be thought of as paid out of consumer expenditures, that is, as personal income taxes assessed on an expenditure basis. This procedure permits a measurement of their contribution to the flexibility of the tax structure but it does not account for the complications arising from the fact that excise taxes are reflected in the price level of output. These complications, however, do not bear significantly upon the major argument here developed and can be neglected for simplicity's sake.

[3] For the simplest case where transfer expenditures are assumed constant, the decline in (r_1) would be offset by an increase in the value for (E) leaving (Er_1), the marginal tax rate, unaffected.

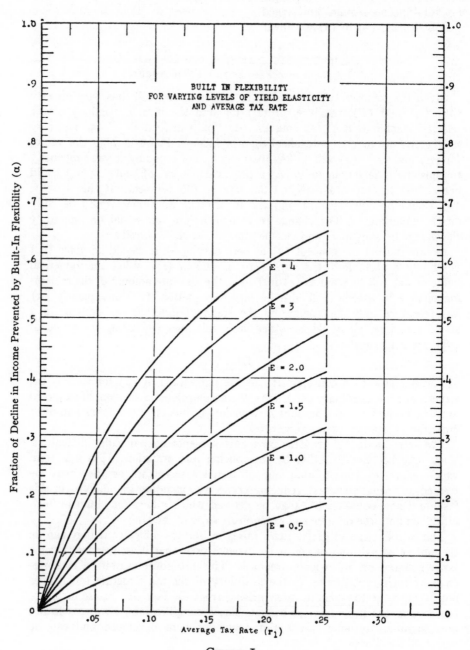

BUILT IN FLEXIBILITY
FOR VARYING LEVELS OF YIELD ELASTICITY
AND AVERAGE TAX RATE

CHART I

Corporate profits and corporate income taxes may be introduced with a minimum of complication by treating corporations as unincorporated businesses. Total income is then defined as personal income plus corporate profits before tax (but after dividends which are already included in personal income) and (c) becomes the marginal propensity to consume out of disposable personal income plus retained corporate profits. The values for (E) and (r_1) would apply to the tax system as a whole, and (α) would measure the effect of "built-in flexibility" on the entire private sector of the economy.[4]

Chart I shows the value of (α) for the United States under normal conditions at various levels of tax yield (r_1) and for various degrees of yield elasticity (E), using what may be considered a "normal" value for (c) of 0.65.[5] In reading the chart, (E) should be interpreted as a weighted average of the elasticities of the separate tax sources and a change in (E), as a change in the composition of the tax yield. An increase in (E), for example, would represent an increase in the proportion of tax revenue derived from taxes based on the more volatile income shares (such as corporate profits) or from taxes with progressive rates (such as the personal income tax). A decrease in (E) would represent increased reliance on taxes whose bases are relatively insensitive (such as excises and estate taxes) or a reduction in the degree of progressivity of the sensitive taxes. As a reference point, it may be noted that for the present federal tax system (r_1) is about 0.20 and (E) about 1.5.[6] The yield is

[4] The redefinition of (c) as the propensity to consume out of disposable income plus retained corporate profits has the disadvantage of making (c) more subject to changes in (Y) and more dependent upon the particular tax structure in use. Thus (c) will be lower if the corporation tax is lower and changes in the corporation tax share in total receipts will affect the value of (c). To a lesser extent, the same problem arises with respect to differences in the consumption impact of, say, highly progressive income taxes and highly regressive spending taxes. For a fuller discussion of the implications of the differences in the consumption impact of various taxes see R. A. Musgrave, "Alternative Budgets for Full Employment," *Am. Econ. Rev.*, Vol. XXXV, No. 3 (June, 1945), p. 387.

[5] This value of (c) was obtained by correlating total net private saving with disposable income plus corporate saving for the period 1929-1941. This thirteen-year period was found to be divided into three distinct sub-periods 1930-1932 ($[c] = 0.74$); 1933-1936 ($[c] = 0.63$); and 1937-1941 ($[c] = 0.54$), giving 0.65 as an average. All data used were from the new Commerce series.

At the present time, the value for (c) is, of course, very much higher and for consumption out of disposable income is probably greater than 1. Under such abnormal conditions (α) becomes much higher than the numerical values shown on the chart even for relatively inelastic tax system. The same tendency would result if an acceleration factor is allowed for. However, as has been indicated above, (α) should not be compared for different values of (c). In view of the abnormality and instability of present (c) values, the discussion of "built-in flexibility" is confined to some more "normal" post-transition period.

Attention is also called to the fact, not here allowed for, that (c) will differ with the rate and amplitude of income fluctuations. Instead of working with a fixed value of (c) a more elaborate analysis could be made in terms of consumption functions showing cyclical variations or time lags in adjustments.

[6] In 1946, personal income averaged 177.2 billion dollars and corporate profits (before inventory adjustment) 21.1 billion dollars. For 1947, the corresponding figures based on data for the first half year are 197.2 billion and 29.0 billion dollars. Federal personal income tax *liabilities* for 1946 at current tax rates and size of labor force may be put at 17.8 billion dollars

composed of corporation taxes 24 per cent; income taxes 50 per cent and other taxes 26 per cent.

The chart shows that for an (r_1) of 0.20 and an (E) of 1.5, (α) will be 0.358, that is, somewhat more than a third of the change in income due to a change in investment will be offset by "built-in flexibility" at that yield level. Should revenues be reduced uniformly by 50 per cent to an (r_1) of 0.10 without changing the composition of the yield, (α) will fall to 0.218. On the other hand, the effectiveness of "built-in flexibility" could be maintained at the lower level of yield by raising the average elasticity to 3.0.

IV

These preliminary considerations suggest that "built-in flexibility" may be an important factor in maintaining stability over the long run if taxes take a large proportion of income and if income elastic taxes are relied upon. But the analysis here provided lends no justification to the view now growing in popularity that "built-in flexibility" can do the job alone and that deliberate countercyclical fiscal policy can be dispensed with. The computations of the value for (α), despite their roughness, show that even under optimistic assumptions as to yield flexibility, the automatic movement of tax yields can not offset the major portion of a decline in income and employment.[7] Moreover, it should be noted that "built-in flexibility" cuts two ways: If it is helpful in cushioning the downswing in a depression, it also serves to delay the return to a full-employment level of income.

Actually there is every prospect that the value for (Er_1) will decline in the post-transition period. The level of (r_1) will be determined largely by average budget needs over the cycle. These will tend to decline as a per cent of income, although remaining higher than the prewar average. It is unlikely that much can be done to offset the fall in (r_1) by raising (E) through qualitative changes in the tax structure or its composition. In fact it is probable that (E)

(after adjustment for changes in the composition of income payments since 1946, mainly the decline in tax-exempt military pay and certain transfer payments). At the personal income level of 197.2 billion dollars assumed for 1947, income tax liabilities would be very close to 21.5 billion dollars. Federal corporation income taxes under the levels of profits assumed for the two years would be 7.3 billion dollars and 10.4 billion dollars respectively. Other federal taxes (consisting of estate and gift taxes, excises and social security taxes) would increase from 10.7 billion dollars to 11.2 billion dollars. The total change in tax revenue is therefore estimated at 7.7 billion dollars, from 35.4 billion dollars to 43.1 billion dollars.

For measuring (E), "total income" should be defined as personal income plus corporate profits before tax (but after dividends which are already included in personal income) giving 220.0 billion dollars for 1947 and 192.7 billion dollars for 1946. On this basis, (E) for the present federal tax system works out to be 1.46. It may be noted that this estimate for (E) would not be too greatly affected by moderate errors in estimates of the level of tax yields under the assumed income conditions. An underestimate by as large an amount as 2 billion dollars (which is rather unlikely) would raise (E) to about 1.8.

[7] Changing levels of unemployment benefit are the major item of flexibility on the expenditure side of the budget. If these are taken into account and using present rates of benefit payments, the value for (d) might be raised by from 5 to 10 points. The results would thus not be changed greatly.

will be lowered somewhat as the tax system is modified to reduce the impact on "investment incentives."[8] The flexibility of the tax system might be increased if provision was made for automatic adjustments in tax *rates* with changes in income but this could hardly be called "built-in flexibility" in the usual sense of the term. Rather, it is a way of applying deliberate countercyclical adjustments in the rate of taxation and expenditures. Such adjustments must remain the primary reliance of fiscal policy when it appears (as it most certainly will) that the actual level of fluctuations passes tolerable limits.

RICHARD A. MUSGRAVE*

MERTON H. MILLER*

[8] Much will depend upon what happens to the corporation tax rate and the share of the corporate tax in total receipts. Reduction of the corporate share in taxes will reduce (E) but reduction in the corporate rate applicable to dividends only would reduce (E) less than an equivalent reduction in the present uniform rate on profits because of the greater stability of dividends in comparison with total profits.

The value for (E) will also be decreased if weight is shifted from the personal income tax to the estate tax and if present exemption levels are maintained while upper surtax bracket rates are reduced faster than lower bracket rates. In the other direction, decreased reliance on excises would tend to raise (E) somewhat. To the extent that the various adjustments described are successful in raising the average level of investment and hence income over the cycle, this will tend to compensate for decreased flexibility as well as lessen the need for deliberate countercyclical adjustment.

* Mr. Musgrave is associate professor of economics at the University of Michigan and Mr. Miller is economist, Division of Research and Statistics, Board of Governors, Federal Reserve System.

[18]

TAXES, INCOME DETERMINATION, AND THE BALANCED BUDGET THEOREM

William A. Salant

THE proposition that a tax-financed change in expediture will lead to an equal change in income has been subjected to critical examination in two recent articles.[1] Both emphasize that the proposition, which has been christened the "balanced budget theorem," applies only when certain conditions are fulfilled, and they dismiss it as a special case of little interest because of the restrictive character of these conditions.

There is undoubtedly a danger that conclusions drawn from simplified models will be applied beyond the context in which they are valid and will be invested with the aura of universal truths. By defining and calling attention to the limitations on the validity of the balanced budget theorem, the articles cited serve as a useful corrective against this danger in this case. There is, however, some danger that in two respects they may be the source of confusion rather than clarification. In the first place, they concentrate attention on the limitations of the balanced budget theorem in such a way that the reader may easily lose sight of its essential core of truth. Second, they may create a somewhat inaccurate impression as to the exact location of those limits. The first danger is discussed in the succeeding paragraphs; the second in the later portions of the present paper.

It may well be that the balanced budget theorem has little direct application to the world of reality because the necessary preconditions to its validity are rarely fulfilled in that world. Nevertheless, it does not follow that the theorem is completely uninteresting and that it provides no insight whatever into the real world. In order to recognize its role in the evolution of income theory, it is only necessary to recall that, until the balanced budget theorem was advanced, it was generally believed that, under exactly the same general conditions that are assumed in the development of the theorem, a change in expenditures balanced by a change in taxes had no effect on income whatever. That is, it was believed that the multiplier for a balanced budget was zero. Whatever its limitations, the balanced budget theorem represents an important refinement of this earlier view.

That view followed from the assumption (or impression) that taxes could be treated simply as deductions from expenditure. In the balanced budget analysis, it was recognized that, while expenditures (on currently produced domestic goods and services) generate income directly, taxes do not directly reduce expenditure and income. Instead, they reduce the flow of funds available either for spending *or nonspending*. If this flow is subject to further leakages (after the taxes have been paid), such as through saving, the distinction becomes significant.

The balanced budget theorem can best be regarded as a corollary of this treatment of taxes. In a still more refined analysis, it is true, the effect upon spending of different kinds of taxes would be distinguished (and the substitution effect as well as the income effects of taxes might be considered, as Baumol and Peston have suggested). Nevertheless, it remains true that the first step was to introduce taxes explicitly as a distinct entity in the analysis and to formulate some hypothesis, however simple, as to their effect on the flow of income.

Turvey has pointed out that, in his model, the balanced budget multiplier is unity when household saving is the only leakage.[2] Does this mean, as he seems to imply, that the balanced budget multiplier will *not* be unity if there are any other leakages, or, to put it more precisely, if there are any dependent variables other than household saving and consumption? Here we must distinguish between taxes themselves and other variables. The case in which taxes are a dependent variable, assumed to be a function of income, is considered

[1] Ralph Turvey, "Some Notes on Multiplier Theory," *American Economic Review*, XLIII (June 1953), 282–86; and W. J. Baumol and M. H. Peston, "More on the Multiplier Effects of a Balanced Budget," *American Economic Review*, XLV (March 1955), 140.

[2] Turvey, loc. cit., 285–86.

TAXES, INCOME DETERMINATION, BUDGET THEOREM   153

in section III below. In section IV, new dependent variables, such as induced investment, imports, and business saving are introduced, and the effect of tax changes and balanced budget changes is considered in these enlarged systems. We shall find that the application of the balanced budget theorem is not limited to the simple model for which it was first developed.

Before we proceed to these enlarged systems, it will be useful to place the balanced budget analysis in perspective by reviewing briefly, in section I, the earlier treatment of taxes in the theory of income determination. In section II, the model from which the balanced budget theorem was originally deduced is presented.[3]

I: Background

It is a paradoxical fact that, although Keynes's *General Theory* was highly influential in directing attention to the role of governmental fiscal operations in determining the level of income, government as such plays no explicit part in the formal Keynesian model. That model divides the economy into two sectors, firms and households. Expenditures of households (consumption) are regarded as a function of income, while net expenditures of firms for goods and services (i.e., output less sales to households, or investment) are taken to be determined by other factors. Thus, given the consumption function, income is determined by investment.

In discussions based on this formulation, deficit spending by the government was considered equivalent, in its effect on income, to investment.[4] Tax-financed expenditure was assumed by implication to have no effect on income. It was sometimes mentioned, perhaps as an after-thought, that tax remission was equivalent in its effect to deficit spending. Thus taxes were treated, again by implication, as equivalent to negative investment (or to saving).[5]

Subsequent refinement of the theory brought about two major changes in the treatment of taxes.

1. It was recognized quite early that it is unrealistic to treat tax receipts or collections as an autonomous or exogenous variable, since, with a given structure of tax rates, tax collections tend to vary with income. Consequently, tax receipts were treated as a function of income.

2. It was recognized, though considerably later, that taxes cannot correctly be treated as equivalent to negative spending (or to saving) in their effect on income. Tax remission does not in itself involve any change in income or expenditure. It merely reduces the receipts of government and puts additional disposable income into the hands of the private sectors, income which they are free to save or to spend. If government expenditure and investment are considered autonomous, tax remission can raise income only by inducing an increase in consumption. As a first approximation, particularly appropriate in the case of income taxes, it seemed reasonable to assume that decisions about the division of income between consumption and saving are based on income after taxes, that is, to regard consumption as a function of *disposable* income.

---

[3] It may be noted at this point that Baumol and Peston characterize the balanced budget analysis as "misleading in that it appears by a feat of magic to be able to determine an empirical magnitude (the value of the multiplier) without the use of any empirical material" (loc. cit., 140). This complaint is difficult to understand. The balanced budget theorem is, in this respect, formally equivalent to (a) the proposition that *if* the numerator and denominator of a fraction are equal, the value of that fraction will be 1, regardless of the magnitude of numerator and denominator; or (b) the proposition that *if* the elasticity of demand for a commodity is unity, a change in supply will cause no change in the value of sales regardless of the magnitude of the shift in the supply function or the elasticity of supply. The validity of these statements is a matter of logic, not of fact. Whether either proposition is applicable to a particular situation, however, cannot be determined without the empirical knowledge, in the case of proposition (a), that the numerator and denominator of the fraction are in fact equal or unequal, or, in the case of proposition (b), that the demand function does or does not have unit elasticity. See also Prof. Alvin Hansen's comment on the Baumol and Peston paper in "More on the Multiplier Effects of a Balanced Budget: Comment," *American Economic Review*, XLVI (March 1956), 157; and the "Reply" by Baumol and Peston, *ibid.*, 160.

[4] In Robertson's phrase, the government deficit was regarded as "honorary investment." See "Mr. Clark and the Foreign Trade Multiplier," *Economic Journal*, XLIX (June 1939), 354.

[5] The only explicit reference to taxes in the *General Theory* is the observation that they might influence the aggregate consumption function by redistributing income among individuals or by affecting the net return on savings. See *General Theory of Employment, Interest and Money* (New York, 1936), 94–95.

These two refinements meant the introduction into the Keynesian model of one new equation, the tax-income function, and the modification of an old one, the consumption equation, to make consumption a function of disposable income instead of national income. These changes in the model altered the conclusions that it yields as to (1) the effect on income of changes in investment, government, or consumption expenditure with a *given* set of tax rates, and (2) the effect of changes in the tax structure itself.

With respect to the effect of changes in investment or government expenditure, or shifts in the consumption function, the recognition of tax receipts as a function of income meant that an autonomous change in spending would cause an income-induced change in taxes. Thus an increase in government spending would cause taxes to rise, and the resulting deficit would be smaller than the spending itself.[6]

Moreover, the increase in tax receipts would be a leakage that reduces the multiplier effect of the spending. The multiplier adjusted to allow for the marginal tax-income ratio is smaller than the simple Keynesian multiplier which allowed only for the leakage into saving.[7]

When we consider the effect on income of autonomous changes in taxes themselves, we find that much of the discussion does not appear to incorporate the second refinement mentioned above, the treatment of tax receipts as a function of income. For example, the two most explicit algebraic statements of the balanced budget theorem treat taxes as an independent variable.[8] On that assumption, it was concluded that:

1. Dollar for dollar, changes in taxes have a weaker income-generating effect than changes

[6] While this point was frequently mentioned in the late 1930's, especially by advocates of expansionist fiscal policies, it is interesting to note that it was also recognized in Kahn's original formulation of the theory of the multiplier. See R. F. Kahn, "The Relation of Home Investment to Unemployment," *Economic Journal*, XLI (June 1931), 171.
[7] See Paul A. Samuelson, "Fiscal Policy and Income Determination," *Quarterly Journal of Economics*, LVI (August 1942), 581.
[8] See Trygve Haavelmo, "Multiplier Effects of a Balanced Budget," *Econometrica*, XIII (October 1945), 311; and Samuelson, "The Simple Mathematics of Income Determination," in Lloyd Metzler et al., *Income, Employment, and Public Policy, Essays in Honor of Alvin H. Hansen* (New York, 1948), 138.

in expenditures (for currently-produced goods and services). Specifically, if the multiplier applicable to expenditures is k, the (negative) tax multiplier is $(k-1)$.

2. As a corollary of (1) it follows that a change in expenditure balanced by an equal change in taxes will have a multiplier of 1.[9]

Whether these conclusions apply when tax receipts are assumed to vary with income is, as indicated above, one of the questions raised by Turvey's discussion and is considered in section III below.

While the treatment of taxes in the Keynesian system was refined along the lines just described, it was shown that the original simple model could be developed and enlarged in numerous other ways, by the addition of new variables, the disaggregation of old ones, and the introduction of new behavior hypotheses. For example, exports, imports, and induced investment could be introduced, or saving could be divided into a business and a household

[9] For early statements of the balanced budget theorem, see references cited in Samuelson, "Simple Mathematics," 140. While the application of the balanced budget theorem to the situation in which an increase in effective demand is considered desirable has often been discussed, the reasoning, of course, applies also to situations verging on inflation. Thus, in order to prevent an inflationary gap when government expenditures are rising, it is not enough for taxes to rise in step with expenditures and keep disposable income from rising. They must increase faster, in order to reduce disposable income and private demand as government demand increases. While this fact was clearly recognized in some wartime studies of the inflationary gap — see e.g. Walter S. Salant's and Milton Friedman's papers on "The Inflationary Gap," *American Economic Review*, XXXII (June 1942), 309 and 318, respectively — it is interesting to note that it was not recognized in the British budget address of April 1941, which introduced the concept of the inflationary gap, and in which Keynes played a central role.

Note: This statement must be drastically amended in the light of R. S. Sayers, *Financial Policy, 1939–1945* (London, 1956), which the writer was able to consult only after the present article was in proof. In his account of the 1941 budget, which he describes as the cornerstone of British wartime financial policy, Professor Sayers quotes an internal memorandum written by Keynes in September 1940, which states that extra taxes of £300 million might reduce consumption by only £150–200 million, the remainder of the taxation falling on saving (op. cit., 71). To effect a £300 million cut in consumption, the additional taxes needed were of the order of £400 million. This is, of course, as clear a statement as could be asked of the principle underlying the balanced budget theorem. It was evidently regarded as a refinement which could be slurred over in the budget address itself, and the language of that address appears to imply that, in order to achieve a specified cut in consumption, it was necessary only to increase taxes by an equal amount.

component.[10] What is the effect of these developments on the conclusions as to the income effects of tax changes? In particular, does the balanced budget theorem apply to such enlarged systems? Section IV is addressed to these questions.

II: Consumption the Only Dependent Variable

The simple model from which the balanced budget theorem was derived contains only the definitional identities:

$$Y = C + I + G \qquad (1)$$
$$X = Y - W \qquad (2)$$

and the single behavior equation

$$C = a + bX \qquad (3)$$

where Y denotes income, C consumption, I investment, G government expenditure on currently produced goods and services, X disposable income (income less taxes plus government transfer payments), and W tax receipts less government transfer payments,[11] all in real terms. Equation (3) is an aggregate consumption function, assumed to be linear.[12] Investment, government expenditures, and taxes less transfer payments are all assumed to be autonomous.[13]

[10] For an excellent summary of these developments, see Samuelson's article on "The Simple Mathematics of Income Determination," cited above.

[11] It will be noted that transfer payments are treated as negative taxes. This treatment implies that the income effect of transfer payments is equal and opposite to that of taxes. Specifically, it is assumed that, although transfer payments do not themselves represent income, they do add to the disposable income available for consumption or saving. On this assumption, which is reasonable for simple models, it is easier to treat transfer payments as negative taxes than as a special category of expenditure. In the text below, we shall, for the sake of brevity, refer to tax receipts less transfer payments of government simply as "taxes" or "tax receipts." Similarly, G, government expenditures, always denotes expenditures for currently-produced goods and services. Thus it excludes transfer payments, purchases of existing capital assets, and purchases that result in disinvestment in inventories. Turvey has pointed out that the balanced budget theorem does not apply to expenditures for these purposes, and Baumol and Peston have dealt with the value of the balanced budget multiplier when part of the additional expenditure is for purposes other than purchase of newly-produced goods and services.

[12] In order to concentrate on the income effect of taxes, we rule out the possibility of a shift in the consumption function arising from redistribution of income by assuming that all individuals have linear consumption functions with identical marginal propensities to consume.

[13] In this model, and in those considered below, the only

Solving for income, we get:

$$Y = \frac{I + G + a - bW}{1 - b} \qquad (4)$$

The multiplier relating a change in income to a change in one of the independent variables, investment or government expenditure (or for that matter a parallel shift in the consumption function denoted by the addition of an amount h to the parameter a), takes the familiar form

$$\frac{\Delta Y}{\Delta I} = \frac{\Delta Y}{\Delta G} = \frac{\Delta Y}{h} = \frac{1}{1 - b}. \qquad (5)$$

The multiplier relating a change in income to a change in tax receipts is

$$\frac{\Delta Y}{\Delta W} = -\frac{b}{1 - b}. \qquad (6)$$

Thus tax changes will have a weaker effect on income, dollar for dollar, than expenditure changes. The ratio of the tax multiplier to the expenditure multiplier is $(-b)$. The effect on income of a change in expenditure accompanied by an equal change in taxes is the algebraic sum of the multipliers (5) and (6):[14]

$$\frac{\Delta Y}{\Delta G} = \frac{\Delta Y}{\Delta W} = 1 \quad \text{when } \Delta G = \Delta W. \quad (7)$$

This is the balanced budget theorem. It means that the increment in income will be equal to the increment in government expenditure and will consist entirely of additional goods and services produced for the government. Consumption will remain unchanged.

The foregoing is familiar ground. Two comments are called for at this point.

1. The values of the expenditure, tax, and balanced budget multipliers follow from the hypothesis in (3) that consumption is a func-

behavior relations considered are simple income effects. That is, the dependent variables are made functions either of aggregate income or of some component of income or expenditure. This treatment excludes the possibility, for example, that changes in marginal tax rates might alter the inducement to invest with unchanged prospective demand, or that government expenditure for a particular purpose might affect private spending for related purposes and thereby shift the consumption function.

[14] It should be noted that the expression ΔY in the lefthand side of (7) refers to the total (or net) change in income resulting from the combined effect of the tax change and the expenditure change, not to that resulting from the expenditure change alone.

tion of disposable income. If instead it had been assumed that taxes were paid entirely out of saving, consumption would be a function of income, Y, and taxes would play no part whatever in income determination. If, on the other hand, it had been assumed that taxes were paid entirely out of consumption, the consumption function would have the form $C = C(Y) - W$, and the effect of taxes on the level of income would be equal and opposite to that of government or investment expenditure. The hypothesis that consumption varies with income after taxes appears most applicable to personal income taxes. Thus the balanced budget theorem applies primarily to these taxes, rather than to indirect taxes or corporate income taxes.[15]

2. The balanced budget theorem can be deduced directly by solving the underlying equations (1), (2), and (3) for disposable income, without going through the intermediate stages of calculating the expenditure multiplier and the tax multiplier. The solution for disposable income is

$$X = \frac{a + I + G - W}{1 - b}. \tag{8}$$

Since a, b, and I are unchanged, and the change in taxes offsets the change in government expenditure, disposable income must be unchanged. Hence the change in income must be equal to the change in the budget.[16] We shall find this short-cut proof useful later in dealing with more complicated models.

III: Taxes a Function of Income

We shall now consider the case in which taxes less transfers are assumed to be a linear function of income: [17]

[15] Somers has considered all three possibilities mentioned above: taxes falling on saving, those falling on consumption, and taxes falling on income that leave the marginal propensity to consume (out of disposable income) unchanged. See Harold M. Somers, "The Impact of Fiscal Policy on National Income," *Canadian Journal of Economics and Political Science* (August 1942), 364, and *Public Finance and National Income* (Philadelphia, 1949), 500–503 and 507–12. E. Cary Brown has analyzed the effect of consumption taxes in "Analysis of Consumption Taxes in Terms of the Theory of Income Determination," *American Economic Review*, XL (March 1950), 74.

[16] This method of demonstrating the balanced budget theorem is due to Samuelson. See "The Simple Mathematics of Income Determination." op. cit., 142.

[17] The reader may, if he finds it convenient, think of this function as representing a proportional income tax

$$W = s + tY. \tag{9}$$

Solving for income, we now get

$$Y = \frac{I + G + a - bs}{1 - b(1 - t)}. \tag{10}$$

With a given tax structure, the multiplier for changes in either investment or government expenditure, or for an increment h to the constant term in consumption, is:

$$\frac{\Delta Y}{\Delta I} = \frac{\Delta Y}{\Delta G} = \frac{\Delta Y}{h}$$

$$= \frac{1}{1 - b(1 - t)}. \tag{11}$$

It should be noted that changes in any of these variables will alter tax receipts. In particular, an increment in G will not result in an equal change in the budget deficit.

Changes in the tax function may be caused by changes in either of the parameters s or t. The former correspond geometrically to parallel vertical shifts in the tax function, the latter to changes in its slope resulting from rotation around its intercept with the vertical axis. We shall consider first parallel shifts resulting from the addition of an increment, denoted by Δs, to the term s. The multiplier will be:

$$\frac{\Delta Y}{\Delta s} = -\frac{b}{1 - b(1 - t)}. \tag{12}$$

The ratio of the tax multiplier to the expenditure multiplier is still $(-b)$, as it was in the first model. The sum of the multipliers, however, which indicates the effect on income of a change in expenditure accompanied by an equal change in the terms of the tax function, is now:

$$\frac{\Delta Y}{\Delta G} = \frac{1-b}{1-b(1-t)} \text{ when}$$

$$\Delta G = \Delta s. \tag{13}$$

This quantity will be less than unity as long as the marginal tax rate t is positive. Consumption, instead of remaining constant, as it does when the marginal tax rate is zero, will decline.

levied at rate t, along with a head tax s. Alternatively, he may think of s as a lump-sum transfer payment or tax exemption, in which case its value would be negative. The assumption of linearity rules out consideration of an income tax with rising marginal rates.

TAXES, INCOME DETERMINATION, BUDGET THEOREM   157

A balanced change in expenditure and in tax receipts *at the initial level of income* will not produce an equal change in income.

This, however, is not the whole story. The ultimate change in tax receipts at the new equilibrium level of income ($\triangle W$ in our notation) will be greater than $\triangle s$, and therefore greater than $\triangle G$. Instead of equal changes in expenditures and taxes, we have an expenditure change accompanied by a somewhat greater change in taxes. The multiplier in (13) can hardly be called a "balanced budget" multiplier.

In order to determine the balanced budget multiplier for this model, we must so adjust the shift in the tax function that, *at the new equilibrium position*, the tax change and the expenditure change are equal. One way to find this multiplier is to set $\triangle W = \triangle G$, solve for the required shift in the tax function $\triangle s$, and then for the resulting change in income $\triangle Y$. We can proceed more directly, however, by solving for disposable income as in (2) of section II above. Since the solution for disposable income is identical with that developed in section II, equation (8), we know at once that disposable income must remain unchanged if $\triangle G = \triangle W$. Thus the change in income again equals the change in expenditures and the ultimate change in tax receipts. The "balanced budget" multiplier is again unity even when tax receipts are assumed to vary with income, but "balance" in the budget change must be understood to refer to the equality of $\triangle G$ with $\triangle W$, the *ultimate* change in tax receipts, rather than $\triangle s$, the initial change.[18]

We turn now to the effect of changes in the marginal tax rate t on income.[19] Denoting the original tax rate t' and the new rate t'' and the original level of income Y' and the new equilibrium level Y'', we first solve for the change in income resulting from a change in the marginal tax rate from t' to t''.[20] The result is a fraction, equation (16) in footnote 20, of which the numerator represents the product of the change in tax yield at the *original* level of income and the marginal propensity to consume, while the denominator is the same expression that appeared in the denominators of the multipliers in equations (11) and (12) above, but calculated at the *new* tax rate t''.

Equation (16) is the first case in which the initial level of income Y' appears in the solution for $\triangle Y$. By dividing through by Y', we can find the *relative* change in income as a function of the marginal propensity to consume and the new and old tax rates. This result is in accordance with common sense; a given change in tax rates (as opposed to tax receipts) will produce a determinate relative change in income, rather than a determinate absolute change.

The conclusions with respect to the balanced budget theorem are similar to those reached above in the case of parallel shifts in the tax function. When the change in tax receipts at the *original* level of income is set equal to the change in expenditure, i.e., when $(t'' - t')Y' = \triangle G$, the resulting change in income will be less than the change in revenues and expenditures. When, however, the *ultimate* change in taxes is set equal to the change in expenditures, i.e., when $\triangle W = \triangle G$, an equal change in income will result. This conclusion can again be derived from inspection of equation (8), the solution for disposable income, which remains unchanged.[21] It might be added that, since the

[18] One loose end remains. While we have assumed a vertical shift, $\triangle S$, in the tax function just sufficient to insure that $\triangle W = \triangle G$, we have yet to determine how great this shift must be. Since we now know that $\triangle Y = \triangle G = \triangle W$, the calculation is simple. Substituting $\triangle G$ for both $\triangle Y$ and $\triangle W$ in the tax equation (9), we get

$$\triangle S = \triangle G (1 - t). \qquad (14)$$

[19] This case has been considered only in geometric terms, so far as I am aware, except for Turvey's article, loc. cit., 285. Geometric treatments include Robert L. Bishop, "Alternative Expansionist Policies: A Diagrammatic Analysis," in *Income, Employment and Public Policy*, 317; E. Cary Brown, loc. cit., 74, in which the effect of consumption taxes is compared to that of income taxes; and J. G. Gurley, "Fiscal Policy for Full Employment," *Journal of Political Economy*, LX (December 1952), 525.

[20] From equation (10) we obtain for the change in income the unwieldy expression

$$\triangle Y = Y'' - Y' = \frac{I + G + a - bs}{1 - b(1 - t'')} - \frac{I + G + a - bs}{1 - b(1 - t')} \qquad (15)$$

which fortunately simplifies to

$$\triangle Y = -\frac{b(t'' - t')Y'}{1 - b(1 - t'')}. \qquad (16)$$

This result corresponds to Turvey's conclusion, loc. cit., 285.

[21] The calculation of the change in the marginal tax rate required to preserve the original state of budgetary balance is somewhat more complicated than before. The change in tax receipts, $\triangle W$, which results from both the change in rates and the change in income, can be expressed as

$$\triangle W = t''Y'' - t'Y'.$$

form of tax and consumption functions does not affect equation (8), this conclusion does not depend on the assumption of linear functions.

We have shown that the treatment of taxes as a dependent variable instead of an independent parameter does not alter the value of the balanced budget multiplier. Similar conclusions apply if government expenditure is treated as a dependent variable.

Up to this point, we have been concerned largely with balanced changes in expenditure and taxation. What can we say about the relative effectiveness of tax changes by themselves, as compared with expenditure changes, in inducing changes in income? The first problem is to decide on the appropriate terms for comparison. We might compare the increase in income resulting from a dollar of expenditure with that resulting from a dollar of tax remission (either at the initial or at the new equilibrium level of income). This, however, does not seem an entirely appropriate comparison, because, in the present model, the expenditure will itself induce a change in tax receipts, and the change in the budget surplus or deficit will be less than the additional expenditure. It would appear to be more interesting to compare the increase in income resulting from one dollar of additional *deficit* caused by expenditure with the increase resulting from a dollar of deficit caused by tax remission.

The result of this comparison is that the increase in income per dollar of deficit resulting from increased expenditure bears a ratio to the increase in income per dollar of deficit caused by tax remission of $1/b\ (1-t)$.[22] Since the

quantity $b(1-t)$ must be less than unity in a stable system,[23] we can conclude that, per unit of deficit, expenditure has a greater impact on income than tax remission, just as it did in the first model.

IV: Additional Dependent Variables Introduced

We have just considered a model in which tax receipts (or expenditures) are considered a function of income, and we have found that the value of the balanced budget multiplier is still unity, provided the "balanced" change in expenditures and taxes is understood to refer to the values of those variables at the new equilibrium position. In this section we shall see what happens to the balanced budget multiplier when new dependent variables (whether leakages like imports or business saving, or expenditures like investment), other than taxes and household saving, are introduced. To anticipate the results, the conclusions will be that (1) the balanced budget multiplier will be unity if the new dependent variables are made functions of disposable income $(Y-W)$ or of private expenditure $(Y-G)$, but not if they are functions of national income (Y); (2) in any event, the balanced budget multiplier will be greater than zero and may be greater or less than unity.

To simplify the analysis, we shall first consider tax receipts an independent variable, as in section II above. We introduce investment as a new dependent variable, which we shall assume initially to be a linear function of national income:[24]

$$I = u + vY. \tag{19}$$

By assumption $\Delta W = \Delta G = \Delta Y$.

Manipulation of these expressions gives the following result for the required change in rates:

$$t'' - t' = \frac{\Delta G(1 - t')}{\Delta G + Y'}$$

[22] The increase in income ΔY resulting from an increment of expenditure ΔG is given by equation (11). The rise in tax receipts is $t\,\Delta Y$, and the change in the deficit (which we may denote as $\Delta G - \Delta W$), is therefore $\Delta G - t\,\Delta Y$. The ratio of the change in income to the change in the deficit is

$$\frac{\Delta Y}{(\Delta G - \Delta W)} = \frac{1}{(1-b)(1-t)} \text{ with } s \text{ and } t \text{ constant. (17)}$$

This result agrees with Samuelson, "Simple Mathematics,"

145, equation (11). The corresponding ratio for changes in the tax function, whether they result from changes in the constant term s or in the marginal tax rate t, is

$$\frac{\Delta Y}{\Delta W} = -\frac{b}{1-b} \text{ with } G \text{ constant.} \tag{18}$$

The value of the ratio $\Delta Y / \Delta W$ is the same as in the first model considered, in which taxes were an independent variable — see equation (6) above. This equality has been pointed out by Thomas C. Schelling, *National Income Behavior* (New York, 1951), 100.

[23] See Schelling, op. cit., 85.

[24] Investment has been selected as the new dependent variable because its introduction requires less change in the system of equations than would that of, say, business saving or imports, and it serves equally well to illustrate the propositions with which we are concerned here.

TAXES, INCOME DETERMINATION, BUDGET THEOREM 159

Solving the new system of equations (1), (2), (3), and (19) for income, we obtain

$$Y = \frac{a + u + G - bW}{1 - b - v}. \qquad (20)$$

It is readily seen that the multiplier for changes in government expenditures, assuming all other parameters constant, is

$$\frac{\triangle Y}{\triangle G} = \frac{1}{1 - b - v} \qquad (21)$$

while the multiplier for tax changes alone is

$$\frac{\triangle Y}{\triangle W} = -\frac{b}{1 - b - v}. \qquad (22)$$

While the ratio of the tax multiplier to the expenditure multiplier remains $(-b)$, as in the first model considered in section II, the balanced budget multiplier, which is equal to the sum of the separate multipliers, is no longer unity but rather $\left(\dfrac{1 - b}{1 - b - v}\right)$, which is greater than unity if v is positive.

Why does the introduction of induced investment affect the balanced budget multiplier? While there are differences between investment and consumption which are vital for other purposes, inspection of the system of equations shows that, in the present context, the only difference is that investment is assumed to be a function of national income (Y), while consumption is made a function of disposable income ($Y - W$). Thus, while a balanced change in G and W will initially (i.e., in the "first round") leave disposable income and hence consumption unchanged, it will affect Y, and hence investment, and will set in motion a multiplier process.

If induced investment were assumed to be a function of disposable income instead of national income, equation (20), the investment function, would be exactly similar in form to equation (3), the consumption function, and the balanced budget multiplier would be unity.[25] Alternatively, investment might be assumed, with equal plausibility, to be a function of private expenditure (i.e., of $C + I$

[25] Smithies has treated investment in this way in his chapter on "Federal Budgeting and Fiscal Policy," in *A Survey of Contemporary Economics* (Philadelphia, 1948), 188.

which equals $Y - G$). The balanced budget multiplier would still be unity (although the government expenditure multiplier would now be reduced to $\dfrac{1 - v}{1 - b - v}$).

More generally, when each of the individual dependent variables is treated as a function of either disposable income ($Y - W$) or private expenditure ($Y - G$), they will be uniquely determined by $G - W$ (assuming the parameters of the behavior equations, such as a, b, v, and u in the present system, and any other independent variables, constant). Since a balanced change in G and W means that $G - W$ remains unchanged, all these dependent variables will also remain constant. Government expenditure will be the only type of expenditure that changes, and $\triangle Y$ will equal $\triangle G$; the balanced budget multiplier will be unity.

If, however, some dependent variable is not uniquely determined by $Y - W$ or $Y - G$ and, in particular, if it is a function of Y, then it cannot be expressed as a unique function of $G - W$, and it will be affected by balanced changes in G and W.

These conclusions can be readily applied to an open system with foreign trade. If, for example, exports are considered an independent variable which remains constant for the present purpose, and imports are made a function of national income (or of total expenditure $C + I + G + E$ where E denotes exports), then the balanced budget multiplier will be less than unity (but greater than zero). If, however, imports were assumed to consist entirely of goods destined for private consumption and investment but not for government use, then the introduction of foreign trade would not affect a balanced budget multiplier which had a value of unity in a closed system.

If business saving is introduced, the "disposable income" available to households is now reduced by the amount of the business saving, and the consumption equation must be adjusted accordingly. Under most conditions, the introduction of business saving reduces the value of the balanced budget multiplier. There is, however, a special case which illustrates the general conclusions stated above. If personal taxes, imports, and investment are all zero or constant, and if business saving is a function of national income less business taxes, then business saving, disposable income, and consumption will all be uniquely determined by national income less taxes. Under these conditions, a change in expenditure fully balanced by a change in business taxes will have a multiplier of unity.

All of the preceding discussion has been based on the assumption that taxes are an independent variable. How are the conclusions altered if taxes are allowed to vary with income? It can be shown that, as in section III above when a tax function was added, the value of the expenditure multiplier will change, but the balanced budget multiplier will not be affected.[26] It also remains true that, per dollar of deficit, the income-generating effect of expenditures is higher than that of taxes.

The foregoing conclusions may be compared with Turvey's remark that the balanced budget multiplier will be unity when "household saving is the only leakage; i.e., business saving, marginal rates of government expenditure, all marginal tax rates, and the marginal propensity to import are all zero."[27] In section III above we concluded that marginal rates of government expenditure (on goods and services) and on personal income tax need not be

[26] The calculation of the value of the balanced budget multiplier when taxes are a function of income, and the balanced budget multiplier is not unity, is rather complex. The difficulty lies in determining how much of a shift in the tax function is required to insure that the change in tax receipts balances the change in expenditure. It will be recalled that in section III above, where taxes were treated as a function of income, we deduced at once by inspection of the equations that the balanced budget multiplier must be unity. Knowing the change in income, we could easily compute the required shift of the tax function. If, however, the value of the balanced budget multiplier cannot be determined by inspection, then it is necessary to calculate the shift in the tax function *before* the change in income can be determined. For example, if a given change in expenditure ΔG is to be balanced by an equal change in taxes ΔW, achieved in part through a vertical shift in the tax function Δs, the determination of the resulting change in income requires the following steps: (1) calculate the change in income resulting from ΔG alone; (2) calculate the change in the budget surplus resulting from ΔG alone, by applying the marginal tax rate to the change in income calculated in (1), and subtracting the result from ΔG; (3) calculate the change in the parameter s required to offset the change in the deficit resulting from ΔG alone, as found in (2); and finally (4) calculate the change in income resulting from the change in s alone, and add it to that resulting from ΔG alone. The sum is the change in income resulting from the balanced change in expenditures and taxes.

[27] Loc. cit., 285–86.

zero if the balanced budget condition is interpreted to refer to the ultimate rather than the initial change in the budget. We can now conclude that the other leakages need not be zero provided the relevant dependent variables are functions of disposable income (or of $Y - G$).[28]

V: Concluding Remarks

The foregoing analysis suggests the following general conclusions about the income effects of personal income taxes (or transfer payments) and of balanced changes in such taxes and government expenditures on goods and services:[29]

1. Per dollar of additional deficit, an increase in expenditures with unchanged tax rates will have a greater income-generating effect than a dollar of deficit arising from a reduction in tax rates.

2. It follows from (1) that an increase in expenditures fully offset by an equal increase in tax receipts will have *some* income-generating effect. The magnitude of this effect will vary in different models.

3. An increase in expenditure fully offset by an equal increase in tax receipts will generate an equal increase in income in a system in which all the income-determining dependent variables, such as consumption, induced investment, and imports, are functions of disposable income $(Y-W)$ or of private expenditure less imports $(Y-G)$, but not when they are functions of national income.

4. The foregoing propositions apply even when income taxes (or for that matter government expenditures) are themselves dependent variables, provided it is understood that the relevant changes in expenditures and tax receipts are the *ultimate* changes at the new

[28] In the particular model used by Turvey, neither imports nor business saving satisfies this condition, but indirect taxes are considered a function of disposable income. For this reason, the balanced budget multiplier will be unity in Turvey's model even if the marginal rate of indirect taxes (which Turvey assumes to fall entirely on consumption) is not zero, as Peston has pointed out. See "A Note on the Balanced Budget Multiplier," *American Economic Review*, XLIV (March 1954), 129.

[29] These conclusions apply to models of the type considered in this paper, in which all functional relations involve only simple income effects. See fn. 13.

TAXES, INCOME DETERMINATION, BUDGET THEOREM   161

equilibrium levels of income, rather than the initial or impact effects of shifts in the tax (or expenditure) function at the original income level.

The balanced budget theorem, in what we may call its strict form, states that a balanced change in taxes and expenditures has a multiplier of exactly unity. As (3) above indicates, this proposition is valid only under certain conditions. In particular, it applies to simple models in which consumption (and taxes themselves) are the only dependent variables (and the hypothesis about the behavior of consumption is that it varies with income after taxes).

Nevertheless, as stated in (2) above, a balanced change in taxes (or transfer payments) and expenditures will always have *some* income-generating effect; the appropriate multiplier may be greater or less than one, depending on the model. The balanced budget theorem, while only an approximation to the truth (like any statement derived from simplified models), is a better approximation than the view it superseded, that the income-generating effects of taxes (or transfer payments) are equal and opposite to those of expenditures on goods and services, and hence that the balanced budget multiplier is zero.

[19]

STABILISATION POLICY AND THE TIME-FORMS OF LAGGED RESPONSES [1]

In an earlier article [2] I used a number of dynamic process models to illustrate the operation of certain types of stabilisation policy. In setting up the models I assumed that each lagged response was of the particular time-form known as an exponential lag. I pointed out [3] that other time-forms would probably give better representations of the real responses in an economic system, but did not introduce these more realistic lag forms into the models owing to the difficulty of solving the high-order differential equations to which they would have led.

Since then the National Physical Laboratory and Short Brothers and Harland, Ltd., have allowed me to use their electronic simulators, by means of which the time responses of quite complex systems with a variety of lag forms can be found very rapidly. [4] In addition, I have become more familiar with the frequency-response method of analysis based on the Nyquist stability criterion. This is a graphical method which not only enables considerable information to be obtained about the dynamic properties of a system without solving the differential equation of the system, but also gives valuable insight into the ways in which the dynamic properties would be altered if the relationships and lag forms in the system were modified or additional relationships included. [5]

A study, using frequency-response analysis and electronic simulators, of the properties of models in which the lags are given more realistic time-forms has shown that the problem of stabilisation is more complex than appeared to be the case when attention was confined to the simpler lag forms used in

[1] I wish the thank Professor R. G. D. Allen, Professor J. E. Meade, Professor Lionel Robbins and Mr. R. H. Tizard for helpful comments on an earlier draft of this paper.

[2] " Stabilisation Policy in a Closed Economy," ECONOMIC JOURNAL, June 1954, pp. 290–323.

[3] *Ibid.*, p. 292.

[4] I am indebted to the Director of the National Physical Laboratory and to Short Brothers and Harland, Ltd., for permission to use the simulators. At the National Physical Laboratory, where most of the work was carried out, Mr. D. V. Blake operated the simulator and gave invaluable help and advice. I benefited greatly from discussions with him and am most grateful to him for his willing co-operation. I also wish to thank Mr. E. Lloyd Thomas, Mr. R. J. A. Paul and Mr. P. A. R. Wright of Short Brothers and Harland, Ltd., for their assistance. The possibility of using electronic simulators for studying problems of economic regulation was suggested to me by Mr. R. H. Tizard.

[5] There is an extensive literature on the use of frequency-response methods in the analysis and synthesis of engineering systems. See, for example, H. M. James, N. B. Nichols and R. S. Phillips, *Theory of Servomechanisms* (New York: McGraw-Hill Book Co., 1947) and G. S. Brown and D. P. Cambell, *Principles of Servomechanisms* (New York: John Wiley and Sons, 1948). For a brief description of the methods with some applications to economic problems see A. Tustin, *The Mechanism of Economic Systems* (London: William Heinemann, Ltd., 1954), especially Chapter III. See also R. G. D. Allen, " The Engineers' Approach to Economic Models," *Economica*, May 1955, and R. G. D. Allen, *Mathematical Economics* (London: Macmillan and Co. Ltd., 1956), Chapters 8 and 9.

my earlier article. In this study a number of alternative models were first analysed by the frequency-response method, and the effects of variations in the lag forms and the values of the parameters on the stability of the models were investigated. Some of the models were then set up on the electronic simulators, disturbances were applied and the resulting time paths of the variables were found. In the present article two of the models which were studied are described and their dynamic properties illustrated by recordings from the electronic simulators.

I. A Multiplier Model with Error Correction

The first model is shown diagrammatically in Fig. 1, which is similar to Fig. 10 of my earlier article [1] except that the accelerator relationship has

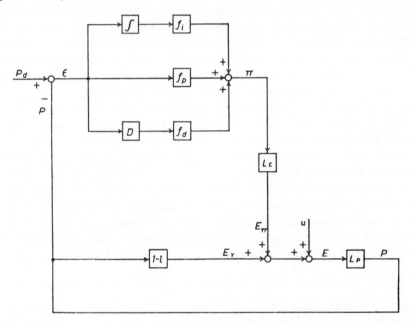

Fig. 1

been omitted. The lines in the diagram represent the variables of the system, measured as deviations from initial equilibrium values. Relationships between variables are indicated by the symbols in the squares, the arrows showing the causal direction of the relationships. The lower closed loop in the diagram represents a simple multiplier model. It is assumed that aggregate real income or production, P, responds to changes in aggregate real demand, E, through the lag relationship L_P. Changes in aggregate demand are analysed into three components, E_Y, E_π and u. E_Y denotes those changes in demand which are related to changes in income through the

[1] *Op. cit.*, p. 306.

marginal propensity to spend $1-l$. We shall give l, the " marginal leakage " from the circular flow of income, the value 0·25, so that the multiplier is 4·0. E_π is the policy demand, *i.e.*, it is the amount by which aggregate demand is increased or decreased as a direct result of action taken by the regulating authorities for the purpose of stabilising the system.   All changes in aggregate demand caused by changes in factors other than income and stabilisation policy are included in the variable u.

The relationships shown at the top of the diagram represent an error-correction type of stabilisation policy. The actual level of production is subtracted from the desired level of production, P_d, giving the error in production,[1] ϵ. It is assumed that the regulating authorities are able to make continuous adjustments in the strength of the correcting action they take but that there is a distributed time lag, L_c, between changes in the strength of the correcting action and the resulting changes in policy demand. The amount by which policy demand would be changed as a direct result of the policy measures if they operated without time lag will be called the potential policy demand, π, the amount by which it is in fact changed as a direct result of policy measures is the actual policy demand E_π.

The basic problem in stabilising production is to relate the actual policy demand to the error in production in such a way that errors caused by un-predicted disturbances are corrected as quickly and smoothly as possible.[2] For a given correction lag the problem reduces to that of finding the most suitable way of relating the potential policy demand to the error in produc-tion.   In my earlier article [3] I argued that to obtain satisfactory regulation of a system it is usually necessary for the potential policy demand to be made the sum of three components, one component depending on the error itself, one depending on the time integral of the error and the third depending on the time derivative (or rate of change) of the error.   That is, the relationship should be of the form $\pi = f_p \epsilon + f_i \int \epsilon dt + f_d \frac{d\epsilon}{dt}$, where f_p, f_i and f_d are parameters which I called respectively the proportional, integral and deriva-tive correction factors.   This relationship is represented by the three loops at the top of Fig. 1, the symbol $\int$ indicating integration with respect to time and D indicating differentiation with respect to time.

We shall consider three different forms of the production lag L_p.   These are illustrated by curves (a), (b) and (c) of Fig. 2, which show hypothetical time paths of the response of production to a unit step fall in demand occur-ring at time $t = 0$.   With lag form (a) the rate of change of production at any

---

[1] The error is here defined to be P_d-P rather than $P-P_d$ as in my earlier article.   In the literature on regulating systems the error in a variable is usually defined as the desired value minus the actual value.

[2] If reliable and frequent measurements of aggregate demand were available the potential policy demand could also be related to the error in demand. This would permit a more rapid correction of errors in production caused by shifts in aggregate demand.

[3] *Op. cit.*, pp. 293–303.

time is proportional to the difference between demand and production at that time.   We call this an exponential lag and define the time constant of the lag as the reciprocal of the factor of proportionality; for the response shown in curve (a) the time constant is 0·25 year.   The exponential lag form is very convenient for mathematical treatment, but it implies a more rapid response in the early stages of an adjustment than is likely to be typical of economic behaviour.   The time path of adjustment shown in curve (b) of Fig. 2 is probably more realistic.   This time path is obtained if the lag is

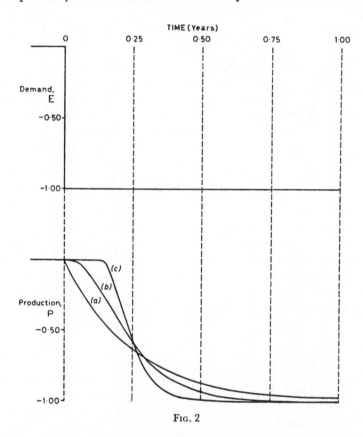

Fig. 2

equivalent to three shorter exponential lags operating in sequence, the time constants of the individual lags being 0·0833 year, so that the total time constant of the composite lag is again 0·25 year.   This triple exponential form of lag is probably a fairly good representation of many economic relationships.   In some cases, however, we should expect that there would be no response at all until some considerable time after a change had occurred, the time path of the adjustment being somewhat like that shown in curve (c) of Fig. 2.   We shall call an interval during which there is no response at all a time delay, to distinguish it from the exponential type of lag in which a continuous gradual adjustment takes place. The adjustment path in curve (c) results from a lag which is equivalent to a sequence consisting of a time delay of 0·125 year and three exponential lags each with a time constant of 0·0417 year, the total time constant of the composite lag again being 0·25 year.

The time forms which we shall use for the correction lag will be similar to those shown in Fig. 2, except that the time scale will be doubled. Thus lag form (a) for the correction lag will be a single exponential lag with a time

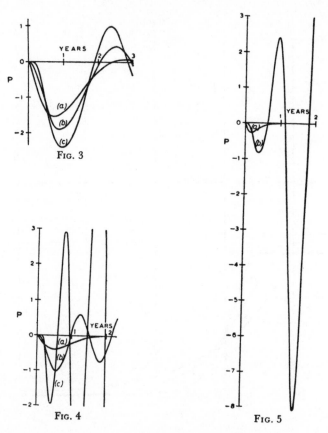

FIG. 3

FIG. 4

FIG. 5

constant of 0·50 year, lag form (b) will be a sequence of three exponential lags, each with a time constant of 0·167 year, and lag form (c) will be a sequence consisting of a time delay of 0·25 year and three exponential lags, each with a time constant of 0·0833 year.

Figs. 3, 4 and 5 reproduce recordings from the electronic simulators showing the response of production to a unit step change in the variable u applied negatively at time $t = 0$, for different combinations of correction factors and lag forms. The responses shown in Fig. 3 are obtained when the proportional correction factor f_p is 0·5, the integral correction factor f_i is

0·5 and the derivative correction factor f_d is zero. When both the production and the correction lags are of form (*a*) the response is that shown in curve (*a*).[1] When the lags are changed to form (*b*), the rest of the system remaining the same, the response is that shown in curve (*b*). When the lags are of form (*c*) the response shown in curve (*c*) is obtained. In the case now being considered, with proportional and integral correction factors of 0·5, the " overshoot " which occurs in the response when the lags are of form (*b*) or (*c*) can be eliminated by introducing a small amount of derivative correction. When the lags are of form (*b*) the overshoot is eliminated if the derivative correction factor is raised from zero to about 0·06; when they are of form (*c*) a derivative correction factor of about 0·09 is required to prevent overshoot in the response.

Curves (*a*), (*b*) and (*c*) of Fig. 4 show the responses obtained with lag forms (*a*), (*b*) and (*c*) respectively when both the proportional and the integral correction factors are 2·0 and the derivative correction factor is 0·5. With the higher values of the proportional and integral correction factors the system has become less stable, and even when the lags are of form (*a*) some derivative correction is needed to prevent an oscillatory response. When the lags are of form (*b*) the system is on the verge of instability. Nor can the response be improved by adjustment of the derivative correction factor. Any appreciable increase or decrease in its value makes the system completely unstable. When the corrective action has some effect fairly quickly, as is the case when the lags are of form (*a*), the use of derivative correction is a powerful method of reducing or eliminating fluctuations. But when the corrective action does not have much effect until some considerable time after it is applied, as is the case when the lags are of form (*b*) and still more when they are of form (*c*), derivative correction is less effective in reducing oscillations, and indeed if used excessively it will introduce an additional cycle of high frequency. When the proportional and integral correction factors are 2·0 and the lags are of form (*c*) the system is unstable for all values of the derivative correction factor.

Curve (*a*) of Fig. 5 shows the response when both the proportional and integral correction factors are raised to 8·0 and the derivative correction factor is 1·0, the lags being of form (*a*).[2] With lags of form (*b*) the response becomes that shown in curve (*b*). With lags of form (*c*) the system is so violently unstable that it proved impossible to obtain a satisfactory recording of the response given by the electronic simulator. Adjustment of the derivative correction factor again fails to stabilise the system in this case when the lags are of form (*b*) or (*c*).

Figs. 3, 4 and 5 show that a comparatively small change in the time-

---

[1] This response was obtained mathematically in my earlier article and was shown as curve (*b*) o Fig. 7, p. 300.

[2] This response was also obtained mathematically in my earlier article and was shown as curve (*e*) of Fig. 7.

forms of the lags may have a great effect on the stability of a closed-loop control system, especially if the values of the correction factors are high.   It is in fact only in the simplest systems in which there are not more than two lags, each of single exponential form, that it is possible to give any value, no matter how large, to one correction factor and then to find values for the other correction factors such that the system is stable and non-oscillatory. Any system in which there is time delay or a sequence of more than two lags of single exponential form, or in which any lag is equivalent to a sequence which includes a time delay or more than two single exponential lags, as is the case with lags of form (*b*) or (*c*), will be stable and non-oscillatory only if the values of the correction factors are kept sufficiently low.   This limitation of permissible values of the correction factors implies a corresponding limit to the speed with which it is possible to correct an error caused by a disturbance.

It is not possible to make any completely general statement about the effect on the response of a closed-loop system of an alteration to one part of the system unless the remainder of the system is fully specified.   It will, however, be found that except in very special cases which are most unlikely to occur in practice a reduction in the length of the correction lag brought about by a reduction in the time scale, the form of the lag remaining unchanged, increases the maximum values of the correction factors that can be used without causing instability, and so permits a more rapid correction of errors.   A similar effect is produced, again except in very special cases, if the form of the correction lag is altered from form (*c*) through form (*b*) to form (*a*).   As can be seen from Fig. 2, this implies that the maximum values of the correction factors that can be used without causing instability are increased if the interval between the time when an error occurs and the time when the corrective action *begins* to take effect is reduced, even if the time required for the full effect of the corrective action to be obtained is simultaneously increased.   Thus it is important, both for obtaining rapid correction and for avoiding instability, that the corrective action should be adjusted continuously and quickly to changes in the error and that it should have some initial effect quickly; whether its full effect is obtained quickly or slowly is comparatively unimportant.[1]

We have seen from Fig. 3 that a cycle with a period of about three years occurs if the lags in our system are of form (*b*) or (*c*) and if the proportional and integral correction factors are 0·5 (which may perhaps be about the order of magnitude of these correction factors that can be attained in actual economic regulation) unless a small amount of derivative correction is also applied.   Since the basic multiplier model which has been used so far is

---

[1] Justification of the above statements would require an extensive use of the frequency-response method of analysis and cannot be given here.   The reader who wishes to acquire sufficient familiarity with the method to convince himself of their truth will find the necessary material in the works cited in footnote 5, p. 265.

non-oscillatory, this may properly be called a control cycle. A more adequate model of an economy might itself have cyclical properties, for example, inventory adjustments are likely to cause cycles with a period of three or four years. The question immediately arises whether the maximum values of the correction factors that can be used without causing instability are not further reduced when the system being controlled has oscillatory tendencies. This question is examined briefly in the next section.

II. An Inventory Model with Error Correction

A model with inventory adjustments is shown in Fig. 6. An "inventory demand," E_V, is now distinguished as an additional component of aggregate demand, total demand for purposes other than inventory adjustment being E_N. Thus $E = E_N + E_V$ and $E_N = E_Y + E_\pi + u$. We assume that any excess of the "non-inventory demand" E_N over aggregate production P is met by drawing on inventories, and any excess of production over non-inventory demand is added to inventories. Then the rate of change of inventories, $\frac{dV}{dt}$, is equal to $P - E_N$. Integration of $\frac{dV}{dt}$ with respect to time gives total inventories, V. Some part of the total inventories will be locked up in work in progress and essential stocks closely related to the level of production. These "minimum working inventories," which we shall call V_1, are assumed to be a constant proportion, w, of production. We shall give w the value 0·2, *i.e.*, we shall assume that minimum working inventories are equal to one-fifth of a year's production. Inventories held in excess of minimum working inventories will be called V_2, so that $V_2 = V - V_1$.[1] From precautionary and speculative motives businesses will wish to hold some inventories in excess of minimum working inventories, but the amount they wish to hold, which we shall call V_{2_d} or the desired value of V_2, will not always be equal to the amount they are holding. In this simplified model we shall assume that V_{2_d} is a lagged function of non-inventory demand and we shall give the magnitude of this dependence, s, the value 0·125 and assume that the lag, L_s, is of form (*b*) with a time constant of 0·75 year. (In fact, of course, V_{2_d} will also be influenced by other factors, in particular by interest rates and expected rates of change of prices.) Subtracting V_2 from V_{2_d} gives the "error in inventories," ϵ_V. We shall assume that the inventory demand, E_V, is a constant proportion, v, of the error in inventories and shall give v the value 2·0.

The only other change from the model shown in Fig. 1 is the addition of the demand lag, L_D, which, because of the fairly rapid adjustment of expenditure by wage-earners when their incomes change, we shall assume

---

[1] It will be noticed that the distinction made here between V_1 and V_2 corresponds closely to the distinction between working capital and liquid capital made by Keynes in Chapters 28 and 29 of the *Treatise on Money*. It is also analogous to his later distinction between M_1 and M_2 in monetary theory.

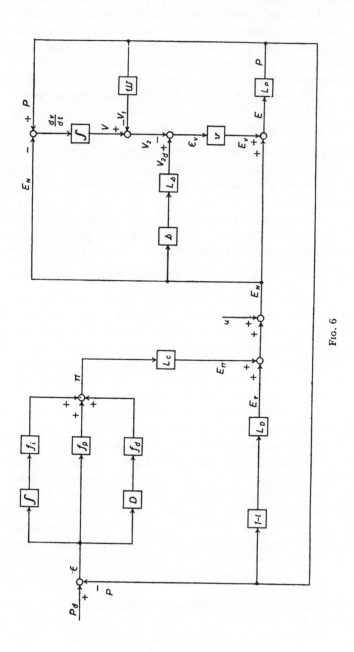

Fig. 6

to be of form (*a*) with a time constant of 0·125 year. We shall, however, give the marginal leakage, *l*, the value 0·4 instead of its previous value 0·25. This reduces the multiplier from 4·0 to 2·5, which is probably a more realistic value, and makes the system more stable. We assume a correction lag of form (*c*) with a total time constant of 0·5 year and a production lag of form (*b*) with a total time constant of 0·25 year.

When all three correction factors are zero the response of production to a unit step change in the variable *u*, applied negatively at time *t* = 0, is the damped inventory cycle shown in curve (*a*) of Fig. 7. If derivative correction only is applied the equilibrium position of the system is unchanged, so the error in production persists. With low values of the derivative correction factor the fluctuations in the response are reduced, but with

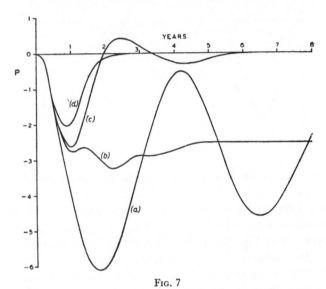

Fig. 7

higher values another cycle appears with a period of just over one year, and if the derivative correction factor is raised above 0·38 this cycle becomes explosive. Curve (*b*) of Fig. 7 shows the response when the derivative correction factor is 0·25.

If proportional correction only is applied, the fluctuations in the response are slightly reduced when the value of the proportional correction factor is very low, but if it is raised above 0·1 the fluctuations become worse again and the system becomes unstable when the proportional correction factor is raised above about 0·28. If any integral correction at all is applied alone the amplitudes of the fluctuations increase and the system becomes unstable if the integral correction factor is raised above about 0·08. Similarly, any combination of proportional and integral correction without the addition of derivative correction reduces the stability of the system and increases the magnitudes of the fluctuations unless the two correction factors have extremely low values, while if the values are extremely low the improvement in the response is negligible.

Even if derivative correction is included in the stabilisation policy, the speed with which an error can be corrected is rather limited. About the best response that can be obtained is that shown in curve (c) of Fig. 7. This response results when $f_p = 0.3$, $f_i = 0.4$ and $f_d = 0.2$. Higher values of the correction factors worsen the response by reducing the stability of the system. If the correction lag is changed from form (c) to form (b), the time constant remaining at 0.5 years, the correction factors can be increased a

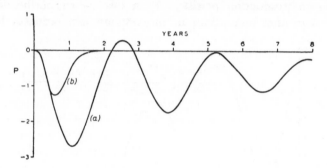

Fig. 8

little. The best response is then that shown in curve (d) of Fig. 7, the correction factors being $f_p = 0.4$, $f_i = 0.5$ and $f_d = 0.3$.

If the correction lag is of form (b) with a total time constant of 0.25 year the best response is obtained when $f_p = 0.9$, $f_i = 0.9$ and $f_d = 0.25$. It is shown as curve (b) of Fig. 8. It is of interest to note that even with this correction lag the stabilisation policy is not satisfactory unless it includes an element of derivative correction. If $f_d = 0$ about the best response that can be obtained is that shown in curve (a) of Fig. 8, the proportional and integral correction factors being 0.4 and 0.1 respectively. With either higher or lower values of f_p and f_i the fluctuations are of greater amplitude.

III. Conclusions

Because of the simplified nature of the models considered in this paper the results that have been obtained cannot be applied directly to the interpretation of actual economic situations. Indeed, one of the first lessons one learns from studying a variety of hypothetical models is that the problem of economic stabilisation is, even in principle, an extremely intricate one, and that a much more thorough investigation of both theoretical principles and empirical relationships would be needed before detailed policy recommendations could be justified. A few very elementary conclusions can, however, be drawn with some confidence.

The first is that the regulation of a system can be improved if the lengths of the time delays operating around the main control loop are reduced. The distinction between delays and lags should here be noticed. What is of primary importance is that the correcting action should be adjusted continuously and with the minimum possible delay to changes in the error and that the adjustments should quickly produce some initial effect. It does not matter very much if it takes a long time for the policy changes to have their full effect. In fact, it can be shown that if there is a long delay before corrective action is taken or before it begins to have an appreciable effect it is better that the effect, when it does come, should be gradual rather than sudden. The worst possible condition for regulating purposes is one in which the adjustment of policy demand to a change in the error is delayed for a considerable time and then effected quickly and abruptly.

A second conclusion is that it is usually necessary to include an element of derivative correction in a stabilisation policy if regulation is to be satisfactory. In other words, the potential policy demand should be made to depend not only on the magnitude of the current error and on the sum of the past errors,[1] but also on the rate of change of the error, or when observations are at discrete intervals on the difference between the last two observed values of the error. The longer the time delays in the responses around the main control loop, the less effective is derivative correction in reducing fluctuations. Nevertheless, the longer the delays, the more desirable it is that some derivative correction be used, since the delays reduce the stability of the system and so make it more important that whatever stabilising effect can still be obtained by derivative correction should not be foregone.

A third conclusion is that if the lags in the real economic system are at all similar to those we have used in the models it is unlikely that the period needed to restore any desired equilibrium conditions after an economy has experienced a severe disturbance could be much less than two years, even assuming that the regulating authorities use the policy which is most appropriate to the real system of relationships existing in the economy. As these relationships are not known quantitively, it is unlikely that the policy applied will be the most appropriate one, it may well cause cyclical fluctuations rather than eliminate them.

It is true that many relationships inherent in the real economic system have been omitted from our models and that some of the omitted relationships seem intuitively to be of a stabilising type. But intuitions about dynamic processes may be dangerously misleading and need to be carefully tested. Most of the inherent relationships which at first sight would seem

---

[1] The quantity to which integral correction is related is the integral, or sum, of all past errors. In practice a good approximation to integral correction would be obtained if the integral component of potential policy demand was made to depend on the sum of the errors over the past four or five years or on a weighted sum of these errors, the earlier errors being given less weight than the later one.

to have stabilising effects can be expressed in forms similar to the policy relationships in the models we have been using. If the lengths and forms of the time lags of these inherent relationships are also similar to those which we have assumed for the correction lag the effects of the inherent relationships will be similar to the effects of the policy relationships which we have already considered. The existence of inherent relationships which appear intuitively to be of a stabilising type may therefore reduce the amount of correction that needs to be applied deliberately by regulating authorities (particularly the proportional and integral elements of correction; it is difficult to think of any inherent relationship which is equivalent to the derivative element of a correction policy), but will not reduce the time required to restore equilibrium after a disturbance unless these relationships operate with shorter time lags and delays than we have been assuming. Nor do the additional inherent relationships make it more likely that cyclical fluctuations will be avoided. In fact, they make it less likely, since it becomes very difficult to judge what quantitative values should be given to the deliberate policy relationships when the system already contains numerous inherent relationships whose magnitudes and speeds of operation are unknown.

The main conclusion that must be drawn from this investigation is that much more research is needed in the general field of economic regulation. To throw light on the practical problems involved in regulating complex economic systems it is necessary to study the properties of more realistic models in which non-linear relationships, growth trends, multiple objectives and multiple disturbances are incorporated. The means for carrying out such studies are now becoming available and should be fully exploited. It is equally important that improved methods should be developed for estimating quantitatively the magnitudes and time-forms of economic relationships in order that the range of permissible hypothesis may be restricted more closely than is at present possible.

A. W. PHILLIPS

London School of Economics.

[20]

THE TAX MIX AND EFFECTIVE DEMAND

by

M. H. PESTON [*]

The typical treatment of the comparative effects of direct and indirect taxes on the level of effective demand and real national product bases the comparison on two situations, one in which direct taxes are zero and the other in which indirect taxes are zero. This is the comparison made in Cary-Brown's article, [1] in Peacock and Williamson's article, [2] and more recently in Peacock and Shaw's book. [3] Nonetheless, these writers conclude from their analysis that, "a given tax yield will have a great 'deflationary impact' if levied in the form of a consumption tax". [4] Although this result is a true consequence of their analysis, strictly speaking it is not the result they have proved. It seems worthwhile, therefore, to set out the derivation of the result correctly.

R is real national product at factor cost

(1) $$R = C + I + G$$

Y is real national product at market prices

(2) $$Y = PC + I + G$$

We assume initially that the "price" of $I + G$ is unity, as is the price of C apart from tax.

The price of consumption goods contains an element for indirect taxes.

[*] The author is Professor of Economics, Queen Mary College, University of London.

[1] E. C. Brown, "Analysis of Consumption Taxes in Terms of the Theory of Income Distribution", American Economic Review, March 1950.

[2] A. T. Peacock and J. Williamson, "Consumption Taxes and Compensatory Finance", Economic Journal, March 1967.

[3] Alan T. Peacock and G. K. Shaw, The Economic Theory of Fiscal Policy, Allen and Unwin, London 1971.

4 Ibid. p. 89—90.

(3) $$1 = (1 - t_i)P$$

Note that the tax rate is calculated at the market price, i.e. the tax per unit is t_iP.

Real personal disposable income is equal to D.

(4) $$D = \frac{(1 - t_d)R}{P}$$

where t_d is the rate of direct taxes.

(5) $$D = (1 - t_d)(1 - t_i)R$$

Assume real consumption is proportionate to D.

(6) $$C = a_1 D$$

(7) $$C = a_1(1 - t_d)(1 - t_i)R$$

Substituting into (1), we obtain

(8) $$R = \frac{I + G}{1 - a_1(1 - t_d)(1 - t_i)}$$

It is at this point that others have noted the identical way in which both t_d and t_i appear in the multiplier. This does not mean that changes in them have the same effect because these changes depend on the level of the other tax rate. Equally, the relevant comparison either theoretically or practically is not simply in terms of effectiveness when the other rate is zero.

Total tax revenue equals T, part derived from direct taxes, T_d, and part from indirect taxes, T_i, i.e.

(9) $$T = T_d + T_i$$

(10) $$T_d = t_d R$$

(11) $$T_i = t_i PC$$

From (3):

(12) $$T_i = \frac{t_i}{1 - t_i}C$$

Note that $\dfrac{t_i}{1 - t_i}$ is the tax rate calculated as a mark-up on factor cost.

From (7):

THE TAX MIX AND EFFECTIVE DEMAND　　　　495

(13)　　　　　　　　　　$$T_i = t_i a_1 (1 - t_d) R$$

Let us consider the effect of changes in t_d and t_i on R.

Differentiating (8) we have

(14)　　　　$$\frac{\delta R}{\delta t_d} = - \frac{(I + G) a_1 (1 - t_i)}{[1 - a_1 (1 - t_d)(1 - t_i)]^2}$$

(15)　　　　$$\frac{\delta R}{\delta t_i} = - \frac{(I + G) a_1 (1 - t_d)}{[1 - a_1 (1 - t_d)(1 - t_i)]^2}$$

Each of these is, of course, negative. Their comparative size in each case depends on the size of the other rate of tax, i.e. if t_d is large relative to t_i, a change in t_d will have a larger absolute effect than a change in t_i. Let us consider the effect of changes in t_d and t_i on T_d and T_i.

(16)　　　　$$\frac{\delta T_d}{\delta t_d} = R \frac{-t_d(I + G) a_1 (1 - t_i)}{[1 - a_1 (1 - t_d)(1 - t_i)]^2}$$

$$= R \left[1 - \frac{t_d a_1 (1 - t_i)}{1 - a_1 (1 - t_d)(1 - t_i)} \right]$$

$$= R \left[\frac{1 - a_1 (1 - t_i)}{1 - a_1 (1 - t_d)(1 - t_i)} \right]$$

(17)　$$\frac{\delta T_i}{\delta t_i} = a_1 (1 - t_d) \left[R - \frac{t_i(I + G) a_1 (1 - t_d)}{[1 - a_1 (1 - t_d)(1 - t_i)]^2} \right]$$

$$= a_1 (1 - t_d) R \left[1 - \frac{t_i a_1 (1 - t_d)}{1 - a_1 (1 - t_d)(1 - t_i)} \right]$$

$$= a_1 (1 - t_d) R \left[\frac{1 - a_1 (1 - t_d)}{1 - a_1 (1 - t_d)(1 - t_i)} \right]$$

In both cases the expression inside the brackets is positive so that $\frac{\delta T_d}{\delta t_d}$ and $\frac{\delta T_i}{\delta t_i}$ are, as expected, positive. Once again their comparative size depends on the other rate of tax. It is impossible to say a priori which is larger than the other. (There is, of course, the trivial point that if $t_i = t_d$, $\frac{\delta T_d}{\delta t_d}$ is greater than $\frac{\delta T_i}{\delta t_i}$. The point is trivial because there is no economic significance in equalising the two rates).

As an arithmetic example, if $a_1 = 0.8$; $t_i = 0.1$; $t_d = 0.3$, $\frac{\delta T_d}{\delta t_d} > \frac{\delta T_i}{\delta t_i}$, i.e. $.565 > .497$. But if $a_1 = 0.8$; $t_i = .05$; $t_d = .375$,

$$\frac{\delta T_i}{\delta t_i} > \frac{\delta T_d}{\delta t_d}, \text{ i.e. } .476 > .457.$$

We must also consider the cross effects of the taxes.

(18) $$\frac{\delta T_d}{\delta t_i} = -\frac{t_d a_1 (1 - t_d)}{1 - a_1 (1 - t_d)(1 - t_i)} \quad R < 0$$

(19) $$\frac{\delta T_i}{\delta t_d} = -\left[\frac{t_i a_1{}^2 (1 - t_d)(1 - t_i)}{1 - a_1 (1 - t_d)(1 - t_i)} + t_i a_1 \right] R < 0$$

$$= -\left[\frac{a_1 (1 - t_d)(1 - t_i) + 1 - a_1 (1 - t_d)(1 - t_i)}{1 - a_1 (1 - t_d)(1 - t_i)} \right] t_i a_1 R$$

$$= -\frac{t_i a_1 R}{1 - a_1 (1 - t_d)(1 - t_i)}$$

We now wish to compare the effects of changes in t_i and t_d on R holding T constant. [5] If T is constant, we have
from (16), (17), (18), and (19)

(20) $$dt_d + a_1 (1 - t_d)^2 dt_i = 0$$

$$\frac{dt_i}{dt_d} = -\frac{1}{a_1 (1 - t_d)^2}$$

Eq. (14) may be rewritten as

(21) $$\frac{\delta R}{\delta t_d} = -RMa_1 (1 - t_i)$$

where M is the multiplier.

Eq. (15) may be rewritten as

(22) $$\frac{\delta R}{\delta t_i} = -RMa_1 (1 - t_d)$$

If we treat t_i as a function of t_d because of (20), we may determine the constrained effect of t_i on R as

(23) $$\frac{\delta R}{\delta t_d} + \frac{\delta R}{\delta t_i} \frac{\delta t_i}{\delta t_d} = -RMa_1 (1 - t_i) + \frac{RM}{1 - t_d} = RM\left[\frac{1}{1 - t_d} - a_1 (1 - t_i) \right]$$

$$= \frac{R}{1 - t_d} > 0$$

In other words, an increase in the direct — indirect tax mix, holding total tax proceeds constant, is expansionary. [6]

[5] Note that T is held constant in money terms. An alternative and more complicated problem arises if it is held constant in real terms.

[6] This indicates once again, therefore, that the balanced budget theorem depends on tax structure and not simply on the relationship between aggregate public expenditure and aggregate taxation.

[21]

Journal of Public Economics 2 (1973) 319–337. © North-Holland Publishing Company

DOES FISCAL POLICY MATTER ? *

Alan S. BLINDER and Robert M. SOLOW

Princeton University and MIT, U.S.A.

First version received September 1972, revised version received May 1973

Perhaps the most fundamental achievement of the Keynesian revolution was the re-orientation of the way economists view the influence of government activity on the private economy. Before Keynes, it was commonplace that government spending and taxation were powerless to affect the aggregate levels of spending and employment in the economy; they could only redirect resources from the private to the public sector. This, of course, is an immediate corollary of Say's Law. In a full-employment context, each dollar of additional government spending can only 'crowd out' exactly one dollar of private spending; it cannot alter the over-all level of aggregate income.

The Keynesian demonstration that with sticky wages unemployment can persist changed all this. Economists began to stress the macro-economic effects of government spending and taxation. It became commonplace that not only would a dollar of additional government spending raise national income by the original dollar but that this expenditure would have multiplier effects of perhaps several dollars more. The old view that government spending simply crowded out private spending was banished. At the same time a new question arose: Does monetary policy matter, or, at least, does it matter much?

Lately, however, the resurgence of the quantity theory of money – under the new name of 'monetarism' – has brought with it both a renewed belief in the power of monetary policy and a resurgence of interest in the crowding out effect. Both the theoretical and empirical

* This paper is an outgrowth of work we are doing for The Brookings Institution. Support from Brookings and from the National Science Foundation under Grant GS 32003X is gratefully acknowledged. We are also indebted to A.B. Atkinson for an important suggestion which led to a substantial revision of this paper.

work of the monetarists has called into question the basic Keynesian principle that government spending can alter the aggregate level of employment. The current question appears to be: Does fiscal policy matter? [1]

The purpose of this note is to re-examine the underlying basis of the Keynesian multiplier in view of the monetarist critique. We hope to show that there are still good theoretical reasons to believe in the efficacy of fiscal policy in an economy with underemployed resources.

1. The problem defined

There are several levels at which crowding out has been alleged to occur. The most obvious is the possibility that government will engage in productive activities which would otherwise be provided by the private sector, so that public spending would simply supplant private investment. It can be argued, for example, that total investment in electrical utilities in the Tennessee Valley area would be much the same today had the government never created the Tennessee Valley Authority. However, for the bulk of government expenditures − on national defense, courts, and the like − it is hard to imagine that public-sector outlays are simply replacing potential private outlays on a *dollar-for-dollar basis*. In any case, this is not the sort of crowding out we wish to discuss, and it would occur whether the spending were financed by taxes, bonds or money.

A second level of crowding out is an integral part of the Keynesian tradition and is, in fact, disputed by almost no one. This is the notion that deficit spending *not accompanied by new issues of money* carries with it the need for the government to float debt issues which compete with private debt instruments in financial markets. The resulting upward pressure on interest rates will reduce any private expenditures which are interest-elastic − which may include some spending by state and local governments as well as private spending on consumer durables, business fixed investment and residential construction. This financial side-effect will partially offset the expansionary effect of the original increase in public spending. Thus in a monetary economy the government spending multiplier is certainly lower than the naive Keynesian

---

[1] See, for example, L.C. Andersen and J.L. Jordan (1968); R.W. Spencer and W.A. Yohe (1970); and many of the writings of Milton Friedman.

formula, multiplier = $1/(1 -$ marginal propensity to spend), and is lower for bond-financed spending than it is for money-financed spending.

There is no theoretical controversy over this second level of crowding out. The only contested issues are empirical. How much will interest rates rise in response to the greater demand for money and supply of bonds engendered by the government spending? How much will investment fall in response to the rise in interest rates? It is by now well-known that only a zero interest-elasticity of the demand for money will give rise to a multiplier of zero, that is, make fiscal policy impotent. While this assumption was formerly associated with the new quantity theorists, [2] there is by now an overwhelming accumulation of empirical evidence against it, and the monetarists have more or less disavowed it. [3]

Yet monetarists still cling to the view that fiscal policy is powerless, that is, that the multiplier for bond-financed government spending is approximately zero. How can this be so? A possible answer is that when there are significant wealth effects the simple Keynesian story (as summarized, say, in the $IS-LM$ model) closes the books too soon. Any government deficit requires the issuance of some sort of debt instrument — outside money or interest-bearing bonds — and this increase in private wealth will have further reverberations in the economy. It is precisely these wealth effects — which provide the rationale for the third level of crowding out — that we wish to investigate in this paper.

Figs. 1 and 2 illustrate the problem. In fig. 1, IS_0 and LM_0 represent the initial equilibrium of the economy in the ordinary Hicks–Hansen model. Government spending is indicated by an outward shift of the IS curve to IS_1. Income rises by $Y_1 - Y_0$. Income does not rise all the way to Y_2 — which represents the naive multiplier effect — because of the second level of crowding out alluded to above.

This is where the usual textbook story ends, and if there are no significant wealth effects, that is correct. However, when wealth effects exist, Y_1 is not an equilibrium position. Greater wealth will, presumably, mean higher levels of consumption out of any given income flow; thus the IS curve will shift out further to IS_2 in fig. 2. This augments the ordinary multiplier. But the greater wealth will also affect the financial markets. Increased household wealth will presumably mean

[2] See Friedman (1956, 1959).
[3] Friedman (1966, 1972), Fand (1970).

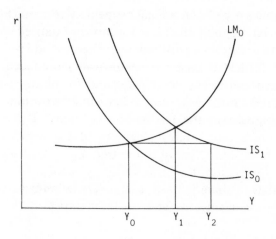

Fig. 1.

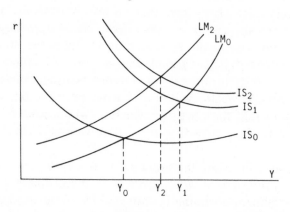

Fig. 2

increased demands for money (and bonds) at any level of income and interest rates, represented by a shift in the *LM* curve to LM_2 in fig. 2.

The outcome of these last two shifts may be either expansionary or contractionary on balance as Silber (1970) has stressed. Advocates of complete crowding out, of course, believe the results to be contractionary. If they are correct, as long as a budgetary deficit exists there will be increases in private wealth which have deflationary impacts on the level of national income. In the long run, the fiscal policy multiplier is negative.

In response to a recent criticism by Tobin (1972), Friedman has indicated that he now believes that these wealth effects, rather than the oft-cited slope of the *LM* curve, constitute the main issue separating monetarists from Keynesians. He contrasts the initial impact of fiscal policy in fig: 1 with the wealth-induced shifts in fig. 2 — shifts which continue as long as the budget is unbalanced — and he asks: 'Is there any doubt that this (latter) effect must swamp the once-for-all shift of the *IS* curve?' (Friedman, 1972, p. 916). He summarizes his new view of the monetarist–Keynesian debate as follows (Friedman, 1972, p. 922):

> One way to characterize the Keynesian approach is that it gives almost exclusive importance to the first-round effect. This leads it to attach importance primarily to flows of spending rather than to stocks of assets. Similarly, one way to characterize the quantity-theory approach is to say that it gives almost no importance to first-round effects.
>
> The empirical question is how important the first-round effects are compared to the ultimate effects. Theory cannot answer that question.

Friedman believes that the answer for deficit spending financed by printing money is that the subsequent asset effects are (a) much larger than and (b) in the same direction as the initial expansionary thrust of government spending. By contrast, if the deficits are financed by floating government bonds, he apparently believes that wealth effects are (a) about equal in magnitude and (b) opposite in direction to the initial movement of the *IS* curve. On the other hand, it has always been a central tenet of Keynesian macroeconomics that bond-financed government spending has a net expansionary impact on the level of economic activity. [4] After all, if this were not so, symmetry would imply that reducing spending in order to pay off part of the national debt would be expansionary.

But is it only faith that supports this view? In this paper, we hope to show that while Friedman may be correct in describing the issue as an empirical one, certain theoretical arguments can be adduced in support of the conventional view that fiscal policy works. Furthermore, we suggest that it is also an empirical question whether the subsequent wealth effects of bond-financed deficits, while less expansionary than money-financed deficits in the short run (Friedman's 'first round'), are actually more expansionary in the long run. [5]

---

[4] There is no controversy over government spending financed by printing money. Both sides agree that it will be expansionary; but one group likes to call it fiscal policy, while the other prefers to call it monetary policy. Nothing much hinges on this distinction. In terms of fig. 2, the *LM* curve would shift outward instead of inward if financing were by money instead of by bonds.

[5] So far as we know, this conclusion was first suggested in a paper by Sean Murray (forthcoming).

In the following section we consider the long-run impact of government spending, under the two alternative modes of financing, in an *IS–LM* model with wealth effects. This analysis, however, utilizes a funny concept of the 'long run' since, in conformity with the *IS–LM* rules, the capital stock is held fixed (despite positive net investment) while the stocks of the other two assets (money and bonds) adjust to their final equilibrium. So, in sec. 3, we rectify this error by considering a true long-run equilibrium where all three asset stocks are free to adjust. We find that, in a sense to be specified later, the case for fiscal policy is somewhat stronger in this more sophisticated model.

2. Crowding out in the simple *IS–LM* model

The conventional *IS–LM* model, [6] with wealth effects added, consists of the following ingredients:

(goods–market equilibrium) $Y \equiv NNP = C + I + G$ (1)

(consumption function) $C = C(Y - T, W)$ (2)

(net investment function) $I = I(r)$ (3)

(tax function) $T = T(Y)$ (4)

(demand for real balances) $M^d/P = L(r, Y, W)$ (5)

(exogenous money supply) [7] $M^s = M$ (6)

(money–market equilibrium) $M^s = M^d$ (7)

(definition of wealth) [8] $W = K + M/P + V(r)/P$.   (8)

---

[6] The *IS–LM* model usually treats the price level as exogenously fixed, and we shall adhere to this convention. However, it should be noted that we do this strictly for simplicity. There are no real difficulties in adding a production function and a labor market and allowing the price level to be endogenously determined. The result would be that expansionary fiscal policy causes some inflation of the price level which reduces the value of the multiplier for (at least) three reasons: (1) With prices higher, the real value of the money stock is lower, which shifts the *LM* curve inward. (2) Higher prices reduce the real wealth of the private sector, which has a negative 'Pigou effect' on consumption, shifting the *IS* curve inward. (3) If taxes are progressive in terms of money income, inflation will increase the real yield of the tax system at each level of real income, again lowering the *IS* curve. While each of these serves to reduce the absolute value of the fiscal multiplier, none of them has any bearing on its sign, which is what is at issue here.

[7] This is again a simplification made solely for the purpose of notational convenience. We here ignore the banking system, and thus the distinction between inside and outside money,

A.S. Blinder, R.M. Solow, Does fiscal policy matter?   **325**

Here $V(r)$ is the nominal market value of the supply of government bonds. The only additions to the classical textbook treatment which we have made are to include wealth as an argument in both the consumption and demand-for-money functions.

To this model, we must append a somewhat different version of what Carl Christ (1967, 1968) has called the 'government budget restraint'. As it usually appears in the work of Christ and others, the restraint is a simple differential (or difference) equation equating the changes in the nominal stocks of bonds and money to the nominal government deficit:

$$P[G - T(Y)] = \dot{B} + \dot{M} ,\tag{9'}$$

where B is the number of bonds (each of face value $\$1$). But (9') commits an oversight: it ignores the fact that interest paid on bonds is an expense item in the government's budgetary accounts along with G. If we assume for simplicity that each bond is a perpetuity paying $\$1$ per year, interest payments will be B and the market value of the stock of bonds will be B/r. The government budget restraint can therefore be written:

$$P[G + B - T] = \dot{B}/r + \dot{M} .\tag{9}$$

Note that the bond term on the righthand side is the change in the number of bonds, evaluated at the current market price. This differs from $(\dot{B}/r)$, which is the change in the market value of the stock of bonds, if there are capital gains or losses on pre-existing bonds.

Two other minor alterations in the model are necessary. First, in the definition of wealth we can write B/r for $V(r)$. Second, both consumption and taxes presumably depend upon personal income, which includes the interest paid on the national debt; thus (2') and (4') become:

$$C = C(Y + B - T, W)\tag{2}$$

and we treat the money stock as exogenous. These complications could all be brought in, and would in no way affect the central conclusions.

[8] This includes government bonds as a net asset to the public. We are well aware of, but not persuaded by, the arguments which hold that such bonds are not seen as net worth by individuals because of the implied future tax liability. If that view were correct, the wealth effects of new bonds, illustrated in fig. 2, would simply not occur.

$$T = T(Y + B) . \tag{4}$$

The first model which we shall study consists of equations (1)–(9). Since we shall treat the price level as fixed throughout, we can set $P = 1$ with no loss of generality and reduce the nine equations to the following three-equation dynamic system:

$$Y = C[Y + B - T(Y + B), \quad M + B/r + K] + I(r) + G \tag{10}$$

$$M = L(r, Y, M + B/r + K) \tag{11}$$

$$\dot{M} + \dot{B}/r = G + B - T(Y + B) . \tag{12}$$

Eqs. (10) and (11) are the static *IS* and *LM* equations which hold at each instant; eq. (12) drives the model from one instantaneous equilibrium to the next by changing the stocks of money and/or bonds.

The unmodified model which ignores interest payments as a budgetary expense item — eqs. (1), (2'), (3), (4'), (5)–(8) and (9') — has an implication which has attracted attention in recent years. Suppose that we ignore the dynamics of the model and look only at the long-run steady-state solution. This means that $\dot{M} = \dot{B} = 0$, so that (9') implies: $G = T(Y)$, that is, the government budget must be balanced in long-run equilibrium. But this immediately implies that the steady-state multiplier for government spending not financed by higher tax rates (but ultimately financed by higher tax revenues at unchanged rates) must be, as Christ has pointed out:

$$\frac{dY}{dG} = \frac{1}{T'(Y)} .$$

Observe that this long-run multiplier expression holds regardless of how the deficit is financed, and is independent of all functional relations in the model except the tax function. In a word, if the model is stable under each mode of financing (so that it actually approaches its steady state), the long-run multipliers for bond and money-financed deficit spending are identical.

What happens when we add interest to the budget constraint? Setting $\dot{B} = \dot{M} = 0$ in (9) gives: $G + B = T(Y + B)$, from which it follows that:

$$\frac{dY}{dG} = \frac{1 + (1 - T')\dfrac{dB}{dG}}{T'} .$$

If deficits are financed by money-creation, so that $dB/dG = 0$, we obtain the same long-run multiplier as before. But if bond financing is used, so that $dB/dG > 0$, the long-run multiplier exceeds $1/T'$. In words, contrary to the usual supposition, the long-run multiplier for bond-financed deficit spending exceeds that for money-financed deficit spending.

What is the reason for this paradoxical result? Simply this: starting from any long-run equilibrium income level with a balanced budget, an initial surge in government spending will cause income to rise as in normal $IS-LM$ analysis. It is well-known that, if the LM curve has positive slope, the impact multiplier will be larger if the deficit is financed by creating money. But, this is only Friedman's 'first round'. Since the budget will be in deficit, new assets will have to be created. If financing is by bonds the subsequent deficit financing will have to be larger than in the money case for two reasons. First, income will rise less so the induced increase in tax receipts will be smaller. Second, a larger outstanding debt will require greater interest payments. Provided that the net impact of the wealth effects is expansionary, the 'second round' increase in income will be greater under bond financing than under money financing, and this will continue to be true in subsequent rounds. The basic intuition is that under bond financing any given budgetary gap is harder to close because every increase in the number of bonds outstanding requires more expenditure on debt service. It therefore takes a greater rise in income to induce tax receipts sufficient to close the budgetary gap.

Thus one is tempted to conclude that Friedman's 'empirical question' can be resolved on purely theoretical grounds after all – not only is deficit spending financed by bonds expansionary in the long run, it is even more expansionary than the same spending financed by the creation of new money. [9] However, this would be jumping too hastily to a conclusion which may not be warranted. Steady state equilibria are of interest only if the system under consideration is stable. And it turns out that the stability of the system of eqs. (10)–(12) may depend on the way in which deficits are financed. As we shall see, the model is always stable under money finance, but there are three possibilities under bond finance:

[9] An interesting corollary of this is that an open-market purchase, i.e. a swap of B for M by the government with G unchanged, will be contractionary! This is because, with less debt service, the existing levels of G and Y will imply a budgetary surplus which, in turn, must lead to a reduction in the supplies of money and/or bonds.

(a) If the parameters of the system are such that the net wealth effect of a new bond issue is contractionary (as depicted in fig. 2), the monetarists will be vindicated; but the more important consequence is that the system will then be unstable.

(b) For some other values of the crucial parameters, bonds will have an expansionary impact on the level of national income (so that the monetarists are wrong), but this impact will not be sufficiently strong to close the budgetary gap. Again the system will be unstable.

(c) Finally, if the parameters are such that the system is stable, additional bonds must have a positive net impact on GNP (Y_2 must lie to the right of Y_1 in fig. 2) so that fiscal policy works as expected. Only in this case can we appeal to the steady-state result that bond-financed deficits are more expansionary than money-financed deficits. And it is an empirical question as to which case actually obtains.

To prove these assertions it will be useful to consider the static equilibrium equations (10)–(11) as defining Y and r as functions of M and B, for given K and G:

$$Y(t) = F(M, B, \overline{K}; G) \tag{13}$$

$$r(t) = H(M, B, \overline{K}; G) . \tag{14}$$

It is a routine exercise in comparative statics to find that the partial derivatives of these functions are:

$$F_M = \mu\alpha \qquad H_M = \mu \frac{\lambda}{L_r} (S' - h) \tag{I}$$

$$F_B = \mu\beta \qquad H_B = -\mu \frac{\lambda}{L_r} \left[\frac{h}{r} + (1 - S')L_y \right]$$

where

$$h \equiv S'L_w + C_w L_y > 0 ;$$

$$0 < S' \equiv 1 - C_y(1 - T') < 1 ;$$

$$\alpha \equiv C_w + (1 - L_w)\sigma > 0 \quad \text{since } 0 < L_w < 1;$$

$$\beta \equiv C_w - L_w \sigma ;$$

$$0 < \lambda \equiv L_r \bigg/ \left(L_r - \frac{B}{r^2} L_w \right) < 1 \; ;$$

$$\sigma = \frac{I_r - (B/r^2)\,C_w}{L_r - (B/r^2)\,L_w} > 0 \; ;$$

and μ is the basic multiplier: [10]

$$\mu \equiv 1/(S' + \sigma L_y) \; .$$

So the short-run multiplier for increases in M is $\partial Y/\partial M = \mu\alpha$, which is unambiguously positive; while the corresponding multiplier for bonds B $\partial Y/\partial B = \mu\beta$ which is ambiguous on a priori grounds. Monetarists, of course, believe $\beta < 0$, but correctly emphasize that the sign of β is an empirical question.

We now turn to the issue of stability. Eqs. (13)–(14) enable us to reduce the dynamic system (10)–(12) to a single nonlinear differential equation:

$$\dot{M} = G + \overline{B} - T[F(M, \overline{B}, \overline{K}) + \overline{B}]$$
under money finance, or $\qquad$ (15a)

$$\dot{B} = H(\overline{M}, B, \overline{K})\{G + B - T[F(\overline{M}, B, \overline{K}) + B]\}$$
under bond finance. $\qquad$ (15b)

Under a regime of pure money finance, the stability condition for differential equation (15a) is simply:

$$\frac{\partial \dot{M}}{\partial M} = -T'F_M = -T'\mu\alpha < 0 \; ,\qquad (16a)$$

which is obviously satisfied. However, if deficits are financed by floating bonds, the corresponding condition is:

---

[10] Note that if, as is typically done in *IS–LM* analysis, we ignored the capital gains on bonds when interest rates change, σ would simplify to I_r/L_r so that μ would be the more familiar $1/(S' + I_r L_y/L_r)$.

$$\frac{\partial \dot{B}}{\partial B} = r\{1 - T'(F_B + 1)\} + H_B\{G + B - T\} < 0$$

$$= r(1 - T' - T'F_B) \text{ in the neighborhood of equilibrium.}$$

So the necessary and sufficient condition for local stability is:

$$F_B = \mu\beta > \frac{1 - T'}{T'}. \tag{16b}$$

We find that the stability of the $IS–LM$ model under bond financing of deficits is indeed an empirical question. However, since $\beta > 0$ is necessary (but not sufficient) for stability, *in a stable system* the discovery of a hitherto unsuspected government bond must lead to a higher level of national income. The three possibilities enumerated above are immediately apparent from condition (16b). If $F_B < 0$ as the monetarists claim, fiscal policy does not work, but the system is unstable. The economy does not return to its initial equilibrium before the deficit spending, as monetarist doctrine holds; instead income falls cumulatively and without limit. If $0 < F_B < (1 - T')/T'$, fiscal policy works as Keynesians have always believed, but the increases in GNP are not sufficient to close the budgetary gap. Each new bond leads to a rise in income of $F_B \, dB$ and a rise in tax revenues of $T'F_B \, dB$, but costs the government $(1 - T')dB$. Only if $T'F_B$ exceeds $(1 - T')$, i.e. only if (16b) is satisfied, will the budget deficit be falling, and thus only in this case will the system approach its new steady state equilibrium. [11]

3. Crowding out when the capital stock may vary

We now wish to make only two small alterations in the $IS–LM$ model of eqs. (10)–(12). First, we recognize that the change in the capital stock (K) is identical to net investment (I). Second, in line with modern investment theory which envisions an equilibrium demand for capital stock and a disequilibrium demand for investment, we alter the investment function of eq. (3) to read:

[11] In a model where interest payments are omitted from the budget restraint, the stability condition turns out to be simply $F_B < 0$, so that there is a direct correspondence between whether fiscal policy works as expected and whether the system is stable.

$$I = I(r, K), \quad I_r < 0, \ I_K < 0; \tag{3'}$$

with the property that $I(r^*, K^*) = 0$ if r^* is the long-run equilibrium interest rate corresponding to any long-run equilibrium capital stock, K^*.

With these modifications, our dynamic system becomes:

$$Y = C[Y + B - T(Y + B), M + \frac{B}{r} + K] + I(r, K) + G \tag{17}$$

$$M = L(r, Y, M + \frac{B}{r} + K) \tag{18}$$

$$\dot{M} + \frac{\dot{B}}{r} = G + B - T(Y + B) \tag{19}$$

$$\dot{K} = I(r, K) . \tag{20}$$

Once again, we can treat the static *IS–LM* eqs. (17) and (18), as defining Y and r as functions of M, B and K, for a given G:

$$Y = F(M, B, K; G) \tag{21}$$

$$Y = H(M, B, K; G) \tag{22}$$

with the following comparative-static derivatives:

$$F_M = \mu \alpha > 0; \qquad H_M = \mu \frac{\lambda}{L_r}(S' - h)$$

$$F_B = \mu \beta; \qquad H_B = -\mu \frac{\lambda}{L_r}[\frac{h}{r} + (1 - S')]L_y > 0$$

$$F_K = \mu(\beta + I_K) < F_B; \quad H_K = -\mu \frac{\lambda}{L_r}(h + I_K L_y) . \tag{II}$$

Note that the derivatives with respect to M and B are the same as in eqs. (I). In particular, $\partial Y / \partial B = \mu \beta$ remains ambiguous. Substitution of (21)–(22) into (19)–(20) reduces our system to two non-linear differential equations:

$$\dot{K} = I[H(M, B, K), K] \tag{23}$$

and either:

$$\dot{M} = G + \bar{B} - T[F(M, \bar{B}, K) + \bar{B}] \tag{24a}$$

in the case of money financing, or:

$$\dot{B} = H(\bar{M}, B, K)\{G + B - T[F(\bar{M}, B, K) + B]\} \tag{24b}$$

in the case of bond financing.

Let us take up the case of monetary finance first. Linearizing the non-linear system (23)–(24a) about its equilibrium:

$$M^*, \bar{B}, K^*, T(Y^* + \bar{B}) = G + \bar{B}, I(r^*, K^*) = 0,$$

gives:

$$\begin{pmatrix} \dot{m} \\ \dot{k} \end{pmatrix} = \begin{pmatrix} -T'F_M & -T'F_K \\ I_r H_M & I_r H_K + I_K \end{pmatrix} \begin{pmatrix} m \\ k \end{pmatrix} \tag{25}$$

where $m \equiv M - M^*$ and $k \equiv K - K^*$. Denoting the matrix in (25) by D, the stability conditions are:

$$\operatorname{tr}(D) < 0 \tag{26a}$$

$$\det(D) > 0 \tag{26b}$$

where $\operatorname{tr}(D)$ and $\det(D)$ denote respectively the trace and determinant of D. Substituting from (II) into (26a) yields:

$$\operatorname{tr}(D) = -T'\mu\alpha - \mu\lambda \frac{I_r}{L_r}(h + I_K L_y) + I_K < 0$$

$$= -T'\mu\alpha - \mu\lambda \frac{I_r}{L_r} h + I_K \left(1 - \mu\lambda \frac{I_r}{L_r} L_y\right) < 0.$$

A sufficient condition is therefore:

$$\lambda \frac{I_r}{L_r} L_y < \frac{1}{\mu} = S' + \sigma L_y,$$

which is true since $\lambda(I_r/L_r) < \sigma$.

The proof that the determinant is positive is as follows. From eqs. (II):

$$\det(D) = -T'\mu \begin{vmatrix} \alpha & \beta + I_K \\ \mu\lambda \dfrac{I_r}{L_r}(S'-h) & I_K(1 - \mu\lambda \dfrac{I_r}{L_r} L_y) - \mu\lambda \dfrac{I_r}{L_r} h \end{vmatrix}$$

So we need to prove:

$$\alpha I_K - \lambda \frac{I_r}{L_r} \mu [\alpha I_K L_y + \alpha h + (\beta + I_K)(S' - h)] < 0.$$

The term in square brackets can be written:

$$I_K(\alpha L y - h) + S'(\beta + I_K) + (\alpha - \beta)h$$

$$= I_K(\alpha L y - h) + S'(\beta + I_K) + \sigma h \qquad \text{since } \alpha - \beta = \sigma.$$

Expanding this by using the definitions of α, β and h yields:

$$I_K[C_w L_y + (1 - L_w)\sigma L_y - S' L_w - C_w L_y]$$

$$+ S'(C_w - \sigma L_w + I_K) + \sigma(S' L_w + C_w L_y)$$

$$= [I_K(1 - L_w + C_w](S' + \sigma L_y)$$

$$= \frac{I_K(1 - L_w) + C_w}{\mu}.$$

Thus the entire expression simplifies to:

$$\alpha I_K - \lambda \frac{I_r}{L_r}(I_K(1 - L_w) + C_w) < 0$$

$$C_w(I_K - \lambda \frac{I_r}{L_r}) + (1 - L_w) I_K(\sigma - \lambda \frac{I_r}{L_r}) < 0$$

which is again true since $\lambda(I_r/L_r) < \sigma$. Q.E.D. This establishes (26b) and thus the stability of the system (25).

Now turn to the system under bond financing of deficits, eqs. (23) and (24b). Linearizing around equilibrium as before results in:

$$
\begin{bmatrix} \dot{b} \\ \dot{k} \end{bmatrix} = \begin{bmatrix} r(1 - T' - T'F_B) & -T'rF_K \\ I_r H_B & I_r H_K + I_K \end{bmatrix} \begin{bmatrix} b \\ k \end{bmatrix} \tag{27}
$$

where $\dot{b} = B(t) - B^*$. Defining Δ as the matrix in (27), the stability conditions for the system are:

$$\text{tr}(\Delta) < 0 \tag{28a}$$

$$\det(\Delta) > 0. \tag{28b}$$

It is not possible, in general, to prove that these inequalities must hold. That is, as in the case where the capital stock was fixed, stability under bond finance is an empirical matter. We can, however, derive a set of intuitively plausible sufficient conditions for stability.

Consider first the trace. The upper left term will be negative if and only if condition (16b) holds. The lower right term is simply the total effect of an increase in the capital stock on investment, including any indirect effects through changing interest rates. It seems intuitively plausible that this should be negative. If this condition is met, then the model with variable capital stock is 'more stable' than the model with fixed capital stock in the sense that (16b) is sufficient but no longer necessary.

Only one other condition is required to insure stability. Let us pose the following question: What would be the effect on aggregate demand of the discovery of an additional dK of capital? First, it would increase consumption through the wealth effect by $C_W dK$. Second, it would decrease investment by $I_K dK$. It seems intuitively plausible that the net effect should be contractionary, that is, $I_K + C_W < 0$. As the reader can verify from (II), this assumption suffices to establish that $H_K < 0$, and thus that (28a) holds. In fact, it proves (28b) as well. From (II) we find that $I_K + C_W < 0$ implies $F_K < 0$, which, in view of the fact that $H_B > 0$ establishes that the determinant is positive.

To recapitulate, two jointly sufficient conditions (neither one necessary) for the stability of the economy under bond finance are:

$$F_B > \frac{1 - T'}{T} \tag{16b}$$

$$I_K + C_w < 0. \tag{29}$$

We would argue that both are likely to be satisfied in practice.

The argument for (29) has already been given: it asserts that the depressing effect of more capital on investment outweighs the expansionary wealth effect on consumption. [12] In considering (16b), the reader is reminded that B is the volume of interest payments on the national debt, so $F_B = dY/dB$ is analogous to an ordinary multiplier for transfer payments. A number between 1.0 and 2.0 seems plausible for F_B, at least for the United States. These limits would imply that T' must exceed some number between 0.33 and 0.50 in order to satisfy (16b). The appropriate interpretation of T' is as the *marginal propensity to tax and reduce income-conditioned transfer payments* as GNP rises. According to Modigliani (1971, p. 30) when U.S. GNP rises by $1, the combined increase in federal income taxes, state and local income taxes, social security contributions and corporate income taxes amounts to about 50¢. Since there are also transfer payments which decline automatically with rising incomes — unemployment insurance, welfare payments of various kinds and farm subsidies are just a few examples — it would appear that $T' > 0.50$. And this would imply that any F_B greater than unity would mean that the system is stable. [13]

4. Summary and conclusions

The cutting edge of monetarism is the assertion that fiscal policy can not affect aggregate spending; otherwise monetarism is hardly distinguishable from an eclectic Keynesian view. The latest version of the monetarist challenge appears to accept the interest-elasticity of the

---

[12] Note that this is not *necessary* for stability since more capital also has a contractionary impact through the *LM* curve.

[13] In the oversimplified model which omits interest payments from the budget restraint, stability under bond finance can be established on purely theoretical grounds in the case where the capital stock varies. The proof is given in the original working draft upon which the present paper is based: 'Does Fiscal Policy Matter?' Econometric Research Program Memorandum No. 144, Princeton, New Jersey, August 1972.

demand for money and to rest, instead, on the perverse wealth effects associated with bond-financed government spending.

We have analyzed the question in the framework of an *IS–LM* model extended to allow for wealth effects and for the need of the government to finance its budget deficit or surplus. The economy can be at rest only when the budget is balanced, else the stock of financial assets in the hands of the private economy will necessarily be changing, and there will be wealth-effects on private spending. In this context, an analysis of the effectiveness of fiscal and monetary policy has to cover both the comparative-static multiplier for bond-financed or money-financed government spending and the stability of the process touched off by an unbalanced government budget.

As a preparatory exercise, we study a conventional 'short-run' model in which the stock of fixed capital is assumed to be constant, although net investment may be going on for as long as it takes the economy to reach a new equilibrium. Our conclusion is that if such an economy is stable at all under bond finance, fiscal policy is normally effective. If the monetarists are right, the system must be unstable. And then fiscal policy is worse than impotent: bond-financed spending drives income down without limit. Both the stability of the economy and the effectiveness of fiscal policy are in principle empirical matters. But eq. (16b) provides an empirically plausible condition that guarantees both. The case of monetarist instability—deficit spending contracts the economy, thus enlarging the deficit and contracting the economy still more, thus... – hardly sounds plausible.

Allowing the capital stock to vary complicates the story, but changes the result only slightly. It remains true that both the stability of the economy and the positivity of the multiplier for bond-financed deficit spending are empirical matters. But (16b) and (29) are a pair of plausible restrictions on the behavior functions that suffice to insure both. In this extended model, $dY/dB > 0$ is no longer a necessary condition for convergence, so that it is logically possible for the economy to be stable and fiscal policy ineffective. However, we regard this as a curiosum rather than as a vindication of monetarism. For the empirical values characteristic of the United States, at least, the evidence seems to require a comfortable 'yes' in answer to the question posed in the title of this paper.

References

Andersen, L.C. and J.L. Jordan, 1968, Monetary and fiscal actions: a test of their relative importance in economic stabilization, Federal Reserve Bank of St. Louis Review 51 (November), 11–24.

Christ, C.F., 1967, A short-run aggregate–demand model of the interdependence of monetary and fiscal policies with Keynesian and classical interest elasticities, American Economic Review 57 (May), 434–443.

Christ, C.F., 1968, A simple macroeconomic model with a government budget restraint, Journal of Political Economy 76, 53–67.

Fand, D.I., 1970, A monetarist model of the monetary process, Journal of Finance 25, 275–289.

Friedman, M., 1956, The quantity theory of money – a restatement, in: Friedman, M., ed., Studies in the quantity theory of money (University of Chicago Press, Chicago), 3–21.

Friedman, M., 1959, The demand for money: some theoretical and empirical results, Journal of Political Economy 67, 327–351.

Friedman, M., 1966, Interest rates and the demand for money, Journal of Law and Economics 9, 71–85.

Friedman, M., 1972, Comments on the critics, Journal of Political Economy 80, 906–950.

Modigliani, F., 1971, Monetary policy and consumption, in: Federal reserve bank of Boston, Consumer spending and monetary policy: the linkages, Conference Series No. 5 (Boston), 9–84.

Murray, S., (forthcoming), Financing the government budget deficit, Journal of Money, Credit, and Banking.

Silber, W.L., 1970, Fiscal policy in *IS–LM* analysis: a correction, Journal of Money, Credit and Banking 2, 461–472.

Spencer, R.W. and W.P. Yohe, 1970, The 'crowding out' of private expenditures by fiscal policy actions, Federal Reserve Bank of St. Louis Review 52 (October), 12–24.

Tobin, J., 1972, Friedman's theoretical framework, Journal of Political Economy 80, 852–863.

Errata (1988)

p. 324 Eqs. (2) and (4) should be labelled (2') and (4')
p. 325 Third line after eq. (9) should be (B'/r) not (B/r)
p. 329, line 3 Should end with 'is' not with 'B'
p. 331, eq. (22) The left-hand side should be 'r' not 'Y'
p. 333 Fourth line of algebra from bottom is missing a parenthesis. It should read

$$[I_k (1 - L_w) + C_w](S' + \sigma Ly)$$

p. 334, eq. (27) The upper left-hand entry in the matrix is missing a parenthesis. It should read

$$r (1 - T' - T' F_B)$$

Journal of Public Economics 5 (1976) 183–184. © North-Holland Publishing Company

DOES FISCAL POLICY MATTER?

A correction

Alan S. BLINDER*

Princeton University, Princeton, NJ 08540, U.S.A.

Robert M. SOLOW

M.I.T., Cambridge, MA 02139, U.S.A.

Received January 1975

There are two errors in our 1973 paper.[1]

First, the expression given in eqs. (I) and (II) for the impact multiplier of the number of bonds (B) on real net national product (Y), denoted by F_B, is incorrect. This affects the quantitative, though not the qualitative, dimensions of our conclusions on the efficacy of bond-financed deficit spending. The correct expression is

$$F_B = \mu[(\beta/r) + C_Y(1 - T')],$$

so that the sign of F_B can no longer simply be equated with the sign of $\beta \equiv C_W - \sigma L_W$.[2] Instead, $\beta > 0$ is sufficient, but not necessary, for $F_B > 0$. On pp. 329–331, where we discuss the sign of β or the size of $\mu\beta$, it is, of course, F_B that really matters.

The necessary and sufficient condition for stability in the fixed-capital model, and one of the jointly sufficient conditions for stability in the variable-capital model, remains as stated in equation (16b) of our paper: $F_B > (1 - T')/T'$.

---

*We are grateful to Martin Baily, Willem Buiter and William Johnson for calling these errors to our attention.

[1]Does fiscal policy matter? Journal of Public Economics 2, no. 4, 319–337.

[2]To review the notation: $C = C(Y-T, W)$ is the consumption function, $M^D/P = L(r, Y, W)$ is the demand function for real balances, $T = T(Y)$ is the tax function, $I = I(r, K)$ is the investment function, and $\sigma > 0$ is defined as

$$\sigma \equiv \frac{I_r - (B/r^2)C_W}{L_r - (B/r^2)L_W},$$

where W is real wealth, defined as the sum of K, M/P and B/rP. The multiplier μ is given by

$$\mu \equiv [1 - C_y(1 - T') + \sigma L_y]^{-1}.$$

$\beta > 0$ is necessary, but not sufficient, for this to hold.[3] If, in fact, β is positive, the correction enhances the prospects for stability since (16b) can be written as

$$\beta > r\left(\frac{1-T'}{T'}\right)(1-C_Y+\sigma L_Y),$$

whereas the corresponding (erroneous) condition implied by our 1973 paper would have been

$$\beta > \left(\frac{1-T'}{T'}\right)(1-C_Y(1-T')+\sigma L_Y).$$

The second error is in the verbal explanation, on p. 334, of the jointly sufficient conditions for stability in the variable-capital model: eqs. (16b) and (29). We should have said that the trace of matrix (27) must be negative if (16b) holds, because we proved earlier (on p. 332) that the lower right-hand element is negative. Given that $H_B > 0$, a sufficient condition for the determinent to be positive is $F_K < 0$, and (29) is sufficient for this. The sign of H_K is irrelevant.

[3]Proof: Suppose $\beta = 0$, then

$$\left(\frac{T'}{1-T'}\right)F_B = \frac{T'C_y}{1-C_y(1-T')+\sigma L_y} < 1.$$

[22]

Journal of Public Economics 7 (1977) 309–328. © North-Holland Publishing Company

'CROWDING OUT' AND THE EFFECTIVENESS OF FISCAL POLICY

Willem H. BUITER*

London School of Economics, London WC2A 2AE, England

Received January 1976, revised version received January 1977

'Crowding out' of private economic activity by public economic activity is a multidimensional concept. A taxonomy is proposed: the degree of crowding out, the time horizon considered, direct and indirect crowding out constitute the four main categories. The latter two each have many subcategories. With direct crowding out government economic activity directly enters as an argument into structural private behavioural relationships. Indirect crowding out refers to crowding out in the reduced form of the model without there being any direct crowding out at the level of the structural private behavioural relationships. A small full employment model is used to analyse the implications of various forms of direct crowding out for the effectiveness of fiscal policy.

1. Introduction

'Crowding out' refers to the displacement of private economic activity by public economic activity. Known as 'diversion' to Keynes (1929), the subject has a long history in macroeconomic theory and policy debate. In recent years the dangers of public borrowing crowding out private borrowing and of public spending crowding out private spending have again been emphasised in the financial press and by government officials.[1] At the same time papers by Barro (1974, 1976), Feldstein (1976), David and Scadding (1974), Kochin (1974) and Peltzmann (1973) have analysed some of the implications of 'ultrarationality' in the relation between the private sector and the public sector.

In section 2 an attempt is made to bring some order into this frequently confused debate by developing a comprehensive taxonomy. Crowding out is shown to be a multidimensional concept.[2] The different notions of crowding out are

---

*This paper is based on chapter 3 of my Ph.D. dissertation 'Temporary equilibrium and long-run equilibrium', Yale, 1975. Comments, criticism and advice from James Tobin, Gary Smith, Katsuhito Iwai, Alan Blinder, A.B. Atkinson and an anonymous referee are gratefully acknowledged

[1]See e.g. the Economic Report of the President (1975, pp. 4, 25).

[2]Crowding out is not of course an all-or-nothing phenomenon. The degree of crowding out can be defined as the ratio of the induced change in the scale of some private activity to the change in the scale of the public economic activity that brought it about. The crowding out debate, in other words, is about the signs and magnitudes of public policy multipliers.

related to the existing literature and their implications for the effectiveness of
fiscal policy are evaluated in some familiar simple macroeconomic models.
The third part of the paper uses a simple closed economy full employment model
to study the short-run and long-run implications of 'direct crowding out',
one of the major categories in the taxonomy developed in section 2. Section 4
touches on three special problem areas.

2. A taxonomy of crowding out

2.1. Short run and long run

The short-run–long-run dichotomy contrasts the impact effect of changes in
government activity – for given values of the short-run exogenous but long-run
endogenous (or predetermined) variables such as asset stocks and expectations
about the future – with the long-run, steady-state effect of such changes when
stocks and expectations have adjusted fully to the change in government policy.
Until fairly recently the neo-Keynesian literature dealt mainly with short-run
crowding out.[3] A number of more recent papers investigate various aspects of
long-run crowding out [e.g. Mundell (1965), Christ (1968), Blinder and Solow
(1973b), Friedman (1972), Tobin and Buiter (1976)]. The slightly older crop of
monetary growth models can also be considered to fall into the long run crowding out category [e.g. Tobin (1955, 1965), Stein (1966), Johnson (1967), Levhari
and Patinkin (1968), Foley and Sidrauski (1971)].

Often neither the impact effect nor the long-run, steady-state effect correspond
to the 'run' one is most interested in for policy purposes. For policy, the real
(i.e. calendar) time effects of policy changes over a period of, say, a few years
tend to be most pertinent. In principle this represents no great problems. The
method of comparative dynamics – solving the dynamic system and comparing
trajectories under different assumptions about initial conditions, other parameter
values or the behaviour of policy control variables – permits one to find the
degree of crowding out for any time interval. In practice explicit analytical
solutions of nonlinear dynamic economic systems tend to be difficult to obtain.
Numerical solutions through computer simulations are required to derive the
interim multipliers [e.g. Chow (1975)].

It is important to realise that the degree of crowding out is not necessarily
greater in the long run than in the short run. Tobin and Buiter (1976) analyse
an extreme case in which complete crowding out of real private spending by
public spending in the short run, because of full employment of all resources

---

[3]The theoretical and empirical literature on this subject is surveyed comprehensively in
Blinder and Solow (1973a); see also Friedman (1970).

and a fixed capital stock, is contrasted with a positive long run effect of government spending on real output because of capital deepening.

2.2. Direct crowding out[4]

The degree of direct crowding out or ultrarationality is the extent to which the government sector can be subsumed under the private sector in specifying the structural behavioural relationships of the economy. Direct crowding out is a multidimensional concept, the dimensions being characterized by the government activities that are crowding out (the denominator of the multiplier) and the private activities that are being crowded out (the numerator of the multiplier).[5] If every action undertaken by the government is neutralised by a corresponding action in the opposite direction by the private sector, the government is but another veil waiting to be removed by probing economists.[6] In the textbook *IS–LM* model direct crowding out would be reflected in the inability of fiscal policy actions to shift the *IS* curve.

The most important dimensions are the following:

(1) *Income.* What is regarded as income by the private sector? Is government spending on final goods and services regarded as part of private income? Free school milk, school lunches, housing subsidies and food stamps are examples of public expenditure constituting private income in kind. Are government deficits excluded, i.e. are current deficits (surpluses) viewed as equivalent to current taxes (transfers) and is public saving a perfect substitute for private saving? Certain kinds of taxes are directly competitive with discretionary private saving: social security contributions and state-run compulsory retirement or health insurance schemes are substitutes for voluntary private saving for old age and sickness. [See e.g. Katona (1965), Cagan (1965), Juster and Lipsey (1967), Taylor (1971)].

(2) *Wealth.* What is regarded as wealth by the private sector? This is the capital account counterpart to the current account question asked above. If the private sector regards current deficits as equivalent to current taxes because the financing of the deficit is regarded as equivalent to taxation – no matter what combination of high-powered money creation, new borrowing and taxation is

---

[4]Alternative descriptions would be 'structural' or 'ex ante' crowding out for direct crowding out and 'reduced form' or 'ex post' crowding out for indirect crowding out. The 'ex ante'–'ex post' nomenclature is found in David and Scadding (1974).

[5]The best single reference on direct crowding out is the 'textbook' by Bailey (1971), esp. ch. 9, pp. 152–164. Another recent textbook that deals with some aspects of ultrarationality is Miller and Upton (1974).

[6]An analogous issue within the private sector is the relationship between households and corporations. Is the corporation merely an extension of the households that own it, i.e. can its actions be entirely subsumed under household decision making or is the corporate veil not quite as easily removed?

actually used to finance the deficit – government interest-bearing debt will not be counted as part of private sector net worth.[7]

(3) *Consumption.* What is regarded as consumption by the private sector, i.e. to what extent is public consumption a substitute for private consumption? Certain types of public consumption expenditure that are directly competitive with private consumption spending are public spending on education, law and order, health care and care for the elderly [Peltzman (1973)].

(4) *Investment.* What is regarded as investment by the private sector, i.e. to what extent is public investment a substitute for private investment?[8]

(5) *Borrowing.* How close substitutes are government bonds for corporate bonds and other private bonds in private portfolios?[9]

Ultimately questions about the presence and strength of various forms of ultrarationality can only be answered by looking at the facts.[10] All I shall attempt here is to indicate the range of theoretical possibilities and the logical implications of certain assumptions. Some casual empirical remarks about the importance of various forms of ultrarationality will occasionally be ventured.

The implications of completely subsuming public sector behaviour under private sector behaviour can be far-reaching. The simple model presented in part 3 shows how in a full employment economy with complete crowding out in all dimensions, fiscal policy is completely powerless if all taxes are lump sum. The public sector has effectively been worked out of the model altogether.

2.3. Indirect crowding out

Indirect or system-wide crowding out refers to the substitution of public economic activity for private economic activity (e.g. the substitution of public

---

[7]This argument has a long history. See e.g. Tobin (1952), Patinkin (1965), Meyer (1974) and Barro (1974). A recent exchange between Barro (1976), Feldstein (1976) and Buchanan (1976) has brought out the importance of population growth and intertemporal inefficiency. There has not yet been a systematic investigation of the intuitively plausible proposition that with imperfect capital markets and binding cash flow or liquidity constraints on spending and borrowing for some private economic agents, the composition of income flows and wealth portfolios will affect behaviour and the mix of financing instruments chosen by the government will affect real economic activity.

[8]The crowding out of consumption and investment can of course be disaggregated by type of consumption good and capital good.

[9]An alternative classification scheme would distinguish forms of direct crowding out that depend on the specific *content* of government spending programmes from those that depend on the *financing* of government spending programmes, irrespective of their specific content. The consumption and investment dimensions fall into the former category. The inclusion of government spending on final goods and services in private income will depend on the specific content of the spending programme. The wealth dimension and the government budget deficit are financing issues. The borrowing dimension fits neatly into neither category.

[10]Some (inconclusive) empirical evidence is already available on various aspects of 'ultra-rationality' [e.g. Denison (1958), David and Scadding (1974), Kochin (1974) and Peltzman (1973)].

spending for private spending or of public saving for private saving) that comes out of the working of the entire model of the economy without there being any 'ultrarationality' at the level of the individual structural relationships. There is indirect crowding out, in other words, when the reduced form derivatives (or multipliers) of the model show that increased government taxation reduces private saving or increased government spending reduces private spending even if the private and public consumption functions cannot be consolidated into a single 'social' consumption function with government economic decision-making subsumed entirely under private economic activity. Indirect crowding out is induced by changes in prices and interest rates resulting from changes in the value of some government policy instrument.

An example of 100% short-run indirect crowding out of private spending by public spending in the simple fixed price, closed economy, unemployment version of the *IS–LM* model is the absence of any effect on real income of changes in public spending when the *LM* curve is vertical or the *IS* curve is horizontal. (No empirical support exists for these two theoretical possibilities.) In general, if the government spending multiplier is positive but less than unity, there is partial short-run crowding out of private investment and/or consumption spending. With a downward sloping *IS* curve and an upward sloping *LM* curve a rise in the interest rate accompanies an increase in real income due to a higher level of government spending. While this reduces the magnitude of the equilibrium increase in real income below the magnitude of the rightward shift of the *IS* curve (which gives the multiplier at a given rate of interest), the equilibrium change in real income is nevertheless positive. The multiplier is reduced by a scarcity not of real resources (labour and capital) but of money, which pushes up interest rates when the economy begins to expand. This situation could therefore be better described as the crowding out of private spending by restrictive monetary policy than by public spending.

In the open economy version of the same model under a flexible exchange rate regime with perfect capital mobility, changes in government spending will have no (short-run) effect on real income [Mundell (1962), Fleming (1962)]. Government spending crowds out export demand (and 'crowds in' import demand) dollar for dollar.

In the closed economy, full employment version of the *IS–LM* model with a classical labour market there will be 100% crowding out of private spending by public spending in the short run. With real output fixed, each unit of output appropriated by the government means one less unit of output available for private consumption and investment. When the cause of 'spending' crowding out is competition for limited funds in an economy with unemployed real resources, expansionary monetary policy can help bring the economy to its production possibility frontier where the real scarcities set in. No such easy way of obtaining something for nothing exists when the economy is already operating on its efficient boundary: the allocation of scarce resources among alternative uses applies to the allocation of resources between the public and private sector as much as to the allocation of resources within the private sector [Ott and Korb (1973)]. Expansionary monetary policy has only inflationary consequences in an economy operating at or near full employment.[11]

Competition between the public and the private sector is not limited to the demand side of the market for final goods and services. In a fully employed economy, a government wishing to engage in productive activity of its own will compete with the private sector in factor markets and intermediate product

Table 1

	Direct	Indirect
Short run	Spencer and Yohe (1970) Bailey (1971) Peltzman (1973) David and Scadding (1974) Kochin (1974) Miller and Upton (1974) Carlson and Spencer (1975)	Hicks (1937) Keynes (1929, 1936) Friedman (1970) Blinder and Solow (1973b)
Long run	Barro (1974, 1976) Feldstein (1976)	Christ (1960) Johnson (1967) Foley and Sidrauski (1971) Friedman (1972) Blinder and Solow (1973a) Tobin and Buiter (1976)

markets for labour and other resources. Many other examples of indirect crowding out could be given, but the small sample offered here is sufficient to illustrate the point that short-run indirect crowding out has been a mainstream macro-economic theory and policy issue for at least four decades.

The taxonomy developed here is summarised in table 1 together with some of the contributions to each of the categories.

In section 3 the short-run and long-run effects of direct crowding out will be discussed in greater detail using a simple closed economy full employment model.

---

[11]Note that the public spending on final goods and services considered under indirect crowding out was assumed not to affect private consumption and investment directly. This does not require us to assume that governments purchase goods and services and proceed to throw them into the sea, although that would be a possible rationalization. Government spending that directly affects private utility functions or opportunity sets was considered under direct crowding out.

3. Some examples of direct crowding out in a full employment model and their implications for fiscal policy

A full employment *IS–LM* model will be used in this section to analyse some of the forms of direct crowding out discussed in part 2. Labour force growth, technical change and depreciation are ignored. The long run equilibrium of the model will therefore be a stationary state. In a stationary state real asset stocks are constant and expectations are realised (or at least no longer revised).

The notation is as follows:

M = nominal quantity of money,

B = nominal quantity of bonds,

K = stock of real reproducible capital $K = K^P + K^G$,

K^P = privately owned capital stock,

K^G = publicly owned capital stock,

P = money price level,

x = expected rate of inflation,

C^P = private consumption,

C^G = public consumption,

I^P = private investment,

I^G = public investment,

T = real taxes,

R = nominal rate of return on bonds.

For concreteness I shall assume that an adaptive expectations mechanism characterises the formation of price expectations and that expectations about capital gains on claims to real reproducible capital are static. The constant labour force is scaled to 1. Taxes are lump sum. The production function is a constant returns to scale neo-classical production function $f(K)$; $f' > 0$, $f'' < 0$. Private consumption (C^P) depends on income (Y), with a marginal propensity to consume between zero and one, and on (nonhuman) net worth (W), with $C_W^P > 0$. The demand for real money balances (L) depends on the aftertax real rate of return differential between money and other assets. It is essential, for bond financing of government spending to be equivalent to tax financing, that the public sector interest-bearing financial liability be a perfect substitute in private sector portfolios for some private sector claim. Thus, in our model with only one private sector asset, government bonds and claims to the earnings of existing capital are assumed to be perfect substitutes in private portfolios. If, in the eyes of private economic agents, government bonds were qualitatively different from claims to private capital (e.g. because of different risk properties) the real trajectory of the economy will not be invariant under different choices of bond and tax financing policies. Private economic agents could then not, in general, 'undo' changes in government financing policies by borrowing or lending on personal account.[12] The nominal rate of return on money balances is institutionally fixed at zero. Bonds are fixed nominal face value, variable interest rate claims. The demand for real balances also depends on wealth,

$$L = L(R, W), \qquad L_R < 0, \quad 0 < L_W < 1.$$

The momentary equilibrium is given by the *IS* curve and the *LM* curve

$$C^P + C^G + I^P + I^G = f(K), \qquad (IS) \tag{1}$$

$$L = \frac{M}{P}. \qquad (LM) \tag{2}$$

The dynamic equations are

$$\dot{K} = I^P, \tag{3}$$

$$\dot{K}^G = I^G, \tag{4}$$

$$\frac{d}{dt}\left(\frac{B}{P}\right) = \gamma\left(C^G + I^G + \frac{RB}{P} - T - f'(K)K^G\right) - \frac{\dot{P}}{P}\frac{B}{P}, \tag{5}$$

$$\frac{d}{dt}\left(\frac{M}{P}\right) = (1-\gamma)\left(C^G + I^G + \frac{RB}{P} - T - f'(K)K^G\right) - \frac{\dot{P}}{P}\frac{M}{P}, \tag{6}$$

$$\dot{x} = \beta\left(\frac{\dot{P}}{P} - x\right), \qquad \beta > 0. \tag{7}$$

Eqs. (5) and (6) are derived from the government budget identity. γ is the share of the deficit financed by borrowing. The change in the real value of private sector holdings of a government debt instrument is the real value of current changes in the nominal stock of the instrument plus capital gains on existing holdings. Pure fiscal policy is commonly defined as changes in some parameter(s) of public spending or taxation with any resulting deficit (or surplus) financed by borrowing (or retiring bonds), i.e. $\gamma = 1$. Eqs. (3) and (4) reflect the simplifying assumptions that there are no sales of capital between the public and the private sectors and no depreciation.

Without direct crowding out of investment, we assume private investment to be an increasing function of q, the ratio of the market value of claims to the existing stock of capital to the value of the stock of capital at current reproduc-

[12]See Barro (1974).

tion costs, or equivalently, the ratio of the rate of return obtainable by investing a dollar in the production of new capital goods to the rate of return obtainable by investing a dollar in existing capital goods,

$$q = \frac{f'(K)}{R-x}.$$

Thus without direct crowding out along the investment dimension,

$$I^P = I[f'(K)/(R-x)], \qquad I' > 0, \quad I(1) = 0. \tag{8}$$

If public investment is a substitute for private investment we can specify private investment as follows

$$I^P = I^P(I^G, f'(K)/(R-x)), \qquad -1 \le I_1^P \le 0. \tag{8'}$$

Perfect substitutes would be characterised by $I_1^P = -1$. Another way of representing the perfect substitutes case would be to use eq. (8'')

$$I^P = I[f'(K)/(R-x)] - I^G. \tag{8''}$$

If complementarity relations exist between private and public investment the private investment function is given by (8') with $I_1^P \ge 0$.

The private consumption function without direct crowding out along the consumption dimension can be written as:

$$C^P = C(Y, W), \qquad 0 < C_1 < 1, \quad C_2 > 0. \tag{9}$$

Direct substitutability or complementarity relations between public and private consumption can be represented by:

$$C^P = C^P(C^G, Y, W), \qquad C_1^P \lessgtr 0. \tag{9'}$$

The perfect substitutes case is $C_1^P = -1$. This could also be written as:

$$C^P = C(Y, W) - C^G. \tag{9''}$$

Two other forms of direct crowding out that can be conveniently analyzed in this simple model are direct crowding out along the income and wealth dimensions. Y and W are arguments in the private consumption function and the money demand function. Y and W go through a sequence of transformations as different forms and degrees of direct crowding out are assumed.

c

In models that ignore all forms of direct crowding out, real private income (including expected capital gains due to inflation) is given by:

$$Y = f(K) + \frac{RB}{P} - x\left(\frac{M+B}{P}\right) - T - f'(K)K^G. \tag{10}$$

Let $1-\alpha$ denote the fraction of the private sector's holdings of public sector interest-bearing debt that is offset by the present discounted value of the future taxes 'required' to service that debt: after the future taxes implied by current deficits are taken into account, only a fraction α of private sector holdings of public sector bonds will be part of private sector net worth and therefore subject to capital gains or losses due to expected inflation. On the income side a fraction $(1-\alpha)$ of the bond-financed part of the deficit will be subtracted from the initial concept of real private income in (10),

$$Y' = f(K) + \frac{RB}{P} - x\frac{(M+\alpha B)}{P} - T - f'(K)K^G$$

$$- (1-\alpha)\gamma\left(C^G + I^G + \frac{RB}{P} - T - f'(K)K^G\right). \tag{10'}$$

If, in addition, government spending is counted as an addition to private income to the extent indicated by fractions $0 \leq \varepsilon_1, \varepsilon_2 \leq 1$, multiplying C^G and I^G respectively, real private income becomes

$$Y'' = f(K) + \frac{RB}{P} - x\frac{(M+\alpha B)}{P} - T - f'(K)K^G$$

$$- (1-\alpha)\gamma\left(C^G + I^G + \frac{RB}{P} - T - f'(K)K^G\right) + \varepsilon_1 C^G + \varepsilon_2 I^G. \tag{10''}$$

Complete crowding along the income dimensions requires $\alpha = 0$ and $\varepsilon_1 = \varepsilon_2 = 1$. The final private real income concept, perhaps better labelled real social income, is $f(K) + (1-\gamma)[C^G + I^G + (RB/P) - T - f'(K)K^G] - x(M/P)$, or

$$Y''' = f(K) + \frac{\dot{M}}{P} - x\frac{M}{P}. \tag{10'''}$$

Private sector nonhuman marketable wealth, W, goes through an analogous sequence of transformations. In the absence of any ultrarationality, we have

$$W = \frac{M+B}{P} + qK^P. \tag{11}$$

When the future taxes 'required' to service the debt are taken into account, this becomes

$$W' = \frac{M+\alpha B}{P} + qK^{P}. \tag{11'}$$

When in addition a fraction ε_2 of public investment is counted as part of private income, we get

$$W'' = \frac{M+\alpha B}{P} + qK^{P} + q\,\varepsilon_2 K^{G}. \tag{11''}$$

Complete crowding out ($\alpha = 0$, $\varepsilon_2 = 1$) gives

$$W''' = \frac{M}{P} + qK. \tag{11'''}$$

It could be argued that with the consolidation of the private and the public sectors having gone this far, the distinction between inside and outside assets has become blurred. There appears to be little rationale left for counting expected capital gains or losses on the stock of outside money as part of net worth. Carrying the consolidation to its logical conclusion would reduce real income to real output and net worth to the value of the stock of capital.

The ultrarational version of the *IS–LM* model with bond-financed deficits or surpluses (complete direct crowding out along the investment, consumption, income and net worth dimensions, given by eqs. (1)–(4), (5) and (6) with $\gamma = 1$, (7), (8''), (9''), (10''') and (11''') can be summarised as follows:

$$C\left(f(K)-x\frac{M}{P},\frac{f'(K)}{R-x}K+\frac{M}{P}\right)+I\left(f'(K)/(R-x)\right)=f(K), \quad (IS)$$

$$\tag{12a}$$

$$L\left(R,\frac{f'(K)}{R-x}K+\frac{M}{P}\right)=\frac{M}{P}, \quad (LM)$$

$$\tag{12b}$$

$$\dot{K} = I(f'(K)/R-x), \tag{12c}$$

$$\frac{d}{dt}\left(\frac{M}{P}\right) = -\frac{\dot{P}}{P}\frac{\dot{M}}{P}, \tag{12d}$$

$$\dot{x} = \beta\left(\frac{\dot{P}}{P}-x\right), \tag{12e}$$

The distinction between publicly owned capital and privately owned capital has disappeared. Government deficits and surpluses are bond-financed but the bond debt of the public sector has effectively disappeared from the model. It is irrelevant whether or not the budget balances, since neither private income nor private portfolios are affected by the government's financing policy. The equation giving the change in the real value of the stock of bonds is irrelevant for the rest of the model and has been omitted. The private sector is indifferent about the amount of bonds the government wishes to issue, because with every bond that is issued a perfectly equivalent tax liability is imposed. The net effect is equivalent to the complete absence of government bonds from the economy.[13] The government as an independent spending and revenue-raising agent has been consolidated out of the model. In this model there is, trivially, complete crowding out of private spending by government spending and of private saving by lump sum taxation both in the short run, given by the IS and LM curves for given values of stocks and expectations, and in the long run, given by the IS and LM curves and the values of K, M/P and x obtained by setting $\dot{K} = d/dt(M/P) = \dot{x} = 0$. The government can influence neither real nor nominal magnitudes by operating on C^G, I^G and T.

Two points should be made about this result. First, it depends on the tax being a lump sum tax. If there were, say, a tax at a rate θ on factor incomes and debt service, $R(1-\theta)$ rather than R would be an argument in the money demand function and the government could influence the real economy by varying the tax *rate*.[14]

Second, 100% direct crowding out of private consumption by public consumption (or of private investment by public investment) is not sufficient to guarantee the absence of long-run effects of changes in public consumption (or public investment). In addition, government bonds should not appear as an argument in any private sector behavioural relationship.

Consider the general model (eqs. (1)–(4), (5) and (6) with $\gamma = 1$, (7), (8'), (9') (10'') and (11'')). When $C^P = -1$ there is complete direct crowding out of private consumption by public consumption: in the short run an increase in C^G will merely displace an equal amount of C^P. Even if there were no direct crowding out of C^P by C^G, the full employment assumption would ensure complete short-run indirect crowding out of private spending by public spending through increases in the price level and the rate of interest. With complete direct crowding out even the price level and the interest rate are unaffected in the short run.

---

[13] It is unfortunate that there is no convenient analytical way of differentiating between the effect of financial intermediation in saving real resources and facilitating saving and accumulation and the effect of increasing the quantity of some financial claim, given a financial system of a given degree of sophistication.

[14] The point that changes in non-lump-sum taxes will virtually always affect behaviour in a way that will not be cancelled out is of course a more general one. The effect of changes in wage tax rates on labour supply and demand is another example.

If, however, government bonds constitute private net worth to any extent ($\alpha \neq 0$), financing the deficit or surplus resulting from the change in public spending by issuing or retiring debt will gradually change private net worth; eq. (5), describing the rate of change of the stock of real government debt, again becomes an integral part of the dynamics of the model, and the balanced budget condition is again a relevant steady state condition. Thus, even if ultra-rationality prevails in all dimensions except for private sector behaviour not being invariant under different amounts of government interest-bearing debt held in private portfolios, changes in government spending or taxing behaviour will have real long-run effects when bonds are used to finance the resulting budget imbalance.

If the government deficit or surplus is exclusively money-financed, the ultra-rational version of the model is given by eqs. (1)–(4), (5) and (6) with $\gamma = 0$, (7), (8''), (9''), (10'') and (11''')

$$C\left(f(K)+C^G+I^G+\frac{RB}{P}-T-f'(K)K^G-x\frac{M}{P},\frac{f'(K)}{R-x}K+\frac{M}{P}\right)$$

$$+I[f'(K)/(R-x)] = f(K), \quad (IS) \tag{13a}$$

$$L\left(R,\frac{f'(K)}{R-x}K+\frac{M}{P}\right)=\frac{M}{P}, \quad (LM) \tag{13b}$$

$$\dot{K} = I[f'(K)/(R-x)], \tag{13c}$$

$$\frac{d}{dt}\left(\frac{B}{P}\right) = -\frac{\dot{P}}{P}\frac{B}{P}, \tag{13d}$$

$$\frac{d}{dt}\left(\frac{M}{P}\right) = C^G+I^G+\frac{RB}{P}-T-f'(K)K^G-\frac{\dot{P}}{P}\frac{M}{P}, \tag{13e}$$

$$\dot{x} = \beta\left(\frac{\dot{P}}{P}-x\right). \tag{13f}$$

Even though bonds are not part of private sector net worth, the volume of bonds affects the size of the government deficit and therefore the rate of change of M. Eq. (13d) can therefore not be ignored. For simplicity take $I^G = K^G = 0$. The long-run equilibrium (*IS* and *LM* with $\dot{K} = d/dt(B/P) = d/dt(M/P) = \dot{x} = 0$) is again a zero rate of inflation equilibrium if $B \neq 0$. Changes in C^G and T will have short-run effects on the price level and the rate of interest. Across steady states an increase in C^G or a decrease in T will cause equiproportionate increases in the nominal stock of money and the price level. K and R are un-affected. If there were no bonds in the model ($B = 0$) the rate of inflation could be nonzero in long-run equilibrium. In that case changes in C^G and T will cause changes in the steady-state rate of inflation. There would be long-run real effects of such fiscal policy changes because the nominal rate of return on money balances is institutionally fixed. The real rate of return differential between money and capital would therefore be altered.

The analysis developed so far can be applied to a variety of issues. In what follows I shall use it to develop a possible interpretation of the *Newsweek* statement by Milton Friedman (1975) that the true cost of government is measured by government spending, not by explicit taxes. My interpretation of this statement is that real private income consists of net national product plus capital gains minus government spending on goods and services. (Alternatively – but not in the context in which it was written – one could interpret the statement as simply referring to the indirect crowding out of private spending by public spending in the short run in a fully employed economy.) In our notation

$$Y = f(K) - x\frac{M}{P} - (C^G + I^G). \tag{13}$$

This is the real private income concept one obtains when the entire government budget deficit is subtracted from the conventional measure of real private income (and government bonds do not constitute private net worth to any extent). For simplicity, public investment and capital are again ignored in what follows.

The *Newsweek* model is a special case of our general model eqs. (1)–(9). (10′) and (11′) with $\alpha = I^G = K^G = 0$, under bond-financed deficits ($\gamma = 1$), It can be summarised as follows

$$C^G + C^P\left(f(K) - x\frac{M}{P} - C^G, \frac{M}{P} + \frac{f'(K)}{R-x}K\right) + I[f'(K)/(R-x)] = f(K) \tag{14a}$$

$$L\left(R, \frac{M}{P} + \frac{f'(K)}{R-x}K\right) = \frac{M}{P}, \tag{14b}$$

$$\dot{K} = I[f'(K)/(R-x)], \tag{14c}$$

$$\frac{d}{dt}\left(\frac{M}{P}\right) = -\frac{\dot{P}}{P}\frac{M}{P}, \tag{14d}$$

$$\frac{d}{dt}\left(\frac{B}{P}\right) = C^G + \frac{RB}{P} - T - \frac{\dot{P}}{P}\frac{B}{P}, \tag{14e}$$

$$\dot{x} = \beta\left(\frac{\dot{P}}{P} - x\right). \tag{14f}$$

The long-run equilibrium values of R, P, K and B are determined by

$$C^G + C^P\left(f(K) - C^G, \frac{M}{P} + K\right) = f(K), \tag{15a}$$

$$L\left(R, \frac{M}{P} + K\right) = \frac{M}{P}, \tag{15b}$$

$$f'(K) = R, \tag{15c}$$

$$C^G + \frac{RB}{P} - T = 0. \tag{15d}$$

The stock of bonds only enters eqs. (14e) and (15d), and does not affect the behaviour of R, P and K.

The impact effect of an increase in C^G is to shift the IS curve to the right in $R-P$ space, raising R and P and crowding out private consumption and investment to the extent required to make room for the larger amount of government consumption. Solving eq. (15c) for K as a function of R, $K = g(R)$, $g' = 1/f'' < 0$

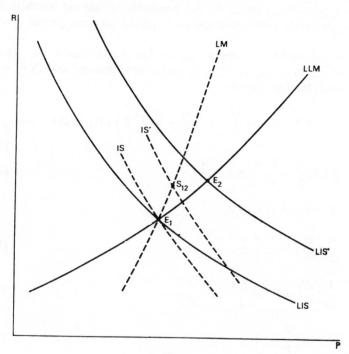

Fig. 1

and substituting this into (15a) and (15b) we can represent the long-run equilibrium in $R-P$ space

$$C^G + C^P\left(f(g(R)) - C^G, \frac{M}{P} + g(R)\right) = f(g(R)), \quad (LIS \text{ curve}) \quad (16a)$$

$$L\left(R, \frac{M}{P} + g(R)\right) = \frac{M}{P}. \qquad\qquad (LLM \text{ curve}) \quad (16b)$$

Short-run IS and LM curves corresponding to the long-run equilibrium E and the long-run LIS and LLM curves are drawn in fig. 1 above. (the LLM curve could be steeper than the LM curve). The short-run result of an increase in C^G is to create a new momentary equilibrium at S_{12}. In the long run, an increase in government consumption spending will reduce real output (raise R and P) as drawn in fig. 1, if the LIS curve is downward sloping or if it is upward sloping and steeper than the LLM curve, and raise real output otherwise.[15]

Thus, even if the full government deficit is viewed as equivalent to current taxation and government interest-bearing debt is not counted as private sector net worth to any extent, changes in public consumption spending will have real long-run effects unless there also happens to be complete direct crowding out along the consumption dimension.

4. Caveats

The results established so far are subject to three broad qualifications.

[15]

$$\left.\frac{dR}{dp}\right|_{LIS} = \frac{C_W^P \frac{M}{P^2}}{[(C_Y^P - 1)f' + C_W^P]/f''} < 0 \quad \text{if} \quad (C_Y^P - 1)f' + C_W^P > 0,$$

$$\left.\frac{dR}{dp}\right|_{IS} = \frac{-C_W^P \frac{MR}{P^2}}{KC_W^P + I'} < 0, \quad \text{(at the long-run equilibrium)},$$

$$\left.\frac{dR}{dp}\right|_{LLM} = \frac{(L_W - 1)\frac{M}{P^2}}{L_R + L_W/f''} > 0,$$

$$\left.\frac{dR}{dp}\right|_{LM} = \frac{(L_W - 1)\frac{M}{P^2}}{L_R - L_W\frac{K}{R}} > 0.$$

4.1. Corners

Consider the case of complete direct crowding out of private consumption of some commodity by public consumption – a change in the level of public consumption causing merely a change in the *composition* of total (private + public) consumption of that commodity without changing its level. For this crowding out of private spending to be possible, it has to be assumed that no individual consumer is 'at a corner' beyond which consumption cannot be reduced for technical or physiological reasons. As an example, with the consumption of private education constrained to lie in the nonnegative orthant, no dollar-for-dollar offset of an increase in public spending on education is possible with private spending already at the origin. Mutatis mutandis the same applies to the other forms of direct crowding out. As another example, private portfolio reshuffles and changes in borrowing and lending behaviour can only negate an increase in the volume of public debt if private agents hold sufficient amounts of government bonds to begin with [Barro (1974)].

In an overlapping generations model changes in the volume of public debt will have no real effect only if current generations are connected to future generations by a chain of operative intergenerational transfers. An increase in forced intergenerational transfers can only be offset by a reduction in voluntary inter-generational transfers, if voluntary intergenerational transfers are not zero initially [Barro (1974)].

The importance of corner solutions for economic activities in which crowding out is potentially important is an empirical issue on which little hard evidence is available.

4.2. Substitutes and complements

A specific commodity or service supplied (competitively or otherwise) by the government may be a substitute for a privately supplied commodity or service. At the level of theoretical possibilities with some empirical plausibility, comple-mentarity relations between certain categories of public and private spending also ought to be considered. Public investment, for example, may be competitive with private investment in certain instances (as in public housing construction) but complementarity relations between certain categories of investment in social overhead capital and private investment are certainly possible. Public investment in projects with increasing returns or massive overheads such as the construction of a dam come to mind.

4.3. Effective demand and notional demand

Even when there is complete direct crowding out of, say, private consumption by public consumption in terms of *notional* private demand, there need not be complete crowding out of *effective* private demand. In a Clower–Barro and Grossman world with households unable to execute their notional consumption plans because they are quantity-constrained in the labour market and firms unwilling to execute their notional labour hiring plans because they are quantity-constrained in the output market, an increase in public consumption might well cause a smaller reduction in effective private consumption demand than in notional private consumption demand. [Clower (1965), Barro and Grossman (1971)].

The same fundamental problem arises with indirect crowding out of private spending by public spending in the presence of involuntary unemployment of labour and idle capital. The textbook neo-Keynesian model with unemployment permits, at least temporarily, the existence of insufficient private effective demand at current (non-market-clearing) prices and interest rates and given the current state of expectations. This can then be remedied by increasing public spending or reducing taxation. Two fundamental issues are whether such a state of affairs requires private behaviour to be irrational and whether the information available to the public sector is assumed to be superior to that available to the private sector. It is beyond the scope of this paper to deal with these problems[16] [see Gordon (1976)].

5. Conclusion

The model developed in section 3 offers considerable scope for further analysis of alternative combination of types and degrees of direct crowding out. More useful, at this stage, would be careful empirical analysis of the existence and importance of the many types of direct crowding out. The analysis of section 3 was conducted using a full employment model. The important issues associated with indirect crowding out under conditions of involuntary unemployment of labour and idle capital were only mentioned in passing.

The conditions under which changes in public spending have no long-run effect on real variables are very stringent indeed. Complete direct crowding out of private spending by public spending and full equivalance between taxes and public sector deficits are required. The fact that even complete direct crowding out along any one dimension does not prevent fiscal policy from having real long-run effect does not imply that direct crowding out is unimportant for policy purposes. Some degree of direct (and indirect) crowding out is definitely a theoretical and a practical possibility – along each of the many dimensions.

---

[16]A complete solution will, in our opinion, have to incorporate the following two elements: First, the assumption that prices clear labour and output markets continuously – or in each market period – must be abandoned. (This is not the same as assuming permanent price rigidity.) Second, the unique position of the government as the 'spender of last resort' – not subject to the same budget constraints as private agents because of its monopoly in the issue of legal tender, its ability to tax and its resulting lower risk of default – must be recognized.

A number of examples were given in section 2 and others can undoubtedly be thought of. The degree of crowding out along each dimension is an empirical matter that will have to be settled if accurate policy-oriented models are to be constructed. It is important to beware of jumping from accepting the plausibility of some degree of direct (or indirect) crowding out to presenting the (on a priori and empirical grounds) implausible case of 100% crowding out as the only relevant one.

References

Bailey, M.J., 1971, National income and the price level: A study in macroeconomic theory, 2nd edition (McGraw–Hill, New York).

Barro, R.J. and H.I. Grossman, 1971, A general disequilibrium model of income and employment, American Economic Review 61, 82–93.

Barro, R.J., 1974, Are government bonds net wealth?, Journal of Political Economy 82, 1095–1117.

Barro, R.J., 1976, Reply to Feldstein and Buchanan, Journal of Political Economy 84, 343–349.

Blinder, A.S. and R.M. Solow, 1973a, Analytical foundations of fiscal policy, in: A.S. Blinder, R.M. Solow et al., The economics of public finance (The Brookings Institution, Washington DC) 3–119.

Blinder, A.S. and R.M. Solow, 1973b, Does fiscal policy matter?, Journal of Public Economics 2, 319–337.

Buchanan, J.M., 1976, Barro on the Ricardian equivalence theorem, Journal of Political Economy 84, 337–342.

Cagan, P., 1965, The effect of pension plans on aggregate saving, N.B.E.R. Occasional Paper No. 95.

Carlson, K.M. and R.W. Spencer, 1975, Crowding out and its critics, Federal Reserve Bank of St. Louis Review 47, 2–17.

Christ, C., 1968, A simple macroeconomic model with a government budget restraint, Journal of Political Economy 76, 53–67.

Chow, G., 1975, Analysis and control of dynamic economic systems (John Wiley, New York).

Clower, R.W., 1965, The Keynesian counter revolution: A theoretical appraisal, in: F.H. Hahn and F.P.R. Brechling, eds., The theory of interest rates (Macmillan, London) 103–125.

David P.A. and J.L. Scadding, 1974, Private savings: 'Ultrarationality', aggregation and Denison's Law, Journal of Political Economy 82, 225–249.

Denison, E.F., 1958, A note on private saving, Review of Economics and Statistics 40, 261–267.

Economic Report of the President, 1975.

Feldstein, M., 1976, Perceived wealth in bonds and social security: A comment, Journal of Political Economy 84, 331–336.

Fleming, J.M., 1962, Domestic financial policies under fixed and floating exchange rates, I.M.F. Staff Papers 9, 369–379.

Foley, D.K. and M. Sidrauski, 1971, Monetary and fiscal policy in a growing economy (Macmillan, London).

Friedman, M., 1970, A theoretical framework for monetary analysis, in: M. Friedman et al. (1974).

Friedman, M., 1972, Comments on the critics, Journal of Political Economy 80, 906–950.

Friedman, M. et al., 1974, Milton Friedman's monetary framework: A debate with his critics (University of Chicago Press, Chicago, IL).

Friedman, M., 1975, Wonderland scheme, Newsweek, January 27, 24–25.

Gordon, R.J., 1976, Recent developments in the theory of inflation and unemployment, Journal of Monetary Economics 2, 185–221.

Hicks, J.R., 1937, Mr. Keynes and the classics, Econometrica 5, 147–159.

328   *W.H. Buiter, 'Crowding out' and fiscal policy*

Johnson, H.G., 1967, Money in a neo-classical one-sector growth model, in: H.G. Johnson, Essays in monetary economics (Allen and Unwin, London) 143–178.

Juster, T.F. and R.E. Lipsey, 1967, A note on consumer asset formation in the U.S., Economic Journal 77, 834–847.

Katona, G., 1965, Private pensions and individual saving, University of Michigan Survey Research Center, Monograph 40 (Ann Arbor, MI).

Keynes, J.M. and H.D. Henderson, 1929, Can Lloyd George do it? in: J.M. Keynes, Essays in persuasion (Macmillan, London) 118–134.

Keynes, J.M., 1936, The general theory of employment, interest and money (Macmillan, London).

Kochin, L.A., 1974, Are future taxes anticipated by consumers?, Journal of Money, Credit and Banking 6, 385–394.

Levhari, D. and D. Patinkin, 1968, The role of money in a simple growth model, American Economic Review 68, 713–753.

Meyer, L.H., 1974, Wealth effects and the effectiveness of monetary and fiscal policy, Journal of Money, Credit and Banking 6, 481–503.

Miller, M.H. and C.W. Upton, 1974, Macroeconomics: A neoclassical introduction (Richard D. Irwin, Homewood, IL).

Mundell, R.A., 1962, The appropriate use of monetary and fiscal policy for internal and external stability, I.M.F. Staff Papers, 9, 70–79.

Mundell, R.A., 1965, A fallacy in the interpretation of macroeconomic equilibrium, Journal of Political Economy 73, 61–65.

Ott, D.J. and L.J. Korb, 1973, Public claims on U.S. output (American Enterprise Institute for Public Policy Research, Washington DC).

Patinkin, D., 1965, Money, Interest and Prices, 2nd edition (Harper and Row, New York).

Peltzman, S., 1973, The effect of public subsidies-in-kind on private expenditures: The case of higher education, Journal of Political Economy 81, 1–27.

Spencer, R.W. and W.P. Yohe, 1970, The 'crowding out' of private expenditures by fiscal policy actions, Federal Reserve Bank of St. Louis Review 52, 12–24.

Stein, J.L., 1966, Money and capacity growth, Journal of Political Economy 74, 451–465.

Taylor, L.D., 1971, Saving out of different types of income, Brookings Institution Papers on Economic Activity 2, 283–407.

Tobin, J., 1952, Asset holdings and spending decisions, American Economic Review, Papers and Proceedings 42, 109–126.

Tobin, J., 1955, A dynamic aggregative model, Journal of Political Economy 63, 103–115.

Tobin, J., 1965, Money and economic growth, Econometrica 33, 671–684.

Tobin, J. and .W.H Buiter, 1976, Long run effects of fiscal and monetary policy on aggregate demand, in: J.L. Stein, ed., Monetarism (North-Holland, Amsterdam) 273–309.

[23]

THE ECONOMIC JOURNAL

JUNE 1985

The Economic Journal, **95** (*June* 1985), 285–306
Printed in Great Britain

MACROECONOMIC POLICY DESIGN AND CONTROL THEORY – A FAILED PARTNERSHIP?*

David Currie

My subject is the applicability of control theory to the pressing questions of macroeconomic policy design that face us, both domestically and in the international arena. I approach the issue with some trepidation, conscious that I am a relative amateur in control matters. I am also mindful of the dangers of claiming too much in the field of policy design. Those were nicely stated in a broader context by that eminent biologist, Sir Peter Medawar (1984), when he wrote:

> It is not their wrongness so much as their pretensions to rightness that have brought economic predictions and the theory that underlies them into well-deserved contempt. The dogmatic self-assurance and the asseverative confidence of economists are additional causes of grievance – self-defeating traits among people eager to pass for scientists.

I have no wish to pass myself off as a scientist, but I do hope that I am not guilty of dogmatism and unreasonable pretensions in arguing my main theme – that we have made important advances in the application of control theory to macroeconomic policy design, which are yielding important insights and should continue to do so.

The control theory that has mostly been applied in economics has been taken over from engineering. This theory tells us how best to control a physical system (a space-ship, for example) in order to achieve certain objectives (to reach and return from the moon) by appropriate adjustment of the instruments of control (the rockets and stabilisers of the space ship), subject to the physical laws constraining the behaviour of the system. These control techniques have been applied with considerable success in a wide range of physical and engineering applications – the control of chemical process plants, electronic systems, rockets, to name just three. The problem of control in economics is often posed in similar

* This is a slightly revised version of an inaugural lecture presented at Queen Mary College on 22 May 1984 and draws on many formal and informal discussions with economists too numerous to acknowledge, even if I were able to attribute my general intellectual debts. I should, however, specifically thank Gerald Kennally of the National Institute of Economic and Social Research for drawing my attention to the work of Axelrod and related research.

terms. Thus, in macroeconomics, for example, policymakers may wish to ensure that the economy progresses, without undue fluctuations in output, unemployment, prices and other key variables, along a course that yields the most prosperous outcome for society, by suitable adjustment of instruments – interest rates, taxes, government spending and so on – subject to the constraints imposed by the structure of the macroeconomy, as expressed in a suitable macroeconometric model. The essential problem – the design of control rules for the instruments that best meet the preferences of the controller given the structure of the system to be controlled – appears to be common with that already solved in the field of engineering. With techniques available from the engineering literature it is not surprising that economists took these over and applied them to the design of macroeconomic policy.

Control methods entered economics quite early on, most notably through the work of Bill Phillips (1954; 1957) at the London School of Economics. But I think it is fair to say that their influence was only fully felt in the 1970s, when computational techniques caught up and the theory of control entered the tool-kit, albeit the specialised one, of economists. In the UK, the QMC based Programme of Research into Econometric Methods was important in hastening this process. By 1976, matters had developed so far that an official committee was established under the chairmanship of Professor Jim Ball, to investigate the usefulness of optimisation techniques for policy formulation.

The report of that Committee, Ball (1978), gave a cautious welcome to control methods as an additional weapon in the armoury of policy formulation. It gave little support to those – and I regret there were some – who naïvely conveyed the impression that control techniques were the answer to policymakers' dreams, that all one needed to do was to take the Treasury model, apply control methods, and after a process in which the preferences of policy makers would be established, the budget could be read straight from the computer printout.

Now there are a variety of reasons why the use of control theory in economics is likely to be less straightforward than in engineering applications, and some of these I shall touch on later. But there is one in particular on which I wish to focus. It is distinctive to economics, and social systems more generally. Essentially it arises from the fact that the analogy between engineering and economic systems which inspired much of the early work on control theory in economics is, quite simply, misleading. Economic systems, like all systems of social interaction, are intelligent in a way that engineering systems are not. In economics, we are concerned with the control of intelligent systems that think about what policymakers do to them and act accordingly.

This distinction is so obviously important once it is stated that it is surprising how little it figures in the report of the Ball Committee. That reflects not on the quality of the report, but rather on the state of thinking about these issues within the profession at the time. It is this feature of economic systems – that the components of the economic system that we wish to control reflect upon and react to economic policy in an intelligent, non-mechanical manner – that has made us rethink our approach to macropolicy making. In the process, the subject has become much richer, greatly exciting, and, I believe, more useful. I want to try to give a flavour of the subject, of the issues with which we have been grappling and our attempts to resolve them. Unfortunately it can only be a flavour, for it is a subject that can properly be expressed only in rather forbidding mathematics.

Let me give two simple examples of how the control problem is complicated by intelligent private sector behaviour. My examples concern the two main instruments of policy – fiscal and monetary. My first is the use of tax changes – fiscal policy – to control the economy. This was the standard fare of the annual budget, at least until a recent fetish with the Public Sector Borrowing Requirement overthrew all that. The standard view was that, to raise the level of demand and output and reduce unemployment, the Chancellor should cut taxes. Conversely to reduce overheating – inflationary pressures – he should raise taxes. This policy will indeed work, at least in the short to medium run, in all the current main macromodels; and it operates by regulating the level of aggregate consumption in the economy. Now at the same time, our theories of consumption emphasise the wish of consumers to spread out unevenness in their flow of income so as to achieve a rather smoother pattern of consumption. If we take this permanent income or life cycle view of consumption as it has come to be known, and I think the evidence supports it, we are forced to think with greater care about the consequences of tax changes. In particular, we must think about whether the tax change is permanent or temporary. A cut in income tax that is perceived to be permanent will increase the future stream of income, and lead to a rise in consumption. But a temporary cut has very limited effects on life-time earnings, and consumers are likely to spread out its benefits over a considerable time. Hence a transitory cut in income tax may do very little to affect consumption. But if the object of the tax cut is to offset a temporary fall in aggregate demand, this argument suggests that a cut in income tax, necessarily temporary, will not be effective. To engineer a temporary boost to consumption, the Chancellor needs an alternative: thus a cut in indirect taxes, which lowers prices temporarily, will make it advantageous to buy now rather than later. This example illustrates the point that the effects of a tax cut depend very much on whether consumers see it as temporary or permanent, and this depends in turn on what policy is perceived to lie behind the tax cut.

My second example concerns monetary policy and the exchange rate. Suppose one is asked what effect an increase in the money supply has on the exchange rate – a simple straightforward question to which one might think a simple answer should be possible, if we have our wits about us. But I have at least two contradictory views to offer. On one view, a larger money supply implies higher domestic prices, so that a *depreciation* of the exchange rate will occur, maintaining the relationship between domestic and foreign prices when expressed in a common currency.[1] Indeed the overshooting hypothesis suggests that, if prices adjust slowly to the money supply change, the exchange rate depreciation may be exaggerated, overshooting its final equilibrium and then appreciating back.[2] But on an alternative view, the money supply increase will cause an exchange

[1] This is emphasised by the monetary approach. See, for example, Frenkel and Johnson (1976).
[2] Dornbusch (1976), Buiter and Miller (1981; 1982).

rate *appreciation*. This is because the foreign exchange market expects the Bank of England to raise interest rates to dampen monetary growth and bring the money supply back onto target.[1]

This is the sort of contradiction that gives economists a bad press. But it is apparent, not real, for the arguments apply to quite different circumstances. The first argument rests on the assumption that changes in the money supply tend not to be reversed – the money supply, for example, follows a random walk. In the second, monetary changes are reversed, and the authorities pursue a policy of monetary targets. Two distinct policies underlie the two cases. What my argument illustrates is not that economists can never agree, but rather that to ask how the foreign exchange market reacts to a money supply change is not a well-defined question. The answer to the question depends crucially on how the market expects the authorities to react. Once again the behaviour of the system depends on the perceived policy or control rule of the authorities. In designing policy, we must take account of this dependence.

This is a very general proposition that applies in almost every area of macro-economics. Its consequences are pervasive. It blurs the usual distinction between technical advice on 'how the economy works' on the one hand and policy advice on the other. One cannot discuss how the economy works without first specifying a background of what policy is in force; and it is then a very natural question to lead on to ask how changes in that policy influence the behaviour of the system.

I hope by now that I have persuaded you that there is an extra complication, a new dimension, to the control problem in economics. As in engineering applications, the design of the control rule depends on the structure of the system to be controlled; but unlike engineering, the structure of the system depends on what control rule is perceived to be in force.

To get a grip on this problem, it is clear that we must model the way in which people form their expectations about the future. We therefore need a theory of the economy in which people's expectations about the future enter as explanatory variables; and we need a theory (or theories) of how people think about economic events and form expectations of the future. The natural way to progress is, of course, to use direct observations of expectations drawn from surveys. Unfortunately such data are rather sparse, available only for relatively short time periods, and usually relate only to the very short term future, not the one, two or five years or longer that are all too often relevant for economic decisions. Cross-sectional panel data on expectations would be an invaluable aid to research in this area. It is therefore regrettable that we are not actively seeking new sources of expectations data – instead Rayner's axing of the general database available to economists offers little encouragement in this.

In the absence of satisfactory expectations data, economists have proceeded in one of two ways. The first is to assume that expectations are formed by some rule of extrapolation, more or less complicated, based on the past. Thus inflation may be forecast from observation of past inflation using some type of adaptive or Box–Jenkins forecasting procedure. Conventional methods of this kind may serve quite well for forecasting a variable such as inflation or output over a one

[1] Currie (1984).

or two year period provided present developments are not very different from the past. But it serves rather badly if circumstances change markedly – for example if the price of oil alters dramatically as in 1973 and 1978, or if policy shifts abruptly as in 1979/80. Moreover, it is most unlikely to perform well in financial or foreign exchange markets, where conventional rules of thumb cannot be expected to produce profits.

The second approach is what has come to be known as 'rational or consistent expectations'.[1] This cuts through the problem of having two distinct models – one for how the economy works and the other for how people form expectations – by assuming that people form their expectations on the basis of knowledge of the true structure of the economy. Thus when testing an economic theory, we also assume that people's expectations are formed consistently with that same theory, and the quantitative estimates of the model used in forming expectations coincide with those of the model itself. If the theory is correct, this amounts to assuming that expectations are optimal predictors, in the sense of being unbiassed and having minimum variance.

Now the assumption that people form their expectations rationally is rather breathtaking in its range, and may remind you of Sir Peter Medawar's dictum that I cited earlier. After all, the experiments of psychologists reveal that most people are ignorant of even the most elementary principle of statistical inference. We find it particularly difficult, so the work of Kahnemann, Tversky and other experimental psychologists indicates, to make rational decisions where the problem is too open-ended.[2] In so far as they admit the term 'rational', psychologists typically characterise our mode of reasoning as taking the form of *bounded rationality*. Whether consciously or unconsciously, people limit the range of options to be considered at any particular time. We all, no doubt, can give instances of such behaviour, of course in others, never ourselves. Inevitably, this form of decision-making can be severely suboptimal, particularly when having to cope with new circumstances that need novel decisions.

Despite this, I hope you will not dismiss the assumption of rational forecasts too easily. One way in which each of us can come to terms with our lack of even elementary skills in forecasting is to draw on outside advisers. A number of groups forecast key macroeconomic variables regularly, and these are available for only the price of a newspaper. Of course, such forecasts have a bad name – I recall, in particular, Sir John Mason's comparison, in his British Association Presidential address last year, between economic forecasting and weather forecasting.[3] Sir John spoke of weather forecasting from the informed position of a former Director of the Met Office. But he overstated, I think, the inaccuracy of macroeconomic forecasts, which have indeed a reasonable success rate.[4] Provided that their models are well estimated, and provided the models are allowed to influence the forecasts (both of which conditions I emphasise for they are by no

---

[1] See the papers collected in Lucas and Sargent (1981). For excellent surveys, see Begg (1982) and Sheffrin (1983).
[2] Kahnemann *et al.* (1982). On the notion of bounded rationality in economics, see particularly Simon (1982; 1983).
[3] Mason (1983).
[4] See, for example, the National Institute (1983; 1984), Kmenta and Ramsey (1981).

means always met), those who use these forecasts may well behave as though they are making careful forecasts, even though they have no knowledge of economics and statistics. Of course, the extent to which people draw on macro forecasts depends not only on their accuracy, but also on the costs of being wrong, and one might well expect these to be greater in financial markets than other markets. It is no surprise to find, therefore, that the assumption of rational expectations seems to work much better in financial and foreign exchange markets than elsewhere.

My second defence of the assumption of rationality in forecasting, and decision-making more generally, is that it may be a reasonable aggregate approximation. Even if individuals are subject to bounded rationality, divergences from full rationality at the individual level may cancel out in the aggregate, so that aggregate behaviour is such that it is as if individuals can forecast rationally.

This idea has been developed formally in the work of John Cross on adaptive strategies of behaviour.[1] He demonstrates that in a stable environment, adaptive behaviour, based on repeating more frequently those successful strategies and shifting away from those unsuccessful ones, leads to a distribution of individuals around the rational outcome in a wide class of problems. Suboptimal strategies persist, though because in a large population, some ill-conceived strategies will pay-off and some well-conceived strategies fail in any particular experiment; so that non-rational strategies can survive. This view is helpful since it means that we do not have to accept that each and every one of us forms our expectations rationally in order to apply the theory in the aggregate. It also emphasises the need to understand processes of learning, and the importance of the flourishing literature that is currently integrating the analysis of learning and expectations, as well as relaxing the extreme informational assumptions that underlay the early analysis of behaviour under rational expectations.[2]

There is, I think, an even more compelling reason for adopting the assumption of rational expectations in policy appraisal, though in this context the term consistent expectations is probably better. In assessing policies under consistent expectations, one is testing them under conditions where their effects are understood. I submit that a good performance under these conditions is a *necessary* condition for a satisfactory policy. For if a policy performs badly under these circumstances, but well under different ones, it can only be because it works through systematic forecasting errors by the private sector. But since there will be an incentive for the private sector (or its forecasting agents) to alter its forecasting method if it generates systematic error, this is a rather weak and vulnerable basis for policy. A policy that performs badly when its effects are understood must be unsatisfactory. To be sure, we must be sensitive to our uncertainty about model structure, but this can be handled within the framework of consistent expectations by methods of robustness testing to check that our policy advice is not too model dependent.

[1] Cross (1983).
[2] For models of learning, see Bray (1982), Bray and Savin (1983), and Frydman and Phelps (1983). For analysis of partial information, see Frydman and Phelps (1983), Minford and Peel (1983), Pearlman *et al.* (1983) and Townsend (1983). See also Barro and Gordon (1983*a; b*), Kreps and Wilson (1982) and Backus and Driffill (1984*a; b*) for consideration of credibility and reputation.

I hope that I have persuaded you that the notion of rational or consistent expectations is useful in the control setting. There is no doubt that it has revolutionised our way of thinking about macroeconomics. This is because, notwithstanding the severe technical problems it poses for analytical and empirical macroeconomics, it provides the simplest possible way of incorporating intelligent behaviour on the part of the private sector, and this is essential for most policy problems in macroeconomics. But initially rational expectations were thought to be destructive for the use of control theory in economics. This was for two quite separate reasons. The first has a long pedigree stretching back to Adam Smith's invisible hand – the notion that perfect markets and intelligent individuals will lead to an optimal outcome, without any need for government intervention. Essentially the private sector can act as controller, making government control superfluous. This appeared in the early work on rational expectations in the form of a class of models in which government could influence the real economy only by fooling the private sector.[1] Since rational expectations imply that such fooling cannot be systematic, government could only add extra unsystematic noise to the system, not assist in stabilisation. To be sure, one might object that government may be better informed than the private sector – the Civil Service would hardly be doing its job otherwise – but then the answer is to make public that better information. Stabilisation policy becomes the province of the Press Office, not the Treasury.

But this argument will not wash. It requires us to believe that the problems of co-ordination and adjustment within the private sector are negligible, so that each of us can enter into flexible contracts for wages, financial transactions and other dealings, with clauses contingent upon each possible macroeconomic state of the world.[2] Just imagine how long the negotiations between Ian McGregor and Arthur Scargill would last in that sort of world. Consider the earnings that this would give to lawyers in drawing up complicated contracts, and I am sure you will agree that such a world would be severely suboptimal. We all resent government for some reason or other, just as we curse traffic lights, particularly when they go wrong. But how many of us would really welcome the abolition of traffic lights as the resolution of our traffic problems?

But although consistent expectations do not dispose of the control problem they greatly complicate and enrich it. This is because in order to assess the performance of control rules we must take into account their effect on the way the private sector forecasts and behaves.[3] There is, moreover, an extra dimension to the control problem. For different control rules alter the informational content of variables such as interest rates and the exchange rate.[4] Intelligent agents make inferences about disturbances to the system from observations of such variables, and their behaviour will depend on these inferences. Policy may operate through these informational channels, as well as through more conventional control mechanisms. For those of a theoretical bent of mind, there is also the possible

[1] See, for example, Lucas (1972), Sargent and Wallace (1976), Barro (1976).
[2] For the consequences of less flexible contracts, see, for example, Fischer (1977), Phelps and Taylor (1977) and Taylor (1980).
[3] Lucas (1976).
[4] See Pearlman *et al.* (1983).

need for government to intervene to avoid forms of structural instability and chaotic motion that may arise in rational expectations models.[1]

The second objection to control with rational expectations was equally erroneous, but highlighted an important problem in the control of intelligent systems which has come to be known as time-inconsistency.[2] It is a quite general phenomenon in social decision-making, and will be familiar to those who have decisions imposed upon them, even if decision-makers themselves tend to have a blind spot for it. I shall refer to government in what follows, but you may equally well think of management, head of department, examiner, dean, governor – whatever you will.

Consider how government should respond to an inflationary disturbance, such as a surge in wages. Before the event, a government concerned with inflation should give the impression that it will not accommodate the wage increase by maintaining aggregate demand and output. For by so threatening that wage rises will result in loss of jobs and unemployment, it may persuade those bargaining over wages to limit their demands. This notion of a threat effect undoubtedly underlies current policy, and is also a plank, though only one of several, in the New-Keynesian policies advocated by James Meade.[3]

Before the wage push, therefore, government should be hawkish. After the event, however, the threat effect has served its purpose. Bygones being bygones, the government should consider how best to respond to the wage surge. Under quite general conditions, the optimal response is partially to accommodate the wage surge, so that the effects on unemployment are mitigated, though at the expense of a rise in the price level. The optimal response, it seems then, is to renege on the initial hawkish stance.

It is paradoxical that this problem was first analysed in a two period setting, where, correctly analysed, the problem disappears. For the private sector, if it is bright enough, can figure out that the government will renege, for government has no reason not to do so. The private sector will, therefore, entirely discount the government's hawkish stance. You may be aware of similar chains of reasoning that prove a rational government could not use the UK nuclear deterrent.[4] The only way the government can retain any credible threat in this situation is by appearing irrational in its decision making.

With nuclear war, the world as we know it may end if the threat is called; but fortunately the effects of a wage surge are less drastic. It is therefore much more natural to consider the problem as a continuing game, not in the restricted two period setting. This simplifies matters. For it is clear that government cannot go on reneging on its commitments and continue to retain its credibility. Yet it is the credibility of government announcements that gives them their usefulness for control purposes.

There is, therefore, a choice between two types of policy. The first type, called *time-consistent* policies, are where the government has no credibility. The private

[1] See Currie (1985), Begg (1984), van der Ploeg (1984).
[2] See Kydland and Prescott (1977), Prescott (1977), Calvo (1978), Driffill (1980), Buiter (1981), Miller and Salmon (1983).
[3] Meade (1982a), Vines *et al.* (1983).   [4] McMahon (1981).

sector assumes that the government will succumb to short-run temptation, and calculates its expectations of the future on that basis. Government then formulates policy subject to this lack of credibility. Thus in my example the private sector calculates that the government will accommodate wage surges, and ignores all government pronouncements to the contrary. In the stylised history of the post-war period, it is suggested that such was the pre-Thatcher state – before the Flood. Given that no one believes what it says, the best that the government can then do is, indeed, to accommodate.

The second type of policy is *time-inconsistent*. Government has credibility, because it does not succumb to any short run incentive to renege. Because of this, government policy does influence private sector behaviour through the private sector's expectations of the future, as well as through more conventional control mechanisms. In our example, a policy of not accommodating wage surges, despite the short run temptation so to do, is time-inconsistent.

The view is sometimes expressed that time-inconsistent policies are not feasible, because government cannot credibly commit itself to succumb to temptation. I find this hard to accept. It is clear that a government with credibility has a wider range of policy options available to it than if it lacked credibility; and it can therefore expect a better policy performance.[1] The cost of reneging on a well-chosen time-inconsistent policy is that you end up without credibility with a time-consistent policy yielding worse results. Some of the QMC PRISM (Programme of Research into Small Macromodels) Group's results suggest that this cost can be very high.[2] A government that is concerned with more than the very short term has a real incentive to adhere to time-inconsistent policies, and is therefore credible in so doing.

Those who feel that the chain of reasoning has now become tortuously theoretical, a feature of much of the game theoretic reasoning of this kind, may be reassured by a more down-to-earth argument. Mrs Thatcher has demonstrated the feasibility of sticking to your guns, with only rather minor wavering in the face of strong temptations to renege. The oft-repeated slogan TINA – there is no alternative – was recognised, of course, even (or perhaps especially) within government, to have no intellectual basis. But it served to raise the political costs of a U-turn, and hence to make politically credible the time-inconsistent policy that has been pursued. In this sense Mrs Thatcher has done much to restore the credibility of the notion that government can stick to policies through thick and thin. Unfortunately, time inconsistency is not a sufficient condition for a good policy, and Mrs Thatcher has restored credibility to the policy domain by pursuing what I shall suggest later has been a severely suboptimal time inconsistent policy, so suboptimal that there must be time consistent policies that would have dominated it. But, if such costly strategies can be made credible, a better designed policy should be all the more credible.

Now if you expect me at this point to reveal the nature of that better designed policy, I must disappoint you. I have untried prototypes, and many ideas on what

[1] Buiter (1981).

[2] Levine and Currie (1983). What we here refer to as the time-inconsistent policy may be rendered time-consistent if reputations are explicitly analysed (see Backus and Driffill 1984*a*; *b*) or if a threat strategy is followed (see Oudiz and Sachs, 1984).

not to do, but I have no streamlined policy to wheel on shining and gleaming, fully tested, with knobs and whistles. But what we do now have are control methods available to us much better suited to the problems of policy design in economics. We can devise optimal time inconsistent or time consistent policies in rational expectations models, whether in a deterministic or a stochastic setting.[1] We can alter the information assumptions in such analysis, permitting us to analyse properly for the first time questions of indicator and intermediate target regimes.[2] We can analyse the bargaining, game theoretic aspects of policy that I discuss later. And we have developed experience of the use of these methods that suggests that they are powerful tools for policy appraisal.[3]

There is, of course, the worry that our control technology is in danger of outstripping the capabilities of the models available to us, and that is a concern which I share. After all, in engineering applications of control theory, the laws of motion of the system are usually well known; and if they are not, some experimentation can usually reveal the salient features for control purposes. In macroeconomics, our understanding is much poorer, and I say that despite being firmly of the view that the area of common ground between macroeconomists is much larger than is generally appreciated. Moreover, experimentation is not an attractive option. To make matters worse, the large macroeconometric models (with hundreds or sometimes even thousands of equations) to which control methods have usually been applied do not necessarily incoporate the latest state of understanding. This is not surprising given their sheer size relative to the staff resources available for their support. A frequently recurring analogy in this area, particularly with those like myself who favour smaller models, is with painting the Forth Bridge. But in view of the large number of equations in these models that are just inadequate – whether because they fit very badly, have features that fly in the face of commonsense, have not been updated, or have been imposed in violence to the data – this image does not go far enough. Instead I invite you to think of a Forth Bridge made up in sections of the latest engineering design, while in other places we have sections made of wood, or even, in the case of the monetary sector so crucial to the present government's strategy, submerged stepping stones. Worse still, some would argue, all of this is built across a narrow stretch of river, so that a simpler, smaller design would suffice. Not surprisingly, the heavy technology of control theory reveals all the weaknesses of model construction. Moreover, these models appear more vulnerable in the light of rational expectations, which sheds doubt on the stability of their structure and on the nature of the dynamics that they embody.

However, this far from being a necessary state of affairs – on the contrary, it is changing fast. Applied econometrics has advanced enormously in the past decade, and good econometric technique is now the norm, rather than the exception. In the past few years, we have had studies which systematically compare the sectors of different models, and which have been most helpful in

---

[1] Buiter and Dunn (1982), Chow (1981), Driffill (1980; 1982), Currie and Levine (1983), Levine and Currie (1984).
[2] Pearlman *et al.* (1983), Currie and Levine (1984).
[3] Miller and Salmon (1983; 1984); Currie and Levine (1984; 1985*a*).

identifying best, and worst, practice.[1] Increasingly expectations are being modelled seriously, with corresponding gains in understanding – to cite just two examples, work at the National Institute has highlighted the importance of forward looking expectations in understanding the stock-led recession of 1980/81, and productivity movements in the recent past.[2] I have no doubt that the next generation of models will incorporate the modelling of expectations quite generally. An important extra element is the creation of the new Macro-Modelling Bureau at the University of Warwick, funded by the Economic and Social Research Council, which is making the large forecasting models available to the academic community. If the Bureau takes the process of model comparison further and more systematically, as it should, in a few years' time we shall, I think, have better models and considerably greater convergence of model properties. My own guess is that in the process models will become smaller, sleeker and fitter.

But policy design cannot, and should not, await these developments. We will never have the perfect model, the state of knowledge in macroeconomics being what it is, and if we did we probably would not agree on it. What we need is an approach to policy design that is ever alert to these uncertainties and differences. This has been by no means so in the past. For example, the control methods that we have applied have often treated the macromodel as a rather precise representation of the economy, instead of being vague and uncertain. In consequence, the resulting control rules may lean far too heavily on quirky and unsatisfactory features of the model. Techniques that avoid these pitfalls are, of course, familiar, but they are computationally expensive, particularly when applied to the very large forecasting models.[3] Moreover, they require knowledge of the system properties of the estimates of the model; and this is simply not available for the large models which are generally estimated separately equation by equation, or at best block by block, rather than as a system. This is yet another reason why the future for policy appraisal may well lie in a new generation of small scale macromodels, to which systematic robustness tests can be applied.

Perhaps a more serious problem has been that control techniques have all too often been used to show what policy performs best in each model separately. This is despite the fact that these so-called best policies may perform rather badly in other models. Consider the problem from the policy-maker's point of view. He has available to him a variety of views of the world represented by each of the models and supported by, usually, highly intelligent and persuasive arguments from each of our very articulate and numerate modelling teams. It is not very helpful for him to know that a certain policy performs well in one model, when it performs badly in another. What instead would be of considerable interest would be to know that a certain policy performs tolerably well in all the models. Such policies might be agreed upon by the different modelling groups despite their important differences in outlook. What the racehorse owners at the Treasury and the Bank

[1] See the set of papers from the National Institute dealing with comparisons of models of exports, bank lending, wages and employment; a useful summary is given in Henry (1983).
[2] See Hall *et al.* (1983), Wren-Lewis (1984).
[3] Åström (1970), Holly *et al.* (1979).

of England should be looking for is 'a horse for all courses', not a well refined pure-bred capable of performing well only in special circumstances.[1] At the moment, the sheer diversity of models means that robust policies of this kind are probably not available. No policy could satisfy simultaneously the Merseyside Monetarism of Patrick Minford and the Cambridge Keynesianism of Wynne Godley. But we can reasonably expect to see a narrowing of these differences under the joint imperatives of the ESRC and Warwick as part of the process of model evaluation and selection that I alluded to before. It would not surprise me then if a robust policy, a horse for all courses, could be found.

This is part of a more general argument that our advocacy of particular policies should be sensitive to the important gaps in our knowledge. This may seem evident enough, but it is not taken seriously in practice. A standard question for all who advocate particular policies should be: What if the world is different, in plausible respects, from that which you assume? And this approach needs to be formally assimilated into our control theory. Control engineers have led the way in this, motivated by similar considerations, and there is a whole body of design theory drawing upon general, rather than specific, features of structure, that could well guide us in this task. There are some remaining technical barriers here – the complications introduced by rational expectations make it hard to take this body of knowledge over wholesale – but there is no reason to suppose that these problems will not be resolved. If we can systematically and routinely examine the robustness of our conclusions to those features of the control problem about which we are most uncertain, I have no doubt that the quality and usefulness of our policy advice will be greatly enhanced.

So far my discussion of the control problem incorporates an important asymmetry. Government is aware that its actions modify private sector behaviour, and takes this interdependence into account in determining its best course of action; but the private sector does not take into account any dependence of government strategy on its, the private sector's, actions. Were it to do so, so that the asymmetry disappears, we would be in a world of bilateral bargaining, in which the private sector thinks strategically.

The usual justification for this asymmetry is that the private sector is made up of many separate agents who cannot act together. For many applications I suppose that assumption will do; though sceptics can point to the co-ordinating role of the business lunch, the conformity to fashions of opinion in the City that so strikes the outsider, as well as to the more well-worn example of trade union behaviour. But the sphere in which strategic thinking becomes all important is in the international arena, when questions of international policy co-ordination between governments come under scrutiny.

For much of the post-war era up to the late 1960s, macroeconomic policy was conducted within the international constraints of the system established by Keynes and White at Bretton Woods. But that system showed increasing signs of strain in the late 1960s, as the adjustable peg mechanism for the exchange rate, entailing discrete adjustments to the exchange rate parity, became incompatible

[1] Chow (1980), Currie and Levine (1983).

with the increasing mobility of financial capital internationally. In the consequent move to generalised floating in the early 1970s, the rules of the game were swept away. Each country has pursued its own individual macroeconomic objectives with little regard for its international consequences. Although we have seen within Europe the framework for co-ordination under the auspices of the European Monetary System, the actual degree of co-ordination has been limited, in part because of the acute pressures from unco-ordinated policy in the rest of the world.

Now there is a view that these matters are best left to individual governments. That view is well expressed in the work of Milton Friedman, who emphasises the role of the exchange rate in insulating domestic from foreign developments and conversely, and control of the money supply to stabilise domestic developments.[1] Such results, it is true, can be derived from a rather primitive international monetarist model of the early 1970s vintage. But once one takes account of the full interdependencies between countries – through prices, real demands, asset prices and the flow of funds – it becomes very clear that such independence does not hold. We cannot sidestep the question of how best to formulate policy in an interdependent world. These issues are currently high on the agenda of debate and the PRISM group at QMC is much concerned with them as part of a broader programme of research under the auspices of the newly formed Centre for Economic Policy Research.[2]

How then should we address this problem? One approach – the hard-nosed realistic one – would be to accept that we are in a world where co-operation is limited, and design the best type of policy that one can for the United Kingdom. In other words, we design our policy treating the behaviour of other countries as given. This, it should be noted, is the standard approach to policy design, since almost all our models are of the single open economy, treating the rest of the world as exogenous. If all countries do the same, we arrive (perhaps iteratively) at a non-co-operative solution to the policy problem. The second approach – the soft-headed idealist one – is to assume a world of co-operation, and design policy internationally in such a way as to secure the best overall performance, subject to the co-operating members sharing in the resulting benefits. To do this, of course, requires a model of many economies, specifying the interdependencies between them.

The difficulty is that the non-co-operative solution, hard-nosed though it is, may yield pretty disastrous outcomes. Let me give an example of this. Consider a government that wishes to stabilise the trend of prices in the economy (it could equally well be nominal income), in the face of aggregate demand or aggregate supply disturbances. It turns out that in a wide class of models it is not very difficult to do that using monetary policy. What one makes use of is the fairly strong and well established linkage from the exchange rate through to prices, using the fact that import prices figure directly in consumer prices because of the import component of the price index, as well as indirectly through domestic costs and wages. Essentially government responds to rising inflationary pressures

---

[1] Friedman (1953; 1968).
[2] See Currie and Levine (1985a; b).

by raising interest rates and inducing an exchange rate appreciation, which acts to dampen the rise in prices. Pursued vigorously enough, such a policy can stabilise variations in prices and other nominal magnitudes fairly effectively. Moreover, some recent PRISM work suggests that one can devise a rule of this kind for targeting the price level that is robust in the multiple sense that it stabilises the system well in the face of a variety of disturbances, wide parameter variation, and model variation.[1] From the standard perspective of single country optimisation, it looks a good buy. But, if all countries wish to reduce inflation and all seek to do so by appreciating their exchange rate, they must fail, simply because of the elementary fact that one country's appreciation is another's depreciation. The aggregate consequence of such policies is an interest rate war, of the kind that we have seen in the last five years internationally.[2]

Thus single country policy design is prone to generate beggar-my-neighbour policies. This points to the need to examine policy in the inter-dependent, global setting, searching for policies that perform satisfactorily in the aggregate as well as being able to cope with country specific disturbances that generate divergences between one country and the rest of the world. We have some elementary analysis of such problems, and one or two blueprints for a possible international policy design, notably that of James Meade.[3] But we have, as yet, no systematic appraisal of policy in this area. Given its importance in the international debate, it is perhaps fortunate that this issue is now the object of intense research and I expect the next year or two to see the flow of important and useable research results.

But the hard-nosed realist will respond by asking what is the point of devising elaborate policy designs that would work well if all countries adhered to them, but will *not* be implemented because all countries have an incentive to renege, to carry out a different, free-riding policy. The problem is, after all, like the so-called prisoners' dilemma in game theory: there is a co-operative outcome that is best all round, but each player has an incentive to choose a different strategy, since that seems to improve his pay-off irrespective of the strategy chosen by the other players. Yet if everyone acts in this way, all are left worse off. Thus the problem is one of co-ordination, given the private incentive to renege on co-operative behaviour.

Had Keynes and White taken this sceptical view, and with the background of the 1930s there was every reason for them to do so, we would never have seen Bretton Woods and the post-war settlement. Fortunately the problem is not as intractable as it first appears, for we are concerned with a *repeated* prisoners' dilemma game, not an isolated one. In this context, the question is whether one can devise a set of threats of penalties to be imposed on those players or countries who renege. That sounds an impossibly complicated task. But recent advances in the theory of non-co-operative game theory suggest that it may be much more amenable than it appears.[4] Rather than attempt to describe and motivate the complicated theorems that have been thrown up in the past few years, let me

[1] Levine and Currie (1983), Currie and Levine (1983).
[2] Currie and Levine (1985a; b).   [3] Meade (1982b; 1984).   [4] Basar and Olsder (1982).

instead describe a revealing experiment that was conducted several years ago.[1] Game theorists were invited to submit computer programs to play a game of the repeated prisoners' dilemma kind that I described earlier, in a league play-off against all other entries. The winner was very simple and familiar – tit for tat – you are nice to people until they are nasty to you, and then you are nasty to them until they are nice to you again. On the second round, competitors were invited to resubmit, having the benefits of a comprehensive analysis of the results of the first round. Once more tit-for-tat came out ahead of the other strategies, some of them enormously complex, devious and Macchiavellian in design.

I find this result, which has been confirmed by subsequent analysis suggested by the experiment as well as other work, most reassuring. The notion that simple, nice strategies of the type that we all commonly use are robust, effective strategies suggests that the co-operation on which all aspects of our social life depend is not as fragile as analysis sometimes suggests. Tit-for-tat's strength lies in its capacity to elicit and reward co-operation in other players – the key to success in games of the repeated prisoners' dilemma type. It does this by offering co-operation, retaliating speedily to non-co-operation, but forgiving equally rapidly; and in all this being transparent, clear and predictable throughout. Results of this kind being generated by non-co-operative game theory have important implications throughout social science, in particular in the theories of social institutions and social conventions, as well as in other areas such as biology.[2] In the field of international economic co-operation, it suggests that the design of a threat system to sustain a co-operative policy design need not be as hard as at first it seems, and that the crucial question that faces us is rather whether we can devise a satisfactory co-operative policy that copes with the problems of inter-dependence. The design of a new international order is a formidable task, particularly in the changed balance of forces that now prevails in the world, but it is a challenge to which economists as a profession should, and I believe can, rise.

On the basis of the review that I have given of developments in the field of economics and control, you will perceive that I am optimistic of the future. Unfortunately, and this takes me to my final theme, I am not optimistic that these developments will be translated into a more effective economic policy, at least in the foreseeable future. I base this pessimism on the experience of the past few years, when we have seen a policy implemented that flies in the face of what we know, and knew then, and that seems almost wilfully designed to provide an object lesson in how not to manage our macroeconomic affairs. The points that I wish to argue are not new – they have been argued repeatedly, forcefully and at great length both inside and outside Whitehall. But there has been an absence of interest in taking these arguments seriously, to engage in rigorous policy appraisal in their light.

Lest I be misunderstood, let me emphasise that it is not part of my case to argue that the government was wrong to embark upon a policy of reducing inflation by sole reliance on monetary and fiscal retrenchment. That view can be

[1] Axelrod (1980a; b; 1981; 1984), Axelrod and Hamilton (1981); for a convenient summary, see Hofstadter (1983).
[2] Schotter (1981), Axelrod and Hamilton (1981), Maynard Smith (1982), Dawkins (1982).

argued, and has been argued many times, and I sympathise with it. But it was the government's prerogative to take that decision and make it stick; and it is the electorate's prerogative to judge whether it was right. What I wish to argue instead is this: that had it opened its ears to the technical advice available to it, this government might well have managed its basic strategy much more effectively, with less cost in terms of output foregone, investment and employment.

Since 1979, policy has been conducted in accordance with the principles of the Medium Term Financial Strategy, MTFS for short, formally unveiled in the budget of 1980. This laid down target ranges for the growth of the money supply, initially £M3, and a supporting stance for fiscal policy in the form of targets for the Public Sector Borrowing Requirement. At the heart of the strategy was the notion (drawn from Friedman, and developed by Laidler and in the United Kingdom context most notably by Ball, Burns and their colleagues at the London Business School) that the best way to reduce inflation was to do so gradually by means of a phased reduction in the money supply.[1] Once a low inflation rate is established, continued targeting of the money supply at a low constant rate was hoped to prevent any resurgence of inflation.

Now the conception behind the MTFS – that if one is to embark on a dis-inflationary programme, it should be gradualist – is a good one. Because of the sluggishness of wage and price inflation in adjusting downwards, for which there is overwhelming evidence, deflation is best administered slowly to smooth the effects on output. This intuition is formally confirmed by the optimal control based analysis of a number of researchers.[2] But while the conception may have been right, the delivery went sadly wrong. For while a phased reduction in the money supply may deliver gradualism in the financially closed economy of Friedman's mind, it has a very different effect in the open economy that is the United Kingdom. The error was to neglect the consequences of intelligent behaviour in the foreign exchange market. It was clear that the strict imple-mentation of the MTFS gave the prospect of higher UK interest rates for a run of years, which together with lower domestic inflation made sterling a more attractive investment. Funds flowed into sterling and the exchange rate therefore showed a marked appreciation, resulting in an historically unprecedented loss of international competitiveness. So-called gradualism inflicted a sudden sustained contractionary blow to the traded goods sector, notably manufac-turing, with consequences for jobs and output that we observe today. Matters were made still worse by an inauspicious rise in indirect taxes, proclaimed in the Alice-in-Wonderland economics of the time as non-inflationary. This pushed up prices, and exacerbated the upward pressure on interest rates and the fall in output.

This suggests that the MTFS was a poorly designed, high risk strategy. In saying this, I am not speaking with the advantage of hindsight. The essence of the analysis was set out in the work of Rudiger Dornbusch (1976) on exchange rate overshooting. And there were papers circulating widely in both academic

[1] Friedman (1975), Ball *et al.* (1977; 1979), Laidler (1982). For a recent assessment of the work of Ball *et al.* from a sympathetic background, see Budd and Longbottom (1984).
[2] Driffill (1982), Currie and Levine (1983).

and official circles in 1979 and 1980 that spelt out these points most clearly – notably in the symposium organised by *Oxford Economic Papers*.[1] Moreover, the most obvious resolution of these problems – to engage in the popular pastime of rate-capping, but in the context of the foreign exchange market to stem the rise in sterling, or at the very least to relax monetary stringency in the face of a rising exchange rate – these policies had a highly respectable pedigree, with the Swiss Central Bank following such a course only the year before.[2]

Equally damaging has been the straitjacket in which the MTFS has placed fiscal policy. A long-standing feature of the fiscal system has been the operation of automatic fiscal stabilisers. By this is meant the tendency of the fiscal deficit to fall as demand rises, and conversely to rise as demand falls, because of the link of revenues and expenditures – income tax and unemployment benefit, for example – to demand. By allowing this effect to operate, fluctuations in demand are dampened, helping to stabilise output movements. But over the period in question, the government has been pursuing an absolute target for the deficit, expressed in terms of the Public Sector Borrowing Requirement. Fiscal stabilisers have therefore been switched off, and in consequence the ride has been bumpier – the unusual severity of the stock cycle through which we have just been owes much to this feature of policy.

Now it is true that there are problems in operating fiscal stabilisers alongside short run monetary targets. It is a feature of a great many models, sometimes not always appreciated by their originators, that this policy combination generates stochastic instability.[3] This is because the need to finance by bond sales residual budget imbalances arising from demand fluctuations generates a rising level of volatility in interest rates, demand and output. The Treasury model, amongst others, shares this feature. But if that is the reason for this bizarre policy of PSBR targeting, it does not stand up. It would not be hard to devise low frequency fiscal adjustments that permit automatic fiscal stabilisers to operate while avoiding such instabilities One might equally look at the many alternatives to short run monetary targeting that provide assurances about longer run inflation without emasculating fiscal policy

The consequences of this fiscal conservatism have been severe. With the economy in deep recession, with unemployment well above estimates of the level at which inflation is non-accelerating, the United Kingdom has been running a substantially contractionary fiscal policy [4] With other EEC countries following the United Kingdom example, it is no surprise that eminent economists should be calling for some fiscal relaxation to help the European economy out of the trap of depressed demand and rising unemployment [5] But our policy-makers seem set to disregard the strong case that has been advanced for a supply-side-friendly policy of demand expansion

[1] Eltis and Sinclair (1981). See particularly Buiter and Miller (1981), Artis and Currie (1981), and the suggestively titled paper by Scott (1981).
[2] Artis and Currie (1981), Schiltknecht (1981).
[3] Blinder and Solow (1973), Currie (1976; 1978), Christ (1979), Currie and Gazioglou (1983), Whittaker and Wren-Lewis, (1983) Blackburn and Currie (1984).
[4] Buiter and Miller (1984), Buiter (1984).
[5] Layard *et al.* (1984).

But perhaps the most bizarre aspect of the whole strategy is its centrepiece – the targeting of the money supply It may seem heretical to challenge such ideas – clearly I must be of unsound mind – but let me remind you that we managed without monetary targeting for most of our country's history; and that indeed there has been almost no period in which the money supply has not been free to vary within reasonable limits in response to movements over the business cycle. We are, after all, not interested in the money supply as such, but rather with prices and output. The attention given to the money supply is usually justified in terms of its being an intermediate target or indicator, containing useful information about the future course of prices and output. But no one has shown that the money supply, however one defines it, is the sole variable that should be used in that way, or that it is very satisfactory in that role: supposed relationships involving money break down as quickly as they are discovered. I am not asserting that the money supply, suitably defined, is unimportant – even though we do not have compelling evidence in its favour, we would be most unwise to disregard money supply movements. But my point is that there are many other variables that are important as well. And one of the damaging features of over-concern with the money supply has been the consequent neglect of international considerations, notably the exchange rate. United Kingdom policies have, as a result, been of a severely beggar-my-neighbour character.

But questions of this kind are, I am afraid, of little interest to our current masters. Most recently, we observed the Chancellor of the Exchequer dismissing David Hendry's demolition of Friedman's empirical work for the United Kingdom with the lofty words 'I am not interested really in the arcane quibbles of econometricians', and then saying in the next moment 'the basic concept is very clear'.[1] There is no empirical regularity involving money that has stood up for more than a brief time that can justify the current naïve approach to policy making. The latest in a string of fads is the targeting of Mo, cash plus bank reserves. The recent study by Barry Johnston – a fine piece of econometrics incidentally, but widely misinterpreted – has been said to be the econometric basis of the reformulated MTFS.[2] Yet we expect in advance that it will not stand up for long, that it will collapse as the latest victim of Goodhart's Law. The study itself made clear just how much financial innovation – the spread of branches credit cards and cash tills – has altered the demand for Mo over the past decade, and this in a period when no one was concerned with Mo. How much greater and faster can we expect innovation to be when government is creating an incentive so to economise by tracking the cash available to the public and banks and with the spread of electronic cash management If the banks are not busy considering strategies for expanding their business without Mo, they are failing as bankers. Can we really expect to control the activities of the financial institutions, amongst the most powerful, innovative and creative of our industries, by devices of this kind?

All of this should be a matter of deep concern to us For these policies, wished on us by those for whom 'the basic concept is very clear', are laid at the door of

[1] Hendry and Ericsson (1983), Brown (1983), Treasury and Civil Service Committee (1984).
[2] Johnston (1984), Treasury and Civil Service Committee (1984).

the economics profession when they fail And those advances in our understanding of which I mentioned earlier will, I think, go untapped so long as this intellectual climate prevails. We must insist that those who would experiment with the British economy and our fellow citizens should first subject their favoured schemes to a process of rigorous scrutiny and appraisal against available alternatives. But I am not hopeful that we will see this happen. My title refers to a failed partnership, but left matters open with a question mark. We must, I fear, take down that question mark: the partnership, rich, rewarding and exciting though its potential may be, is foundering on a failure to listen and to learn.

Queen Mary College

Date of receipt of final typescript: November 1984

REFERENCES

Artis, M. J. and Currie, D. A. (1981). 'Monetary targets and the exchange rate: a case for conditional targets.' In Eltis and Sinclair (1981).

Åström, K. J. (1970). *Introduction to Stochastic Control Theory*. London: Academic Press.

Axelrod, R. (1980a). 'Effective choice in the prisoner's dilemma.' *Journal of Conflict Resolution*, vol. 24, pp. 3–25.

—— (1980b). 'More effective choice in the prisoner's dilemma.' *Journal of Conflict Resolution*, vol. 24, pp. 379–403.

—— (1981). 'The emergence of cooperation among egoists.' *American Political Science Review*, vol. 75, pp. 306–18.

—— (1984). *The Evolution of Cooperation*. New York: Basic Books.

—— and Hamilton, W. D. (1981). 'The evolution of cooperation.' *Science*, no. 211, pp. 1390–6.

Ball, R. J. (1978). *Report of the Committee on Policy Optimisation*. H.M.S.O., Cmnd. 7148.

——, Burns, T. and Laury, J. S. E. (1977). 'The role of exchange rate changes in balance of payments adjustment: the UK case.' ECONOMIC JOURNAL, vol. 87, pp. 1–29.

—— —— and Warburton, P. J. (1979). 'The London Business School model of the UK economy: an exercise in international monetarism.' In *Economic Modelling* (ed. P. Ormerod). London: Heinemann.

Backus, D. and Driffill, J. (1984a). 'Inflation and reputation.' Mimeo.

—— and —— (1984b). 'Rational expectations and policy credibility following a change in regime.' Mimeo.

Barro, R. J. (1976). 'Rational expectations and the role of monetary policy.' *Journal of Monetary Economics*, vol. 2, pp. 1095–117.

—— and Gordon, D. B. (1983a). 'A positive theory of monetary policy in a natural rate model.' *Journal of Political Economy*, vol. 91, pp. 589–610.

—— and —— (1983b). 'Rules, discretion and reputation in a model of monetary policy.' *Journal of Monetary Economics*, vol. 12, pp. 101–21.

Basar, T. and Olsder, G. J. (1982). *Dynamic Noncooperative Game Theory*. London: Academic Press.

Begg, D. K. H. (1982). *The Rational Expectations Revolution in Macroeconomics*. Oxford: Philip Allan.

—— (1984). 'Rational expectations and bond pricing: modelling the term structure with and without certainty equivalence.' ECONOMIC JOURNAL, vol. 94, Supplement, pp. 45–58.

Blackburn, K. and Currie, D. A. (1984). 'Stability in an open economy model: a comparison of adaptive and rational expectations in the foreign exchange market.' PRISM Discussion Paper no. 22.

Blinder, A. S. and Solow, R. M. (1973). 'Does fiscal policy matter?' *Journal of Public Economics*, vol. 2, pp. 319–37.

Bray, M. M. (1982). 'Learning, estimation and the stability of rational expectations.' *Journal of Economic Theory*, vol. 26, pp. 318–39.

—— and Savin, N. N. (1983). 'Rational expectations equilibrium, learning and model specification.' Mimeo.

304   THE ECONOMIC JOURNAL   [JUNE

Brown, A. J. (1983). 'Friedman and Schwartz on the United Kingdom.' Bank of England Panel of
    Academic Consultants, Panel Paper No. 22, October.
Budd. A. and Longbottom, A. (1984). 'International monetarism and the London business School
    model, a re-assessment.' London Business School, Centre for Economic Forecasting, Discussion
    Paper No. 123.
Buiter, W. H. (1981). 'The superiority of contingent rules over fixed rules in models with rational
    expectations.' ECONOMIC JOURNAL, vol. 91, pp. 647-70.
—— (1984). 'Allocative and stabilisation aspects of budgetary and financial policy.' Centre for
    Economic Policy Research, Discussion Paper No. 2.
—— and Dunn, R. (1982). 'A program for solving and simulating discrete time linear rational
    expectations models.' LSE Centre for Labour Economics, Discussion Paper No. 127.
—— and Miller, M. H. (1981). 'Monetary policy and international competitiveness: the problems of
    adjustment.' In Eltis and Sinclair (1981).
—— and —— (1982). 'Real exchange rate overshooting and the output cost of bringing down
    inflation.' *European Economic Review*, vol. 18, pp. 85-123.
—— and —— (1984). 'The macroeconomic consequences of a change of regime: the UK under
    Mrs Thatcher.' *Brookings Papers on Economic Activity*.
Calvo, G. A. (1978). 'On the time inconsistency of optimal policy in a monetary economy.' *Econo-
    metrica*, vol. 46, pp. 1411-28.
Chow, G. C. (1980). 'Comparison of econometric models by optimal control techniques.' In *Evaluation
    of Econometric Models* (ed. J. Kmenta and J. B. Ramsey). New York: Academic Press.
—— (1981). *Econometric Analysis by Control Methods*. New York: John Wiley.
Christ, C. (1979). 'On fiscal and monetary policies and the government budget restraint.' *American
    Economic Review*, vol. 69, pp. 526-38.
Cross, J. G. (1983). *A Theory of Adaptive Behaviour*. Cambridge: Cambridge University Press.
Currie, D. A. (1976). 'Optimal stabilisation policies and the government budget constraint.' *Economica*.
—— (1978). 'Macroeconomic policy and government financing: a survey of recent developments.'
    In *Studies in Contemporary Economic Analysis* (ed. M. J. Artis and A. R. Nobay), vol. 1. Croom Helm.
—— (1982). 'The monetarist policy rule: A critique.' *Banca del Lavoro Nazionale Quarterly Review*.
—— (1984). 'Monetary overshooting and the exchange rate.' *The Manchester School*, vol. 52,
    pp. 28-48.
—— (1985). 'Structural instability in a rational expectations model of a small open economy.'
    Economica.
—— and Gazioglou, S. (1983). 'Wealth effects, treasury bill financing and stability.' *Journal of Public
    Economics*, vol. 21, pp. 397-403.
—— and Levine, P. (1983). 'An evaluation of alternative indicator regimes for monetary policy.'
    QMC PRISM Discussion Paper No. 9, CEPR Discussion Paper No. 4.
—— and —— (1984). 'Exchange rate and price level volatility under partial information.' *Greek
    Economic Review*.
—— and —— (1985a). 'Simple macropolicy rules for the open economy.' ECONOMIC JOURNAL,
    vol. 95, Supplement.
—— and —— (1985b). 'Macroeconomic policy design in an interdependent world.' In *The Inter-
    national Coordination of Economic Policy* (ed. W. H. Buiter and R. Marston).
Dawkins, R. (1982). *The Extended Phenotype*. Oxford: Oxford University Press.
Dornbusch, R. (1976). 'Expectations and exchange rate dynamics.' *Journal of Political Economy*, vol. 84,
    pp. 1161-76.
Driffill, E. J. (1980). 'Time inconsistency and "rules versus discretion" in macroeconomic models with
    rational expectations.' Mimeo.
—— (1982). 'Optimal money and exchange rate policy.' *Greek Economic Review*.
Eltis, W. A. and Sinclair, P. J. N. (1981). *The Money Supply and the Exchange Rate*. Oxford: Oxford
    University Press.
Fischer, S. (1977). 'Long-term contracts, rational expectations and the optimum money supply rule.'
    Journal of Political Economy, vol. 85, pp. 191-205.
Frenkel, J. A. and Johnson, H. G. (eds) (1976). *The Monetary Approach to the Balance of Payments*.
    London: Allen and Unwin.
Friedman, M. (1953). 'The case for flexible exchange rates.' In *Essays in Positive Economics*. Chicago:
    University of Chicago Press.

—— (1968). 'The role of monetary policy.' *American Economic Review*, vol. 58, pp. 1–17.

—— (1975). *Unemployment versus Inflation*. Institute for Economic Affairs, London.

Frydman, R. and Phelps, E. S. (eds) (1983). *Individual Forecasting and Aggregate Outcomes*. Cambridge: Cambridge University Press.

Hall, S. G., Henry, S. G. B. and Wren-Lewis, S. (1983). 'Manufacturing stocks and forward looking expectations in the UK.' NIESR Discussion Paper No. 64.

Hendry, D. F. and Ericsson, N. R. (1983). 'Assertion without empirical basis: an econometric appraisal of Friedman and Schwartz, "Monetary Trends in...the United Kingdom."' Bank of England Panel of Academic Consultants, Panel Paper No. 22, October.

Henry, S. G. B. (1983). 'Systematic econometric comparisons: an outline of the project and summaries of its results.' NIESR Discussion Paper.

Hofstadter, D. R. (1983). 'Metamagical Themas.' *Scientific American* (May).

Holly, S., Rustem, B. and Zarrop, M. B. (1979). *Optimal Control for Econometric Models*. London: Macmillan.

Johnston, R. B. (1984). 'The demand for non interest bearing money in the United Kingdom.' Government Economic Service Working Paper No. 66.

Kahnemann, D., Slovic, P. and Tversky, A. (1982). *Judgement under Uncertainty: Heuristics and Biases*. Cambridge: Cambridge University Press.

Kmenta, J. and Ramsey, J. B. (1981). *Large Scale Macrocononometric Models*. Amsterdam: North-Holland.

Kreps, D. M. and Wilson, R. (1982). 'Sequential equilibrium.' *Econometrica*, vol. 50, pp. 863–94.

Kydland, F. E. and Prescott, E. C. (1977). 'Rules rather than discretion: the inconsistency of optimal plans.' *Journal of Political Economy*, vol. 85, pp. 473–91.

Laidler, D. (1982). 'On the case for gradualism.' In *Monetarist Perspectives*. Oxford: Philip Allan.

Layard, R., Basevi, G., Blanchard, O., Buiter, W. and Dornbusch, R. (1984). 'Europe: the case for unsustainable growth.' Centre for European Policy Studies, Paper No. 819.

Levine, P. and Currie, D. A. (1983). 'Optimal feedback rules in an open economy model.' QMC PRISM Discussion Paper No. 5, *European Economic Review*, forthcoming 1985.

—— and —— (1984). 'The design of feedback rules in stochastic rational expectations models.' Presented to the Nice Conference on Economic Dynamics and Control, QMC PRISM Discussion Paper No. 20.

Lucas, R. E. (1972). 'Expectations and the neutrality of money.' *Journal of Economic Theory*, vol. 4, pp. 103–24.

—— (1976). 'Econometric policy evaluation: a critique." In *The Phillips Curve and Labour Markets* (ed. K. Brunner and A. H. Meltzer). Carnegie–Rochester Conference Series on Public Policy. Amsterdam: North-Holland.

—— and Sargent, T. J. (eds) (1981). *Rational Expectations and Econometric Practice*. London: Allen and Unwin.

Mason, B. J. (1983). 'Predictability in science and society.' *Meteorological Magazine*, vol. 112, pp. 361–7.

Maynard Smith, G. (1982). *Evolution and the Theory of Games*. Cambridge: Cambridge University Press.

McMahon, J. (1981). *British Nuclear Weapons*. London: Junction Books.

Meade, J. E. (1982a). *Wage-Fixing*. London: Allen and Unwin.

—— (1982b). 'Domestic stabilization and the balance of payments.' *Lloyds Bank Review* (January).

—— (1984). 'A New Keynesian Bretton Woods.' *Three Banks Review* (June).

Medawar, P. (1984). 'Expectation and prediction.' In *Plato's Republic*. Oxford: Oxford University Press.

Miller, M. H. and Salmon, M. (1983). 'Dynamic games and the time inconsistency of optimal policy in open economies.' Mimeo.

—— and —— (1984). 'Policy coordination and dynamic games.' Paper presented to the 1984 Bath AUTE Conference.

Minford, A. P. L. and Peel, D. (1983). 'Some implications of partial current information sets in macroeconomic models embodying rational expectations.' *The Manchester School*.

National Institute (1983). 'The assessment of the National Institute's forecasts of GDP, 1959–82.' *National Institute Economic Review*, August, No. 105.

—— (1984). 'The National Institute's forecasts of inflation, 1964–82.' *National Institute Economic Review*, February, No. 107.

Oudiz, G. and Sachs, J. (1984). 'International policy coordination in dynamic macroeconomic models.' Paper presented to the CEPR/NBER Conference on International Policy Coordination, London, June.

Pearlman, J., Currie, D. A. and Levine, P. (1983). 'Rational expectations models with partial information.' Presented to the 1984 Nice Conference on Economic Dynamics and Control, and the Fourth International Symposium on Forecasting, London, 1984; PRISM Discussion Paper No. 15.

Phelps, E. S. and Taylor, J. B. (1977). 'The stabilizing powers of monetary policy under rational expectations.' *Journal of Political Economy*, vol. 85, pp. 163–90.

Phillips, A. (1954). 'Stabilisation policy in a closed economy', ECONOMIC JOURNAL, vol. 64, pp. 290–323.

—— (1957). 'Stabilisation policy and the time form of lagged responses.' ECONOMIC JOURNAL, vol. 67, pp. 265–77.

Prescott, E. C. (1977). 'Should control theory be used for economic stabilisation?.' In *Optimal Policies, Control Theory and Technology Exports* (ed. K. Brunner and A. H. Meltzer). Carnegie–Rochester Conference Series on Public Policy. Amsterdam: North-Holland.

Sargent, T. J. and Wallace, N. (1976). 'Rational expectations and the theory of economic policy.' *Journal of Monetary Economics*, vol. 2.

Schotter, A. (1981). *The Economic Theory of Social Institutions*. Cambridge: Cambridge University Press.

Scott, M. FG. (1981). 'How best to deflate the economy.' In Eltis and Sinclair (1981).

Sheffrin, S. M. (1983). *Rational Expectations*. Cambridge: Cambridge University Press.

Simon, H. A. (1982). *Models of Bounded Rationality*, vols. 1 and 2. Cambridge, Massachusetts: MIT Press.

—— (1983). *Reason in Human Affairs*. Oxford: Basil Blackwell.

Schiltknecht, K. (1981). 'Targeting the base – the Swiss experience.' In *Monetary Targets* (ed. B. Griffiths and G. E. Wood (1981)). London: Macmillan.

Taylor, J. B. (1980). 'Aggregate dynamics and staggered contracts.' *Journal of Political Economy*, vol. 88, pp. 1–23.

Townsend, R. B. (1983). 'Forecasting the forecasts of others.' *Journal of Political Economy*, vol. 91.

Treasury and Civil Service Committee (1984). *Fourth Report: the 1984 Budget*, Minutes of evidence. London: H.M.S.O.

Van der Ploeg, F. (1984). 'Rational expectations, risk and chaos in financial markets.' Mimeo.

Vines, D., Maciejowski, J. and Meade, J. E. (1983). *Demand Management*. London: Allen and Unwin.

Whittaker, R. and Wren-Lewis, S .(1983). 'The stability of financial policy rules and the long run effects of policy changes in an open economy with asset accumulation: some analytical, numerical and simulation resuts.' H.M. Treasury. Mimeo.

Wren-Lewis, S. (1984). 'The roles of output expectations and liquidity in explaining recent productivity movements.' *National Institute Economic Review*, May.

Name Index